Why You Need This New Edition

We have written this book for college students who are seeking to enhance their interpersonal communication and relationships. Retaining the strengths that readers seem to value most—an easily accessible style, our other-oriented approach, and a balance of theory and skills—this new edition provided us the opportunity to add fresh examples and research throughout and to fine-tune every feature, activity, and illustration. Here are five good reasons to give this new edition a close look!

① Our other-oriented approach: We have strengthened and highlighted the other-orientation theme through new features that help you apply an other-orientation to your own communication and relationships. A new Being Other-Oriented feature will help connect this approach to your everyday communication experiences, and a new Applying an Other-Orientation section will help you tie interpersonal concepts to the skill of being other-oriented in your own life.

② Increased emphasis on technology: Updated and expanded coverage now includes the differences between EMC and face-to-face communication and the implications of new technologies for our interactions and relationships. New Relating to Others in the 21st Century features discuss the influence of new technology on interpersonal communication and cover topics ranging from self-disclosure on Facebook to texting to Twitter!

③ Increased emphasis on diversity: We need to understand each other's differences and find common links in order to establish meaningful interpersonal relationships with others. We have significantly revised

and expanded Chapter 4, Interpersonal Communication and Diversity, and have incorporated the latest research on differences in gender, age, culture, sexual orientation, and points of view. We also include new Understanding Others: Adapting to Differences features that include practical suggestions and strategies for overcoming barriers to competent intercultural communication.

④ New built-in Study Guide at the end of each chapter: New end-of-chapter material, including brief chapter summaries, key terms with page numbers, critical thinking questions and questions about ethics, application activities, and lists of relevant resources help you review, apply, and explore key chapter concepts.

⑤ New and updated discussions, research findings, and examples: New material throughout the book covers such provocative topics as emotional intelligence and how to measure it, hate speech, listening in the 21st century, the dark side of the Internet, meta-messages and online communication, and networked families and coworkers.

PEARSON

SIXTH EDITION

Interpersonal Communication

Relating to Others

Steven A. Beebe

Texas State University–San Marcos

Susan J. Beebe

Texas State University–San Marcos

Mark V. Redmond

Iowa State University

Allyn & Bacon

Boston   Columbus   Indianapolis   New York   San Francisco   Upper Saddle River
Amsterdam   Cape Town   Dubai   London   Madrid   Milan   Munich   Paris   Montreal   Toronto
Delhi   Mexico City   Sao Paulo   Sydney   Hong Kong   Seoul   Singapore   Taipei   Tokyo

DEDICATED TO OUR FAMILIES
Mark and Matthew Beebe
Peggy, Nicholas, and Eric Redmond, and Beth Maroney

Acquisitions Editor: Jeanne Zalesky
Assistant Editor: Megan Lentz
Media Producer: Megan Higginbotham
Development Manager: David Kear
Development Editor: Hilary Jackson
Associate Development Editor:
    Angela G. Pickard
Marketing Manager: Blair Tuckman
Project Coordination, Text Design,
    and Electronic Page Makeup:
    Nesbitt Graphics, Inc.

Art Director: Anne Nieglos/Pat Smythe
Cover Designer: Wanda Espana
Cover Art: Image Source/Getty Images, Inc.
    RF
Photo Researcher: Pearson Image Resource
    Center/Kathy Ringrose
Image Permission Coordinator: Cynthia
    Vincenti
Operations Specialist: Mary Ann Gloriande
Printer and Binder: Courier Corporation
Cover Printer: Coral Graphic Services, Inc.

For permission to use copyrighted material, grateful acknowledgment is made to the copyright holders listed on page 402, which are hereby made part of this copyright page.

Library of Congress Cataloging-in-Publication Data
Beebe, Steven A.
  Interpersonal communication: relating to others/Steven A. Beebe, Susan J. Beebe, Mark V. Redmond. –6th ed.
    p. cm.
  Includes bibliographical references and index.
  ISBN 978-0-205-67453-4
1. Interpersonal communication—Textbooks. I. Beebe, Susan J. II. Redmond, Mark V. III. Title.
  BF637.C45B43 2009
  153.6—dc22

                            2009045267

1 2 3 4 5 6 7 8 9 10—CRK—13 12 11 10

Allyn & Bacon
is an imprint of

www.pearsonhighered.com

ISBN 10: 0-205-67453-4
ISBN 13: 978-0-205-67453-4

Brief Contents

Contents

PART TWO
Interpersonal Communication Skills   117

The world does not revolve around you. We believe that this unprofound observation has profound implications for the study of interpersonal communication: **At the heart of quality interpersonal relationships is an emphasis on others.** A focus on others rather than on oneself has been the hallmark of most volunteer, community, and faith movements in the world for millennia. Yet this book is not about religion or philosophy. It's about how to enhance the quality of your interpersonal communication with others.

An Other-Oriented Approach

Becoming other-oriented is not a single skill, but rather a collection of skills and principles that are designed to increase your sensitivity to and understanding of others. Being other-oriented doesn't mean you abandon your own thoughts, ignore your feelings, and change your behavior only to please others; that would not only be unethical, it would also be an ineffective approach to developing genuine, honest relationships with others. An other-oriented person is self-aware as well as aware of others. As we stress throughout the book, true empathy, emotional intelligence, and sensitivity are possible only when we feel secure about our own identities.

Becoming other-oriented is a mindful process of considering the thoughts, needs, feelings, and values of others, rather than focusing exclusively on oneself. This process involves all the classic principles and skills typically taught in interpersonal communication courses—listening, providing feedback, using conflict management skills and verbal and nonverbal skills—and places additional emphasis on the importance of the perceptions, thoughts, attitudes, beliefs, values, and emotions of others.

> **BEING Other-ORIENTED**
>
> The healthiest relationships are those in which both partners have an agreed-on and clear understanding of the relationship. Think about some of your closest relationships. How close do you think those partners would say the relationship is? In what ways do they communicate the level of intimacy and the feelings they have about the relationship? What nonverbal cues do they send? Are those clear or ambiguous? What have your partners said to let you know their assessment of the relationship?

New to This Edition

The importance of being other-oriented was the foundation of the first five well-received editions of *Interpersonal Communication: Relating to Others,* and it continues to be the central theme of the sixth edition. In this new edition, you will find that this other-orientation has been more fully explored and integrated throughout the book in numerous text discussions and examples, and it is highlighted by several new features that emphasize its importance and its application to everyday communication. We have introduced a new margin feature called **Being Other-Oriented** that appears throughout the book and connects the other-orientation theme to specific discussions, often presenting thought-provoking questions to get students thinking about how other-oriented their own communication is. We have also added a new summary section to the end of each chapter, called **Applying an Other-Orientation to . . . ,** which discusses essential applications and specifically applies the other-orientation to the chapter content.

> **APPLYING AN OTHER-ORIENTATION**
> to Friends and Romantic Partners
>
> As you develop friendships and romantic relationships, you continue to gain more information about your partners—about their beliefs, values, attitudes, needs, interests, desires, fears, and hopes. This accumulation of knowledge provides the foundation for a better understanding and ability to predict your partners behaviors and reactions and creates the expectation that you will anticipate and to adapt to the person's behaviors and needs. From a partner's perspective, it is a failure event when you don't incorporate your accumulated knowledge and understanding of your partner into your actions. For example, forgetting that your friend dislikes horror movies when you rent a horror movie for your weekly Friday night movie is likely to evoke a comment such as "But you know I hate horror movies; I can't believe you rented it anyway." Imagine the impact on a relationship of frequently committing such failure events. Your partner might interpret your failure to be other-oriented and to adapt as a lack of caring and concern for his or
>
> her needs and desires, or as a move toward withdrawing from the relationship.
>
> On the other hand, increasing knowledge of your friends and romantic partners improves your ability to adapt to their behavior and to anticipate responses. Knowledge of your closest same-sex friend and closest cross-sex friend should lead you to unique interpretations of their behaviors and to adaptation of your behavior, particularly in your selection of relevant communication strategies. Such empowerment does not necessarily mean greater relational satisfaction. For example, understanding that your romantic partner's discomfort with physical affection is a result of his or her upbringing won't necessarily offset your own desire for physical affection.
>
> The most significant challenge to being other-oriented in our friendships and romances is overcoming egocentric biases or distorted perceptions of our friends and lovers. In essence, we make errors in our mind-reading of others. The perceptual barriers identi-
>
> fied in Chapter 3 undermine your ability to gain the accurate information needed to be other-oriented. Another error occurs when you assume similarities between you and your partner that don't really exist. Assuming similarity leads to projecting your feelings, motivations, and needs your partner, which leads to errors when relevant differences are unaccounted for. On the other hand, when you and your partner are indeed similar, then such projecting can provide accurate understanding. A final barrier to effective other-orientation occurs when your perspective and your feelings are so strong that they prevent you from accurately recognizing your partner's perspective and feelings.[133] For example, after discovering that your partner has cheated on you, the weight of your emotional pain can prevent you from understanding your romantic partner's perspective. As a matter of fact, you might not even be motivated to try. Ultimately, the application of any other-orientation to your friendships and romantic relationships will require a motivation to do so.

A Balance of Interpersonal Communication Principles and Skills

Reviewers continue to praise our balanced presentation of both principles and skills. We provide a clear and cogent overview of interpersonal communication theory and principles to help students understand how they communicate, coupled with strategies to help students improve their interpersonal communication skill. Every chapter includes both classic and contemporary research conclusions that document essential interpersonal communication principles. Theory that helps explain the interpersonal communication behavior of others also helps students predict how best to enhance their own interpersonal communication.

Yet theory without practical application can leave students wondering how to develop interpersonal skills. That is why we also offer research-based skills and practical suggestions to help students apply interpersonal communication principles and improve such skills as listening, conflict management, and verbal and nonverbal communication.

An Emphasis on Diversity

Inherent in our other-oriented approach is the understanding that people differ in significant ways. It is because of those differences that we need skills and principles that allow us to develop links to other people and encourage us to establish meaningful interpersonal relationships with them. The last two decades have brought a significant expansion of our understanding of the role of differences in culture, age, gender, sexual orientation, religion, political perspectives, and other points of view in people's ability to connect with others.

Communication occurs when people find commonalities in meaning that transcend their differences. In this book, we do more than simply identify such differences. **Using a competency-based approach, we present practical, research-based strategies for increasing understanding when interacting with those who are different from us.** Using examples, illustrations, and research conclusions that are liberally woven throughout each chapter, we identify ways to become other-oriented despite differences we encounter in people of the other gender or of other cultures, ethnicities, or ideologies.

- In a significantly revised and expanded Chapter 4, Interpersonal Communication and Diversity: Adapting to Others, we not only identify barriers to competent intercultural communication but also present strategies to bridge the chasm of differences that still too often divide rather than unite people.

- **Understanding Others: Adapting to Differences** features in every chapter present research findings as well as communication strategies for understanding differences.

An Emphasis on Technology and Interpersonal Relationships

The line between face-to-face and electronically mediated communication has become increasingly blurred as we text, e-mail, and Skype with our friends and share the latest news and views via Facebook, MySpace, LinkedIn, Twitter, and blogs. In this edition, we explore the ever-increasing role of technology in interpersonal communication and the implications of technology for our daily communication and our relationships with others. We have significantly updated and expanded the introductory discussion of electronically mediated communication (EMC) in Chapter 1 and have included the latest research findings about how our electronic connections affect our face-to-face interactions throughout the book. In addition, we have developed a new feature in this edition: **Relating to Others in the 21st Century** focuses on research conclusions about the ways in which technology is changing how we relate to and interact with others and offers practical applications of such research relating to such issues as online stereotyping, what to self-disclose on Facebook, and the increasingly pervasive influence of Twitter.

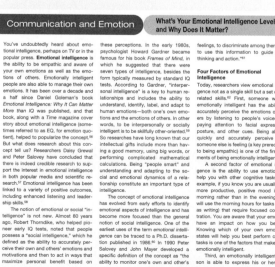

Relating to Others in the 21st Century — Text Me

Nobody is txting me
Im troubld & im stressd
Wen no one even thinks of me
It makes me feel d?pressd[51]

You don't need a textbook to tell you that texting is an important way to keep in touch with others. Like the author of the above poem, you may even feel stress if you're not receiving an e-bushel basket full of text messages. At the end of the first decade of the twenty-first century, text messages may be the most ubiquitous way of interacting with others who are not physically present. One study found that 80 percent of people under 25 tended to text rather than phone a friend and leave a short message.[52] Texting is a worldwide practice, in part because in most countries it's much cheaper to text than to call someone on the phone. According to Cheil Communications, in 2006 over 93 percent of teenagers in Britain between the ages of 17 and 19 sent or received at least one text message per day.[53] In Norway, even just a few years ago, more than 85 percent of teens and young adults (up to about age 25) sent text messages every day.[54] Faye Siytangco, a young sales representative from the Philippines, said she wasn't surprised to see people bowing their heads at a funeral for a friend's father. But she was shocked when she realized they weren't bowing in prayer, but were texting their friends. According to contemporary Philippine custom, texting while something else important is going on is not a breach of etiquette; it's just what people do now.[55]

Texting seems to be more for the young. Research has found that only 2.7 percent of people over the age of 67 send a text message a day.[56] Statistics also tell us about the kind of messages you are likely to text someone. Women tended to write longer text messages, to use more emoticons, to use more formal salutations ("Dear Mark") and farewell statements ("Sincerely, Sue"), and to write more grammatically complex messages than men.[57]

Why are so many people, especially young people, communicating via text messages? If you frequently send text messages, you can answer the question yourself: It's fast, cheap, easy, and always available. There's no need to open a laptop or be near a computer. And you don't have to worry about playing "telephone tag"—the recipient will read and respond to your message when he or she has time. And there's no need for small talk—text messaging lends itself to getting to the point.

Here's one set of text etiquette rules that have been posted on the Internet.[58]

Don't text when you're with someone else, without apologizing.
Don't text if you've had too much to drink.
Don't text while driving.
Don't say anything in text you wouldn't say in person.
Don't send bad news by text.

Norman Silver wrote ten "txt commandments" that humorously summarize the power and influence of text messages in his life:

U shall LUV ur mobil fone with all ur hart.

U & ur fone shall neva b apart.
U shall nt lust aftr ur neibrs fone nor thiev.
U shall be prepard @ al times 2 tXt & 2 recv.
U shall use LOL & othr acronyms in conversatns.
U shall be zappy with ur ast*r*sks & exclmatns!!
U shall abbrevi8 & rite words like thyr sed.
U shall nt speak 2 sum 1 face2face if u cn msg em insted.
U shall nt shout wth capitls XEPT IN DIRE EMERGNCY.
U shall nt consult a ninglish dictnry.[59]

Research evidence suggests that you will keep texting. It's cheap, easy, convenient, and it keeps you in touch with others. But don't forget the joys of having a good face-to-face conversation with someone now and then.

An Emphasis on Relationships

As the book's subtitle, *Relating to Others*, suggests, we highlight the importance of enhancing interpersonal relationships by developing an increased awareness of and sensitivity to how we relate to others. Our emphasis on relationships is reflected in the wide range of relationship types we discuss, including relationships with friends, romantic partners, family members, and coworkers, as well as relationships formed and developed over the Internet.

- A significant change in this edition is a reorganization of the relationship chapters to focus first on fundamental interpersonal theory and skills directly related to relationships and on theories of the stages of relationship development (Chapters 9 and 10). Subsequently we explore in detail specific types of relationships: friendships, romance, family relationships, and those in the workplace (Chapters 11 and 12).

- While we emphasize the positive nature of relationships, we also provide a glimpse into the challenging "dark side" of relating to others, including such issues as deception, jealousy, and the influence of technology on our interactions and communication.

- Revised **Communication and Emotion** boxes throughout help students see how emotions affect their relationships with others.

Communication and Emotion — What's Your Emotional Intelligence Level and Why Does It Matter?

You've undoubtedly heard about emotional intelligence, perhaps on TV or in the popular press. **Emotional intelligence** is the ability to be empathic and aware of your own emotions as well as the emotions of others. Emotionally intelligent people are also able to manage their own emotions. It has been over a decade and a half since Daniel Goleman's book *Emotional Intelligence: Why It Can Matter More than IQ* was published, and that book, along with a *Time* magazine cover story about emotional intelligence (sometimes referred to as EQ, for emotion quotient), helped to popularize the concept.[56] But what does research about this concept tell us? Researchers Daisy Grewal and Peter Salovey have concluded that there is indeed credible research to support the interest in emotional intelligence in both popular media and scientific research.[57] Emotional intelligence has been linked to a variety of positive outcomes, including enhanced listening and leadership skills.[58]

The notion of emotional or social "intelligence" is not new. Almost 80 years ago, Robert Thorndike, who helped pioneer early IQ tests, noted that people possess a "social intelligence," which he defined as the ability to accurately perceive their own and others' emotions and motivations and then to act in ways that maximize personal benefit based on these perceptions. In the early 1980s, psychologist Howard Gardner became famous for his book *Frames of Mind*, in which he suggested that there were seven types of intelligence, besides the form typically measured by standard IQ tests. According to Gardner, "interpersonal intelligence" is a key to human relationships and includes the ability to understand, identify, label, and adapt to human emotions—both one's own emotions and the emotions of others. In other words, to be interpersonally or socially intelligent is to be skillfully other-oriented.[59] So researches have long known that our intellectual gifts include more than having a good memory, using big words, or performing complicated mathematical calculations. Being "people smart" and understanding and adapting to the social and emotional dynamics of a relationship constitute an important type of intelligence.

The concept of emotional intelligence has evolved from early efforts to identify emotional aspects of intelligence and has become more focused than the general notion of social intelligence. One of the earliest uses of the term *emotional intelligence* can be traced to a Ph.D. dissertation published in 1986.[60] In 1990 Peter Salovey and John Mayer developed a specific definition of the concept as "the ability to monitor one's own and other's feelings, to discriminate among them, and to use this information to guide one's thinking and action."[61]

Four Factors of Emotional Intelligence

Today, researchers view emotional intelligence not as a single skill but a set of four related skills.[62] First, someone who is emotionally intelligent has the ability to accurately perceive the emotions of others by listening to people's voices and paying attention to facial expressions, posture, and other cues. Being able to quickly and accurately perceive what someone else is feeling (a key prerequisite to being empathic) is one of the first elements of being emotionally intelligent.

A second factor of emotional intelligence is the ability to use emotions to help you with other cognitive tasks. For example, if you know you are usually in a more productive, positive mood in the morning rather than in the evening, you will use the morning hours for tasks (such as writing) that require focused concentration. You are aware that your emotions have an impact on how you behave. Knowing which of your own emotional states will help you best perform certain tasks is one of the factors that makes you emotionally intelligent.

Third, an emotionally intelligent person is able to express his or her own

A Partnership with Students and Instructors

RECAP Categories of Movement and Gestures

Category	Definition	Example
Emblems	Behaviors that have specific, generally understood meaning within a given culture	Raising a hitchhiking thumb
Illustrators	Cues that accompany verbal messages and add meaning to the message	Pounding the lectern to emphasize a point
Affect displays	Expressions of emotion	Hugging someone to express love
Regulators	Cues that control and manage the flow of communication between two people	Looking at someone when you wish to speak
Adaptors	Behaviors that help you adapt to your environment	Scratching; combing your hair

Building Your Skills   Practicing Nonverbal Perception Checking

We have identified several strategies to improve your skill at interpreting the nonverbal messages of others, including being able to check your perceptions of others. Accurately perceiving others gets to the heart of becoming other-oriented.

Look at the photographs. First, note the nonverbal behavior of the target person in the picture. Next, form a mental impression of what you think the person is thinking and feeling. Finally, compose a perception-checking question that the other person in the photo could ask to confirm the target person's thoughts and feelings.

Photo 1
A. Describe the student's nonverbal behavior.
B. What do you think the student is thinking and feeling?
C. What is a perception-checking question the teacher could ask her student?

Photo 2
A. Describe the customer's nonverbal behavior.
B. What do you think the customer is thinking and feeling?
C. What is a perception-checking question the salesman could ask the customer?

STUDY GUIDE
Review, Apply, and Explore

Conflict Defined, Myths, and Types
(pages 216–226)

Interpersonal conflict is an expressed struggle between at least two interdependent people who perceive incompatible goals, scarce resources, or interference, and who are attempting to achieve a specific goal. Conflict is a process, with a beginning, a middle, an end, and an aftermath. Conflict can be constructive if it airs differences and helps build new insights and establish new patterns that lead to a more satisfying relationship. But it can also be destructive if people have a win–lose perspective and don't look for solutions. Being aware of potential conflict triggers can help you avoid or manage sensitive topics. Most conflict fits into one of three categories: pseudoconflict, simple conflict, or ego conflict.

Key Terms

Interpersonal conflict 216	Pseudoconflict 223
Interdependent 217	Simple conflict 223
Constructive conflict 219	Ego conflict 223
Destructive conflict 220	Expressive conflict 224
Conflict triggers 220	Instrumental conflict 224
Dialectical tension 220	

Critical Thinking Questions

1. Think of a recent communication exchange with a friend, spouse, or coworker that began as a seemingly casual conversation but escalated into a conflict. Can you identify a reason for this, such as one or both of you feeling tired, stressed, or anxious? Is there anything you could have done to avoid the conflict? What cues might you each have looked for to understand the other's mood?
2. Melissa and Jake always seem to end up making personal attacks and calling each other names when they get into a disagreement. What type of conflict are they experiencing when they do this, and how can they avoid it?
3. Ethics: Is it ethical to mask your true emotions in order to get along with others? Is honesty in a relationship always the best policy? Explain your response.

Activities

Based on the discussion of conflict presented on pages 218–219, think of a recent conflict you had with someone or a conflict that is still ongoing. To help you better understand and manage the process, answer the following questions:

Prior Conditions Stage
• What were the prior conditions that led to the conflict?
• How long were some of the prior conditions simmering in the background?

Frustration Awareness Stage
• When did you become aware that you were frustrated and that your needs weren't being met or that there was an issue to resolve?

• When did you perceive that the other person was aware that a conflict might exist?

Active Conflict Stage
• What caused the conflict to move from frustration to active conflict?
• What type of conflict was(is) it—pseudoconflict, simple conflict, or ego conflict?

Resolution Stage
• What conflict management skills did you use (or are you and the other person using) to manage emotions, information, goals, or the problem?
• What conflict management skills could you have used, but didn't?

Follow-Up Stage
• Has the conflict been truly managed and resolved, or not? What leads you to that conclusion?
• Did you or the other person explicitly indicate that the conflict is over?

Web Resources
http://www.cios.org.encyclopedia/conflict/index.htm This conflict management site provides an introduction to the study of conflict management through links that explain why the study of conflict is important, key elements of conflict, the nature of conflict and conflict variables, and skills for conflict managers, and offers a self-test to check your conflict management understanding.

Conflict and Power
(pages 227–231)

Conflict and power are often connected because people use interpersonal power to influence or control others. Interpersonal power is a fundamental element of our personal relationships. Understanding principles of power and sources of power can provide insight into how you and others are using power to influence the outcome of disagreements. Five sources of power suggested by researchers are legitimate power, referent power, expert power, reward power, and coercive power. Being able to negotiate and renegotiate power in a relationship can lead to a more rewarding and productive relationship.

Key Terms

Interpersonal power 227	Expert power 229
Dependent relationship 228	Reward power 229
Legitimate power 229	Coercive power 229
Referent power 229	Compliance gaining 229

Critical Thinking Questions

1. Examine several recent interpersonal conflicts for unresolved power issues. (For example, consider conflicts that have focused on managing money, household tasks, or

249

To use a music metaphor, we have provided the "notes," but the instructor is the one who makes the music, in concert with the student reader. We provide the melody line, but the instructor adds harmony, texture, and color to make the instructional message sing. In this new edition, we continue our tradition of providing a wide array of instructional resources to help instructors teach, as well as numerous pedagogical aids to help students review, apply, and master the fundamental principles and skills of interpersonal communication. Built into the book is a vast array of pedagogical features:

- A chapter-opening quotation to provide a provocative focal point for the chapter.

- Chapter learning objectives.

- A comprehensive chapter-opening outline of key content.

- Highly praised **Recap** features that periodically summarize key concepts and terms for the reader.

- **Building Your Skills** boxes throughout that offer practical strategies for applying chapter content.

- An expanded margin glossary of all boldface terms in the text.

- New to this edition: A **Study Guide** at the end of each chapter, which gives students the opportunity to review, apply, and explore the key chapter concepts through critical thinking questions, questions about ethics, classroom and group activities, and lists of web sites.

- A striking new design has been created to make the material as interesting, accessible, and engaging as possible. We have also included new cartoons and photos throughout, to freshen the overall look and emotional impact of the book.

In addition to the learning resources built into the book, we offer a wealth of instructor and student supplements.

Resources in Print and Online

Name of Supplement	Available in Print	Available Online	Instructor or Student Supplement	Description
Skillbuilder Workbook	✓		Student Supplement	This guide, by *Interpersonal Communication* co-author, Mark V. Redmond, helps students reinforce their understanding of the principles of interpersonal communication and enhance their skills. Filled with exercises, activities, and study aids, it provides students with a wealth of opportunities to review and apply concepts introduced in the text.
Instructor's Manual and Test Bank	✓	✓	Instructor Supplement	Prepared by Matt Vos, Covenant College, this comprehensive Instructor's Manual and Test Bank has the following resources for each chapter: Chapter-at-a-Glance grids (that correlate with all available book-specific ancillary resources), Learning Objectives, Chapter Overview, Chapter Lecture Outline, Discussion/Journal Questions, and Chapter Activities and Assignments. The Test Bank portion contains a blend of approximately 1000 fully reviewed assessments (multiple choice, true/false, and essay questions), which are referenced by page and skill. Available for download at www.pearsonhighered.com/irc; access code required.
MyTest Computerized Testbank		✓	Instructor Supplement	This flexible, online test-generating software includes all questions found in the Test Bank section of the printed Instructor's Manual and Test Bank. The software allows instructors to create their own personalized exams, to edit any or all of the existing test questions, and to add new questions. Other special features of this program include random generation of test questions, creation of alternate versions of the same test, scrambling of question sequence, and test preview before printing. Available at www.pearsonmytest.com; access code required.
PowerPoint™ Presentation Package		✓	Instructor Supplement	This text-specific package, prepared by Jill Harms, Iowa State University, provides a basis for your lecture with PowerPoint™ slides for each chapter of the book. New to this edition are additional discussion launching questions and suggested class activities embedded right in the presentations for each chapter! Available for download at www.pearsonhighered.com/irc; access code required.
The Blockbuster Approach: Teaching Interpersonal Communication with Video	✓		Instructor Supplement	This guide by Thomas E. Jewell, Marymount College, provides lists and descriptions of commercial videos that can be used in the classroom to illustrate interpersonal concepts and complex interpersonal relationships. Sample activities are also included.
Pearson Allyn & Bacon Interpersonal Communication Video Library	✓		Instructor Supplement	Pearson Allyn & Bacon's Interpersonal Communication Video Library contains a range of videos for adopters to choose from. Each of the the videos features a variety of scenarios that illustrate interpersonal concepts and relationships. Some topics included in the library are nonverbal communication, perception, conflict, and listening. Contact your Pearson representative for details; some restrictions apply.
Allyn & Bacon Digital Media Archive for Communication	✓		Instructor Supplement	The Digital Media Archive CD-ROM contains electronic images of charts, graphs, maps, tables, and figures, along with media elements such as video clips, audio clips, and related web links. These media assets are fully customizable to use with our pre-formatted PowerPoint™ outlines or to import into instructors' own lectures. (Available for Windows and Mac.)
Pearson Allyn & Bacon Interpersonal Communication Study Site (Open access)		✓	Student Supplement	The Pearson Allyn & Bacon Interpersonal Communication Study Site features practice tests, learning objectives, web links, and selected media. The site is organized around the major topics typically covered in an interpersonal communication course. Available at www.abinterpersonal.com.
Study Card for Interpersonal Communication	✓		Student Supplement	Colorful, affordable, and packed with useful information, Pearson Allyn & Bacon Study Cards make studying easier, more efficient, and more enjoyable. Course information is distilled down to the basics, helping you quickly master the fundamentals, review a subject for understanding, or prepare for an exam. Because they're laminated for durability, you can keep these Study Cards for years to come and pull them out whenever you need a quick review. Available for purchase.
MyCommunicationLab		✓	Instructor & Student Supplement	MyCommunicationLab is a state-of-the-art, interactive, and instructive solution for communication courses. Designed to be used as a supplement to a traditional lecture course or as a complete online course, MyCommunicationLab combines a Pearson eText, multimedia, video clips, activities, research support, tests, and quizzes to completely engage students. See next page for more details.

Save time and improve results with
mycommunicationlab.com

Designed to amplify a traditional course in numerous ways or to administer a course online, **MyCommunicationLab** for interpersonal communication courses combines pedagogy and assessment with an array of multimedia activities—videos, assessments, research support, multiple newsfeeds—to make learning more effective for all types of students. Now featuring more resources, this new release of **MyCommunicationLab** is visually richer and even more interactive than the previous version—a leap forward in design with more tools and features to enrich learning and aid students in classroom success.

Teaching and Learning Tools

NEW VERSION! Pearson eText: Identical in content and design to the printed text, a Pearson eText provides students access to their text whenever and wherever they need it. In addition to contextually placed multimedia features in every chapter, our new Pearson eText allows students to take notes and highlight, just as they can with a printed book.

Videos and Video Quizzes: Interactive videos provide students with the opportunity to watch portrayals of different communication scenarios, interviews with well-known communication scholars, contemporary television shows, and more. Many videos are annotated with critical thinking questions or include short, assignable quizzes that report to the instructor's gradebook.

Self-Assessments: Online self assessments including SCAM, PRCA-24, and assessments that test introversion, shyness, and communication competence, as well as pre- and post-tests for every chapter help students to learn about different communication styles and assess their own. The tests generate a customized study plan for further assessment and focus students on areas in which they need to improve. Instructors can use these tools to show learning over the duration of the course.

NEW! ABC News RSS feed: MyCommunicationLab provides an online feed from ABC news, updated hourly, to help students choose and research group assignments and speeches.

NEW! MySearchLab: Pearson's MySearchLab™ is the easiest way for students to start a research assignment or paper. Complete with extensive help on the research process and four databases of credible and reliable source material, MySearchLab™ helps students quickly and efficiently make the most of their research time.

Online Administration

No matter what course management system you use—or if you do not use one at all, but still wish to easily capture your students' grades and track their performance—Pearson has a **MyCommunicationLab** option to suit your needs. Contact one of Pearson's Technology Specialists for more information and assistance.

A **MyCommunicationLab** access code is provided at no additional cost when packaged with selected Pearson Communication texts. To get started, contact your local Pearson Publisher's Representative at **www.pearsonhighered.com/replocator.**

Acknowledgments

This book is not only a collaboration among the three of us, but also a collaboration with a host of others. Without the research conclusions of the talented, creative scholars who have studied interpersonal communication and published their results, a book of this scope would not be possible. We also thank our students, who are a constant source of questions, ideas, inspiration, and challenges that enrich our teaching and writing.

We are especially thankful for the continuing outstanding editorial support and leadership that kept our multi-author team collaborating with aplomb. Editor in Chief Karon Bowers, who has worked with us for a decade, continues to be a source of inspiration and unwavering support. Our talented development editor, Hilary Jackson, has skillfully guided us through every step of the revision process. We appreciate her new ideas and fresh insights.

We also appreciate the dozens of gifted interpersonal communication instructors and scholars who read the manuscript and offered suggestions that have made this a better book. We thank the following people for sharing their information, ideas, and ingenuity with us as they reviewed this edition or previous editions of the book.

Sixth Edition Reviewers

Carolyn Clark, *Salt Lake Community College*

Rebecca E. Dunn, *Westmoreland County Community College*

Traci Letcher, *University of Kentucky*

Douglas H. Stewart, *Lake Washington Technical College*

Dennis Sutton, *Grand Rapids Community College*

R. Weylin Sternglanz, *Nova Southeastern University*

Reviewers of Previous Editions

Rebecca Anderson, *Johnson County Community College*

Leonard Barchak, *McNeese University*

Cameron Smith Basquiat, *Community College of Southern Nevada*

Judyth Betz-Gonzales, *Delta College*

Marion Boyer, *Kalamazoo Community College*

Scott E. Caplan, *University of Delaware*

Norman Clark, *Appalachian State University*

Carolyn P. DeLeCour, *Palo Alto College*

Carol Z. Dolphin, *University of Wisconsin–Waukesha*

Terrence Doyle, *Northern Virginia Community College*

Reginald E. Ecarma, *Campbellsville University*

David L. Edwards, *South Central Technical College*

Janie Harden Fritz, *Duquesne University*

Patricia M. Harris-Jenkinson, *Sacramento City College*

Sherry J. Holmen, *Albuquerque Technical Vocational Institute*

Adna G. Howell, *Delta College*

David D. Hudson, *Golden West College*

Diana K. Ivy, *Texas A&M University–Corpus Christi*

Thomas E. Jewell, *Marymount College*

Elizabeth R. Lamoureux, *Buena Vista University*

Heidi McGrew, *Sinclair Community College*

Charles R. McMahan, *Vincennes University*

Timothy P. Mottet, *Texas State University–San Marcos*

Lisa M. Orick, *Albuquerque Technical Vocational Institute*

James R. Pauff, *Bowling Green State University*

Nan Peck, *Northern Virginia Community College*

Terry Perkins, *Eastern Illinois University*

Narissra Punyanunt-Carter, *Texas Tech University*

Susan Richardson, *Prince George's Community College*

Michael Schliessman, *South Dakota State University*

Cheri Simonds, *Illinois State University*

Anntarie Lanita Sims, *Trenton State College*

Heather A. Smith, *Santa Monica College*

Vincent Scott Smithson, *Purdue University North Central*

Dickie Spurgeon, *Southern Illinois University*

Glen H. Stamp, *Ball State University*

Claire Sullivan, *University of Maine*

James J. Tolhuizen, *Indiana University Northwest*

Sally Vogl-Bauer, *University of Wisconsin–Whitewater*

Sheryl L. Williams, *University of Wisconsin–Whitewater*

Lori Wisdom-Whitley, *Everett Community College*

Richard L. Wiseman, *California State University–Fullerton*

We are blessed with the support and ideas of our many colleagues and friends. Sue and Steve thank Thompson Biggers, a valued friend and colleague who helped conceptualize this book. Mary Jeanette Smythe, Tom Willett, Tim Mottet, and Diana Ivy are long-time educators and friends who inspired us with their knowledge and gift of friendship. Phil Salem, Lee Williams, Cathy Fleuriet, and Maureen Keeley are friends and colleagues at Texas State University–San Marcos who have positively influenced our work. John Masterson, a valued friend and colleague, also greatly influenced our teaching and writing about interpersonal communication. Special thanks go to the late Michael Argyle at Oxford University, Oxford, England, who sponsored Steve as a Visiting Scholar at Oxford's Wolfson College and generously shared his research findings. Thanks, too, to Peter and Jill Collett, friends and colleagues from Oxford, for their assistance, support, and friendship. Thane McCollough, from Gonzaga University, also provided valuable support for this project.

We have outstanding support from many people. Sue Hall, senior administrative assistant in the Department of Communication Studies at Texas State, continues to be an invaluable assistant and friend. Meredith Clayton, Malinda Murry, and Bob Hanna are other valued colleagues and staff members who provided skilled support. We thank our good friend Kosta Tovstiadi for his skillful research assistance in helping us secure the most contemporary research we could find about interpersonal communication.

Mark has used the textbook for many years in teaching the introduction to interpersonal communication course at Iowa State and owes a debt to hundreds of students, both for their feedback on the text and for teaching him through their own interpersonal experiences. For example, it was his students who first introduced him to the term and meaning of "friends with benefits." Beth Lamoureux at Buena Vista University continues to be an extraordinary supporter of our text, as well as a supportive friend, and we particularly appreciate the detailed suggestions she provided for improving this edition. Specific colleagues at Iowa State have provided moral support and encouragement as well as feedback from their use of the text: they include Denise Vrchota, Todd Jenks, Jill Harms, and Kay Mueller. Mark would also like to acknowledge and thank a group of colleagues he met years ago when they were all graduate students at the University of Denver and with whom he developed life-long treasured friendships: Rich Arthur, Slippery Rock University; John Masterson, Texas Lutheran University; Diane Ritzdorf, Arapahoe High School; Marc Routhier, Frostburg State University; Jim Tolhuizen, Indiana University Northwest; and especially Phil Backlund, Central Washington University.

Finally, our families provide ongoing love and support to each of us. Mark thanks his parents, Jack and Alice Redmond; his brother, Jack; and his sisters, Ruthann, Mary Lynn, and Tina, who helped shape a family environment that planted the seeds for studying and appreciating interpersonal communication. Those seeds have been nurtured into a full-grown fascination with how communication shapes our lives and personal development by his wife, Peggy, his daughter Beth, and his sons, Nicholas and Eric. On a practical level, Mark owes a lot of his understanding of chat rooms and instant messaging to them.

Steve and Sue want especially to thank their parents, Russell and Muriel Beebe, who have recently celebrated their 68th wedding anniversary, and Herb and Jane Dye, who have been married for more than 60 years. These humble, loving, and dedicated mentors were our first and finest teachers of interpersonal communication. We also thank our son Mark, who continues to teach us that the power of love can overcomes life's challenges, and our son Matt, who teaches us about the importance of finding music in days filled with both sunshine and clouds.

Steven A. Beebe
Susan J. Beebe
San Marcos, Texas

Mark V. Redmond
Ames, Iowa

About the Authors

Steven A. Beebe is Regent's Professor and Chair of the Department of Communication Studies and Associate Dean of the College of Fine Arts and Communication at Texas State University–San Marcos. Steve is the author or co-author of eleven widely used communication books, most of which have been through multiple editions, as well as of numerous articles, book chapters, and conference presentations. He has been a Visiting Scholar at both Oxford University and Cambridge University in England, has traveled widely in Europe and Asia, and has played a leadership role in establishing new communication curricula in Russian universities. In 1996 he was named Outstanding Communication Professor by the National Speaker's Association. He has also received the President's Award for Research as well as the President's Award for Service at Texas State. His passions in life include his family and a life-long love of music; he is a pianist and organist and is currently struggling to learn the cello.

Susan J. Beebe's professional interests and expertise encompass both oral and written communication. Currently serving as Acting Director of Lower-Division Studies in the Department of English at Texas State University–San Marcos, Sue has co-authored three books and has published a number of articles and teaching materials in both English and communication studies. She has received both the Texas State Presidential Award for Excellence in Service and the College of Liberal Arts Award for Excellence in Scholarly/Creative Activities. An active volunteer in the community of San Marcos, Texas, Sue was the founding coordinator of the San Marcos Volunteers in Public Schools Program and has served on the San Marcos School Board and the Education Foundation Board. In 1993 she was named the statewide Friend of Education by the Texas Classroom Teachers' Association; in 2000 the San Marcos school district presented her with its Lifetime Achievement Award. Sue enjoys reading, traveling, and caring for the Beebe family cats, Luke and Bouncer. Sue and Steve have two sons: Mark, a graduate of Rice University; and Matt, a graduate of Southwestern University.

Mark V. Redmond is an Associate Professor of Communication Studies at Iowa State University. Besides this book, Mark has authored an introductory text on communication theory and research, edited an upper-level text in interpersonal communication, and co-authored a public speaking text. His research focuses on social decentering (taking into account another person's thoughts, feelings, perspectives, etc.), one of the themes incorporated in this text. His studies have included an examination of initial interactions between strangers, adaptation in interpersonal interactions, interpersonal influence, and intercultural communication competence. He is a Cyclone sports fan with an avocation for playing basketball at least three times a week (despite an aging hook shot). An unaccomplished piano and guitar player, he loves composing and writing songs and vows to someday complete the musical he's been working on for twenty years. Mark and his wife Peggy have three children: Beth, continuing her nursing education while a nurse at the University of Iowa Hospitals; Nicholas, a graduate of Iowa State University, now completing a Master of Divinity; and Eric, completing his degree at Iowa State.

Chapter-by-Chapter Changes

Here's a brief chapter-by-chapter summary of new or significantly revised and updated chapter material:

PART ONE
Interpersonal Communication Foundations

Chapter 1
- Significantly expanded and revised discussion of electronically mediated interpersonal communication
- New research about texting and interpersonal communication
- Revised discussion of metacommunication
- Updated discussion of emotional contagion and interpersonal communication

Chapter 2
- New discussion of attachment styles
- Expanded discussion of face and facework
- New discussion of self-presentation online
- New and revised discussion of self and interaction with others
- Revised discussion of self and communication social style

Chapter 3
- Revised discussion of how we form impressions of others
- New discussion of intercultural communication and perception
- New discussion of how people stereotype others online
- New and expanded discussion of personal perception barriers

Chapter 4
- Updated statistics in our diversity almanac
- New clarification of the differences between sex and gender
- New and updated discussion of Hofstede's dimensions of cultural values
- New discussion of making intercultural e-connections
- Updated discussion of how to improve intercultural competence
- Revised discussion of how to decenter and develop empathy

PART TWO
Interpersonal Communication Skills

Chapter 5
- Expanded discussion of listener styles
- Revised discussion of listening and gender differences
- Revised discussion of the role of self talk in improving listening skill
- New discussion of listening in the 21st century
- New and revised discussion of enhancing empathic listening skills
- New discussion of emotional intelligence
- Revised discussion of enhancing responding skills

Chapter 6
- New discussion of onomatopoeia, profanity, euphemisms, and hate speech
- Revised discussion of how words influence thoughts
- New information about words, meaning, and the brain
- Revised discussion of gender differences and similarities and verbal messages
- New discussion of verbal messages and communication online

Chapter 7
- New research about how to interpret nonverbal messages
- New discussion of metamessages and online communication
- New information about nonverbal messages and deception
- New discussion of skills in expressing nonverbal messages

Chapter 8

- Revised discussion of the definition of interpersonal conflict
- New discussion of conflict triggers
- New discussion of conflict and intercultural communication
- New section on conflict and power, including power negotiation
- Expanded discussion of demand-withdrawal pattern of conflict management
- New discussion of managing conflict online
- Revised discussion of communicating with prickly people

PART THREE
Interpersonal Communication in Relationships

Chapter 9

- Reorganized chapter includes stages and theories of relational development
- New discussion of the biological aspects of interpersonal attraction
- Revised discussion of social exchange theory
- New discussion of relational development and social penetration theory
- New discussion of self-disclosure as part of relational development
- New discussion on the reciprocity of self-disclosure
- New discussion of online self-disclosure in the 21st century

Chapter 10

- Repositioned in the text to precede specific relationship chapters
- New discussion of relational transgressions
- New discussion on how to achieve forgiveness
- New discussion on interracial, interethnic, and intercultural relationships
- Discussion of deception enhanced by addition of Burgoon and Bueller's interpersonal deception theory
- Revised discussion of jealousy and addition of cognitive and emotional jealousy
- Revised discussion on managing obsessive relational intrusion
- New discussion of female and male responses to relationship challenges

Chapter 11

- Reorganized to focus on friendship and romance
- New discussion of the meaning of intimacy
- New discussion on making friends
- New discussion of adolescent, young adult, adult, and late adulthood friendships
- New section on same-sex friendships
- New discussion on developing intercultural and interracial friendships
- Revised discussion of romantic relationships and love
- New sections on commitment and physical affection and sex
- New section on the movement of relationships from friendship to romance
- New section on first dates and dating
- New section on unrequited romantic interest
- New section on friendship, romance, and the Internet
- Revised discussion of strategies and skills for developing relationships

Chapter 12

- Expanded discussion on blended families and single-parent families
- New section on family communication patterns
- New discussion of committed partners, including benefits, satisfaction, and conflict
- Revised and expanded discussion of parent-child communication
- New discussion of sibling relationships throughout the lifetime
- New discussion of the values and functions of workplace friendships
- New discussion of the deterioration of workplace friendships
- New discussion of the reasons for and values of workplace romances
- New discussion of the dark side of workplace romances and management's response
- New section on guidelines for workplace romances
- Revised discussion of upward and downward communication with managers
- New discussion of leader-member exchange theory

Introduction to Interpersonal Communication

1

> # Communication is to a relationship what breathing is to maintaining life.
>
> **Virginia Satir**

Interpersonal communication is like breathing; it is a requirement for life. And, like breathing, interpersonal communication is inescapable. Unless you live in isolation, you communicate interpersonally every day. Listening to your roommate, talking to a teacher, meeting for lunch with a friend, and talking to your parents or your spouse are all examples of interpersonal communication.

It is impossible *not* to communicate with others.[1] Even before we are born, we respond to movement and sound. With our first cry, we announce to others that we are here. Once we make contact with others, we communicate, and we continue to do so until we draw our last breath. Even though many of our messages are not verbalized, we nonetheless send messages to others—intentionally and sometimes unintentionally. Whatever our intentions, people draw conclusions from our behavior. Without interpersonal communication, a special form of human communication that occurs as we manage our relationships, people suffer and even die. Recluses, hermits, and people isolated in solitary confinement dream and hallucinate about talking with others face to face.

Human communication is at the core of our existence. Think of the number of times you communicated with someone today, as you worked, ate, studied, shopped, or went about your other daily activities. Most people spend between 80 and 90 percent of their waking hours communicating with others.[2] It is through these interactions with others that we develop interpersonal relationships.[3]

Because these relationships are so important to our lives, later chapters will focus on the communication skills and principles that explain and predict how we develop, sustain, and sometimes end relationships. We'll explore such questions as the following: Why do we like some people and not others? How can we interpret other people's unspoken messages with greater accuracy? Why do some relationships blossom and others deteriorate? How can we better manage disagreements with others? How can we better understand our relationships with our family, friends, and coworkers?

This chapter charts the course ahead, addressing key questions about what interpersonal communication is and why it is important. We will begin by seeing how our understanding of the interpersonal communication process has evolved. And we will conclude by examining how we initiate and sustain relationships through interpersonal communication.

What Is Interpersonal Communication?

communication Process of acting on information.

human communication Process of making sense out of the world and sharing that sense with others by creating meaning through the use of verbal and nonverbal messages.

To understand interpersonal communication, we must begin by understanding how it relates to two broader categories: communication in general and human communication. Scholars have attempted to arrive at a general definition of communication for decades, yet experts cannot agree on a single one. One research team counted more than 126 published definitions.[4] In the broadest sense, **communication** is the process of acting on information.[5] Someone does or says something, and others think or do something in response to the action or the words as they understand them.

To refine our broad definition, we can say that **human communication** is the process of making sense out of the world and sharing that sense with others by creating meaning through the use of verbal and nonverbal messages.[6] We learn about the world by listening, observing, tasting, touching, and smelling; then we share our conclusions with others. Human communication encompasses many media: speeches, e-mail, songs, radio and television broadcasts, online discussion groups, letters, books, articles, poems, and advertisements.

Interpersonal communication *is a distinctive, transactional form of human communication involving mutual influence, usually for the purpose of managing relationships.* The three essential elements of this definition differentiate the unique nature of interpersonal communication from other forms of human communication.[7]

Interpersonal Communication Is a Distinctive Form of Communication

For years, many scholars defined interpersonal communication simply as communication that occurs when two people interact face to face. This limited definition suggests that if two people are interacting, then they are engaging in interpersonal communication. Today, interpersonal communication is defined not just by the number of people who communicate, but also by the quality of the communication. Interpersonal communication occurs not simply when you interact with someone, but when you treat the other person as a unique human being.[8]

Think of all human communication as ranging on a continuum from impersonal to interpersonal communication. **Impersonal communication** occurs when you treat people as objects, or when you respond to their roles rather than to who they are as unique people. When you ask a server in a restaurant for a glass of water, you are interacting with the role, not necessarily with the individual. You know nothing personal about this individual, and he or she knows nothing personal about you (unless this person eavesdrops on your conversation).

Philosopher Martin Buber influenced our thinking about human communication when he presented the concept of honest dialogue as the essence of true, authentic communication.[9] He described communication as consisting of two different qualities of relationships. He discussed an "I–It" relationship as an impersonal one; the other person is viewed as an "It" rather than as an authentic, genuine person. When you buy a pair of socks at a clothing store, you have a two-person, face-to-face, relatively brief interaction with someone. You communicate. Yet that interchange could hardly be described as intimate or personal.

Interpersonal communication occurs when you interact with another person as a unique, authentic individual rather than as an object or an "It." Buber calls this kind of relationship an "I–Thou" relationship. In this kind of relationship, there is true dialogue. An "I–Thou" relationship is not self-centered. The communicators have developed an attitude toward each other that is honest, open, spontaneous, nonjudgmental, and based on equality rather than superiority.[10]

We're not suggesting that the goal of every communication transaction is to develop a personal, intimate dialogue. That would be unrealistic and inappropriate. It's possible to go through an entire day communicating with others but not be involved in interpersonal communication. As we noted earlier, interpersonal communication is a distinctive form of communication because it focuses on the uniqueness of others; it does not occur just because two people are communicating.

Additionally, although interpersonal communication is more intimate and reveals more about the people involved than does impersonal communication, not all interpersonal communication involves sharing closely guarded personal information. As we discuss later in the book, there are degrees of intimacy when interacting with others.

interpersonal communication
A distinctive, transactional form of human communication involving mutual influence, usually for the purpose of managing relationships.

impersonal communication
Process that occurs when we treat others as objects or respond to their roles rather than to who they are as unique persons.

RECAP   The Continuum Between Interpersonal Communication and Impersonal Communication

Interpersonal Communication	Impersonal Communication
• People are treated as unique individuals.	• People are treated as objects.
• People communicate in an "I–Thou" relationship. Each person is treated as special, and there is true dialogue and honest sharing of self with others.	• People communicate in an "I–It" relationship. Each person has a role to perform.
• Interpersonal communication often involves communicating with someone you care about, such as a good friend or cherished family member.	• There is mechanical, stilted interaction, rather than honest sharing of feelings.
	• Impersonal communication involves communicating with people such as sales clerks and servers—you have no history with them, and you expect no future with them.

Interpersonal Communication Involves Mutual Influence Between Individuals

Every interpersonal communication transaction influences us. Mutual influence means that *all* partners in the communication are affected by a transaction. Interpersonal communication may or may not involve words. The degree of mutual influence varies a great deal from transaction to transaction. You probably would not be affected a great deal by a brief smile that you received from a traveling companion on a bus, but you would be greatly affected by your lover telling you he or she was leaving you. Sometimes interpersonal communication changes our lives dramatically, sometimes in small ways. Long-lasting interpersonal relationships are sustained not by one person giving and another taking, but by a spirit of mutual equality. Both you and your partner listen and respond with respect for each other. There is no attempt to manipulate others.

Buber's concept of an "I–Thou" relationship includes the quality of being fully "present" when communicating with another person.[11] To be present is to give your full attention to the other person. The quality of interpersonal communication is enhanced when both you and your partner are simultaneously present and focused on each other.

Interpersonal Communication Helps Individuals Manage Their Relationships

Question: What is neither you nor I, but always you and I? Answer: a relationship.[12] A **relationship** is a connection established when you communicate with another person. When two individuals are in a relationship, what one person says or does influences the other person. As in dancing, people in relationships are affected by the beat of the music (that is, the situation in which they are communicating), their ability to interpret the music and move accordingly (the personal skills they possess), and the moves and counter-moves of their partner.

You initiate and form relationships by communicating with others whom you find attractive in some way. You seek to increase your interactions with people with whom you wish to develop relationships, and you continually communicate interpersonally to maintain the relationship. You also use interpersonal communication to end or redefine relationships that you have decided are no longer viable or need to be changed. In summary, to relate to someone is to "dance" with them. We dance with them in a specific time and place, with certain perceptions and expectations. Over time, this dance becomes an ongoing interpersonal relationship.

relationship A connection established with another person through communication.

In this book, we define interpersonal communication as a unique form of human communication. There are other forms of communication, as well. **Mass communication** occurs when someone communicates the same message to many people at once, but the creator of the message is usually not physically present, and listeners have virtually no opportunity to respond immediately to the speaker. Messages communicated via radio and TV are examples of mass communication. **Public communication** occurs when a speaker addresses an audience in person. **Small group communication** occurs when a group of from three to fifteen people meet to interact with a common purpose and mutually influence one another. The purpose of the gathering could be to solve a problem, make a decision, learn, or just have fun. While communicating with others in a small group, it is also possible to communicate with others interpersonally—to communicate to manage a relationship with one or more individuals in the group. Finally, **intrapersonal communication** is communication with yourself. Thinking is perhaps the best example of intrapersonal communication. In our discussion of self and communication in Chapter 2, we discuss the relationships between your thoughts and your interpersonal communication with others.

In face-to-face encounters, we simultaneously exchange both verbal and nonverbal messages that result in shared meanings. Through this kind of interrelation, we build relationships with others.

Why Is Interpersonal Communication Important to Your Life?

Why learn about interpersonal communication? Because it touches every aspect of our lives. It is not only pleasant or desirable to develop quality interpersonal relationships with others, it is vital for our well-being. We have a strong need to communicate interpersonally with others. Learning how to understand and improve interpersonal communication can improve relationships with family, loved ones, friends, and colleagues and can enhance the quality of physical and emotional health.

Improved Relationships with Family

Relating to family members can be a challenge. The divorce statistics in the United States document the difficulties that can occur when people live in relationships with others: About half of all marriages end in divorce. We don't claim that you will avoid all family conflicts or that your family relationships will always be harmonious if you learn principles and skills of interpersonal communication. You can, however, develop more options for responding when family communication challenges come your way. You will be more likely to develop creative, constructive solutions to family conflict if you understand what's happening and can promote true dialogue with your spouse, partner, parent, brother, or sister. Furthermore, family relationships play a major role in determining how you interact with others. Family communication author Virginia Satir calls family communication "the largest single factor determining the kinds of relationships [people make] with others."[13] Being able to have conversations with family members and loved ones is the fundamental way of establishing close, personal relationships with them.

mass communication Process that occurs when one person issues the same message to many people at once; the creator of the message is usually not physically present, and there is virtually no opportunity for listeners to respond immediately to the speaker.

public communication Process that occurs when a speaker addresses an audience in person.

small group communication Process that occurs when a group of from three to fifteen people meet to interact with a common purpose and mutually influence one another.

intrapersonal communication Communication with yourself; thinking.

Improved Relationships with Friends and Lovers

For unmarried people, developing friendships and falling in love are the top-rated sources of satisfaction and happiness in life.[14] Conversely, losing a relationship is among life's most stressful events. Most people between the ages of 19 and 24 report that they have had from five to six romantic relationships and have been "in love" once or twice.[15] Studying interpersonal communication may not unravel all the mysteries of romantic love and friendship, but it can offer insight into behaviors.[16]

Improved Relationships with Colleagues

In many ways, colleagues at work are like family members. Although you choose your friends and lovers, you don't always have the same flexibility in choosing those with whom or for whom you work. Understanding how relationships develop on the job can help you avoid conflict and stress and increase your sense of satisfaction. In addition, your success or failure in a job often hinges on how well you get along with supervisors and peers.

Several surveys document the importance of quality interpersonal relationships in contributing to success at work.[17] The abilities to listen to others, manage conflict, and develop quality interpersonal relationships with others are usually at the top of the list of the skills employers seek in today's job applicants.[18]

Improved Physical and Emotional Health

Research has shown that the lack or loss of a close relationship can lead to ill health and even death. Physicians have long observed that patients who are widowed or divorced experience more medical problems such as heart disease, cancer, pneumonia, and diabetes than do married people.[19] Grief-stricken spouses are more likely than others to die prematurely, especially around the time of the departed spouse's birthday or near their wedding anniversary.[20] Being childless can also shorten one's life. One study found that middle-aged, childless wives were almost two-and-one-half times more likely to die in a given year than those who had at least one child.[21] Terminally ill patients with a limited number of friends or no social support die sooner than those with stronger ties.[22] Without companions and close friends, opportunities for intimacy and stress-minimizing interpersonal communication are diminished. Although being involved in intimate interpersonal relationships can lead to conflict and feelings of anger and frustration, researchers suggest that when all is said and done, having close relationships with others is a major source of personal happiness.[23] Studying how to enhance the quality of your communication with others can make life more enjoyable and enhance your overall well-being.[24]

Interpersonal Communication Myths

Although we've made impressive claims about the importance of interpersonal communication in enhancing our relationships and health, you shouldn't get the idea that interpersonal communication principles and skills are like a magic elixir that, when applied, will solve all relationship problems. That's unrealistic. There are benefits to learning about interpersonal communication and applying your knowledge, but there is no technique or set of skills that will cure *all* relational problems. That's a myth. As we embark on our study of interpersonal communication, it's just as important to unlearn some commonly held misconceptions as it is to learn research conclusions and time-tested principles of interpersonal communication. Don't believe the following myths about interpersonal communication.

More Words Will Make the Meaning Clearer

More is not necessarily better. Piling on more words when your interpersonal communication partner is already baffled by what you are talking about can make matters worse. There is a time to stop talking, take a calming breath, and just listen.

Meanings Are in Words

In and of itself, whether spoken or written, a word has no meaning. It's just a sound, marks on paper, or images on a computer screen. Other people provide the meaning to "connect the dots" between the words you've spoken and the meaning you intend to create. (Of course, sometimes people connect the dots in ways you had not intended.) Words are simply symbols we use to communicate with others. Remember, meanings are in people, not in words.

Information Equals Communication

"How many times do I have to tell you not to surf the Internet while you're on the job?" "Can't you read? It's in the syllabus." "Are you deaf? I've already told you that I love you a hundred times!" Each of these exasperated communicators seems to believe that information is the same thing as communication. But information is *not* communication. Presenting information doesn't make people "get" your meaning. Like the proverbial tree that falls silently in the forest because no one is there to hear it, a message is not necessarily communication just because you've expressed it.

Interpersonal Relationship Problems Are Always Communication Problems

"You don't understand me!" shouts Paul to his exasperated partner, Pat. "We just can't communicate anymore!" Paul seems to think that the problem he and Pat are having is a communication problem. But Paul and Pat may understand each other perfectly; they may simply disagree. Although it's certainly true that conflict and discord in interpersonal relationships can occur because of misunderstandings, not all conflict and bumpy relationships stem from misunderstandings. People can be self-centered or grumpy, or they may just disagree. The problem in the relationship may not be communication, but a non–other-oriented, self-absorbed communicator.

Studying interpersonal communication is undoubtedly a way to enhance the quality of your relationships with others. But it's not a magic cure-all for relationship woes. If you know unicorns don't exist, then you don't look for them. Knowing the myths of interpersonal communication can help you avoid unrealistic expectations about the virtues of mastering interpersonal communication principles and skills.

"Gary, we need to not talk."

▶ **RECAP** Interpersonal Communication Myths

Myth	Reality
More words will make the meaning clearer.	Sometimes it's best to stop talking, take a deep breath, and listen.
Meanings are in words.	Meanings are in people, not in words.
Information equals communication.	Information is not communication. Saying, writing, or expressing a thought or feeling doesn't mean someone else will make sense of the message merely because we've created it.
Interpersonal relationship problems are always communication problems.	We may understand what someone means but just disagree with them.

The Communication Process

Interpersonal communication involves more than simply transferring or exchanging messages; it is a complex process of creating meaning in the context of an interpersonal relationship. So that we can understand this process more fully, it is useful to see how perspectives on the human communication process have evolved over the past half century.[25] We will begin with the simplest and oldest model of the human communication process and then discuss more contemporary models.

Human Communication as Action: Message Transfer

"Did you get my message?" This simple sentence summarizes the communication-as-action approach to human communication. Communication takes place when a message is sent and received. Period. It is a way of transferring meaning from sender to receiver.

Figure 1.1 shows a basic model that depicts communication as a linear input/output process. Today, although they view the process as more complicated, researchers still define most of the key components in this model in basically the same way.

Source. The **source** for communication is the originator of a thought or an emotion, who expresses ideas and feelings as a code that can be understood by a receiver. Translating ideas, feelings, and thoughts into a code is called **encoding.** Vocalizing a word, gesturing, and establishing eye contact are signals that we use to encode our thoughts into a message that can be decoded by someone. **Decoding,** the opposite process of encoding, occurs when the words or unspoken signals are interpreted by the receiver.

Message. **Messages** are the written, spoken, and unspoken elements of communication to which people assign meaning. You can send a message intentionally (talking to a professor before class) or unintentionally (falling asleep during class); verbally ("Hi. How are you?"), nonverbally (a smile and a handshake), or in written form (this book).

Channel. A message is communicated from sender to receiver via some pathway called a **channel.** Channels correspond to your senses. When you call your mother on the telephone, the channel is an auditory one. When you talk with your mother face to

source Originator of a thought or emotion, who puts it into a code that can be understood by a receiver.

encode To translate ideas, feelings, and thoughts into code.

decode To interpret ideas, feelings, and thoughts that have been translated into a code.

message Written, spoken, and unspoken elements of communication to which people assign meaning.

channel Pathway through which messages are sent.

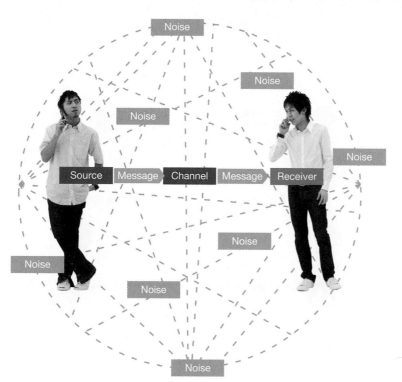

FIGURE 1.1

A Simple Model of Human Communication as Action

face, the channels are many. You see her: the visual channel. You hear her: the auditory channel. You may smell her perfume: the olfactory channel. You may hug her: the tactile channel. And when you're apart from your mom, tasting a warm, gooey cinnamon roll may trigger memories of her homemade treats.

Receiver. The **receiver** is the person who decodes and attempts to make sense of what the source encoded. Think of a radio station as a source broadcasting to a receiver that picks up the station's signal. In human communication, however, there is something in between the source and the receiver: People filter messages through past experiences, attitudes, beliefs, values, prejudices, and biases.

Noise. **Noise** is anything that interferes with a message and keeps it from being understood and achieving its intended effect. Without noise, all messages would be communicated with sublime accuracy. But noise is always present. It can be literal (the obnoxious roar of a neighbor's lawn mower), or it can be psychological (instead of concentrating on your teacher's lecture, you may start thinking about the chores you need to finish before the end of the day). Whichever kind it is, noise gets in the way of the message and may even distort it. Communicating accurate messages involves minimizing both external and psychological noise.

The action approach is simple and straightforward, but it has a key flaw: Human communication rarely, if ever, is as simple and efficient as "what we put in is what we get out." Others cannot automatically know what you mean just because you think you know what you mean. Although by the early 1940s, when the action approach was formulated, communication scholars had already begun identifying an array of key elements in the communication process, the action approach overlooked the complexity of those elements.

receiver Person who decodes a message and attempts to make sense of what the source has encoded.

noise Anything literal or psychological that interferes with accurate reception of a message.

FIGURE 1.2

A Model for Communication as Interaction

Interaction models of communication include feedback, as a response to a message sent by the communication source, and context, as the environment for communication.

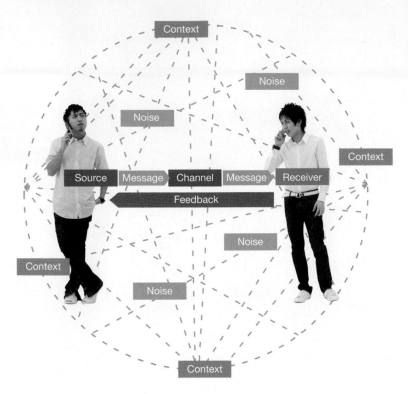

Human Communication as Interaction: Message Exchange

The communication-as-interaction perspective used the same elements as the action model but added two new ones: feedback and context.

Feedback is the response to the message. Think of a Ping-Pong game. Like a Ping-Pong ball, messages bounce back and forth. We talk; someone listens and responds; we listen and respond to this response. This perspective can be summarized using a physical principle: For every action, there is a reaction.

Without feedback, communication is rarely effective. When you order a black olive pizza and the server says in response, "That's a black olive pizza, right?" he has provided feedback to ensure that he decoded the message correctly. Like other messages, feedback can be intentional (your mother gives you a hug when you announce your engagement) or unintentional (you yawn as you listen to your uncle tell his story about bears again), verbal ("That's a black olive pizza, right?") or nonverbal (blushing after being asked to dance).

Context, a second component recognized by the interaction perspective, is the physical and psychological environment for communication. All communication takes place in some context. As the cliche goes, "Everyone has to be somewhere." A conversation on the beach with your good friend would likely differ from a conversation the two of you might have in a funeral home. Context encompasses not only the physical environment but also the number of people present and their relationships with the communicators, the communication goal, and the culture of which the communicators are a part.[26]

The communication-as-interaction perspective, as shown in Figure 1.2, is more realistic than the action perspective, but it still has limitations. Although it emphasizes feedback and context, it does not quite capture the complexity of interpersonal

feedback Response to a message.

context Physical and psychological environment for communication.

communication, which typically takes place simultaneously. The interaction model of communication still views communication as a linear, step-by-step process. But in interpersonal situations, both the source and the receiver send and receive messages at the same time.

Human Communication as Transaction: Message Creation

The communication-as-transaction perspective acknowledges that when you talk to another person face to face, you are constantly reacting to your partner's responses. Most scholars today view the transaction perspective as the most realistic model for interpersonal communication. Like action and interaction, transaction uses various components to describe communication. However, in this model, all the components are simultaneous. As Figure 1.3 indicates, you send and receive messages concurrently. Even as you talk, you are also interpreting your partner's nonverbal and verbal responses.

The transactional approach to communication is based on **systems theory.** A system is a set of interconnected elements in which a change in one element affects all of the other elements. Your body is an example of a system. Key aspects of any system include *inputs* (all of the variables that go in to the system), *throughputs* (which are all of the things that make communication a process), and *outputs* (what the system produces). Systems theory, from a communication perspective, helps us to understand the transactional nature of communication, in that a change in any aspect of the communication system (source, message, channel, receiver, context, feedback) has a potential influence on all of the other elements of the system. Viewing communication as action or interaction does not quite capture the complexity of the communication process as a systems or transactional process does. From a systems theory point of view, all of the elements of communication are connected to every other element of communication.

systems theory Theory that describes the interconnected elements of a system in which a change in one element affects all of the other elements.

FIGURE 1.3

A Model for Communication as Mutual Transaction

The source and receiver of a message experience communication simultaneously.

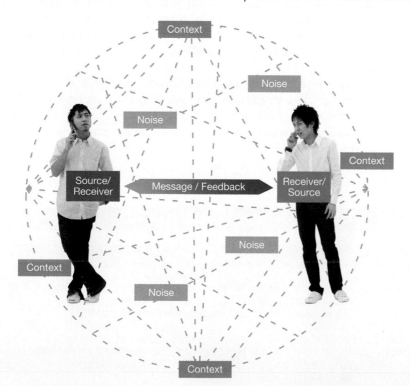

UNDERSTANDING OTHERS
Adapting to Differences   **The World Is Here**

One of our most visionary politicians said that he envisioned a time when the United States could become the brain of the world, by which he meant the repository of all the latest advanced information systems. I thought of that remark when an enterprising poet friend of mine called to say that he had just sold a poem to a computer magazine and that the editors were delighted to get it because they didn't carry fiction or poetry. Is that the kind of world we desire? A humdrum homogenous world of all brains but no heart, no fiction, no poetry; a world of robots with human attendants, bereft of imagination or culture. Or does North America deserve a more exciting destiny? To become a place where the cultures of the world crisscross. This is possible because the United States is unique in the world: The world is here.[27]

These words from Ishmael Reed's essay "The World Is Here" remind us that America is not a one-dimensional culture. You need not travel to far-off places to develop interpersonal relationships with people from other cultures, races, or ethnic backgrounds. America has long been known as a melting pot—a place where people from a variety of cultures and traditions have come together to seek their fortunes. Others think America is more like a tossed salad than a melting pot—in a salad, each ingredient retains its essential character rather than melting together to form a united whole. Focusing on communication and diversity means much more than focusing on cultural differences. Culture consists of the learned values, behaviors, and expectations shared by a group of people. It takes skill and sensitivity to develop quality interpersonal

relationships with others whose religion, race, ethnicity, age, gender, or sexual orientation differs from your own. Throughout the text, we include boxes like this one to help you develop your sensitivity to important issues related to cultural diversity. As you embark on your study of interpersonal communication, consider these questions, either individually or with a group of your classmates:

1. What are the implications of this melting pot or tossed salad culture for your study of interpersonal communication?

2. Is there too much emphasis on being politically correct on college campuses today? Support your answer.

3. What specific interpersonal skills will help you communicate effectively with others from different cultural and ethnic traditions?

A transactional approach to communication suggests that no single cause explains why you interpret messages the way you do. In fact, it is inappropriate to point to a single factor to explain how you are making sense of the messages of others; communication is messier than that. The meaning of messages in interpersonal relationships evolves from the past, is influenced by the present, and is affected by visions of the future.

One researcher says that interpersonal communication is "the coordinated management of meaning" through **episodes,** sequence of interactions between individuals during which the message of one person influences the message of another.[28] Technically, only the sender and receiver of those messages can determine where one episode ends and another begins.

episode Sequence of interactions between individuals, during which the message of one person influences the message of another.

▶ RECAP   An Evolving Model for Interpersonal Communication

Human Communication as Action

Human communication is linear, with meaning sent or transferred from source to receiver.

Human Communication as Interaction

Human communication occurs as the receiver of the message responds to the source through feedback. This interactive model views communication as a linear action–reaction sequence of events within a specific context.

Human Communication as Transaction

Human communication is mutually interactive. Meaning is created based on a concurrent sharing of ideas and feelings. This transaction model most accurately describes human communication.

Electronically Mediated Interpersonal Communication

Can you really communicate *interpersonally* with people on the Internet without meeting them face to face (FtF)? Yes, of course. You probably communicate this way every day, to both initiate and maintain relationships. When you use a medium such as a cell phone or the Internet to carry your message, you are using **electronically mediated communication (EMC)**. When you go on Facebook or text friends and family members, you are using one of the most ubiquitous communication tools you have for maintaining relationships. And with social networking applications such as Twitter now available on cell phones, you have quite sophisticated EMC technology at your fingertips wherever you go. The title of a book by Naomi Baron summarizes the impact of EMC on our lives: Because of EMC we're *Always On*.[29] We use technology to make and keep friends, to self-disclose, to "listen" and respond to and confirm and support others, and to coordinate other interactions. There is evidence that some EMC relationships can be as satisfying as face-to-face relationships.[30] That's why throughout this book we'll discuss research findings about EMC as well as face-to-face interpersonal communication. The new media have a major impact on your real-life relationships.

Comparing Electronically Mediated Communication with Face-to-Face Communication

Mediated communication is not new; people have been communicating without being face to face for centuries; sending letters and other written messages to others is an age-old human way of relating to others. And even before written communication was widespread, humans used smoke signals and drum beats to communicate via long distances. What's new today is that there are so many different ways of *immediately* connecting with someone, such as using a cell phone, social networking applications (such as MySpace, Facebook, and LinkedIn), text messages, e-mail, instant messaging, video messages on YouTube, or a host of other Internet-based ways of developing and maintaining interpersonal relationships. Just a few years ago, e-mail was the hot new way of connecting; then there was instant messaging (IM). There is evidence that these two technologies are declining in use. As we enter the second decade of the twenty-first century, texting from phones or BlackBerrys, as well as connecting via Twitter, Facebook, and MySpace, are among the most popular EMC technologies.

We use EMC to share information that ranges from the dramatic to the routine. By mid-2007, over 70 percent of Americans actively used the Internet (compared to just under 40 percent of Europeans).[31] And we're taking our BlackBerrys and phones with us; more people in the United States have mobile phones than land line phones.[32] We've also dramatically increased our use of text messages. Just a few years ago, in 2006, Americans sent 158 billion text messages, double the number sent in 2005. And the numbers continue to grow: As of 2009, 125 million people were on MySpace or Facebook, 18 million of whom were using these applications on their cell phones.[33]

How is electronically mediated interpersonal communication different from live, face-to-face conversations? There are six key differences, which have to do with (1) time, (2) varying degrees of anonymity, (3) potential for deception, (4) nonverbal cues, (5) role of the written word, and (6) distance.[34]

Time. When you interact with others using EMC, you can do so asynchronously. An **asynchronous message** is a message that is not read, heard, or seen at the same time it is sent; there is a time delay between when you send such a message and when someone

electronically mediated communication (EMC)
Communication that is not face to face, but rather is sent via a medium such as a cell phone or the Internet.

asynchronous message A message that is not read, heard, or seen exactly when it is sent; there is a time delay between the sending of the message and its receipt.

else receives it. A text message sent to a friend's phone or to someone who is not monitoring Facebook or a voicemail message are examples of asynchronous messages.

Synchronous messages are those that are sent and received instantly and simultaneously. Face-to-face conversations are synchronous—there is no time delay between when you send a message and when the other person receives it. A video conference is another example of a synchronous message.

The more synchronous an interaction, the more similar it is to face-to-face interactions. The more a technology simulates a face-to-face conversation, the more social presence it creates. **Social presence** is the feeling we have when we act and think as if we're involved in an unmediated, FtF conversation. Technically, there is always some delay in sending and receiving messages (even in FtF interactions, sound takes time to travel). The key distinction among different forms of EMC and the degree of social presence we experience is whether we *feel* we are in a synchronous interaction. When we send text messages back and forth, or instant-message, we create a shared sense of social or psychological co-presence with our partners. Receiving a Twitter message from a friend letting us know what he or she is doing at that moment gives us the feeling of being instantly connected to that person.

Another time difference between EMC and FtF messages is that it takes longer to tap out a typewritten message than to speak or to convey a nonverbal message. The amount of delay (which corresponds to silence in FtF interactions) can have an impact on the interpretation of a message's meaning. When texting, participants may expect to see a response to their message very quickly. This is one reason text messages are often very short and concise. (Another reason is that it can be tricky to type on smaller keyboards with your thumbs—although some people are quite adept at using tiny keyboards.) A rapid succession of short messages fosters a sense of synchronicity and social presence.

Texting someone allows you time to compose your message and craft it more carefully than you might in an FtF interaction. As a sender of text messages, you have more control over what you say and the impression you create; as the receiver of Internet messages, you no doubt realize that the other person has had the chance to shape his or her message carefully for its greatest impact on you.

Varying Degrees of Anonymity. Maybe you've seen the cartoon of a mutt sitting at a computer and saying to his companion, "On the Internet, nobody knows you're a dog." The cartoon canine communicator has a point: You may not always know precisely with whom you are communicating when you receive an e-mail message or are "friended" or "poked" by someone you don't know. When you are friending someone on Facebook, that person may not know precisely who you are. (One study found seventeen Karl Marxes, four Anne Boleyns, seven Kermit the Frogs, and three people named Socrates of Athens who had Facebook pages.)[35] Because you can be anonymous and there is less chance that anyone will find out who you are, you may say things that are bolder, more honest, or even more outrageous than you would if your audience knew who you were. And being anonymous may also tempt you to say things that aren't true. Yet many of the EMC messages you send and receive are from people you know. So there are varying degrees of anonymity, depending on the technology that you are using and how honest you and your communication partners are.

Potential for Deception. Because with many forms of EMC you can't see or hear others, it's easy to lie. Here's evidence that people are deceptive when using EMC: A survey of 191 students at one college found that 40 percent had lied on the Internet: 15 percent about their age, 8 percent about their weight, 6 percent about appearance, 6 percent about marital status, and 3 percent about what sex they were.[36]

synchronous message
A message that is sent and received simultaneously.

social presence The feeling that communicators have of engaging in unmediated, face-to-face interactions even though messages are being sent electronically.

Online deception is almost as easy as typing. We say "almost," because you *can* assess the content of a written message for clues to deceit. In a study by Katherine Cornetto, college student respondents reported the most common indicator of deception was someone's implausible statement or bragging.[37] As friendships develop over the Internet, to detect deception people come to depend on personal knowledge and impressions of their partners acquired over the course of their correspondence.[38] Interestingly, Cornetto's study also found that those who reported lying most were the people most likely to suspect other users of lying.[39] The ease with which someone can create a false persona means that you need to be cautious in forming relationships with strangers over the Internet.

Nonverbal Cues. Words and graphics become more important in EMC than in FtF communication, because when communicating electronically you must rely solely on words to carry nonverbal messages. Of course, a YouTube video does include nonverbal messages, but even on YouTube some cues may be limited, such as the surrounding context and reactions from others.

There are some basic things text users do to add emotion to their messages, including CAPITALIZING THE MESSAGE (which is considered "yelling"), making letters **bold,** and inserting emoticons—a smiley face :-), a frowning face with glasses 8-(, and so on. In FtF communication, we laugh and smile in direct response to what we or others are saying. In the EMC context, we use emoticons to provide emotional punctuation in our written messages. There are predictable places where we place a smiley face or a frowning face to underscore something we've just written.[40] The ability to tease or make sarcastic remarks is limited with EMC, because there is no tone of voice in the written message—so emoticons must provide information about the intended emotional tone of what is written. You can also write out an accompanying interpretation—for example, "Boy, am I insulted by that! (just kidding)" to compensate for the limited emotional cues.

There is also typically less emphasis on a person's physical appearance online than in FtF situations, unless you're using MySpace or Facebook. In those forums, not only does your appearance help determine how others react to you, but one study found that the physical attractiveness or unattractiveness of your "friends" rubs off on you. If you have friends who are perceived as attractive, you will be perceived as more popular and attractive.[41]

Role of the Written Word. The reliance on the written word also affects EMC interactions. One online scholar suggests that a person's typing ability and writing skills affect the quality of any relationship that is developed.[42] Not everyone is able to encode thoughts quickly and accurately into written words. Not only do writing skills affect your ability to express yourself and manage relationships, they also affect how others perceive you. Your written messages provide insights to others about your personality, skills, sense of humor, and even your values. Consider the following two text messages and think about the impressions you form of the two authors.

Parr: "Hey, babe, whaddup? no what im thinking now we shuld do?"

Chuck: "Hello, Ashley. I have been thinking about some options for our evening's entertainment."

What's your impression of the two texters? What affected your impression? The first example is filled with grammar and spelling shortcuts that might create a negative

People use electronically mediated communication (EMC) to share information that ranges from the dramatic to the routine. EMC can create a shared sense of social or psychological presence between two people, giving them the feeling of being instantly connected to each other.

impression because the author is not particularly skilled at writing—or you might have a positive reaction because you think the author is cool and contemporary. The second author uses correct grammar and spelling, which may produce a positive impression, yet (because text messages are typically brief and casual) you may think author number two is a nerd, or at least older and more traditional. You communicate a message about the nature of a relationship based on the formality or informality of language used and whether your style reflects what the receiver expects.

Distance. Although we certainly can and do send text messages to people who live and work in the same building we're in (or even the same room), there is typically greater physical distance between people who are communicating using EMC. When using the Internet or a cell phone, we can just as easily send a text or a video message to someone on the other side of the globe as we can someone who is on the other side of the room.

In addition to these six differences between EMC and FtF messages, there are questions about who is more likely to use EMC messages. For example, researchers have asked whether people who spend a lot of time online generally have more or less personal contact with other people. A team of researchers led by Robert Kraut and Sara Kiesler made headlines when they published the results of their study, which concluded that the more people use the Internet, the less they will interact with others in person.[43] The researchers also found a correlation between people saying they were lonely and using the Internet. But other research contradicts this finding: Two follow-up studies found that people who use the Internet are more likely to have a greater number of friends, are more involved with community activities, and overall have greater levels of trust in other people. The most recent research seems to suggest that for some people—those who are already prone to being shy or introverted—there may be a link between Internet use and loneliness or feelings of social isolation. However, their isolation may not be because of their use of the Internet, but simply because they are less likely to make contact with others.[44] For those who are generally outgoing and who like to interact with others, the Internet is just another tool to reach out and make contact.

Increasingly people use EMC forums such as Facebook or MySpace not to substitute completely for FtF contact, but to enrich it. In fact, using EMC messages can result in relationships becoming more intimate in less time than they would through FtF interpersonal communication. Researchers have found that people develop hyperpersonal relationships using EMC. **Hyperpersonal relationships** are relationships formed primarily through EMC that become even *more personal* than equivalent face-to-face relationships, in part because of the absence of distracting external cues (such as physical qualities), an overdependence on just a few tidbits of personal information (which increases the importance of the information), and idealization of the partner.[45] Hyperpersonal relationships were first identified in a study in which pairs of students who were initially strangers interacted for up to an hour in a simulated instant-messaging situation, while another group of pairs met face to face for up to 15 minutes. Those in EMC interactions skipped the typical superficial getting-acquainted questions and used more direct questioning and disclosing with their partners.[46] Online pairs engaged in more intimate probes and responses and reached a similar level of understanding and ability to predict their partners' behaviors as those in FtF interactions.

A comprehensive study that investigated whether instant messages and text messages are more like speech or writing concluded that instant messages contain elements of both, but nonetheless differ from speech in grammar, style, syntax, and other

hyperpersonal relationship
A relationship formed primarily through electronically mediated communication that becomes more personal than an equivalent face-to-face relationship because of the absence of distracting external cues, smaller amounts of personal information, and idealization of the communication partner.

language factors. Text messages are more like writing than like spoken messages. There are also gender differences: Women's text and instant messages use more words, longer sentences, and more emoticons and discuss and include more social and relational information than men's messages.[47]

Understanding Electronically Mediated Communication

We've noted that EMC messages have both similarities to and differences from FtF messages. What theories and models of electronically mediated messages help us understand how relationships are developed and make predictions about how we will use EMC messages?

The communication models that we've presented (communication as action, interaction, and transaction) on pages 8–12 are certainly applicable to EMC. There are times when EMC is like the action model of communication. You post a message on a message board, blog, or Facebook wall and you get no immediate response from others. The communication is asynchronous—there's a time delay, so you're not really sure you've communicated with anyone. During some e-mail or text-message exchanges, your communication is more like the communication-as-interaction model; you send a text message and you wait for the response. There's a time delay, but sooner or later you get a response. And then there are instances when you can see and hear the other person simultaneously, such as in a live conversation with someone via a webcam—which is a synchronous interaction. In this instance the EMC resembles the transactional communication model, in that communicating this way is almost like being there in person because of the immediacy of the communication.

Three theories have been developed to further explain and predict how EMC works.

Cues-Filtered-Out Theory. One early theory of communication via the Internet was called **cues-filtered-out theory.** This theory suggested that emotional expression is severely restricted when we communicate using only text messages; nonverbal cues such as facial expression, gestures, and tone of voice are filtered out. The assumption was that text messages were best used for brief, task-oriented communication, such as sharing information or asking questions; text messages were assumed to be less effective in helping people establish meaningful relationships with one another.[48] The cues-filtered-out-theory also suggests that because of the lack of nonverbal cues and other social information, we'll be less likely to use EMC to manage relationships because of its limited ability to carry emotional and relational information. Although Facebook and MySpace present photos and ample personal information, communication through those forums is still not as rich as an FtF conversation.

Media Richness Theory. Another theory helps us make predictions about which form of media we will use to send certain kinds of messages. We use different types of media depending on the richness of a medium—whether it allows us to express emotions and relational messages as well as send information. **Media richness theory** suggests that the richness of a communication channel is based on four criteria: (1) the amount of feedback that the communicator can receive, (2) the number of cues that the channel can convey and that can be interpreted by a receiver, (3) the variety of language that a communicator uses, and (4) the potential for expressing emotions and feelings.[49] Using these four criteria, researchers have developed a continuum of communication channels, from communication-rich to communication-lean. Figure 1.4 illustrates this continuum.

There is some evidence that those wishing to communicate a negative message, such as a message ending a relationship, may select a less rich communication medium—they may be more likely to send a letter or an e-mail rather than sharing the bad news face

cues-filtered-out theory Theory that suggests that communication of emotions is restricted when people send messages to others via e-mail or other electronic means because nonverbal cues such as facial expression and tone of voice are filtered out.

media richness theory Theory that identifies the richness of a communication medium based on the amount of feedback it allows, the number of cues receivers can interpret, the variety of language it allows, and the potential for emotional expression.

FIGURE 1.4

A Continuum of Communication-Rich and Communication-Lean Channels

Adapted from L. K. Trevino, R. L. Draft, and R. H. Lengel, "Understanding Managers' Media Choices: A Symbolic Interactionist Perspective." In *Organizations and Communication Technology,* edited by J. Fulk and C. Steinfield (Newbury Park, CA: Sage, 1990), 71–94. Reprinted by permission of Sage Publications, Inc.

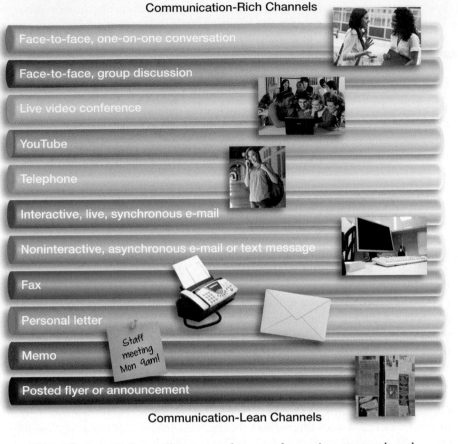

Communication-Rich Channels

- Face-to-face, one-on-one conversation
- Face-to-face, group discussion
- Live video conference
- YouTube
- Telephone
- Interactive, live, synchronous e-mail
- Noninteractive, asynchronous e-mail or text message
- Fax
- Personal letter
- Memo
- Posted flyer or announcement

Communication-Lean Channels

to face.[50] Similarly, people usually want to share good news in person, when they can enjoy the positive reaction to the message.

Both the cues-filtered-out theory and media richness theory suggest that the restriction of nonverbal cues, which provide information about the nature of the relationship between communicators, hampers the quality of relationships that can be established using EMC. But a newer perspective suggests that although EMC may communicate fewer relational cues, eventually we are able to discern relational information.

social information-processing theory Theory that suggests people can communicate relational and emotional messages via the Internet, although such messages take longer to express without nonverbal cues.

Social Information-Processing Theory.

Social information-processing theory suggests that we *can* communicate relational and emotional messages via the Internet, *but it may take longer* to express messages that are typically communicated

with facial expressions and tone of voice. A key difference between face-to-face and computer-mediated communication is the *rate* at which information reaches you. During an in-person conversation, you process a lot of information quickly; you process the words you hear as well as the many nonverbal cues you see (facial expression, gestures, and body posture) and hear (tone of voice and the use of pauses). During text-only interactions, there is less information to process (no audio cues or visual nonverbal cues), so it take a bit longer for the relationship to develop—but it does develop as you learn more about your partner's likes, dislikes, and feelings.

Relating to Others in the 21st Century — Text Me

Nobody is txting me
Im troubld & im stressd
Wen no one even thinks of me
It makes me feel dpressd[51]

You don't need a textbook to tell you that texting is an important way to keep in touch with others. Like the author of the above poem, you may even feel stress if you're not receiving an e-bushel basket full of text messages. At the end of the first decade of the twenty-first century, text messages may be the most ubiquitous way of interacting with others who are not physically present. One study found that 80 percent of people under 25 tended to text rather than phone a friend and leave a short message.[52] Texting is a worldwide practice, in part because in most countries it's much cheaper to text than to call someone on the phone. According to Cheil Communications, in 2006 over 93 percent of teenagers in Britain between the ages of 17 and 19 sent or received at least one text message per day.[53] In Norway, even just a few years ago, more than 85 percent of teens and young adults (up to about age 25) sent text messages every day.[54] Faye Siytangco, a young sales representative from the Philippines, said she wasn't surprised to see people bowing their heads at a funeral for a friend's father. But she was shocked when she realized they weren't bowing in prayer, but were texting their friends. According to contemporary Philippine custom, texting while something else important is going on is not a breach of etiquette; it's just what people do now.[55]

Texting seems to be more for the young. Research has found that only 2.7 percent of people over the age of 67 send a text message a day.[56] Statistics also tell us about the kind of messages you are likely to text someone. Women tended to write longer text messages, to use more emoticons, to use more formal salutations ("Dear Mark") and farewell statements ("Sincerely, Sue"), and to write more grammatically complex messages than men.[57]

Why are so many people, especially young people, communicating via text messages? If you frequently send text messages, you can answer the question yourself: It's fast, cheap, easy, and always available. There's no need to open a laptop or be near a computer. And you don't have to worry about playing "telephone tag"—the recipient will read and respond to your message when he or she has time. And there's no need for small talk—text messaging lends itself to getting to the point.

Here's one set of text etiquette rules that have been posted on the Internet.[58]

Don't text when you're with someone else, without apologizing.

Don't text if you've had too much to drink.

Don't text while driving.

Don't say anything in text you wouldn't say in person.

Don't send bad news by text.

Norman Silver wrote ten "txt commandments" that humorously summarize the power and influence of text messages in his life:

U shall luv ur mobil fone with all ur hart.

U & ur fone shall neva b apart.

U shall nt lust aftr ur neibrs fone nor thiev.

U shall be prepard @ al times 2 tXt & 2 recv.

U shall use LOL & othr acronyms in conversatns.

U shall be zappy with ur ast*r*sks & exclmatns!!

U shall abbrevi8 & rite words like thyr sed.

U shall nt speak 2 sum 1 face2face if u cn msg em insted.

U shall nt shout with capitls XEPT IN DIRE EMERGNCY.

U shall nt consult a ninglish dictnry.[59]

Research evidence suggests that you will keep texting. It's cheap, easy, convenient, and it keeps you in touch with others. But don't forget the joys of having a good face-to-face conversation with someone now and then.

Social information-processing theory also suggests that if you expect to communicate with your electronic communication partner again, you will likely pay more attention to the relationship cues—expressions of emotions that are communicated directly (as when someone writes "I'm feeling bored today") or indirectly (as when an e-mail recipient responds to your long chatty e-mail with only a sentence, which suggests he or she may not want to spend much time "talking" today).

In one study that supported social-information processing theory, communication researchers Joseph Walther and Judee Burgoon found that the kinds of relationships that developed between people who met face to face differed little from those between people who had computer-mediated interactions.[60] The general stages and patterns of communication were evident in both face-to-face and e-mail relationships. But over time, the researchers found that the computer-mediated communication actually developed into *more* socially rich relationships than face-to-face communication did. This finding reinforces the hypothesis that relationship cues *are* present in computer-mediated communication. It also supports the notion that we develop hyperpersonal relationships via EMC. So even though it may take more time for relationships to develop online, they can indeed develop and can be just as satisfying as relationships nurtured through face-to-face conversation.

Research suggests that when using EMC, we ask questions and interact with others to enhance the quality of our relationship with them. A study by W. Scott Sanders found that people who communicated via Facebook enhanced the nature of the relationship and reduced their uncertainty about others by asking questions based on information that was already present on the other person's Facebook page.[61] Lisa Tidwell and Joseph Walther found that people in computer-mediated conversations asked more direct questions, which resulted in people's revealing more information about themselves when online.[62] The pattern of differences between computer-mediated communication and face-to-face communication is still being explored as computer-mediated communication becomes an even more significant part of contemporary life.

In summary, we believe that EMC makes it possible for people to develop interpersonal relationships with others, whether they are miles away or in the next room. Walther and Tidwell use the "information superhighway" metaphor to suggest that EMC is not just a road for moving data from one place to another, but a boulevard where people pass each other, occasionally meet, and decide to travel together. You can't see very much of other drivers unless you do travel together for some time. There are highway bandits, to be sure, who are not what they appear to be—one must drive defensively—and there are conflicts and disagreements when traveling, just as there are in "off-road," or face-to-face, interactions.[63]

▶ RECAP   Theories of Electronically Mediated Communication

Theory	Description
Cues-Filtered-Out Theory	The communication of emotion and relationship cues is restricted in e-mail or text messages because nonverbal cues, such as facial expression and tone of voice, are filtered out.
Media Richness Theory	The richness or amount of information a communication medium has is based on the amount of feedback it permits, the number of cues in the channel, the variety of language used, and the potential for expressing emotions.
Social Information-Processing Theory	Emotional and relationship messages can be expressed via electronic means, although such messages take longer to be communicated without the immediacy of nonverbal cues.

Principles of Interpersonal Communication

As we introduce the study of interpersonal communication in this chapter, it is useful to present fundamental principles that help explain its nature. Underlying our current understanding of interpersonal communication are five principles: Interpersonal communication connects us to others, is irreversible, is complicated, is governed by rules, and involves both content and relationship dimensions.

Interpersonal Communication Connects Us to Others

Unless you are a living in a cave or have become a cloistered monk, you interact with others every day. We agree with author H. D. Duncan, who said, "We do not relate and then talk, but relate in talk." Fundamental to an understanding of interpersonal communication is the assumption that the quality of interpersonal relationships stems from the quality of communication with others. It's been said—and we noted earlier—that people can't *not* communicate. Because people often don't intend to express ideas or feelings, this perspective is debated among communication scholars. However, there is no question that interpersonal communication is inescapable in the twenty-first century.

The ever-present nature of interpersonal communication doesn't mean others will *accurately* decode your messages; it does mean that others draw inferences about you and your behavior—inferences that may be right or may be wrong. Even as you silently stand in a crowded elevator, your lack of eye contact with others communicates your unwillingness to interact with fellow passengers. Your unspoken messages, even when you are asleep, provide cues that others interpret. Remember: *People judge you by your behavior, not your intent.* Your interpersonal communication is how you develop connections to others. Even in well-established interpersonal relationships, you may be evoking an unintended response by your behavior.

Interpersonal Communication Is Irreversible

"Disregard that last statement made by the witness," instructs the judge. Yet the clever lawyer knows that once her client has told the jury that her husband gave her a black eye during an argument, the client cannot really "take it back," and the jury cannot really disregard it. This principle applies to all forms of communication. We may try to modify the meaning of a spoken message by saying something like "Oh, I really didn't mean it." But in most cases, the damage has been done. Once created, communication has the physical property of matter; it can't be uncreated. As the helical model in Figure 1.5 suggests, once interpersonal communication begins, it never loops back on itself. Instead, it continues to be shaped by the events, experiences, and thoughts of the communication partners. A Russian proverb nicely summarizes the point: "Once a word goes out of your mouth, you can never swallow it again."

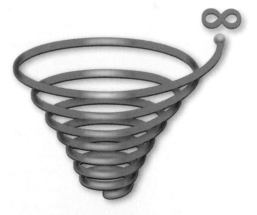

FIGURE 1.5

Interpersonal Communication Is Irreversible

This helical model shows that interpersonal communication never loops back on itself. Once it begins, it expands infinitely as the communication partners contribute their thoughts and experiences to the exchange.

Copyright © F. E. X. Dance in *Human Communication Theory* (Holt, Rinehart and Winston, 1967), 294. Reprinted with permission.

Interpersonal Communication Is Complicated

No form of communication is simple. If any were, we would know how to reduce the number of misunderstandings and conflicts in our world. Because of the variables involved in interpersonal exchanges, even simple requests are extremely complex. Life holds much uncertainty; there are many things we do not know. One of the purposes of communication, according to communication theorists, is to reduce our uncertainty.[64] The process of sharing information and asking questions helps us reduce our uncertainty about what is happening at any given moment. Communication theorists have noted that whenever you communicate with another person, there are really at least six "people" involved: (1) who you think you are; (2) who you think the other person is; (3) who you think the other person thinks you are; (4) who the other person thinks he or she is; (5) who the other person thinks you are; and (6) who the other person thinks you think he or she is.[65] Whew! And when you add more people to the interaction, it becomes even more involved.

Moreover, when humans communicate, they interpret information from others as symbols. A **symbol** is a word, sound, or visual image that represents something else, such as a thought, concept, or object; it can have various meanings and interpretations. Language is a system of symbols. In English, symbols do not resemble the objects they represent. The word (symbol) for *cow* does not look at all like a cow; someone, somewhere, decided that *cow* should mean a beast that chews its cud and gives milk. The reliance on symbols to communicate poses a communication challenge; you are often misinterpreted. Sometimes you don't know the code. Only if you are up to date on contemporary slang will you know, for example, that "fo' shizzle" means "certainly," "wikidemia" is a term paper entirely researched on Wikipedia.org, and "brodown" is a boys' night out.

Messages are not always interpreted as we intend them. Osmo Wiio, a Scandinavian communication scholar, points out the messiness of communicating with others when he suggests the following maxims:

If communication can fail, it will.

If a message can be understood in different ways, it will be understood in just that way which does the most harm.

There is always somebody who knows better than you what you meant by your message.

The more communication there is, the more difficult it is for communication to succeed.[66]

Although we are not as pessimistic as Professor Wiio, we do suggest that the task of understanding each other is challenging.

Interpersonal Communication Is Governed by Rules

According to communication researcher Susan Shimanoff, a **rule** is a "followable prescription that indicates what behavior is obligated, preferred, or prohibited in certain contexts."[67] The rules that help define appropriate and inappropriate communication in any given situation may be *explicit* or *implicit*. For your interpersonal communication class, explicit rules are probably spelled out in your syllabus. But your instructor has other rules that are more implicit. They are not written or verbalized, because you learned them long ago: Only one person speaks at a time, you raise your hand to be called on, you do not send text messages during class.

Interpersonal communication rules are developed by the people involved in the interaction and by the culture in which the individuals are communicating. Many times, we learn communication rules from experience, by observing and interacting with others.

symbol Word, sound, or visual image that represents something else, such as a thought, concept, or object.

rule Followable prescription that indicates what behavior is obligated, preferred, or prohibited in certain contexts.

British researcher Michael Argyle and his colleagues asked people to identify general rules for relationship development and maintenance and then rate their importance. The study yielded the following most important rules:[68]

Respect each other's privacy.

Don't reveal each other's secrets.

Look the other person in the eye during conversation.

Don't criticize the other person publicly.

Although we may modify rules to achieve the goals of our relationships, and although there may be cultural differences, these general rules remain fairly constant. The rules of interpersonal relationships are mutually defined and agreed on. Most of us don't like to be told what to do or how to behave all the time. Expectations and rules are continually renegotiated as the relationship unfolds. Few of us learn relationship rules by copying them from a book. Most of us learn these rules from experience, through observing and interacting with family members and friends. Individuals who grow up in environments in which these rules are not observed may not know how to behave in close relationships.

For many of us, friendships are vital to our personal well-being. By improving our interpersonal communication skills, we can learn how to improve our friendships.

Interpersonal Communication Involves Both Content and Relationship Dimensions

What you say (your words) and how you say it (your tone of voice, amount of eye contact, facial expression, and posture) can reveal much about the true meaning of your message. If one of your roommates loudly and abruptly bellows, "HEY, DORK! CLEAN THIS ROOM!" and another roommate uses the same verbal message but more gently and playfully says, "Hey, dork. Clean this room," both are communicating a message aimed at achieving the same outcome. But the two messages have different relationship cues. The shouted message suggests that roommate number one may be frustrated that the room is still full of leftovers from last night's pizza party, whereas roommate number two's teasing request suggests he or she may be fondly amused by your untidiness. What you say and how you say it provide information not only about content but also about the relationship you have with the other person.

Content Message.   The **content** of a communication message consists of the information, ideas, or suggested action that the speaker wishes to share. You may think that your messages to others are primarily about content, but that's not the whole story. You also provide clues about your relationship with others.

Relationship Message.   The **relationship dimension** of a communication message is usually more implied; it offers cues about the emotions, attitudes, and amount of power and control the speaker feels with regard to the other person. This distinction between the content of a message (what is said) and relationship cues (how the message is expressed) explains why reading a transcript of what someone said can seem to reveal quite a different meaning from actually hearing the person say the message.

Metacommunication Message.   Because messages have both content and relationship dimensions, one dimension can modify or even contradict the other dimension.

content Information, ideas, or suggested actions that a speaker wishes to share.

relationship dimension The implied aspect of a communication message, which conveys information about emotions, attitudes, power, and control.

metacommunication Verbal or nonverbal communication about communication.

mood A conscious, subjective state of mind.

emotional contagion The process whereby people mimic the emotions of others after watching and hearing their emotional expressions.

Communication theorists have a word that describes how we can communicate about our communication: metacommunication. Stated in the simplest way, **metacommunication** is communication about communication, and it can be nonverbal or verbal. Accurately decoding unspoken or verbalized metamessages helps you understand what people really mean and can help you "listen between the lines" of what someone is expressing.

You can express an idea nonverbally (for example, by smiling to communicate that you are pleased), and you can also express your positive feeling verbally (for example, by saying, "I'm happy to be here"). But sometimes your nonverbal communication can contradict your verbal message. You can say "Oh, that's just great" and use your voice to provide relational cues that express just the opposite of what the verbal content of the message means. The sarcasm communicated by the tone of your voice (a relationship cue) modifies the meaning of your verbal message (the content of your message).

Communication and Emotion

The Role of Emotions in Our Relationships with Others

Emotions don't literally come from our hearts, yet for thousands of years poets, authors, and songwriters in Western culture have identified the heart as a metaphor for the source of human emotions. (In some cultures, it's the liver rather than the heart that serves as a metaphorical source of emotions. But to us Westerners, this just doesn't sound right, does it?) Perhaps it's because the human heart is vital for survival that it has become an important metaphor for our emotions: If it stops beating, we die. Similarly, without experiencing emotions, we are not truly alive. And our emotions are related to everything—from how fast our heart beats to the intensity of our blood pressure and our breathing. Throughout this book we highlight the importance of emotion in a feature called Communication and Emotion.

What is emotion? How do emotions work? Precisely what causes us to experience emotions? There are various theories, but scholars don't agree on any one specific answer to each of these questions. One researcher described an emotion as a biological, cognitive, behavioral, and subjective affective reaction to an event.[69] A closer look at that definition suggests that an emotional reaction includes four things: biological or physiological reactions (heart rate increases, changes in breathing); cognitive responses (angry thoughts, happy thoughts); behavioral reactions to our thoughts and feelings (frowning, laughing); and subjective affective responses (either mild or strong experiences of joy, panic, anger, pleasure, and the like).[70]

How does an emotion differ from a mood? **Moods** are typically longer lasting than emotions, and a mood often doesn't have a single, specific, identifiable cause. You can be in a bad mood or good mood and not know precisely why you're feeling the way you're feeling. Sometimes you can pinpoint what has put you in a particular mood, but it's often several things, not just one, that determine your mood.

Your emotions and your moods play an important role in how you communicate with others. To provide an introduction to the role emotions play in our relationships, consider the following general principles:

We are more likely to discuss our emotions in an *interpersonal* **relationship than in an** *impersonal* **relationship.** Research supports our common intuition: We are more likely to talk about our personal feelings with people we know, care about, and feel a unique relationship with (friends, lovers, and family members) than with people we don't know or don't particularly care about.[71]

We express our emotions both verbally and nonverbally, yet our nonverbal messages often communicate our emotions more honestly. We sometimes explicitly tell people how we are feeling ("I'm feeling sad," "I'm angry with you," or "I love you"). But it's often through our nonverbal behavior (facial expression, tone of voice, or body posture) that our true feelings are communicated to others. We'll explore the role of nonverbal communication and emotion in greater detail in Chapter 7.

Our culture influences our emotional expression. It may seem that we express our feelings of happiness, joy, or sadness spontaneously, yet there is evidence that we often learn what is and is not appropriate in expressing emotions.[72] The culture in which we were raised has a major influence on how we learn to both express emotions and respond to emotions expressed by others. In Western cultures, for example, males are sometimes encouraged not to express emotions ("Boys don't cry"). One study found that Japanese students express fewer negative emotions than American students.[73]

Emotions are contagious. When you watch a funny movie in a crowded movie theatre, you are more likely to laugh when other people around you laugh (that's why TV shows sometimes have laugh tracks, to help people "catch" the humor). You are also more likely to cry when you see others experiencing sadness or pain. The process called **emotional contagion** occurs when we mimic the emotions of others after watching and hearing their emotional expression.[74] So being around positive, upbeat people can have an impact on your emotions. And, in turn, your emotional expression can affect others.

In summary, emotions include four things: biological/physiological reactions, cognitive responses, behavioral reactions to our thoughts and feelings, and subjective affective responses. To experience emotion is to experience life.

In addition to nonverbal cues, which provide communication about communication, you can also use words to explicitly talk about your message. For example, you can ask, "Is what I'm saying bothering you?" Your question is seeking information about the communication. We use metacommunication to check on how our message is being understood or to make sure we understand what someone else is saying. When you say, "I'm not sure what you said is clear to me," you are using a metamessage to help you better understand the communication; it's a metamessage because you are talking about your talk. Here's another example of verbal metacommunication: "I'd like to talk with you about the way we argue." Again, you are using communication to talk about communication. Talking about the way you talk can help clarify misunderstandings. Being aware of the metamessage, in both its verbal and its nonverbal forms, can help improve the accuracy of your interpretations of the meaning of message content as well as enhance the quality of your relationships with others.

Improving Your Interpersonal Communication Competence

Now that we have previewed the study of interpersonal communication, you may be saying to yourself, "Well, that's all well and good, but is it possible to improve my own interpersonal communication? Aren't some people just born with better interpersonal skills than others?" Just as some people have more musical talent or greater skill at throwing a football, evidence does suggest that some people may have an inborn, biological talent for communicating with others.[75]

A growing body of research on what is called the **communibiological approach** to communication suggests that some people inherit certain traits or characteristics that affect the way they communicate with others. There may be a genetic basis for why people communicate as they do.[76] For example, perhaps someone you know may be a born introvert, always shy, and thus have more stage fright or anxiety when communicating with others.[77] And some people may not be as comfortable interacting in interpersonal situations as others are.

So what are the implications of the communibiological approach to communication? Does it mean you can't improve your interpersonal communication? *Absolutely not!* Some researchers and teachers believe that the communibiological approach puts too much emphasis on biology and not enough on how we can learn to compensate for what nature did not give us.[78] The underlying premise of our study of interpersonal communication is that you can learn ways to enhance your interpersonal communication competence.

Social learning theory suggests that we can learn how to adapt and adjust our behavior toward others; how we behave is not solely dependent on our genetic makeup. By observing and interacting with others (hence the term *social* learning), we discover that we can adapt and adjust our behavior.[79] Although biology unquestionably plays a key role in how we behave, we can't blame biology for all aspects of our behavior. We believe that people can learn how to enhance their communication competence.

To be a competent communicator is to communicate in ways that are perceived to be both *effective* and *appropriate*.[80] You communicate effectively when your message is understood by others and achieves its intended effect. For example, if you want your roommate to stop using your hair dryer, and after you talk to your roommate, he stops using your hair dryer, your message has been effective.

Competent communication should also be appropriate. By *appropriate*, we mean that the communicator should consider the time, place, and overall context of the message and should be sensitive to the feelings and attitudes of the listener. Who

communibiological approach
Theoretical perspective that suggests communication behavior can be predicted based on personal traits and characteristics that result from people's genetic or biological background.

social learning theory Theory of human behavior that suggests we can learn how to adapt and adjust our behavior toward others; how we behave is not solely dependent on our genetic or biological makeup.

determines what is appropriate? Communication scholar Mary Jane Collier suggests that competence is a concept based on privilege; to label someone as competent means that another person has made a judgment as to what is appropriate or inappropriate behavior. Collier asks the following questions: ". . . competence and acceptance for whom? Who decides the criteria? Who doesn't? Competent or acceptable on the basis of what social and historical context?"[81] What Collier points out is that we have to be careful not to insist on one approach (our own approach) to interpersonal communication competence. *There is no single best way to communicate with others.* There are, however, avenues that can help you become both more effective and more appropriate when communicating with others.[82] We suggest a two-part strategy for becoming a more competent communicator. First, competent communicators are knowledgeable, skilled, and motivated.[83] Second, they draw on their knowledge, skill, and motivation to become other-oriented.

Become Knowledgeable, Skilled, and Motivated

Become Knowledgeable. By reading this chapter, you have already begun improving your interpersonal communication competence. Effective communicators are knowledgeable. They know how communication works. They understand the components, principles, and rules of the communication process. As you read further in this book, you will learn theories, principles, concepts, and rules that will help you explain and predict how humans communicate interpersonally.

Understanding these things is a necessary prerequisite for enhancing your interpersonal effectiveness, but this kind of knowledge alone does not make you an effective communicator. You would not let someone fix your car's carburetor if he or she had only read a book. Knowledge must be coupled with skill. And we acquire skill through practice.

Become Skilled. Effective communicators know how to translate knowledge into action.[84] You can memorize the characteristics of a good listener but still not listen well. To develop skill requires practice and helpful feedback from others who can confirm the appropriateness of your actions.[85]

It has been suggested that learning a social skill is not much different from learning how to drive a car or operate a computer.[86] To learn any skill, you must break it down into subskills that you can learn and practice. "Hear it, see it, do it, correct it" is the formula that seems to work best for learning any new behaviors. In this book, we examine the elements of complex skills (such as listening), offer activities that let you practice the skills, and provide opportunities for you to receive feedback and correct your application of the skills.

Become Motivated.   Practicing skills requires work. You need to be motivated to use your knowledge and skill. You must want to improve, and you must have a genuine desire to connect with others if you wish to become a competent communicator. You may know people who understand how to drive a car and have the skill to drive, yet hesitate to get behind the wheel. Or maybe you know someone who took a course in public speaking but is reluctant to stand in front of a crowd. Similarly, someone may pass a test about interpersonal communication principles with flying colors, but unless that person is motivated to use those newfound skills, his or her interactions with others may not improve.

Become Other-Oriented

It's not always about you. Lucy Van Pelt, in the Peanuts cartoon on page 27, seems startled to learn that the world does not revolve around her. Perhaps you know some-

one like Lucy. Sometimes we may need someone like Linus to remind us that we're not the center of the universe. The signature concept for our study of interpersonal communication is the goal of becoming other-oriented in relationships. To be an other-oriented communicator is to consider the thoughts, needs, experiences, personality, emotions, motives, desires, culture, and goals of your communication partners, while still maintaining your own integrity. The choices we make in forming our messages, in deciding how best to express those messages, and in deciding when and where to deliver those messages will be made more effectively when we consider the other person's thoughts and feelings. *To emphasize the importance of being an other-oriented communicator, throughout this book we will offer sidebar comments and questions to help you apply the concept of being other-oriented to your own interpersonal relationships.*

Being other-oriented involves a conscious effort to consider the world from the point of view of those with whom you interact.[87] This effort occurs almost automatically when you are communicating with those you like or who are similar to you. Thinking about the thoughts and feelings of those you dislike or who are different from you is more difficult and requires more effort and commitment.

Sometimes, we are **egocentric communicators;** we create messages without giving much thought to the person who is listening. To be egocentric is to be self-focused and self-absorbed. Scholars of evolution might argue that our tendency to look out for Number One ensures the continuation of the human species and is therefore a good thing.[88] Yet, it is difficult to communicate effectively when we focus exclusively on ourselves. Research suggests that being egocentric is detrimental to developing healthy relationships with others.[89] If we fail to adapt our message to our listener, we may not be successful in achieving our intended communication goal. Other people can often perceive whether we're self-focused or other-oriented (especially if the person we're talking with is a sensitive, other-oriented communicator).

Are people more self-focused today than in the past? Sociologist Jean Twenge suggests that people today are increasingly more narcissistic (self-focused) than they have been in previous generations—she dubs today's narcissistic generation the "me generation." Her research found that "in the early 1950s, only 12 percent of teens aged 14 to 16 agreed with the statement 'I am an important person.' By the late 1980s, an incredible 80 percent—almost seven times as many—claimed they were important."[90] Using the Narcissistic Personality Inventory, an instrument designed to assess egocentrism and self-focus, Twenge and two of her colleagues found corroborating evidence for an increased self-focus among contemporary students.[91]

We may find ourselves speaking without considering the thoughts and feelings of our listener when we have a need to purge ourselves emotionally or to confirm our sense of self-importance, but doing so usually undermines our relationships with others. A self-focused communicator often alienates others. Research suggests

BEING Other-ORIENTED

Being other-oriented means focusing on the interests, needs, and goals of another person. Think about a person who is important to you—it could be a family member, close friend, lover, or colleague. Consider the other-oriented nature of the relationship you have with this person. Are there specific things you say, gifts you have given, or activities that you do with this person that demonstrate your focus on *his* or *her* interests, needs, and desires? What things does this person do that reflect his or her other-orientation toward you?

egocentric communicator
Person who creates messages without giving much thought to the person who is listening; a communicator who is self-focused and self-absorbed.

Building Your Skills · Practice Being Other-Oriented

At the heart of our study of interpersonal communication is the principle of becoming other-oriented. To be other-oriented means that you are aware of others' thoughts, feelings, goals, and needs and respond appropriately in ways that offer personal support. It does not mean that you abandon your own needs and interests or that you diminish your self-respect. To have integrity is to behave in a thoughtful, integrated way toward others while being true to your core beliefs and values. To be other-oriented is to have integrity; you don't just agree with others or give in to the demands of others in encounters with them.

Do you know a sycophant? A *sycophant* is a person who praises others only to manipulate emotions so that his or her needs are met. Sycophants may look as though they are focused on others, but their behavior is merely self-serving. A sycophant is not other-oriented. A person who is truly other-oriented is aware of the thoughts, feelings, and needs of others and then mindfully and honestly chooses to respond to those needs. To enhance your other-oriented awareness and skill takes practice. Throughout the book, we offer both principles and opportunities to practice the skill and mindset of being other-oriented.

To develop an awareness of being other-oriented with a communication partner, role-play the following interpersonal situations in two ways. First, role-play the scene as a communicator who is not other-oriented but rather self-focused. Then re-enact the same scene as a communicator who is other-oriented—someone who considers the thoughts and feelings of the other person while maintaining his or her own integrity.

Suggested situations:

- Return a broken DVD player to a department store salesperson.
- Correct a grocery store cashier who has scanned an item at the wrong price.
- Meet with a teacher who gave your son or daughter a failing grade.
- Ask your professor for a one-day extension on a paper that is due tomorrow.
- Ask someone for a donation to a worthy cause.
- Ask a professor for permission to get into a class that has reached its maximum enrollment.
- Accept an unappealing book as a gift from a friend.
- Remind your son or daughter that he or she needs to practice the cello.

that fortunately, almost by necessity, we adapt to our partner in order to carry on a conversation.[92]

How do you become other-oriented? Being other-oriented is really a collection of skills rather than a single skill. We devote considerable discussion throughout the book to developing this collection of essential communication skills, including being self-aware, being aware of others, using and interpreting verbal messages, using and interpreting nonverbal messages, and listening and responding to others.[93] Being empathic—able to experience the feelings and emotions of others—is especially important in becoming other-oriented. After listening to and empathizing with others, someone who is other-oriented is able to appropriately adapt messages to them.

To appropriately adapt messages to others is to be flexible. In this book, we do not identify tidy lists of sure-fire strategies that you can always use to win friends and influence people. The same set of skills is not effective in every situation, so other-oriented communicators do not assume that "one size fits all." Rather, they assess each unique situation and adapt their behavior to achieve the desired outcome. Adaptation includes such things as simply asking questions in response to a communication partner's disclosures, finding topics of mutual interest to discuss, selecting words and examples that are meaningful to our partner, and avoiding topics that we don't feel comfortable discussing with another person. Adapting messages to others does *not* mean that we tell them only what they want to hear; that would be unethical.

Other-oriented communicators are ethical. **Ethics** are the beliefs, values, and moral principles by which we determine what is right or wrong. To be an ethical communicator means to be sensitive to the needs of others, to give people choices rather than forcing them to act a certain way. Unethical communicators believe that they know what other people need, even without asking them for their preferences. As we

ethics The beliefs, values, and moral principles by which a person determines what is right or wrong.

discuss in Chapter 6, being manipulative and forcing opinions on others usually results in a climate of defensiveness. Effective communicators seek to establish trust and reduce interpersonal barriers, rather than erect them. Ethical communicators keep confidences; they keep private information that others wish to be kept private. They also do not intentionally decrease others' feelings of self-worth. Another key element in being an ethical communicator is honesty. If you intentionally lie or distort the truth, then you are not communicating ethically or effectively. Ethical communicators also don't tell people only what they want to hear. At the end of each chapter, in our Study Guide section, we pose ethical questions to help you explore the ethics of interpersonal relationships.

In addition to appropriately and ethically adapting to others, being other-oriented includes developing positive, healthy attitudes about yourself and others. In 1951, Carl Rogers wrote a pioneering book called *Client-Centered Therapy*, which transformed the field of psychotherapy. In it, Rogers explains how genuine positive regard for another person and an open supportive communication climate lay the foundation for trusting relationships. But Rogers did not invent the concept of developing a positive, healthy regard for others. The core principles of every religion and faith movement in the last 5000 years include a focus on the needs of others. Our purpose is certainly not to promote a specific religion or set of spiritual beliefs. What we suggest is that becoming other-oriented, as evidenced through knowledge, skill, and motivation, can enhance your interpersonal communication competence and the quality of your life.

APPLYING AN OTHER-ORIENTATION
to Being a Competent Interpersonal Communicator

To be a competent interpersonal communicator is to be an other-oriented communicator—to focus on the needs, interests, values, and behaviors of others while being true to your own principles and ethical credo. In this chapter we've previewed some of the knowledge, provided a rationale for being motivated to master interpersonal competencies, and offered a glimpse of the skills that enhance an other-orientation.

Knowledge. When you view communication as a transactive process rather than as a simplistic action or even an interactive process, you gain realistic insight into the challenge of communicating with others and the potential for misunderstandings. Knowing the messiness and dynamic nature of communication, as well as the various components of the process (source, message, channel, receiver, context, and feedback) can help you better diagnose communication issues in your own relationships and improve your ability to accurately decode the messages of others.

Motivation. Why learn how to be other-oriented? As we've noted, learning about interpersonal communication has the potential to enhance both the quality of your relationships with others and your health. Developing your skill and knowledge of interpersonal communication can enhance your confidence to improve your relationships with family members, friends, lovers, and colleagues.

Skill. To be competently other-oriented takes more than knowledge of the elements and nature of communication (although that's a good start), and more than a strong motivation to enhance your abilities. It takes skill. As you begin your study of interpersonal communication, you can be confident that in the chapters ahead you will learn how to listen, respond, use, and interpret verbal messages, express and interpret emotional meanings of messages, more accurately use and interpret nonverbal messages, manage conflict, and adapt to human differences. To be other-oriented is to have the knowledge, nurture the motivation, and develop the skill to relate to others in effective and ethical ways.

What Is Interpersonal Communication, Why Is It Important to Your Life, and What Communication Myths Should Be Dispelled?
(pages 2–7)

It is impossible *not* to communicate with others. In fact, human communication is at the core of our existence, in our daily interactions and the relationships we develop. Human communication can be seen as a continuum, with impersonal communication on one end, which treats people as objects, and interpersonal communication on the other, through which you interact with others as unique individuals. Interpersonal communication touches every aspect of our lives and is vital in developing and improving relationships with family, loved ones, friends, and colleagues, as well as contributing to our physical and emotional well-being.

Key Terms

Communication *2*

Human communication *2*

Interpersonal communication *3*

Impersonal communication *3*

Relationship *4*

Mass communication *5*

Public communication *5*

Small group communication *5*

Intrapersonal communication *6*

Critical Thinking Questions

1. Draw a relationship scale on a piece of paper, and label it "impersonal" at one end and "intimate" at the other. Place your family members, friends, and work colleagues on the scale. Why do some fall toward the "impersonal" end? What makes those relationships less personal than others? Discuss and compare your entries with those of classmates.

2. Ethics: Think about your primary goal for this course. Is it to develop communication strategies to help you achieve personal goals? Is it to develop sensitivity to the needs of others? What is behind your goal? Is your purpose ethical?

3. Do you know someone who seems to subscribe to one or more of the myths on pages 6–7? How does that tendency affect his or her communication?

Activities

Briefly describe a recent interpersonal communication exchange that was *not* effective. Analyze the exchange. Write down some of the dialogue if you remember it. Did the other person understand you? Did your communication have the intended effect? Was your message ethical?

Web Resources

www.natcom.org/nca/ This is the home page of the National Communication Association, the largest professional association in the world. The site offers information, references, and resources about human communication.

The Communication Process
(pages 8–12)

Interpersonal communication is a complex process of creating meaning in messages in the context of an interpersonal relationship. In order to understand this process, various perspectives and models have been developed over the years. Human communication as action is the oldest and most basic model, describing communication as a linear input/output process of transferring meaning from sender to receiver. Newer communication models include communication as interaction, which includes feedback as a crucial element in the communication process, and human communication as transaction, based on systems theory, which views source and receiver as experiencing the communication simultaneously.

Key Terms

Source *8*

Encode *8*

Decode *8*

Message *8*

Channel *8*

Receiver *9*

Noise *9*

Feedback *10*

Context *10*

Systems theory *11*

Episode *12*

Critical Thinking Questions

1. What makes interpersonal communication a complex process? Explain, drawing on some of your own everyday communication exchanges.

2. Think of some recent interpersonal communication exchanges you've had. Which communication model best captures the nature of each exchange? Analyze each exchange, identifying the components of communication discussed in this section of the chapter. Was feedback an important component? Were you and your partner experiencing the communication simultaneously? What was the context? What were sources of internal and external noise? Did you or your partner have problems encoding or decoding each other's messages?

Activities

Working with a group of your classmates or individually, develop your own model of interpersonal communication. Include all of the components that are necessary to describe how communication between people works. Your model could be a drawing or an object that symbolizes the communication process. Share your model with the class, describing the decisions you made in developing it. Illustrate your model with a conversation between two people, pointing out how elements of the conversation relate to the model.

Web Resources

www.wcaweb.org The home page of the World Communication Association includes a wealth of information, references, and resources about human communication.

Electronically Mediated Interpersonal Communication
(pages 13–20)

Interpersonal communication can still take place even when people are not face to face. In the past, non–face-to-face messages, from smoke signals to mailed letters, allowed humans to communicate over long distances. Today, much of our communication is electronically mediated through a variety of devices that carry our messages, from cell phones to the Internet and more. Electronically mediated communication (EMC) differs from face-to-face (FtF) communication with regard to six key factors: time, varying degrees of anonymity, potential for deception, nonverbal cues, role of the written word, and distance. Several theories and models of electronically mediated messages help us understand the similarities and differences between EMC and FtF communication.

Key Terms

Electronically mediated
 communication (EMC) *13*
Asynchronous message *13*
Synchronous message *14*
Social presence *14*

Hyperpersonal relationship *16*
Cues-filtered-out theory *17*
Media richness theory *17*
Social information-processing
 theory *18*

Critical Thinking Questions

1. Does electronically mediated communication make us more or less other-oriented than face-to-face communication? Explain. Think of the different types of EMC that you use in your daily life. How does each of these affect your social presence?

2. Ethics: There is a greater potential for deception with EMC than with face-to-face communication. What other ethical issues arise with EMC? What are some steps you can take to be sure that you are communicating ethically via electronic media? And how do you evaluate the credibility and reliability of the electronically mediated communication you receive?

Activities

Keep a one-day log of your electronically mediated interactions (e.g., phone calls, Facebook messages, text messages, etc.). Describe each one, noting whether there was a greater emphasis on the content or the relational elements of the messages you exchanged during the interaction.

Principles of Interpersonal Communication and Improving Your Communication Competence
(pages 21–29)

Five fundamental principles help explain interpersonal communication and enhance our understanding of how it works:

- Interpersonal communication connects us to others.
- Interpersonal communication is irreversible.
- Interpersonal communication is complicated.
- Interpersonal communication is governed by rules.
- Interpersonal communication involves both content and relational dimensions.

Although recent research suggests that some people may, in fact, be born with better interpersonal skills than others, you *can* learn ways to enhance your communication competence. Competent communicators are knowledgeable, skilled, and motivated, and they draw on their knowledge, skill, and motivation to become other-oriented. Other-oriented communicators are also ethical: honest, trustworthy, and sensitive to the needs of others.

Key Terms

Symbol *22*
Rule *22*
Content *23*
Relationship dimension *23*
Metacommunication *24*
Mood *24*

Emotional contagion *24*
Communibiological approach *25*
Social learning theory *25*
Egocentric communicator *27*
Ethics *28*

Critical Thinking Questions

1. What rules govern your relationship with your mother? Your father? Your communication teacher? Your roommate? Your coach? Your spouse? Your siblings?

2. Ethics: Your parents want you to visit them for the holidays. You would rather spend the time with a friend. You don't want to hurt your parents' feelings, so you tell them that you are working on an important project and you won't be able to come home for the holidays. Your message is understood. It achieves the intended effect: Your parents don't seem to have hurt feelings, and you don't go home. Explain whether your message is ethical or unethical.

Activities

Review the discussion of principles of interpersonal communication that begins on page 21. Give an example from your own relationships that illustrates each principle.

Web Resources

www.khake.com/page66.html This web site offers a host of resources and links to other sites that provide information about human communication.

Interpersonal Communication and Self

Philosophers suggest that there are three basic questions to which all people seek answers: (1) "Who am I?" (2) "Why am I here?" and (3) "Who are all these others?" In this chapter, we focus on these essential questions about the self. We view them as progressive. Grappling with the question of who you are and seeking to define a purpose for your life are essential to understanding others and becoming other-oriented in your interpersonal communication and relationships.

> ❝People tell themselves stories and then pour their lives into the stories they tell.❞
>
> **Anonymous**

Fundamentally, all your communication starts or ends with you. When you are the communicator, you intentionally or unintentionally code your thoughts and emotions to be interpreted by another. When you receive a message, you interpret the information through your own frame of reference. Your self-image and self-worth, as well as your needs, values, beliefs, and attitudes, serve as filters for your communication with others. As you establish and develop relationships, you may become more aware of these filters and perhaps want to alter them. A close relationship often provides the impetus for change.

To understand the role that self-concept plays in interpersonal communication, we will explore the first two basic questions—"Who am I?" and "Why am I here?"—in an effort to discover the meaning of self. We will examine the multifaceted dimensions of self-concept, learn how it develops, and compare self-concept to self-esteem. Then we will move to the third basic question, "Who are all these others?" What you choose to tell and not tell others about yourself reveals important clues about who you are, what you value, and how you relate to another person.

Self-Concept: Who You Think You Are

You can begin your journey of self-discovery by doing the exercise in Building Your Skills: Who Are You?

How did you answer the question "Who are you?" Perhaps you listed activities in which you participate, or groups and organizations to which you belong. You may have listed some of the roles you assume, such as student, child, or parent. All these things are indeed a part of your self, the sum total of who you are. Psychologist Karen Horney defines **self** as "that central inner force, common to all human beings and yet unique in each, which is the deep source of growth."[1]

Your answers are also part of your **self-concept**. Your self-concept is your subjective description of who you *think* you are—it is filtered through your own perceptions. For example, you may have great musical talent, but you may not believe in it enough to think of yourself as a musician. You can view self-concept as the labels you consistently use to describe yourself to others.

Who you are is also reflected in the attitudes, beliefs, and values that you hold. These are learned constructs that shape your behavior and self-image. An **attitude** is a learned predisposition to respond to a person, object, or idea in a favorable or unfavorable way. Attitudes reflect what you like and what you don't like. If you like school, butter pecan ice cream, and your brother, you hold positive attitudes toward these things. You were not born with a fondness for butter pecan ice cream; you learned to like it, just as some people learn to enjoy the taste of snails, raw fish, or pureed turnips.

Beliefs are the way in which you structure your understanding of reality—what is true and what is false for you. Most of your beliefs are based on previous experience.

self Sum total of who a person is; a person's central inner force.

self-concept A person's subjective description of who he or she is.

attitude Learned predisposition to respond to a person, object, or idea in a favorable or unfavorable way.

belief Way in which you structure your understanding of reality—what is true and what is false for you.

Building Your Skills   Who Are You?

Consider this question: Who are you? More specifically, ask yourself this question ten times. Write your responses in the spaces provided here or on a separate piece of paper. It may be challenging to identify ten aspects of yourself. The Spanish writer Miguel de Cervantes said, "To know thyself . . . is the most difficult lesson in the world." Your answers will help you begin to explore your self-concept and self-esteem in this chapter.

I am _____

I am _____

I am _____

I am _____

I am _____

I am _____

I am _____

I am _____

I am _____

I am _____

You believe that the sun will rise in the morning and that you will get burned if you put your hand on a hot stove.

How are attitudes and beliefs related? They often function quite independently of each other. You may have a favorable attitude toward something and still believe negative things about it. You may believe, for example, that your school football team will not win the national championship this year, although you may be a big fan. Or you may believe that God exists, yet not always like what you think God does or does not do. Beliefs have to do with what is true or not true, whereas attitudes reflect likes and dislikes.

Values are enduring concepts of good and bad, right and wrong. Your values are more resistant to change than either your attitudes or your beliefs. They are also more difficult for most people to identify. Values are so central to who you are that it is difficult to isolate them. For example, when you go to the supermarket, you may spend a few minutes deciding whether to buy regular or cream-style corn, but you probably do not spend much time deciding whether you will steal the corn or pay for it. Our values are instilled in us by our earliest interpersonal relationships; for almost all of us, our parents shape our values.

The model in Figure 2.1 illustrates that values are central to our behavior and concept of self and that what we believe to be true or false stems from our values; that's why values are in the center of the model. Attitudes are at the outer edge of the circle because they are the most likely to change. You may like your coworker today

value Enduring concept of good and bad, right and wrong.

▶ **RECAP**   Who You Are Is Reflected in Your Attitudes, Beliefs, and Values

	Definition	Dimensions	Example
Attitude	Learned predisposition to respond favorably or unfavorably to something	Likes–Dislikes	You like ice cream, incense, and cats.
Belief	The way in which you structure reality	True–False	You believe that your parents love you.
Value	Enduring concepts of what is right and wrong	Good–Bad	You value honesty and truth.

but not tomorrow, even though you *believe* the person will come to work every day and you still *value* the concept of friendship. Beliefs are between attitudes and values in the model because they are more likely to change than our core values but don't change as much as our attitudes (likes and dislikes).

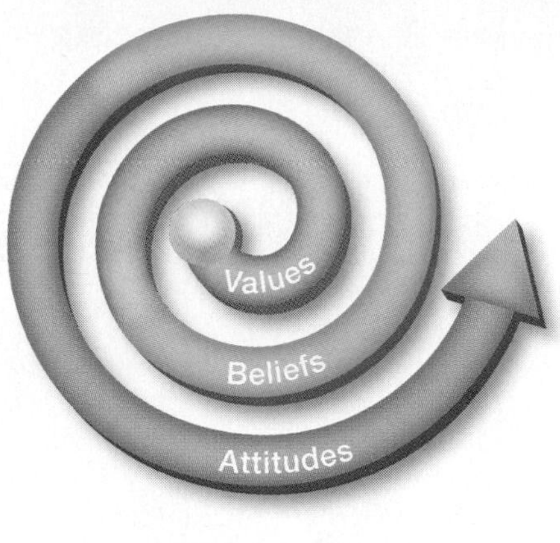

Are You Conscious of Who You Are?

Do you know what you're doing right now? "Of course," you may think, "I'm reading this textbook." But are you *really* aware of all of the fleeting thoughts bouncing in your head, whether you're truly happy or sad, or even whether you may be twiddling a pencil, jiggling your leg, or in need of a snack? To be aware of who you are and what you may be thinking about is a more involved process than you may think. To be self-aware is to be mindful. **Mindfulness** is the ability to consciously think about what you are doing and experiencing, rather than responding out of habit or intuition.[2] If you've ever talked on the phone while driving (something illegal in many states), you may not have been mindful of, or consciously thinking about, where you were driving. Researchers have described three ways of being self-aware, or conscious of who you are and what you are doing: subjective self-awareness, objective self-awareness, and symbolic self-awareness.[3]

Subjective Self-Awareness. **Subjective self-awareness** is the ability that people have to differentiate themselves from their environment. You are a separate being apart from your surroundings. It is so basic an awareness that it may even seem not worth talking about. You know, for example, that you're not physically attached to the chair you may be sitting in. You are a separate entity from all that is around you.

Objective Self-Awareness. **Objective self-awareness** is the ability to be the object of our own thoughts and attention. You have the ability to think about your own thoughts as you are thinking about them. (Some research suggests that some primates also have this ability.) Not only are you aware that you're separate from your environment (subjective self-awareness), but you can also ponder the distinct thoughts you are thinking. Of course, objective self-awareness, like subjective self-awareness, can be "turned on" and "turned off." Sometimes you are aware of what you are thinking, sometimes you're unaware of what you are thinking or on what you are focusing.

Symbolic Self-Awareness. **Symbolic self-awareness,** unique to humans, is our ability not only to think about ourselves but to use language (symbols) to represent ourselves to others. For example, you have the ability to think about how to make a good impression on others. In an effort to make a positive impression on someone, you may say, "Good evening, Mrs. Cleaver. You look nice this evening" rather than just saying, "Hi ya." You make conscious attempts to use symbols to influence the way you want to be perceived by others.

A four-stage model of how aware or unaware we are of what we are doing at any given moment has been attributed to psychologist Abraham Maslow. This framework has also been used to explain how individuals develop communication skills.

Stage 1: *Unconscious incompetence.* You are unaware of your own incompetence. You don't know what you don't know. For example, at one point in your life you didn't know how to ride a bicycle and you didn't even realize that you were missing this skill. You were unconsciously incompetent about bicycle-riding skills.

FIGURE 2.1

Values, Beliefs, and Attitudes in Relation to Self

mindfulness The ability to consciously think about what you are doing and experiencing.

subjective self-awareness Ability to differentiate the self from the social and physical environment.

objective self-awareness Ability to be the object of one's own thoughts and attention—to be aware of one's state of mind and that one is thinking.

symbolic self-awareness Uniquely human ability to think about oneself and use language (symbols) to represent oneself to others.

Peter Blake sought to explore his self-dimensions by painting his self-portrait. What qualities does this self-portrait reveal about the artist?

Stage 2: *Conscious incompetence.* At this level, you become aware or conscious that you are not competent: You know what you don't know. Continuing our example, at some point you realized that others could ride a bike and you could not. You became conscious of your incompetence with regard to bicycle-riding.

Stage 3: *Conscious competence.* You are aware that you know something, but applying it has not yet become a habit. When you first learned to ride a bike, if you're like most people, you had to concentrate on keeping your balance and focus on riding forward without falling over.

Stage 4: *Unconscious competence.* At this level, your skills become second nature to you. Now you don't have to mentally review how to ride a bike every time you hop on one. You are unconsciously competent of how to ride a bicycle; you just get on and automatically start pedaling. The same could be said about tying your shoes; you don't have to think about how to tie your shoes; you just do it without thinking about each step. These same four stages explain how you learn any skill, from riding a bike to enhancing the interpersonal communication skills we discuss in this book.

One or Many Selves?

Shakespeare's famous line "To thine own self be true" suggests that you have a single self to which you can be true. But do you have just one self? Or is there a more "real you" buried somewhere within? Most scholars conclude that each of us has a core set of behaviors, attitudes, beliefs, and values that constitutes our self—the sum total of who we are. But our *concept* of self can and does change, depending on circumstances and influences.

In addition, our self-concept is often different from the way others see us. We almost always behave differently in public than we do in private. Sociologist Erving Goffman suggests that, like actors and actresses, we have "on-stage" behaviors when others are watching and "backstage" behaviors when they are not.[4] Goffman writes that "often what talkers undertake to do is not to provide information to a recipient but to present dramas to an audience. Indeed, it seems that we spend most of our time not engaged in giving information but in giving shows."[5] With an audience present, whether it's one person or several, you adapt and "perform."

Perhaps the most enduring and widely accepted framework for describing who we are was developed by the philosopher William James. He identified three classic components of the self: the material self, the social self, and the spiritual self.[6]

The Material Self. Perhaps you've heard the statement "You are what you eat." The concept of the **material self** goes a step further by suggesting that "You are what you have." The material self is a total of all the tangible things you own: your body, your possessions, your home. As you examine your list of responses to the question "Who are you?" note whether any of your statements refer to one of your physical attributes or something you own.

One element of the material self gets considerable attention in this culture: the body. Do you like the way you look? Most of us, if we're honest, would like to change something about our appearance. When there is a discrepancy between our desired material self and our self-concept, we may respond to eliminate the discrepancy. We may try to lose weight, develop our muscles, or acquire more hair. The

material self Concept of self as reflected in a total of all the tangible things you own.

multibillion-dollar diet industry is just one of many that profit from our collective desire to change our appearance.

The Social Self. Look at your "Who are you?" list once more. How many of your responses relate to your **social self,** the part of you that interacts with others? William James believed that you have many social selves—that, depending on the friend, family member, colleague, or acquaintance with whom you are interacting, you change the way you are. A person has, said James, as many social selves as there are people who recognize him or her. For example, when you talk to your best friend, you are willing to "let down your hair" and reveal more thoughts and feelings than you would in a conversation with your communication professor, or even your parents. Each relationship that you have with another person is unique because you bring to it a unique social self.

"I don't want to be defined by who I am."

The Spiritual Self. Your **spiritual self** consists of all your thoughts and introspections about your values and moral standards. It does not depend on what you own or with whom you talk; it is the essence of who you *think* you are and your *feelings* about yourself, apart from external evaluations. It is an amalgam of your religious beliefs and your sense of who you are in relationship to other forces in the universe. Whether you believe in intelligent design or Darwinian evolution (or both),

social self Concept of self as reflected in social interactions with others.

spiritual self Concept of self based on thoughts and introspections about personal values, moral standards, and beliefs.

UNDERSTANDING OTHERS
Adapting to Differences

The "Golden Rule": A Universal Value?

It's clear that there are cultural differences among the world's people, including differences in language, food preferences, housing preferences, and a host of other elements; these differences have existed as long as there have been people. Anthropologists and communication scholars who study intercultural communication, a topic we'll discuss in more detail in Chapter 4, teach the value of adapting to cultural differences in order to understand others better. But is it possible that despite their clear differences, there is a universally held principle that influences the behavior of all people? The question is not a new one. Scholars, theologians, and many others have debated for millennia whether there are any universal values that inform all human societies.

The importance of being other-oriented rather than self-absorbed is not a new idea.

Most world religions emphasize some version of the same spiritual principle, known in Christianity as the Golden Rule: Do unto others as you would have others do unto you. There is convincing evidence that this rule has been the foundation of most ethical codes throughout the world. The following principles underlying various religious traditions emphasize the universal importance accorded to being other-oriented.[7]

Hinduism This is the sum of duty: Do nothing to others that would cause pain if done to you.

Buddhism One should seek for others the happiness one desires for one self.

Taoism Regard your neighbor's gain as your own gain, and your neighbor's loss as your loss.

Confucianism Is there one principle that ought to be acted on throughout one's whole life? Surely it is the principle of

loving-kindness: do not unto others what you would not have them do unto you.

Zoroastrianism The nature alone is good that refrains from doing unto another whatsoever is not good for itself.

Judaism What is hateful to you, do not do to others. That is the entire law: all the rest is but commentary.

Islam No one of you is a believer until he desires for his brother that which he desires for himself.

Christianity Do unto others as you would have others do unto you.

Do you find this list of variations on the Golden Rule from different world religions convincing evidence that being other-oriented is a universal value? Are there other underlying values or principles, such as how the poor or the elderly should be treated, that should inform our interactions with others?

your beliefs about the ultimate origins of the world (and about your own origins and ultimate destination) are embedded in your spiritual self. Your spiritual self is the part of you that answers the question "Why am I here?"

▶RECAP   William James's Dimensions of Self

	Definition	Examples
Material Self	All the physical elements that reflect who you are	Body, clothes, car, home
Social Self	The self as reflected through your interactions with others; actually, a variety of selves that respond to changes in situations and roles	Your informal self interacting with your best friend; your formal self interacting with your professors
Spiritual Self	Introspections about values, morals, and beliefs	Belief or disbelief in God; regard for life in all its forms

BEING Other-ORIENTED

One of the ways we develop our self-concept is by interacting with others. Who are the others in your life who have had the most profound impact on who you are? Most people would say their parents and members of their family. Who besides family members have helped to shape your concept of self? In what ways?

How Your Self-Concept Develops

Some psychologists and sociologists have advanced theories that suggest you learn who you are through five basic means: (1) interactions with other individuals, (2) associations with groups, (3) roles you assume, (4) self-labels, and (5) your personality. Like James's framework, this one does not cover every base in the study of self, but its constructs can provide some clues about how your own self-concept develops.

Interaction with Individuals.   In 1902, Charles Horton Cooley first advanced the concept of the **looking-glass self,** which was his term for the notion that we form our self-concept by seeing ourselves in a kind of figurative looking glass: We learn who we are by interacting with others, much as we look into a mirror and see our reflection.[8] Like Cooley, George Herbert Mead also believed that our sense of who we are is a consequence of our relationships with others.[9] And Harry Stack Sullivan theorized that from birth to death our selves change primarily because of how people respond to us.[10] One sage noted, "We are not only our brother's keeper; we are our brother's maker."

The process begins at birth. Our names, one of the primary ways we identify ourselves, are given to us by someone else. During the early years of our lives, our parents are the key individuals who reflect who we are. If our parents encouraged us to play the piano, we probably play now. As we become less dependent on our parents, our friends become highly influential in shaping our attitudes, beliefs, and values. And friends continue to provide feedback on how well we perform certain tasks. This, in turn, helps us shape our sense of identity as adults—we must acknowledge our talents in math, language, or art in our own minds before we say that we are mathematicians, linguists, or artists.

Fortunately, not *all* feedback affects our sense of who we think we are. We are likely to incorporate the comments of others into our self-concept under three conditions.

First, we are more likely to believe another's statement if he or she repeats something we have heard several times. If one person casually tells you that you have a good singing voice, you are not likely to launch a search for an agent and a recording contract. But if several individuals tell you on many different occasions that you have a talent for singing, you may decide to do something about it.

Second, we are more likely to value another's statements if we perceive him or her to be credible. If we believe the individual is competent, trustworthy, and qualified to make a judgment about us, then we are more likely to believe the person's assessment.

Third, we are likely to incorporate another's comments into our own concept of self if the comments are consistent with other comments and our own experience. If your boss tells you that you work too slowly, but for years people have been urging

looking-glass self Concept that suggests you learn who you are based on your interactions with others, who reflect your self back to you.

you to slow down, then your previous experience will probably encourage you to challenge your boss's evaluation.

Not surprisingly, your parents or early caregivers played an important role in influencing your self-concept. Researchers have found that the emotional and relational bond that you developed early on with your parents—or, to phrase this another way, how *attached* you felt to one or both of your parents or primary caregiver—influenced your concept of self, and that continues to influence how you relate to others.[11] According to several researchers, you develop an **attachment style** based on how secure, anxious, or uncomfortable you felt in relating to one or both of your parents.[12] Research suggests that you developed one of three different types of attachment styles: secure, anxious, or avoidant.[13]

You have a **secure attachment style** if you are comfortable giving and receiving affection, experiencing intimacy, and trusting other people. If you have a secure attachment style, then you probably developed a strong, trusting, close, predictable, and positive emotional bond with your parents. Research suggests the majority of people, about 60 percent, develop a secure attachment style.[14]

You may have developed an **anxious attachment style** if you received some affection but not quite enough, and so you may feel uncomfortable in some relationships; the affection you received from your parents was not always predictably present. It's not that you received *no* affection from your caregivers, but you didn't receive all that you felt you needed and therefore you may experience some anxiety about intimacy and giving and receiving affection. About 10 percent of the population develops an anxious attachment style.[15]

Finally, you may have an **avoidant attachment style** if you consistently received too little nurturing. People who had this type of upbringing may feel considerable discomfort and awkwardness when expressing or receiving intimacy. Because they didn't receive adequate affection and emotional connections as children, such people may tend to avoid relational intimacy with others. About 25 percent of the population fits this attachment style profile.[16]

Your concept of yourself as someone who enjoys strong emotional connections with other people, or as someone who is anxious or avoids relational intimacy, is thus influenced by the degree of attachment you felt during your formative years. Obviously, you should neither blame nor congratulate your parents for *everything* about the way you relate to people today. But research suggests that early relationship connections with our parents do influence the way we relate to others.

Associations with Groups. Reflect once more on your responses to the "Who are you?" question. How many responses associate you with a group? Religious groups, political groups, ethnic groups, social groups, study groups, and occupational and professional groups play important roles in determining your self-concept. Some of these groups you are born into; others you choose on your own. Either way, these group associations are significant parts of your identity.

Associating with groups is especially important for people who are not part of the dominant culture. Gays and lesbians, for example, find the support provided by associating with other gays and lesbians to be beneficial to their well-being. The groups you associate with not only provide information about your identity, but also provide needed social support.

Roles You Assume. Look again at your answers to the "Who are you?" question. Perhaps you see words or phrases that signify a role you often assume. Father, aunt, sister, uncle, manager, salesperson, teacher, and student are labels that imply certain expectations for behavior, and they are important in shaping self-concept. Couples who live together before they marry often report that marriage alters their

attachment style A style of relating to others that develops early in life, based on the emotional bond one forms with one's parents or primary caregiver.

secure attachment style The style of relating to others that is characteristic of those who are comfortable giving and receiving affection, experiencing intimacy, and trusting other people.

anxious attachment style The style of relating to others that is characteristic of those who experience anxiety in some intimate relationships and feel uncomfortable giving and receiving affection.

avoidant attachment style The style of relating to others that is characteristic of those who consistently experience discomfort and awkwardness in intimate relationships and who therefore avoid such relationships.

relationship. Before, they may have shared domestic duties such as doing dishes and laundry. But when they assume the labels of "husband" and "wife," they slip into traditional roles. Husbands don't do laundry. Wives don't mow the grass. These stereotypical role expectations that they learned long ago may require extensive discussion and negotiation. Couples who report the highest satisfaction with marriage agree on their expectations regarding roles ("We agree that I'll do laundry and you'll mow the grass").[17]

One reason we assume traditional roles automatically is that our gender group asserts a powerful influence from birth on. As soon as parents know the sex of their children, many begin placing them in that gender group by following cultural rules. They paint the nursery pink for a girl, blue for a boy. Boys get catcher's mitts, train sets, or footballs for their birthdays; girls get dolls, frilly dresses, and tea sets. These cultural conventions and expectations play a major role in shaping our self-concept and our behavior.

Relating to Others in the 21st Century | Your "Online Self" and Your "Offline Self"

If you have a MySpace or Facebook page, would people who only know you online have the same impression of you if they met you in person? Would people with whom you communicate via e-mail or a blog have the same image of you if they met you in person? Electronically mediated communication (EMC) makes it easier to control what information people learn about us. Because you have more control, does your online presentation of yourself differ from your live-and-in-person presentation of self? Do you try to enhance your "face" on Facebook in ways that are different from techniques you use when communicating face to face? The ease and prevalence of EMC communication in the twenty-first century has spurred communication researchers to investigate these and other questions about how we present ourselves online.[18]

Communication researchers Lisa Tidwell and Joseph Walther wanted to know whether there are differences between face-to-face conversations and EMC conversations in the amount of information people share with others, their projection of confidence, and the overall effectiveness of communication. They found that when people communicate via e-mail, they exchange information more directly with each other and perceive themselves and others to be more "conversationally effective" because they are more direct. Perhaps people perceive their communication as more effective because they can

edit and revise what they say online and have more control than when talking face to face. E-mail conversation partners also reported that they were more confident when communicating online than they were in their face-to-face encounters.[19]

In addition to perceiving ourselves as more effective and confident as well as sharing more personal information when communicating via e-mail, we may be less truthful about ourselves when we are online compared with face-to-face communication. Two Internet researchers found strong evidence that people are much more likely to misrepresent themselves in cyberspace than in "realspace" relationships.[20] As we noted in Chapter 1, we're most likely to lie about our age, weight, and personal appearance when communicating online.[21]

Researchers have also found that people report their face-to-face relationships were more serious in tone than their exclusively online relationships. And even though people made more expressions of commitment in their realspace relationships compared to their cyberspace relationships, research participants reported about the same levels of satisfaction with both types of relationships and similar potential for emotional growth in their romantic relationships, whether in realspace or cyberspace.

With our increased use of EMC, researchers have found that our sense of self is derived not only from face-to-face

interactions but also from the amount, kind, and quality of relationships we develop with people online. Canadian psychologist M. Kyle Matsuba examined how our self-concept (what he labeled "ego identity") is influenced by EMC.[22] He found that the more clear college students are about their own identity (self-concept), the less they develop online relationships. Or, stated the other way around, the *less* clear a person is about his or her own identity the *more* likely he or she is to develop relationships online. (Note that this is a correlation rather than a cause-and-effect relationship.) Perhaps if we are not totally certain about who we are, we develop relationships with others online to help explore who we are. Matsuba also found a strong correlation between being a heavy user of the Internet and reporting greater feelings of loneliness. (Again, he found a correlation rather than a cause-and-effect link between Internet use and loneliness; Internet use doesn't *cause* loneliness, but more people who feel lonely may use the Internet to connect with others.)

Because we can control our online persona more readily than our realspace presentation of self, we're more confident about what we're saying about ourselves online. The Internet, which offers the opportunity to develop many relationships with others quickly and efficiently, especially on social networking sites, can help us explore facets of ourselves and clarify our self-concept.

Although it is changing, American culture is still male-dominated. What we consider appropriate and inappropriate behavior is often different for males and for females. For example, in group and team meetings, task-oriented, male-dominated roles are valued more than relationship-building roles.[23] Some may applaud fathers who work sixty hours a week as diligent and hard-working but criticize mothers who do the same as neglectful and selfish.

Although our culture defines certain roles as masculine or feminine, we still exercise individual choices about our gender roles. One researcher developed an inventory designed to assess whether we play traditional masculine, feminine, or androgynous roles.[24] Because an **androgynous role** is both masculine and feminine, such a role encompasses a greater repertoire of actions and behaviors.

In American culture, behavior among girls is in many ways quite distinct from that among boys.

Self-Labels. Although our self-concept is deeply affected by others, we are not blank slates for them to write on. The labels we use to describe our own attitudes, beliefs, values, and actions also play a role in shaping our self-concept.

Where do our labels come from? We interpret what we experience; we are self-reflexive. **Self-reflexiveness** is the human ability to be objectively self-aware—that is—to think about what we are doing while we are doing it. We talk to ourselves about ourselves. We are both participants and observers in all that we do. This dual role encourages us to use labels to describe who we are.

When you were younger, perhaps you dreamed of becoming an all-star basketball player. Your coach may have told you that you were a great player, but as you matured, you probably began observing yourself more critically. You scored no points. So you self-reflexively decided that you were not, deep down, a basketball player, even though others may have labeled you as "talented." But sometimes, through this self-observation, people discover strengths that encourage them to assume new labels. One woman we know never thought of herself as "heroic" until she went through seventy-two hours of labor before giving birth!

Your Personality. The concept of personality is central to **psychology,** the study of how your thinking influences how you behave. According to psychologist Lester Lefton, your **personality** consists of a set of enduring internal predispositions and behavioral characteristics that describe how you react to your environment.[25] Understanding the forces that shape your personality is central to increasing your awareness of your self-concept and how you relate to others.

Does nature or nurture play the predominant role in your personality? As we noted in Chapter 1, the **communibiological approach** to communication suggests that a major factor affecting how people communicate with others is genetic makeup.[26] Others argue that although it's true that communication behavior is influenced by genes, we should not forget that humans can learn to adjust and adapt.[27]

One personality characteristic that communication researchers have spent considerable time studying is the level of comfort or discomfort individuals experience when interacting with other people. Some people just don't like to talk with others.[28] We may say such a person is shy. **Shyness** is the behavioral tendency not to talk with others. One study found that about 40 percent of adults reported they were shy.[29] In public-speaking situations, we say a person has stage fright; a better term to describe this feeling is *communication apprehension*. **Communication apprehension,** according to communication experts James McCroskey and Virginia Richmond, is "the fear

androgynous role Gender role that includes both masculine and feminine qualities.

self-reflexiveness Ability to think about what you are doing while you are doing it.

psychology Study of how thinking influences behavior.

personality Enduring internal predispositions and behavioral characteristics that describe how people react to their environment.

communibiological approach Perspective that suggests that genetic and biological influences play a major role in influencing communication behavior.

shyness Behavioral tendency not to talk or interact with other people.

communication apprehension Fear or anxiety associated with either real or anticipated communication with other people.

41

Communication and Emotion

Self and Emotion: How We Influence How We Feel

In Chapter 1, we defined an emotion as a biological, cognitive, behavioral, and subjective affective reaction to an event. Emotions are reactions to what we experience. What continues to be debated is the specific sequence of events that results in an emotional response. Are we in control of our emotions, or do our emotions control us? We present three different theories that describe the chain of events that cause us to experience emotions.

Commonsense Theory of Emotion: Emotions Happen

The commonsense approach is so named because it seems to be a description of the way many people would describe how emotions occur. The commonsense theory, shown in Figure 2.2, suggests the following order of emotional experience: (1) Something happens, (2) you have an affective (that is, an emotional) reaction to the event (you feel sad or happy), and finally, (3) you respond physiologically by blushing, experiencing an increased heart rate, or having another

biological reaction to your emotion.[30] Here's an example: (1) You meet your new boss for the first time, (2) you feel nervous, and (3) your heart rate increases and you begin to perspire. This sequence is typically the way many people think about emotions occurring—emotions just happen, and we really have no choice in how we feel. But there are other theories about what causes emotions.

James-Lange Theory of Emotion: Physiological Response Determines Emotional Response

Another theory of emotion, developed by psychologists William James and Carl Lange, is called the James-Lange theory of emotion.[31] Note the difference in the sequence of events in this theory in Figure 2.3: (1) Something happens, (2) you respond physiologically, and then (3) you experience

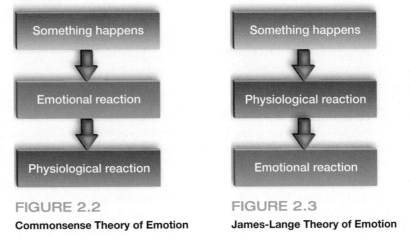

FIGURE 2.2
Commonsense Theory of Emotion

FIGURE 2.3
James-Lange Theory of Emotion

or anxiety associated with either real or anticipated communication with another person or persons."[33] One study found that up to 80 percent of the population experiences some degree of nervousness or apprehension when they speak in public.[34] Another study found that about 20 percent of people are considerably anxious when they give a speech.[35] What makes some people apprehensive about communicating with others? Again, we get back to the nature–nurture issue. Heredity plays an important role in whether you are going to feel nervous or anxious when communicating with someone else. But so does whether you were reinforced for talking with others as a child, as well as other experiences that are part of your culture and learning.

Your overall **willingness to communicate** with others is a general way of summarizing the likelihood that you will talk with others in a variety of situations. If you are unwilling to communicate with others, you will be less comfortable in a career such as sales or customer service that forces you to interact with other people.

Understanding the factors that influence your self-concept—such as your interactions with individuals and groups, the roles you assume, your self-labels, and your personality, including your overall comfort level in communicating with others—can help you understand who you are and why you interact (or don't interact) with others. But it's not only who you are that influences your communication; it's also your overall sense of self-esteem or self-worth that affects how you express yourself and respond to others.

willingness to communicate
General term for the likelihood that an individual will communicate with others in certain situations.

an emotion. This theory suggests that we respond physiologically *before* we experience an emotion. The physiological responses tell us whether or not to experience an emotion. When you meet your new boss, you begin to perspire, and your heart starts beating more rapidly; this, in turn, *causes* you to feel nervous.

Appraisal Theory of Emotion: Labels Determine What Emotions Are Experienced

Yet a third view suggests that you are more in control of your emotions than you might think. You can change the emotion you are feeling by the way you decide to label or describe your experiences to yourself. This theory is called the appraisal theory, which means we appraise and label what we feel; the labels we use to describe what we experience have a major effect on what we feel as an emotional response.[32] Here's the suspected sequence according to this theory: (1) Something happens, (2) you respond physiologically, (3) you decide how you will react to what is happening to you, and then (4) you experience the emotion. (See Figure 2.4.) Do you see the difference in this last approach? *It suggests that you have control over how you feel, based in part on what you tell yourself about what you are experiencing.*

According to the appraisal theory of emotion, you actively participate in determining what emotion you experience by labeling your experiences. For example, (1) you meet your new boss, (2) your heart rate increases and you start to perspire, (3) you tell yourself that this is an important and fear-inducing event, so (4) you feel nervous and anxious. Or you could tell yourself, "This is no big deal" and not feel nervous but enjoy your conversation with your new boss.

Although researchers continue to debate precisely how events trigger our emotions, we know that our emotional reaction to what we experience has a profound impact on how we relate to others.

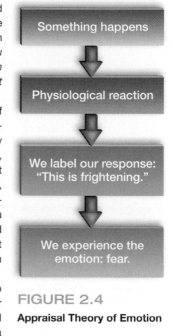

FIGURE 2.4

Appraisal Theory of Emotion

Self-Esteem: Your Self-Worth

Your self-esteem is closely related to your self-concept. Your self-concept is a *description* of who you are. Your self-esteem is an *evaluation* of who you are. The term **self-worth** is often used interchangeably with *self-esteem*. There is evidence that your overall feeling of self-worth is related to feeling and expressing positive messages toward others as well as being supportive of other people.[36] You feel better about yourself if you behave in ways that researchers call being *prosocial,* which means your behaviors benefit others. Research has also found a positive relationship between high self-esteem and happiness.[37] And although evidence suggests that having high self-esteem doesn't mean you'll perform better in school, or be more likely to be a leader, there is evidence that people with high self-esteem tend to speak up more in groups and share information with others.[38]

People derive their sense of self-worth from comparing themselves to others, a process called **social comparison.** Social comparison helps people measure how well they think they are doing compared to others. I'm good at playing soccer (because I beat others); I can't cook (because others cook better than I do); I'm not good at meeting people (most people I know seem to be more comfortable interacting with others); I'm not handy (but my brothers and sisters can fix a leaky faucet). Each of these statements implies a judgment about how well or badly you can perform

self-worth (self-esteem) Your evaluation of your worth or value based on your perception of such things as your skills, abilities, talents, and appearance.

social comparison Process of comparing yourself to others who are similar to you, to measure your worth and value.

"My self-esteem was so low I just followed her around everywhere she would go."

certain tasks, with implied references to how well others perform the same tasks. A belief that you cannot fix a leaky faucet or cook like a chef may not in itself lower your self-esteem. But if there are *several* things you can't do well or *many* important tasks that you cannot seem to master, these shortcomings may begin to color your overall sense of worth. At times we may need to be reminded that our value as a human being is not equivalent to our cooking ability, our grade-point average, or the kinds of clothes we wear. Our self-worth is more precious than money, grades, or fashion.

In the 1960s, psychologist Eric Berne developed the concept of a **life position** to describe people's overall sense of their own worth and that of others.[39] He identified four life positions: (1) "I'm OK, you're OK," or positive regard for self and others; (2) "I'm OK, you're not OK," or positive regard for self and low regard for others; (3) "I'm not OK, you're OK," or low self-regard and positive regard for others; and (4) "I'm not OK, you're not OK," or low regard for both self and others. Your life position is a driving force in your relationships with others. People in the "I'm OK, you're OK" position have the best chance for healthy relationships because they have discovered their own talents and also recognize that others have been given talents different from their own.

Facework: Communicating Your Positive Image of Yourself to Others

life position Feelings of regard for self and others, as reflected in one's sense of worth and self-esteem.

Your face is important to you. It's something you look at several times a day, whether you catch a fleeting glimpse of yourself as you pass a mirror or purposefully check to make sure you are looking your best. Your face is a focal point of your self-image. The amount of money spent on plastic surgery to enhance the face is clear evidence that facial appearance is important to most people. In addition, such common expressions as "in your face" or communicating "face to face" confirm that the face is a key part of everyone's identity. But, *face* can refer to more than just the eyes, nose, and mouth. **Face** is a person's positive perception of himself or herself in interactions with others.[40] A related term, **facework,** refers to using communication to maintain your own face (your positive perception of who you are) or to support, reinforce, or challenge someone else's face (or self-perception).

Projecting Your Face

If you are typical, you spend considerable effort to project a positive face—a positive image of yourself to others. You are using positive facework, for example, when you announce to your parents or friends that you made the dean's list during the recent college semester. By telling them the good news about your academic success, you're using communication to maintain a positive image of yourself and thus reinforce your own positive self-image. To have a positive face is to be approved of and liked by others. Some researchers speculate that the concept of face originated with the ancient Chinese, but no doubt they merely gave a name to something that is a characteristic of being human.

We use **preventative facework** to avoid developing a negative impression of ourselves—we actively work to maintain and enhance our positive perception of ourselves. For example, if you think you may be late for a meeting, you may tell a coworker, "If I'm late it's because there may be heavy traffic on the road during rush hour." Even before the event you're trying to save face. We engage in **corrective facework** when we "save face" by correcting what we perceive as a negative perception of us, as when we say, "Oh, I'm sorry I was late. I got stuck in heavy traffic."[41] To "save face" is a metaphor for instilling a positive perception of yourself in others. Sociologist Erving Goffman suggests that saving face is important for most people.[42] The effort you expend to save face (to protect your positive image) reflects the kind of perception you want others to have of you.

What are strategies for projecting a positive face? One of the best things to do is to simply be mindful of what you do to communicate positive information about yourself. Monitor how you talk to others, and consider the needs and expectations of others (be other-oriented) as you interact with them.

Besides being aware of how you are communicating a positive self-image to others, make sure your words are consistent with your actions. If you tell your family that you're getting good grades, but your final grades don't correspond to your story, it's your actions, not your words, they will believe.

Since it's others, not just you, who will assess whether you have a positive image, by observing what others value, you can mindfully decide whether you want to conform to what others expect of you. This is always a delicate balance. If you know, for example, that your friend likes people to dress up when dining in a restaurant, you can accommodate your friend by dressing more formally than you typically do. We're not suggesting that you should *always* conform to the expectations of others, only that you should be aware of their expectations so that you can make a mindful decision about whether you will meet their expectations.

face A person's positive perception of himself or herself in interactions with others.

facework Using communication to maintain your own positive self-perception or to support, reinforce, or challenge someone else's self-perception.

preventative facework Efforts to maintain and enhance one's positive self-perceptions.

corrective facework Efforts to correct what one perceives as a negative perception of oneself on the part of others.

Projecting a positive image of yourself—positive face—means being mindful of how you talk to and interact with others.

Protecting Others' Face

Communication researchers Kathy Domenici and Stephen Littlejohn suggest that there are several things we can do to actively help others maintain a positive face.[43] Underlying each of their prescriptions is the value of being other-oriented. For example, you can honor others by addressing them as they wish to be addressed. Some of your teachers want to be called "doctor" if they have a doctoral degree or "professor" if they hold that academic rank. Yet others may say, "Call me Steve."

Being polite is another way of enhancing the face of others. Saying "please," "thank you," or "excuse me" are common courtesies that are valued in virtually every culture.

Being generous and supportive are other ways you enhance the face of others. Spending time with someone who enjoys your company, offering positive and affirming messages to the person, and interacting in appropriately attentive and supportive ways also help to build face. An other-oriented communicator considers what the other person would like.

We engage in **face-threatening acts** when we communicate in a way that undermines or challenges someone's positive face.[44] We may not intend for something we say or do to threaten someone else's face, but any interaction we have with someone has the potential to be face-threatening to them. It's the other person, not you, who determines whether a statement or behavior is face-threatening. Being aware of how we may threaten someone's face can help us develop greater sensitivity toward others.

Social psychologists Penelope Brown and Stephen Levinson suggest that people from all cultures have a universal need to be treated politely.[45] Brown and Levinson developed a theory, called **politeness theory,** that suggests not only that people have a tendency to promote a positive image of themselves (a positive face) but also that people will have a positive perception of others who treat them politely and respectfully. Politeness theory makes intuitive sense. We want our image of our self to be positive. And when others are polite to us, we will have a positive perception of their face.

Although people from different cultures have varying levels of need to be treated politely, what seems clear is that everyone needs to be valued and appreciated. Offering compliments, behaving respectfully, and showing concern for others are all ways of using politeness to help others project a positive face.

According to politeness theory, when we have a negative message to communicate, we make a choice regarding how much we threaten someone else's face. The statements in the following list are arranged from most face-threatening to least face-threatening

1. Bluntly communicating a negative message: "Your office is a mess."

2. Delivering the negative message but also communicating a face-saving message: "Your office is a mess, but perhaps messy is the look you want."

3. Delivering the negative message but offering a counter-explanation to help the person save face: "Your office is a mess, but that's understandable, given how much work you do around here."

4. Communicating the negative message but doing so "off the record" or in such an indirect way that the other person saves face: "I'm not supposed to tell you this; even though your office is a mess, the boss is impressed with how well you seem to find everything."

5. Finally, not communicating any message that would cause someone to lose face.

When someone threatens your face ("Because you were late to the meeting, I missed picking my daughter up from school"), you have choices to make. You can

face-threatening acts
Communication that undermines or challenges someone's positive face.

politeness theory Theory that people have positive perceptions of others who treat them politely and respectfully.

respond by defending yourself or by denying what the other person has said ("No, I wasn't late to the meeting yesterday"), or you can offer an explanation, an excuse, or an apology ("I'm so sorry. The elevator was broken so I had to walk up the stairs"). Or, by simply saying and doing nothing you can communicate a range of responses. As researchers Dominici and Littlejohn suggest, being silent can mean (1) I'm thinking about what you said, (2) I'm ignoring what you said because it's not worth my time or effort, or (3) I'm simply not going to respond in kind to the way you've treated me.[46] The effort you expend to save face (to protect your positive image) reflects the kind of perception you want others to have of you. The more effort you expend to protect your face, the more you want others to have a positive perception of you.

Although positive self-talk will never be able to make all of us become champion cyclists like Lance Armstrong, it can help us focus on our own goals and improve our performance levels.

How to Improve Your Self-Esteem

We have mentioned that low self-esteem can affect our own communication and interactions. In recent years, teachers, psychologists, ministers, rabbis, social workers, and even politicians have suggested that many societal problems also stem from collective feelings of low self-esteem. Feelings of low self-worth may contribute to choosing the wrong partners; to becoming dependent on drugs, alcohol, or other substances; or to experiencing problems with eating or other vital activities. So people owe it to society, as well as to themselves, to maintain or develop a healthy sense of self-esteem.

Although no simple list of tricks can easily transform low self-esteem into feelings of being valued and appreciated, you can improve how you think about yourself and interact with others. We'll explore seven proven techniques that have helped others.

Engage in Self-Talk

Cycling champion Lance Armstrong is also a cancer survivor. When he got sick, he told a friend, "Cancer picked the wrong guy. When it looked around for a body to hang out in, it made a big mistake when it chose mine. Big mistake."[47] The positive self-talk reflected in his words undoubtedly helped Armstrong to overcome the challenge of cancer and go on to win the Tour de France seven times.

Intrapersonal communication is communication within yourself—self-talk. Realistic, positive self-talk can have a reassuring effect on your level of self-worth and on your interactions with others.[48] Conversely, repeating negative messages about your lack of skill and ability can keep you from trying and achieving.

Of course, blind faith without hard work won't succeed. Self-talk is not a substitute for effort; it can, however, keep you on track and help you ultimately to achieve your goal.

Visualize a Positive Image of Yourself

Visualization takes the notion of self-talk one step further. Besides just telling yourself that you can achieve your goal, you can actually try to "see" yourself conversing effectively with others, performing well on a project, or exhibiting some other desirable

intrapersonal communication Communication within yourself; self-talk.

visualization Technique of imagining that you are performing a particular task in a certain way; positive visualization can enhance self-esteem.

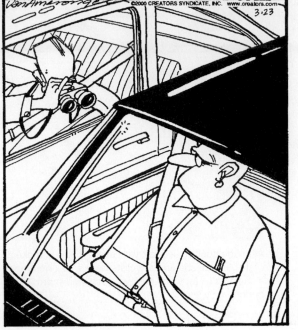

Michael continually measures himself against others.

behavior. Being able to visualize completing a goal (thinking positively rather than thinking you won't achieve your goal) adds to your overall sense of happiness and well-being.[49] Recent research suggests that an apprehensive public speaker can manage his or her fears not only by developing skill in public speaking, but also by visualizing positive results when speaking to an audience.[50] The same technique can be used to boost your sense of self-worth about other tasks or skills. If, for example, you tend to get nervous when meeting people at a party, imagine yourself in a room full of people, glibly introducing yourself to others with ease. Visualizing yourself performing well can yield positive results in changing long-standing feelings of inadequacy. Of course, your visualization should be realistic and coupled with a plan to achieve your goal.

Avoid Comparing Yourself with Others

Even before we were born, we were compared with others. The latest medical technology lets us see sonograms of fetuses still in the womb, so parents may begin comparing their children with other babies before birth. For the rest of our lives, we are compared with others, and rather than celebrating our uniqueness, comparisons usually point up who is stronger, brighter, or more beautiful. Many of us have had the experience of being chosen last to play on a sports team, being passed over for promotion, or standing unchosen against the wall at a dance.

In North American culture, we may be tempted to judge our self-worth by our material possessions and personal appearance. If we know someone who has a newer car (or simply a car, if we rely on public transportation), a smaller waistline, or a higher grade point average, we may feel diminished. Comparisons such as "He has more money than I have" or "She looks better than I look" are likely to deflate our self-worth.

Rather than finding others who seemingly are better off, focus on the unique attributes that make you who you are. Avoid judging your own value by comparing yourself with others. A healthy, positive self-concept is fueled not by judgments of others, but by a genuine sense of worth that you recognize in yourself.

Reframe Appropriately

Reframing is the process of redefining events and experiences from a different point of view. Just as reframing a work of art can give the picture a whole new look, reframing events that cause you to devalue your self-worth can change your perspective. For example, if you get a report from your supervisor that says you should improve one area of your performance, instead of listening to the self-talk that says you're bad at your job, reframe the event within a larger context: Tell yourself that one negative comment does not mean you are a hopeless employee.

Of course, not all negative experiences should be tossed off and left unexamined, because you can learn and profit from your mistakes. But it is important to remember that your worth as a human being does not depend on a single exam grade, a single response from a prospective employer, or a single play in a football game.

reframing Process of redefining events and experiences from a different point of view.

Develop Honest Relationships

Having at least one other person who can help you objectively and honestly reflect on your virtues and vices can be extremely beneficial in fostering a healthy, positive self-image. As we noted earlier, other people play a major role in shaping your self-concept and self-esteem. The more credible the source of information, the more likely you are to believe it. Later in the chapter, we discuss how honest relationships are developed through the process of self-disclosure. Honest, positive support can provide encouragement for a lifetime.

Let Go of the Past

Your self-concept is not fixed. It was not implanted at birth to remain constant for the rest of your life. Things change. You change. Others change. Individuals with low self-esteem may be fixating on events and experiences that happened years ago and tenaciously refusing to let go of them. Perhaps you've heard religious and spiritual leaders suggest that it's important to forgive others who have hurt you in the past. There is research evidence that suggests it's important to your own mental health and sense of well-being to let go of old wounds and forgive others.[51] Someone once wrote, "The lightning bug is brilliant, but it hasn't much of a mind; it blunders through existence with its headlight on behind." Looking back at what we can't change only reinforces a sense of helplessness. Constantly replaying negative experiences in our mind only serves to make our sense of worth more difficult to change. Becoming aware of the changes that have occurred and can occur in your life can help you develop a more realistic assessment of your value. Look past your past.

Seek Support

You provide **social support** when you express care and concern as well as listen and empathize with others. Perhaps you just call it "talking with a friend." Having someone who will be socially supportive is especially important when we experience stress and anxiety or are faced with a vexing personal problem.[52]

Social support from a friend or family member can be helpful, but some of your self-image problems may be so ingrained that you need professional help. A trained counselor, clergy member, or therapist can help you sort through them. The technique of having a trained person listen as you verbalize your fears, hopes, and concerns is called **talk therapy.** You talk, and a skilled listener helps you sort out your feelings and problems. There is power in being able to put your thoughts, especially your negative thoughts and emotions, into words. By saying things out loud to an open, honest, empathic listener, we gain insight and can sometimes figure out why we experience the hurts and difficulties that we do. If you are not sure to whom to turn for a referral, you can start with your school counseling services. Or, if you are near a medical-school teaching hospital, you can contact the counseling or psychotherapy office there for a referral.

Because you have spent your whole lifetime developing your self-esteem, it is not easy to make big changes. But talking through problems can make a difference. As communication researchers Frank E. X. Dance and Carl Larson see it, "Speech communication empowers each of us to share in the development of our own self-concept and the fulfillment of that self-concept."[53]

BEING Other-ORIENTED

We all need support and encouragement from others from time to time. When have other people helped you manage a difficult situation or period of your life? What are the qualities in others that you look for when you need social support? What are talents and skills that you possess that will help you provide useful social support to others?

social support Expression of empathy and concern for others that is communicated while listening to them and offering positive and encouraging words.

talk therapy Technique in which a person describes his or her problems and concerns to a skilled listener in order to better understand the emotions and issues that are creating the problems.

▶ **RECAP**   Strategies for Improving Your Self-Esteem

Engage in Self-Talk	If you're having a bad hair day, tell yourself that you have beautiful eyes and lots of friends who like you anyway.
Visualize	If you feel nervous before a meeting, visualize everyone in the room congratulating you on your great ideas.
Avoid Comparison	Focus on your positive qualities and on what you can do to enhance your own talents and abilities.
Reframe Appropriately	If you experience one failure, keep the larger picture in mind, rather than focusing on that isolated incident.
Develop Honest Relationships	Cultivate friends in whom you can confide and who will give you honest feedback for improving your skills and abilities.
Let Go of the Past	Talk yourself out of your old issues; focus on ways to enhance your abilities in the future.
Seek Support	Talk with professional counselors who can help you identify your gifts and talents.

BEING Other-ORIENTED

You develop your perception of yourself as an "I" based on your self-talk or the messages you tell yourself. Your perception of "me" is based on what you believe others say about you. Are you aware of your own perceptions of yourself ("I") compared with how others see you ("me")? Compare and contrast the information you use to develop your concept of yourself and your self-esteem with the information others use to form their perceptions of you.

Self and Interpersonal Relationships

Your self-concept and self-esteem filter every interaction with others. They determine how you approach, respond to, and interpret messages. Specifically, your self-concept and self-esteem affect your ability to be sensitive to others, your self-fulfilling prophecies, your interpretation of messages, your own social needs, and your typical communication style.

Self and Interaction with Others

Your image of yourself and your sense of self-worth directly affect how you interact with others. Who you think you are affects how you communicate with other people.

We defined human communication as the way we make sense of the world and share that sense with others by creating meaning through verbal and nonverbal messages. A theory called **symbolic interaction theory** is based on the assumption that we make sense of the world based on our interactions with others. We interpret what a word or symbol means based, in part, on how other people react to our use of that word or symbol. We learn, for example, that certain four-letter words have power because we see people react when they hear the words. Even our own understanding of who we think we are is influenced by who others tell us we are. For example, you don't think you're a good dancer, but after several of your friends tell you that you have dazzling dance moves, you start believing that you *do* have dancing talent. Central to understanding ourselves is understanding the importance of other people in shaping our self-understanding. Symbolic interaction theory has had a major influence on communication theory because of the pervasive way our communication with others influences our very sense of who we are.

George Herbert Mead is credited with the development of symbolic interaction theory, although Mead did not write extensively about his theory.[54] One of Mead's students, Herbert Blumer, actually coined the term *symbolic interaction* to describe the

symbolic interaction theory
Theory that people make sense of the world based on their interpretation of words or symbols used by others.

process through which our interactions with others influence our thoughts about others, our life experiences, and ourselves. Mead believed that we cannot have a concept of our own self-identity without interactions with other people.

Because the influence of others on your life is so far-reaching, it's sometimes hard to be consciously aware of how other people shape your thoughts. One of the ways to be more mindful of the influence of others is to become increasingly other-oriented—sensitive to the thoughts and feelings of others—which is essential for developing quality relationships with others. Becoming other-oriented involves recognizing that your concept of self (who *you* think you are) is different from how others perceive you—even though it's influenced by others, as suggested by symbolic interaction theory. Mead suggests that we come to think of ourselves both as "I," based on our own perception of ourselves, and as "me," based on the collective responses we receive and interpret from others. Being aware of how your concept of self ("I") differs from the perceptions others have of you ("me") is an important first step in developing an other-orientation.

Although it may seem complicated, it's really quite simple: You affect others and others affect you. Your ability to predict how others will respond to you is based on your skill in understanding how your sense of the world is similar to and different from theirs. To enhance your skill in understanding this process, you need to know yourself well. But understanding yourself is only half the process; you also need to be other-oriented. One of the best ways to improve your ability to be other-oriented is to notice how others respond when you act on the predictions and assumptions you have made about them. If you assume that your friend, who is out of work and struggling to make ends meet, will like it if you pick up the check for lunch, and she offers an appreciative "Thank you so much," you have received confirmation that your generosity was appreciated and that your hunch about how your friend would react to your gesture was accurate.

BEING Other-ORIENTED

By becoming a detective, you can find clues in the behavior of others to determine if the assumptions you've made about them are accurate. Reflect on times when you have accurately identified the emotions of another person and compare those instances to other times when you weren't as accurate. What kinds of clues help you accurately predict others' moods and feelings?

Self and Your Future

What people believe about themselves often comes true because they expect it to come true. Their expectations become a **self-fulfilling prophecy.** If you think you will fail the math quiz because you have labeled yourself inept at math, then you must overcome not only your math deficiency, but also your low expectations of yourself. The theme of George Bernard Shaw's *Pygmalion* is "If you treat a girl like a flower girl, that's all she will ever be. If you treat her like a princess, she may be one." Research suggests that you can create your own obstacles to achieving your goals by being too critical of yourself.[55] Or you can increase your chances for success by having a more positive mindset.[56] Your attitudes, beliefs, and general expectations about your performance have a powerful and profound effect on your behavior.

The medical profession is learning the power that attitudes and expectations have for healing. Physician Howard Brody's research suggests that in many instances, just giving patients a placebo—a pill with no medicine in it—or telling patients that they have been operated on when they haven't had an operation can yield positive medical results. In his book *The Placebo Response,* Brody tells of a woman with debilitating Parkinson's disease who made a miraculous recovery; her only treatment was the doctors' telling her that they had completed a medical procedure.[57] They hadn't. Yet before the "treatment," she could barely walk; now she can easily pace around the room. There is a clear link, suggests Dr. Brody, between mental state and physical health. Patients who believe they will improve are more likely to improve.

self-fulfilling prophecy
Prediction about future actions that is likely to come true because the person believes that it will come true.

Your image of yourself and your sense of self-worth in part determine whether your expectations are fulfilled, but that sense of self-worth is shaped to a great degree by your interactions with others.

Self and Interpretation of Messages

Although it may have been many years since you've read A. A. Milne's classic children's stories about Winnie-the-Pooh, you probably remember Eeyore, Winnie-the-Pooh's donkey friend. Eeyore lives in the gloomiest part of the Hundred Acre Wood and has a self-image to match. In one story, all the animals congregate on a stormy night to check on Eeyore:

> . . . they all came to the part of the forest known as Eeyore's gloomy place. On this stormy night it was terribly gloomy indeed—or it would have been were it not for Christopher Robin. He was there with a big umbrella.
>
> "I've invited Eeyore to come and stay with me until the storm is over," said Christopher Robin.
>
> "If it ever is," said Eeyore, "which doesn't seem likely. Not that anybody asked me, you understand. But then, they hardly ever do."[58]

Perhaps you know or have known an Eeyore—someone whose low self-esteem colors how he or she interprets messages and interacts with others. According to research, such people are more likely to

- Be more sensitive to criticism and negative feedback from others.

- Be more critical of others.

- Believe they are not popular or respected by others.

- Expect to be rejected by others.

- Prefer not to be observed while performing.

- Feel threatened by people who they feel are superior.

- Expect to lose when competing with others.

- Be overly responsive to praise and compliments.

- Evaluate their overall behavior as inferior to that of others.[59]

The Pooh stories offer an antidote to Eeyore's gloom in the character of the optimistic Tigger, who assumes that everyone shares his exuberance for life:

> . . . when Owl reached Piglet's house, Tigger was there. He was bouncing on his tail, as Tiggers do, and shouting to Piglet. "Come on," he cried. "You can do it! It's fun!"[60]

If, like Tigger, your sense of self-worth is high, research suggests you will

- Have higher expectations for solving problems.

- Think more highly of others.

- Be more likely to accept praise and accolades from others without feeling embarrassed.

- Be more comfortable having others observe you when you perform.

- Be more likely to admit you have both strengths and weaknesses.

- Prefer to interact with others who view themselves as highly competent.

- Expect other people to accept you for who you are.

- Be more likely to seek opportunities to improve skills that need improving.

- Evaluate your overall behavior more positively than would people with lower self-esteem.[61]

Self and Interpersonal Needs

According to social psychologist Will Schutz, our concept of who we are, coupled with our need to interact with others, profoundly influences how we communicate with others. Schutz identifies three primary social needs that affect the degree of communication we have with others: the need for inclusion, the need for control, and the need for affection.[62]

Inclusion. Each of us has a **need for inclusion**—the need to be included in the activities of others and to experience human contact and fellowship. We need to be invited to join others, and perhaps we need to invite others to join us. Of course, the level and intensity of this need differ from person to person, but even loners desire some social contact. Our need to include others and be included in activities may stem, in part, from our concept of ourselves as either a "party person" or a loner.

Control. We also have a **need for control:** We need some degree of influence over the relationships we establish with others. We may also have a need to *be* controlled because we desire some level of stability and comfort in our interactions with others.

Affection. Finally, we each have a **need for affection.** We need to give and receive love, support, warmth, and intimacy, although the amounts we need vary enormously from person to person. The greater our needs for inclusion, control, and affection, the more likely it is that we will actively seek others as friends and initiate communication with them.

Self and Disclosure to Others

When we interact with others, we reveal information about ourselves—we self-disclose. **Self-disclosure** occurs when we purposefully provide information to others about ourselves that they would not learn if we did not tell them. Self-disclosure ranges from revealing innocuous information about yourself, such as where you were born, to admitting your deepest fears and most private fantasies. Disclosing personal information not only provides a basis for another person to understand you better, it also conveys your level of trust and acceptance of the other person. Because others self-disclose, you are able to learn information about them and

need for inclusion Interpersonal need to be included and to include others in social activities.

need for control Interpersonal need for some degree of influence in our relationships, as well as the need to be controlled.

need for affection Interpersonal need to give and receive love, support, warmth, and intimacy.

self-disclosure Purposefully providing information about yourself to others that they would not learn if you did not tell them.

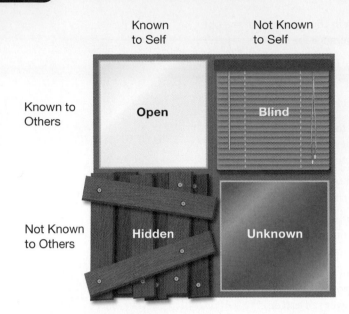

Known to Self

Not Known to Self

Known to Others

Open

Blind

Not Known to Others

Hidden

Unknown

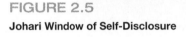

FIGURE 2.5

Johari Window of Self-Disclosure

deepen your interpersonal relationships with them.[63] We introduce the concept of self-disclosure in this chapter because it's an important element in helping us understand ourselves. Because self-disclosure is the primary way we establish and maintain interpersonal relationships, we'll discuss self-disclosure in considerable detail in Chapter 9.

In order to disclose personal information to others, you must first be aware of who you are. Your **self-awareness** is your understanding of who you are. In addition to just thinking about who you are, asking others for information about yourself and then listening to what they tell you can enhance your self-awareness.

A variety of personality tests, such as the Myers-Briggs personality inventory, may give you additional insight into your interests, style, and ways of relating to others. Most colleges and universities have a career services office where you can take vocational aptitude tests to help you identify careers that fit who you are.

The **Johari Window model** nicely summarizes how your awareness of who you are is influenced by your own level of disclosure, as well as by how much information others share *about* you *with* you. (The name "Johari Window" sounds somewhat mystical and exotic, but it is simply a combination of the first names of the creators of the model, Joseph Luft and Harry Ingham.[64]) As Figure 2.5 shows, the model looks like a set of windows, and the windows represent your self. This self includes everything about you, including things even you don't yet see or realize. One axis is divided into what you have come to know about yourself and what you don't yet know about who you are. The other axis represents what someone else may know about you and not know about you. The intersection of these categories creates four windows, or quadrants.

BEING Other-ORIENTED

Some things about ourselves we learn from others: elements of our personality (both positive and negative characteristics), talents that we possess, as well as other pieces of information that others share. What aspects of your personality or talents you have did you learn about from others, and might not have known about if someone had not shared them with you? How have others helped you learn about yourself?

---

self-awareness A person's conscious understanding of who he or she is.

Johari Window model Model of self-disclosure that summarizes how self-awareness is influenced by self-disclosure and information about yourself from others.

Open: Known to Self and Known to Others. Quadrant 1 is an *open area*. The open area contains information that others know about you and that you are also aware of—such as your age, your occupation, and other things you might mention about yourself. At first glance, all four quadrants appear to be the same size. But that may not be the case (in fact, it probably isn't). In the case of quadrant 1, the more information that you reveal about yourself, the larger this quadrant will be. Put another way, the more you open up to others, the larger the open area will be.

Blind: Not Known to Self but Known to Others. Quadrant 2 is a *blind area*. This window contains information that other people know about you, but that you do not know. Perhaps when you were in grade school, as a joke someone put a sign on your back that said, "Kick me." Everyone was aware of the sign but you. The blind window represents much the same situation. For example, you may see yourself as generous, but others may see you as a tightwad. As you learn how others see you, the blind window gets smaller. Generally, the more accurately you know yourself and perceive how others see you, the better your chances to establish open and honest relationships with others.

Hidden: Known to Self but Not Known to Others. Quadrant 3 is a *hidden area*. This area contains information that you know about yourself, but that others do not know about you. You can probably think of many facts, thoughts, feelings, and fantasies that you would not want anyone else to know. They may be feelings

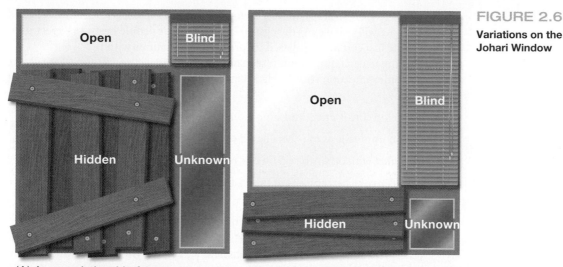

FIGURE 2.6

**Variations on the
Johari Window**

(A) A new relationship for someone
who is very self-aware

(B) An intimate relationship

you have about another person or something you've done privately in the past that you'd be embarrassed to share with others. The point here is not to suggest you should share all information in the hidden area with others. It is useful to know, however, that part of who you are is known by some people, but remains hidden from others.

Unknown: Not Known to Self or Others.   Quadrant 4 is an *unknown area.* This area contains information that is unknown to both you and others. These are things you do not know about yourself *yet.* Perhaps you do not know how you will react under certain stressful situations. Maybe you are not sure what stand you will take on a certain issue next year or even next week. Other people may also not be aware of how you would respond or behave under certain conditions. Your personal potential, your untapped physical and mental resources, are unknown. You can assume that this area exists, because eventually some (though not necessarily all) of these things will become known to you, to others, or to both you and others. Because you can never know yourself completely, the unknown quadrant will always exist; you can only guess at its current size, because the information it contains is unavailable to you.

We can draw Johari Windows to represent each of our relationships; see Figure 2.6. Part A shows a new or restricted relationship for someone who knows himself or herself very well. The open and blind quadrants are small, but the unknown quadrant is also small. Part B shows a very intimate relationship, in which both individuals are open and disclosing.

Self and Communication Social Style

Over time we develop general patterns or styles of relating to others based on several factors, including our personality, self-concept, self-esteem, and what we choose to disclose to others. Our general style of relating to others is called our **communication social style;** it is an identifiable way of habitually communicating with others. The concept of communication social styles originates in the work of Carl Jung who, in his book *Psychological Types,* described people according to four types: thinkers, feelers, intuiters, and sensors.[65] (The Myers-Briggs personality inventory, which in part assesses ways of relating to others, is based on Jung's types.) Communication researchers built on Jung's pioneering work to identify communication social styles.

communication social style An
identifiable way of habitually
communicating with others.

The communication social style we develop helps others interpret our messages and predict how we will behave. As they get to know us, other people begin to expect us to communicate in a certain way, based on previous associations with us.[66]

According to communication researchers William Snavely and John McNeill, the notion of communication social style is based on four underlying assumptions about human behavior:

1. We develop consistent communication behavior patterns over time.

2. We form impressions of others based on their verbal and nonverbal behavior.

3. We interact with others based on our perceptions of them.

4. We develop our perceptions of others based primarily on two dimensions: assertiveness and responsiveness.[67]

A variety of different communication social style models have been developed during the past 30 years. Regardless of the specific model (some models describe four styles, others include just two), there is general agreement on the two fundamental dimensions of assertiveness (which focuses on accomplishing a task) and responsiveness (which emphasizes concern for relationships) as anchoring elements in determining a person's social style.[68]

assertiveness Tendency to make requests, ask for information, and generally pursue one's own rights and best interests.

Assertiveness is the tendency to accomplish a task by making requests, asking for information, and generally looking out for one's own rights and best interests. An assertive style is sometimes called a "masculine" style. By masculine, we don't mean that only males can be assertive, but that in many cultures, males are expected to be assertive. You are assertive when you seek information if you are confused or direct others to help you get what you need.

responsiveness Tendency to be sensitive to the needs of others, including being sympathetic to others' feelings and placing the feelings of others above one's own feelings.

Responsiveness is the tendency to focus on the dynamics of relationships with others by being sensitive to their needs. Being other-oriented and sympathetic to the

Building Your Skills

What's Your Communication Social Style?

Directions: The following questionnaire lists 20 personality characteristics. Please indicate the degree to which you believe each of these characteristics applies to you, as you normally communicate with others, by marking whether you (5) strongly agree that it applies, (4) agree that it applies, (3) are undecided, (2) disagree that it applies, or (1) strongly disagree that it applies. There are no right or wrong answers. Work quickly; record your first impression.

_____ 1. helpful

_____ 2. defends own beliefs

_____ 3. independent

_____ 4. responsive to others

_____ 5. forceful

_____ 6. has strong personality

_____ 7. sympathetic

_____ 8. compassionate

_____ 9. assertive

_____ 10. sensitive to the needs of others

_____ 11. dominant

_____ 12. sincere

_____ 13. gentle

_____ 14. willing to take a stand

_____ 15. warm

_____ 16. tender

_____ 17. friendly

_____ 18. acts as a leader

_____ 19. aggressive

_____ 20. competitive

Scoring: Items 2, 3, 5, 6, 9, 11, 14, 18, 19, and 20 measure assertiveness. Add the scores on these items to get your assertiveness score. Items 1, 4, 7, 8, 10, 12, 13, 15, 16, and 17 measure responsiveness. Add the scores on these items to get your responsiveness score. Scores range from 50 to 10. The higher your scores, the higher your orientation toward assertiveness and responsiveness.

Source: James C. McCroskey and Virginia P. Richmond, *Fundamentals of Human Communication: An Interpersonal Perspective* (Prospect Heights, IL: Waveland Press, 1996), 91. Reprinted with permission of James C. McCroskey and Virginia P. Richmond.

TABLE 2.1   Identifying Assertive Behaviors in Others[69]

	More Assertive People Tend To	Less Assertive People Tend To
Speech	• Talk more • Talk faster • Talk loudly	• Talk less • Talk more slowly • Talk softly
Body	• Move faster • Appear more energetic • Lean forward	• Move more slowly • Appear less energetic • Lean backward

feelings of others, and placing others' feelings above your own are examples of being responsive. Researchers sometimes label responsiveness a "feminine" quality. Again, this does not mean that only women are or should be responsive, only that many cultures stereotype being responsive as a traditional and expected behavior of females.

To assess your style on the assertiveness and responsiveness dimensions, take the sociocommunicative orientation test by James McCroskey and Virginia Richmond in the Building Your Skills box. You may discover that you test higher on one dimension than on others. It's also possible to be high on both or low on both. Assertiveness and responsiveness are two different dimensions; you need not have just one or the other.

Another way to identify your communication social style is to ask your friends, family members, and colleagues who know you best to help you assess your style. They are in the best position to determine your overall behavior that contributes to their perceptions of you as assertive or nonassertive, responsive or nonresponsive.

It's all well and good to understand your own communication social style and know how your self-concept, self-esteem, personality, and even your biology contribute to a predominant way of interacting with others. But as we've noted before: *It's not always about you.* At the heart of interpersonal communication is relating to *others.* Understanding your self in relationship to the style of other people can help you make mindful decisions about how to relate to them. But let us be clear: We're not talking about how to manipulate other people—we're talking about how to ethically and sensitively enhance the quality of your communication with others.

How can you assess another person's communication social style? Although you're probably not going to have your friends, family members, colleagues, and acquaintances take a test to assess their communication style, you can look for behaviors that indicate their levels of assertiveness and responsiveness.

The longer you know someone, the more likely you are to be able to accurately identify another person's social style. Tables 2.1 and 2.2 list a few behaviors that may indicate assertiveness or responsiveness. The tables are based on research on the

TABLE 2.2   Identifying Responsive Behaviors in Others[70]

	More Responsive People Tend To	Less Responsive People Tend To
Speech	• Use more pitch variation • Take a brief time to respond • Use more vocal energy	• Use less pitch variation • Take a longer time to respond • Use less vocal energy
Body	• Show more facial animation when talking • Use more head nods • Use smoother, flowing gestures	• Show less facial animation when talking • Use fewer head nods • Use more hesitant, nonflowing gestures

majority population of North Americans, so there are cultural and ethnic limitations to these lists. And we certainly don't claim that by observing these few cues, you can definitively determine someone's communication social style. But the tables will give you some initial ideas that you can use to later refine your impressions.

Experts who study and apply communication social style research suggest that the simplest way to adapt your style to enhance communication quality is to communicate in ways that more closely match the style of the other person. Keep the following principles in mind as you consider your communication social style and the social styles of others:

- Most people have a dominant communication social style (a primary way of interacting with others) that includes the two dimensions of assertiveness and responsiveness.

- There is no single best communication social style to use in all situations—there are advantages and disadvantages to every style, and the specific circumstances should help you determine whether you should be more assertive or more responsive toward others.

- To enhance interpersonal communication, it's useful to understand both your style and the style of the other person and then decide whether to adapt your communication social style.

APPLYING AN OTHER-ORIENTATION
to Self and Interpersonal Communication

"To thine own self be true." In this famous line from Act I, Scene iii of *Hamlet*, Polonius is providing advice to his son Laertes as Laertes prepares to travel abroad. Polonius gives Laertes a number of suggestions, and concludes with this wise fatherly advice: "This above all, to thine own self be true,/And it must follow, as the night the day,/Thou canst not then be false to any man."

In this chapter we've discussed the significance of your self-perception and self-esteem and how these self-perceptions affect your relationships with others. Although we've emphasized the importance of being other-oriented, we conclude the chapter by echoing Polonius's advice to his son: *Be true to yourself*.

To be other-oriented doesn't mean only behaving in people-pleasing ways in order to ingratiate yourself to them.

Rather, as an other-oriented communicator, you are aware of the thoughts and feelings of others, but remain true to your own ethics and beliefs. For example, if you object to watching violent movies, and a group of your friends invites you to see a "slasher" movie, you don't have to attend with them. Nor do you have to make a self-righteous speech about your feelings about violent movies; you simply can excuse yourself after calmly saying you don't like those kinds of movies. You don't have to do what others do simply to be popular. As your mother may have said when you were growing up, "If all of your friends jumped off a cliff, would you jump too?" In essence, your mother was echoing Polonius's counsel to be true to yourself rather than blindly following the herd to be popular.

The word *credo* means belief. What's your personal credo or set of beliefs? Being aware of your personal beliefs—whether those beliefs are about things philosophical, or spiritual, about human nature, or about the political and social issues of the day—can serve as an anchoring point for your interactions with others. Without knowing where your "home" is—your personal credo—you'll not know how far away from "home" you travel as you make your way in the world and relate to others.

There is sometimes a tension between being true to yourself and being true to others. Consider drafting your own personal credo, your statement of core beliefs, so that you might more mindfully follow Polonius's advice to be true to yourself as you relate to others.

Self-Concept: Who You Think You Are
(pages 33–43)

Self-concept plays an important role in interpersonal communication. Understanding who you are is essential to understanding others and becoming other-oriented in your interpersonal communication and relationships. Self-concept is your subjective description of who you think you are. It is filtered through your own perceptions and is different from the way others see you. A classic framework for describing who you are identifies three components of the self: the material self, the social self, and the spiritual self. Self-concept is also reflected in the attitudes, beliefs, and values you hold. You develop your self-concept and the different dimensions of self in five ways: through interactions with other individuals, association with groups, roles you assume, self-labels, and your personality.

Key Terms

Self *33*

Self-concept *33*

Attitude *33*

Belief *33*

Value *34*

Mindfulness *35*

Subjective self-awareness *35*

Objective self-awareness *35*

Symbolic self-awareness *35*

Material self *36*

Social self *37*

Spiritual self *37*

Looking-glass self *38*

Attachment style *39*

Secure attachment style *39*

Anxious attachment style *39*

Avoidant attachment style *39*

Androgynous role *41*

Self-reflexiveness *41*

Psychology *41*

Personality *41*

Communibiological approach *41*

Shyness *41*

Communication apprehension *41*

Willingness to communicate *42*

Critical Thinking Questions

1. Make a list of all the groups, clubs, and organizations to which you belong. Rank them from most important to you to least important. What does your ranking tell you about these groups in reference to your self-concept? For example, which groups have you joined more from a desire to belong or for the prestige of the group than because of an interest in or passion for the group's cause?

2. Ethics: Considering again Shakespeare's line "To thine own self be true," can you think of instances when you have not been true to yourself, in your actions, the role(s) you assumed, and/or your interactions with others? Did you know at the time that you were behaving in a way that was not compatible with your values? Do you think others were aware of this? Explain.

Activities

Rank the following list of values from 1 to 12 to reflect their importance to you. In a group with other students, compare your answers. Discuss how your ranking of these values influences your interactions with others.

_____Honesty

_____Salvation

_____Comfort

_____Good health

_____Human rights

_____Peace

_____Justice

_____Wealth

_____Beauty

_____Equality

_____Freedom

_____Mercy

Web Resources

http://www.queendom.com Assess your personality and other communication-related variables.

Self-Esteem
(pages 43–49)

Your self-esteem is closely related to your self-concept. Your self-concept is a *description* of who you are, whereas your self-esteem is an *evaluation* of who you are. This sense of self-worth (self-esteem) is often derived from comparing yourself to others, in terms of skills, personal appearance, material possessions, or other qualities or characteristics. In a process called facework, we use communication to maintain a positive self-perception, as well as to reinforce or challenge others' perceptions. Through various techniques such as visualization, talk therapy, and avoiding social comparisons, you can improve your self-esteem, not only in terms of how you think about yourself, but also in terms of how you interact with others.

Key Terms

Self-worth/self-esteem *43*

Social comparison *43*

Life position *44*

Face *45*

Facework *45*

Preventative facework *45*

Corrective facework *45*

Face-threatening acts *46*

Politeness theory *46*

Intrapersonal communication *47*

Visualization *47*

Reframing *48*

Social support *49*

Talk therapy *49*

Critical Thinking Questions

1. Describe a recent event or communication exchange that made you feel better or worse about yourself. What happened that made you feel good? Or, what made you feel bad—inadequate, embarrassed, or unhappy? In general, how do your communication exchanges influence your self-esteem? Explain. How might visualization or other strategies help?

2. Do you find that you make social comparisons with others that affect your self-esteem? If so, what qualities of others most influence your own view of yourself: appearance, material possessions, skills/talent, something else? Explain.

3. How does electronically mediated communication (EMC) influence the comparisons you described in Question 3, and in turn, your self-esteem? Do Facebook profiles play a role? Do the mass media play a role in creating those comparisons?

4. Ethics: Many self-help books claim to provide sure-fire techniques for enhancing self-esteem and thus enrich your social life. Do you think these claims are ethical? Why or why not?

Activities

Briefly describe an upcoming situation that makes you anxious, such as working on a group project, calling a prospective employer about a job, or competing in a sporting event. What strategies are you employing to deal with your nervousness? Describe how visualization might help. Share with your classmates a positive scenario, describing the successful outcome.

Web Resources

http://www.social-anxiety.com Go to this site to learn more about shyness and social phobias; the site also offers case studies.

Self and Interpersonal Relationships (pages 50–58)

Your self-concept and self-esteem have a direct impact on your interactions with others—both how you respond to and interpret messages and the communications style you develop and employ. At the same time, other people have a central impact on your self-understanding. Being aware of how your concept of self ("I") differs from the perceptions others have of you ("me") is an important first step in becoming other-oriented. Being other-oriented is being mindful of others' influence on you and your self-concept, as well as being sensitive to the thoughts and feelings of others. This mindfulness, in turn, influences how you communicate with others. Self-disclosure, sharing information about yourself with others, is a key component of that communication and is how we establish and maintain relationships. This becomes our communication style.

Key Terms

Symbolic interaction theory *50*	Self-awareness *54*
Self-fulfilling prophecy *51*	Johari Window model *54*
Need for inclusion *53*	Communication social style *55*
Need for control *53*	Assertiveness *56*
Need for affection *53*	Responsiveness *56*
Self-disclosure *53*	

Critical Thinking Questions

1. Provide an example of a recent communication exchange with a friend, classmate, family member, or work colleague that revealed that some aspect of your perception of yourself differed from how the other person perceived you. Why do you think the perceptions differed? Did knowing the other person's perception change your behavior and/or your own perceptions, or not? Explain.

2. Describe a situation in which your expectations of the outcome became a self-fulfilling prophecy. Was the outcome positive or negative? Did your self-esteem have an impact? Explain.

3. Have you ever shared personal information and found that what you revealed wasn't well received or received as you intended? How did you handle the situation?

4. Ethics: Is it always best to be honest when self-disclosing? What types of self-disclosure might be inappropriate? Are there times when it would be appropriate to withhold information? Is that ethical? Explain.

5. Ethics: Carmelita would like to become better friends with Hector. She decides to disclose some personal information to Hector, hoping that this self-disclosure will increase feelings of intimacy between them. Is it ethical to self-disclose to others as a strategy to enhance intimacy in a relationship?

Activities

Create a Johari Window that includes in square 3 ("hidden," or known to self but not to others) five or six adjectives that best describe your personality as you see it. Then ask a close friend to fill in square 2 ("blind," or known to others but not known to self) with five or six adjectives to describe your personality. Separately, ask a classmate you've just met to fill in square 2 as well. Compare and contrast. Are the adjectives used by your close friend and the acquaintance you've just met similar or different? Is there any overlap? Now fill in square 1 ("open," or known to self and others) with any adjectives that both you and either of the other participants chose. What does this tell you about what you disclose about yourself to others?

Go through your library of music downloads and CDs and identify a selection that best symbolizes you, based on either the lyrics or the music. Bring your selection to class to play for your classmates. Tell why this music symbolizes you. Discuss with classmates how your choice of music provides a glimpse of your attitudes and values, as well as a vehicle for self-expression.

Web Resources

http://abacon.com/commstudies/interpersonal/indisclosure.html Want to learn more about the Johari Window? This site about self-disclosure helps explain the Johari Window and gives you an opportunity to complete an interactive activity and take a short quiz to test your understanding of the concept.

http://www.winning-solutions.com/Training/interpersonal.html Check out this site to assess your personality type. Explore relationships between your personality and interpersonal communication.

Interpersonal Communication and Perception

3

1 Define perception and interpersonal perception.

2 Identify and explain the three stages of interpersonal perception.

3 Describe the relationship between interpersonal communication and interpersonal perception.

4 Explain how we form impressions of others, describe others, and interpret others' behavior.

5 Identify the eight factors that distort the accuracy of our interpersonal perceptions.

6 Offer five suggestions for improving interpersonal perceptions.

Outline

- Understanding Interpersonal Perception
- How We Form Impressions of Others
- How We Interpret the Behavior of Others
- Barriers to Accurate Interpersonal Perception
- How to Improve Interpersonal Perception Skills

> "What you see and what you hear depends a good deal on where you are standing. It also depends on what sort of person you are."
>
> **C. S. Lewis**

Look at the Norman Rockwell painting. What is happening, and what has happened? What is the relationship among the individuals in the painting? You probably have deduced that the boy was running away from home, the policeman found him, and then he took the boy into the local coffee shop for ice cream or some other treat. Perhaps you think that the man behind the counter is wistfully recalling his own days of running away as a child. What are your feelings about the policeman? Do you see him as a friendly and caring person who has a good understanding of kids?

In Chapter 1, we defined human communication as the process of making sense of the world and sharing that sense with others by creating meaning through the use of verbal and nonverbal messages. In this chapter, we discuss the first half of that definition—the process of making sense of our world. How we make sense out of what we experience is the starting point for what we share with others. As human beings, we interpret and attribute meaning to what we observe or experience, particularly if what we are observing is other people. We tend to make inferences about their motives, personalities, and other traits based on their physical qualities and behaviors. Those who are skilled at making observations and interpretations have a head start in developing effective interpersonal relationships. Those who are other-oriented, who are aware of and sensitive to the communication behaviors of others, will likely be better at accurately perceiving others.

perception Process of experiencing the world and making sense out of what you experience.

interpersonal perception Process of selecting, organizing, and interpreting your observations of other people.

Before we turn to the role that perception plays in interpersonal communication, let's first take a closer look at the interpersonal perception process itself.

Saturday Evening Post cover, September 20, 1958. Old Corner House Collection, Stockbridge, Massachusetts.

Understanding Interpersonal Perception

What is perception? **Perception** is the process of experiencing your world and then making sense out of what you experience. You experience your world through your five senses. Your perceptions of people, however, go beyond simple interpretations of sensory information. **Interpersonal perception** is the process by which you decide what people are like and give meaning to their actions. It includes making judgments about personality and drawing inferences from what you observe.[1]

When you meet someone new, you *select* certain information to attend to: For example, you note whether the person is male or female, has an accent, smiles, and uses a friendly tone of voice, as well as particular personal information (she is from Boone, Iowa). You then *organize* the information into some category that is recognizable to you, such as "a friendly Midwesterner." Then you *interpret* the organized perceptions: This person is trustworthy, honest, hardworking, and likable.

Stage 1: Selecting

Sit for a minute after you read this passage and tune in to all the sensory input you are receiving: Consider the feel of your socks against your feet, the pressure of the floor on your heels, the pressure of the piece of furniture against your body as you sit, the sounds from various sources around you—"white noise" from a refrigerator, personal computer, fluorescent lights, water in pipes, voices, passing traffic, or your own heartbeat or churning stomach. What do you smell? What do you see? Without moving your eyes, turn your awareness to the images you see in the corner of your vision. What colors do you see? What shapes? What taste is in your mouth? How do the pages of this book feel against your fingertips? Now stop reading and consider all these sensations. Try to focus on all of them at the same time. You can't.

You are selective as you attempt to make sense out of the world around you. The number of sensations you can attend to at any given time is limited. Perhaps you close your eyes or sit in the dark as you listen to music. This allows you to select more auditory sensations because you have eliminated visual cues.

We Perceive and Remember Selectively. Why do we select certain sounds, images, and sensations and not others? Four principles frame the process of how we select what we see, hear, and experience: selective perception, selective attention, selective exposure, and selective recall.

Selective perception occurs when we see, hear, or make sense of the world around us based on a host of factors such as our personality, beliefs, attitudes, hopes, fears, and culture, as well as what we like and don't like. We literally see and don't see things because of our tendency to perceive selectively. Your eyes and your brain do not work like a camera, which records everything in the picture. When you develop film, you capture what was in the viewfinder. Your brain doesn't necessarily process everything you see through your viewfinder. Similarly, your ear is not a microphone that consciously picks up every sound.

In a court of law, eyewitness testimony often determines whether someone is innocent or guilty of a crime. Recent research suggests, however, that a witness's powers of observation are not flawless. In fact, researchers have discovered several perceptual errors in eyewitness testimony. Many innocent people have been convicted because of what a witness thought he or she saw or heard. As this evidence documents, our eyes are not cameras; our ears are not microphones. We perceive selectively.

Selective attention is the process of focusing on specific stimuli; we selectively lock on to some things in our environment and ignore others. As in the selective perception process, we have a tendency to attend to those things around us that relate to our needs and wants. When you're hungry, for example, and you're looking for a place to grab a quick bite of lunch, you'll probably be more attentive to fast-food advertising and less focused on ads for cars. We also attend to information that is moving, blinking, flashing, interesting, novel, or noisy. Web page designers, for example, give a lot of thought to ways of catching our attention with advertisements.

Selective exposure is our tendency to put ourselves in situations that reinforce our attitudes, beliefs, values, or behaviors. The fact that we're selective about what we expose ourselves to means that we are more likely to be in places that make us feel comfortable and support the way we see the world than in places that make us uncomfortable. Whom do you usually find at a Baptist church on Sunday mornings? Baptists. Who attends a Democratic Party convention? Democrats. If you perceive yourself to be a good student who does everything possible to get high grades, you will do your best to attend class. We expose ourselves to situations that reinforce how we make sense out of the world.

selective perception Process of seeing, hearing, or making sense of the world around us based on such factors as our personality, beliefs, attitudes, hopes, fears, and culture, as well as what we like and don't like.

selective attention Process of focusing on specific stimuli, locking on to some things in the environment and ignoring others.

selective exposure Tendency to put ourselves in situations that reinforce our attitudes, beliefs, values, or behaviors.

When we observe others, we gather information about them and ascribe motives and causes to their behaviors—sometimes incorrectly. What do you perceive about this couple's relationship? What might they be discussing?

selective recall Process that occurs when we remember things we want to remember and forget or repress things that are unpleasant, uncomfortable, or unimportant to us.

thin slicing Observing a small sample of someone's behavior and then making a generalization about what the person is like, based on the sample.

Selective recall occurs when we remember things we want to remember and forget or repress things that are unpleasant, uncomfortable, or unimportant to us. Because our brains don't operate like cameras or microphones, not all that we see or hear is recorded in our memories so that we can easily retrieve it. Some experiences may simply be too painful to remember. Or we just don't remember some information because it's not relevant or needed (like the address of the web page you clicked on yesterday).

We Thin Slice. Have you ever gone to a grocery store and enjoyed the free samples that are sometimes offered to get you to buy various products? The grocer hopes that if you like the small sample, you'll want to purchase more. Perhaps after tasting a thin slice of cheese, you'll buy a pound of it. The concept of **thin slicing** in the perception process works the same way. You sample a little bit of someone's behavior and then generalize as to what the person may be like, based on the brief information you have observed. Journalist Malcolm Gladwell wrote a popular book called *Blink: The Power of Thinking Without Thinking,* in which he pointed to several examples of how people thin slice to make judgments of others.[2] For example, Gladwell reviewed research that found that a patient was less likely to sue a physician for malpractice if the doctor had effective "people skills." Doctors who took the time to listen, respond positively, empathize, and, in short, be other-oriented were less likely to be sued than doctors who were not other-oriented. As patients, we thin slice when we make a judgment about the overall credibility of a doctor based on just one aspect of the doctor's behavior—his or her bedside manner. Later in this book, we'll review the research of John Gottman, another researcher who has evidence of the accuracy of thin slicing; he has done extensive research about marriage and divorce. Gottman has been able to thin slice behaviors in marriage to be able to predict with 94 percent accuracy whether a couple will divorce.[3] He has found that when he watches videotapes of couples having conversations and discussing real issues and problems in their marriage, he can make very accurate guesses as to whether the couple will stay together. Gottman has developed a way of thin slicing these marriage relationships. The four behaviors that predict divorce if all are present are defensiveness, stonewalling (not responding), criticism, and contempt—with contempt being the most corrosive.

Some people are better at thin slicing than others. There is evidence, for example, that women are better than men in interpreting nonverbal cues. Can you improve your ability to thin slice with accuracy? Yes, but it takes time and practice. It took marriage researcher John Gottman many years and a significant amount of research to be able to know what to look for in order to predict a successful or unsuccessful marriage. Learning how to be more perceptive and being more other-oriented, the focus of this book, can improve your ability to thin slice accurately.

Stage 2: Organizing

Look at the four items in Figure 3.1. What does each of them mean to you? If you are like most people, you will perceive item A as a rabbit, item B as a telephone number, item C as the word *interpersonal,* and item D as a circle. Strictly speaking, none of those perceptions is correct. We discuss why after we explore the second stage of perception, organizing.

We organize our world by creating categories, linking together the categories we've created, and then seeking closure by filling in any missing gaps in what we perceive.

We Create Categories. After we perceive certain stimuli, we organize them into convenient, understandable, and efficient categories that let us make sense of what we have observed. Organizing, or chunking, what we perceive makes it easier to process complex information because it lets us impose the familiar on the unfamiliar, and because we can more easily store and recall simple patterns.

One of the ways we create categories is by **superimposing** a familiar structure on information we select. To superimpose is to use a framework we're already familiar with to interpret information that may, at first, look formless. We look for the familiar in the unfamiliar. For example, when you looked at item A in Figure 3.1, you saw the pattern of dots as a rabbit because *rabbit* is a concept you know and to which you attach various meanings. The set of dots would not have meaning for you in and of itself, nor would it be meaningful to you to attend to each particular dot or to the dots' relationships to one another. It would be possible to create a mathematical model of the dots indicating their placement on the *x-y* grid, but such a model would be extremely complex and difficult to observe and remember. It's much easier to organize the dots by superimposing something that is stored in your memory: a rabbit. For similar reasons, people have organized patterns of stars in the sky into the various constellations and have given them names that reflect their shapes, like the Bear, the Crab, and the Big and Little Dippers.

People also search for and apply patterns to their perceptions of other people. You might have a friend who jogs and works out at a gym. You put these together to create a pattern and label the friend as "athletic." That label represents a pattern of qualities you use in relating to your friend, a pattern that we discuss later in the chapter.

We Link Categories. Once we have created categories, we link them together as a way of further making sense of how we have chunked what we experience. We link the categories though a process called *punctuation*. **Punctuation** is the process of making sense out of stimuli by grouping, dividing, organizing, separating, and further categorizing information.[4]

Just as punctuation marks on this page tell you when a sentence ends, punctuation in the perception process makes it possible for you to see patterns in information. To many Americans, item B in Figure 3.1 looks like a telephone number because it has three numbers followed by four numbers. However, the digits could just as easily represent two totally independent numbers: five hundred fifty-five followed by the number four thousand, four hundred thirty-three. How we interpret the numbers depends on how we punctuate or separate them. When we record information, we use commas, periods, dashes, and colons to signal meanings and interpretations. In our minds, we sometimes impose punctuation marks where we believe they should be. For example, perhaps you mentally put a dash between 555 and 4433, even though no dash appears there.

When it comes to punctuating relational events and behaviors, people develop their own separate sets of standards. You will sometimes experience difficulties and disagreements because of differences in how you and your communication partner choose to punctuate a conversational exchange or a shared sequence of events.[5] One classic example of relational problems resulting from differences in punctuation involves a husband who withdraws and a wife who nags.[6] The husband punctuates their interactions in such a way that he sees his withdrawing as a reaction to her nagging. The wife, in contrast, sees herself as nagging her husband because he keeps

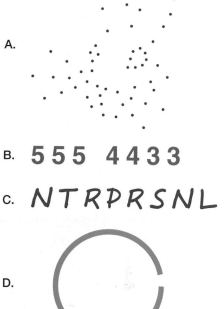

FIGURE 3.1
What Do You See?

superimpose To place a familiar structure on information you select.

punctuation Process of making sense out of stimuli by grouping, dividing, organizing, separating, and categorizing information.

withdrawing. The husband and wife punctuate their perceptions differently because they each perceive different starting points for their interactions. Resolving such conflicts involves having the parties describe how they have punctuated the event and agree on a common punctuation.

We Seek Closure.   Another way we organize information is by seeking closure. **Closure** is the process of filling in missing information or gaps in what we perceive. Looking again at Figure 3.1, you can understand people's inclination to label the figure in item D a circle, even though circles are continuous lines without gaps. We apply the same principles in our interactions with people. When we have an incomplete picture of another human being, we impose a pattern or structure, classify the person on the basis of the information we do have, and fill in any missing information. For example, when meeting someone for the first time who looks and acts like someone you already know, you may make assumptions about your new acquaintance, based on the characteristics of the person you already know. You close the gaps in the missing information about your new acquaintance, based on the characteristics of the person well known to you. Many of us are uncomfortable with uncertainty; creating closure is a way of helping us make better sense out of what is new and unfamiliar.

Stage 3: Interpreting

Once you have selected and organized stimuli, you next typically interpret the stimuli. You see your best friend across a crowded room at a party. He waves to you, and you say to yourself, "He wants to talk with me." Or you nervously wait as your British literature teacher hands back the results of the last exam. When the professor calls your name, she frowns ever so slightly; your heart sinks. You think, "I must have bombed on the test." Or, while you are out, your administrative assistant leaves you a note that your sister called. You're worried. You reflect, "My tightwad sister never uses her daytime cell phone minutes to call during the day. There must be something wrong." In each of these situations, you're trying to make sense out of the information you hear or see. You're attempting to interpret the meaning of the verbal and nonverbal cues you experience.

closure Process of filling in missing information or gaps in what we perceive.

RECAP   The Interpersonal Perception Process

Term	Explanation	Example
Selecting	The first stage in the perceptual process, in which we select certain sensations to focus awareness on	Sitting in your apartment where you hear lots of traffic sounds and car horns, but attending to a particular rhythmic car honking that seems to be right outside your door
Organizing	The second stage in the perceptual process, in which we assemble stimuli into convenient and efficient patterns	Putting together the car honking with your anticipation of a friend's arrival to pick you up in her car to drive to a movie that starts in five minutes
Interpreting	The final stage in perception, in which we assign meaning to what we have observed	Deciding the car honking must be your friend signaling you to come out to the car quickly because she's running late

We form impressions of others both passively and actively, and our own implicit assumptions and expectations color those impressions.

How We Form Impressions of Others

Impressions are collections of perceptions about others that we maintain and use to interpret their behaviors. Impressions tend to be very general: "She seems nice," "He was very friendly," or "What a nerd!" According to **impression formation theory,** we form these impressions based on our perceptions of physical qualities (what people look like), behavior (what people do), what people tell us, and what others tell us about them. When we first meet someone, we form a first impression without having much information, and we often hold on to this impression (even if it's an inaccurate one) throughout the relationship. So it's important to understand how we form impressions of others. Researchers have found that we often give special emphasis to the first things we see or the last things we observe about another person. We also generalize from specific positive or negative perceptions we hold.

Our perceptions of others affect how we communicate with them, and their perceptions of us affect the way they interact with us. It's through our perceptions that we develop general as well as specific impressions of other people. (And they do the same—they rely on their perceptions to develop impressions of us.) How much we notice about another person relates to our level of interest and need. We perceive others either passively or actively.

Passive perception occurs simply because we are alive and our senses are operating. We see, hear, smell, taste, and feel things around us without any conscious attempt

impression Collection of perceptions about others that you maintain and use to interpret their behaviors.

impression formation theory Theory that explains how you develop perceptions about people and how you maintain and use those perceptions to interpret their behaviors.

passive perception Perception that occurs without conscious effort, simply in response to one's surroundings.

to do so. No one teaches you to be passively perceptive; you simply respond to your surroundings. Similarly, you don't have to think about perceiving others, you just do it because you're alive.

Active perception doesn't just happen. It is the process of actively finding out specific information by intentionally observing and sometimes questioning others. We're engaged in active perception when we make a conscious effort to figure out what we are observing. Do you like to "people watch?" If you have some time on your hands while waiting for a friend, you may start just looking at people and making guesses about what these strangers do for a living, whether they are friendly, grumpy, peaceful, or petulant, where they are from, or whether they are married. When people watching, you are involved in active perception. You consciously make assumptions about the personalities and circumstances of those you observe.

As we make these assumptions and form impressions of others, most of us rely on an **implicit personality theory,** our personal set of assumptions and expectations or a pattern of associated qualities that we attribute to people, which allows us to understand them—whether we met them 10 minutes ago or 10 years ago. An implicit personality theory provides a way of organizing the vast array of information we have about people's personalities.[7]

Although an implicit personality theory describes how we organize and interpret our perceptions of people's personalities in general, we develop specific categories for people, called constructs. A **construct,** according to psychologist George Kelly, is a bipolar quality (that is, a quality with two opposite categories) or a continuum that we use to classify people.[8] We may pronounce someone good or bad, athletic or nonathletic, warm or cold, funny or humorless, selfish or generous, beautiful or ugly, kind or cruel, and so on. So we don't necessarily classify people in absolute terms—they are categorized in degrees.

As we meet and observe people, we draw on our own implicit personality theory to help us reduce our uncertainty about others. **Uncertainty reduction theory** suggests that one of the primary reasons we communicate at all is to reduce our uncertainty about what we see and experience. By making guesses and assumptions about people, we reduce our uncertainty. If we can reduce our uncertainty about other people, then we can predict their reactions and behaviors, adapt our behaviors and strategies, and therefore maximize the likelihood of fulfilling our own social needs.[9] Being able to reduce uncertainty and increase predictability gives us greater control when communicating with others. Although this might sound calculating, it really isn't. If you enjoy outdoor activities such as camping and hiking, one of your goals in establishing social relationships is probably to find others who share your interest. So actively observing, questioning, and consciously processing information to determine a potential friend's interests can help you assess whether the relationship will meet your goals. And in the spirit of being other-oriented, you will also be able to assess whether you can meet the goals and interests of the other person. In Chapter 5, we discuss ways to improve your ability to gain information through more effective listening.

Now let's take a closer look at several typical ways most of us form impressions of others: our tendency to emphasize what we see first or what we observe last when interacting with others, and our tendency to generalize from our perceptions of them as positive or negative.

We Emphasize What Comes First: The Primacy Effect

There is evidence that when we form impressions of others, we pay more attention to our first impressions. The tendency to attend to the first pieces of information that we observe about another person is called the **primacy effect.** The primacy effect was

---

BEING Other-ORIENTED

By listening to and observing others, we reduce our uncertainty about how they will interact with us. Think about a person you first met in school who is now a good friend. What type of active perception activities did you engage in to get to know this person better—to reduce your uncertainty about him or her? How would you assess your skill level in observing, questioning, and processing information to get to know other people?

---

active perception Perception that occurs because you seek out specific information through intentional observation and questioning.

implicit personality theory Your unique set of beliefs and hypotheses about what people are like.

construct Bipolar quality used to classify people.

uncertainty reduction theory Theory that claims people seek information in order to reduce uncertainty, thus achieving control and predictability.

primacy effect Tendency to attend to the first pieces of information observed about another person in order to form an impression documented in a famous study conducted by Solomon Asch.[10] Individuals were asked to evaluate two people based on two lists of adjectives. The list for the first person had the following adjectives: *intelligent, industrious, impulsive, critical, stubborn,* and *envious.* The list for the other person had the same adjectives, but in reverse order. Although the content was identical, respondents gave the first person a more positive evaluation than the second. One explanation for this is that the first words in each list created a first impression that respondents used to interpret the remaining adjectives. In a similar manner, the first impressions we form about someone often affect our interpretation of subsequent perceptions of that person.

We Emphasize What Comes Last: The Recency Effect

Not only do we give more weight to our first impressions, we also give considerable attention to our most recent experiences and impressions. The tendency to put a lot of stock in the last thing we observe is called the **recency effect.**[11] For example, if you have thought for years that your friend is honest, but today you discover that she lied to you about something important, that lie will have a greater impact on your impression of her than the honest behavior she has displayed for years. Similarly, if, during a job interview, you skillfully answered all of the interviewer's questions yet your last answer to a question was not the answer the interviewer was looking for, you may not get the job. If you're going to make mistakes in an interview, it's best not to do it at the beginning of the interview (primacy effect) or at the end of the conversation (recency effect).

We Generalize Positive Qualities to Others: The Halo Effect

One feature common to most of our implicit personality theories is the tendency to put people into one of two categories: people we like and people we don't like. Categorizing people as those we like often creates a **halo effect,** in which we attribute a variety of positive qualities to them without personally confirming the existence of these qualities. If you like me, you will add a "halo" to your impression of me and then apply to me those qualities from your implicit personality theory that apply to people you like, such as being considerate of other people, warm, caring, fun to be with and having a great sense of humor.

We Generalize Negative Qualities to Others: The Horn Effect

Just as we can use the halo effect to generalize about someone's positive qualities, the opposite can also happen. We sometimes make many negative assumptions about a person because of one unflattering perception. This is called the **horn effect,** named for the horns associated with medieval images of a devil. If you don't like the way someone looks, you might also decide that person is selfish or stingy and attribute a variety of negative qualities to that individual, using your implicit personality theory. As evidence of the horn effect, research suggests that during periods of conflict in our relationships, we are more likely to attribute negative behaviors to our feuding partner than we are to ourselves.[12] A little bit of negative information can affect how we perceive other attributes of a person.

In support of the premise underlying the horn effect, researchers Dominic Infante and Andrew Rancer observed that some people have a tendency to see the worst in others, which causes them to lash out and be verbally aggressive.[13] There is also evidence that some people interpret any negative feedback they receive as a personal attack, no matter how carefully the feedback is worded.[14] For many

recency effect Tendency to attend to the most recent information observed about another person in order to form or modify an impression.

halo effect Attributing a variety of positive qualities to those you like.

horn effect Attributing a variety of negative qualities to those you dislike.

people, there is no such thing as "constructive criticism." Like a sunburned sunbather, such people perceive even a mild suggestion presented with a light touch as a stinging rebuke.

How We Interpret the Behavior of Others

"I know why Alicia hasn't arrived at our meeting yet. She just doesn't like me. She is always late," says Cathy. "I'll bet she just wants people to think she's too busy to be on time for our little group meetings. She is so stuck up." Cathy seems not only to have formed a negative impression of Alicia, but also to harbor a hunch about why Alicia is typically late. Cathy is attributing meaning to Alicia's behavior. Even though Alicia could have just forgotten about the meeting, may have another meeting that always runs overtime right before her meeting with Cathy, or is from a culture in which meetings almost always start after the announced meeting time, Cathy thinks Alicia's absence is caused by feelings of superiority and contempt. Cathy's assumptions about Alicia can be explained by several theories about the way we interpret the behavior of others. Based on a small sample of someone's behavior, we develop our own explanations of why people do what they do. Attribution theory, standpoint theory, and intercultural communication theory can offer perspectives on how we make sense on what we perceive.

We Attribute Motives to Others' Behavior: Attribution Theory

Attribution theory explains how we ascribe specific motives and causes to the behaviors of others. It helps us interpret what people do. For example, suppose the student sitting next to you in class gets up in the middle of the lecture and walks out. Why did the student leave? Did the student become angry at something the instructor said? It seems unlikely—the lecturer was simply describing types of cloud formations. Was the student sick? You remember noticing that the student looked a little flushed and occasionally winced. Maybe the student has an upset stomach. Or maybe the student is just a bit of a rebel and often does strange things like leaving in the middle of a class.

Social psychologist Fritz Heider says that we are "naive psychologists,"[15] because we all seek to explain people's motives for their actions. We are naive because we do not create these explanations in a systematic or scientific manner, but rather by applying

attribution theory Theory that explains how you generate explanations for people's behaviors.

common sense to our observations. Developing the most credible explanation for the behavior of others is the goal of the attribution process.

Causal attribution theory identifies three potential causes for any person's action: circumstance, a stimulus, or the person herself or himself.[16] Attributing behavior to *circumstance* means that you believe a person acts in a certain way because the situation leaves no choice. This way of thinking places responsibility for the action outside of the person. There is interesting research that suggests that during times when you feel lonely and isolated from others, you are more likely to attribute your feelings of loneliness to your specific circumstance rather than to any flaws in your personality.[17]

You would be attributing to circumstance if you believed the student quickly left the classroom because of an upset stomach. Concluding that the student left because the instructor said something inappropriate would be attributing the student's action to the *stimulus* (the instructor). But if you knew the instructor hadn't said anything out of line and that the student was perfectly healthy, you would place the responsibility for the action on the student. Attributing to the *person* means that you believe there is some quality about the person that caused the observed behavior.

To explore how attributions to a person affect us, interpersonal communication researchers Anita Vangelisti and Stacy Young wanted to know whether intentionally hurtful words inflict more pain than unintentionally hurtful comments.[18] As you might suspect, if we think someone intends to hurt us, spiteful words have more sting and bite than if we believe someone does not intend to hurt our feelings. Our attributions are factors in our impressions.

We Use Our Own Point of Reference About Power: Standpoint Theory

Standpoint theory is yet another framework that seeks to explain how we interpret the behavior of others. The theory is relatively simple: We each see the world differently because we're each viewing it from a different position. Some people

causal attribution theory Theory of attribution that identifies the cause of a person's actions as circumstance, a stimulus, or the person himself or herself.

standpoint theory Theory that a person's social position, power, or cultural background influences how the person perceives the behavior of others.

UNDERSTANDING OTHERS
Adapting to Differences | The Power of Perspective

As noted in our discussion of standpoint theory, where you stand makes a difference in what you see and how you interpret human behavior. Following the September 11, 2001, terrorist attacks on the United States, discussions about the perceptions of the power and influence of different cultural groups and countries became more common.

Men and women, Blacks and Whites, Jews and Christians, Muslims and Hindus, Hispanics and Asians, gay and straight individuals, all experience life from their own cultural standpoints, which means they all have perceptions about their influence on others. To become more other-oriented is to become aware of your own perceived place in society and to be more sensitive to how that position of power or lack of power affects how you perceive others with a different standpoint.

To explore applications of standpoint theory in your life, consider the following questions:

1. How would you describe your standpoint in terms of power and influence in your school or at work, or in your family? Have you ever experienced rejection, alienation, or discrimination based on how others perceived you?

2. How would other people in your life (parents, siblings, children, coworkers, employer, or friends) describe your power and influence on them?

3. How does your standpoint influence your relationship with others? Identify a specific relationship with a teacher, coworker, or family member in which different standpoints influence the quality of the relationship in either positive or negative ways.

4. What can you do to become more aware of how your standpoint influences your interactions with others? How can your increased awareness enhance the quality of your interpersonal communication with others?

have positions of power, and others do not; the resources that we have to help us make our way through life provide a lens through which we view the world and the people in it.

Standpoint theory explains why people with differing cultural backgrounds have different perceptions of others' behavior. In the early nineteenth century, German philosopher Georg Hegel noted this simple but powerful explanation of why people see and experience the world differently.[19] Hegel was especially interested in how one's standpoint was determined in part by one's power and influence. For example, people who have greater power and more influence in a particular culture may not be aware of their power and influence and how this power affects their perceptions of others. A person with less power (which in many cultures includes women and people of color) may be acutely aware of the power he or she doesn't have.

As evidence of standpoint theory, one team of researchers found that people who perceived that they were the victims of someone's lying to them or cheating them had an overall more negative view of the communication with their lying or cheating communication partner than with someone who they perceived did not lie or cheat.[20] This makes sense, doesn't it? If our point of view is that a certain person can't be trusted in one situation, we are less likely to trust the person in other situations. C. S. Lewis was right: What we see and hear depends a good deal on where we are standing.

▶ RECAP   How We Organize and Interpret Interpersonal Perceptions

Theory	Description	Example
Impression Formation Theory	We form general impressions of others based on general physical qualities, behaviors, and disclosed information.	Categorizing people as nice, friendly, shy, or handsome
Implicit Personality Theory	We use a personal set of assumptions to draw specific conclusions about someone's personality.	"If she is intelligent, then I believe she must be caring, too."
Attribution Theory	We develop reasons to explain the behaviors of others.	"I guess she didn't return my call because she doesn't like me." "He's just letting off steam because he had a bad week of exams."
Causal Attribution Theory	We ascribe a person's actions to circumstance, a stimulus, or the person himself or herself.	"He didn't go to class because his alarm didn't go off." "He didn't go to class because it was a makeup session." "He didn't go to class because he is bored by it."
Standpoint Theory	We interpret the behavior of others through the lens of our own social position, power, or cultural background.	"He won't join the fraternity because he doesn't understand how important that network can be to his professional career."

We Draw on Our Own Cultural Background: Intercultural Communication Theory

When Cathy thought Alicia was rude and thoughtless because she always arrived at their meetings late, Cathy was attributing meaning to Alicia's behavior based on Cathy's cultural assumptions about when meetings usually begin. According to Cathy, if a meeting is supposed to start at 10:00 A.M., it's important to be prompt and be ready to begin on time. But Alicia comes from a culture with a different approach to time; in Alicia's culture, meetings *never* begin on time. In fact, it's polite, according to Alicia, to be fashionably late so that the meeting leader can greet people and make any last-minute preparations for the meeting. To show up on time would be disrespectful. Both Alicia and Cathy are making sense out of their actions based on their own cultural framework. Alicia and Cathy aren't the only ones who interpret behavior through their cultural lens—we all do.

Culture is a learned system of knowledge, behaviors, attitudes, beliefs, values, and norms that is shared by a group of people. Our culture is reflected not only in our behavior but in every aspect of the way we live our lives. The categories of things and ideas that identify the most profound aspects of cultural influence are known as *cultural elements*. According to one research team, cultural elements include the following:[21]

- Material culture: housing, clothing, automobiles, and other tangible things

- Social institutions: schools, governments, religious organizations

- Belief systems: ideas about individuals and the universe

- Aesthetics: music, theatre, art, dance

- Language: verbal and nonverbal communication systems

As you can see from the list, cultural elements are not only things we can see and hear, but also ideas and values. And because these elements are so prevalent, they have an effect on how we interpret all that we experience.

Our culture is like the air we breathe, in that we're often not aware that it's there—we simply go about our daily routines, usually not conscious that we are breathing. Because our culture is ever-present and is constantly influencing our thoughts and behavior, it has a profound impact on how we experience the world. If

Our own cultural framework has a profound effect on how we interpret everything we experience, including our interactions with others. Do people in your own culture typically behave like those in this photo? If not, what is your reaction to what you see here?

you come from a culture in which horsemeat is a delicacy, you'll likely savor each bite of your horse steak, because you've learned to enjoy it. Yet if eating horsemeat is not part of your cultural heritage, you will have a different perception if you're invited to chow down on filet of horse. So it is with how we interpret the behavior of other people who have different cultural expectations than we do. In some countries, men kiss each other on the cheek when greeting one another, or they may walk arm in arm down the sidewalk when conversing. These are considered normal and natural aspects of human interaction. Yet in North America, these behaviors may be perceived differently because of different cultural expectations.

In a study investigating whether people from a variety of cultural backgrounds used their own culture to make sense out of the behavior of others, researchers found that *stereotyping*—making rigid judgments of others based on a small bit of information—is rampant in many cultures.[22] In this study, participants from Australia, Botswana, Canada, Kenya, Nigeria, South Africa, Zambia, Zimbabwe, and the United States all consistently formed stereotypical impressions of others. Culture strongly influences how we interpret the actions of others.

Barriers to Accurate Interpersonal Perception

Think about the most recent interaction you had with a stranger. Do you remember the person's age, sex, race, or physical description? Did the person have any distinguishing features, such as a beard, tattoos, or a loud voice? The qualities you recall

culture Learned system of knowledge, behaviors, attitudes, beliefs, values, and norms shared by a group of people.

will most likely serve as the basis for attributions you make about that person's behavior. But these attributions, based on your first impressions, might be wrong. Each person sees the world from his or her own unique perspective. That perspective is clouded by a number of distortions and barriers that contribute to inaccurate interpersonal perception.

We Stereotype

Preconceived notions about what they expect to find may keep people from seeing what's before their eyes and ears. We see what we want to see, hear what we want to hear. We stereotype others. To **stereotype** someone is to attribute a set of qualities to the person because of his or her membership in some category. The word *stereotype* was originally a printing term, referring to a metal plate that was cast from type set by a printer. The plate would print the same page of type over and over again. When we stereotype people, we place them into inflexible, all-compassing categories. We "print" the same judgments on anyone placed in a given category.

Stereotyping other people and then treating them unfairly is a significant problem in modern society. There is clear evidence that this problem is especially acute for socially marginalized groups such as gays and lesbians and Blacks.[23] Being aware of the problem is the first step to overcoming it.

We are more likely, according to communication researchers, to maintain our stereotypes of others if we believe that the people with whom we typically interact also share our stereotype.[24] Why? People who hold a common stereotype reinforce one another's thinking.

When we stereotype others, we overgeneralize. To *overgeneralize* is to treat small amounts of information as if they were highly representative. This tendency also leads people to draw inaccurate, prejudicial conclusions.[25] For example, a professor may talk to two students and then generalize the impression he or she develops of those two students to the entire student population. In a similar way, most people tend to assume that the small sampling of another person's behavior is a valid representation of who that person is. As you saw in Figure 3.1, you might perceive a rabbit even when you have only a few dots on which to base your perception.

To overgeneralize is similar to the concept of thin slicing that we discussed earlier in the chapter. Although we each thin slice—use a small sample of information to reach a conclusion—a problem occurs when the conclusion we reach from a brief observation is inaccurate. Overgeneralization occurs when the thin-sliced information we use to reach a conclusion is wrong. When making snap judgments from only bits of information, realize the potential for drawing an inaccurate conclusion.

We also stereotype others when we *oversimplify*—which is a human tendency to prefer a simple explanation to a more complex one. When Imelda picks you up late to go to a movie, she says, "Sorry, I lost track of the time." The next day, Mary also picks you up late to go to a movie. She says, "Sorry. You wouldn't believe how busy I've been. I ran out of hot water when I was showering, and my hair dryer must be busted. It kept shutting off. Then I stopped to get something to eat, and it took forever to get my order. And then it turned out they had it all messed up and had to redo it." Whose explanation can you accept more easily, Imelda's or Mary's?

Usually, people prefer simple explanations; they tend to be more believable and easier to use in making sense of another's actions. But in reality, our behaviors are affected by a multitude of factors, as Mary's explanation indicates. Unfortunately, it takes a lot of effort to understand what makes another person do what he or she does—more effort than we are typically willing to give.

stereotype To attribute a set of qualities to a person because of the person's membership in some category.

Relating to Others in the 21st Century   Stereotyping Others Online

We've identified several theories that explain how we form impressions of other people when communicating via electronically mediated communication (EMC). These theories can help you explain and predict how others develop stereotypical impressions of you and how you may stereotype others based on your EMC. As we noted in Chapter 1, researchers first thought that because communicating via e-mail, text message, Facebook, Twitter, or phone offers fewer nonverbal cues, these media allow only limited expressions of relationship cues and feelings. This theory is called the *cues-filtered-out theory*.[26] But more recently, researchers have found support for *social information-processing theory*. This theory suggests that EMC *does* include relationship cues and additional information that communicates feelings and emotions (such as emoticons), as well as more subtle cues embedded in the message, (such as how long someone takes to respond to a message, the formality of a message, use of all capital letters for emphasis, or even attention to spelling). It just takes longer for those cues to be evidenced as we interact online.[27] So although there may be fewer cues available to help us form impressions of others when we communicate online, those that do exist may be even more potent in influencing the impressions we form and impressions others form of us.

Regardless of which theory explains how we form impressions of others online, there is evidence that we use what cues are present online to stereotype others, just as we do in face-to-face interactions. In fact, we may be *more* likely to stereotype others online than in person, because we have to make more inferences about the other person—because there are fewer cues and because it takes longer for relationship cues to emerge. This theory is called the **social identity model of deindividuation effects (SIDE)**.[28] We are more likely to reduce someone to a stereotype or, to use a technical term, to *deindividuate* someone, online because we have fewer cues to help us develop a clear impression of others.

One study found that Asian American women were stereotypically perceived as shyer and more introverted compared to African American women when communicating via e-mail but not when communicating by telephone.[29] The fewer cues available, the more likely stereotypical perceptions of the other person were to emerge. Since e-mail offers fewer cues than the telephone (the telephone is a richer medium), stereotyping is more likely in the media-lean e-mail context. Another study found that people make stereotypical judgments about another person's gender when communicating via e-mail when they aren't certain whether the person they are interacting with is a male or female.[30] We use whatever cues we have, such as language style, and even topics discussed, to help us form a stereotypical impression of the other person.

Another interesting study suggests that people may form stereotyped impressions about you based on the perceived physical attractiveness of the friends you have posted on your MySpace or FaceBook pages.[31] We apparently use all of the information we can get to help us form impressions of others when interacting online, including how attractive we perceive other people's friends to be. If the friends whose photos appear on your page are attractive, research suggests *you* will be perceived as more attractive and have a more positive impression on others than if your friends are perceived as less attractive in appearance.[32] In short, you look good if you have friends who look good. This suggests that people form stereotypes not only on the basis of the qualities of other people but also by using context cues about those with whom others associate.

What are the implications of these research studies? They suggest that in the twenty-first century, we are *more* likely rather than less likely to stereotype others when communicating online. We are more likely to overgeneralize and to oversimplify because we have limited information available. The problem is that with less relational information or fewer cues in general, we may be even more inaccurate in making stereotypical judgments of others online. So be mindful of the potential for developing inaccurate stereotypes online. Being aware of the problem is the first step in avoiding the problem.

We Ignore Information

People sometimes don't focus on important information, because they give too much weight to information that is obvious and superficial.[33] Why do we ignore important information that may be staring us in the face? It's because, as you learned in the discussion about attribution theory, we tend to explain a person's motives on the basis of the most obvious information rather than on in-depth information we might have. When meeting someone new, we perceive his or her physical qualities first: color of skin, body size and shape, age, sex, and other obvious characteristics. We overattribute to these qualities, because they are so vivid and available, and ignore other

social identity model of deindividuation effects (SIDE) Theory that people are more likely to stereotype others with whom they interact online, because such interactions provide fewer relationship cues and the cues take longer to emerge than they would in face-to-face interactions.

Stereotypes can help us make sense out of the wide range of stimuli we encounter every day. But we also need to be sure that we don't overuse stereotypes and thus fail to see people as individuals.

details. We have all been victims of these kinds of attributions, some of us more than others. Often, we are unaware that others are making biased attributions, because they do not express them openly. But sometimes we can tell by the way others react to us and treat us. We may even choose to ignore contradictory information that we receive directly from the other person. Instead of adjusting our conception of that person, we adjust our perception.[34] The halo and horn effects discussed earlier reflect this tendency. For example, if an instructor gets an excellent paper from a student who the instructor has concluded is not particularly bright or motivated, she may tend to find errors and shortcomings that are not really there, or she may even accuse the student of plagiarism.

There is evidence that we make stereotypical judgments of others even when we may not be fully aware that we are making such judgments. Researchers have found that we hold what are called *implicit attitudes* that affect how we perceive others.[35] Since these implicit attitudes operate below our level of awareness, it's important to monitor our behavior and reactions to others to ensure that we are not unfairly, inaccurately, or inappropriately making stereotypical judgments of them.

Categorizing individuals is not an inherently bad thing to do, but it is harmful to hang on to an inflexible image of another person in the face of contradictory information. For example, not all mothers are responsible or loving. But because American culture typically reveres motherhood, we may not easily process our perceptions of a mother who is abusive or negligent. Researchers have suggested that when we categorize and stereotype others, we do so to meet our own needs for power, authority, and structure.[36] And it's the minority group with less social and political power that tends to be marginalized and to get lost in the power shuffle.[37]

To become more other-oriented is to become aware of your own perceived place in the power hierarchy in our society and to be more sensitive about how that position of power or lack of power affects your perceptions of others with a different level of power. Where are you in the power structure in your school, family, workplace, and in society in general? Whether you perceive yourself to have power or not, understanding your relative power level can help explain and predict how others will interact with you.

In the next chapter, we will explore how cultural differences have an impact on our interactions with others and identify strategies to more mindfully bridge cultural barriers that may contribute to negative perceptions of others.

We Impose Consistency

People overestimate the consistency and constancy of others' behaviors. When we organize our perceptions, we also tend to ignore fluctuation in people's behaviors and instead see them as consistent. We believe that if someone acted a certain way one day, he or she will continue to act that way in the future. Perhaps you have embarrassed yourself in front of a new acquaintance by acting foolish and silly. At another encounter with this new acquaintance, you realize that the person is continuing to see your behavior as foolish, even though you don't intend it to be seen that way. The other person is imposing consistency on your inconsistent behavior.

In fact, everyone's behavior varies from day to day. Some days, we are in a bad mood, and our behavior on those days does not represent what we are generally like. As intimacy develops in relationships, we interact with our partners in varying circumstances that provide a more complete picture of our true nature.

We Focus on the Negative

People give more weight to negative information than to positive information.[38] Job interviewers often ask you to describe your strengths and weaknesses. If you describe five strengths and one weakness, it is likely that the interviewer will attend more to the one weakness you mention than to the strengths. We seem to recognize this bias and compensate for it when we first meet someone by sharing only positive information about ourselves.

In another of Solomon Asch's experiments on impression formation, participants heard one of the following two lists of terms to describe a person: (1) *intelligent, skillful, industrious, warm, determined, practical, cautious;* or (2) *intelligent, skillful, industrious, cold, determined, practical, cautious.*[39] The only difference in these two lists is the use of *warm* in the first list and *cold* in the second. Despite the presence of six other terms, those who heard the "cold" list had a much more negative impression of the person than those who heard the "warm" list. One piece of negative information can have a disproportionate effect on our impressions and negate the effect of several positive pieces of information. Perhaps you've noticed that following a near-flawless Olympic ice skating performance, the TV commentator, rather than focusing on the best executed leaps, twists, and turns, will first replay the one small error the skater made in the performance. In our own lives, we may have a tendency to do the same thing; we may focus on what we didn't do well rather than emphasizing what we've done skillfully.

We Blame Others, Assuming They Have Control

People are more likely to believe that others are to blame when things go wrong than to believe that the problem was beyond their control. Your parents were looking forward to celebrating their twenty-fifth wedding anniversary. They planned a quiet family celebration at a restaurant. You set your personal digital assistant to remind you one week before the anniversary dinner to buy them a present to give to them at the dinner. You hadn't anticipated, however, that you'd lose your PDA. When the phone rang and your mom asked, "Where are you?" it all came jarringly back to you: Today was their anniversary, and you'd forgotten it! Not only did you forget to buy them a present, you forgot to attend the dinner. Your parents were hurt. Your mother's quivering "How could you forget?" still sears your conscience. Your parents' hurt feelings evolved into anger. They think you just didn't care enough about them to remember such an important day. Rather than thinking that there might be an explanation for why you forgot their important day, they blame you for your thoughtlessness. Although they certainly have a right to be upset, their assuming that you don't care about them is an example of what researchers call a fundamental attribution error.

A **fundamental attribution error** occurs when a person blames a problem on something that is personally controllable (such as forgetting an important date because you don't care about your parents) rather than something uncontrollable (losing your personal digital assistant and having no back-up system to remind you of the event).[40] Stated simply: We are likely to think that a person's behavior is influenced by his or

fundamental attribution error
Error that arises from attributing another person's behavior to internal, controllable causes rather than to external, uncontrollable causes.

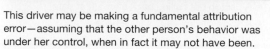
This driver may be making a fundamental attribution error—assuming that the other person's behavior was under her control, when in fact it may not have been.

her actions and choices rather than by external causes. We assume that people are responsible for their own actions. For example, the fundamental attribution error would predict that you're more likely to assume that the person who cuts you off in traffic is a jerk rather than to assume he's trying to get out of the way of the truck that's tailgating him. If you assume another person made a conscious choice to hurt you instead of considering that there may be other reasons for the person's behavior that are beyond the person's control, you've made a fundamental attribution error. You can avoid making a fundamental attribution error by honestly examining your role in the communication process. There is also evidence that the more empathic or other-oriented we are, the less likely we are to blame the other person for any problem or mistake.[41] For example, if we can empathize with someone over the recent death of a loved one or a recent divorce, we may "cut that person some slack" and excuse behavior that otherwise might strike us as rude or self-centered. When you've made a mistake about a person's behavior, admit it. You can enhance the quality of your relationships when you own up to making perceptual errors.

We Avoid Responsibility

People are more likely to save face by believing that they are not the cause of a problem; people assume that other people or events are more than likely the source of problems or events that may put them in an unfavorable light. In one classic episode of *The Simpsons*, Bart Simpson created a popular catch phrase by saying, "I didn't do it" when he clearly was the cause of a calamity. Whether it was lighting Lisa's hair on fire, calling Moe's tavern asking for Al Coholic, or putting baby Maggie on the roof, Bart would simply say, "I didn't do it." We chuckle at Bart's antics and would never stoop to such juvenile pranks. Yet there is evidence that when we *do* cause a problem or make a mistake, we are more likely to blame someone else rather than ourselves. Bart's "I didn't do it" approach to life represents self-serving bias.

When we avoid taking responsibility for our own errors and mistakes, we are guilty of what researchers call the self-serving bias. **Self-serving bias** is the tendency to

self-serving bias Tendency to perceive our own behavior as more positive than others' behavior.

Building Your Skills	Assuming the Best or the Worst About Others: Identifying Alternative Explanations

Do you give people the benefit of the doubt when they do something that irritates you or make a mistake, or do you tend to assume the worst about their intentions? The fundamental attribution error is the human tendency to believe that the cause of a problem or a personal slight is something that is within the other person's control, rather than external to the person. This tendency to blame others rather than considering that there may be an alternative explanation for a problem or a behavior can result in developing a judgmental, negative attitude toward others. For each of the following, think about what your first explanation was when the event happened to you:

- A person not calling back after a first date
- A server giving you lousy service

- A customer service person promising your car would be fixed by 5:00 P.M., but it isn't
- A teacher being late for class
- A teacher not returning grades when he or she promised
- A student copying test answers from the student next to him
- A sales clerk ignoring you when you need assistance
- A friend not remembering your birthday

Now go back and generate several additional possible explanations for each behavior. How can you be sure which explanation is accurate? How often do you commit the fundamental attribution error? How often do you give someone the benefit of the doubt?

perceive our own behavior as more positive than others' behavior. Sociologist Erving Goffman was one of the first to note this tendency when he wrote his classic book *The Preservation of Self in Everyday Life*.[42] As the title of Goffman's book reveals, we work hard to preserve our own selves. We strive to preserve not only our physical existence, but our psychological health as well. We sometimes may try to preserve a positive image of ourselves by not taking responsibility for our mistakes and by telling ourselves that we are skilled and effective. We are likely, for example, to attribute our own personal success to our hard work and effort rather than any to external, uncontrollable causes. You get an A on your anthropology paper because, you think, "I'm smart." When you get an F on your history paper, it's because your neighbor's loud party kept you up all night and you couldn't study. Self-serving bias is the tendency to take credit for the good things that happen to you and to say "I didn't do it" or "It's not my fault" when bad things happen to you.[43] Simply being aware of the self-serving bias may help you become more objective and accurate in identifying the causes of calamities in your own life.

▶ RECAP Barriers to Accurate Interpersonal Perception

Ignoring Information	We don't focus on important information because we give too much weight to obvious and superficial information.
Stereotyping	We allow our pre-existing rigid expectations about others to influence our perceptions.
Imposing Consistency	We overestimate the consistency and constancy of others' behavior.
Focusing on the Negative	We give more weight to negative information than to positive information.
Blaming Others by Assuming They Have Control	We are more likely to believe that others are to blame when things go wrong than to assume that the cause of the problem was beyond their control.
Avoiding Responsibility	We save face by believing that other people, not ourselves, are the cause of problems; when things go right, it's because of our own skills and abilities rather than help from others.

How to Improve Interpersonal Perception Skills

With so many barriers to perceiving and interpreting other people's behavior accurately, what can you do to improve your perception skills? Increasing your awareness of the factors that lead to inaccuracy will help initially, and you will find additional suggestions in this section. Ultimately, your improvement will depend on your willingness to expand your experiences, to communicate about your perceptions with others, and to seek out and consider others' perceptions of you. Realize that you have had a lifetime to develop these barriers and that it will take time, commitment, and effort to overcome their effects.

Be Aware of Your Personal Perception Barriers

Don't get the idea that you (and everybody else) are automatically doomed to enact the various perception barriers that we've described. We presented them so that you can spot them and work to minimize them as you form impressions of and interact with others. But before you can minimize these perception barriers, you need to be aware of which ones are most likely to affect you. Go back over the descriptions of the perception barriers and identify those that you've found yourself doing most often. Specifically, which of the barriers are you most susceptible to? Do you tend to ignore information, to think in terms of stereotypes, or to blame others as your first response? After identifying the barrier or barriers that you most often encounter, it may be helpful to think of a specific situation in which you perceived someone else inaccurately. What could you have done differently to gain additional information before drawing an inaccurate conclusion? Although making perceptual errors is a natural human tendency, by being aware of these barriers you can be on the lookout for them in your own interactions with others and more actively work to minimize their impact.

Be Mindful of the Behaviors That Create Meaning for You

To be **mindful** is to be conscious of what you are doing, thinking, and sensing at any given moment. In Chapter 2 we noted that you are sometimes unconsciously incompetent—you may not even realize when you are making a perceptual error. A way to increase your perceptual accuracy is to make an effort to be less on "automatic pilot" when making judgments of others and more aware of the conclusions that you draw. The opposite of being mindful is to be mindless—not attuned to what is happening to you. Have you ever walked into a room and then forgotten why you were going there? (Trust us: If this hasn't happened to you, it will happen as you get older.) Or have you ever misplaced your keys, even though you just had them in your hand minutes earlier? How could you forget what you were directly experiencing just moments ago? The answer is, you were mindless rather than mindful. We sometimes aren't paying attention to what we are doing. When you interact with others, try to identify one new thing to focus on and observe each time. Watch gestures, eyes, the wrinkles around eyes, foot movements; listen to tone of voice. Try to notice as much detail as possible, but keep the entire picture in view, being mindful of what you are observing.

Just by reading this chapter, you've gained greater understanding of how the perception process affects your relationships with others. Use your knowledge of the perceptual process to sharpen your own perceptions and conclusions. Here are additional strategies to help you become a more accurate perceiver.

mindful Conscious of what you are doing, thinking, and sensing at any given moment.

Link Details with the Big Picture

Any skilled detective knows how to take a small piece of information or evidence and use it to reach a broader conclusion. Skilled perceivers keep the big picture in mind as they look for clues about a person. Just because someone may dress differently from you, or have a pronounced accent, don't rush to judgment about the person based on such few snatches of information. Look and listen for other cues about your new acquaintance that can help you develop a more accurate understanding of who that person is. Try not to use early information to form a quick or rigid judgment that may be inaccurate. Look at all the details you've gathered.

Become Aware of Others' Perceptions of You

The best athletes don't avoid hearing criticism and observations from their coaches. Instead, they seek out as much feedback as they can about what they are doing right

BEING Other-ORIENTED

Being willing not only to accept criticism from others but also to seek it can enhance a relationship, if both people are sensitive when sharing and listening. Can you think of criticism that a close friend or family member has shared with you that strengthened the quality of your relationship with that person? Have you heard criticism that caused a relationship to deteriorate? What kind of shared information makes a relationship stronger? What kinds of criticism may be damaging to a relationship?

and wrong. It is difficult to be objective about our own behavior, so feedback from others can help us with our self-perceptions. The strongest relationships are those in which the partners are willing both to share their perceptions and to be receptive to the perceptions of the other.

Check Your Perceptions

Throughout this chapter we've encouraged you to be more mindful of your communication with others. It may seem like we're expecting you to be a mind reader—to just look at someone and know precisely what he or she is thinking. Mind reading may be a good circus act, but it's not a well-documented way of enhancing your perception of others. What does seem to work is to check your perceptions of others.

You can check out the accuracy of your perceptions and attributions in two ways: indirectly and directly. **Indirect perception checking** involves seeking additional information through passive perception, either to confirm or to refute your interpretations. If you suspect someone is

Do you think this woman is using direct perception checking, indirect perception checking, or a combination of the two?

angry at you but is not admitting it, for example, you could look for more cues in his or her tone of voice, eye contact, and body movements to confirm your suspicion. You could also listen more intently to the person's words and language.

Direct perception checking involves asking straight out whether your interpretation of what you perceive is correct. Asking someone to confirm a perception shows that you are committed to understanding his or her behavior. If your friend's voice sounds weary and her posture is sagging, you may assume that she is depressed or upset. If you ask, "I get the feeling from your tone of voice and the way you're acting that you are kind of down and depressed; what's wrong?" your friend can then either provide another interpretation: "I'm just tired; I had a busy week"; or expand on your interpretation: "Yeah, things haven't been going very well. . . ." Your observation might also trigger a revelation: "Really? I didn't realize I was acting that way. I guess I am a little down."

indirect perception checking
Seeking through passive perception such as observing and listening additional information to confirm or refute interpretations you are making.

direct perception checking
Asking for confirmation from the observed person of an interpretation or a perception about him or her.

Become Other-Oriented

Effective interpersonal perception depends on the ability to understand where others are coming from, to get inside their heads, to see things from their perspectives.

Becoming other-oriented involves a two-step process: social decentering (consciously *thinking* about another's thoughts and feelings) and empathizing (*responding emotionally* to another's feelings).[44] What does your boss think and feel when you arrive late for work? What would your spouse think and feel if you brought a dog home as a surprise gift? Throughout this book we offer suggestions for becoming other-oriented, for reminding yourself that the world does not revolve around you. Being other-oriented enables you to increase your understanding of others and improve your ability to predict and adapt to what others do and say.

To improve your ability to socially decenter and to empathize, strive for two key goals: (1) Gather as much information as possible about the circumstances that are affecting the other person; and (2) gather as much information as possible about the other person.

BEING Other-ORIENTED

Being other-oriented may sound like a simple set of techniques that can solve all relationship problems. But it's not that simple. And we don't claim that if you *are* other-oriented, all your relational challenges will melt away. Can you think of situations in which you believed you were being other-oriented, yet the relationship continued to experience turbulence and challenges? What are the limitations of being other-oriented?

Communication and Emotion

How to More Accurately Perceive the Emotions of Others

One barrier to effective interpersonal communication is inaccurately perceiving the emotional expressions of others. Misreading someone's emotional response can impede effective and appropriate communication with that person. If, for example, you think your friend is angry with you because of something that you did, when in reality, he is upset because of his poor performance on a test, your misattribution of your friend's emotion could create relational turbulence between the two of you. Inaccurately jumping to conclusions, either about what emotion someone may be experiencing or about the cause of that emotion, reduces communication effectiveness.

In this chapter we've discussed the role of attribution theory as a framework for understanding how we interpret the behavior of others, including emotional expression. Attribution theory explains why we may think someone is angry, upset, frustrated, or delighted because of something we said or did.

How can we improve our ability to accurately perceive what others may feel or express? One way is to use the perception checking skills we've presented. You can try the indirect perception checking approach by simply withholding your interpretation until you spend more time observing your partner. Or you can use direct perception checking. Rather than trying to read someone's mind and make an assumption about what the person may be feeling, you can check your perceptions directly by asking that person what she or he is feeling.

- Step one is to observe what someone is expressing nonverbally (the person's facial expression, tone of voice, movement, posture, and gestures).
- Step two is to make a mindful guess as to what the person may be feeling. But don't stop there.
- Step three is to ask a question to check whether your impression is accurate.

Besides using perception checking, it's useful to keep the following principles in mind when trying to accurately perceive others' emotions.

- Seek to interpret someone's emotion by considering the overall context of the communication.
- Don't consider just one bit of behavior, such as only facial expression or only tone of voice; look for a variety of cues, both spoken and unspoken, to increase the accuracy of your perception of your partner's emotions.
- Consider how your partner has responded to information and events in the past to help you interpret emotional responses.

Being conscious of attribution theory, effectively using perception checking skills, and being mindful of general strategies for accurately interpreting emotions can help enhance the quality of your interpretations of the emotional expressions of others.

APPLYING AN OTHER-ORIENTATION
to Interpersonal Perception

We continue to stress the importance of considering the thoughts and feelings of others as a way to enhance the quality of our interpersonal relationships. When forming impressions of others and striving to perceive them accurately, it's especially important to consider what the other person may be thinking and feeling. To help you become more other-oriented, we offer several questions you could ask yourself. You don't need to ponder each question every time you meet someone new—that would be unrealistic. But in situations in which it's especially important to form an accurate impression of

someone (whether you're interviewing the person for a job or thinking about asking the person out on a date), consider these questions:

- What factors or circumstances are affecting the other person right now?
- How can I determine whether there are factors I don't know about or don't fully understand about the other person? Should I ask specific questions?
- What do I know about this person that explains his or her behaviors?
- What might be going on in the other person's mind right now?

- What might the other person be feeling right now?
- What other possible explanations could there be for the person's actions?
- What would I be thinking if I were in the same situation as this person?
- How would I be feeling if I were in the same situation as this person?
- What would most other people think if they were in that situation?
- How would most other people feel if they were in that situation?

Understanding Interpersonal Perception
(pages 62–66)

Interpersonal perception is a fundamental element of interpersonal communication. It is the process by which you decide what people are like and give meaning to their actions, including selecting information about them and forming impressions about their personalities and behavior. We select information, make judgments, organize, and create categories to help us make sense of what we observe and interpret what we see, hear, and experience.

Key Terms

Perception 62
Interpersonal perception 62
Selective perception 63
Selective attention 63
Selective exposure 63
Selective recall 64
Thin slicing 64
Superimpose 65
Punctuation 65
Closure 66

Critical Thinking Questions

1. Describe your current environment. What is going on around you at the moment? Is there noise in the room? Noise outside the room? What do you see? What can you smell? Are you being distracted by technology—TV, radio, iPod, cell phone, etc.? Are there other people around? What are you attending to most closely? What sensory input are you selecting? Are you perceiving other things that you are able to ignore or tune out? Explain.

2. Do you ever "people watch"? If so, do you find that you thin slice, or make judgments about the people you are observing? What cues do you tend to focus on?

Activities

Find a magazine ad or illustration, a photograph, or a painting that shows a group of people, and bring it to class. In groups of four or five, pass around the pictures. For each picture, write down a few words to describe your perceptions of what you see. What are the people doing? What is their relationship to one another? What is each person like? How is each person feeling? Why are they doing what they are doing? After you have finished, share what you wrote with the others in your group. Try to determine why people's descriptions of what they saw differed. What factors influenced your perceptions?

Web Resources

http://novaonline.nv.cc.va.us/eli/spd110td/interper/siteindex .html Learn more about the perception process at this site; explore how the way you make sense out of the world affects the way you communicate with others.

http://lynn_meade.tripod.com/id38.htm Visit this site and explore the meaning of self-concept and perception while gaining knowledge about yourself through an assortment of tests.

How We Form Impressions of Others and Interpret Their Behaviors
(pages 67–73)

Our perceptions and the impressions we form of others affect how we communicate with them, and their perceptions of us affect the way they interact and communicate with us. Attribution theory, standpoint theory, and intercultural communication theory offer perspectives on how to make sense of what we perceive.

Key Terms

Impressions 67
Impression formation theory 67
Passive perception 67
Active perception 68
Implicit personality theory 68
Construct 68
Uncertainty reduction theory 68
Primacy effect 68
Recency effect 69
Halo effect 69
Horn effect 69
Attribution theory 70
Causal attribution theory 71
Standpoint theory 71
Culture 73

Critical Thinking Questions

1. Describe a recent situation in which your first impression of someone turned out to be inaccurate. What led you to form this initial impression? What were your initial perceptions? What then led you to change those perceptions?

2. Think of a recent interaction with a friend, family member, or work colleague in which you interpreted the person's behavior incorrectly. Did you attribute specific motives to the person's behavior? What led you to ascribe these motives? What was the outcome of the exchange?

Activities

Pair up with someone in class whom you do not know and with whom you have not interacted before. Without saying anything to each other, write down ten words that you think apply to the other person. Now chat together for five minutes. On a separate section of your paper, write down any additional words that you believe apply to the person; you can also go back and cross out any of the words in the first list that you now think don't apply. Share both lists of words with each other. Discuss the reasons each of you chose each word.

Barriers to Accurate Interpersonal Perception
(pages 73–79)

Each person sees the world from his or her own unique perspective. That perspective is clouded by a number of distortions or barriers that contribute to inaccurate interpersonal perceptions. One of the primary and most common barriers is stereotyping, the tendency to attribute certain qualities to someone because of the person's membership in a particular category. We tend to ignore information that doesn't mesh with our preconceived notions. We may also overgeneralize, focus on negative information, or avoid responsibility for a problem in our interaction or communication with another person.

Key Terms

Stereotype *74*

Social identity model of
   deindividuation effects
   (SIDE) *75*

Fundamental attribution
   error *77*

Self-serving bias *78*

Critical Thinking Questions

1. What do you think contributes to the tendency to perceive others inaccurately? How might the effects of those factors be minimized or eliminated?

2. Think about some of your recent interpersonal conflicts. How would you describe your perception of the problem in each conflict? How do you think the others would describe their perceptions of the problem? What role did perception play in contributing to or resolving the conflict?

3. Choose several "friends" from Facebook or another social networking site—people you don't know well but who have nonetheless "friended" you. What impressions do you have of these people? Do you tend to place them into a category based on their profile information, wall posts, or photos? What factors lead you to categorize them in this way? Are your perceptions positive or negative? What attribution errors might you be making?

4. Ethics: Do you have a right in an intimate relationship to expect your partner to share his or her perceptions of you, whether those perceptions are positive or negative? Explain your reasoning.

Activities

Make a list to share with classmates of between five and ten stereotypes of different groups or categories of people. Compare and contrast your list and your classmates' lists. What factors contribute to the forming of these stereotypes?

Ask a classmate to make a list of adjectives that he or she would use to describe you. Then discuss with the classmate how many of these characteristics are based on stereotypes. How many are based on other perceptual barriers such as lack of information?

Web Resources

https://implicit.harvard.edu/implicit/demo/ At this site you can test your implicit attitudes to explore prejudices and stereotypes that you might have.

How to Improve Interpersonal Perception Skills
(pages 79–82)

Despite the barriers to perceiving and interpreting others' behavior accurately, there are a number of things you can do to improve your perception skills. The first step is to be aware of these barriers and mindful of what you are doing, thinking, sensing, and observing. Other strategies to improve the accuracy of your perceptions include

- Linking details and clues about a person with the big picture.
- Becoming aware of others' perceptions of you.
- Checking your perceptions directly and indirectly.
- Becoming other-oriented.

Key Terms

Mindful *80*

Indirect perception checking *81*

Direct perception checking *81*

Critical Thinking Questions

1. Describe a recent communication exchange in which you needed to be other-oriented. How did you "step back" to understand what the other person was thinking and feeling? Did you express empathy? Explain how you did so.

2. Ethics: If you are aware of how you are distorting your own perceptions and attributions, should you try to change? Are people morally obligated to perceive others accurately? Explain your reasoning.

Activities

Think of a person in your life whose recent behavior and/or communication has puzzled or angered you. Put yourself in the person's place and analyze why he or she is behaving in this way. List the questions you need to ask yourself to help understand your perceptions and determine whether these perceptions are accurate. What perception-checking steps do you need to take? What, specifically, do you need to do to adjust your perceptions and have more effective communication with this person?

Web Resources

http://www.selfgrowth.com/index.html This is a site devoted to personal growth, self-improvement, and self-help. You can also sign up to receive a free newsletter.

http://sds.hss.cmu.edu/risk Make better decisions by understanding the domain in which they take place. The Center for Risk Perception and Communication will help you measure perceptions and evaluate communication.

Interpersonal Communication and Diversity: Adapting to Others

> "Strangers, people different from us, stir up fear, discomfort, suspicion, and hostility. They make us lose our sense of security just by being 'other'."
>
> **Henri J. M. Nouwen**

His Indonesian-American half sister was there along with her Chinese-Canadian husband. Another family member, the rabbi, was there, too. If all family members from his past could have attended, you would have heard English, Indonesian, French, Cantonese, German, Hebrew, Swahili, Luo, Igbo, and Gullah, a Creole dialect of South Carolina's Low Country.[1] His Black father from Kenya, who was a Muslim, and his White Methodist mother from Kansas, both of whom had passed away, would no doubt have been proud to attend. The event? The inauguration of the 44th President of the United States, Barack Obama.

Diversity of culture, language, religion, and a host of other factors is increasingly commonplace in contemporary society. This diversity creates the potential for misunderstanding and even conflict stemming from the different ways we make sense out of the world and share that sense with others. In their book *Communicating with Strangers,* intercultural communication researchers William Gudykunst and Young Yun Kim point out that strangers are "people who are different and unknown."[2] Although as human beings we share many things in common, our interpersonal interactions with others make it obvious that many people look different from us and communicate in ways that are different from ours.

In the first three chapters, we acknowledged the influence of diversity on interpersonal relationships. In this chapter, we examine in more detail the impact that people's differences have on their lives and suggest some communication strategies for bridging those differences in our interpersonal relationships. Our premise for this discussion of diversity is that in order to live comfortably in the twenty-first century, people must learn to appreciate and understand our differences instead of ignoring them, suffering because of them, or wishing that they would disappear.

Some people may be weary of what they perceive as an overemphasis on diversity. One student overheard a classmate say, "I've had it with all this diversity stuff. It seems like every textbook in every class is obsessed with it. I'm tired of all this politically correct nonsense. I mean, we're all Americans. We're not all going off to live in China. Why don't they just teach us what we need to know and cut all of this diversity garbage?" Perhaps you've encountered this kind of "diversity backlash" among some of your classmates (or maybe you hold this attitude yourself). It may seem unsettling to some that textbooks are emphasizing cultural diversity. But this emphasis is not motivated by an irrational desire to be politically correct, but by the fact that the United States and other countries are becoming increasingly diverse.[3] With this diversity comes a growing awareness that learning about differences, especially cultural differences, can affect every aspect of people's lives in positive ways. You need not travel the world to interact with people who may seem strange to you; the world is traveling to you.

A central goal of your study of interpersonal communication is to learn how better to relate to others. Some of the differences that contribute to diversity and may interfere with developing relationships include differences in age, learning style, gender, religion, race and ethnicity, sexual orientation, social class, and culture. We will emphasize the role of cultural differences and how those differences affect our interpersonal communication while also noting a variety of ways in which we may seem strange to one another.

BEING Other-ORIENTED

Communicating with people who are different from you is something you likely do every day. Even people who are our close friends and family members differ from us in many ways. Reflect on one or two interpersonal relationships you have and note the similarities and differences between you and the other person. How have the differences (such as in age, ethnicity, gender, religion, or culture) affected the way you interact with this person?

UNDERSTANDING OTHERS
Adapting to Differences

A Diversity Almanac

1. Two-thirds of the immigrants on this planet come to the United States.[4]

2. In the United States, there are "minority majorities" (where minorities outnumber traditional European Americans) in Miami; Laredo, Texas; Gary, Indiana; Detroit; Washington, DC; Oakland, California; Atlanta; San Antonio; Los Angeles; Chicago; Baltimore; Houston; New York; Memphis; San Francisco; Fresno, California; and San Jose, California.[5]

3. It is estimated that more than forty million U.S. residents have a non-English first language, including eighteen million people whose first language is Spanish.[6]

4. Almost one-third of U.S. residents under age thirty-five are members of minority groups, compared with one-fifth of those age thirty-five or older. According to U.S. Bureau of the Census population projections, by the year 2025 nearly half of all young adults in this country will come from minority groups.[7]

5. If the current trend continues, by the year 2050 the percentage of the U.S. population that is White will decrease to 53 percent, down from a current 79 percent. Asians will increase to 16 percent, up from 1.6 percent; Hispanics will more than triple their numbers to over 25 percent, up from just over 7.5 percent; and African Americans will increase their proportion slightly from the current 12 percent.[8]

6. More than 30 percent of graduate assistants teaching in universities in the United States are foreign born.[9]

7. Studies of gay and lesbian populations in the United States estimate that gay men make up from 1 to 9 percent of the general male population and lesbians make up from 1 to 5 percent of the general female population.[10]

8. There are more "Millennials" (people born between 1982 and 2002) in the U.S. population than any other age group. In 2004 the U.S. population included 100 million Millennials, 44 million Generation Xers (born 1961–1981), and 78 million Baby Boomers (born 1943–1960).[11]

9. One out of every eight U.S. residents speaks a language other than English at home, and one-third of children in urban U.S. public schools speak a first language other than English.[12]

10. During the past decade, the combined population of African Americans, Native Americans, Asians, Pacific Islanders, and Hispanics grew thirteen times faster than the non-Hispanic White population.[13]

11. Non-Hispanic Whites constitute a minority of the population in Texas, New Mexico, and California.[14]

12. Sixty percent of the residents of Miami are foreign-born.[15]

Understanding Diversity: Describing Our Differences

How are we different? Let us count the ways. No, let's not—that would take up too much space! There are an infinite number of ways in which we are different from one another. Unless you have an identical twin, you look different from everybody else, although you may have some things in common with a larger group of people (such as skin color, hair style, or clothing choice). Communication researchers have, however, studied several major differences that affect the way we interact with one another. To frame our discussion of diversity and communication, we'll note differences in gender, sexual orientation, race and ethnicity, age, and social class. Each of these differences—some learned, some based on biology, economic status, or simply on how long someone has lived—has an effect on how we perceive others and interact with them. Following our discussion of some classic ways in which we are diverse, we'll turn our attention to cultural differences and then note the barriers that cultural differences can create. We'll conclude the chapter by identifying strategies to enhance the quality of interpersonal communication with others, despite our differences.

Sex and Gender

Perhaps the most obvious form of human diversity is the existence of female and male human beings.[16] A person's **sex** is determined by biology; only men can impregnate; only women can menstruate, gestate, and lactate. In contrast to sex differences, *gender differences* reflect learned behavior that is culturally associated with being a man or a woman. Gender role definitions are flexible: A man can adopt behavior associated with a female role in a given culture, and vice versa. **Gender** refers to psychological and emotional characteristics that cause people to assume masculine, feminine, or androgynous (having a combination of both feminine and masculine traits) roles. Your gender is learned and socially reinforced by others, as well as by your life experiences and genetics. Some researchers prefer to study gender as a co-culture (a subset of the larger cultural group). We view gender as one of many basic elements of culture.

In the predominant culture of the United States, someone's gender is an important thing to know. Yet how different are men and women? John Gray, author of the popular book *Men Are from Mars, Women Are from Venus,* would have us believe that the sexes are so different from each other that we approach life as if we lived on two different planets.[17] Communication researchers have challenged many of Gray's stereotypical conclusions.[18] Although researchers have noted some differences in the way men and women interact, to label *all* men and *all* women as acting in prototypical ways may cause us to assume differences that aren't really there. Researchers who study gender and communication have found that gender differences are complex and not easily classified into tidy categories of "masculine" and "feminine" behaviors.[19]

Deborah Tannen, author of several books on communication between the sexes, views men and women as belonging to different cultural groups.[20] She suggests that female–male communication is cross-cultural communication, with all of the challenges of communicating with people who are different from us.

Research conclusions can result in uncertainty about sex and gender differences. Are there really fundamental differences in the way men and women communicate? Yes, some differences have been documented by researchers. But the differences may have more to do with *why* we communicate than *how.* There is evidence that men tend to talk in order to accomplish something or to complete a task. Women are often more likely to use conversation to establish and maintain relationships. There is a short way of summarizing this difference: *Men often communicate to report; women often communicate to establish rapport.*[21] Research suggests that many men tend to approach communication from a content orientation, meaning that they view the purpose of communication as primarily information exchange. You talk when you have something to say. Women, research suggests, tend to use communication for the purpose of relating or connecting to others. So the point of difference isn't in the way the sexes actually communicate but in their motivations or reasons for communicating. Note, however, that although gender differences account for considerable variation in how men and women view the world and the assumptions they hold about the nature of relationships, research suggests that cultural background is an even more powerful influence on some key assumptions about relationships.[22]

sex Biologically based differences that determine whether one is male or female.

gender Socially learned and reinforced characteristics that include one's biological sex and psychological characteristics (femininity, masculinity, androgyny).

Sexual Orientation

During the past two decades, gays and lesbians have become more assertive in expressing their rights within American society. Questions of whether gays and lesbians should participate in the military, the clergy, and the teaching profession have stirred the passions of many. Being gay or lesbian has become a source of pride

DONNELLY

for some, but it is still a social stigma for others. The incidence of suicide among gay and lesbian teenagers is significantly higher than among heterosexual teens.[23] Although gay people are gaining legal rights and protections, they are still subject to discriminatory laws and social intolerance. Yet the gay and lesbian communities are important co-cultures within the larger U.S. culture.

There is evidence that gay and lesbian individuals continue to be judged negatively based solely on their sexual orientation.[24] Research further suggests that heterosexuals who have negative perceptions of gays and lesbians are more likely to have rigid views about gender roles and to assume that their peers also hold such rigid views and negative impressions of gays and lesbians.[25] In addition, those who hold negative attitudes toward gays and lesbians are less likely to have interpersonal communication with gays or lesbians.[26] It is because of the existence of these negative attitudes as well as anti-gay violence and harassment, that some gays and lesbians continue to conceal their sexual orientation.

An effective and appropriate interpersonal communicator is aware of and sensitive to issues and attitudes about sexual orientation in contemporary society. Homophobia, the irrational fear of, aversion to, or discrimination against homosexuality and gays or lesbians, continues to exist among many people. Just as you have been taught to avoid biased expressions that degrade someone's race or ethnicity, it is equally important to avoid using language that demeans a person's sexual orientation. Telling stories and jokes whose points or punch lines rely on cruelly ridiculing a person because of his or her sexual orientation lowers perceptions of your credibility not only among gay and lesbian people, but also among people who dislike any show of bias against gays and lesbians.

Although we may not intend anything negative, sometimes we unintentionally offend someone through more subtle use and misuse of language.[27] For example, usually gays and lesbians typically prefer to be referred to as "gay" or "lesbian" rather than "homosexual." In addition, the term *sexual orientation* is preferred over *sexual preference*

when describing a person's sexual orientation. Our language should reflect and acknowledge the range of human relationships that exist. Our key point is this: Be sensitively other-oriented as you interact with those whose sexual orientation is different from your own.

Race and Ethnicity

Racial and ethnic differences are often discussed and sometimes debated. According to *Random House Webster's Unabridged Dictionary,* **race** is based on the genetically transmitted physical characteristics of a group of people who are also classified together because of a common history, nationality, or geographical location.[28] A person's racial classification is typically based on visible physiological attributes— *phenotypes*— which include skin color, body type, hair color and texture, and facial attributes. Skin color and other physical characteristics affect our responses and influence the way people of different races interact.

Although it may seem neat and tidy to classify individuals genetically as belonging to one race or another, it's not quite that simple. One geneticist has concluded that there is much more genetic variation *within* a given racial category than *between* one race and another.[29] There really aren't vast genetic differences among people who have been assigned to racial categories. That's why many scholars suggest that we think of race as a category that not only emphasizes biological or genetic characteristics, but also includes cultural, economic, social, geographic, and historical elements.[30] The term *race,* therefore, is a fuzzy, somewhat controversial way of classifying people.

Ethnicity is a related term, yet scholars suggest it is different from race. **Ethnicity** is a *social classification* based on a variety of factors, such as nationality, religion, language, and ancestral heritage (race), that are shared by a group of people who also share a common geographic origin. Simply stated, an ethnic group is a group of people who have labeled themselves an ethnic group based on a variety of factors that may or may not include race. In making distinctions between race and ethnicity, Brenda Allen suggests that ethnicity refers to "a common origin or culture based on shared activities and identity related to some mixture of race, religion, language and/or ancestry."[31] Although ethnicity may include race, race is a separate category that is based on genetic or biological factors. But research has found those genetic or biological distinctions are not clear-cut. A key distinction between race and ethnicity is that one's ethnicity is a *socially constructed* category

race Genetically transmitted physical characteristics of a group of people.

ethnicity Social classification based on nationality, religion, language, and ancestral heritage, shared by a group of people who also share a common geographical origin.

that emphasizes culture and a host of other factors other than one's racial or genetic background. Not all Asians (race), for example, have the same cultural background (ethnicity).[32] Nationality and geographical location are especially important in defining an ethnic group. Those of Irish ancestry are usually referred to as an ethnic group rather than as a race. The same could be said of Britons, Norwegians, and Spaniards.

Ethnicity, like race, fosters common bonds that affect communication patterns. On the positive side, ethnic groups bring vitality and variety to American society. On the negative side, members of these groups may experience persecution or rejection by members of other groups in society.

One of the most significant problems that stem from attempts to classify people by racial or ethnic type is the tendency to discriminate and unfairly, inaccurately, or inappropriately ascribe stereotypes to racial or ethnic groups. **Discrimination** is the unfair or inappropriate treatment of other people based on their group membership.[33] One of the goals of learning about diversity and becoming aware of both differences and similarities among groups is to eliminate discrimination and stereotypes that cause people to rigidly and inappropriately pre-judge others.

Age

Different generations, because they have experienced different cultural and historical events, tend to view life differently. If your grandparents or great-grandparents experienced the Great Depression of the 1930s, they may have different attitudes about savings accounts than you or even your parents do. Today's explicit song lyrics may shock older Americans who grew up with such racy lyrics as "makin' whoopee." The generation gap is real and has implications for the relationships we develop with others.

Generational differences have an effect not just on communication with your parents or other family members, but on a variety of relationships, including those with teachers, merchants, bosses, and mentors. There is considerable evidence that people hold stereotypical views of others based on others' perceived age.[34] In addition, a person's age has an influence on his or her communication with others. For example, one study found that older adults have greater difficulty in accurately interpreting the nonverbal messages of others than younger people do.[35] Older adults also don't like to be patronized or talked down to (who does?).[36] And younger people seem to value social support, empathic listening, and being mentored more than older people do.[37]

Authors Neil Howe and William Strauss, two researchers who have investigated the role of age and generation in society, define a generation as "a society-wide peer group, born over a period roughly the same length as the passage from youth to adulthood, who collectively possess a common persona."[38] *Baby Boomers* is the label for one such generation, people born between 1943 and 1960. Perhaps your parents or grandparents are Boomers. *Generation X* is the term used for people born between 1961 and 1981. If you were born between 1982 and 2002, you and your generation have been labeled *Millennials*.[39] Researchers Howe and Strauss suggest that, as a group, "Millennials are unlike any other youth generation in living memory. They are more numerous, more affluent, better educated, and more ethnically diverse. More importantly, they are beginning to manifest a wide array of positive social habits that older Americans no longer associate with youth, including a focus on teamwork, achievement, modesty, and good conduct."[40] Table 4.1 summarizes labels for and common characteristics and values of several generational groups.

discrimination Unfair or inappropriate treatment of people based on their group membership.

Table 4.1	**Summary of Generational Characteristics**

Generation Name	Birth Years	Typical Characteristics
Matures	1925–1942	• Work hard • Have a sense of duty • Are willing to sacrifice • Have a sense of what is right • Work quickly
Baby Boomers	1943–1960	• Value personal fulfillment and optimism • Crusade for causes • Buy now, pay later • Support equal rights for all • Work efficiently
Generation X	1961–1981	• Live with uncertainty • Consider balance important • Live for today • Save • Consider every job as a contract
Millennials	1982–2002	• Are close to their parents • Feel "special" • Are goal-oriented • Are team-oriented • Focus on achievement

Source: Information summarized from N. Howe and W. Strauss, *Millennials Rising: The Next Great Generation* (New York: Vintage Books, 2000).

Your generation has important implications for interpersonal communication, especially as you relate to others in both family and work situations. Each generation has developed its own set of values, which are anchored in social, economic, and cultural factors stemming from the times in which the generation has lived. Our values, core conceptualizations of what is fundamentally good or bad, right or wrong, color our way of thinking about and responding to what we experience.

Generational and age differences may create barriers and increase the potential for conflict and misunderstanding.[41] For example, one team of researchers who investigated the role of generations in the workforce suggests that Generation X workers are paradoxically both more individualistic (self-reliant) and more team-oriented than Boomers are.[42] In contrast, Boomers are more likely to have a sense of loyalty to their employers, expect long-term employment, value a pension plan, and experience job burnout from overwork. Generation Xers, on the other hand, seek more of a balance between work and personal life, expect to have more than one job or career, value good working conditions over other job factors, and have a greater need to feel appreciated.[43] Of course, these are broad generalizations and do not apply to all people in these categories.

Social Class

The Constitution of the United States declares that all people are created equal, but there is dramatic evidence that class differences exist and affect communication patterns. Social psychologist Michael Argyle reports that the cues we use to identify class distinctions are (1) way of life, (2) family, (3) job, (4) money, and (5) education.[44]

Brenda Allen suggests, "Social class encompasses a socially constructed category of identity that involves more than just economic factors; it includes an entire socialization process."[45] Such a socialization process influences the nature and quality of the interpersonal relationships we have with others. Although sociologists are the primary academic group of scholars who study social class, psychologists, business professionals, marketing specialists, and communication scholars also are interested in how a person's social class has an effect on his or her thoughts and behavior. Class differences influence whom we talk with, whether we are likely to invite our neighbors over for coffee, and whom we choose as our friends and lovers. And research suggests that social class is used by advertisers to target sales pitches to specific types of people.[46]

Some principles that describe how social classes emerge from society include the following:[47]

1. Virtually every organization or group develops a hierarchy that makes status distinctions.

2. We are more likely to interact with people from our own social class. There seems to be some truth to the maxim "Birds of a feather flock together."

3. People who interact with one another over time tend to communicate in similar ways; they develop similar speech patterns and use similar expressions.

4. Members of a social class develop ways of communicating class differences to others by the way they dress, cars they drive, homes they live in, schools they attend, and other visible symbols of social class.

5. It is possible to change one's social class through education, employment, and income.

Differences in social class and the attendant differences in education and lifestyle affect whom we talk with and even what we talk about.[48] These differences influence our overall cultural standpoint, from which we perceive the world.

Understanding Culture: Dimensions of Our Mental Software

We have noted a few of the fundamental ways people differ. Differences in gender, sexual orientation, race and ethnicity, age, and social class contribute to an overall cultural perspective that influences on a fundamental level how we relate to others. As we discussed in Chapter 3, **culture** is a learned system of knowledge, behaviors, attitudes, beliefs, values, and norms that is shared by a group of people. In the broadest sense, culture includes how people think, what they do, and how they use things to sustain their lives. Researcher Geert Hofstede describes culture as the "mental software" that touches every aspect of how we make sense out of the world and share that sense with others.[49] Just like software in a computer, our culture influences how we process information. To interact with other people is to be touched by the influence of culture and cultural differences.

Your culture and your life experiences determine your **worldview**—the general cultural perspective on such key issues as death, God, and the meaning of life that shapes how you perceive and respond to what happens to you. Your cultural worldview shapes your thoughts, language, and actions; it permeates all aspects of how you interact with society. *You cannot avoid having a worldview.* Our personal worldview is so pervasive

culture Learned system of knowledge, behavior, attitudes, beliefs, values, and norms that is shared by a group of people.

worldview Individual perceptions or perceptions by a culture or group of people about key beliefs and issues, such as death, God, and the meaning of life, which influence interaction with others.

that we may not even be aware of it. Just as a fish may not be aware of the water in its fish bowl, you may not be aware of how your worldview influences every aspect of your life—how you see and what you think. Your worldview is one of the primary ways you make sense out of the world—it's how you interpret what happens to you.

Sometimes when we speak of culture, we may be referring to a co-culture. A **co-culture** is a distinct culture within a larger culture. The differences of gender, sexual orientation, race and ethnicity, age, and social class that we discussed earlier are co-cultures within the predominant culture. For example, about 80 percent of the population of the United States is classified as White, European, American, or Caucasian. Members of minority groups such as African Americans, Latinos, and Asians develop a co-culture, or what is sometimes called a *microculture.* The Amish, Mennonite, Mormon, Islamic, and Jewish religious groups are additional examples of important religious co-cultures. Often, because they are in the minority, members of a co-culture not only *feel* marginalized, they *are* marginalized in employment, education, housing, and other aspects of society. To enhance their power and self-identity, members of co-cultures may develop their own rules and norms. For example, teens develop their own slang, wear certain kinds of clothing, value certain kinds of music, and engage in other behaviors that make it easier for them to be identified apart from the larger culture.

co-culture A microculture; a distinct culture within a larger culture (such as the gay and lesbian co-culture).

enculturation The process of transmitting a group's culture from one generation to the next.

Researchers and scholars who study culture have identified various dimensions or elements, of culture. These dimensions provide a framework to describe how our culture influences us. These dimensions are not rooted in biology but are learned, passed on from parents to children. **Enculturation** is the process of transmitting a group's culture from one generation to the next. You are not born with a certain taste in music, food, or automobiles. You *learn* to behave in accordance with the elements that characterize your culture and to appreciate the dimensions of your culture, just as you learn anything: through observing role models and receiving positive reinforcement.

Individualism is a strong cultural dimension in the United States. Individual achievements are rewarded, often quite publicly.

The six dimensions of culture that we discuss here have been identified by researchers who have found them in all cultures that they have studied. Think of these dimensions as general ways of describing how culture is expressed in the behavior of groups of people. The six dimensions are (1) individualism (an emphasis on the individual) versus collectivism (an emphasis on the group); (2) an emphasis on the surrounding context, including nonverbal behaviors, versus little emphasis on context; (3) masculine values that emphasize accomplishment versus feminine values that emphasize nurturing; (4) degree of tolerance for uncertainty; (5) approaches to power; and (6) short- or long-term approaches to time.

Individualism: One and Many

One of the most prominent dimensions of a culture is the dimension of individualism versus collectivism. Individualistic cultures, such as those in North America, value individual achievement and personal accomplishment. Collectivistic cultures, including many Asian cultures, value group and team achievement. One researcher summed up the American goal system this way:

> Chief among the virtues claimed . . . is self-realization. Each person is viewed as having a unique set of talents and potentials. The translation of these potentials into actuality is considered the highest purpose to which one can devote one's life.[50]

Conversely, in a collectivistic culture, people strive to attain goals for all members of the family, group, or community. In Kenyan tribes, for example,

> [N]obody is an isolated individual. Rather, his [or her] uniqueness is a secondary fact. . . . In this new system group activities are dominant, responsibility is shared, and accountability is collective. . . . Because of the emphasis on collectivity, harmony and cooperation among the group tends to be emphasized more than individual function and responsibility.[51]

Individualistic cultures tend to be more loosely knit socially; individuals feel responsible for taking care of themselves and their immediate families.[52] In collectivistic cultures, individuals expect more support from others; they also experience more loyalty to and from the community. Because collectivistic cultures place more value on "we" than "I," teamwork approaches usually succeed better in their workplaces. U.S. businesses have tried to adopt some of Japan's successful team strategies for achieving high productivity.

Context: High and Low

Individuals from different cultures use cues from the **cultural context** to varying degrees to enhance messages and meaning. This insight led anthropologist Edward T. Hall to categorize cultures as either high- or low-context.[53] In **high-context cultures,** nonverbal cues are extremely important in interpreting messages. **Low-context cultures** rely more explicitly on language and use fewer contextual cues to send and interpret information. Individuals from high-context cultures may perceive people from low-context cultures as less attractive, knowledgeable, and trustworthy, because they violate unspoken rules of dress, conduct, and communication. Individuals from low-context cultures often are not skilled in interpreting unspoken, contextual messages.[54]

Gender: Masculine and Feminine

Some cultures emphasize traditional male values, whereas others place greater value on female perspectives. These values are not really about biological sex differences but about overarching approaches to interacting with others.

People from **masculine cultures** tend to value more traditional roles for both men and women. Masculine cultures also value achievement, assertiveness, heroism, and material wealth. Research reveals that men tend to approach communication from a content orientation, meaning that they view communication as functioning primarily for information exchange. Men talk when they have something to say. This is also consistent with the tendency of men to base their relationships, especially their male friendships, on sharing activities rather than talking.

Men and women from **feminine cultures** tend to value such things as caring for the less fortunate, being sensitive toward others, and enhancing the overall quality of life.[55] Women, as research suggests, tend to approach communication for the purpose of relating or connecting to others, of extending themselves to other people in order to know them and be known by them.[56] What women talk about is less important than the fact that they're talking, because talking implies relationship.

Of course, rarely is a culture on the extreme end of the continuum; many are somewhere in between. For centuries, most countries in Europe, Asia, and the Americas have had masculine cultures. Men and their conquests dominate history books; men have been more prominent in leadership and decision making than women. But

cultural context Aspects of the environment and/or nonverbal cues that convey information that is not explicitly communicated through language.

high-context culture Culture in which people derive much information from nonverbal and environmental cues.

low-context culture Culture in which people derive much information from the words of a message and less information from nonverbal and environmental cues.

masculine culture Culture in which people tend to value traditional roles for men and women, achievement, assertiveness, heroism, and material wealth.

feminine culture Culture in which people tend to value caring, sensitivity, and attention to quality of life.

Many cultures have traditionally put a high value on masculine domination of women, but today there is a gradual trend toward greater equality between male and female roles.

today many of these cultures are moving slowly toward the middle—legal and social rules are encouraging more gender balance and greater equality between masculine and feminine roles.

Uncertainty: High and Low Tolerance

Some cultures tolerate more ambiguity and uncertainty than others. Cultures in which people need certainty to feel secure are more likely to create and enforce rigid rules for behavior and to develop more elaborate codes of conduct. People from cultures with a greater tolerance for uncertainty have more relaxed, informal expectations for others. "Go with the flow" and "It will sort itself out" are phrases that describe their attitudes. Research suggests that people from Portugal, Greece, Peru, Belgium, and Japan have high certainty needs, but people from Scandinavian countries tend to tolerate uncertainty.[57]

Power: Centralized and Decentralized

Some cultures value an equal, or decentralized, distribution of power, whereas others accept a concentration of hierarchical power in a centralized government and other organizations. In cultures in which people prefer a more centralized approach to power, hierarchical bureaucracies are common, and people expect some individuals to have more power than others. Russia, France, and China are all high on the concentrated power scale. Those that often strive for greater equality and distribution of power and control include many (but not all) citizens of Australia, Denmark, New Zealand, and Israel. People from these latter countries tend to minimize differences in power between people.

Time: Short-Term and Long-Term

A culture's orientation to time falls on a continuum between long-term and short-term.[58] People from a culture with a long-term orientation to time place an emphasis on the future and tend to value perseverance and thrift, because these are virtues that pay off over a long period of time. A long-term time orientation also implies a greater willingness to subordinate oneself for a larger purpose, such as the good of society or the group. In contrast, a culture that tends to have a short-term time orientation values spending rather than saving (because of a focus on the immediate rather than the future), tradition (because of the value placed on the present and the past), and preserving "face" of both self and others (making sure that an individual is respected and that his or her dignity is upheld) and has an expectation that results will soon follow the actions and effort expended on a task. Short-term cultures also place a high value on social and status obligations.

Cultures or societies with a long-term time orientation include many Asian cultures such as China, Hong Kong, Taiwan, and Japan. Short-term time orientation cultures include Pakistan, the Czech Republic, Nigeria, Spain, and the Philippines. Both Canada and the United States are closer to the short-term time orientation than the long-term time orientation, which suggests an emphasis on valuing quick results from projects and greater pressure toward spending rather than saving, as well as a respect for traditions.[59]

> **RECAP** Understanding Culture: Dimensions of Our Mental Software

Cultural Dimension	Countries That Score Higher on This Cultural Dimension	Countries That Score Lower on This Cultural Dimension
Individualism: Societies that place greater emphasis on individualism generally value individual accomplishment more than do societies that value collective or collaborative achievement.	United States, Australia, Great Britain, Canada, Netherlands, New Zealand, Italy, Belgium, Denmark, Sweden, France	Guatemala, Ecuador, Panama, Venezuela, Colombia, Indonesia, Pakistan, Costa Rica, Peru, Taiwan, South Korea
Context: High-context societies prefer to draw information from the surrounding context, including nonverbal messages. Low-context societies tend to prefer information to be presented explicitly, usually in words.	Japan, China, Saudi Arabia, Italy, Greece	Switzerland, Germany, Sweden, Denmark, Finland, United States, Australia
Gender: Societies with greater emphasis on masculinity value achievement, assertiveness, heroism, material wealth, and more clearly differentiated sex roles. People from more feminine cultures tend to value caring, sensitivity, and attention to quality of life.	Japan, Australia, Venezuela, Italy, Switzerland, Mexico, Ireland, Jamaica, Great Britain	Sweden, Norway, Netherlands, Denmark, Costa Rica, Finland, Chile, Portugal, Thailand
Uncertainty: People in societies with less tolerance for uncertainty generally like to know what will happen next. People in other societies are more comfortable with uncertainty.	Greece, Portugal, Guatemala, Uruguay, Belgium, Japan, Peru, France, Argentina, Chile	Singapore, Jamaica, Denmark, Sweden, Hong Kong, Ireland, Great Britain, Malaysia, India, Philippines, United States, Canada
Power: Societies with a more centralized power distribution generally value greater power differences between people; people in such societies are generally more accepting of fewer people having authority and power than are people from societies in which power is more decentralized.	Malaysia, Guatemala, Panama, Philippines, Mexico, Venezuela, Arab countries, Ecuador, Indonesia, India	Austria, Israel, Denmark, New Zealand, Ireland, Sweden, Norway, Finland, Switzerland, Great Britain
Time: People in societies with a long-term orientation to time tend to value perseverance and thrift. People in societies with a short-term orientation to time value both the past and the present, tradition, saving "face," and spending rather than saving.	China, Hong Kong, Taiwan, Japan, Vietnam, South Korea, Brazil, India, Thailand, Hungary, Singapore, Denmark, Netherlands	Pakistan, the Czech Republic, Nigeria, Spain, Philippines, Canada, Zimbabwe, Great Britain, United States, Portugal, New Zealand

Barriers to Effective Intercultural Communication

Intercultural communication occurs when individuals or groups from different cultures communicate. The transactional process of listening and responding to people from different cultural backgrounds can be challenging. The greater the difference in culture between two people, the greater the potential for misunderstanding and mistrust. Research suggests that culture has a direct effect on how we communicate with one another.[60] When we communicate with people who have different cultural backgrounds than our own, we tend to share less information with them than we do with people who share our cultural heritage.[61]

intercultural communication
Communication between or among people who have different cultural traditions.

Relating to Others in the 21st Century — Making Intercultural E-Connections

You don't have to travel the globe to communicate with people who live on the other side of the world. It's increasingly likely that you will interact electronically with others who have cultural or ethnic perspectives different from yours. Research suggests that you or one or more of your work colleagues will work in an international location: According to a *Business Week* survey, most workers thought that by 2017 they would have a colleague with whom they would work closely but who lived in another country.[62] Social networking sites like Facebook or MySpace, as well as other Internet-based or phone-based connections, make it easy to interact with international friends and colleagues. As more companies are outsourcing customer service to international venues, it's also increasingly likely that you may be speaking to someone in another country when making a call about a problem with your computer or your TV or some other customer-service need. It's challenging enough bridging cultural differences when we're interacting face to face. It can be even more challenging communicating electronically with others who have different cultural perspectives than you do.

Here are some tips and strategies for enriching electronic intercultural connections with others.

- If you are communicating with someone who is from a high-context culture (such as someone from Japan or another Asian country) in which nonverbal messages are especially important and you are using a leaner communication medium such as texting, consider providing more explicit references to your feelings and emotions by using emoticons or more explicitly stating your feelings and emotional reactions to messages.

- Consider asking more questions than you normally would if you were interacting face to face to clarify meanings and the interpretation of messages.

- Use "small talk" and comments about the weather, what your typical day is like, and other low-level disclosures to build a relationship. Then look for reciprocal responses from your communication partner that indicate a relationship is naturally evolving.

- Summarize and paraphrase messages that you receive more often than you might normally, in order to increase the accuracy of message content.

- Remember the difference between your time zone and the other person's time zone.

- If you find a relationship is awkward or you notice an increase in conflict, use the richest medium you can—use the phone instead of texting or sending e-mail, or use a web cam instead of the phone. If you're merely sharing routine, noncontroversial information, a lean medium (such as texting) should be fine.

Misunderstanding and miscommunication occur between people from different cultures because of different coding rules and cultural norms, which play a major role in shaping patterns of interaction. The greater the difference between the cultures, the more likely it is that they will use different verbal and nonverbal codes. When you encounter a culture that has little in common with your own, you may experience **culture shock,** or a sense of confusion, anxiety, stress, and loss. If you are visiting or actually living in the new culture, your uncertainty and stress may take time to subside as you learn the values and codes that characterize the new culture. But if you are simply trying to communicate with someone from a background very different from your own—even on your home turf— you may find the suggestions in this section helpful in closing the communication gap.[63]

The first step to bridging differences between cultures is to find out what hampers effective communication. What keeps people from connecting with those from other cultures? Sometimes it is different meanings created by different languages or by different interpretations of nonverbal messages. Sometimes it is the inability to stop focusing on oneself and begin focusing on the other. We'll examine some of these barriers first, then discuss strategies and skills for overcoming them.

Ethnocentrism

All good people agree,
And all good people say,
All nice people like Us, are We,
And everyone else is They.

culture shock Feelings of stress and anxiety a person experiences when encountering a culture different from his or her own.

In a few short lines, Rudyard Kipling captured the essence of what sociologists and anthropologists call ethnocentric thinking. Members of all societies tend to believe that "All nice people like Us, are We. . . ." They find comfort in the familiar and often denigrate or distrust others. Of course, with training or experience in other climes, they may learn to transcend their provincialism, placing themselves in others' shoes. Or, as Kipling put it,

> . . . if you cross over the sea,
> Instead of over the way,
> You may end by (think of it!)
> Looking on We
> As only a sort of They.

In a real sense, a main lesson of intercultural communication is to begin to "cross over the sea," to learn to understand why other people think and act as they do and to be able to empathize with their perspectives.[64]

Marilyn had always been intrigued by Russia. Her dream was to travel the country by train, spending time in small villages as well as exploring the cultural riches of Moscow, Pyatigorsk, and St. Petersburg. Her first day in Russia was a disappointment, however. When she arrived in Moscow, she joined a tour touting the cultural traditions of Russia. When the tour bus stopped at Sparrow Hills, affording the visitors a breathtaking hilltop view of the Moscow skyline, she was perplexed and mildly shocked to see a woman dressed in an elegant wedding gown mounted on horseback and galloping through the parking lot. Men in suits were cheering her on as a crowd of tipsy revelers set off fireworks and danced wildly to a brass band. "What kind of people are these?" sniffed Marilyn.

"Oh," said the tour guide, "it is our custom to come here to celebrate immediately following the wedding ceremony."

"But in public, with such raucousness?" queried Marilyn.

"It is our tradition," said the guide.

"What a backward culture. They're nothing but a bunch of peasants!" pronounced Marilyn, who was used to more refined nuptial celebrations at a country club or an exclusive hotel.

For the rest of the tour, Marilyn judged every Russian behavior as inferior to that of Westerners. That first experience colored her perceptions, and her ethnocentric view served as a barrier to effective interpersonal communication with the Russian people she met.

Ethnocentrism stems from a conviction that our own cultural traditions and assumptions are superior to those of others. It is the opposite of an other-orientation that embraces and appreciates the elements that give another culture meaning. This kind of cultural snobbism is one of the fastest ways to create a barrier that inhibits rather than enhances communication.

The concept of ethnocentrism is not new. One hundred years ago, W. G. Sumner defined it as "the technical name of this view of things in which one's own group is the center of everything and all others are scaled and rated with reference to it."[65] Many scholars have found that virtually all cultural groups are ethnocentric to some degree.[66] Some even argue that it's not always bad to see one's own cultural group as superior; an ethnocentric tendency enhances group pride and patriotism and encourages cultural traditions.[67] A problem occurs, however, when a group views its own preferences as *always* the best way. Extreme ethnocentrism creates a barrier between the group and others.

Colorful celebrations like this local festival in Bali can reinforce healthy ethnic pride. But if ethnic pride is taken to extremes, the resulting ethnocentrism may act as a barrier between groups.

ethnocentrism Belief that your cultural traditions and assumptions are superior to those of others.

BEING **Other**-ORIENTED

Most people are ethnocentric to some degree. But extreme ethnocentrism can be a major interpersonal communication barrier. What symptoms may indicate when an ethnocentric mindset may be interfering with the quality of communication with another person? What are examples of comments that might signal that someone believes his or her cultural approaches are superior to another person's culture?

99

Different Communication Codes

You are on your first trip to Los Angeles. As you step off the bus and look around for Hollywood Boulevard, you realize you have gotten off at the wrong stop. You see what looks like an old-fashioned corner grocery store with "Bodega" painted on a red sign. So you walk in and ask the man behind the counter, "How do I get to Hollywood Boulevard, please?"

"*No hablo inglés,*" says the man, smiling and shrugging his shoulders. But he points to a transit map pasted on the wall behind the counter.

Today, even when you travel within the United States, you are likely to encounter people who do not speak your language. Obviously, this kind of intercultural difference poses a formidable communication challenge. And even when you do speak the same language as someone else, he or she may come from a place where the words and gestures have different meanings. But, as William Gudykunst wisely noted, "If we understand each others' languages, but not their cultures, we can make fluent fools of ourselves."[68] Research has found that your culture and ethnic background have a direct effect on the way you listen to information from others.[69] Ultimately, your ability to communicate effectively and appropriately depends on whether you can understand each other's verbal and nonverbal codes.

In the preceding example, although the man behind the counter did not understand your exact words, he noted the cut of your clothing, your backpack, and your anxiety, and he deduced that you were asking directions. And you could understand what his gesture toward the transit map meant. Unfortunately, not every communication between speakers of two different languages is this successful.

Even when language is translated, meaning can be missed or mangled. Note the following examples of mistranslated advertisements:

- "Body by Fisher" in a General Motors auto ad became "Corpse by Fisher" in Flemish.

- A Colgate-Palmolive toothpaste named "Cue" was advertised in France before anyone realized that *Cue* also happened to be the name of a widely circulated pornographic book about oral sex.

- Pepsi-Cola's "Come Alive with Pepsi" campaign, when it was translated for the Taiwanese market, conveyed the unsettling news that "Pepsi brings your ancestors back from the grave."

- Parker Pen could not advertise its famous "Jotter" ballpoint pen in some languages because the translation sounded like "jockstrap" pen.

- One American airline operating in Brazil advertised that it had plush "rendezvous lounges" on its jets, unaware that in Portuguese (the language of Brazil), *rendezvous* implies a special room for making love.[70]

Building Your Skills　　Assessing Your Ethnocentrism

The following measure of ethnocentrism was developed by communication researchers James Neuliep and James McCroskey. Answer the following questions honestly.

Directions: This instrument is composed of twenty-four statements concerning your feelings about your culture and other cultures. In the space provided to the left of each item, indicate the degree to which the statement applies to you by marking whether you (5) strongly agree, (4) agree, (3) are neutral, (2) disagree, or (1) strongly disagree with the statement. There are no right or wrong answers. Work quickly and record your first response.

_____ 1. Most other cultures are backward compared with my culture.

_____ 2. People in other cultures have a better lifestyle than we do in my culture.

_____ 3. Most people would be happier if they didn't live like people do in my culture.

_____ 4. My culture should be the role model for other cultures.

_____ 5. Lifestyles in other cultures are just as valid as those in my culture.

_____ 6. Other cultures should try to be more like my culture.

_____ 7. I'm not interested in the values and customs of other cultures.

_____ 8. It is not wise for other cultures to look up to my culture.

_____ 9. People in my culture could learn a lot from people in other cultures.

_____ 10. Most people from other cultures just don't know what's good for them.

_____ 11. People from my culture act strange and unusual when they go into other cultures.

_____ 12. I have little respect for the values and customs of other cultures.

_____ 13. Most people would be happier if they lived like people in my culture.

_____ 14. People in my culture have just about the best lifestyles of anywhere.

_____ 15. My culture is backward compared with most other cultures.

_____ 16. My culture is a poor role model for other cultures.

_____ 17. Lifestyles in other cultures are not as valid as those in my culture.

_____ 18. My culture should try to be more like other cultures.

_____ 19. I'm very interested in the values and customs of other cultures.

_____ 20. Most people in my culture just don't know what is good for them.

_____ 21. People in other cultures could learn a lot from people in my culture.

_____ 22. Other cultures are smart to look up to my culture.

_____ 23. I respect the values and customs of other cultures.

_____ 24. People from other cultures act strange and unusual when they come into my culture.

Scoring: To determine your ethnocentrism, *reverse* your score for items 2, 3, 5, 8, 9, 11, 15, 16, 18, 19, 20, and 23. For these items, 5 = 1, 4 = 2, 3 = 3, 2 = 4, and 1 = 5. That is, if your original score was a 5, change it to a 1. If your original score was a 4, change it to a 2, and so forth. Once you have reversed your score for these twelve items, add up all twenty-four scores. This is your generalized ethnocentrism score. Scores greater than 80 indicate high ethnocentrism. Scores of 50 and below indicate low ethnocentrism.

Source: J. W. Neuliep and J. C. McCroskey, "The Development of a U.S. and Generalized Ethnocentrism Scale," *Communication Research Reports* 14 (1997): 393.

Stereotyping and Prejudice

All Europeans dress fashionably.

All Asians are good at math.

All Americans like to drive big cars.

These statements are stereotypes. They are all inaccurate. As we discussed in Chapter 3, to **stereotype** someone is to push him or her into an inflexible, all-encompassing category. Our tendency to simplify sensory stimuli can lead us to adopt stereotypes as we interpret and label the behavior of others.[71] As we also noted in Chapter 3, there is evidence that we thin slice—make judgments about others in just seconds based on nonverbal cues. One

stereotype To place a person or group of persons into an inflexible, all-encompassing category.

study found that after viewing just 20 seconds of silent videotape, subjects made stereotypical, biased racial judgments of others.[72] Stereotypes become a barrier to effective intercultural communication when we fail to consider the uniqueness of individuals, groups, or events. Two anthropologists suggest that every person is, in some respects, (1) like all other people, (2) like some other people, and (3) like no other people.[73] The challenge when meeting others is to sort out how they are alike and how they are unique.

Can stereotypes play any useful role in interpersonal communication? It may sometimes be appropriate to draw on stereotypes, or generalizations drawn from limited instances. If, for example, you are alone and lost in a large city at two o'clock in the morning and another car aggressively taps your rear bumper, it would be prudent to try to drive away as quickly as possible, rather than to hop out of your car to make a new acquaintance. You would be wise to pre-judge that the other driver might have some malicious intent. In most situations, however, **prejudice**—a judgment or opinion of someone formed on the basis of stereotypes or before you know all the facts—inhibits effective communication, especially if your labels are inaccurate or assume superiority on your part.[74]

Communication author and consultant Leslie Aguilar notes that whether or not we intend to perpetuate stereotypes and prejudice, we do so in seemingly innocent ways.[75] Here are some of the ways we may inadvertently stereotype others: telling jokes ("Have you heard the one about the minister and the rabbi?"); using labels (she's a real "blue hair" or he's "trailer trash") or rigid descriptions ("crotchety old man" or "bad woman driver"); making assumptions (assuming, for example, that a woman's career is less important than a man's career, that men are insensitive, or that women are physically weak); relying on "spokesperson syndrome" ("Don, what do Hispanic people think about this topic?"); or making statistical overgeneralizations ("Statistics show that Chinese do well in math").

Certain prejudices are widespread. Although there are slightly more females than males in the world, one study found that even when a male and a female hold the same type of job, the male's job is considered more prestigious than the female's.[76] Today, gender and racial discrimination in hiring and promotion is illegal in the United States. But some people's opinions have not kept pace with the law.

Assuming Similarities

Just as it is inaccurate to assume that all people who belong to another social group or class are worlds apart from you, it is usually erroneous to assume that others act and think just as you do. Cultural differences *do* exist. Research and our own observations support the commonsense conclusion that people from different cultural and ethnic backgrounds do speak and behave differently.[77] Even if they appear to be like you, all people are not alike. Although this statement is not profound, it has profound implications. People often make the mistake of assuming that others value the same things they do, maintaining a self-focused perspective instead of an other-oriented one. As you saw in Chapter 3, focusing on superficial factors such as appearance, clothing, and even a person's occupation can lead to false impressions. Instead, you must take the time to explore a person's background and cultural values before you can determine what you really have in common.

Assuming Differences

Although it may seem to contradict what we just noted about assuming similarities, another barrier to intercultural communication is to automatically assume that another person is different from you. It can be just as detrimental to communication to assume someone is different from you as it is to assume that others are similar to you. The fact is, human beings *do* share common experiences, while at the same time there are differences.

prejudice A judgment or opinion of someone, formed before you know all of the facts or the background of that person.

The point of noting that humans have similarities as well as differences is not to diminish the role of culture as a key element that influences communication, but to recognize that despite cultural differences, we are all members of the human family. The words *communication* and *common* resemble one another. We communicate effectively and appropriately when we can connect to others based on what we hold in common. Identifying common cultural issues and similarities can also help us establish common ground with others.

How are we all alike? Cultural anthropologist Donald Brown has compiled a list of hundreds of "surface" universals of behavior and language use that have been identified. According to Brown, people in all cultures[78]

- Have beliefs about death.

- Have a childhood fear of strangers.

- Divide labor on the basis of sex.

- Experience envy, pain, jealousy, shame, and pride.

- Use facial expressions to express emotions.

- Have rules for etiquette.

- Experience empathy.

- Value some degree of collaboration or cooperation.

- Experience conflict and seek to manage or mediate conflict.

Of course, all cultures do not have the same beliefs about death, or divide labor according to sex in the same ways, but all cultures address these issues. Communication researcher David Kale believes that all humans seek to protect the dignity and worth of other people.[79] Thus, he suggests, all people can identify with the struggle to enhance their own dignity and worth, although different cultures express that in different ways. A second common value that Kale notes is the search for a world at peace. Intercultural communication scholars Larry Samovar and Richard Porter suggest that there are other elements that cultures share.[80] They note that people from all cultures seek physical pleasure as well as emotional and psychological pleasure and avoid personal harm. It's true that each culture and each person decide what is pleasurable or painful; nonetheless, Samovar and Porter argue, all people operate within this pleasure–pain continuum.

Linguist and scholar Steven Pinker is another advocate of common human values. Drawing on the work of anthropologists Richard Shweder and Alan Fiske, Pinker suggests that the following value themes are universally present in some form or degree in societies across the globe:

- It is bad to harm others and good to help them.

- People have a sense of fairness; we should reciprocate favors, reward benefactors, and punish cheaters and those who do harm.

- People value loyalty to a group and sharing in a community or group.

- It is proper to defer to legitimate authority and to respect those with status and power.

- People should seek purity, cleanliness, and sanctity while shunning defilement and contamination.[81]

In summary, " . . . avoidance of harm, fairness, community (or group loyalty), authority, and purity . . . are the primary colors of our moral senses."[82]

What are the practical implications of trying to identify common human values or characteristics? Here's one implication: If you are speaking about an issue on which

BEING **Other**-ORIENTED

We build bridges with others who are different from us when we can identify something we may have in common with them. Can you think of times when you've been communicating with someone who was quite different from you, but you sought to identify something you both had in common? What are some common human experiences that can create bridges as we seek to establish common ground with others?

you and another person fundamentally differ, identifying a larger common value—such as the value of peace, prosperity, or the importance of family—can help you find a foothold so that the other person will at least listen to your ideas. It's useful, we believe, not just to categorize our differences but also to explore how human beings are similar to one another. Discovering how we are alike can provide a starting point for human understanding. Yes, we are all different, but we share things in common as well. Communication effectiveness is diminished when we assume we're all different from one another in *every* aspect, just as communication is affected negatively if we assume we're all alike.[83] We're more complicated than that.

Improving Intercultural Communication Competence

Eleanor Roosevelt once said, "We have to face the fact that either all of us are going to die together or we are going to live together, and if we are to live together we have to talk."[84] In essence, she was saying that to overcome differences people need effective communication skills. It is not enough just to point to the barriers to effective intercultural communication and say, "Don't do that." Although identifying the causes of misunderstanding is a good first step to becoming interculturally competent, most people need help with specific strategies to help them overcome these barriers. In this book and in this chapter, we want to focus attention on the interpersonal communication strategies that can lead to intercultural communication competence.

Intercultural communication competence is the ability to adapt your behavior toward another in ways that are appropriate to the other person's culture.[85] To be interculturally competent is to be more than merely aware of what is appropriate or simply sensitive to cultural differences. To be interculturally competent is to *behave* toward others in ways that are appropriate. But prior to behaving appropriately, an individual needs to have knowledge about another culture and the motivation to adapt or modify his or her behavior.

Although we've identified stages in the process of becoming interculturally competent, the question remains: How do you achieve intercultural communication competence? The remaining portion of this chapter presents specific strategies to help you bridge differences between you and people who have a different cultural perspective from yours.

You enhance your intercultural competence by doing what we introduced in Chapter 1: You become knowledgeable, motivated, and skilled.[86]

- *Develop Appropriate Knowledge.* One of the barriers to effective intercultural communication is having different communication codes. Improving your knowledge of how others communicate can reduce the impact of this barrier. We offer strategies to help you learn more about other cultures by actively pursuing information about others.

- *Develop Motivation.* **Motivation** is an internal state of readiness to respond to something. A competent communicator *wants* to learn and improve. Developing strategies to appreciate others who are different from you may help you appreciate different cultural approaches to communication and relationships. We suggest you endeavor to be tolerant of uncertainty and to avoid knee-jerk negative evaluations of others.

- *Develop Skill.* Developing **skill** in adapting to others focuses on specific behaviors that can help overcome barriers and cultural differences. As we discussed in Chapter 1, becoming other-oriented is critical to the process of relating to others.

intercultural communication competence Ability to adapt one's behavior toward another in ways that are appropriate to the other person's culture.

motivation Internal state of readiness to respond to something.

skill Behavior that improves the effectiveness or quality of communication with others.

Communication and Emotion   Are There Universal Emotions?

Do all of us experience and express emotions in the same way? The question of whether there are universal emotions or universal ways of expressing emotions has been studied and debated by scholars for decades.

One widely debated analysis, developed by psychologist Robert Plutchik and shown in Figure 4.1, suggests that there are eight primary human emotions: joy, acceptance, fear, surprise, sadness, disgust, anger, and anticipation.[87] These eight primary emotions can combine to produce eight secondary emotions. Although not all researchers agree that the eight primary emotions are the definitive set of human emotions, a host of scholars argue that yes, there is a set of basic emotions that all humans experience.[88] They believe that through the biological process of evolution, all humans have a core set of emotional experiences. The debate about whether there are universal emotions boils down to whether you believe that nature (biology) or nurture (culture) determines common, core emotions. Those who think we are "wired" or programmed for common emotions believe that biology is the predominant influence in determining how we both interpret emotional expression and respond emotionally.

Researcher Paul Ekman has spent many years working with several colleagues to determine if people from a wide variety of cultures all interpret facial expressions of emotion in the same way. His conclusion: "Our evidence, and that of others, shows only that when people are experiencing strong emotions, are not making any attempt to mask their expressions, the expression will be the same regardless of age, race, culture, sex and education. That is a powerful finding."[89]

Other researchers have reached a different conclusion.[90] When critically examining the evidence of Paul Ekman and others, they have found that culture does play an important role in determining how facial expressions are displayed and interpreted.[91] There is some evidence, for example, that people from collectivistic cultures are socialized to not express emotions that would disrupt harmony in the group. Specifically, people with collectivist values may work harder at regulating how they express such emotions as anger, contempt, and disgust—emotions that would hinder group peace.[92] And people from individualistic cultures may feel that they have greater cultural license to express these emotions more freely.

Why is it important to know whether emotional expression and interpretation are common to all humans or are learned, just as other elements of culture are learned? If there are indeed universal human attributes common to all people, their existence provides powerful additional evidence for the theory of evolution. It also has implications for the development of a truly human theory of communication.

So are there universal expressions and interpretations of human emotions? Among experts, consensus is emerging that all humans have in common a biologically based tendency to express emotions, while cultural differences exist in how some emotions are interpreted.

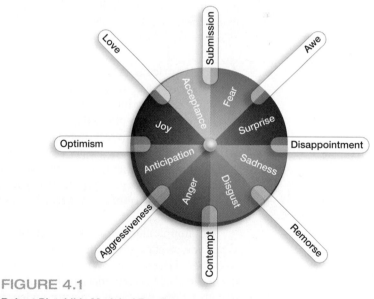

FIGURE 4.1

Robert Plutchik's Model of Emotions

From Robert Plutchik, *Emotion: A Psychoevolutionary Synthesis,* © 1980. Published by Allyn & Bacon, Boston, MA. Copyright © by Pearson Education. By permission of Pearson Education, Inc..

Develop Knowledge

Knowledge is power. To increase your knowledge of others who are different from you, we suggest that you actively seek information about others, ask questions and listen for the answers, and establish common ground.

Seek Information. Seeking information about a culture or even about a specific communication situation enhances the quality of intercultural communication. Why?

Because seeking information helps manage the uncertainty and anxiety that we may feel when we interact with people who are different from us.[93] Sometimes we feel uncomfortable in intercultural communication situations because we just don't know how to behave. We aren't sure what our role should be; we can't quite predict what will happen when we communicate with others because we're in a new or strange situation. Seeking new information can help counter inaccurate information and prejudice.

As we've noted, every person has a worldview based on cultural beliefs about the universe and key issues such as death, God, and the meaning of life.[94] These beliefs shape our thoughts, language, and behavior. Only through intercultural communication can we hope to understand how each individual views the world. As you speak to a person from another culture, think of yourself as a detective watching for implied, often unspoken messages that provide information about the values, norms, roles, and rules of that person's culture.

You can also prepare yourself by studying the culture. If you are going to another country, courses in the history, anthropology, art, or geography of that place can give you a head start on communicating with understanding. Learn not only from books and magazines, but also from individuals whenever possible.

Given the inextricable link between language and culture, the more you learn about another language, the more you will understand the traditions and customs of the culture. Politicians have long known the value of using even a few words of their constituents' language. President Kennedy impressed and excited a crowd in Berlin by proclaiming, "Ich bin ein Berliner" ("I am a Berliner"). Even though his diction was less than perfect, he conveyed the message that he identified with his listeners. Speaking even a few words can signify your interest in learning about the language and culture of others.

Ask Questions and Listen Effectively. When you encounter a person from another background, asking questions and then pausing to listen is a simple technique for gathering information and also for confirming the accuracy of your expectations and assumptions. For example, some cultures, such as the Japanese culture, have clear expectations regarding gift giving. It is better to ask what these expectations are than to assume that your good old down-home manners will see you through.

When you ask questions, be prepared to share information about yourself, too. Otherwise, your partner may feel that you are interrogating him or her as a way to gain power and dominance rather than from a sincere desire to learn about cultural rules and norms.

Communication helps to reduce the uncertainty that is present in any relationship.[95] When you meet people for the first time, you may be uncertain about who they are and what they like and dislike. When you communicate with someone from another culture, the uncertainty level is particularly high. As you begin to interact, you exchange information that helps you develop greater understanding. If you continue to ask questions, eventually you will feel less uncertain about how the person is likely to behave.

Just asking questions and sharing information about yourself are not sufficient to bridge differences in culture and background. It is equally important to listen to what others share. In the next chapter, we provide specific strategies for improving your listening skills.

Create a "Third Culture."   Several researchers suggest that one of the best ways to enhance understanding when communicating over a period of time with someone from a different cultural background is to develop a **third culture.** This is created when the communication partners join aspects of separate cultures to create a third, "new" culture that is more comprehensive and inclusive than either of the two separate cultures.[96]

According to one intercultural communication researcher, F. L. Casmir, a third-culture approach to enhancing the quality of intercultural communication occurs

third culture Common ground established when people from separate cultures create a third, "new," more comprehensive and inclusive culture.

when the people involved in the conversation construct "a mutually beneficial interactive environment in which individuals from two different cultures
can function in a way beneficial to all involved."[97]

How do you go about developing a third culture? In a word: talk. A third
culture does not just happen all at once; it evolves from dialogue. The communicators construct a third culture *together*. After they realize that cultural differences may divide them, they may develop a third culture by making a conscious
effort to develop common assumptions and common perspectives for the relationship. Dialogue, negotiation, conversation, interaction, and a willingness to
let go of old ways and experiment with new frameworks are the keys to developing a third culture as a basis for a new relationship.

Developing a third-culture mentality can reduce our tendency to approach cultural differences from an "us-versus-them" point of view. Rather
than trying to eliminate communication barriers stemming from two different sets of experiences, adopting a third-culture framework creates a new understanding of the other on the part of both participants.[98]

Consider the example of Marsha, a businesswoman from Lincoln, Ne-
braska, and Tomiko, a businesswoman from Tokyo, Japan. In the context of
their business relationship, it would be difficult for them to develop a comprehensive understanding of each other's cultural traditions. However, if they
openly acknowledged the most significant of these differences and sought to create a third culture by identifying explicit rules and norms for their interaction,
they might be able to develop a more comfortable relationship with each other.

As described by communication researcher Benjamin Broome, the third
culture "is characterized by unique values and norms that may not have existed
prior to the dyadic [two-person] relationship."[99] Broome labels the essence of this new
relationship **relational empathy,** which permits varying degrees of understanding,
rather than requiring complete comprehension of another's culture or emotions.

The cultural context includes all the elements of the culture (learned behaviors
and rules, or "mental software") that affect the interaction. Do you come from a culture that takes a tea break each afternoon at 4 P.M.? Does your culture value hard work
and achievement, or relaxation and enjoyment? Creating a third culture acknowledges
the different cultural contexts and interactions participants have experienced and
seeks to develop a new context for future interaction.

Studying interpersonal communication
helps us learn to bridge differences in age,
gender, race, or ability that might act as
barriers to effective communication.

Develop Motivation: Strategies to Accept Others

Competent communicators want to learn and improve. They are motivated to enhance their ability to relate to others and to accept others as they are. A key to accepting others is to develop a positive attitude of tolerance and acceptance of those who
are different from you. We suggest three strategies to help improve your acceptance
and appreciation of others who differ from you: Tolerate ambiguity, become mindful,
and avoid negative judgments of others.

Tolerate Ambiguity.   Communicating with someone from another culture pro-
duces uncertainty. It may take time and several exchanges to clarify a message. Be patient and try to expand your capacity to tolerate ambiguity if you are speaking to
someone with a markedly different worldview.

When Ken and Rita visited Miami from Peoria, they asked their hotel concierge
to direct them to a church of their faith, and they wound up at one with a predominantly Haitian congregation. They were not prepared for the exuberant chanting and
verbal interchanges with the minister during the sermon. They weren't certain
whether they should join in or simply sit quietly and observe. Ken whispered to Rita,

---

BEING Other-ORIENTED

Being motivated to establish
positive relationships with others
who are different from us is a
key aspect of communicating in
interculturally competent ways.
What are "self-talk" messages
that you could tell yourself (such
as "I may feel uncomfortable
right now, but I will keep
listening to this person") to
motivate you to increase your
intercultural competence?

---

relational empathy Essence of
a relationship that permits varying
degrees of understanding, rather than
requiring complete comprehension
of another's culture or emotions.

"I'm not sure what to do. Let's just watch and see what is expected of us." In the end, they chose to sit and clap along with the chanting rather than to become actively involved in the worship. Rita felt uncomfortable and conspicuous, though, and had to fight the urge to bolt. But after the service, several members of the congregation came up to greet Ken and Rita, invited them to lunch, and expressed great happiness in their visit. "You know," said Rita later in the day, "I'm so grateful that we sat through our discomfort. We might never have met those terrific people. Now I understand why their worship is so noisy—they're just brimming with joy."

Be Mindful. "Our life is what our thoughts make it," said Marcus Aurelius in *Meditations*. As we noted in Chapter 3, to be mindful is to be consciously aware of what you are doing, thinking, and sensing. With regard to cultural differences, to be **mindful** is to acknowledge that there is a connection between thoughts and deeds when you interact with a person from a background different from your own. William Gudykunst suggests that being mindful is one of the best ways to approach any new cultural encounter.[100] Remember that there are and will be cultural differences, and try to keep them in your consciousness. Also try to consider the other individual's frame of reference, or worldview, and to use his or her cultural priorities and assumptions when you are communicating.[101] Adapt your behavior to minimize cultural noise and distortion.

You can become more mindful through self-talk, something we discussed in Chapter 2. Self-talk consists of messages you tell yourself to help you manage your emotions or discomfort with a certain situation. Imagine that you are working on a group project with several classmates. One classmate, Suji, was born in Iran. When interacting with you, he consistently stands about a foot away from you, whereas you are more comfortable with three or four feet between you. When Suji encroaches on your space, you could be mindful of the reason for this behavior by mentally noting, "Suji sure likes to get close to people when he talks to them. This may be how they do things in his culture." This self-talk message makes you consciously aware that there may be a difference in your interaction styles. If you still feel uncomfortable, instead of blurting out, "Hey, man, why so close?" you could express your own preferences with an "I" message: "Suji, I'd prefer a bit more space between us when we talk."

Avoid Negative Judgments.

American tourist on her first visit to France:	Can you believe it? How repulsive! These people actually eat horse meat and think it's a delicacy.
Black teenager watching his White classmates dance:	Man, they don't know anything about good music! And those dances are so dumb. I don't call this a party.
Japanese businessperson visiting Argentina:	These people are never on time. No wonder they can never catch up to us.
German student, after watching a documentary about life in Japan:	No wonder they work so hard. They have dinky little houses. I'd work long hours too if I had to live like that.

mindful Aware of cultural differences and the connection between thoughts and deeds in one's interactions with someone from a background different from one's own.

The kind of ethnocentrism that underlies judgments like these is a communication barrier. It is also an underlying cause of suspicion and mistrust and, in extreme cases, a spark that ignites violence. Instead of making judgments about another culture, try simply to acknowledge differences and to view them as interesting challenges rather than as obstacles to be eradicated.

It's clear that there are cultural differences among the world's people and that these differences have existed since there have been people. Anthropologists and communication scholars who study intercultural communication teach us the value of adapting to cultural differences in order to understand others better. But are there any universal values that are or have been embraced by all humans? The question is not a new one; scholars, theologians, and many others have debated for millennia whether there are any universal underpinnings for all human societies. In Chapter 3 we noted that social psychologists Penelope Brown and Stephen Levinson suggest that people from all cultures have a universal need to be treated with politeness.[102] Are there other needs and values that all humans share? To uncover such commonalities is to develop a truly human communication theory rather than a theory that applies to a specific cultural context.

C. S. Lewis, a British scholar, author, and educator who taught at both Oxford University and Cambridge University, argued that there are universal ethical and moral principles that undergird all societies of civilized people, regardless of

their religious beliefs, cultural background, or government structure. He suggested that the existence of Natural Laws, or what he called a *Tao*—a universal moral code—informs human ethical decisions. In his book *The Abolition of Man*, Lewis presented eight universal principles, or laws.[103] He did not claim that all societies have followed these laws—many of them have been clearly violated and continue to be violated today—but he did suggest they provide a bedrock of values against which all societies may be measured. Here are his eight laws:

1. The Law of General Beneficence: Do not murder, be dishonest, or take from others what does not belong to us.

2. The Law of Special Beneficence: Value your family members.

3. Duties to Parents, Elders, and Ancestors: Especially hold your parents, those who are a generation older than you, and your ancestors with special honor and esteem.

4. Duties to Children and Posterity: We have a special obligation to respect the rights of the young and to value those who will come after us.

5. The Law of Justice: Honor the basic human rights of others; each person is of worth.

6. The Law of Good Faith and Veracity: Keep your promises, and do not lie.

7. The Law of Mercy: Be compassionate to those less fortunate than you are.

8. The Law of Magnanimity: Avoid unnecessary violence against other people.

To support his argument that these are universal values, Lewis offered quotations from several well-known sources, including religious, historical, and political writings, both contemporary and centuries old. Lewis implied that these eight laws may be viewed as a universal Bill of Rights, and that they constitute an underlying set of principles that either implicitly or explicitly guide all civilized society. Do you agree? Is it useful to search for underlying principles of humanness? Despite cultural differences, are there underlying values or principles that should inform our interactions with others? Is there truly a universal human theory of communication? Or might it do more harm than good to suggest that universal principles underlie what it means to behave and communicate appropriately and effectively?

Develop Skill

To be skilled is to be capable of putting into action what you know and want to achieve. The skills underlying being interculturally competent are the ability to be flexible, to be other-oriented, and to adapt your communication to others. We discuss these crucial skills as an introduction to the communication skills that we present in the next four chapters.

Develop Creative Flexibility. When you encounter someone who comes from a very different background, remember Dorothy's famous line from *The Wizard of Oz* and remind yourself that you're "not in Kansas anymore." You can no longer rely on the assumptions of your own cultural heritage. Rather than relying on "scripts" you would use "back home in Kansas," it's important to be flexible and respond in creative and inventive ways. You may read guidebooks to prepare you for new cultural experiences, but you can only learn so much from books; you must be willing to learn as you communicate on the spot. Although in this chapter we've identified generalizations about different cultural groups, we caution you that these are only generalizations. Every individual is unique, so generalizations that you learn from research will not always apply. For example, it would be inappropriate to automatically assume that someone from Japan will value collectivism instead of individual achievement. Many members of minority groups in the United States find it tiresome to correct these generalizations in their encounters with others. If you're

It's important to be flexible in your responses to other cultures and people with different backgrounds. Traveling in other countries can hone your intercultural communication skills.

African American, gay, lesbian, or from a rural community, you may be weary of someone asking what "you people" think about a particular issue, as if you spoke for all members of your cultural or co-cultural group. Because each person is unique, it's important to treat each person not as a representative of a monolithic group, but as someone with a distinct perspective.

The skill of observing and responding with creative flexibility enhances your intercultural competence. It also calls on your ability to do a variety of things simultaneously. While you're listening to someone, you're also adapting your behavior to respond to the person's cultural expectations. To multitask takes both creativity and flexibility. There is evidence that as you gain experience and skill in interacting with people from other cultural backgrounds, you develop an expanded repertoire of behaviors to enhance your intercultural competence. Research further suggests that the amount of culture shock you experience when communicating with someone from a different culture decreases as you develop skills in interacting with people from that culture.[104]

How do you develop these skills? By developing the knowledge, motivation, and behaviors that enhance the quality of your relationships with others. You'll need to pay close attention to the other person's nonverbal cues when you begin conversing (Is the person attentive? Does the person look interested? Confused?); then adjust your communication style and language, if necessary, to put the person at ease. Listen and respond and, if necessary, as we noted earlier, create a new culture—a third culture—to forge a new way of interacting. You may, for example, prefer direct eye contact when you speak with another person, but someone from a different culture may prefer less direct eye contact. So you may need to modify the amount of eye contact you have with that person. As communication researchers Kathy Domenici and Stephen Littlejohn advocate, "Good intercultural communication requires a certain creativity, an ability to create new forms that bridge established cultural patterns."[105]

Don't go on "automatic pilot" when interacting with anyone—but, especially people from a different cultural context.

Become Other-Oriented. Throughout the book, we have emphasized the importance of becoming other-oriented—focusing on others rather than yourself—as an important way to enhance your interpersonal competence.[106] We have also discussed the problems ethnocentrism can create when you attempt to communicate with others, especially with people whose culture differs from yours.

Although our focus in this discussion is on how to increase other-orientation in intercultural interactions, the principles apply to *all* interpersonal interactions. The major difference between intercultural interactions and those that occur within your own culture is primarily the obviousness of the differences between you and the other person.

To become other-oriented is to do two things: first, to take into account another person's thoughts and perspective, and second, to consider what the other person may be experiencing emotionally. These are skills we've emphasized before. The first skill is called social decentering. The second skill is empathy.

Social decentering is a *cognitive process* in which you take into account the other person's thoughts, values, background, and overall perspective. The greater the difference between you and another person, the more difficult it is to accomplish social decentering. As you meet someone from a different culture, ask yourself, "What might this person be thinking right now?" Of course, since you're not a mind reader, you won't be able to know definitively what someone is thinking. But you can think about what most people that you know might be thinking, or draw on your own experiences. But keep the other person's worldview and cultural values in mind as you make inferences about his or her cognitive perspective. After considering his or her cognitive point of view, consider what the person may be experiencing emotionally.

Empathy is an *emotional reaction* that is similar to the one being experienced by another person.[107] Empathy is about *emotions,* whereas social decentering is about

BEING **Other**-ORIENTED

Being other-oriented does not mean becoming a "wishy-washy" person who only says or does what the other person wants. When you are other-oriented, you maintain your own sense of ethics and values while considering the needs and interests of others. Identify situations in which you have thought about what another person might want, yet have mindfully chosen to do something contrary to what the other person may have wanted. Do you think you can be other-oriented but not always do what another person wants you to do?

social decentering Cognitive process in which we take into account another person's thoughts, feelings, values, background, and perspective.

empathy Emotional reaction that is similar to the reaction being experienced by another person; empathizing is feeling what another person is feeling.

Building Your Skills

Identifying and Adapting to Cultural Rules and Norms

What are the typical norms and rules that you expect when communicating with people in your own cultural and ethnic group in the following situations?

Norms and rules regarding punctuality at meetings:

_____

_____

Norms and rules regarding greetings between good friends:

_____

_____

Norms and rules regarding giving and receiving gifts among friends:

_____

_____

Norms and rules regarding giving and receiving gifts among business associates:

_____

_____

Norms and rules regarding typical times for daily meals:

_____

_____

Norms and rules regarding appropriate use of someone's first name:

_____

_____

Share your answers with your classmates. Note the similarities and differences in your responses, both among people who share common cultural and ethnic backgrounds and among people who have different cultural and ethnic backgrounds.

Which of the skills for enhancing intercultural competence discussed on pages 109–112 would help you adapt to the different rules and expectations?

cognitive processes. You develop empathy as you draw on your own experiences (what you might be feeling), your knowledge of other people in general, and what you know about the specific person you are interacting with. Some suggest that it's impossible to ever experience the emotions of another person with complete confidence and accuracy. We agree. But to be empathic is to do your best to put yourself in someone else's place emotionally and consider what that person is feeling. Being in touch emotionally is hard work, and some people are just naturally more empathic toward others.

Appropriately Adapt Your Communication. The logical extension of being flexible and becoming other-oriented is to adapt your communication to enhance the quality and effectiveness of your interpersonal communication. To **adapt** means to adjust your behavior to others to accommodate differences and expectations. Appropriate adaptation occurs in the context of the relationship you have with the other person and what is happening in the communication environment. **Communication accommodation theory** suggests that all people adapt their behavior to others to some extent. Those who adapt to others appropriately and sensitively are more likely to experience more positive communication.[108] Adapting to others doesn't mean you only tell others what they want to hear and do what others want you to do. Nor are we suggesting that you adapt your behavior only so that you can get your way; the goal is effective communication, not manipulation. We are suggesting, rather, that you be aware of what your communication partner is doing and saying, especially if there are cultural differences between you, so that your message is understood and you don't unwittingly offend the other person. Although it may seem to be common sense, being sensitive to others and adapting behaviors to others are not as common as you might think.

Sometimes people adapt their behavior based on what they think someone will like. At other times, they adapt their communication after realizing they have done something wrong. When you modify your behavior in anticipation of an event, you **adapt predictively.** For example, you might decide to buy a friend flowers to soften the news about breaking a date because you know how much your friend likes flowers. When you modify your behavior after an event, you **adapt reactively.** For example, you might buy your friend flowers to apologize after a fight.

You often adapt your messages to enhance message clarity. There are at least four reasons that explain why you may adapt your communication with another person.

- *Information:* You adapt your message in response to specific information that you already know about your partner, such as what he or she may like or dislike, or information that your partner has shared with you.

- *Perceived Behavior:* You adapt your communication in response to what you think the other person is thinking, what you see the person doing, and your observations of the person's emotional expressions and moods.

- *History:* You adapt your messages to others based on previous conversations, past shared experiences, and personal information that others have shared with you.

- *Communication Context:* You adapt your message depending on where you are; you may whisper a brief comment to someone during a movie, yet shout a comment to someone when attending a loud rock concert.

In intercultural interactions, people frequently adapt communication in response to the feedback or reactions they are receiving during a conversation. An other-oriented communicator is constantly looking at and listening to the other person in order to appropriately adapt his or her communication behavior. Table 4.2 describes how we adapt our verbal messages to others and provides some examples.

People in conversations also adapt to nonverbal cues. Many times, they raise or lower voice volume in response to the volume of a partner, or lean toward people in response to their leaning toward the speaker. We talk more about such nonverbal cues in Chapter 7.

adapt To adjust one's behavior in accord with what someone else does. We can adapt based on the individual, the relationship, and the situation.

communication accommodation theory Theory that all people adapt their behavior to others to some extent.

adapt predictively To modify or change behavior in anticipation of an event.

adapt reactively To modify or change behavior after an event.

BEING Other-ORIENTED

At the heart of being other-oriented is adapting your behavior toward others in mindful and ethical ways. Review the adaptation strategies that are presented in Table 4.2. Identify other examples of various ways of adapting to others. Which strategies are easiest for you to use, and which are the most challenging for you?

TABLE 4.2	**How Do We Adapt to Others?**

Type of Adaptation	Examples
Adapting the Topic and Level of Intimacy of Your Conversation Choosing topics of conversation because of shared interests or things you have in common with your partner, including sharing information about yourself	• Talking about a class you both attend • Mentioning an article you read about a TV show your partner really likes • Telling someone about your depression because you believe he or she cares
Adapting How You Explain or Describe Something Providing additional information or detail because you recognize that your communication partner has certain gaps in his or her information	• Telling a story about Ike, whom your partner doesn't know, and explaining that Ike is your uncle • Describing Facebook to your grandparent, who doesn't know what the Internet is • Telling someone, "I know my behavior might seem a little erratic, but I'm under a lot of pressure at work right now and my parents are on my case"
Adapting by Withholding or Avoiding Information Not providing explanations of something your partner already knows; not providing information to avoid an anticipated undesired reaction from your partner; or not providing information because of a fear of how your partner might potentially use the information (such as sharing the information with other people)	• Not elaborating on the parts of an auto engine when describing a car problem because you know your partner is knowledgeable about cars • Not telling someone you saw his or her lover with someone else because he or she would be hurt • Not mentioning your interest in a mutual friend because you know the listener would blab about it to the mutual friend
Adapting Your Use of Examples, Comparisons, and Analogies Choosing messages you believe your partner will find relevant	• Describing a person your partner doesn't know by comparing the person to someone your partner knows • Explaining roller blading by comparing it to ice skating because your partner is an avid ice skater
Adapting Through Your Choice of Language Choosing or avoiding specific words because of the anticipated effect on your partner; consciously selecting words that you believe are understandable to your partner; or using words that have a unique meaning to you and your partner	• Using formal address in response to status differences: "Thank you, Professor Smith" • Using slang when the relationship is perceived as informal • Using nicknames, inside jokes, or teasing comments with close friends

Source: © Mark V. Redmond, "Interpersonal Content Adaptation in Everyday Interactions," paper presented at the annual meeting of the National Communication Association, Boston (2005).

Adaptation across intercultural contexts is usually more difficult than adaptation within your own culture. Imagine shaking hands with a stranger and having the stranger hold on to your hand as you continue to talk. In the United States, hand holding between strangers violates nonverbal norms. But in some cultures, maintaining physical contact while talking is expected. Pulling your hand away from this person would be rude. What may be mannerly in one culture is not always acceptable in another. Adapting to these cultural differences means developing that "third culture" that we talked about earlier in the chapter.

Taking an other-oriented approach to communication means considering the thoughts, feelings, background, perspectives, attitudes, and values of your partners and adjusting your interaction with them accordingly. Other-orientation leads to more effective interpersonal communication, regardless of whether you are dealing with someone in your family or a person from another country.

In an effective interpersonal relationship, your partner is also orienting himself or herself to you. A competent communicator has knowledge of others, is motivated to enhance the quality of communication, and possesses the skill of being other-oriented.

If you learn the skills and principles we have presented here, will it really make a difference in your ability to relate to others? Evidence suggests that the answer is yes. A study by communication researcher Lori Carrell found that students who had been exposed to lessons in empathy linked to a study of interpersonal and intercultural communication improved their ability to empathize with others.[109] There is evidence that if you master these principles and skills, you will be rewarded with greater insight and ability to relate to others who are different from you.

> **RECAP** How to Improve Your Intercultural Communication Competence
>
> **Develop Knowledge**
>
> | | |
> |---|---|
> | Actively Seek Information | Learn about the worldview of someone from another culture |
> | Listen and Ask Questions | Reduce uncertainty by asking for clarification and listening to the answer |
> | Create a Third Culture | Create common ground by merging aspects of both cultural traditions to develop a common understanding |
>
> **Develop Motivation**
>
> | | |
> |---|---|
> | Tolerate Ambiguity | Take your time, and expect some uncertainty |
> | Be Mindful | Be conscious of cultural differences, rather than ignoring the differences |
> | Avoid Negative Judgments | Resist thinking that your culture has all the answers |
>
> **Develop Skill**
>
> | | |
> |---|---|
> | Be Creatively Flexible | Learn as you interact, and be willing to adjust your behavior as you learn |
> | Become Other-Oriented | Put yourself in the other person's mental position (social decentering) and emotional mindset (empathizing) |
> | Adapt Your Communication | Adjust your behavior to others to ethically accommodate differences and expectations |

APPLYING AN OTHER-ORIENTATION
to Diversity: The Platinum Rule

When interacting with someone who is dramatically different from you, if you want to be truly other-oriented, you may need to go beyond what is known to most Westerners as "The Golden Rule": "Do unto others as you would have others do unto you." Or, as succinctly stated by the Buddha, "Consider others as yourself." In Chapter 2 on page 37 we identified additional interpretations of the same principle from a variety of religious traditions. But when interacting with someone who is quite different from you, treating him or her as you'd like to be treated may not achieve relational benefits. If you like hip-hop music but your friend prefers Mozart, taking her to a Mos Def concert may make you feel good about following the Golden Rule (that's how *you'd* like to be treated)—but the concert might be painful for her if she'd rather

be listening to Mozart's Horn Quintet in E flat, K. 407. Whether it's taste in music or food, greeting rituals, or a host of other culturally determined behaviors, the ultimate other-oriented behavior would be what communication researcher Milton Bennett calls the Platinum Rule: Do to others as they themselves would like to be treated.[110] Rather than treating people as *you* would like to be treated, interact with others the way you think *they* would like to be treated. According to Bennett, at its essence, empathy is "the imaginative, intellectual and emotional participation in another person's experience."[111] The goal, according to Bennett, is to attempt to think and feel what another person thinks and feels and to go beyond that by taking positive action toward others in response to your empathic feelings.

But is the Platinum Rule always helpful, or even possible? As you ponder the virtues and challenges of becoming other-oriented and adapting your communication behavior to enhance your intercultural communication competence, consider the following questions:

- Is the Platinum Rule always desirable? Are there situations when it would be inappropriate to follow the Platinum Rule? Explain your answer.
- What are some obstacles to applying the Platinum Rule, especially with people who are culturally different from you?
- How can the Platinum Rule be useful when you are having a disagreement with another person?
- Think about a time when you applied the Platinum Rule. What was the effect on the person with whom you were communicating?

Understanding Diversity: Describing Our Differences
(pages 87–93)

As we increasingly interact and communicate with people who are different from us, we must learn ways to appreciate and understand those differences and to bridge them in our interpersonal relationships. Our everyday world presents us with differences in gender, sexual orientation, race, ethnicity, age, and social class, all of which can influence how we communicate with and relate to others.

Key Terms

Sex 88   Ethnicity 90

Gender 88   Discrimination 91

Race 90

Critical Thinking Questions

1. What type of diversity do you find on campus? In the workplace? In your community? Do you find that you communicate differently with people from different groups and cultures? Explain.

2. How have gender differences played a role in your own communication or interactions with others? Explain.

3. Ethics: When Wayne, a Catholic Polish American, went to visit Dave, who was from an old Southern Baptist family, Dave's dad made a bigoted statement about African Americans. This upset Wayne, and he wondered whether Dave's father was prejudiced against Catholics, too. Should Wayne have spoken up and told Dave's dad that he did not like the remark? What would be the best way to approach such a discussion?

Activities

How well do you think you could predict someone's reactions to finding out that a parent or another close relative had just died? Rank-order each of the following from 1 (the person whose reaction you could predict most confidently) to 6 (the person whose reaction you'd be least confident about predicting).

a. _____ A close friend of your own sex, age, race, and cultural background

b. _____ A sixty-year-old male Chinese farmer

c. _____ A college student twenty years older than you, but of your own race, sex, and cultural background

d. _____ A ten-year-old girl from California who is the daughter of Asian and Latino parents

e. _____ A college student of a different race but your own age, cultural background, and sex

f. _____ A college student of the opposite sex but your own age, race, and cultural background

Which characteristics of each person do you believe provide the best information on which to base your judgments? Why? What would you need to know about each person to feel comfortable in making a prediction? How could you get that information?[112]

Web Resources

http://www.yforum.com Visitors to the National Forum on People's Differences can ask questions about religion, culture, gender, ethnicity, sexual preference, or other topics that might be too personal or embarrassing to ask someone in person.

Understanding Culture: Dimensions of Our Mental Software
(pages 93–97)

Culture is a learned system of knowledge, behaviors, attitudes, beliefs, values, and norms shared by a group of people. Culture influences how we process information and make sense of the world. Researchers have identified six dimensions common to all cultures they have studied: individualism versus collectivism, reliance on context, masculinity versus femininity, comfort with uncertainty, approach to power, and approach to time.

Key Terms

Culture 93   High-context culture 95

Worldview 93   Low-context culture 95

Co-culture 94   Masculine culture 95

Enculturation 94   Feminine culture 95

Cultural context 95

Critical Thinking Questions

1. Name the co-cultures to which you belong. Would you describe your co-cultures as low- or high-context, masculine or feminine? Explain. What beliefs and norms characterize these co-cultures? What does your culture or co-culture value?

2. Ethics: Is it ethical or appropriate for someone from one culture to attempt to change the cultural values of someone from a different culture? For example, consider the case in which children living on a Texas ranch owned by a polygamous religious sect were taken from their families for suspected abuse, which was in the news in 2008: Is it right for others to attempt to make someone from another culture or with a different value system change his or her ways?

Activities

Bring to class a fable, folktale, or children's story from a culture other than your own. As a group, analyze the cultural values implied by the story or characters in the story.

Barriers to Effective Intercultural Communication and Improving Intercultural Communication Competence
(pages 97–114)

Research indicates that culture has a direct effect on how we communicate with one another. The greater the difference in culture, the greater the potential for misunderstanding and miscommunication. Different communication codes, including different languages and interpretations of verbal and nonverbal messages, can be barriers to effective communication with those from cultures different from our own. Likewise, an ethnocentric view that one's own culture is superior to others can be a barrier. You can improve your intercultural communication competence by developing knowledge about others, developing motivation to understand others, and developing skill and adapting your communication and behavior with others in appropriate ways.

Key Terms

Intercultural communication 97

Culture shock 98

Ethnocentrism 99

Stereotype 101

Prejudice 102

Intercultural communication
    competence 104

Motivation 104

Skill 104

Third culture 106

Relational empathy 107

Mindful 108

Social decentering 111

Empathy 111

Adapt 112

Communication accommodation
    theory 112

Adapt predictively 112

Adapt reactively 112

Critical Thinking Questions

1. What is the problem in assuming that other people are like us? How does this create a barrier to effective intercultural communication?

2. Jonna, an American, has just been accepted as a foreign exchange student in Germany. What potential cultural barriers may she face? How should she manage these potential barriers?

3. Ethics: What are appropriate ways to deal with someone who consistently utters racial slurs and displays prejudice toward racial and ethnic groups?

Activities

In small groups, identify examples from your own experiences of each barrier to effective intercultural communication discussed in the text. Use one of the examples as the basis for a skit to perform for the rest of the class. See whether the class can identify which intercultural barrier your group is depicting. Also, suggest how the skills and principles discussed in the chapter might have improved the communication in the situation you role-play.

Web Resources

http://chocd.umsl.edu The Center for Human Origin and Cultural Diversity provides suggestions for the development of social justice and cultural awareness curricula.

5

Listening and Responding Skills

Objectives

1 Describe five elements of the listening process.

2 Identify characteristics of four listening styles.

3 Understand why we listen, and list several important barriers to effective listening.

4 Identify ways to improve your other-orientation and listening skills.

5 Identify responding skills and understand strategies for improving them.

Outline

- Listening Defined
- Listening Styles
- Listening Barriers
- Enhancing Listening Comprehension Skills
- Enhancing Empathic Listening Skills
- Enhancing Critical Listening Skills
- Enhancing Responding Skills
- Enhancing Empathic Responding Skills
- Enhancing Skills in Confirming Others

Think about your best friend. What are some of the qualities you most admire in your friend? Many people would respond that one of the most valued qualities in a friend is his or her just being there—supporting, comforting, and listening. As theologian Henri Nouwen eloquently put it:

> Listening is much more than allowing another to talk while waiting for a chance to respond. Listening is paying full attention to others and welcoming them into our very beings. . . . Listening is a form of spiritual hospitality by which you invite strangers to become friends, to get to know their inner selves more fully, and even dare to be silent with you.[1]

Simply stated, friends listen. They listen even if we sometimes say foolish things. Again, Nouwen describes it well: "True listeners no longer have an inner need to make their presence known. They are free to receive, to welcome, to accept."[2] As we consider the essential skills of interpersonal communication, the skill of listening to others would be at or near the top of the list in terms of importance.[3] Skilled communicators do more than impassively listen—they appropriately respond to what we say. They confirm that they understand and care for us by providing both verbal and nonverbal feedback. There is also evidence that listening is the quintessential skill of an effective leader.[4]

Listening and responding skills are important for several reasons. Some researchers suggest that because listening is the first communication skill that we learn (because we respond to sounds even while in our mother's womb), it's also the most important skill. Listening plays a key role in helping us learn to speak.

Another reason listening is important: You spend more time listening than participating in any other communication activity. In fact, you spend more time listening to others than doing almost anything else. Typical college students spend more than 80 percent of an average day communicating with other people, and as the pie chart in Figure 5.1 shows, of the total time they spend communicating, 50 percent is spent listening to others.[5] Ironically, most people's formal communication training focuses on writing, the activity to which they devote the least amount of communication time. Chances are that until now you have had no formal training in listening. In this chapter, we focus on this often neglected, yet crucial, skill for developing quality interpersonal relationships. Listening is the process by which people learn the most about others. In addition, we explore ways to respond appropriately to others.

listening Process of selecting, attending to, creating meaning from, remembering, and responding to verbal and nonverbal messages.

hearing Physiological process of decoding sounds.

FIGURE 5.1

What You Do with Your Communication Time

Read 13%
Write 12%
Speak 20%
Listen 50%

Listening Defined

"Hey, did you hear me? Where would you like to go for dinner tonight?" Shawn asks Pat. In fact, Pat probably did *hear* the question, but he may not have been *listening*. **Listening** is a complex process of selecting, attending to, constructing meaning from, remembering, and responding to verbal and nonverbal messages.[6] When we listen, we hear words and try to make sense out of what we hear. The essence of being a good listener is being able to accurately interpret the messages expressed by others.[7] **Hearing** is the physiological process of decoding sounds. You hear when sound vibrations reach your eardrum and cause the middle ear bones—the hammer, anvil, and stirrup—to move. Eventually, these sound vibrations are translated into electrical impulses that reach the brain. In order to listen to something, you must first select that sound from competing sounds. Then you must attend to it, understand it, and remember it. A fifth activity—responding—confirms that listening has occurred.[8]

PEARLS BEFORE SWINE

PEARLS BEFORE SWINE © Stephan Pastis/Dist. by United Feature Syndicate, Inc.

Selecting

Selecting a sound is the process of choosing one sound as you sort through the various sounds competing for your attention. As you listen to someone in an interpersonal context, you focus on the words and nonverbal messages of your partner. Even now, as you are reading this book, there are undoubtedly countless noises within earshot. Stop reading for a moment and sort through the various sounds around you. Do you hear music? Is there noise from outside? How about the murmur of voices, the tick of a clock, the hum of a computer, the whoosh of an air conditioner or furnace? To listen, you must select which of these sounds will receive your attention.

Attending

After selecting a sound, you then **attend** to or focus on it. Attention can be fleeting. You may attend to the sound for a moment and then move on or return to other thoughts or other sounds. As we discussed in Chapter 3, your attention is sometimes selective. Either consciously or unconsciously, you are more likely to attend to those messages that meet your needs and are consistent with your attitudes or interests. Information that is novel or intense, or that somehow relates to you, may capture your attention. And conflict, humor, new ideas, and real or concrete things command your attention more easily than abstract theories that do not relate to your interests or needs. Finally, because listening is a transactional rather than a linear process (which means that you are both sending and receiving information *at the same time*), your listening skill is linked to your ability to attend to specific messages, especially during conversations when you're both talking and listening.[9]

Understanding

Whereas hearing is a physiological phenomenon, **understanding** is the process of assigning meaning to the sounds you select and to which you attend; to understand a message is to construct meaning from what you hear and see. There are several theories about how you assign meaning to words you hear, but there is no universally accepted notion of how this process works. We know that people understand best if they can relate what they are hearing to something they already know.

A second basic principle about how people understand others is this: The greater the similarity between individuals, the greater the likelihood of more accurate understanding. Individuals from different cultures who have substantially different religions, family lifestyles, values, and attitudes often have difficulty understanding each other, particularly in the early phases of a relationship.

selecting Process of choosing one sound while sorting through various sounds competing for your attention.

attending Process of focusing on a particular sound or message.

understanding Process of assigning meaning to sounds.

Healthy family relations result when parents and children are able to develop people-oriented listening styles.

You understand best that which you also experience. Perhaps you have heard the Montessori school philosophy: I hear, I forget; I see, I remember; I experience, I understand. Hearing alone does not create understanding. People hear over one billion words each year, but understand only a fraction of that number. Understanding happens when we derive meaning from the words we hear.

Remembering

Remembering is the process of recalling information. Some researchers theorize that you store every detail you have ever heard or witnessed; your mind operates like a hard drive on a computer. But you cannot retrieve or remember all the information. Sometimes you were present at events, yet have no recollection of what occurred.

Human brains have both short-term and long-term memory storage systems. Short-term memory is where you store almost all the information you hear. You look up a phone number in the telephone book, mumble the number to yourself, then dial the number, only to discover that the line is busy. Three minutes later, you have to look up the number again because it did not get stored in your long-term memory. Short-term storage is very limited. Just as airports have just a few short-term parking spaces, but lots of spaces for long-term parking, brains can accommodate only a few things of fleeting significance, but acres of important information. Most of us forget hundreds of bits of insignificant information that pass through our brains each day.

The information stored in long-term memory includes events, conversations, and other data that are significant. People tend to remember dramatic and vital information, as well as seemingly inconsequential details connected with such information. What were you doing on the morning of September 11, 2001, when you first heard that a plane had flown into the World Trade Center in New York? Chances are you remember precisely what you were doing. Information makes it to long-term memory because of its significance to us.

Responding

Interpersonal communication is transactive; it involves both talking and responding. You are **responding** to people when you let them know you understand their messages. Responses can be nonverbal; direct eye contact and head nods let your partner know you're tuned in. Or you can respond verbally by asking questions to confirm the content of the message: "Are you saying you don't want us to spend as much time together as we once did?" or by making statements that reflect the feelings of the speaker: "So you are frustrated that you have to wait for someone to drive you where you want to go." We discuss responding skills in more detail later in the chapter.

remembering Process of recalling information.

responding Process of confirming your understanding of a message.

Listening Styles

What's your listening style? Do you focus more on the content of the message than on the feelings being expressed by the speaker? Or do you prefer brief sound bites of

120

information that you can hear quickly? Your **listening style** is your preferred way of making sense out of the spoken messages you hear. Listening researchers Kitty Watson, Larry Barker, and James Weaver found that listeners tend to fall into one of four listening styles: people-oriented, action-oriented, content-oriented, or time-oriented.[10] There are a variety of factors that influence your listening style, including your personality and social style.[11] Researchers Randy Dillon and Nelya McKenzie suggest that your culture and ethnicity are powerful forces that affect how you listen to others.[12]

People-Oriented Listeners

As you might suspect from the label, **people-oriented listeners** tend to be comfortable with and skilled at listening to people's feelings and emotions. They are likely to empathize and search for common areas of interest. People-oriented listeners embody many of the attributes of being other-oriented that we've discussed throughout the book—they seek strong interpersonal connections when listening to others. Research suggests that those who strongly prefer the people-oriented listening style will be less anxious or apprehensive about listening to other people, especially when listening to just one other person.[13] There is also evidence that people-oriented listeners may be more empathic; they have greater skill in understanding the thoughts and feelings of others.[14] One study also found that jurors who are people-oriented listeners tend to find the plaintiffs less at fault in civil court trials.[15]

Action-Oriented Listeners

An **action-oriented listener** prefers information that is well organized, brief, and error-free. An action-oriented listener doesn't like the speaker to tell lengthy stories and digress. The action-oriented listener may think "Get to the point" or "What am I supposed to do with this information?" when hearing a message filled with too many anecdotes or rambling, disorganized bits of information. Whereas a people-oriented listener would be more likely to focus on the feelings of the person telling the story, the action-oriented listener wants to know the point or the punch line. There is new evidence to suggest that action-oriented listeners are more likely to be more skeptical when listening to information. Researchers call this skepticism **second-guessing**— questioning the ideas and assumptions underlying a message. Rather than taking the information they hear at face value, action-oriented listeners are more likely to reinterpret or evaluate the literal message to determine whether it is true or false—they make another guess (hence the term *second-guessing*) about whether the information they are listening to is accurate.[16]

Content-Oriented Listeners

If you are a **content-oriented listener,** you are more comfortable listening to complex, detailed information than are people with other listening styles. A content-oriented listener homes in on the facts, details, and evidence in a message. In fact, if a message does not include ample supporting evidence and specific details, the content-oriented listener is more likely to reject the message. Like the action-oriented listener, content-oriented listeners are likely to make second guesses about the messages they hear. Content-oriented listeners are also less apprehensive when communicating with others in group and interpersonal situations.[17] People who have listening style preferences for both high content and high action are more likely to have a precise and attentive style of arguing with others; they leave a strong impression on others when trying to persuade them.[18] Content-oriented listeners would make good judges or lawyers; they focus on issues and arguments and listen to see whether a speaker's conclusion is accurate or credible.

listening style Preferred way of making sense out of spoken messages.

people-oriented listener Listener who is comfortable with and skilled at listening to people's feelings and emotions.

action-oriented listener Listener who prefers information that is well-organized, brief, and error-free.

second-guessing Questioning the ideas and assumptions underlying a message; assessing whether the message is true or false.

content-oriented listener Listener who is more comfortable listening to complex, detailed information than are those with other listening styles.

Time-Oriented Listeners

You're a **time-oriented listener** if you like your messages delivered succinctly. Time-oriented listeners are keenly aware of how much time they have to listen. They have many things on their "to-do" list; their "in basket" often overflows, so they want messages delivered quickly and briefly. Whereas a people-oriented listener might enjoy spending time over a cup of coffee catching up on the day's activities, a time-oriented listener is more like a drive-by listener—a time-oriented listener may think, "Give me what I need so I can keep on moving to my next task or hear my next message. Don't ramble, don't digress, just get to the point quickly."

Understanding Your Listening Style

Now that we've identified the four listening styles, you may wonder, "Do I have just one listening style, or do I have more than one style?" According to Watson and Barker, about 40 percent of all listeners use one primary listening style, especially if they are under stress.[19] Another 40 percent of listeners prefer to use more than one style—for example, sometimes they may prefer to listen to content, and they may also want the information delivered in a short amount of time (content- and time-oriented listening styles). And about 20 percent of people do not have a specific listening style preference; these individuals may just want to avoid listening altogether, either because they are shy and don't like to be around others in social situations, they have listener apprehension, or they are simply weary of listening to other people. There is also evidence that your listening style varies depending on what you are listening to—which is a good thing.[20] Adapting to others is an important skill in being other-oriented. Having a flexible style suggests you are aware of both your own listening style and the listening styles of others.

Knowing your listening style can help you better understand how to adapt to various listening situations. If, for example, you know that you are a time-oriented or action-oriented listener and your friend or companion is a people-oriented listener, you and your friend will need to adjust your speaking and listening styles. When speaking to an action-oriented listener, give the listener a brief preview of what you will be talking about. You could say, "Phil, there are three things I'd like to share with you." Stick to that structure. When speaking to a people-oriented listener, realize that he or she will feel rushed or hurried if you skip information about feelings or relationships. A people-oriented listener prefers to spend more time talking about emotions than do those with other listening styles. A time-oriented listener would like information summarized as in a concisely written business memo punctuated with bullets and lists of essential information.

What is the best listening style? It depends on the listening situation and the communication context and objectives. In a high-pressure, fast-paced job such as stock trading, you don't have time to listen to stories about clients' families or the latest TV show; you need information delivered quickly and efficiently. A father listening to a daughter talk about her rotten day at school would find a people-oriented listening style better for listening to his daughter pour her heart out. Being aware of your own preferred listening style and the needs of your communication partner can help you adopt a listening style that best suits the situation.

BEING Other-ORIENTED

It's important not only to know your own preferred listening style but also to understand the listening style of your communication partner. How? Look for clues that help you identify the listening style of others. People-oriented listeners are likely to tell more stories and anecdotes about others. Action-oriented listeners will perk up if you use more action verbs. Content-oriented listeners will like lists of information. Time-oriented listeners will often tell you they can only listen for a short period of time (e.g., "I've got two minutes").

Listening Barriers

Even though people spend so much of their communication time listening, most don't listen as well as they should. Twenty-four hours after you hear a speech, a class lecture, or a sermon, you have forgotten more than half of what was said. And it gets

time-oriented listener Listener who likes messages delivered succinctly.

worse. In another twenty-four hours, you have forgotten half of what you remembered, so you really remember only a quarter of the lecture.

Interpersonal listening skills may be even worse. When you listen to a speech or lecture, you have a clearly defined listening role; one person talks, and you are expected to listen. But in interpersonal situations, you may have to alternate quickly between speaking and listening. This takes considerable skill and concentration. Often you are thinking of what you want to say next, rather than listening.

One surprising study found that we sometimes listen better to strangers than to intimate friends or partners. Married couples in the study tended to interrupt each other more often and were generally less polite to each other than were strangers involved in a decision-making task.[21] Apparently, we take listening shortcuts when communicating with others in close relationships. As the Understanding Others: Adapting to Differences feature suggests, the problem may be gender-related.

Inattentive listening is a bit like channel surfing when we watch TV—pushing the remote control button to switch from channel to channel, avoiding commercials and focusing for brief periods on attention-grabbing programs. When we listen to others, we may tune in to the conversation for a moment, decide that the content is uninteresting, and then focus on a personal thought. These thoughts are barriers to communication, and they come in a variety of forms.

Are we more attentive listeners to TV? Apparently not. One research team phoned TV viewers as soon as the evening news program was over. On average, most people remembered only about 17 percent of what they heard. And even when they were reminded of some of the news coverage, most averaged no better than 25 percent recall.[22] Even though more highly educated viewers did a little better, the overall conclusion is not good: We often don't "catch" what we hear, even a few moments after hearing it. Let's explore several listening barriers that keep us from catching others' meaning.

Being Self-Absorbed

You're in your local grocery store during "rush hour." It appears that most of your community has also decided to forage for food at the same time. You want to get in and out of the store quickly, but many shoppers are oblivious to those around them. They stop in the aisle, blocking the path for others. They elbow their way into crowded checkout stands. And the "express lane" that limits customers to ten items or fewer is backed up because some shoppers have difficulty counting to ten. You find yourself becoming tense—not just because you are hungry, but because it seems the grocery store is filled with people who are self-absorbed; they are focused on getting their needs met and are oblivious to the needs of others.

UNDERSTANDING OTHERS
Adapting to Differences

Who Listen Better, Men or Women?

Research provides no definitive answer to the question "Who listen better, men or women?" There is evidence, however, that men and women may listen somewhat differently and have different expectations about the functions of listening and talking. Language expert Deborah Tannen suggests that two of the most common complaints wives have about their husbands are "He doesn't listen to me any more" and "He doesn't talk to me any more." Complaints about lack of communication are usually at the top of women's lists of reasons for divorce but are mentioned much less often by men. Why are women more often dissatisfied with the listening and talking process than men are? Tannen's explanation: Women expect different things from conversations than men do. There appear to be gender differences in attention styles, listening goals, and listening focus. But in the end, both men and women may listen equally well; it may be that different expectations on the part of each gender explain perceptual differences between the sexes about the quality of listening.

Different Attention Styles

Research suggests that men and women may have different attention styles.[23] When men listen, they may be looking for a new structure or an organizational pattern for what they are hearing or trying to separate bits of information they hear. They continually shape, form, observe, inquire, and direct energy toward a goal. Men's attention style is sometimes reported to be more emotionally controlled than women's attention style. Women have sometimes been described as being more subjective, empathic, and emotionally involved as they listen. They are perceived as more likely to search for relationships among a pattern and to rely on more intuitive perceptions of feelings. They are also more easily distracted by competing details. Females may hear more of the message because they reject less of it. In summary, men often focus on the big picture (the forest), while women are more likely to focus on the details (the trees). These differences in attention styles and the way men and women may process information can potentially affect listening, even though we have no direct evidence linking attention style to listening skill.

Different Listening Goals

There also may be differences in listening goals. There is evidence that when men listen, they listen to solve a problem; men are more task-oriented.[24] Women may listen to seek new information to enhance understanding about the relationship. The difference in listening goals has been summarized this way: Men listen to report, women listen to establish rapport.

What do these research studies imply about both attention styles and listening goals? They may mean that men and women focus on different parts of messages and have different listening objectives. These differences can affect relationship development. Males may need to recognize that while they are attending to a message and looking for structure to solve a problem or achieve a goal, they may hear less of the message and therefore listen less effectively. And even though many females may hear more of the message, they may need to make connections between the parts of the information they hear to look for major ideas, rather then just focusing on the details. In any case, gender-based differences in attention style and information processing may account for some of the relational problems that husbands and wives, lovers, siblings, and male and female friends experience.[25]

---

conversational narcissism
A focus on personal agendas and self-absorption rather than on the needs and ideas of others.

BEING Other-ORIENTED

When someone "pushes your hot buttons" and you find yourself becoming emotionally upset, what can you do to calm yourself and remain centered? First, simply be aware that you are becoming emotionally upset. Then take action (such as focusing on your breathing) to lower the tension you are feeling. What are other strategies to help you remain calm when someone "pushes your buttons"?

Self-absorbed listeners are focused on their needs rather than on yours; the message is about *them,* not *you.* During conversations with a self-absorbed communicator, you have difficulty sustaining the conversation about anything except your self-absorbed partner's ideas, experiences, and stories. This problem is also called **conversational narcissism.** To be narcissistic is to be in love with oneself, like the mythical Greek character Narcissus, who became enamored with his reflection in a pool of water.[26]

The self-absorbed listener is actively involved in doing several things other than listening. The self-absorbed person is much more likely to interrupt others in mid-sentence, as he or she is seeking ways to focus the attention on himself or herself. The self-absorbed listener is also not focusing on his or her partner's message but thinking about what he or she is going to say next. This focus on an internal message can keep a listener from selecting and attending to the other person's message.

How do you short-circuit this listening problem in yourself? First, diagnose it. Note consciously when you find yourself drifting off, thinking about your agenda rather than concentrating on the speaker. Second, throttle up your powers of concentration when you find your internal messages are distracting you from listening well.

Different Listening Focus

There also may be gender differences in the way people focus on a listening task. To be able to multitask—to work on several tasks simultaneously—is a valued skill for administrative assistants, but some people can do two things at once, and some people can't. When it comes to listening to more than one message at a time, research suggests that men are more likely to have difficulty attending to multiple messages; when they are focused on one message, they may have more difficulty than women in carrying on a conversation with another person.[27] Men have a tendency to lock on to a message, whereas women seem more adept at shifting between two or more simultaneous messages. For example, sometimes when men watch a TV program, they may seem lost in the program and oblivious to other voices around them. Women, on the other hand, are more likely to be carrying on a conversation with one person and also focusing on the television program or a message they may hear nearby. We're not saying that women are more likely to eavesdrop intentionally—simply that some women have greater potential to listen to two things at once.

What are the implications of this research? It may be especially important for women to stop and focus on the message of others, rather than on either internal or external competing messages. And men may need to be sensitive to others who may want to speak to them, rather then becoming oblivious to their surroundings and fixated on their own internal message or on a single external message. Being able to stop competing thoughts and focus on a single message can enhance comprehension of the message on which you are focused. It's useful, however, to make sure this message is the most important one to which you should be attending.

Different Listening Perceptions

Although it may seem that men and women have somewhat different approaches to listening, it is still not clear whether men and women are really that different when it comes to relating to one another. Communication researchers Stephanie Sargent and James Weaver suggest that pop psychology, which alleges dramatic differences between the way men and women listen, may simply be perpetuating stereotypes based on the way men and women

think they are supposed to listen.[28] Although some research suggests that men and women may differ somewhat in the way they respond to information, the difference may not be based in a person's biological sex; it is more likely a reflection of differences in gender (socially constructed, cultural or co-cultural, learned behavior).

When it comes to enhancing communication and listening to one another, it is best to start, not from the position that men and women are from different planets, but rather from the position that they share common needs.[29]

Unchecked Emotions

Words are powerful symbols that affect people's attitudes, behavior, and even blood pressure. Words arouse people emotionally, and your emotional state can affect how well you listen. **Emotional noise** occurs when emotional arousal interferes with communication effectiveness. If you grew up in a home in which R-rated language was never used, then four-letter words may be distracting to you. Words that insult your religious or ethnic heritage can be fighting words. Most people respond to certain trigger words like a bull to a waving cape; they want to charge in to correct the speaker or perhaps even do battle with him or her.

Sometimes, it is not specific words but rather concepts or ideas that cause an emotional eruption. Some talk-radio hosts try to boost their ratings by purposely using words that elicit passionate responses. Although listening to such shows can be interesting and entertaining, when your own emotions become aroused, you may lose your ability to converse effectively. Unchecked emotions can interfere with focusing on the message of another. Note that we're primarily concerned here with negative emotions that can sap your ability to listen accurately to others. Research suggests that being in a positive emotional state can actually make you a better listener because you are able to be more attentive and focused when you are in a good mood.[30]

emotional noise Form of communication interference caused by emotional arousal.

If you are listening to someone who is emotionally distraught, you will be more likely to focus on his or her emotions than on the content of the message.[31] Communication author R. G. Owens advises that when you are communicating with someone who is emotionally excited, you should remain calm and focused and try simply to communicate your interest in the other person.[32]

Your listening challenge is to avoid emotional sidetracks and keep your attention focused on what others are saying. When you find yourself distracted by emotional noise brought on by objectionable words or concepts, or by an emotional speaker, use self-talk (tell yourself to remain calm) to quiet the noise and steer back to the subject at hand.

Criticizing the Speaker

The late Mother Teresa once said, "If you judge people, you have no time to love them." Being critical of the speaker may distract a listener from focusing on the message. Do you remember seeing villains in movies about the Old West, waiting in the bushes, ready to jump out and ambush an unsuspecting passerby? Perhaps you know someone who is an **ambush listener.** This is a person who eagerly pounces on the speaker to argue, criticize, or find fault with what the other person has said. Although the ambush listener may look as if she or he is listening, in reality this type of listener is just waiting to critique the speaker for a variety of reasons.

Superficial factors such as clothing, body size and shape, age, and other aspects of personal appearance all affect our interpretation of a message. Monitor your internal dialogue to make sure you are focusing on the message rather than on judging the messenger. Good listeners say to themselves, "While it may be distracting, I am simply not going to let the appearance of this speaker keep my attention from the message."

Differing Speech Rate and Thought Rate

Your ability to think faster than people speak is another listening pitfall. The average person speaks at a rate of 125 words a minute. Some folks talk a bit faster, others more slowly. In contrast, you have the ability to process up to 600 or 800 words a minute. The difference between your mental ability to handle words and the speed at which they arrive at your cortical centers can cause trouble, giving you time to daydream and to tune the speaker in and out and giving you the illusion that you are concentrating more attentively than you actually are.[33]

You can turn your listening speed into an advantage if you use the extra time instead to summarize what a speaker is saying. By periodically sprinkling in mental summaries during a conversation, you can dramatically increase your listening ability and make the speech-rate/thought-rate difference work to your advantage.

Information Overload

We live in an information-rich age. We are all constantly bombarded with sights and sounds, and experts suggest that the volume of information competing for our attention is likely to become even greater in the future. BlackBerrys, satellite radio, cell phones, MP3 players, and other technological devices can interrupt conversations and distract us from listening to others.

Be on the alert for interruptions from such sources when you are talking with others. Don't assume that because you are ready to talk, the other person is ready to listen. If your message is particularly sensitive or important, you may want to ask your listening partner, "Is this a good time to talk?" Even if he or she says yes, look for eye contact and a responsive facial expression to make sure the positive response is genuine.

ambush listener Person who is overly critical and judgmental when listening to others.

External Noise

As you will recall, all the communication models in Chapter 1 include the element of noise—distractions that take your focus away from the message. Many households seem to be addicted to noise. Often, there is a TV on (sometimes more than one), a computer game beeping, and music emanating from another room. These and other sounds compete for your attention when you are listening to others.

Besides literal noise, there are other potential distractors. A headline in your evening paper about a lurid sex scandal may "shout" for your attention just when your son wants to talk with you about the science fiction story he's trying to write. A desire to listen to your recent download of *Pacific Overtures* may drown out your spouse's overtures to have a heart-to-heart talk about your family's budget problems. The lure of music, TV, books, or your computer can all distract you from your listening task.

Information overload can prevent us from being able to communicate effectively with people around us.

Distractions make it difficult to sustain attention to a message. You have a choice to make. You can attempt to listen through the competing distractions, or you can modify the environment to reduce them. Turning off the stereo, setting down the paper, and establishing eye contact with the speaker can help minimize the noise barrier.

Listener Apprehension

Not only do some people become nervous and apprehensive about speaking to others, but some are anxious about listening to others. **Listener apprehension** is the fear of misunderstanding or misinterpreting, or of not being able to adjust psychologically to messages spoken by others.[34] Because some people are nervous or worried about missing the message, they *do* misunderstand the message; their fear and apprehension keep them from absorbing it.[35] President Franklin Roosevelt's admonition that "The only thing we have to fear is fear itself" implies correctly that fear can become "noise" and keep people from listening to messages accurately. If you are one of those people who are nervous when listening, you may experience difficulty understanding all you hear.

If you're an apprehensive listener, you will have to work harder when you listen to others. When listening to a public speech, it may be acceptable to use a tape or digital recorder or to start taking notes; it's not appropriate or even always possible to have a recorder or paper and pencil to take notes during interpersonal conversations. If you're on the phone, you can take notes when you listen to help you remember the message content, but taping phone conversations without the other speaker's consent is not ethical. Whether you're face to face with the speaker or on the phone, what you can do is try to mentally summarize the message as you're listening to it. Concentrating on the message by mentally summarizing what you hear can help take your mind off your anxiety and help you focus on the message.

listener apprehension The fear of misunderstanding, misinterpreting, or being unable to adjust to the spoken messages of others.

▶RECAP Listening Barriers

Listening Barrier	To Overcome the Barrier
Self-Absorption	Consciously become aware of the self-focus and shift attention.
Unchecked Emotions	Use self-talk to manage emotions.
Criticism of the Speaker	Focus on the message, not the messenger.
Differing Speech and Thought Rate	Use the time difference between speech rate and thought rate to mentally summarize the message.
Information Overload	Realize when you or your partner is tired or distracted and not ready to listen.
External Noise	Take charge of the listening environment by eliminating distractions.
Listener Apprehension	Concentrate on the message as you mentally summarize what you hear.

Enhancing Listening Comprehension Skills

Many of the listening problems that we have identified stem from focusing on one's self rather than on the messages of others. Dale Carnegie, in his classic book *How to Win Friends and Influence People,* offered this tip to enhance interpersonal relationships: "Focus first on being interested, not interesting."[36] In essence, he was affirming the importance of being other-oriented when listening to others.

You can become a more other-oriented listener by following three steps you probably first encountered in elementary school: (1) stop, (2) look, and (3) listen. Although these steps may seem simplistic and just common sense, they are not always common practice. They can provide the necessary structure to help you refocus your mental energies and improve your ability to comprehend the messages of others. These steps to improved listening are supported by a considerable body of listening research. Let's consider each step separately.

Stop

Stop what? What should you *not* do in order to be a better listener? You should not be attending to off-topic "self-talk." Your internal, self-focused messages may distract you from giving your undivided attention to what others are saying.

Most interpersonal listening problems can be traced to a single source—ourselves. While listening to others, we also "talk" to ourselves. Our internal thoughts are like a play-by-play sportscast. We mentally comment on the words and sights that we select and to which we attend. If we keep those mental comments focused on the message, they may be useful. But we often attend to our own internal dialogues instead of others' messages. Then our listening effectiveness plummets.

Two listening researchers conducted a study to identify the specific behaviors that good listeners perform when listening. What they discovered supports our admonition that the first thing you have to do to be a better listener is to stop focusing on your own mental messages and be other-oriented. Specifically, you should take the following actions during what the researchers called the "pre-interaction phase" of listening.

- Put your own thoughts aside.
- Be there mentally as well as physically.
- Make a conscious, mindful effort to listen.
- Take adequate time to listen; don't rush the speaker; be patient.
- Be open-minded.[37]

BEING **Other**-ORIENTED

At the heart of being a good listener is focusing on the other person instead of on your own thoughts and feelings. Being aware of whether your mind is truly centered on the other person or on your own internal messages is the first step to effective listening. When you are listening to others, what topics or behavior on the part of the speaker are most likely to trigger a self-oriented focus rather than an other-oriented focus in you?

It boils down to this: When you listen, you are either on-task or off-task. When you are on-task, you are concentrating on the message; when you're off-task, your mind may be a thousand miles away. What's important is to be mindful of what you are doing. Research suggests that you can increase your motivation to listen by reminding yourself why listening is important; sprinkling in a few on-task "self-talk" reminders of why the information you are listening to is important can enhance your listening skill.[38]

Two researchers studied how to enhance the performance of "professional listeners" who work in call centers, places where customers call to order products, make product suggestions, or lodge complaints.[39] They found that customers preferred listeners who were focused and communicated that they were devoting their full attention to the caller. Training listeners to avoid distractions, home in on the essence of a caller's message, and stop and focus on what the callers were telling them increased customers' confidence and satisfaction in the speaker–listener relationship. The researchers also concluded that the ability to stop and focus on the comments of others can be taught. People who learn how to stop mental distractions can improve their listening comprehension.

Look

Nonverbal messages are powerful. As the primary ways we communicate feelings, emotions, and attitudes, they play a major role in the total communication process, particularly in the development of relationships. Facial expressions and vocal cues, as well as eye contact, posture, and use of gestures and movement, can dramatically color the meaning of a message. When the nonverbal message contradicts the verbal message, people almost always believe the nonverbal message. In listening to others, it is vital to focus not only on the words, but also on the nonverbal messages.

Accurately interpreting nonverbal messages can help you "listen between the lines" by noting what someone is not saying verbally but expressing nonverbally. By attending to your partner's unspoken message, you are looking for the **meta-message**—the message about the message. Metacommunication, as you learned in Chapter 1, is communication about communication. The nonverbal meta-message provides a source of information about the emotional and relational impact of what a speaker may be expressing with the verbal message. For example, a friend may not explicitly say that he or she is angry, upset, or irritated, but his or her nonverbal cues let you know that your friend is not happy. The essence of the "look" step is to listen with your eyes as well as your ears.

Another reason to look at the other person is to establish eye contact, which signals that you are focusing your interest and attention on him or her. If your eyes are darting over your partner's head, looking for someone else, or if you are constantly peeking at your watch, your partner will rightly get the message that you're not really listening. Researcher Jinni Harrigan found that people telegraph desire to change roles from listener to speaker by increasing eye contact, using gestures such as a raised finger,

meta-message A message about a message; the message a person is expressing via nonverbal means (such as by facial expression, eye contact, and posture) about the message articulated with words.

Building Your Skills

Identifying Message Details and Major Ideas

How skilled are you at noting both the details of a message and its major ideas? To become a skilled listener, you must know how to identify both of these aspects of what someone is telling you. Here's a chance to practice your skill in identifying and remembering bits of information, as well as the main meaning of a message.

Read each of the following statements. After you have read each statement, cover it with your hand or a piece of paper. First, list as many of the details as you can recall from the message. Second, summarize your understanding of the major idea or key point of the message. As a variation on this activity, rather than reading the statement, have someone read the statement to you and then identify the details and major idea.

Statement 1: "I'm very confused. I reserved our conference room for 1 P.M. today for an important meeting. We all know that conference space is tight. I reserved the room last week with the administrative assistant. Now I learn that you are planning to use the conference room at noon for a two-hour meeting. It's now 11 A.M. We need to solve this problem soon. I have no other option for holding my meeting. And if I don't hold my meeting today, the boss is going to be upset."

Statement 2: "Hello, Marcia? I'm calling on my cell phone. Where are you? I thought you were supposed to meet me at the circle drive 45 minutes ago. You know I can't be late for my seminar this evening. What do you mean, you're waiting at the circle drive? I don't see you. No, I'm at Switzler Hall circle drive. You're where? No, that's not the circle drive I meant. I thought you'd know where I meant. Don't you ever listen? If you hurry, I can just make it to the seminar."

Statement 3: "Oh, Mary, I just don't know what to do. My daughter announced that when she turns 18 next week she's going to shave her head, get a large tattoo, and put a ring in her nose and eyebrow. She said it's something she's always wanted to do and now she can do it without my permission. She's always been such a sweet, compliant girl, but she seems to have turned wacky. I've tried talking with her. And her father isn't much help. He thinks it may look 'cool.' I just don't want her to look like a freak when she has her senior picture taken next month."

and shifting posture.[40] So it is important to maintain eye contact and monitor your partner's nonverbal signals when you are listening as well as when you are speaking.

The tricky part of the Look step is not to be distracted by nonverbal cues that may prevent you from interpreting the message correctly. A research team asked one group of college students to listen to a counselor, and another group both to watch the counselor and to listen.[41] The students then rated the counselor's effectiveness. Students who both saw and heard the counselor perceived him as *less* effective, because his distracting nonverbal behaviors affected their evaluations. So, look to discern the emotional meaning behind the words, but don't let a speaker's delivery distract you from what the speaker is saying.

Listen

After making a concerted effort to stop distracting internal dialogue and to look for nonverbal cues, you will be in a better position to understand the verbal messages of others. To listen is to do more than focus on facts and message details; it is to search for the essence of the speaker's thoughts.

Research suggests that effective listeners are active rather than passive when listening. For example, during the normal course of actively listening to another person, effective listeners[42]

- just listen—they do not interrupt.

- respond appropriately and provide feedback—both appropriate verbal feedback ("yes, I see," "I understand") and nonverbal feedback (eye contact, nodding, appropriate facial expressions).

- appropriately contribute to the conversation.

Effective listeners are not only goal-oriented (listening for the point of the message) but are also people-oriented (listening to appropriately affirm the person). To maximize your listening effectiveness, we offer several more specific strategies and tips.

Determine Your Listening Goal. You listen to other people for several reasons—to learn, to enjoy yourself, to evaluate, or to provide empathic support. With so many potential listening goals and options, it is useful to decide consciously what your listening objective is.

If you are listening to someone give you directions to the city park, then your mental summaries should focus on the details of when to turn left and how many streets past the courthouse you go before you turn right. The details are crucial to achieving your objective. If, in contrast, your neighbor is telling you about her father's triple bypass operation, then your goal is to empathize. It is probably not important that you be able to recall when her father checked into the hospital or other details. Your job is to listen patiently and to provide emotional support. Clarifying your listening objective in your own mind can help you use appropriate skills to maximize your listening effectiveness.

Transform Listening Barriers into Listening Goals. If you can transform into listening goals the listening barriers you read about earlier, you will be well on your way to improving your listening skill. Make it a goal not to focus on your personal agenda. Make it a goal to use self-talk to manage emotional noise. Set a goal not to criticize the speaker. Remind yourself before each conversation to create mental summaries that capitalize on the differences between your information processing rate and the speaker's verbal delivery rate.[43] And make it your business to choose a communication environment that is free of distraction from other incoming information or noise.

Mentally Summarize the Details of the Message. This strategy may seem to contradict the suggestion to avoid focusing only on facts; but if your goal is to be able to recall information, it is important to grasp the details that your partner provides. As we noted earlier, you can process words much more quickly than a person speaks. So periodically summarize the names, dates, and locations in the message. Organize the speaker's factual information into appropriate categories or try to place events in chronological order. Without a full understanding of the details, you will likely miss the speaker's major point.

Mentally Weave These Summaries into a Focused Major Point or a Series of Major Ideas. Facts usually make the most sense when you can use them to help support an idea or major point. So, as you summarize, try to link the facts you have organized in your mind with key ideas and principles. Use facts to enhance your critical thinking as you analyze, synthesize, evaluate, and finally summarize the key points or ideas your listening partner is making.[44]

Practice Listening to Challenging Material. To improve or even maintain any skill, you need to practice it. Listening experts suggest that listening skills deteriorate if people do not practice what they know. Listening to difficult, challenging material can sharpen listening skills, so good listeners practice by listening to documentaries, debates, and other challenging material.

> **RECAP** How to Improve Your Listening Comprehension Skills

Step	Listening Skill	Action
Stop	Tune out distracting competing messages.	Become conscious of being distracted; use on-task self-talk to remain focused.
Look	Become aware of the speaker's nonverbal cues; monitor your own nonverbal cues to communicate your interest in the speaker.	Establish eye contact; avoid fidgeting or performing other tasks when someone is speaking to you; listen with your eyes.
Listen	Create meaning from your partner's verbal and nonverbal messages.	Mentally summarize details; link these details with main ideas.

Relating to Others in the 21st Century | Overcoming Contemporary Listening Challenges

Listening may be an even more important skill in the twenty-first century than in the past.[45] Why? There are two reasons: recorded messages and noise. Today's technology makes it increasingly likely that you will be listening to recorded messages. This is called **asynchronous listening**—listening to a message communicated at another time, when no one is available to receive it. Retrieving messages through voicemail or an answering machine are examples of asynchronous listening. Listening to recorded messages can be tricky, because you can't stop the person to ask for clarification or to have information repeated. Without immediate feedback, there is greater potential for you to misunderstand a message. Yes, you can replay a message one or more times to make sure you understand it—but no matter how often you replay it, you'll never be able to ask for more details or for an example to help you understand the message. Yet another problem with asynchronous listening is that you are only *listening* to these recorded messages; you aren't *seeing* the person delivering the message. Without the nonverbal cues that you pick up when you can see the sender of a message, the true meaning of the message may be more elusive.

Another contemporary listening challenge is noise. The prevalence of iPods and Bluetooth technology means that you may have more sounds competing for your attention, and this can sap your listening effectiveness. Perhaps even now, as you're reading this book, you hear music—either something you've selected as background for your reading or music booming from an out-of-sight but not out-of-earshot source. In addition, melodious ring tones (from hip-hop to Handel), electronic beeps from machines announcing that your clothes and dishes are washed, and other e-reminders punctuate our days and can be potential distractions as we listen to others. Whether it's noise or recorded messages, there are strategies that can help tame technology and enhance listening accuracy.

Overcoming Asynchronous Listening Barriers. One of the things you can do to help manage the recorded messages you receive is to customize the recorded message that invites a caller to leave you a message. For example, your recorded message could remind callers to speak slowly or to repeat key information, such as phone numbers or e-mail addresses. In addition, when you listen to your messages, do so when you're not distracted by other tasks. Trying to remember key information when you're zipping down the highway in your car or puttering around the living room doing other things compounds the listening problem. Listen to your messages in a quiet place with pen and notepad ready to capture key details that you'll need later. Of course, you can replay a message to make sure you get key information or to confirm that you've heard the message accurately.

Although recorded messages can be an efficient way of sharing simple information or confirming appointments, without feedback and the opportunity to seek clarification, a voice message is not conducive to managing relational conflict, especially when the topic under discussion is an emotional one. It is best to use the richest possible communication medium when dealing with difficult or sensitive topics.

Overcoming Noise Barriers. Often the solution to noise distractions is simple: Get away from the noise. Turn off the music, shut off your cell phone, or move away from the distracting noise. In order to do that, you first need to be aware that noise is indeed noise. Because music and other audio distractions are ubiquitous, you may not be cognizant of their power to distract you. If someone else is the source of the noise, when appropriate, consider making a polite request to have the person reduce the volume. Sometimes just being aware that there's ambient noise causing a listening distraction allows you to take evasive action and return to a calmer environment.

Enhancing Empathic Listening Skills

asynchronous listening
Listening to a message (on an answering machine, via voicemail, or on a cell phone) communicated at another time.

empathy The emotional reaction of feeling what another person is feeling.

Listening involves more than merely comprehending the words of others; it's also about understanding and experiencing the feelings and emotions expressed. As we noted in Chapter 4, at the core of being other-oriented is cultivating **empathy**—feeling what someone else is feeling.[46] The word *empathy* comes from a Greek word for "passion" and is related to the German word *einfuhlung*, which means "to feel with." When a friend has "one of those days," perhaps he or she seeks you out to talk about it. There may not be a specific problem to solve—perhaps it was just a day filled with miscommunication and squabbles with partners or coworkers. But the person wants to tell you the details. Your friend is seeking a listener who focuses attention on him or her and cares about what he or she is saying. The friend is seeking someone who will empathize.

How do you enhance your empathic listening skills? First, you think about what the other person may be thinking by socially decentering; second, you focus on the feelings and emotions of your partner—truly empathizing with the other person.

Socially Decenter: Imagine What Your Partner Is Thinking

We're not advocates of mindreading, yet those people who are more skilled in empathizing with others give some effort to pondering what their communication partners may be thinking and experiencing when communicating with them. **Social decentering** is a *cognitive process* in which you take into account another person's thoughts, values, background, and perspectives as you interact with the person. This process involves viewing the world from the other person's point of view. The greater the difference between you and your communication partner, the more difficult it is to accomplish social decentering.

Developing empathy requires more than simply understanding someone's situation. A person who is truly empathic "feels with" the other person—he or she experiences the emotions the other person is feeling.

There are three ways to socially decenter: (1) Develop an understanding of another person based on how you have responded when something similar has happened to you, (2) base your understanding on knowledge you have about the specific person, or (3) make generalizations about someone based on your understanding of how you think most people would feel or behave.[47]

Decenter by Thinking About How You Would React. When you draw on your direct experience, you use your knowledge of what happened to you in the past to help you guess how someone else may feel. To the degree that the other person is similar to you, your reactions and those of the other person will be similar. For example, suppose you are talking to a friend who has just failed a midterm exam in an important course. You have also had this experience. Your own reaction was not to worry about the failed midterm because you had confidence you could still earn a passing grade in the course. You might use this self-understanding to predict your friend's reactions. To the degree that you are similar to your friend, your prediction will be accurate. But suppose your friend comes from a culture with high expectations for success. He might believe he has dishonored his family by his poor performance. In this situation, your understanding of your own reaction needs to be tempered by your awareness of how similar or dissimilar you and the other person are.

Decenter by Reflecting on What You Know About the Other Person. The second way to socially decenter is based on the specific knowledge we have of the person with whom we are interacting. Your memory of how your friend reacted to failing a midterm exam once before gives you a basis to more accurately predict his reaction this time. And even if you have not observed your friend's reaction to this particular situation, you can project how you think he feels based on what you know about his personality. As relationships become more intimate, you have more information to allow you to socially decenter with greater confidence.

Decenter by Thinking About How Most People Would React. The third way to socially decenter is to apply your understanding of people in general, or of categories of people. Each of us develops personal theories about how people act. You might have a general theory to explain the behavior of men and another for that of women. You might have general theories about Mexicans, Japanese, Canadians,

social decentering The cognitive process of taking into account another person's thoughts, values, background, and perspective as you interact with the person.

Slovenians, Texans, or Iowans. As you meet someone who falls into one of your categories, you draw on that concept to socially decenter. The more you can learn about a given culture, the stronger your general theories can be, and the more effectively you can use this method of socially decentering. The key, however, is to avoid developing inaccurate, inflexible stereotypes of others and basing your perceptions of others only on those generalizations. Making snap judgments based only on past associations may lead you to inaccurate conclusions. That's why it's so important to become other-oriented by being a good listener, learning all you can about the other person, and not just relying on generalizations.

Besides *thinking* about how another may feel (socially decentering), using one or all of the three approaches we've described here, you can have an *emotional* reaction to what others do or tell you.

Empathize: Imagine What Your Partner Is Feeling

As we've noted, empathy is an *emotional reaction* that is similar to the one being experienced by another person. In contrast to social decentering, which is a cognitive reaction to what the other person is experiencing, empathizing is feeling what the other person feels.

Developing empathy is not a single skill but a collection of skills that help you predict how others will respond. There is clear evidence that being empathic is linked to being a better listener.[48] Your ability to empathize with others is influenced by your personality and how you were raised, as well as by your listening habits and your skill level. There is evidence, for example, that boys whose fathers are affectionate and nurturing grow up with a greater capacity for empathy. There is also evidence that boys whose fathers are less affectionate toward them may have a tendency to compensate for the lack of close nurturing from their dads by expressing more affection toward their sons.[49] So your capacity for empathy is both learned, based on your experiences, especially with your parents, and part of your nature.

Your sensitivity and ability to empathize with others are based, according to some researchers, on your level of emotional intelligence.[50] The Communication and Emotion feature on page 136 may give you some insight into your skill in connecting emotionally with others as well as understanding your own emotions.

But precisely how do you empathize with others? The essential empathy action steps are the same as those needed to be an effective listener: You stop, look, and listen. Although these steps may seem quite basic, they are nonetheless crucial to making emotional connections with others.

Stop, Look, and Listen. Before you can accurately empathize with another person you must first focus on the person's thoughts (socially decenter). As best you can, stop focusing on your own thoughts and needs and think about what your partner may be thinking or experiencing. View the world from the other person's perspective.

After stopping to focus on your partner's point of view, you look for nonverbal clues that provide information about the emotions the person is experiencing. As we noted earlier in the chapter, emotions—even those we may be trying to suppress— are communicated through nonverbal behavior. So looking for emotional cues in facial expressions and tone of voice is vital when attempting to empathize with another person.

Then, after stopping and looking, listen to the meaning of what someone is expressing. Listening is essential when identifying the underlying emotions that another person is feeling. Although your partner may not explicitly say "I'm feeling so frustrated right now," based on the words the person *does* use, you may be able to identify the emotion behind the words.

Listen Actively. Good listening, especially listening to empathize with another, is active, not passive. To listen passively is to sit with a blank stare or a frozen facial expression. A passive listener's thoughts and feelings could be anywhere, for all the speaker knows.[51] Those who engage in active listening, in contrast, respond mentally, verbally, and nonverbally to a speaker's message and to what the speaker is doing. Responding to what others say and do serves several specific functions in empathizing with others. First, your responses can be a measure of how accurately you understood the message. If you misunderstand a message, it will be difficult to empathize. If you burst out laughing as your friend tells you about losing his house in a flood, he'll know you either misunderstood or you weren't listening to what he was saying, or he'll think you are an insensitive oaf for not caring about his plight. Second, your responses indicate whether you agree or disagree with the comments others make. If you tell your friend that you do not approve of her comments on abortion, she'll know your position on the information she shared. Although you don't have to have the same attitudes and beliefs as others in order to empathize with them, knowing whether your positions are similar to or different from those of your partner can help you more accurately connect to that person. Finally, your responses tell speakers how they are affecting you. Monitoring your emotional reactions also gives you insight into your own emotional state. When you get tears in your eyes as you listen to your friend describe how lonely he has felt since his father died, he will know that you are affected by his pain. You will sense an empathic connection with him and may also realize that you, too, are feeling down or emotional for other reasons. On the other hand, your emotional reaction need not be of the same intensity as the emotions the other person is experiencing in order to be genuine. You may experience mild pity for your friend who has failed the midterm, in contrast to his stronger feeling of anguish and dishonor.

Some emotional reactions are almost universal and cut across cultural boundaries. You may experience empathy when seeing photos or videos depicting emotion-arousing events occurring in other countries. Seeing a mother crying while holding her sick or dying child in a refugee camp might move you to tears and a sense of sadness or loss. Empathy can enhance interpersonal interactions by creating a bond between you and the other person: When you empathize, you are confirming, comforting, and supporting the other person. Empathy can also increase your understanding of others.

Developing empathy is different from sympathizing with others. When you offer **sympathy,** you tell someone you are sorry he or she feels what he or she is feeling: "I'm sorry your Uncle Joe died" or "I'm sorry to hear you failed your test." When you sympathize with others, you *acknowledge* their feelings. But when you empathize, you *experience* an emotional reaction that is similar to that of the other person; you, too, feel grief or sadness, elation or joy, excitement or apprehension— or whatever the other person is experiencing. Can people be taught to be more empathetic? Research suggests that the answer is a clear yes.[52] One goal of this book is to enhance your skill in being other-oriented—and empathy is at the heart of being other-oriented.[53]

Listening to empathize does not need to be the goal of *every* listening encounter you have; that would be tedious for both you and your listening partners. But when you do want to listen empathically, it's important to focus on your partner to understand and experience the message from his or her perspective.[54] Psychologist and counselor Carl Rogers summarized the value of empathy when he said, "A high degree of empathy in a relationship is possibly the most potent factor in bringing about change and learning."[55] The short test to assess your empathy included at the end of this chapter can help you determine how effectively you empathize with others.

sympathy Acknowledgment of someone else's feelings.

▶ RECAP   How to Be an Empathic Listener

What to Do	How to Do It
Social decentering: A cognitive process of thinking about the other person's thoughts, values, background, and perspectives	• Think how you would react in the given situation • Think how the other person would react, based on what you know about his or her previous experiences and behavior • Think how most people would react
Empathizing: An emotional reaction similar to the emotion being experienced by another person	• Stop focusing on your own thoughts and needs and imagine what the other person is feeling • Look for nonverbal cues that express emotion • Listen for the meaning of words and the meaning behind the words • Respond actively, not passively • Experience the emotion of the other person

Communication and Emotion   What's Your Emotional Intelligence Level and Why Does It Matter?

You've undoubtedly heard about emotional intelligence, perhaps on TV or in the popular press. **Emotional intelligence** is the ability to be empathic and aware of your own emotions as well as the emotions of others. Emotionally intelligent people are also able to manage their own emotions. It has been over a decade and a half since Daniel Goleman's book *Emotional Intelligence: Why It Can Matter More than IQ* was published, and that book, along with a *Time* magazine cover story about emotional intelligence (sometimes referred to as EQ, for emotion quotient), helped to popularize the concept.[56] But what does research about this concept tell us? Researchers Daisy Grewal and Peter Salovey have concluded that there is indeed credible research to support the interest in emotional intelligence in both popular media and scientific research.[57] Emotional intelligence has been linked to a variety of positive outcomes, including enhanced listening and leadership skills.[58]

The notion of emotional or social "intelligence" is not new. Almost 80 years ago, Robert Thorndike, who helped pioneer early IQ tests, noted that people possess a "social intelligence," which he defined as the ability to accurately perceive their own and others' emotions and motivations and then to act in ways that maximize personal benefit based on

these perceptions. In the early 1980s, psychologist Howard Gardner became famous for his book *Frames of Mind,* in which he suggested that there were seven types of intelligence, besides the form typically measured by standard IQ tests. According to Gardner, "interpersonal intelligence" is a key to human relationships and includes the ability to understand, identify, label, and adapt to human emotions—both one's own emotions and the emotions of others. In other words, to be interpersonally or socially intelligent is to be skillfully other-oriented.[59] So researches have long known that our intellectual gifts include more than having a good memory, using big words, or performing complicated mathematical calculations. Being "people smart" and understanding and adapting to the social and emotional dynamics of a relationship constitute an important type of intelligence.

The concept of emotional intelligence has evolved from early efforts to identify emotional aspects of intelligence and has become more focused than the general notion of social intelligence. One of the earliest uses of the term *emotional intelligence* can be traced to a Ph.D. dissertation published in 1986.[60] In 1990 Peter Salovey and John Mayer developed a specific definition of the concept as "the ability to monitor one's own and other's

feelings, to discriminate among them, and to use this information to guide one's thinking and action."[61]

Four Factors of Emotional Intelligence

Today, researchers view emotional intelligence not as a single skill but a set of four related skills.[62] First, someone who is emotionally intelligent has the ability to accurately perceive the emotions of others by listening to people's voices and paying attention to facial expressions, posture, and other cues. Being able to quickly and accurately perceive what someone else is feeling (a key prerequisite to being empathic) is one of the first elements of being emotionally intelligent.

A second factor of emotional intelligence is the ability to use emotions to help you with other cognitive tasks. For example, if you know you are usually in a more productive, positive mood in the morning rather than in the evening, you will use the morning hours for tasks (such as writing) that require focused concentration. You are aware that your emotions have an impact on how you behave. Knowing which of your own emotional states will help you best perform certain tasks is one of the factors that makes you emotionally intelligent.

Third, an emotionally intelligent person is able to express his or her own

Enhancing Critical Listening Skills

After putting it off for several months, you've decided to buy a new cell phone. As you begin to talk to your friends, you find a bewildering number of factors to consider: Do you want a prepaid plan? A plan that includes text messaging? Do you want to be able to check e-mail and surf the web? Receive TV signals? How many weekend minutes, evening minutes, or daily minutes of calling time do you need? You decide to head to a store to see if a salesperson can help you sort through the maze of options. The salesperson is friendly enough, but you become even more overwhelmed with the number of options, bells, and whistles to consider. As you try to make this decision, your listening goal is not to empathize with those who extol the virtues of cell phones. Nor do you need to take a multiple-choice test on the information they share. To sort through the information, you need to listen critically.

Critical listening involves listening to evaluate the quality, appropriateness, value, or importance of the information you hear. *The goal of a critical listener is to use information*

emotional intelligence The ability to be aware of, to understand, and to manage one's own emotions and those of other people.

critical listening Listening to evaluate and assess the quality, appropriateness, value, or importance of information.

emotions—to use words to accurately describe feelings, moods, and emotions. Knowing that you are nervous, happy, anxious, joyful, or whatever it may be is an important element of being emotionally intelligent. By being able to express an emotion using precise and accurate words, you demonstrate that you understand what is happening to you; you aren't simply experiencing a vague, inexpressible feeling. In addition, being able to differentiate between similar types of emotions (such as being sad and being depressed) is a key element of being able to understand emotions.

If you understand your own emotions, you have the ability to manage them, rather than letting them manage you, which is the fourth factor of emotional intelligence. If you're in a negative emotional state and you consciously decide to do something pleasant, such as take a walk, call a friend, or listen to music to manage the emotion, you have taken a positive action to address your emotional state. There are negative and destructive ways of managing your emotions, such as abusing alcohol or drugs. An emotionally intelligent person makes conscious choices of constructive rather than destructive ways to manage emotions. Furthermore, emotionally intelligent people can not only influence their own emotions, but also the emotions of others. A

skilled public speaker, for example, knows how to use motivational appeals to persuade or motivate others. Of course, using one's emotional intelligence to manipulate others is unethical, just as it is unethical to use one's cognitive intelligence to be deceptive and trick others. Many thieves and con artists are quite emotionally intelligent, but they focus this intelligence on duping their victims. Being emotionally intelligent, like being cognitively intelligent, is a gift that can be used for either good or bad purposes.

Why Is Emotional Intelligence Important?

Why does it matter what your EQ is? Research has documented that people who are emotionally intelligent are better listeners and are overall more socially skilled than people who are not emotionally intelligent.[63] One study found that people who were identified as more emotionally intelligent had higher job ratings from both their supervisors and their peers. Emotionally intelligent people are also perceived to be better leaders. In addition, peers report fewer conflicts with emotionally intelligent colleagues and assert that overall, they help create a positive work climate. Emotionally intelligent people also generally achieve higher positions as well as higher salaries than people who are less emo-

tionally intelligent.[64] Another study found that emotionally intelligent people had better relationships with their spouses and romantic partners.[65]

Emotional intelligence is a construct that is here to stay. Research continues to explore how our ability to be aware of our own emotions and the emotions of others has an impact on our relationships with others. Developing listening skills and being able to stop focusing on your own thoughts and emotions, to look (being aware of the nonverbal cues that provide clues to the emotions of others), and then to listen accurately to the messages of others are important to your interpersonal relationships.

What's Your EQ?

Measuring emotional intelligence has been a topic of much debate and discussion among researchers who assess social skills. Some suggest it is a much too elusive and ill-defined concept to measure accurately. Yet several emotional intelligence measures have been created. One version that has received positive reviews from several researchers may be found *at http://www.queendom.com*.

Daniel Goleman summarizes the centrality of emotions in developing empathy by quoting Antoine de Saint-Exupéry: "It is with the heart that one sees rightly; what is essential is invisible to the eye."[66]

Effective critical listening skills are crucial in a business environment.

to make a choice. Whether you're selecting a new phone, deciding whom to vote for, choosing a potential date, or evaluating a new business plan, you will be faced with many opportunities to use your critical listening skills in interpersonal situations.

Assess Information Quality

A critical listener does not necessarily offer negative comments. A critical listener seeks to identify both good information and information that is flawed or less helpful. We call this process *information triage. Triage* is a French term that usually describes the process used by emergency medical personnel to determine which of several patients is the most severely ill or injured and needs immediate medical attention. **Information triage** is a process of evaluating and sorting out information. An effective critical listener performs information triage; he or she is able to distinguish useful and accurate information and conclusions from information that is less useful, as well as conclusions that are inaccurate or invalid.

How do you develop the ability to perform information triage? Initially, listening critically involves the same strategies as listening to comprehend, which we discussed earlier. Before you evaluate information, it's vital that you first *understand* the information. Second, examine the logic or reasoning used in the message. And finally, be mindful of whether you are basing your evaluations on facts (something observed or verifiable) or inference (a conclusion based on partial information). Although courses in logic, argumentation, and public speaking often present skills to help you evaluate information, it's also important to listen critically during interpersonal conversations.

Avoid Jumping to Conclusions

Imagine that you are a detective investigating a death. You are given the following information: (1) Leo and Moshia are found lying together on the floor; (2) Leo and Moshia are both dead; (3) Leo and Moshia are surrounded by water and broken glass; (4) on the sofa near Leo and Moshia is a cat with its back arched, apparently ready to defend itself.

Given these sketchy details, do you, the detective assigned to the case, have any theories about the cause of Leo and Moshia's demise? Perhaps they slipped on the water, crashed into a table, broke a vase, and died (that would explain the water and broken glass). Or maybe their attacker recently left the scene, and the cat is still distressed by the commotion. Clearly, you could make several inferences (conclusions based on partial information) as to the probable cause of death. Oh yes, there is one detail we forgot to mention: Leo and Moshia are fish. Does that help?

People often spin grand explanations and hypotheses based on sketchy details. Making inferences, people may believe the "facts" clearly point to a specific conclusion. Determining the difference between a fact and an inference can help you more accurately use language to reach valid conclusions about what you see and experience.

What makes a fact a fact? Most students, when asked this question, respond by saying, "A fact is something that has been proven true." If that is the case, *how* has something been proven true? In a court of law, a **fact** is something that has been observed or witnessed. Anything else is speculation or inference.

"Did you see my client in your house, taking your jewelry?" asks the defendant's clever attorney.

"No," says the plaintiff.

"Then you do not know for a fact that my client is a thief."

"I guess not," the plaintiff admits.

information triage Process of evaluating information to sort good information from less useful or less valid information.

fact Something that has been directly observed to be true and thus has been proven to be true.

Problems occur when we respond to something as if it were a fact (something observed), when in reality it is an **inference** (a conclusion based on speculation):

"It's a fact that you will be poor all of your life."
"It's a fact that you will fail this course."

Both of these statements, although they may very well be true, misuse the term *fact.* If you cannot recognize when you are making an inference instead of stating a fact, you may give your judgments more credibility than they deserve. Being sensitive to the differences between facts and inferences can improve both critical listening and responding skills.

Enhancing Responding Skills

We've offered several strategies for responding to others when your goal is to comprehend information, empathize with others, or evaluate messages. Regardless of your communication goal, the quality of your communication will be enhanced when you effectively and appropriately respond to others. Responding to what you hear is natural and normal. You don't need a textbook to tell you to respond. To be alive is to respond to stimuli that come your way. But there are some specific strategies and skills that can help you respond to others *skillfully,* so as to enhance the overall quality of your interpersonal relationships with others. Sometimes the best response is not a verbal response—it can be better to just keep listening. Your ability to ask appropriate questions and paraphrase what you hear can dramatically improve your understanding of a message. In addition, the timing of your responses, the usefulness of the information, the amount of detail, and the descriptiveness of your responses are important.

Don't Interrupt

We noted earlier that one of the listening barriers people face is thinking about what they want to say next rather than just listening. And our own thoughts may lead us to blurt out a response, finish someone's sentence, or impose our own ideas on the speaker. Resist those temptations. Before you make your point, let the other person finish his or her point. You don't need to be a passive listener and endure a long, rambling, inarticulate verbal barrage from someone. But if interrupting others is your default listening response, you'll likely miss much of the meaning as well as disconfirm your partner. If you do need to stop someone from talking in order to make a point, do so mindfully rather than habitually and thoughtlessly.

Ask Appropriate Questions

One of the first things to do after listening to someone share information is to ask appropriate questions to get additional details you may have missed and to make sure you understood the message.

Asking appropriate questions can help not only you but also the person sharing information with you. One research study by communication researchers Janet Bavelas, Linda Coates, and Trudy Johnson found that speakers did a better job of sharing a story if listeners asked appropriate questions and made appropriate responses to the story rather than offering no observation about what they heard.[67] These researchers first asked a speaker to tell a story about a time when she or he had experienced a close call—such as narrowly missing being hurt or injured. The listener was just to listen and make no comments. In the second phase of the research study,

> **BEING Other-ORIENTED**
>
> A key to providing useful responses to another person is to think about the other person's needs rather than your own needs. Although it may feel liberating to express your own thoughts or feelings, consider whether your response is in the best interest of your communication partner. What are strategies you can use to identify the needs of others?

inference Conclusion based on speculation.

the listener was told to ask questions and very briefly summarize the gist of what the speaker was saying. In the third phase, the listener was to actively paraphrase what the speaker was saying—to summarize key points. Finally, in the fourth phase, listeners were to listen while mentally counting how many days it was until Christmas. Although this last condition sounds like a bizarre task, the purpose was to explore the effects of having a listener supposedly listening but not paying attention to what the speaker was saying.

Here's what the researchers found: When the listener made no responses to the speaker, the speaker told the story *less* effectively. When speakers had a listener who asked questions and made specific responses in meaningful ways, the speakers were better at telling their story—they used richer details and clearer descriptions. The results suggest that an effective listener is really a "co-narrator," or an active participant in the communication process, rather than merely a passive listener. It's not that specific comments are better than general comments; what's important is that the responses the listener makes should be *appropriate*—comments that fit the story can actually help the speaker gauge how effectively he or she is telling the story. So when you ask appropriate questions and make appropriate comments, you can help your communication partner tell a story better. Asking appropriate and thoughtful questions also communicates that you were indeed listening and interested in what your partner had to say.

Accurately Paraphrase

The only way to know whether you understand another person's message is to check your understanding of the facts and ideas by paraphrasing your understanding. Verbally reflecting what you understood the speaker to say can dramatically minimize misunderstanding. Respond with a statement such as

"Are you saying . . ."

"You seem to be describing . . ."

"So the point you are making seems to be . . ."

"Here is what I understand you to mean . . ."

"So here's what seems to have happened . . ."

Then summarize the events, details, or key points you think the speaker is trying to convey. Your summary need not be a word-for-word repetition of what the speaker has said, nor do you need to summarize the content of *each* phrase or minor detail. Rather, you will **paraphrase** to check the accuracy of your understanding. Here is an example:

Juan: This week I have so much extra work to do. I'm sorry if I haven't been able to help keep this place clean. I know it's my turn to do the dishes tonight, but I have to get back to work. Could you do the dishes tonight?

Brigid: So you want me to do the dishes tonight and for the rest of the week. Right?

Juan: Well, I'd like you to help with the dishes tonight. But I think I can handle it for the rest of the week.

Brigid: OK. So I'll do them tonight and you take over tomorrow.

Juan: Yes.

paraphrase Verbal summary of the key ideas of your partner's message that helps you check the accuracy of your understanding.

An effective listener uses questions and paraphrasing to make sure he or she understands what someone else has been saying.

Research conducted in clinical counseling settings found that when a listener paraphrases the content and feelings of a speaker, the speaker is more likely to trust and value the listener.[68] Paraphrasing to check understanding is also a vital skill to use when you are trying to reconcile a difference of opinion. Chapter 8 shows you how to use it in that context.

Provide Well-Timed Responses

Feedback is usually most effective when you offer it at the earliest opportunity, particularly if your objective is to teach someone a skill. For example, if you are teaching your friend how to make your famous egg rolls, you provide a step-by-step commentary as you watch your pupil. If he makes a mistake, you don't wait until the egg rolls are finished to tell him that he left out the cabbage. He needs immediate feedback to finish the rest of the sequence successfully.

Sometimes, however, if a person is already sensitive and upset about something, delaying feedback can be wise. Use your critical thinking skills to analyze when feedback will do the most good. Rather than automatically offering immediate correction, use the just-in-time (JIT) approach and provide feedback just before the person might make another mistake. If, for example, your daughter typically rushes through math tests and fails to check her work, remind her right before her next test to double-check her answers, not immediately after the one she just failed. To provide feedback about a relationship, select a mutually agreeable place and time when both of you are rested and relaxed; avoid hurling feedback at someone "for his own good" immediately after he offends you.

141

Provide Usable Information

Perhaps you've heard this advice: Never try to teach a pig to sing. It wastes your time. It doesn't sound pretty. And it annoys the pig. When you provide information to someone, be certain that it is useful and relevant. How can you make sure your partner can use the information you share? Try to understand your partner's mindset. Ask yourself, "If I were this person, how would I respond to this information? Is it information I can act on? Or is it information that may make matters worse?" Under the guise of providing effective feedback, you may be tempted to tell others your complete range of feelings and emotions. But research suggests that selective feedback is best. In one study, married couples who practiced selective self-disclosure were more satisfied than couples who told everything they knew or were feeling.[69] Immersing your partner in information that is irrelevant or that may be damaging to the relationship may be cathartic, but it may not enhance the quality of your relationship or improve understanding.

Avoid Unnecessary Details

When you are selecting meaningful information, also try to cut down on the volume of information. Don't overwhelm your listener with details that obscure the key point of your feedback. Hit only the high points that will benefit the listener. Be brief.

Be Descriptive Rather Than Evaluative

"You're an awful driver!" shouts Doris to Frank, her husband. Although Doris may feel she has provided simple feedback to her spouse about his skills, Frank will probably not respond warmly or even listen closely to her feedback. If Doris were to be more descriptive and less evaluative, then he might be inclined to listen: "Frank, you are traveling 70 miles an hour in a 50 miles an hour zone," or "Frank, I get very nervous when you zigzag so fast through the freeway traffic" is a less offensive comment. It describes Frank's behavior rather than rendering judgments about him that are likely to trigger a defensive response.

Enhancing Empathic Responding Skills

When your listening and responding goal is to empathize with another person, just imagining the emotional response of another person may not lead you to an appropriate response. Paraphrasing not only the content of what someone says but also the emotion behind the words may be helpful. And your partner may be seeking more than understanding: He or she may be seeking social support. Your listening partner may want and need to know that you care about him or her. There are ways of responding that can enhance empathy and provide meaningful emotional support.

Paraphrase Emotions

The bottom line in empathic responding is to make certain that you accurately understand how the other person is feeling. You can paraphrase, beginning with such phrases as

"So you are feeling . . ."

"You must feel . . ."

"So now you feel . . ."

In the following example of empathic responding, the listener asks questions, summarizes content, and summarizes feelings.

David: I think I'm in over my head. My boss gave me a job to do, and I just don't know how to do it. I'm afraid I've bitten off more than I can chew.

Mike: (Thinks how he would feel if he were given an important task at work but did not know how to complete the task, then asks for more information.) What job did she ask you to do?

David: I'm supposed to do an inventory of all the items in the warehouse on the new computer system and have it finished by the end of the week. I don't have the foggiest notion of how to start. I've never even used that system.

Mike: (Summarizes feelings.) So you feel panicked because you may not have enough time to learn the system *and* do the inventory.

David: Well, I'm not only panicked; I'm afraid I may be fired.

Mike: (Summarizes feelings.) So your fear that you might lose your job is getting in the way of just focusing on the task and seeing what you can get done. It's making you feel like you made a mistake in taking this job.

David: That's exactly how I feel.

Note that toward the end of the dialogue, Mike has to make a couple of tries to summarize David's feelings accurately. Also note that Mike does a good job of listening and responding without giving advice. Just by being an active listener, you can help your partner clarify a problem.

Researcher John Gottman summarizes several specific ways to make listening active rather than passive:[70]

- Start by asking questions.

- Ask questions about the speaker's goals and visions of the future.

- Look for commonalities.

- Tune in with all your attention.

- Respond with an occasional brief nod or sound.

- From time to time, paraphrase what the speaker says.

- Maintain the right amount of eye contact.

- Let go of your own agenda.

We have discussed responding empathically and listening actively using a tidy step-by-step textbook approach. In practice, you may have to back up and clarify content, ask more questions, and rethink how you would feel before you attempt to summarize how someone else feels. Conversely, you may be able to summarize feelings *without* asking questions or summarizing content if the message is clear and it relates to a situation with which you are very familiar. Overusing paraphrasing can slow down a conversation and make the other person uncomfortable or irritated. But if you use it judiciously, paraphrasing can help both you and your partner keep focused on the issues and ideas at hand.

Reflecting content or feeling through paraphrasing can be especially useful in the following situations:

- Before you take an important action
- Before you argue or criticize
- When your partner has strong feelings or wants to talk over a problem
- When your partner is speaking "in code" or using unclear abbreviations
- When your partner wants to understand your feelings and thoughts
- When you are talking to yourself
- When you encounter new ideas[71]

Sometimes, however, you truly don't understand how another person really feels. At times like this, be cautious of telling others, "I know just how you feel." It may be more important simply to let others know that you care about them than to grill them about their feelings.

If you do decide to use paraphrasing skills, keep the following guidelines in mind:

- Use your own words.
- Don't go beyond the information communicated by the speaker.
- Be concise.
- Be specific.
- Be accurate.

Do *not* use paraphrasing skills if you aren't able to be open and accepting, if you do not trust the other person to find his or her own solution, if you are using these skills as a way of hiding yourself from another, or if you feel pressured, hassled, or tired. And as we have already discussed, overuse of paraphrasing can be distracting and unnatural.

Don't be discouraged if your initial attempts to use these skills seem awkward and uncomfortable. Any new skill takes time to learn and use well. The instructions and samples you have read should serve as guides, rather than as hard-and-fast prescriptions to follow during each conversation.

Express Helpful Social Support

There are times when it is clear that a communication partner is experiencing stress, pain, or a significant life problem. Just by listening and empathizing you can help ease the pain and help the person manage the burden. Specifically, you provide **social support** when you offer positive, sincere, supportive messages, both verbal and nonverbal, when helping others deal with stress, anxiety, or uncertainty. Providing social support isn't the same as expressing pity for another person; it's providing a response that lets the other person know that he or she is both understood and valued. Nor does offering social support mean giving advice to solve the problem or take away the fear. Giving social support is providing messages that help the person seek his or her own solution.

Most people don't need or want dramatic, over-the-top expressions of support when experiencing pain or loss. On the other hand, mild or timid expressions of support from others are not satisfying either. One research study suggests that when we are experiencing stress, we prefer what researchers called a mid-level amount of social support.[72] Genuine, sincere support that is not overly expressive is usually best. Research also suggests that females prefer a bit higher level of comforting response than males.

social support Positive, sincere, supportive messages, both verbal and nonverbal, offered to help others deal with stress, anxiety, or uncertainty.

An ability to listen empathically is important when you discern that someone needs social support. What do researchers suggest are the best ways to provide supportive, empathic, comforting messages to others? Although there are no magic words or phrases that will always ease someone's stress and anxiety, here's a summary of social support messages that seem to be appreciated by others.[73]

- Clearly express that you want to provide support. ("I would really like to help you.")

- Appropriately communicate that you have positive feelings for the other person; explicitly tell the other person that you are a friend, that you care about or love him or her. ("You mean a lot to me." "I really care about you.")

- Express your concern about the situation that the other person is in right now. ("I'm worried about you right now because I know you're feeling _____ [stressed, overwhelmed, sad, etc.].")

- Indicate that you are available to help, that you have time to support the person. ("I can be here for you when you need me.")

- Let the other person know how much you support her or him ("I'm completely with you on this." "I'm here for you, and I'll always be here for you because I care about you.")

- Acknowledge that the other person is in a difficult situation. ("This must be very difficult for you.")

- It may be appropriate to paraphrase what the other person has told you about the issue or problem that is causing stress. ("So you became upset when she told you she didn't want to see you again.")

- Consider asking open-ended questions to see if the other person wants to talk. ("How are you doing now?")

- Let the other person know that you are listening and supportive by providing conversational continuers such as "Yes, then what happened?" or "Oh, I see," or "Uh-huh."

- After expressing your compassion, empathy, and concern, just listen.

Some types of responses are less helpful when providing social support. Here are a few things *not* to do, based on the conclusions of communication researchers:

- Don't tell the other person that you know exactly how he or she feels.

- Don't criticize or negatively evaluate the other person; he or she needs support and validation, not judgmental comments.

- Don't tell the other person to stop feeling what he or she is feeling.

- Don't immediately offer advice. First, just listen.

- Don't tell the other person that "it's going to get better from here" or that "the worst is over."

- Don't tell the other person that there is really nothing to worry about or that "it's no big deal."

- Don't tell the other person that the problem can be solved easily. ("Oh, you can always find another girlfriend.")

- Don't blame the other person for the problem. ("Well, if you didn't always drive so fast, you wouldn't have had the accident.")

- Don't tell the other person that it is wrong to express feelings and emotions. ("Oh, you're just making yourself sick. Stop crying.")

Enhancing Skills in Confirming Others

Couple A:

Wife to husband: "I just don't feel appreciated any more."

Husband to wife: "Margaret, I'm so very sorry. I love you. You're the most important person in the world to me."

Couple B:

Wife to husband: "I just don't feel appreciated any more."

Husband to wife: "Well, what about my feelings? Don't my feelings count? You'll have to do what you have to do. What's for dinner?"

It doesn't take an expert in interpersonal communication to know that Couple B's relationship is not warm and confirming. Researchers have studied the specific kinds of responses people offer to others.[74] Some responses are confirming; other responses are disconfirming. A **confirming response** is an other-oriented statement that causes others to value themselves more; Wife A is likely to value herself more after her husband's confirming response. A **disconfirming response** is a statement that causes others to value themselves less. Wife B knows firsthand what it's like to have her feelings ignored and disconfirmed. Are you aware of whether your responses to others confirm them or disconfirm them? To help you be more aware of the kinds of responses you make to others, we'll review the results of studies that identify both confirming and disconfirming responses.[75]

Provide Confirming Responses

The adage "People judge us by our words and behavior rather than by our intent" summarizes the underlying principle of confirming responses. Those who receive your messages determine whether they have the effect you intended. Formulating confirming responses requires careful listening and attention to the other person. Does it really matter whether we confirm others? Marriage researcher John Gottman used video cameras and microphones to observe couples interacting in an apartment over an extended period of time. He found that a significant predictor of divorce was neglecting to confirm or affirm one's marriage partner during typical, everyday conversation—even though couples who were less likely to divorce spent only a few seconds more confirming their partner than couples who eventually did divorce. His research conclusion has powerful implications: Long-lasting relationships are characterized by

confirming response Statement that causes another person to value himself or herself more.

disconfirming response Statement that causes another person to value himself or herself less.

supportive, confirming messages.[76] The everyday kinds of confirmation and support we offer need not be excessive—sincere moderate, heart-felt support is evaluated as the most positive and desirable kind.[77] We will describe several kinds of confirming responses in this section.

Direct Acknowledgment. When you respond directly to something another person says to you, you are acknowledging not only the statement, but also that the person is worth responding to.

Joan: It certainly is a nice day for a canoe trip.

Mariko: Yes, Joan, it's a great day to be outside.

Agreement About Judgments. When you confirm someone's evaluation of something, you are also affirming that person's sense of taste and judgment.

Nancy: I think the steel guitar player's riff was fantastic.

Victor: Yes, I think it was the best part of the performance.

Supportive Response. When you express reassurance and understanding, you are confirming a person's right to his or her feelings.

Lionel: I'm disappointed that I only scored 60 on my interpersonal communication test.

Sarah: I'm sorry to see you so frustrated, Lionel. I know that test was important to you.

Clarifying Response. When you seek greater understanding of another person's message, you are confirming that he or she is worth your time and trouble. Clarifying responses also encourage the other person to talk in order to explore his or her feelings.

Larry: I'm not feeling very good about my family situation these days.

Tyrone: Is it tough with you and Margo working different shifts?

Expression of Positive Feeling. We feel confirmed or valued when someone else agrees with our expression of joy or excitement.

Lorraine: I'm so excited! I was just promoted to associate professor.

Dorette: Congratulations! I'm so proud of you! Heaven knows you deserve it.

Compliment. When you tell people you like what they have done or said, what they are wearing, or how they look, you are confirming their sense of worth.

Jean-Christophe: Did you get the invitation to my party?

Manny: Yes! It looked so professional. I didn't know you could do calligraphy. You're a talented guy.

In each of these examples, note how the responder provides comments that confirm the worth or value of the other person. But keep in mind that confirming responses should be sincere. Offering false praise is manipulative, and your communication partner will probably sniff out your phoniness.

Avoid Disconfirming Responses

Some statements and responses can undermine another person's self-worth. We offer these categories so that you can avoid using them and also recognize them when someone uses them to chip away at your self-image and self-esteem.

Impervious Response. When a person fails to acknowledge your statement or attempt to communicate, even though you know he or she heard you, you may feel a sense of awkwardness or embarrassment.

Rosa:	I loved your speech, Harvey.
Harvey:	(No response, verbal or nonverbal.)

Interrupting Response. Interrupting another person is one of the most corrosive, disconfirming responses you can make. Why is interrupting so irritating? Because when you interrupt someone, you are implying that what you have to say is more important than what the other person has to say. In effect, your behavior communicates that *you* are more important than the other person is. You may simply be enthusiastic or excited when the words tumble out of your mouth, interrupting your communication partner. Nonetheless, be especially mindful of not interrupting others. An interrupting response is a powerful disconfirming behavior, whether you are aware of its power or not.

Anna:	I just heard on the news that . . .
Sharon:	Oh yes. The stock market just went down 100 points.

Irrelevant Response. An irrelevant response is one that has nothing at all to do with what you were saying. Chances are your partner is not listening to you at all.

Arnold:	First we're flying down to Rio, and then to Quito. I can hardly wait to . . .
Peter:	They're predicting a hard freeze tonight.

The real message Peter is sending is "I have more important things on my mind."

Tangential Response. A tangential response is one that acknowledges you, but that is only minimally related to what you are talking about. Again, it indicates that the other person isn't really attending to your message.

Richard:	This new program will help us stay within our budget.
Samantha:	Yeah. I think I'll save some bucks and send this letter by regular mail.

Impersonal Response. A response that intellectualizes and uses the third person distances the other person from you and has the effect of trivializing what you say.

Diana:	Hey, Bill. I'd like to talk with you for a minute about getting your permission to take my vacation in July.
Bill:	One tends to become interested in recreational pursuits about this time of year, doesn't one?

Incoherent Response. When a speaker mumbles, rambles, or makes some unintelligible effort to respond, you may end up wondering if what you said was of any value or use to the listener.

Paolo:	George, here's my suggestion for the merger deal with Techstar. Let's make them an offer of forty-eight dollars a share and see how they respond.
George:	Huh? Well . . . so . . . well . . . hmmm . . . I'm not sure.

Incongruous Response. When a verbal message is inconsistent with nonverbal behavior, people usually believe the nonverbal message, but they usually feel confused as well. An incongruous response is like a malfunctioning traffic light with red and green lights flashing simultaneously—you're just not sure whether the speaker wants you to go or stay.

Sue:	Honey, do you want me to go grocery shopping with you?
Steve:	(Shouting) OF COURSE I DO! WHY ARE YOU ASKING?

Although it may be impossible to eliminate all disconfirming responses from your repertoire, becoming aware of the power of your words and monitoring your conversation for offensive phrases may help you avoid unexpected and perhaps devastating consequences.

APPLYING AN OTHER-ORIENTATION
to Listening and Responding Skills

It's impossible to be other-oriented without listening and observing others. Listening to comprehend information, empathize, or critically evaluate what others are saying is the quintessential other-oriented skill. The following poem by an anonymous author, simply called *Listen,* nicely summarizes the reason listening is such an important interpersonal skill.

Listen
When I ask you to listen to me and
  you start giving advice, you have
  not done what I asked.
When I ask you to listen to me and
  you begin to tell me why I
  shouldn't feel that way, you are
  trampling on my feelings.

When I ask you to listen to me and
  you feel you have to do
  something to solve my problems,
  you have failed me, strange as
  that may seem.
Listen! All I asked was that you listen.
  Not talk or do—just hear me.
Advice is cheap: 50 cents will get you
  both Dear Abby and Billy Graham
  in the same newspaper.
And I can do for myself; I'm not
  helpless. Maybe discouraged and
  faltering, but not helpless.
When you do something for me that I
  can and need to do for myself,
  you contribute to my fear and
  weakness.
But when you accept as a simple fact
  that I do feel what I feel, no matter

how irrational, then I quit trying to
  convince you and can get about
  the business of understanding
  what's behind this irrational feeling.
And when that's clear, the answers are
  obvious and I don't need advice.
Irrational feelings make sense when we
  understand what's behind them.
Perhaps that's why prayer works,
  sometimes, for some people—
  because God is mute, and doesn't
  give advice or try to fix things,
God just listens and lets you work it
  out for yourself.
So, please listen and just hear me,
  and, if you want to talk, wait a
  minute for your turn, and I'll listen
  to you.

  Anonymous

Listening Defined
(pages 118–120)

Listening and responding with verbal and nonverbal feedback are crucial parts of effective interpersonal communication. We spend more time listening than participating in any other communication activity. Listening is a complex process that involves selecting, attending to, constructing meaning from, remembering, and responding to verbal and nonverbal messages.

Key Terms

Listening *118*

Hearing *118*

Selecting *119*

Attending *119*

Understanding *119*

Remembering *120*

Responding *120*

Critical Thinking Questions

1. Describe two recent communication exchanges in which you were an effective or ineffective listener. What factors contributed to your listening skill (or lack of skill)?

2. Ethics: If you weren't really listening when someone was speaking to you, should you admit you weren't listening and ask the person to repeat what he or she said? Or should you say you couldn't hear or got distracted? Is it best to be honest in such a situation?

Activities

Over the next week, in your numerous communication exchanges with friends, family members, professors, and work colleagues, make an effort to listen carefully and effectively. Then, following each exchange, make a list of at least five items that you remember (things you discussed). Is there a difference in what you remember in each case? What factors contribute to your ability to listen, attend to, and remember details of each communication?

Web Resources

http://communication.learnhub.com/test/take/1409-test-your-listening-skills This site offers a self-test of your knowledge of listening and responding to others.

Listening Styles
(pages 120–122)

Your listening style is your preferred way of making sense of the spoken messages you hear. Researchers have found that there are four distinct listening styles: people-oriented, action-oriented, content-oriented, and time-oriented. You may use one primary listening style or several different styles, depending on the communication context and objectives. Culture and ethnicity can also influence how you listen to others. Understanding your own listening styles and others' styles can help you adapt to others and become a more effective listener.

Key Terms

Listening style *121*

People-oriented listener *121*

Action-oriented listener *121*

Second guessing *121*

Content-oriented listener *121*

Time-oriented listener *122*

Critical Thinking Questions

1. What is your primary listening style? How do you know?

2. Describe several situations in which you might modify or adapt your primary listening style. Do you find that you consciously adapt your communication to others' listening styles? When and why? What factors contribute to the need to adapt your listening style?

Activities

Consider others with whom you frequently communicate. How would you characterize their listening styles? Make a list of people you know who are primarily people-oriented, action-oriented, content-oriented, and time-oriented listeners. Do some of these people use different styles at different times? What cues help you to identify their styles? With which type of listeners do you find it easiest to communicate? Explain.

Web Resources

www.nasua.org/pdf/TipSheet1ActiveListening.pdf Provides tips and suggestions for being a better listener and for providing helpful feedback to others.

www.highgain.com/SELF/index.php3 Visit this site to try an interactive "Listening Self-Assessment" to learn about your current listening skills and what areas you may need to improve.

Listening Barriers
(pages 122–127)

Most of us don't listen as well as we should because we tend to be self-absorbed rather than other-oriented. Also, we often focus more on how we are going to respond rather than actually listening to what the other person is saying. Barriers to effective listening include being self-absorbed, being distracted by unchecked emotions, criticizing the speaker, not taking advantage of the difference between speech rate and thought rate, being distracted by information overload and external noise, and experiencing listener apprehension.

Key Terms

Conversational narcissism *124*

Emotional noise *125*

Ambush listener *126*

Listener apprehension *127*

Critical Thinking Questions

1. What daily challenges do you encounter in listening, and especially, attending to messages? Pause to consider some of the "noise" around you right now, including electronic

and internal (emotional) or external distractions. What effect does this noise have on your ability to listen to others?

2. In this age of communication technologies, what strategies can you use to reduce information overload and listen more effectively to others' messages?

3. Jason and Chris are roommates. They both work hard each day and come home exhausted. What suggestions would you offer to help them listen to each other effectively, even when they are tired?

Enhancing Listening and Responding Skills (pages 128–149)

To become a better and more other-oriented listener, you can follow three simple steps: Stop, look, and listen. After you complete these three steps, you should ask questions and reflect content by paraphrasing the speaker's message. You can further improve your ability to listen and respond empathically by seeking to understand your partner's feelings, paraphrasing his or her emotions, and providing confirming responses. Becoming a competent listener also involves listening and responding *critically* by looking for faulty logic and distinguishing facts from inferences. And you can enhance your responding skills further by providing well-timed responses and usable information, by avoiding unnecessary details, and by being descriptive rather than evaluative.

Key Terms

Meta-message *129*	Information triage *138*
Asynchronous listening *132*	Fact *138*
Empathy *132*	Inference *139*
Social decentering *133*	Paraphrase *140*
Sympathy *135*	Social support *144*
Emotional intelligence *136*	Confirming response *146*
Critical listening *137*	Disconfirming response *146*

Critical Thinking Questions

1. Miranda and Salvador often disagree about who should handle some of the child-rearing tasks in their home. What are some effective listening skills and strategies that they can use in discussing these tasks and making sure they understand each other?

2. Ethics: Your roommate (or partner or spouse) wants to tell you about his day. You are tired and really don't want to hear all the details. Should you fake attention so that you won't hurt his feelings, or simply tell him you are tired and would rather not hear the details right now?

Activities

Test Your Empathy. Take this short test to assess your empathy. Respond to each statement by indicating the degree to which it reflects how you typically communicate with others. Is the statement (1) Always false, (2) Usually false, (3) Sometimes false and sometimes true, (4) Usually true, or (5) Always true?

_____ 1. I try to understand others' experiences from their perspectives.

_____ 2. I follow the Golden Rule ("Do unto others as you would have them do unto you") when communicating with others.

_____ 3. I can "tune in" to emotions others are experiencing when we communicate.

_____ 4. When trying to understand how others feel, I imagine how I would feel in their situation.

_____ 5. I am able to tell what others are feeling without being told.

_____ 6. Others experience the same feelings I do in any given situation.

_____ 7. When others are having problems, I can imagine how they feel.

_____ 8. I find it hard to understand the emotions others experience.

_____ 9. I try to see others as they want me to see them.

_____ 10. I never seem to know what others are thinking when we communicate.

To find your score, first reverse the response for the five even-numbered items: If you wrote 1, make it 5; if you wrote 2, make it 4; if you wrote 3, leave it as 3; if you wrote 4, make it 2; if you wrote 5, make it 1. Next, add the numbers next to each statement. Scores range from 10 to 50. The higher your score, the more you are able to empathize.

Source: William Gudykunst, *Bridging Differences,* 3rd ed. (Thousand Oaks, CA: Sage, 1998), 234. Reprinted by permission of Sage Publications, Inc.

Web Resources

http://www.selfgrowth.com/test.html Visit this site and take a short, ten-question quiz to assess your ability to manage your emotions and be empathic toward others.

http://discoveryhealth.queendom.com/eiq_abridged_access.html This online test provided by Discovery Health will help you assess your emotional intelligence.

http://www.listen.org/Templates/trynew.htm The home page of the International Listening Association includes tips and resources to enhance listening skill.

6
Verbal Communication Skills

Words are powerful. Those who use them skillfully can exert great influence with just a few of them. Consider these notable achievements:

> Lincoln set the course for a nation in a 267-word speech: the Gettysburg Address.

> Shakespeare expressed the quintessence of the human condition in Hamlet's famous "To be, or not to be" soliloquy—363 words long.

> Two billion people accept a comprehensive moral code expressed in a mere 297 words: the Ten Commandments.

Words have great power in private life as well. In this chapter, we will examine ways to use them more effectively in interpersonal relationships. We'll investigate how to harness the power of words to affect emotions, thoughts, and actions, and we'll describe links between language and culture. We will also identify communication barriers that may keep you from using words effectively and note strategies and skills for managing those barriers. Finally, we will examine the role of speech in establishing supportive relationships with others.

According to one study, a person's ability to use words—more specifically, to participate in conversation with others—is one of the best predictors of communication competence.[1] One study found that people who simply didn't talk much were perceived as being less interpersonally skilled than people who spent an appropriate amount of time engaged in conversation with others.[2] This chapter is designed to help you better understand the power of words and to use them with greater skill and confidence.

Throughout our discussion of the power of verbal messages, we invite you to keep one important idea in mind: *You are not in charge of the meaning others derive from your messages.* Meaning is created in others. You don't determine what other people think. That is, words don't have meaning; people create meaning.

> "Words can destroy. What we call each other ultimately becomes what we think of each other, and it matters.
>
> **Jeanne J. Kirkpatrick**

How Words Work

As you read the printed words on this page, how are you able to make sense out of these black marks? When you hear words spoken by others, how are you able to interpret those sounds? Although several theories attempt to explain how people learn language and ascribe meaning to both printed and uttered words, there is no single universally held view that neatly clarifies the mystery.

Words Are Symbols

As we noted in Chapter 1, words are **symbols** that represent something else. A printed or spoken word triggers an image of an object, a sound, a concept, or an experience. Take the word *cat,* for instance. The word may conjure up in your mind's eye a hissing creature with bared claws and fangs. Or perhaps you envision a cherished pet curled up by a fireplace.

The classic model in Figure 6.1 was developed by Charles Ogden and Ivor Richards to explain the relationships between *referents, thought,* and *symbols.*[3] **Referents** are the things the symbols (words) represent. **Thought** is the mental

symbol Word, sound, or visual device that represents an object, sound, concept, or experience.

referent Thing that a symbol represents.

thought Mental process of creating an image, sound, concept, or experience triggered by a referent or symbol.

FIGURE 6.1
Triangle of Meaning

process of creating an image, sound, concept, or experience triggered by the referent or the symbol. So the three elements—referents, thought, and symbols—are inextricably linked. Although some scholars find this model too simplistic to explain how people link all words to meaning, it does illustrate the process for most concepts, people, and tangible things.

Words Symbolize Denotative and Connotative Meaning. Language creates meaning on two levels: the denotative and the connotative. The **denotative meaning** of a word creates content: It is the word's restrictive or literal meaning. For example, here is one dictionary definition for the word *school:*

> An institution for the instruction of children; an institution for instruction in a skill or business; a college or a university.[4]

This definition is the literal, or denotative, definition of the word *school;* it describes what the word means in American culture.

The **connotative meaning** of a word creates feelings. Words have personal and subjective meanings. To you, the word *school* might mean a wonderful, exciting place where you meet your friends, have a good time, and occasionally take tests and perform other tasks that keep you from enjoying your social life. To others, *school* could be a restrictive, burdensome obligation that stands in the way of making money and getting on with life. The connotative meaning of a word is more individualized. Whereas the denotative, or objective, meaning of the word *school* can be found in any dictionary, your subjective, personal response to the word is probably not contained there.

The denotative and connotative meanings of words made headlines in 2008, when the U.S. Supreme Court considered whether a well-known, four-letter word is obscene if it is used connotatively rather than denotatively.[5] The Federal Communication Commission doesn't permit the word to be used on public airways (although it can be used on cable TV or satellite radio). TV broadcasters were fined for allowing the word to be used in a live, on-air broadcast. The broadcasters fought back, arguing that the word is not obscene if it is used to express frustration or that things are a mess (one of its connotative meanings) rather than to describe the act of sex

denotative meaning Restrictive or literal meaning of a word.

connotative meaning Personal and subjective meaning of a word.

▶ RECAP (Denotative and Connotative Meaning

Meaning	Definition	Examples
Denotative	Literal, restrictive definition of a word	Mother: the female person who gave birth to you
Connotative	Personal, subjective reaction to a word	Mother: the warm, caring woman who nurtured and loved you; or the cold, distant woman who always implied that you were not measuring up to her standards

(its denotative meaning). The fact that the highest court in the country heard arguments to determine if a word was obscene depending on its denotative and connotative meaning suggests that both the denotative and the connotative symbolic meanings of words are important.

Words Symbolize Concrete or Abstract Meaning. Words can be placed along a continuum from abstract to concrete. People call a word *concrete* if they can experience its referent with one of their senses; if you can see a word's referent, or touch it, smell it, taste it, or hear it, then the word is concrete. If you cannot do these things with the referent, then the word is abstract. You can visualize the continuum from abstract to concrete as a ladder. Language specialist S. I. Hayakawa first developed the concept of a ladder of abstraction in his classic book *Language in Thought and Action.*[6]

In Figure 6.2, the term at the bottom, *red Mercedes 500,* is quite specific and concrete. You're more likely to have a clear mental picture of a red Mercedes than you are a clear image of the word *transportation*—which could mean anything from walking to jetting across the Atlantic. As you move up the ladder of abstraction, the terms become broader and more general. In general, the more concrete the language, the more likely it is that the precise meaning of a word will be communicated to a listener.

Most of us can agree on the denotative meaning of the word *school*. But the connotative meaning will be different for each person.

FIGURE 6.2

A Ladder of Abstraction

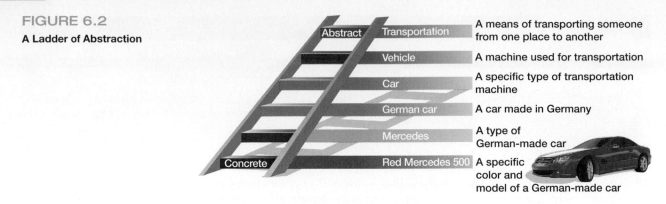

Abstract Transportation — A means of transporting someone from one place to another

Vehicle — A machine used for transportation

Car — A specific type of transportation machine

German car — A car made in Germany

Mercedes — A type of German-made car

Concrete Red Mercedes 500 — A specific color and model of a German-made car

Words Are Arbitrary

American linguist (a linguist is a person who studies the origin and nature of language) Charles Hockett suggested that words are, for the most part, arbitrary.[7] There's not an obvious reason many words represent what they refer to. The word *dog*, for example, does not look like a dog or sound like a dog. Yet there is a clear connection in your mind between your pet pooch and the symbol *dog*. The words we use have agreed-on general meanings, but there is not typically a logical connection between a word and what it represents. Yes, some words, such as *buzz, hum, snort,* and *giggle*, do recreate the sounds they represent. Words that, when pronounced, sound like the event or thing they are signifying are called onomatopoetic words. You probably learned about **onomatopoeia** in an English class. And many words can trace their origin to other languages.[8] But most of the time words have an arbitrary meaning. A linguistic group, such as all the people who speak the English language, has agreed that the word *tree*, for example, will represent the thing with bark, branches, and leaves growing in your yard or a nearby park. The arbitrary nature of most words means that there is no inherent meaning in a word. Therefore, unless we develop a common meaning for a word, misunderstanding and miscommunication may occur.

Words Are Context-Bound

Your English or communication teacher has undoubtedly cautioned you that taking something out of context partially changes its meaning. Symbols derive their meaning from the situation in which they are used. The phrase *old man* could refer to a male over the age of seventy, your father, your teacher, your principal, or your boss. You need to know the context of the phrase in order to decipher its specific meaning. The transactional nature of communication emphasizes how meaning is created in a context.

Words Are Culture-Bound

As you learned in Chapter 4, culture consists of the rules, norms, values, and mores of a group of people, which have been learned and shaped by successive generations. The meaning of a symbol such as a word can change from culture to culture. To a European, for example, a "Yankee" is someone from the United States; to a player on the Boston Red Sox, a "Yankee" is an opponent; and to someone from the American South, a "Yankee" is someone from the American North. A few years ago, General Motors sold a car called a Nova. In English, *nova* means bright star—an appropriate name for a car. In Spanish, however, the spoken word *nova* sounds like the words "no va," which translate "It does not go." As you can imagine, this name was not a great sales tool for the Spanish-speaking market.

onomatopoeia A word that imitates a sound associated with what is named; also, the use of such a word.

One way to measure how words reflect culture is to consider the new words that become entries in dictionaries. Here are some new words that are finding their way into people's conversations:[9]

Crackberry: Nickname for a BlackBerry, a personal digital assistant that can become quite addictive

Webisode: A video clip designed for the Internet

Vlog: A web log (blog) of videos

Bromance: A close but nonsexual relationship between two males

Frenemy: Someone who has a close personal relationship with you but who also hurts you

Crunk: A type of hip-hop music

Ridonkulous: Over-the-top ridiculous

The study of words and meaning is called *semantics.* One important semantic theory known as **symbolic interaction theory** suggests that a society is bound together by the common use of symbols. As we discussed in Chapter 2, the theory was originally developed by sociologists as a way of making sense out of how societies and groups are linked together.[10] The theory of symbolic interaction also illuminates how we use our common understanding of symbols to form interpersonal relationships. Common symbols foster links in understanding and therefore lead to satisfying relationships. Of course, even within a given culture people misunderstand each other's messages. But the more similar the cultures of the communication partners, the greater the chance for a meeting of meanings.

Some researchers, such as linguist Deborah Tannen, suggest that gender plays a major role in how we interpret certain verbal messages.[11] Women tend to interpret messages based on how personally supportive they perceive the message to be. Men, according to Tannen, are more likely to interpret messages based on issues related to dominance and power. Research confirms that psychological gender is a better predictor than biological sex of the general framework we use to interpret messages.[12] Clearly, our life experiences help us interpret the words we hear.

The Power of Words

> Sticks and stones may break my bones,
> But words can never hurt me.

This old schoolyard chant may provide a ready retort for the desperate victim of name-calling, but it is hardly convincing. With more insight, the poet Robert Browning wrote, "Words break no bones; hearts though sometimes." And in his book *Science and Sanity,* mathematician and engineer Alfred Korzybski argued that the words we use (and misuse) have tremendous effects on our thoughts and actions.[13] Browning and Korzybski were right. As we said at the beginning of this chapter, words have power.

Words Create Perceptions

"To name is to call into existence—to call out of nothingness," wrote French philosopher Georges Gusdorff.[14] Words give you a tool to create how you perceive the world

symbolic interaction theory
Theory that members of a society are bound together through common use of symbols.

by naming and labeling what you experience. You undoubtedly learned in your elementary science class that Sir Isaac Newton discovered gravity. It would be more accurate to say that he *labeled* rather than discovered it. His use of the word *gravity* gave us a cognitive category; we now converse about the pull of the earth's forces that keeps us from flying into space. Words give us the symbolic vehicles to communicate our creations and discoveries to others.

When you label something as "good" or "bad," you are using language to create your own vision of how you experience the world. If you tell a friend that the movie you saw last night was vulgar and obscene, you are not only providing your friend with a critique of the movie; you are also communicating your sense of what is appropriate and inappropriate.

You create your self-worth largely with self-talk and with the labels you apply to yourself. Psychologist Albert Ellis believes that you also create your moods and emotional state with the words you use to label your feelings.[15] Although emotions may sometimes seem to wash over you like ocean waves, there is evidence that you have the ability to control your emotions based on your ability to control what you think about, as well as the choice of words you use to describe your feelings. In Chapter 2, we talked about the appraisal theory of emotions, which suggests that we exert considerable control over our emotions based on how we frame what is happening to us.[16] If you get fired from a job, you might say that you feel angry and helpless, or you might declare that you feel liberated and excited. The first response might lead to depression, and the second to happiness. One fascinating study conducted over a thirty-five-year period found that people who described the world in pessimistic terms when they were younger were in poorer health during middle age than those who had been optimistic.[17] Your words and corresponding outlook have the power to affect your health. The concept of reframing, discussed in Chapter 2 as a way to improve self-concept, is based on the power of words to "call into existence" whatever we describe with them.

Words Influence Thoughts

If someone says, "Don't think about a pink elephant," it's hard *not* to think about a pink elephant, because just thinking the words *pink elephant* more than likely triggers an image of a pink pachyderm. Words and thoughts are inextricably linked. Words influence our thoughts.

Is it possible to think without using linguistic symbols (words or numbers)? Yes, we can certainly experience emotions without describing them in words and enjoy music without lyrics. Artists paint, dancers dance, and architects dream new structures, all without words. Yet words are what transmit our dreams and our emotions to others when we verbalize what we feel. Words have tremendous power to influence what we think about, just as our thinking influences the words we use.

There is scientific evidence that words influence our thoughts. As Figure 6.3 illustrates, the process of hearing, seeing, or saying words influences different parts of the brain. How we use words literally changes our brain activity.

Because words have the power to influence our thoughts, the meaning of a word resides within us, rather than in the word itself. Words *symbolize* meaning, but the precise meaning of a word originates in the mind of the sender and the receiver. The meaning of a word is not static; it evolves as a conversation evolves. Your meanings for words and phrases change as you gain additional experiences and have new thoughts about the words you use.[18]

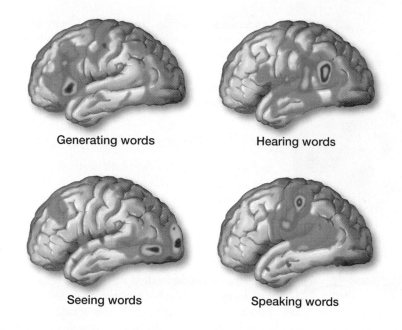

FIGURE 6.3
Words Influence Brain Activity

Generating words   Hearing words

Seeing words   Speaking words

Words Influence Actions

A paraphrase of a well-known verse from the book of Proverbs in the Bible tells us, "As a person thinks, so is he or she." Words not only have the power to create and influence your thoughts, they also influence your actions—because your thoughts, which are influenced by words, affect how you behave. Advertisers have long known that slogans and catch phrases sell products. Political candidates also know that the words they use influence whether they will get your vote.

In the late 1960s, a California sociology professor conducted an experiment to demonstrate that words have the power to affect behavior.[19] He divided his class into two groups. To one group, he distributed a bumper sticker that boldly displayed the words "I support the Black Panthers." At that time, many members of the students' local community thought the Panthers were using unnecessary force to promote their agenda. Students in this first group had to drive around for a week with the stickers on their cars. The other group drove around as usual, without stickers.

It took only a few hours to demonstrate the professor's point: Words do affect attitudes and behavior. Students who had the stickers were harassed by other motorists and issued traffic tickets at an alarming rate. The other group experienced no increase in hassles. By the end of the study, seventeen days later, the "Panther" group had received thirty-three traffic citations. Although this classic example happened decades ago, words are just as powerful today in influencing behaviors. Bumper stickers about gay marriage and abortion refer to contemporary issues that pack an emotional wallop and generate intense reactions. What other words that appear on bumper stickers today might elicit strong reactions?

Research suggests that the very way we use language can communicate the amount of power we have in a conversation with others.[20] We use language in ways that are both powerful and powerless. When we use powerless speech, we are less persuasive and have less influence on others. Powerless speech is characterized by more frequent use of pauses, which may be filled with "umm," "ahhh," and "ehh." We also express our lack of power by using more hesitation and unnecessary verbal fillers like "you know," and "I mean." We communicate our low power when we hedge our

Surfers have created their own special language as part of the culture they share.

conclusions by saying "I guess" and "sort of." Another way of communicating a lack of power is by tacking on a question at the end of a statement, such as "I'm right, aren't I?" or "This is what I think, OK?" So, the very way in which you speak can influence the thoughts and actions of others.[21]

Words Affect and Reflect Culture

In the early part of the twentieth century, anthropologists Edward Sapir and his student Benjamin Whorf worked simultaneously to refine a theory called **linguistic determinism.**[22] The essence of linguistic determinism is that language shapes the way we think. Our words also reflect our thoughts and our culture. A related principle, called **linguistic relativity,** states that each language has unique elements embedded within it. Together these two principles form the underlying elements in the **Sapir–Whorf hypothesis,** which suggests that language shapes our culture and culture shapes our language. To support the theory, Benjamin Whorf studied the languages of several cultures, particularly that of Hopi Native Americans. He discovered that in Hopi, one word (the word *masa'ytaka*) is used for every creature that flies, except for birds. While this seems odd to an English speaker, because the English language has many different words for different flying creatures (and things such as airplanes, balloons, and rockets), for the Hopi, flying creatures (or objects) constitute a single category. Whorf saw this as support of his hypothesis that the words we use reflect our culture and our culture influences our words. Similarly, today's highly developed technological culture has given rise to many new words that reflect the importance we place on technology; terms such as *PC, hard drive,* and *gigabytes* weren't part of your grandparents' language. And the fact that a certain type of behavior is now labeled attention-deficit/hyperactivity disorder (ADHD) is an example of how words can create a reality in a culture. Grandpa might argue that there weren't any ADHD kids in his day—some kids were just "rowdy."[23]

Words not only reflect your culture; there is evidence that they mold it. When Wendell Johnson, a speech therapist, noticed that very few Native Americans in a certain tribe stuttered, he also found that their language had no word for stuttering.[24] He concluded that few people had this affliction because it never entered their minds as a possibility. Perhaps you've heard that Eskimos have forty-nine different words for snow. Even though they really don't have quite that many, there is evidence that they have more words for snow than does someone native to Miami, Florida.[25]

These examples also show that the words people use affect their **worldview**—how they interpret what they experience. The words you use to describe your view of the world, including those you use in your everyday interpersonal conversations with your friends, reflect and further shape your perspective.[26] And you, in turn, help to shape your culture's collective worldview through your use of language.

Words Make and Break Relationships

What you say and how you say it have a strong impact on how you relate to others. Relationships are the connections we make with others. As we noted in Chapter 1, to relate to another person is like dancing with the person. When you dance with a partner, your moves and countermoves respond to the rhythm of the music and the

linguistic determinism Theory that describes how use of language determines or influences thoughts and perceptions.

linguistic relativity Theory that each language includes some unique features that are not found in other languages.

Sapir–Whorf hypothesis Based on the principles of linguistic determinism and linguistic relativity, the hypothesis that language shapes our thoughts and culture, and our culture and thoughts affect the language we use to describe our world.

worldview Culturally acquired perspective for interpreting experiences.

moves your partner makes. In our interpersonal relationships with others, we "dance" as we relate to our communication partners with both language and nonverbal cues (something we'll discuss in more detail in the next chapter). A good conversation has a rhythm, created by both communicators as they listen and respond to each other. Even our "small talk," which is our everyday, sometimes brief, responses and exchanges with others ("Nice weather we're having" or, simply, "Oh, that's nice"), is important in establishing how we feel about others.[27] The words we use, especially in our daily conversations, are directly related to the quality of the relationships we have with others.

Interpersonal communication researcher Steve Duck suggests that we literally talk a relationship into being.[28] It is through our talk that we establish our relationships with other people. And what do we talk about? One research team simply looked at what satisfied couples talked about with each other during the course of a week. The team found that the most frequent topic was the couples themselves—what they did during the day and how they were feeling—followed by general observations, and then responses to each other such as, "Yes, I see," and "Uh huh"—what researchers call *backchannel talk*. The researchers also found we're more likely to have conflict with our partners on the weekend, as well as to use humor, to talk about household tasks, and to make general plans about the future.[29] Couples were least satisfied with their partners on Saturdays and Wednesdays; Monday was the day they were most satisfied. What this means is that what we talk about and the way we talk to others form the basis of how we relate to others.

The use of **profanity,** words that people consider obscene, rude, or insensitive, has an impact on our relationships with others. If you grew up in a home where profanity was never uttered, you may simply have not developed a habit of using such words. Or, you may have made a conscious decision not to use profanity because of your religious or moral convictions. Yet profanity is ever-present in everyday conversations and the media. If you have heard the late comedian George Carlin's monologue "Seven Dirty Words You Can't Say on Television," then you have an idea of the words that form the bedrock of profane speech.

Whether or not something is profanity is determined by context and culture. If you have British friends, then you know the word *bloody* is an obscene word synonymous in profane power with the "F word." Yet you may see nothing wrong with using the word *bloody* in your conversations. Dog breeders know that a female dog is a *bitch,* yet using that term to describe a female classmate would be considered using profanity.

Remember that the other person, not you, determines the effect of the use of profanity on the relationship. Some people might be highly offended if you were to use one or more of George Carlin's seven "dirty" words in a conversation. Yet using profanity may signal your comfort with being yourself when you're with another person.

profanity Words considered obscene, blasphemous, irreverent, rude, or insensitive.

Your use of profanity provides important information about your perception of the relationship you have with the other person.

Another clue to the nature of the relationship you have with someone is your use of euphemism. A **euphemism** is an expression that describes something vulgar or profane (or something people prefer not to talk about directly) but uses less explicit language. Just above, when we referred to "the F word" rather than spelling it out, we were using a euphemism. Not using euphemisms and more directly and explicitly describing your thoughts and feelings provides relational cues that you trust the other person to accept your blunt language. Politicians use euphemisms to soften the impact of an event. Rather than saying innocent people were killed, the spokesperson may say "there was collateral damage." Noting your use of euphemisms and the use and frequency of euphemisms in the speech of others can give you insights about the nature of your relationship with them.

Word Barriers

According to theologian and educator Ruel Howe, a communication barrier is "something that keeps meaning from meeting."[30] Words have the power to create monumental misunderstandings as well as deep connections.[31] Although it is true that meanings are in people, not in words, sometimes assumptions or inaccurate use of words hinders understanding. Let's identify some of the specific barriers to understanding that people sometimes create through language.

Bypassing: One Word, Multiple Meanings

A student pilot was on his first solo flight. When he called the tower for flight instructions, the control tower asked, "Would you please give us your altitude and position?" The pilot replied, "I'm five feet ten inches, and I'm sitting up front."

Bypassing occurs when the same words mean different things to different people. Meaning is fragile. And the English language is imprecise in many areas. One researcher estimated that the 500 words used most often in daily conversations have more than 14,000 different dictionary definitions. And this number does not take into account personal connotations. So it is no wonder that bypassing is a common communication problem. Consider the unsubstantiated story about a young FBI employee who was put in charge of the supply department. In an effort to save money, he reduced the size of memo paper. One of the smaller sheets ended up on J. Edgar Hoover's desk. The director didn't like the small size and wrote on the narrow margin of the paper, "Watch the borders." For the next six weeks, it was extremely difficult to enter the United States from Canada or Mexico.

euphemism A mild or indirect word that is substituted for one that describes something vulgar, profane, unpleasant, or embarrassing.

bypassing Confusion caused by the fact that the same word can mean different things to different people.

Pavlov's dog salivated when he heard the bell that he had learned to associate with food. Sometimes we respond to symbols the way Pavlov's dog did to the bell, forgetting that symbols (words) can have more than one meaning.

How do you avoid bypassing and missing someone's meaning? Using the listening and responding skills we talked about in the previous chapter is key to enhancing communication accuracy. Ask questions if you're uncertain of the meaning. Listen and paraphrase your understanding of the message.

Lack of Precision: Uncertain Meaning

Alice Roosevelt Longworth writes about a merchant seaman who was being investigated under the McCarran Act. "Do you," asked the interrogator, "have any pornographic literature?"

"Pornographic literature!" the sailor burst out indignantly. "I don't even have a pornograph!"

At a ceremony in the Princeton University chapel, an old lady buttonholed an usher and commanded, "Be sure you get me a seat up front, young man. I understand they've always had trouble with the agnostics in the chapel!"

Each of these examples illustrates a **malapropism,** a confusion of one word or phrase for another that sounds similar to it. You have probably heard people confuse such word pairs as *construction* and *instruction,* and *subscription* and *prescription.* Although this confusion may at times be humorous, it may also result in failure to communicate clearly. So, too, can using words out of context, using inappropriate grammar, or putting words in the wrong order. Confusion is the inevitable result, as illustrated by these notes written to landlords:

> The toilet is blocked and we cannot bathe the children until it is cleared.

> Will you please send someone to mend our cracked sidewalk? Yesterday my wife tripped on it and is now pregnant.

These are funny examples, but in fact, incorrect or unclear language can launch a war or sink a ship. We give symbols meaning; we do not receive inherent meaning *from* symbols. If you are other-oriented, you will assess how someone else will respond to your message and try to select those symbols that he or she is most likely to interpret as you intend.

For most communication, the object is to be as correct, specific, and concrete as possible. Vague language creates confusion and frustration. Consider this example:

Derrick: Where's the aluminum foil?

Pam: In the drawer.

Derrick: What drawer?

Pam: In the kitchen.

Derrick: But where in the kitchen?

Pam: By the fridge.

Derrick: But which one? There are five drawers.

Pam: Oh, the second one from the top.

Derrick: Why didn't you say so in the first place?

malapropism Confusion of one word or phrase for another that sounds similar to it.

But is it possible to be too precise? It is if you use a restricted code that has a meaning your listener does not know. A **restricted code** is a set of words that have a particular meaning to a subgroup or culture. Sometimes, we develop abbreviations or specialized terms that make sense and save time when we speak to others in our group. Musicians, for example, use special terms that relate to reading and performing music. Most computer users know that "a screamer" is someone who sends e-mail messages typed in ALL CAPITAL LETTERS. Ham radio operators use codes to communicate over the airwaves. Yet, in each instance, this shorthand language would make little sense to an outsider. In fact, groups that rely on restricted codes may have greater cohesiveness because of this shared "secret" language, or **jargon.** Whatever your line of work, guard against lapsing into phrases that can only be interpreted by a few.

Dot Mobile is a British cell phone service for students that uses a restricted code to summarize classic literary phrases in a text-message format. Can you break the code of the following phrases from literature?[32]

1. 2B?NTB? = ????

2. Ahors, m'kindom 4 Ahors

3. 2morrow &"&"

4. WenevalUFeelLykDissinNel,jstMembaDatADaOoubDaWrldHvntHdDaVantg-stU vAd

5. IfURlyWnt2HrBoutit,Da1stFingUlProbWnt2NolsWhereIWsBorn&WotMy Lousy ChldhdWsLyk&HwMyRetsWerOcupyd&AlB4TheyHdMe&ThtDave CopafieldKi ndaCr"p,BtIDnFeelLykGolnintaltifUWannaNoDaTruf

Here are the answers:

1. "To be or not to be? That is the question."(William Shakespeare, *Hamlet*)

2. "A horse, a horse, my kingdom for a horse." (William Shakespeare, *Richard III*)

3. Tomorrow and tomorrow and tomorrow." (William Shakespeare, *Macbeth*)

4. "Whenever you feel like criticizing anyone . . . just remember that all the people in this world haven't had the advantages that you've had." (F. Scott Fitzgerald, *The Great Gatsby*)

5. "If you really want to hear about it, the first thing you'll probably want to know is where I was born, and what my lousy childhood was like, and how my parents were occupied and all before they had me, and all that David Copperfield kind of crap, but I don't feel like going into it, if you want to know the truth." (J. D. Salinger, *The Catcher in the Rye*)

When people have known one another for a long time, they may also use restricted codes for their exchanges. Often married couples communicate using shorthand speech that no outsider could ever interpret. To enhance the clarity of your messages with others, especially people who don't know you well, be as clear as you can to reduce uncertainty. For example, rather than saying, "I may go to town today," one research team suggests you should be more specific by saying, "There's a 50 percent chance I may go to town today."[33] Be precise to be clear.

Allness: Overgeneralized Meaning

The tendency to use language to make unqualified, often untrue generalizations is called **allness.** Allness statements deny individual differences or variations. Statements such as "All women are poor drivers" and "People from the South love iced tea" are

restricted code Set of words that have particular meaning to a person, group, or culture.

jargon Another name for restricted code; specialized terms or abbreviations whose meanings are known only to members of a specific group.

allness Tendency to use language to make unqualified, often untrue generalizations.

generalizations that imply that the person making the pronouncement has examined all the information and has reached a definitive conclusion. Although the world would be much simpler if we *could* make such statements, reality rarely, if ever, provides evidence to support sweeping generalizations.

One way to avoid untrue generalizations is to remind yourself that your use and interpretation of a word are unique. Saying the words "to me" either to yourself or out loud before you offer an opinion or make a pronouncement can help communicate to others (and remind yourself) that your view is uniquely yours. Rather than announcing, "Curfews for teenagers are ridiculous," you could say, "To me, curfews for teenagers are ridiculous."

Indexing your comments and remarks is another way to avoid generalizing. To index is to acknowledge that each individual, each situation, or each example is unique. Rather than announcing that all doctors are abrupt, you could say, "My child's pediatrician spends a lot of time with me, but my internist never answers my questions." This helps you remember that doctor number one is not the same as doctor number two.

Static Evaluation: Rigid Meaning

You change. Your world changes. An ancient Greek philosopher said it best: "You can never step in the same river twice." A **static evaluation** is a statement that fails to recognize change; labels in particular have a tendency to freeze-frame our awareness. Ruby, known as the class nerd in high school, is today a successful and polished businessperson; the old label does not fit.

In addition, some people suffer from "hardening of the categories." Their world view is so rigid that they can never change or expand their perspective. But the world is a technicolor moving target. Just about the time you think you have things neatly figured out and categorized, something moves. Your labels may not reflect the buzzing, booming, zipping process of change. It is important to acknowledge that perception is a process, and to avoid trying to nail things down permanently into all-inclusive categories.

General semanticists use the metaphorical expression "the map is not the territory" to illustrate the concept of static evaluation. Like a word, a map symbolizes or represents reality. Yet the road system is constantly changing. New roads are built, old ones are closed. If you were to use a 1949 map to guide you on your cross-country trip from Washington, D.C., to Kansas City, Missouri, you would probably lose your way because the interstate highway system would not even be on it. Similarly, if you use old labels and do not adjust your thinking to accommodate change, you will get lost semantically.

To avoid static evaluation, try dating your observations and indicate to others the time period from which you are drawing your conclusion. For example, if your second cousin comes to town for a visit, say, "When I last saw you, you loved to listen to The Dixie Chicks." This allows for the possibility that your cousin's tastes may have changed during the last few years. But most importantly, try to observe and acknowledge changes in others. If you are practicing what you know about becoming other-oriented, you are unlikely to erect this barrier.

Polarization: Extreme Meaning

Describing and evaluating what you observe in terms of extremes, such as good or bad, old or new, beautiful or ugly, brilliant or stupid, is known as **polarization.** General semanticists remind us that the world is not black and white but comes in a variety of colors, hues, and shades. If you describe things in extremes, leaving out

indexing Avoiding generalizations by using statements that separate one situation, person, or example from another.

static evaluation Pronouncement that does not take the possibility of change into consideration.

polarization Description and evaluation of what you observe in terms of extremes such as good or bad, old or new, beautiful or ugly.

the middle ground, then your language does not accurately reflect reality. And because of the power of words to create, you may believe your own pronouncements.

"You either love me or don't love me," says Jerome.

"You're either for me or against me," replies Lisa.

Both people are overstating the case, using language to polarize their perceptions of experience.

Family counselors who listen to family feuds find that the tendency to see things from an either/or point of view is a classic symptom of a troubled relationship. Placing the entire blame on your partner for a problem in your relationship is an example of polarizing. Few relational difficulties are exclusively one-sided.

Biased Language: Insensitivity Toward Others

Using words that reflect your biases toward other cultures or ethnic groups, the other gender, people with a different sexual orientation, or people who are different from you in some other way can create a barrier for your listeners. Because words, including the words used to describe people, have power to create and affect thoughts and behavior, they can affect the quality of relationships with others. Although TV and radio shows and magazine articles may debate the merits of political correctness, there is no doubt that sexist or racially stereotypical language can offend others.

Hate speech is any word or phrase that is intended to offend and show disrespect for another person because of his or her race, ethnicity, cultural background, gender, age, sexual orientation, disability, social class, occupation, personal appearance, mental capacity, or any other personal aspect that could be perceived as demeaning. Some people use words to *intentionally* express their prejudice, bias, ignorance, or just plain meanness toward other people, hoping to hurt someone. Like the sticks and stones that are hurled at others to intentionally inflict harm, hate speech is uttered with the explicit purpose of hurting someone. In the United States, the Second Amendment to the Constitution provides for freedom of speech. Yet do people have the legal right to direct hurtful, venomous comments toward others, knowing that such comments will create mental anguish? Your college or university may have a speech code that prohibits hate speech, yet critics of such codes argue that it's impossible to prove the motivation or intent of someone who uses such language.

An other-oriented communicator avoids language that would intentionally hurt someone. We'll address three issues in language use that can reflect poorly on the speaker and affect interpersonal relationship with others: sexist language, ethnic or racially biased language, and demeaning language.

Avoid Sexist Language. Sexist language is the use of words that reflect stereotypical attitudes or that describe roles in exclusively male or female terms.

Words such as congress*man*, mail*man*, and *man*kind ignore the fact that women are part of the workforce and the human race. Contrast these with *member of Congress, letter carrier,* and *humankind,* which are gender-neutral and allow for the inclusion of both men and women. Or, rather than eliminating the word *man* from your vocabulary, try to use appropriate labels when you know the gender of the subject. A male police officer is a *policeman;* a female police officer is a *policewoman.* Rather than *salesperson,* you could say *salesman* or *saleswoman,* depending on the gender of the seller.

The term *policeman* fails to accurately describe the person shown here. A more inclusive term would be *police officer.*

hate speech Words or phrases intended to offend or show disrespect for someone's race, ethnicity, cultural background, gender, or some other aspect of their personality.

H. S. O'Donnell found that even dictionaries fall into the trap of describing men and women with discriminatory language.[34] Included in the *Oxford English Dictionary* definition of *woman* are (1) an adult female being, (2) a female servant, (3) a lady-love or mistress, and (4) a wife. Men are described in more positive and distinguished terms: (1) a human being, (2) the human creation regarded abstractly, (3) an adult male endowed with many qualities, and (4) a person of importance or position.

Many of our social conventions also diminish or ignore the importance of women:

Sexist	**Unbiased**
I'd like you to meet Dr. and Mrs. John Chao.	I'd like you to meet Dr. Sue Ho and Dr. John Chao. They are husband and wife.
	or I'd like you to meet John Chao and Sue Ho. They're both doctors at Mercy Hospital.
Let me introduce Mr. Tom Bertolone and his wife, Beverly.	Let me introduce Beverly and Tom Bertolone.

Language has, however, made more substantial progress in reflecting changes and changed attitudes toward women in the professional arena. Compare the terms used to describe workers now with those used in the 1950s:

Terms Used Today	**Terms Used in 1950s**
Flight attendant	Stewardess
Firefighter	Fireman
Police officer	Policeman
Physician	Female doctor
Women at the office	Girls at work
Ms.	Miss/Mrs.
People/humans	Mankind

Consciously remembering to use nonsexist language will result in several benefits.[35] First, nonsexist language reflects nonsexist attitudes. Your attitudes are reflected in your speech, and your speech affects your attitudes. Monitoring your speech for sexist remarks can help you monitor your attitudes about sexist assumptions you may hold. Second, using nonsexist language will help you become more other-oriented. Monitoring your language for sexist remarks will reflect your sensitivity to others. Third, nonsexist language will make your speech more contemporary and unambiguous. By substituting the word *humankind* for *mankind,* for example, you can communicate that you are including all people, not just men, in your observation or statement. And finally, your

PEARLS BEFORE SWINE © Stephan Pastis/Dist. by United Feature Syndicate, Inc.

BEING Other-ORIENTED

You don't determine whether a word or phrase is offensive—the person who's been called the name does. How can you assess whether terms, phrases, or labels that you use may be offensive to someone?

nonsexist language will empower others. By eliminating sexist bias from your speech, you will help confirm the value of all the individuals with whom you interact.

In addition to the debate over language that refers to gender, there is considerable discussion about the way people talk about sexual orientation. The principle of being other-oriented suggests that you can be sensitive in the way you speak of someone's sexual orientation. Labeling someone a *fag, queer,* or *dyke* not only may be offensive and hurtful to the person being labeled but also reflects on the sensitivity of the person doing the labeling. We're not suggesting that certain words be expunged from dictionaries or never uttered; we are suggesting that when describing others, people should be sensitive to how the others wish to be addressed and discussed.

Avoid Ethnically or Racially Biased Language. In addition to monitoring your language for sexual stereotypes, avoid racial and ethnic stereotypes. Using phrases such as "She's an Indian giver," or "I jewed him down on the price," or "He doesn't have a Chinaman's chance" demonstrates an insensitivity to members of other cultural groups. Monitor your speech so that you are not, even unconsciously, using phrases that depict a racial group or ethnic group in a negative, stereotypical fashion.

Is Supreme Court Justice Clarence Thomas Black or African American? Is labor leader Dolores Huerta Hispanic or Latina? Given the power of words, the terms we use to label ethnic groups reflect perceptions of culture and identity. Using the wrong word can result in your being labeled "politically incorrect," or worse, a "bigot." In 1995, the U.S. Bureau of Labor Statistics surveyed 60,000 households, asking what ethnic label they liked best. More than 44 percent of households then called "Black" by the government preferred the term "Black," and 28 percent preferred "African American." Twelve percent preferred "Afro-American" and a little more than 9 percent had no preference. In another ethnic category, "Hispanic" was the choice of 58 percent of those currently labeled "Hispanics," rather than terms such as "Latino/Latina" or the generic "of Spanish origin." More than 10 percent had no preference. The survey also reported that the label "American Indian" was the term of choice for slightly fewer than half of the respondents, whereas 37 percent preferred "Native American." Most of those currently designated "White" preferred that term, although 16 percent liked the term "Caucasian" and a very small percentage liked the term "European American."[36] Some of these preferences may surprise you, in that they may have changed since this survey was conducted. A sensitive, other-oriented communicator keeps abreast of such changes and adopts the designations currently preferred by members of the ethnic groups themselves.

Avoid Demeaning Language. Language barriers are created not only when a speaker uses sexist or racially biased language, but also when a speaker disparages a person's age, mental or physical ability, or social standing. Calling someone a "geezer," "retard," or "trailer trash" is disparaging.[37]

Discrimination based on age is a growing problem in the workplace. In some occupations, as a worker moves into his or her fifties, it may be difficult to change jobs or find work. Despite laws designed to guard against age discrimination, such discrimination clearly exists. As we have noted, the language that people use has power to affect attitudes and behavior. That's why using negative terms to describe the elderly can be a subtle—or sometimes not-so-subtle—way of expressing disrespect toward the older generation.

"Actually, I prefer the term Arctic-American."

▶ RECAP Word Barriers and How to Overcome Them

Barrier	Example	What to Do
Bypassing: Confusion caused by the fact that the same word may evoke different meanings for different people	*W. C.* might mean "wayside chapel" to a Swiss person and "water closet" to a British person. (Americans know this as "the bathroom.")	• When speaking, provide specific examples. • When listening, ask questions to clarify the meaning.
Lack of clarity: Inappropriate or imprecise use of words	Sign in Acapulco hotel: "The manager has personally passed all the water served here."	• When speaking, use precise language whenever possible; provide short, specific examples or indicate the probability of something happening: "There's a 40 percent chance I won't go shopping today." • When listening, paraphrase the message to ensure you understand it accurately.
Allness: Tendency to lump things or people into all-encompassing categories	"All Texans drive pick-up trucks and hang rifles in their back windows."	• When speaking, say "To me" before you offer a generalization to indicate that the idea or perception is your own. Index a generalized statement by using phrases that separate one situation, person, or example from another. • When listening, ask the speaker whether he or she means to say that *all* or *every* situation or person fits the generalization presented.
Static evaluation: Labeling people, objects, or events without considering change	You still call your twenty-eight-year-old nephew a "juvenile delinquent" because he spray-painted your fence when he was eleven.	• When speaking, place your observation in a time frame: "I thought he was a difficult child when he was in elementary school." • When listening, ask the speaker whether the observation remains true today or if the same generalization applies now.
Polarization: Use of either/or terms (good or bad, right or wrong)	"You're either for me or against me."	• When speaking, avoid either/or terms and blaming something on a specific cause. • When listening, ask the speaker whether a statement really reflects an all-or-nothing, either/or proposition.
Biased language: Use of language that reflects gender, racial, ethnic, age, ability, or class bias	"His mom is a mailman."	• When speaking, be mindful of how insensitive language can hurt someone. Avoid using labels or derogatory terms. • When listening, try to keep your emotions in check when others use inappropriate words or derogatory phrases. You can't control what others do or say, only what *you* do and say and how *you* react. Consider appropriately but assertively communicating that a word, label, or phrase offends you.

UNDERSTANDING OTHERS
Adapting to Differences

Do Men and Women Speak the Same Language?

In Chapter 4 we noted that gender makes a difference in how we interact with others. John Gray's popular self-help book *Men Are from Mars, Women Are from Venus*[38] has been heralded by some as "the book that saved our relationship," yet other communication scholars have concluded that Gray has overstated his case in claiming that there are vast differences in the ways men and women speak to each other.[39] The thing to keep in mind is that although there are differences, the differences are not so vast that they cannot be bridged. Men and women do indeed speak the same language, but they may have different assumptions about the function of talk in the development of relationships.

Julia Wood is a communication researcher who has criticized John Gray for oversimplifying the differences in how men and women talk to one another. She acknowledges that women tend to use talk to establish and maintain relationships more so than men. In reviewing the literature on women's speech, Wood found the following characteristics of the way women interact with others:[40]

- Women tend to seek to establish equality between themselves and others by using such phrases as "I know just how you feel" or "Yes, the same thing has happened to me."

- Women are more likely to show emotional support for others using statements such as "How wonderful" or "Oh, that sounds very frustrating. You must feel tired."

- Women often spend time conducting conversational "maintenance work," by, for example, trying to keep the conversation from lagging by asking open-ended questions that prompt a more detailed response.

- Women not only tend to work at keeping conversations going, they are more likely to be inclusive—to make sure everyone present is invited to talk.

- Women also have been found to be more tentative in the way they use language. They may use more qualifiers and hedges when they talk, saying things like "*I thought* it was kind of boring" (rather than just saying "It was boring"). Tentativeness is also expressed by ending a phrase with a question—called a tag question—such as "That was a good class, wasn't it?" or "She was a good speaker, wasn't she?"

In contrast, men tend to use their verbal messages for "proving oneself and negotiating prestige."[41] Rather than talking about a relationship, men are more likely to engage in mutual activities to communicate friendship, such as going to a movie together or participating in sports or other activities of mutual interest. Wood's literature review suggests:[42]

- Men are less likely to present information that indicates their vulnerabilities. Men talk to establish their power, status, and worth.

- Men also talk to accomplish tasks rather than to express feelings—they are more instrumental in the way they use language. Men talk to seek information, share information, and solve problems.

- Men tend to use speech to sustain and even dominate a conversation; there is evidence that they interrupt others more than women do.

- Men are, according to research, more assertive and less tentative when talking with others.

- Men speak in more general, abstract ways and often are less concrete and specific when describing situations and events.

- Men tend to provide fewer responsive cues such as "I'm listening," "yes," "uh-hum," and "I'm with you."

Yet, despite differences, researchers have also found much similarity, which is why many communication researchers and educators suggest that it's not help-ful to compare and contrast the way men and women speak as if they were from separate planets. For example, one research study suggests that it's not true that women talk more than men; both men and women use about the same number of words during a typical day of conversation.[43] Communication researcher Anthony Mulac has concluded that although there are some differences between the speech of men and women, the differences are not significant enough to explain why conflicts may occur. Mulac found that when reading written transcripts of conversations, it was difficult for readers to identify whether the speakers were men or women.[44] The differences that emerge from research on the way men and women talk may reveal less about the actual words used and more about the underlying function or assumptions behind the words. Women may pay more attention to the nature of the relationship and men may emphasize the tasks that are to be accomplished. Misunderstandings and misinterpretations may occur because of these underlying assumptions about the function of talk that we harbor as we speak and listen.

Deborah Tannen suggests that differences between men and women can be described as cultural differences.[45] As a linguist, she has focused on how the ways men and women talk to one another shape the cultural differences between them. The strategies for bridging cultural differences that we discussed in Chapter 4 can be useful in enhancing the quality of communication between men and women: Being mindful of different communication assumptions, tolerating some uncertainty and ambiguity in communication, asking questions, seeking more information before reacting (or overreacting) to messages, being other-oriented, and adapting communication messages are strategies that can enhance communication quality between the sexes.

Similarly, the way someone describes people with disabilities can negatively affect how they may be perceived. A study by researcher John Seiter and his colleagues found that when people with a disability were called demeaning or disparaging names, they were perceived as less trustworthy, competent, persuasive, and sociable than when the same people were described in more positive or heroic terms.[46] At the end of their study, the authors note, "Communicators who want to be effective should avoid using derogatory language." Guard against calling attention to someone as a "cripple," "dim-witted," or "mental"; these terms are offensive. As communication researcher Dawn Braithwaite notes, one preferred term is "people with disabilities."[47]

Also monitor the way you talk about someone's social class. Although some societies and cultures make considerable distinctions among classes, it is nonetheless offensive today to use words that are intended to demean someone's social class. Terms such as "welfare recipient," "manual laborer," and "blue-collar worker" are often used derogatorily. Avoid labeling someone in a way that shows disrespect toward the person's social standing, education, or socioeconomic status.

Words of Support

"I'm going to win this argument."

"You're wrong and I'm right. It's as simple as that."

"You're going to do it my way or else!"

None of these statements is likely to result in a positive communication climate. All three are likely to lead to debate rather than true dialogue. The words you hear and use are central to your establishing a quality or positive relationship with others. Author and researcher Daniel Yankelovich suggests that the goal of conversations with others should be to establish a genuine dialogue rather than to verbally arm-wrestle a partner in order to win the argument.[48] True dialogue requires establishing a climate of equality, listening with empathy, and trying to bring underlying assumptions into the open. Expressing equality, empathy, and openness is more likely to occur if you approach conversations as dialogue rather than debate. As shown in Table 6.1, in true dialogue people look for common ground rather than using a war of words to defend a position.

TABLE 6.1 **Debate and Dialogue Compared**

Debate	Dialogue
There is one right answer, and you assume that you have it.	Many people have pieces of the answer; together, you can find the best solution.
The goal is to win.	The goal is to seek common ground and agreement.
The focus is on combat; you try to prove that you are right and the other person is wrong.	The focus is on collaboration and seeking common understanding.
You search for weaknesses and errors in others' positions.	You search for strengths and value the truth in what others say.
You defend your views.	You use the contributions of others to improve your thinking.

Source: Adapted from Daniel Yankelovich, *The Magic of Dialogue: Transforming Conflict into Cooperation* (New York: Simon & Schuster, 1999), 39–40. Reprinted with the permission of Simon & Schuster Adult Publishing Group.

For more than three decades, Jack Gibb's observational research has been used as a framework for describing verbal behaviors that contribute to feeling either supported or defensive. His research, one of the most cited studies in communication textbooks in the past half century, is so popular because he's identified practical strategies for developing supportive relationships with others—dialogue rather than debate—through the way we talk to each other.[49] Gibb spent several years listening to and observing groups of people in meetings and conversations, noting that some exchanges seem to create a supportive climate, whereas others create a defensive one. Words and actions, he concluded, are tools we use to let someone know whether we support them or not. And an emotional response in one person is likely to trigger an emotional response in another.[50] Now let's consider how you can use words to create a supportive climate rather than an antagonistic or defensive one.

Describe Your Own Feelings, Rather Than Evaluate the Behavior of Others

Most people don't like to be judged or evaluated. Criticizing and name calling obviously can create relational problems, but so can attempts to diagnose others' problems or win their affection with insincere praise. In fact, any form of evaluation creates a climate of defensiveness. As British statesman Winston Churchill declared, "I am always ready to learn, although I do not always like being taught." Correcting others, even when we are doing it "for their own good," can raise their hackles.

One way to avoid evaluating others is to eliminate the accusatory "you" from your language. Statements such as "You always come in late for supper" or "You never pick up the dirty clothes in your room" attack a person's sense of self-worth and usually result in a defensive reaction.

Instead, use the word "I" to describe your own feelings and thoughts about a situation or event:[51] "I find it hard to keep your supper warm when you're late," or "I don't enjoy the extra work of picking up your dirty clothes." When you describe your own feelings instead of berating the receiver of the message, you are, in essence, taking ownership of the problem. This approach leads to greater openness and trust because your listener is less likely to feel rejected or as if you were trying to control him or her. Also, when you express your emotions, make sure you choose the right words to communicate your feelings.

Although we've discussed the importance of using "I" messages, interpersonal communication researchers Amy Bippus and Stacy Young found that simply prefacing an emotionally charged piece of feedback with the word "I" instead of "you" doesn't always melt away relational tension.[52] These researchers had subjects in their research read hypothetical examples in which people used either "I" messages or "you" messages. The researchers found no significant difference in how people thought others would respond to the messages. In other words, an "I" message was not found to be better than a "you" message in all instances. (Of course, the fact that the subjects were reading a message rather than actually involved in their own conversation with a partner may have affected the results.) The researchers concluded that regardless of whether a message is prefaced with "I" or "you," people don't like hearing negative expressions of emotion directed toward them.

A climate of defensiveness left unchecked can escalate into interpersonal conflict. Using descriptive "I" language rather than evaluative "you" language can help you manage tension and disagreement.

Building Your Skills	Practice Using "I" Language and Extended "I" Language

An essential skill in being supportive rather than creating defensiveness is describing what you want with "I" language or extended "I" language rather than "you" language. Rephrase the following "you" statements as "I" statements and extended "I" statements.

"You" Language	"I" Language	Extended "I" Language
You are messy when you cook.		
Your driving is terrible.		
You never listen to me.		
You just lie on the couch and never offer to help me.		
You always decide what we watch on TV.		

Sometimes simply using an "I" message may be too subtle to take the sting out of the negative message you want to express. You may need to add a longer justification when you provide negative, emotional information to another. We call this using **extended "I" language,** which is a brief preface to a feedback statement, intended to communicate that you don't want the person to think that you don't value or care about him or her even though you have a negative message to share. Saying something like, "I don't want you to misinterpret what I'm about to say, because I really do care about you," or "I don't think it's entirely your fault, but I'm feeling frustrated when I experience . . ." may have a better chance of enhancing communication than simply beginning a sentence with the word "I" instead of "You." Remember, *there are no magic words for enhancing communication.* However, strategies of being other-oriented do seem to enhance the quality of communication. Building Your Skills: Practice Using "I" Language and Extended "I" Language will help you practice expressing your feelings accurately and effectively.

Solve Problems Rather Than Try to Control Others

Most of us don't like others' attempts to control us. Someone who presumes to tell us what's good for us, instead of helping us puzzle through issues and problems, is likely to engender defensiveness. Open-ended questions, such as "What seems to be the problem?" or "How can we deal with the issue?" create a more supportive climate than critical comments, such as "Here's where you are wrong" or commands such as "Don't do that!"

Be Genuine Rather Than Manipulative

To be genuine means that you honestly seek to be yourself rather than someone you are not. It also means taking an honest interest in others and considering the uniqueness of

extended "I" language Brief preface to a feedback statement, intended to communicate that you don't want your listener to take your message in an overly critical way.

Communication and Emotion

Expressing Your Emotions to Others

Communication is enhanced if you can clearly express the emotions you are feeling using well-chosen words or phrases. The following list gives you several options for expressing your feelings in positive, neutral, or negative terms. Categorizing these terms as positive, neutral, or negative doesn't mean that you should only use positive or neutral terms and avoid negative terms. What's important is that you select a word that accurately helps you communicate your emotions to others.

Positive		Neutral	Negative	
calm	hopeful	amazed	afraid	helpless
cheerful	interested	ambivalent	alone	horrible
comfortable	joyful	apathetic	angry	humiliated
confident	loving	bashful	annoyed	hysterical
content	optimistic	bored	bitter	intimidated
delighted	passionate	detached	confused	listless
ecstatic	peaceful	hurried	defeated	mad
elated	playful	lukewarm	defensive	mean
enthusiastic	pleased	numb	depressed	miserable
excited	refreshed	possessive	devastated	paranoid
flattered	romantic	sentimental	disappointed	rebellious
free	sexy	vulnerable	disgusted	regretful
friendly	tender		disturbed	resentful
glad	warm		empty	restless
grateful	willing		exhausted	sad
happy	wonderful		fearful	shocked
high			frustrated	suspicious
			furious	terrified
			guilty	ugly

each individual and situation, avoiding generalizations or strategies that focus only on your own needs and desires. A manipulative person has hidden agendas; a genuine person discusses issues and problems openly and honestly.

Carl Rogers, the founder of person-centered counseling, suggests that true understanding and dialogue occur when people adopt a genuine or honest positive regard for others.[53] If your goal is to look out only for your own interests, your language will reflect your self-focus. At the heart of being genuine is being other-oriented—being sincerely interested in those with whom you communicate. Although it's unrealistic to assume you will become best friends with everyone you meet, Rogers suggests that you can work to develop an unselfish interest, or what he called an unconditional positive regard for others. That's hard to do. But the effort will be rewarded with a more positive communication climate.

Empathize Rather Than Remain Detached from Others

Empathy is one of the hallmarks of supportive relationships. As you learned earlier, empathy is the ability to understand the feelings of others and to predict the emotional responses they will have to different situations. Being empathic is the essence of being other-oriented. The opposite of empathy is neutrality. To be neutral is to be

To practice expressing your emotions, imagine yourself in each of the following situations, and use some of the words listed here to write a response for each situation. Describe your response using either a single word or a short phrase, such as "I feel angry," or express your feelings in terms of what you'd like to do, such as "I'd be so embarrassed I would sink through the floor" or "I would feel like leaving and never coming back to this house."

- You have several thousand dollars charged to your credit cards, and you get fired from your job.
- Your best friend, with whom you spend a lot of time, is moving to another country.
- You have just learned that your adored aunt has died and left you a $35,000 inheritance.
- Even though you do your best to keep your room clean, your roommate is complaining again that you are a slob.
- You have brought your two-year-old son to a worship service, but he talks and runs around during the service and will not sit still. Other worshippers are looking at you with disapproval.
- You arrive at your vacation hotel only to discover that they do not have a reservation for you, and you do not have your room confirmation number.

Another skill to help you accurately and appropriately express your emotions is to use a word picture. A **word picture** is a short statement or story that dramatizes an emotion you have experienced. Using a visual image can add extra power to an expression of your feelings when a simple descriptive word may not suffice. Word pictures can be used to clarify how you feel, to offer praise or correction, and to create greater intimacy. A key goal of a word picture is to communicate your feelings and emotions. An effective way to express your emotions through a word picture is to use a simile. A simile, as you may remember from your English class, is a comparison that uses the word *like* or *as* to clarify the image you want to communicate. "When you forgot my birthday, I felt like crumbs swept from the table," exclaimed Marge to her forgetful husband. Or, after a hard day's work, Jeff told his family, "I feel like a worn-out punching bag—I've been pounded time and time again, and now I feel torn and scuffed. I need a few minutes of peace and quiet before I join in the family conversation." His visual image helped communicate how exhausted he really felt. The best word pictures use an image to which the listener can relate. To practice your skill, try to develop word pictures to express in a powerful and memorable way the feelings you might have in the following situations.

- You have just learned that a cherished family pet has died.
- You want to tell your friends how happy you are when you learn you received an A in a difficult course.
- You've asked your sister not to leave empty milk cartons in the refrigerator, but you discover another empty carton in the fridge.
- Your family is planning a vacation but didn't ask you to be involved in the planning.

indifferent or apathetic toward another. Even when you express anger or irritation toward another, you are investing some energy in the relationship.

Research suggests that one of the most important things we can do to be empathic and supportive is simply what we have been suggesting throughout this book: Be other-oriented. Interpersonal communication researcher Amy Bippus determined that what most people want from others during times of stress are messages of empathy and sensitivity to their feelings, followed by problem solving, relating, refraining from general negativity, and offering a different perspective. The positive interpersonal outcomes that resulted from providing other-oriented messages were a more upbeat mood, feelings of empowerment, and more focused, calmer thoughts.[54]

Be Flexible Rather Than Rigid Toward Others

Most people don't like someone who always seems certain that he or she is right. A "you're wrong, I'm right" attitude creates a defensive climate. This does not mean that you should have no opinions and go through life blithely agreeing to everything anyone else says. And it doesn't mean that there is *never* one answer that is right and others that are wrong. But instead of making rigid pronouncements, you can use phrases such as "I may be wrong, but it seems to me . . ." or "Here's one way to look at this problem." This manner of speaking gives your opinions a softer edge that allows room for others to express a point of view.

BEING **Other**-ORIENTED

Developing empathy is a quintessential skill of being other-oriented. Yet, if you empathize and then feel smug or self-righteous about being empathic, your efforts to relate to another person may appear manipulative. How can you empathize with another person without focusing on yourself or appearing self-serving?

word picture Short statement or story that illustrates or describes an emotion; word pictures often use a simile (a comparison using the word *like* or *as*) to clarify the image.

Present Yourself as Equal Rather Than Superior

You can antagonize others by letting them know that you view yourself as better than they are. You may be gifted and intelligent, but it's not necessary to announce it. And although some people have the responsibility and authority to manage others, "pulling rank" does not usually produce a cooperative climate. With phrases such as "Let's work on this together" or "We each have a valid perspective," you can avoid erecting walls of resentment and suspicion.

Also, avoid using abstract language or professional jargon to impress others. Keep your messages short and clear, and use informal language. When you communicate with someone from another culture, you may need to use an **elaborated code** to get your message across. This means that your messages will have to be more explicit, but they should not be condescending. For example, two of this book's authors vividly remember trying to explain to a French exchange student what a fire ant was. First, we had to translate *ant* into French, and then we had to provide scientific, descriptive, and narrative evidence to help the student understand how these tiny biting insects terrorize people in the southern part of the United States.

Underlying the goal of creating a supportive rather than a defensive communication climate is the importance of providing social and emotional support when communicating with others. A basic principle of all healthy interpersonal relationships is the importance of communicating positive, supportive messages that impart liking or affection.[55] Several researchers have documented that providing verbal messages of comfort and support, not surprisingly, enhances the quality of a relationship.[56] As a relationship develops over time and the communication partners gain more credibility and influence, messages of comfort play an even more important role in maintaining the quality of the interpersonal relationship.[57] We use not only words of comfort but, as you will learn in Chapter 7, nonverbal expressions of comfort as well.[58]

Communication researchers have documented the power of humor in helping to turn a tense, potentially conflict-producing confrontation into a more supportive, positive conversation. Research by communication scholar Amy Bippus found that most people report using humor as a way of providing comfort to others.[59] Humor also was perceived as a productive way to help a distressed person better cope with problems and stress.

elaborated code Conversation that uses many words and various ways of describing an idea or concept to communicate its meaning.

▶ RECAP   Using Supportive Communication and Avoiding Defensive Communication

Supportive Communication Is . . .

Descriptive: Use "I" language that describes your own feelings and ideas.

Problem Oriented: Aim communication at solving problems and generating multiple options.

Spontaneously Genuine: Be honest and authentic rather than fake and phony.

Empathic: Be emotionally involved in the conversation; attempt to understand what your partner is thinking and feeling.

Flexible: Be open to receive new information; demonstrate flexibility in the positions you take.

Equal: Adopt a communication style based on mutual respect, and assume each person has a right to express ideas and share information.

Defensive Communication Is . . .

Evaluative: Avoid using "you" language that attacks the worth of another person.

Controlling: Don't attempt to get others to do *only* what you want them to do in order to control the outcome.

Strategically Manipulative: Avoid planning your conversation in advance to get what you want. Don't develop a script to manipulate the other person and accomplish your goal.

Neutrally Detached: Avoid being emotionally indifferent or creating the impression that you don't care how another person is feeling.

Certain and Rigid: Don't take a dogmatic or rigid position on issues; be willing to listen to others.

Superior: Avoid assuming an attitude or mindset that your ideas are better than those of others.

Words of Apology: When You've Not Been Other-Oriented

In this chapter, we've talked about the power of words and how communication sometimes can create problems and bruise a relationship. There are times, if we're honest with ourselves, that we aren't as other-oriented as we should be, and we may say and do things that we shouldn't. We're human; we make mistakes. Words, however, not only inflict pain but also have power to repair relational damage.

One of the ways to mend a relational rift when we have made a mistake is to offer an **apology**—to explicitly admit that we made an error and to ask the person we offended to forgive us. An apology helps us save face and can repair relational stress. One research team found that people who received an apology felt less anger, were less likely to be aggressive, and had a better overall impression of the offender.[60] In addition, research has found that when we apologize to someone, the person we initially offended has greater empathy toward us and is less likely to avoid us or seek revenge.[61] An apology can calm a turbulent relationship.

Communication researchers Janet Meyer and Kyra Rothenberg found that the seriousness of the offense and the quality of the relationship we have with another person determine whether we are likely to apologize and the kind of apology we should offer.[62] Committing a serious blunder or error is more likely to result in an apology than committing a mild offense—especially if we believe we've hurt someone. We're also more likely to apologize to someone if we feel guilty or embarrassed by something we've said or done.[63] And the more intimate we are with someone, the more likely we are to apologize.[64]

apology Explicit admission of an error, along with a request for forgiveness.

Building Your Skills

How to Assert Yourself If You Are Sexually Harassed

What Is Sexual Harassment?

Any unwelcome sexual advances, requests for sexual favors, or other inappropriate verbal or physical behavior of a sexual nature may be classified as sexual harassment. Examples include

- Repeated and unwanted requests for dates, sexual flirtation, or propositions of a sexual nature
- Unwanted sexual remarks or questions about a person's clothing, body, or sexual activity
- Unnecessary touching, patting, hugging, or brushing against a person's body
- Direct or implied threats that failure to submit to sexual advances will affect employment, work status, grades, letters of recommendation, or residential choice
- Physical assault
- A pattern of conduct that causes humiliation or discomfort, such as inappropriate terms of greeting; sexually explicit or sexist comments, questions, or jokes; or leering at a person's body

What to Do If You Are Sexually Harassed

- Be direct and candid with the person.
- Use "I" messages (for example, "I don't like those kinds of jokes made about me").
- Avoid being overly dramatic; remain confident that the incident will be dealt with.
- If the incident happens at school or work, use the institution's or organization's grievance procedure.
- Report the harasser to your supervisor, department chair, or dean.
- If the harasser is your supervisor or an administrative official, report the incident to his or her supervisor.
- Report the harassment immediately after it occurs. The longer you wait, the less credible your story will be.
- When the harassment occurs, write down important facts.
- Report the incident as if you were a journalist: Give the who, what, when, where, and how; keep to the facts.
- Be prepared to give the interviewer names of witnesses.
- Put aside your anger and embarrassment and be thorough when telling the story.

Source: Information adapted from Texas State University policy and procedure statement on sexual harassment and Vicki West, "Sexual Harassment: Identify, Stop, and Prevent" seminar.

An apology can help you save face when you have made a relationship blunder and can relieve tension between you and another person.

What kind of apologies are most effective? One of the most effective ways to apologize is simply to honestly and sincerely admit that you were wrong. It's not enough just to say, "I'm sorry I hurt you." A true apology acknowledges that the offending individual was wrong. Thus, it's better to say it explicitly: "I was wrong." Assuming responsibility for the error and offering to do something to repair the damage are specific kinds of behaviors that enhance the effectiveness of an apology. Researchers Cynthia McPherson Frantz and Courtney Bennigson found that it may not be best to apologize immediately after you make a mistake; their results indicated that it may be better to wait a short time before apologizing.[65] Your apology will be perceived as more sincere and heartfelt if the other person believes you truly understand how your mistake hurt him or her and that you want to repair the damage. An apology given too quickly may be perceived as insincere—the offended person may think that you're just trying to quickly dismiss the error. Being perceived as sincerely remorseful is one of the keys to an effective apology.

The words we use can hurt others. We can also use words to repair the damage we have done by offering an apology expressing that we were wrong (not simply sorry), we are sincerely remorseful, we want to do something to repair the damage, we understand how much we may have hurt our communication partner. The book of Proverbs says, "Words fitly spoken are like apples of gold in pictures of silver." A well-worded apology can help restore luster to a relationship that may have become tarnished.

Words of Assertion

At times, you run across people who are verbally aggressive, obnoxious, or worse—they may try to coerce or intimidate you into doing things you'd rather not do. Should the other-oriented person just politely accept obnoxious verbal assaults? No—

being other-oriented doesn't mean you should ignore such boorish behavior. Nor do you have to respond in the same way you were treated. Rather than return mean-spirited aggressiveness with an equally inappropriate stream of aggressive words or rude behavior, consider using your verbal skills to be appropriately assertive. To be **assertive** is to make requests, ask for information, stand up for your rights, and generally pursue your own best interests without denying your partner's rights.

Each individual has rights. You have the right to refuse a request someone makes of you, the right to express your feelings as long as you don't trample on the feelings of others, and the right to have your needs met if this doesn't infringe on the rights of others. Assertive people let their communication partners know when a message or behavior is infringing on their rights.

Some people confuse the terms *assertive* and *aggressive*. Being **aggressive** means pursuing your interests by denying the rights of others. Being appropriately assertive is being other-oriented; aggressiveness is exclusively self-oriented. Aggressive people blame, judge, and evaluate to get what they want. We'll expand on our discussion of aggressive behavior when we discuss relationship challenges in Chapter 11. Aggressive communicators use communication tactics that contribute to defensiveness, including such intimidating nonverbal cues as steely stares, a bombastic voice, and flailing gestures. Assertive people can ask for what they want without judging or evaluating their partners.

assertive Able to pursue one's own best interests without denying a partner's rights.

aggressive Expressing one's interests while denying the rights of others by blaming, judging, and evaluating other people.

Relating to Others in the 21st Century

Using Words to Relate to Others Online

Increasingly people are relying on electronically mediated communication to "talk" to each other. In the early part of the twenty-first century, over four-fifths of students and staff at the University of Texas had Facebook accounts. At the University of Michigan the estimate was over 90 percent. We increasingly express ourselves online.[66] It's likely that you texted one or more of your friends today rather than talking to them in person.

Not only do we connect online, but it's important to us to do so. In response to the statement "I feel addicted to Facebook," over one-third of the over 2,850 students who responded to a survey indicated that they "agreed" or "strongly agreed." One survey respondent wrote "Facebook, I hate you!" in acknowledging the pervasive power it had over her life.[67]

Will the fact that we are using the written word in place of the spoken word to connect to others change the very nature of interpersonal relationships? In speculating about how our reliance on EMC will affect the way we use language and relate to others in the future, linguist Naomi Baron suggests the following

consequences of our increased reliance on the written word:

- Informality: We will write more informally as we write more. What we write to one another will continue to take the place of spoken messages, so our written messages will more closely resemble spoken messages.

- Language Use: We will become increasingly uncertain about how we use words, so we'll make up our own rules and not worry about precise language rules or usage in our informal text messages. As we tap out a quick text message, we may not be as careful or thoughtful about, for example, whether we hyphenate words or how we spell and use punctuation.

- Writing Influences Talking: The way we communicate in EMC contexts will influence how we communicate face to face. We'll use more abbreviations.

- Word Control: We will have more control over the messages we receive. Because we can often see who's texting, calling, or e-mailing us, we'll decide when, where, and even if we will receive messages. We will have what Baron calls greater "volume control"

about the number of EMC words that reach us.

- Written Culture: We will increasingly become a "written culture" because of the power and importance of texting, using instant messaging, and other ways of sharing written words.

- More Relationships in Less Depth. We'll know more people but also know less information about them. In an editorial in *The New York Times,* columnist Robert Wright noted, "Twenty years ago I rarely spoke by phone to more than five people in a day. Now I often send e-mail to dozens of people a day. I have so many friends! Um, can you remind me of their names? . . ."[68] We know more people more shallowly.

- Moment-to-Moment Contact: Because we can be in touch with others in real time with our cell phones, text messages, and a variety of other tools, we will be able to experience what others are experiencing in real time. As Baron put it, "When we are always on, we have the ability to live in other people's moments. Relationships can be maintained through running discourse rather than reflective synopsis. Absence may or may not make the heart grow fonder. . . ."[69]

RECAP Assertiveness versus Aggressiveness

Assertiveness . . .	Aggressiveness . . .
Expresses your interests without denying the rights of others.	Expresses your interests and denies the rights of others.
Is other-oriented.	Is self-oriented.
Describes what you want.	Evaluates the other person.
Discloses your needs using "I" messages.	Discloses your needs using "you" messages.

When presenting the dos and don'ts of appropriate verbal communication in this chapter, we've often emphasized strategies for initiating communication with others. Sometimes what's most challenging is to respond appropriately when another person (someone who has not taken a course in interpersonal communication) comes at you with an inappropriately aggressive, argumentative, or defensive message, especially if the inappropriate message that's hurled at you takes you by surprise. You do not have to be passive when you are on the receiving end of such messages. We suggest instead that an effective communicator is appropriately assertive.

Behaving Assertively: Five Steps

Many people have a tendency to withdraw in the face of controversy, even when their rights are being violated or denied. But you can develop skill in asserting yourself by practicing five key behaviors.[70]

Describe. *Describe how you view the situation.* To assert your position, you first need to describe how you view the situation. You need to be assertive because the other person has not been other-oriented. For example, Doug is growing increasingly frustrated with Maria's tardiness for weekly staff meetings. He approaches the problem by first describing his observation: "I have noticed that you are usually fifteen minutes late to our weekly staff meetings." A key to communicating your assertive message is to monitor your nonverbal message, especially your voice. Avoid sarcasm or excessive vocal intensity. Calmly yet confidently describe the problem.

Disclose. *Disclose your feelings.* After describing the situation from your perspective, let the other person know how you feel.[71] Disclosing your feelings will help to build empathy and avoid lengthy harangues about the other person's unjust treatment. "I feel you don't take our weekly meetings seriously," continues Doug as he asserts his desire for Maria to be on time to the meeting. Note that Doug does not talk about how others are feeling ("Every member of our group is tired of your coming in late"); he describes how *he* feels.

Identify Effects. *Identify the effects of the behavior.* Next, you can identify the effects of the other person's behavior on you or others. "When you are late, it disrupts our meeting," says Doug.

Be Silent. *Be silent and wait.* After taking the first three steps, simply wait for a response. Some people find this step hard. Again, be sure to monitor your nonverbal cues. Make sure your facial expression does not contradict your verbal message. Delivering an assertive message with a broad grin might create a double bind for your listener, who may not be sure what the primary message is—the verbal one or the nonverbal one.

Paraphrase. *Paraphrase content and feelings.* After the other person responds, paraphrase both the content and the feelings of the message. Suppose Maria says, "Oh, I'm sorry. I didn't realize I was creating a problem. I have another meeting that usually goes overtime. It's difficult for me to arrive at the start of our meeting on time." Doug could respond, "So the key problem is a time conflict with another meeting. It must make you feel frustrated to try to do two things at once."

If the other person is evasive, unresponsive, or aggressive, you'll need to cycle through the steps again: Clearly describe what the other person is doing that is not acceptable; disclose how you feel; identify the effects; wait; then paraphrase and clarify as needed. A key goal of making an assertive response is to seek an empathic connection between you and your partner. Paraphrasing feelings is a way of ensuring that both parties are connecting.

If you tend to withdraw from conflict, how can you become assertive? Visualizing can help. Think of a past situation in which you wished you had been more assertive and then mentally replay the situation, imagining what you might have said. Also practice verbalizing assertive statements. When you are able to be appropriately assertive, consciously congratulate yourself for sticking up for your rights.

▶ RECAP How to Assert Yourself

Step	Example
1. Describe.	"I see you haven't completed the report yet."
2. Disclose.	"I feel that the work I ask you to do is not a priority for you."
3. Identify effects.	"Without that report, our team will not achieve our goal."
4. Wait.	Be silent, and wait for a response.
5. Use active listening skills:	
Question.	"Do you understand how I feel?"
Paraphrase content.	"So you were not aware the report was late."
Paraphrase feelings.	"Perhaps you feel embarrassed."

APPLYING AN OTHER-ORIENTATION
to Enhancing Your Verbal Skills

The key to shared understanding is a focus on the needs, goals, and mindset of your communication partner. Throughout this chapter, we have emphasized how to develop an other-oriented approach when communicating verbally. In focusing on others, keep the following principles in mind.

Meanings Are in People, Not in Words. Your communication partner creates meaning based on his or her own experiences. Don't assume that other people will always (or even usually) understand what you mean. Words are symbols and the potential for misunderstanding them is high. Meaning is fragile, so handle with care.

Words Have Power to Influence Others. Words have power to determine how people view the world. They also affect thoughts and behaviors. Be mindful of the potency of words for influencing how others react. Words can trigger wars and negotiate peace; they affect how others react to us.

Speak to Others as They Would Like to Be Spoken To. It's not enough to consider how you would react to words and phrases you use; you need to be tuned in to the kinds of messages another person might prefer. You may like "straight talk" and messages that are short and to the point. Your communication partner may prefer a softer tone and a more positive, supportive message than you need.

We're not suggesting that you should be a verbal chameleon and avoid asserting your own ideas and positions. We are suggesting that if you want to be heard and understood, thinking how others will interpret your message can enhance the communication process.

How Words Work
(pages 153–157)

Words are powerful, and they affect emotions, thoughts, and actions. Your ability to use words effectively contributes to the success of your interpersonal relationships and your overall communication competence. Culture, gender, and life experiences also influence words and their meanings. Words are symbols that represent something else—an object, sound, concept, or experience—but the exact meaning of a word originates in the mind of the sender and the receiver. Words can be arbitrary, but they create meaning on two levels: the denotative, or literal, meaning, and the connotative, or more personal and subjective, meaning.

Key Terms

Symbol *153*	Connotative meaning *154*
Referent *153*	Onomatopoeia *156*
Thought *153*	Symbolic interaction theory *157*
Denotative meaning *154*	

Critical Thinking Questions

1. How is language symbolic? How does the arbitrary nature of language and the naming of objects or experiences lead to misunderstandings?

2. How has culture affected your language? Do you use words that seem confusing to others? Have you been in a situation in which someone used a familiar word but with a different meaning than you were accustomed to? How did you resolve the misunderstanding?

Activities

Make a list of from ten to fifteen familiar, everyday words (such as *home*, or *online communication*) and write their denotative and connotative meanings. Working in small groups, share your words with classmates and ask them to write down what the words mean to them. (Have them do the same with their own list of words.) Compare the connotative meanings. Are there differences in what a word means to different people? Is there a wide range of meanings? Can these differences be attributed to culture, gender, or differences in background and past experiences?

Web Resources

http://www.cwebopaedia.com Uncertain about the meaning of a word that you find on the Internet? Look it up on the "Webopaedia." This site will help you interpret words that you don't understand.

http://linguistlist.org/ask-ling/index.html is a service provided by The Linguist List, an Internet network for professional linguists. This site is designed to allow anyone interested in language or linguistics to ask a question and get a response from a panel of professional linguists.

The Power of Words
(pages 157–162)

Words have power. They have enormous influence on our thoughts and actions. They also create perceptions by giving us tools to name and label what we experience, including moods and emotions. Language also affects and reflects our culture, influencing how we describe our world and in turn, how that worldview continuously shapes our culture. Words also have the power to make or break interpersonal relationships, helping us to establish and maintain relationships, manage conflict, and relate to others.

Key Terms

Linguistic determinism *160*	Worldview *160*
Linguistic relativity *160*	Profanity *161*
Sapir–Whorf hypothesis *160*	Euphemism *162*

Critical Thinking Questions

1. Ethics: Do you think the use of profanity in everyday life is increasing? Have new communication technologies, including texting, blogging, IMing, and the like, contributed to this increase? Do mass media contribute to the increase? Can you think of examples? Do you think the media have relaxed their standards for allowing profanity? Explain.

2. Ethics: Make a list of euphemisms used in everyday speech as well as by politicians and other public figures. (Consider, for example, explanations of the Iraq war, discussions of recent elections, and terms used to describe the recession and economic solutions.) Is the use of these words and expressions appropriate? Do they deliberately mislead? Do they diminish the significance of a difficult situation such as economic woes (e.g., *downsizing*) or war?

Activities

Collect print ads that feature catchy slogans or phrases. Make a list of other mass media ads (TV, radio, Internet, billboards, etc.) whose words or phrases grab your attention. Share the ads with your classmates and analyze as a group what makes the words or phrases powerful or memorable. Do the words influence your actions—for example, persuading you to do something or to buy a particular product? Explain.

Web Resources

http:///www.pitt.edu~uclid/tips.htm At this site you'll learn tips about language and examples of good and bad uses of language. You'll be reminded that language reflects, reinforces, and shapes our perceptions of others.

Word Barriers
(pages 162–171)

Words have the power to create misunderstandings as well as deep connections. Potential pitfalls such as the inaccurate use of words, lack of precision, or different meanings ascribed to a word can hinder the understanding of messages. Other language barriers can be created by overgeneralizing, polarization, using biased and sexist language, including hate speech, or using demeaning language.

Key Terms

Bypassing *162*

Malapropism *163*

Restricted code *164*

Jargon *164*

Allness *164*

Indexing *165*

Static evaluation *165*

Polarization *165*

Hate speech *166*

Critical Thinking Questions

1. Rephrase the following statements, using the skill of indexing:
   a. All politicians want power and control over others.
   b. All teachers are underpaid.
   c. All Texans like to brag about how great their state is.

2. Ethics: Is it ethical to correct someone when he or she uses sexist language or makes a stereotyping remark about someone's race, gender, or sexual orientation? What if that person is your boss or your teacher? Explain your answer.

Activities

In small groups, brainstorm lists of "restricted code" words and/or jargon, including "textspeak" (abbreviations used in IMing and texting). Come up with as many words as you can. Share the lists that each group creates. Are the lists similar? Did classmates introduce you to words you hadn't known before? Do the "restricted codes" seem to suggest a particular group or culture? What do people in these subgroups have in common— for example, age, gender, ethnicity?

Words of Support and Words of Assertion
(pages 171–181)

The words you hear and use can ultimately enhance or detract from the quality of the relationships you establish with others. Conversation should be a genuine dialogue that includes expressions of equality, empathy, and openness. You can further create a supportive communication climate by using extended "I" language, being a problem solver, and being flexible and genuine rather than manipulative in the positions you take. Being able to offer an apology is another crucial skill for developing and maintaining relationships and a positive communication climate. Being a competent, other-oriented communicator involves being assertive without becoming aggressive and following five steps: describe, disclose, identify effects, silently wait, and paraphrase.

Key Terms

Extended "I" language *173*

Word picture *174*

Elaborated code *176*

Apology *177*

Assertive *179*

Aggressive *179*

Critical Thinking Questions

1. What is your reaction to the information presented in the Relating to Others in the 21st Century feature? Do you find yourself texting, IMing, or communicating online more often than face to face these days? Do you feel that you have more friends because you use electronically mediated communication? Are your relationships with these "friends" richer or more shallow than your face-to-face relationships? Explain.

2. Ethics: Is it ethical to mask your true feelings of anger and irritation with someone by using supportive statements or confirming statements when what you really want to do is tell the person off in no uncertain terms? Why or why not?

Activities

Assertiveness Practice: Working with a partner, describe a situation in which you could have been more assertive. Ask your partner to assume the role of the person toward whom you should have been more assertive. Now replay the situation, using the assertiveness skills described in the chapter. Ask your classmates to observe the role play and provide feedback, using the following checklist. When you have finished asserting your point of view, reverse roles with your partner.

_____ Clearly describes the problem

_____ Effectively discloses how he or she felt

_____ Clearly describes the effects of the behavior

_____ Pauses or waits after describing the effects

_____ Uses effective questions to promote understanding

_____ Accurately paraphrases content

_____ Accurately paraphrases feelings

_____ Has good eye contact

_____ Leans forward while speaking

_____ Has an open body posture

_____ Has appropriate voice tone and quality

Web Resources

http://www.vandruff.com/artconverse.html Are you a conversational terrorist, or do you know someone who is? In the article *Conversational Terrorism: How NOT to Talk,* you'll discover dos and don'ts for conversing with others and learn how to avoid terrorizing others when you talk with them.

http://www.about-personal-growth.com/verbal-communication. html This is a site dedicated to helping you develop your verbal communication by mastering linguistic skills.

7 Nonverbal Communication Skills

Y ou are being watched. Whether it's an officer of the Transportation Safety Administration carefully scrutinizing your facial expression when you go through airport security, looking for indications that you are not a terrorist, or just the casual observer watching as you walk around campus, people are watching you.[1] People watch you, and you watch other people. You can glean a vast amount of information about others just from their nonverbal behaviors. We rely on nonverbal behavior to help us make predictions about others. **Nonverbal communication** is behavior other than written or spoken language that creates meaning for us. A person's tone of voice, eye contact, facial expressions, posture, movement, general appearance, use of personal space, manipulation of the communication environment, and a host of other nonverbal clues reveal how that person feels about others. All communication has both a content and a relationship dimension. Our nonverbal communication is a primary source of relationship cues.

In this chapter, we focus on how nonverbal communication affects the quality of our interpersonal relationships. Being able to interpret others' unspoken messages and appropriately express our own feelings through nonverbal communication are key components of being other-oriented. To help you become more skilled in both expressing and interpreting nonverbal messages, we'll discuss why nonverbal communication is important in establishing interpersonal relationships with others. We'll also note challenges in trying to accurately interpret the unspoken messages of others. After we discuss several nonverbal communication codes, we'll offer tips that will help you more accurately interpret nonverbal communication.

> " What you are speaks so loudly that I cannot hear what you say. "
>
> **Ralph Waldo Emerson**

Why Learn About Nonverbal Communication?

Wherever You Go, There You Are is the title of a popular book about Zen meditation.[2] The title could easily refer to nonverbal communication: Wherever you go, nonverbal communication is there. Nonverbal communication is an ever-present form of human expression. If you are alive, chances are that people are making inferences about you based on your nonverbal behavior. But are our people-watching guesses about others accurate? Sometimes yes, and sometimes no. This chapter is designed to help you increase your accuracy in evaluating the nonverbal messages of others. And just as you may inaccurately interpret the nonverbal messages of others, other people may misjudge your nonverbal cues. Because much of our nonverbal communication behavior is unconscious, most of us have only a limited awareness or understanding of it. We begin our examination of nonverbal communication by looking at the multiple reasons that nonverbal communication is so important in the total communication process.

Nonverbal Messages Are the Primary Way We Communicate Our Feelings and Attitudes

Daryl knew that he was in trouble the moment he walked into the room. His wife, Sandra, gave him a steely stare. Her brow was furrowed and her arms were crossed. On the table was a dish of cold lobster Newburg, extinguished candles burnt to nubs, and dirty dishes in all but one spot: his. Daryl was in the doghouse for forgetting the special meal his wife had prepared, and he needed no words to sense the depth of her displeasure. Although Daryl was momentarily in trouble for his forgetfulness, his ability to quickly read the nonverbal message in that situation will serve him well in the long run. Marriage partners who are skilled at interpreting the emotional meaning of

nonverbal communication
Behavior other than written or spoken language that creates meaning for someone.

a message are typically more satisfied in their marriages.[3] Nonverbal communication is the primary way in which we communicate feelings, attitudes, and emotions.

Psychologist Albert Mehrabian concluded that as little as 7 percent of the emotional meaning of a message is communicated through explicit verbal channels.[4] The most significant source of emotional communication is the face—according to Mehrabian's study, it channels as much as 55 percent of our meaning. Vocal cues such as volume, pitch, and intensity communicate another 38 percent of our emotional meaning. In all, we communicate approximately 93 percent of the emotional meaning of our messages nonverbally. Although these percentages do not apply to every communication situation, the results of Mehrabian's investigation do illustrate the potential power of nonverbal cues in communicating emotion.[5] Researchers are continuing to find new ways to measure the impact and power of nonverbal messages in the communication of emotions.[6]

Nonverbal Messages Are Usually More Believable Than Verbal Messages

"Honey, do you love me?" asks Brenda.

"OF COURSE I LOVE YOU! HAVEN'T I ALWAYS TOLD YOU THAT I LOVE YOU? I LOVE YOU!" shouts Jim, keeping his eyes glued to his morning newspaper.

Brenda will probably not be totally reassured by Jim's pledge of affection. The contradiction between his spoken message of love and his nonverbal message of irritation and lack of interest will leave her wondering about his true feelings.

Actions speak louder than words. This cliché became a cliché because nonverbal communication is more believable than verbal communication. Nonverbal messages are more difficult to fake. One research team concluded that North Americans use the following cues, listed in order from most to least important, to help them discern when a person is lying.[7]

- Greater time lag in response to a question
- Reduced eye contact
- Increased shifts in posture
- Unfilled pauses
- Less smiling
- Slower speech
- Higher pitch in voice
- More deliberate pronunciation and articulation of words

Because it is difficult to manipulate an array of nonverbal cues, a skilled other-oriented observer can see when a person's true feelings leak out. Social psychologists Paul Ekman and Wallace Friesen have identified the face, hands, and feet as key sources of nonverbal cues.[8] Are you aware of what your fingers and toes are doing as you are reading this book? Even if you become expert at masking and manipulating your face, you may first signal lack of interest or boredom with another person by finger wiggling or toe wagging. Or you may twiddle a pen or pencil. When you become emotionally aroused, the pupils of your eyes dilate, and you may blush, sweat, or change breathing patterns.[9] Lie detectors (polygraphs) rely on these unconscious clues. A polygraph measures a person's heart and breathing rate, as well as the electrical resistance of the skin (called *galvanic skin response*), to determine whether he or she is giving truthful verbal responses.

Nonverbal Messages Work with Verbal Messages to Create Meaning

Although we rely heavily on nonverbal messages, they do not operate independently of spoken messages in our relationships. Instead, verbal and nonverbal cues work together in two primary ways to help us make sense of others' messages: They help us manage the verbal message, and they augment the emotional meaning of what we say.

1. *Nonverbal cues help us manage verbal messages.* Specifically, our nonverbal cues can substitute for verbal messages, as well as repeat, contradict, or regulate what we say. An extended thumb signals that a hitchhiker would like a ride. A circle formed by the thumb and index finger can either signal that everything is A-OK or convey an obscene message. When someone asks, "Which way did he go?" you can silently point to the back door. In these instances, you are substituting nonverbal cues for a verbal message.

   You can also use nonverbal cues to repeat or reinforce your words. "Where is the personnel department?" asks a job applicant.

   "Three flights up. Take the elevator," says the security guard, pointing to the elevator. The guard's pointing gesture repeats her verbal instruction and clarifies the message.

   "Sure, this is a good time to talk about the Henrikson merger," says the business executive, nervously looking at her watch, stuffing papers into her attaché case, and avoiding eye contact with her coworker. In this instance, the nonverbal cues contradict the verbal ones. And as you learned earlier, the nonverbal message is almost always the one we believe.

   We also use nonverbal cues to regulate our participation in verbal exchanges. In most informal meetings, it is not appropriate or necessary to signal your desire to speak by raising your hand. Yet somehow you are able to signal to others when you'd like to speak and when you'd rather not talk. How does this happen? You use eye contact, raised eyebrows, an open mouth, or perhaps a single raised index finger to signal that you would like to make a point. If your colleagues do not see these signals, especially the eye contact, they may think you are not interested in talking.[10]

2. *Nonverbal cues augment the emotional meaning of verbal messages.* Our unspoken cues accent and complement verbal messages to increase or decrease the emotional impact of what we say. "Unless we vote to increase our tax base," bellows Mr. Coddlington, "we will not have enough classroom space to educate our children."

Portrait artists pay close attention to nonverbal cues such as posture, facial expression, and gesture to capture their subjects' personalities. What do the nonverbal cues reveal about this woman?

While delivering his impassioned plea to the school board, Mr. Coddlington also loudly slaps the lectern to accent his message and reinforce its intensity. A scolding mother's wagging finger and an angry supervisor's raised voice are other nonverbal cues that accent verbal messages.

Simultaneous and complementary verbal and nonverbal messages can also help to color the emotion we are expressing or the attitude we are conveying. The length of a hug while you tell your son you are proud of him provides additional information about the intensity of your pride. The firmness of your handshake when you greet a job interviewer can confirm your verbal claim that you are eager for employment.

People Respond and Adapt to Others Through Nonverbal Messages

You sense that your best friend is upset. Even though she doesn't tell you she's angry, you sense her mood by observing her grimacing facial expression and lack of direct eye contact with you. To help lighten the mood, you tell a joke. Many times every day, you "read" the nonverbal cues of others, even before they utter a word, to gain a clue about what to say or how to react. Interpreting others' nonverbal messages helps us appropriately adapt our communication as we interact with them.

Interaction adaptation theory describes how people adapt to the communication behavior of others.[11] The theory suggests that we respond not only to what people say, but also to their nonverbal expressions to help us navigate through our interpersonal conversations each day.[12] If, for example, your friend leans forward to tell a story, you may lean forward to listen. Or if during a meeting you sit with folded arms, unconvinced of what you are hearing, you may look around the conference table and find others with similarly folded arms. As if we were part of an intricate dance, when we communicate, we relate to others by responding to their movements, eye contact, gestures, and other nonverbal cues.

Sometimes, we relate by mirroring the posture or behavior of others. Or we may find ourselves gesturing in sync with someone's vocal pattern. At times, you are conscious of such mirroring of behavior, which is called **interactional synchrony.** At other times, you may not be aware that when your friend folds her arms while talking with you, you also fold your arms across your chest in a similar way. One researcher found that people evaluate such synchrony as positive; somewhat synchronized behavior (but not so synchronized that it feels as though someone is purposefully imitating you) communicates partners' mutual interest and positive regard.[13]

Nonverbal Messages Play a Major Role in Interpersonal Relationships

As you learned in Chapter 1, because of the ubiquitous nature of nonverbal communication, you cannot *not* communicate; psychologist Raymond Birdwhistell suggests that as much as 65 percent of the social, or relational, meaning in messages is based on nonverbal communication.[14] Of course, the meaning that others interpret from your behavior may not be the one you intended, and the inferences they draw based on nonverbal information may be right or wrong.

You learned in Chapter 3 that people begin making judgments about strangers just a fraction of a second after meeting them, based on nonverbal information. Within the first four minutes of interaction, you scope out the other person and draw conclusions about him or her.[15] Another research team found that you may decide whether a date is going to be pleasant or dull during the first thirty seconds of meeting your partner, before your partner has had time to utter more than "Hello."[16] Nonverbal cues, accurate or not, affect first impressions.

interaction adaptation theory
Theory suggesting that people interact with others by adapting to their communication behaviors.

interactional synchrony
Mirroring of each other's nonverbal behavior by communication partners.

Nonverbal expressions of support also are important when providing comforting messages to others during times of stress and anxiety. Communication researchers Susanne Jones and Laura Guerrero found that being nonverbally expressive and supportive is important in helping people cope with stress.[17] Providing empathic, supportive facial expressions and vocal cues, hugs, and positive touch helps to reduce stress and enhance a person's overall well-being.

Nonverbal cues are important not only when people initiate relationships, but also as they maintain and develop mature relationships with others. In fact, the more intimate the relationship, the more people use and understand the nonverbal cues of their partners.

Long-married couples spend less time verbalizing their feelings and emotions to each other than they did when they were first dating; each learns how to interpret the other's subtle nonverbal cues.[18] The researchers who made that observation also found that the more satisfied a person was with his or her marriage, the more accurately he or she was able to interpret the nonverbal emotional expression of the partner.[19] The ability to *express* an emotion was not found to be related to the quality of the marriage, but the ability to accurately *interpret* an emotional expression was better in marriages that were more satisfying to the couple. In addition, a happily married spouse was less likely to assume that a negative emotional expression was specifically directed toward him or her. If your spouse is silent during dinner, you may know that her day was a tough one and you should give her a wide berth. And if, when you put on your new Kelly green pants, your husband grimaces as he asks, "New pants?" you may understand that he does not love them. In fact, all of us are more likely to use nonverbal cues to convey negative messages than to announce explicitly our dislike of something or someone. People also use nonverbal cues to signal changes in the level of satisfaction with a relationship.[20] When we want to cool things off, we may start using a less vibrant tone of voice and cut back on eye contact and physical contact with our partner.

The Challenge of Interpreting Nonverbal Messages

Even though we have made great claims for the value of studying nonverbal behaviors, it is not always easy to decipher unspoken messages.[21] You have dictionaries to help interpret words, but there is no handy reference book to help you decode nonverbal cues. Although the phrase *body language* is often used in casual conversation, there is no universal or agreed-on interpretation for body movements or gestures. To help you with the decoding process, we will classify some common types of nonverbal behaviors. But first you should be aware of some of the difficulties that hinder classification.

Nonverbal Messages Are Often Ambiguous

Most words carry a meaning that everyone who speaks the same language can recognize. But the meaning of nonverbal messages may be known only to the person displaying them. Perhaps even more importantly, that person may not intend for the behavior to have any meaning at all. And some people have difficulty expressing their emotions nonverbally. They may have a frozen facial expression or a monotone voice. Or they may be teasing you, but their deadpan expressions lead you to believe that their negative comments are heartfelt. Often, it is difficult to draw meaningful conclusions about another person's behavior, even if you know him or her quite well.

Nonverbal Messages Are Continuous

Words are discrete entities; they have a beginning and an end. You can circle the first word in this sentence and underline the last one. Nonverbal behaviors are not as easily dissected. Like the sweep of a second hand on a watch, many nonverbal behaviors are continuous. Some, such as a slap or a hand clap, have definite beginnings and endings. But more often than not, nonverbal behavior unfolds without clearly defined starting and stopping points. Gestures, facial expressions, and even eye contact can flow from one situation to the next with seamless ease. Researchers have difficulty studying nonverbal cues because of this continuous stream, so trying to categorize and interpret them will be challenging as well.

Nonverbal Cues Are Multichanneled

Have you ever tried to watch two or more TV programs at once? Some televisions let you see as many as eight programs simultaneously so that you can keep up with three ball games and two soap operas and view commercials on the three other channels. Like the programs on a multichannel TV, nonverbal cues come at us from a variety of sources simultaneously. And just as you can really only pay attention to one channel at a time on your multichannel television—although you can move among them very rapidly—so, too, can you actually attend to only one nonverbal cue at a time.[22] Social psychologist Michael Argyle suspects that negative nonverbal messages (frowns, grimaces, lack of eye contact) command attention before positive messages when the two compete.[23] Moreover, if the nonverbal message contradicts the verbal message, then you may have trouble interpreting either one correctly.[24]

Nonverbal Interpretation Is Culture-Based

There is some evidence that humans from every culture smile when they are happy and frown when they are unhappy.[25] We also all raise, or flash, our eyebrows when meeting or greeting others, and young children in many cultures wave to signal that they want their mothers, raise their arms to be picked up, and suck their thumbs for comfort.[26] All this suggests that there is some underlying basis for expressing emotion. Yet each culture may develop unique rules for displaying and interpreting these gestures and expressions.

For example, unless you grew up there, you might be startled when on a visit to New Orleans you stumble on a handkerchief-waving, dancing, exuberantly singing crowd and discover that it is an African American jazz funeral. What to the uninformed may seem like disrespect for the dead, others recognize as a joyous send-off to a better world.

UNDERSTANDING OTHERS
Adapting to Differences

Cultural and Gender Differences in Interpreting Nonverbal Messages

Culture

Research investigating nonverbal communication in a variety of cultures confirms that individuals interpret nonverbal messages from their unique cultural perspective. Note the following conclusions:[27]

Facial Expression

One research team found that some facial expressions, such as those conveying happiness, sadness, anger, disgust, and surprise, were the same in 68 to 92 percent of the cultures examined.[28] All humans probably share the same neurophysiological basis for expressing emotions but learn different rules for displaying and interpreting the expressions. For example, the Japanese culture does not reinforce the show of negative emotions; it is important for Japanese to "save face" and to help others save face as well.

Eye Contact

There seems to be more eye contact in interpersonal interactions between Arabs, South Americans, and Greeks than between people from other cultures. There is evidence that some African Americans look at others less than Whites do when sending and receiving messages. One of the most universal expressions appears to be the eyebrow flash (the sudden raising of the eyebrows when meeting someone or interacting with others).

Gestures

Hand and body gestures with the most shared meaning among Africans, North Americans, and South Americans include pointing, shrugging, nodding the head, clapping, pointing the thumb down, waving hello, and beckoning. There are, however, regional variations within cultures; it is not wise to assume that all people in a given culture share the same meaning for certain gestures. The "okay" gesture made by forming a circle with the thumb and finger has sexual connotations in some South American and Caribbean countries. In France, the "okay" sign means "worthless."

Space

Arabs, Latin Americans, and Southern Europeans seem to stand closer to others than do people from Asia, India, Pakistan, and northern Europe. If you have been to Britain, you know that people queue or wait for buses in orderly straight lines. In France, however, queuing is less orderly, and individuals are more likely to push forward to be the next customer or to get the next seat on the bus. As with gestures, however, there are regional variations in spatial preferences. One intercultural communication researcher found that Anglo Saxons (Northern Europeans) used the largest zone of personal space when interacting with others, followed by Asians, Caucasians (Central and Eastern Europeans), and those from Mediterranean countries. Hispanics used the smallest amount of personal space.[29]

Touch

Researchers have found that touch is something that is culturally based and learned. High-contact cultures are cultures in which people expect and value a higher degree of human touching than do people in other cultures. People from warmer climates tend to be from high-contact cultures—they prefer closer distances and expect more touching behavior than people from cooler climates.[30] For example, people from Greece and Italy exhibit more touching behavior than people from England. South Americans initiate and receive more touching behavior than North Americans.[31]

Gender

There is evidence that men and women display and interpret nonverbal cues differently.[32]

Eye Contact

Women usually use a more prolonged gaze than do men. Women, however, are less likely just to stare at someone; they break eye contact more frequently than men. In general, women receive more eye contact from others than do men.

Space

Men tend to require more space around them than do women. Women both approach and are approached more closely than men. And when conversing with others, women seem to prefer side-by-side interactions.

Facial Expression

Research suggests that women smile more than men. It is also reported that women tend to be more emotionally expressive with their faces than men; this is perhaps related to the conclusion that women are more skilled at both displaying and interpreting facial expressions.

Gesture and Posture

Overall, women appear to use fewer and less expansive gestures than men. Women are more likely, for example, to rest their hands on the arms of a chair while seated; men are more likely to gesture. Men and women position their legs differently: women cross their legs at the knees or ankles while men are more likely to sit with their legs apart.

Touch

Men are more likely to initiate touch with others than are women. Women are touched more than men. Men and women also attribute different meaning to touch; women are more likely to associate touch with warmth and expressiveness than are men.

Vocal Cues

Vocal patterns may be more related to biological differences in the vocal register than other nonverbal behaviors. Women speak in both higher and softer tones than do men. Women use their voices to communicate a greater range of emotions than do men. Women are also more likely to raise their pitch when making statements; some people interpret the rising pattern (as in asking a question) as an indication of greater uncertainty.

Nonverbal Communication Codes

Keeping in mind all the challenges to our understanding that we've just discussed, we can begin looking at the categories of nonverbal information that researchers have studied: movement and gestures, eye contact, facial expressions, use of space and territory, touch, and personal appearance. Although we will concentrate on the codes that fall within these categories in mainstream Western culture, we will also look at codes for other cultures and subcultures.

Body Movement and Posture

In 1774, when English explorer Captain James Cook arrived in the New Hebrides, he didn't speak the language of the natives. His only way of communicating was sign language. Through gestures, pointing, and hand waving, he established contact with the natives. There is evidence that people have used gestures to communicate since ancient times—especially to bridge cultural and language differences. The first record of the use of sign language to communicate is found in Xenophon's *The March Up Country,* in which he describes unspoken gestures used to help the Greeks cross Asia Minor around 400 B.C. Even when we do speak the same language as others, we use gestures to help us make our point.[33]

Kinesics is the study of human movement and gesture. Francis Bacon once noted, "As the tongue speaketh to the ear, so the hand speaketh to the eye." People have long recognized that movement and gestures provide valuable information to others. Various scholars and researchers have proposed paradigms for analyzing and coding these movements and gestures, just as grammarians have codified spoken or written language.[34]

One paradigm identifies four stages of "quasi-courtship behavior."[35] The first stage is *courtship readiness.* When you are attracted to someone, you may suck in your stomach, tense your muscles, and stand up straight. The second stage includes *preening behaviors:* You manipulate your appearance by combing your hair, applying makeup, straightening your tie, pulling up your socks, and double-checking your appearance in the mirror. In stage three, you demonstrate *positional cues,* using your posture and body orientation to ensure that you will be seen and noticed by others.

One researcher found 52 gestures and nonverbal behaviors that women use to signal an interest in men. Among the top unspoken flirting cues were smiling and surveying a crowded room with the eyes, and moving closer to the object of affection.[36] People intensify these cues in the fourth stage, *appeals to invitation,* using close proximity, exposed skin, open body positions (uncrossed arms and legs), and eye contact to signal availability and interest. Subjects in one study reported that they were aware of using all these techniques to promote an intimate relationship. In fact, people use these quasi-courtship behaviors to some extent in almost any situation in which they are trying to gain favorable attention from another.

Another team of researchers focused on nonverbal behaviors that prompt people to label someone warm and friendly, or cold and distant.[37] The team found that "warm" people face their communication partners directly, smile more, make more direct eye contact, fidget less, and generally make fewer unnecessary hand movements. "Cold" people make less eye contact, smile less, fidget more, and turn away from their partners.

Albert Mehrabian has identified the nonverbal cues that contribute to perceptions of liking.[38] He found that an open body

kinesics Study of human movement and gesture.

Can you identify the quasi-courtship behavior in this movie still from *Brokeback Mountain?*

and arm position, a forward lean, and a relaxed posture communicate liking. When you are attempting to persuade someone, you typically have more eye contact and a more face-to-face body orientation; you are more likely to lean forward and closer to others.

Ekman and Friesen classified movement and gestures according to their function. They identified five categories: emblems, illustrators, affect displays, regulators, and adaptors.[39]

Emblems. Nonverbal cues that have specific, generally understood meanings in a given culture and may actually substitute for a word or phrase are called **emblems.** When you are busy typing a report that is due tomorrow and your young son bounces in to ask for permission to buy a new computer game, you turn from your computer and hold up an open palm to indicate your desire for uninterrupted quiet. To communicate your enthusiastic enjoyment of a violin soloist at a concert, you applaud wildly. You want your children to stop talking in the library, so you put an index finger up to your pursed lips.

Illustrators. People frequently accompany a verbal message with **illustrators** that either contradict, accent, or complement the message. Slamming a book closed while announcing, "I don't want to read this anymore" or pounding a lectern while proclaiming, "This point is important!" are two examples of nonverbal behaviors that illustrate the verbal message. Typically, English speakers use nonverbal illustrators at the beginning of clauses or phrases.[40] TV newscasters, for example, turn a page to signal that they are moving to a new story or topic. Most of us use illustrators to help us communicate information about the size, shape, and spatial relationships of objects. You probably even use them when you talk on the phone, although probably not as many as you use in face-to-face conversation.[41]

Affect Displays. Nonverbal movements and postures used to communicate emotion are called **affect displays.** As early as 1872, when Charles Darwin systematically studied the expression of emotion in both humans and animals,[42] people recognized that nonverbal cues are the primary ways to communicate emotion. Facial expressions, vocal cues, posture, and gestures convey the intensity of your emotions.[43] If you are happy, for example, your face will telegraph your joy to others. The movement of your hands, the openness of your posture, and the speed with which you move will tell others *how* happy you are. Similarly, if you are feeling depressed, your face will probably reveal your sadness or dejection, while your slumped shoulders and lowered head will indicate the intensity of your despair. When you are feeling friendly, you use a soft tone of voice, an open smile, and a relaxed posture.[44] When you feel neutral about an issue, you signal it by putting little expression on your face or in your voice. When you feel hostile, you use a harsh voice, frown with your teeth showing, and keep your posture tense and rigid.

Regulators. People use **regulators** to control the interaction or flow of communication between themselves and another person. When you are eager to respond to a message, you make eye contact, raise your eyebrows, open your mouth, raise an index finger, and lean forward slightly. In a classroom, you may raise your hand to signal overtly that you want to talk. When you do not want to be part of the conversation, you do the opposite: avert your eyes, close your mouth, cross your arms, and lean back in your seat or away from the verbal action in an attempt to regulate the interaction.

Adaptors. When you are cold, you reach for a sweater or wrap your arms around your chest to keep warm. When it's 102 degrees Fahrenheit in the shade without a breeze, you may reach for a fan to make your own breeze. These behaviors are examples

emblems Nonverbal cues that have specific, generally understood meanings in a given culture and may substitute for a word or phrase.

illustrators Nonverbal behaviors that accompany a verbal message and either contradict, accent, or complement it.

affect display Nonverbal behavior that communicates emotions.

regulators Nonverbal messages that help to control the interaction or flow of communication between two people.

RECAP   Categories of Movement and Gestures

Category	Definition	Example
Emblems	Behaviors that have specific, generally understood meaning within a given culture	Raising a hitchhiking thumb
Illustrators	Cues that accompany verbal messages and add meaning to the message	Pounding the lectern to emphasize a point
Affect displays	Expressions of emotion	Hugging someone to express love
Regulators	Cues that control and manage the flow of communication between two people	Looking at someone when you wish to speak
Adaptors	Behaviors that help you adapt to your environment	Scratching; combing your hair

of **adaptors**—nonverbal behaviors that help you satisfy a personal need and adapt to the immediate situation. When you adjust your glasses, scratch a mosquito bite, or comb your hair, you are using movement to help you manage your personal needs and adapt to your surroundings—and you're communicating something about yourself to whoever may be present.

Understanding these five categories of nonverbal behavior can help you understand interpersonal communication by giving you a new and more precise way to think about your own behavior. By noting how often you use emblems instead of words to communicate a message, you can recognize how important emblems are in your relationships with others. The more you rely on emblems that have unique meanings for you and your partner, the more intimate the interpersonal relationship. Also, start to notice whether your nonverbal behavior contradicts what you say. Monitoring your use of illustrators can help you determine whether you are sending mixed signals to others. Be aware of how you display affect. Knowing that your face and voice communicate emotion and that your posture and gestures indicate the intensity of your feelings can help you understand how others make inferences about your feelings and attitudes. If other people have difficulty interpreting your emotional state, you may not be projecting your feelings nonverbally.

Since nonverbal cues are ambiguous, it may not be a good idea to use them to achieve a specific objective. But as you have seen, people are more likely to respond in predictable ways if you use behaviors they can recognize and interpret easily.

Eye Contact

Whether you choose to look at someone or avert your gaze has an enormous impact on your relationship with that person.[45] Researcher Adam Kendon has identified four functions of eye contact in interpersonal interactions.[46]

First, eye contact serves a *cognitive* function because it gives you information about another person's thought processes. For example, if your partner breaks eye contact after you ask him or her a question, you will know that he or she is probably thinking of something to say.

Second, people use eye contact to *monitor* the behavior of others. You receive a major portion of the information you obtain through your eyes. You look at others to determine whether they are receptive to your messages.

Third, eye contact is one of the most powerful *regulatory* cues you use to signal when you want to talk and when you don't. We have noticed that when we ask questions such

adaptors Nonverbal behaviors that satisfy a personal need and help a person adapt or respond to the immediate situation.

as "Who can tell me the four functions of eye contact?" students quickly yet unobtrusively avert their eyes to signal "Don't call on me." When you do want to communicate with others, you make eye contact—as, for example, when standing in line at the bakery, you fix your eyes on the clerk to signal, "My turn next. Please wait on me."

Finally, the area around your eyes serves an *expressive* function. The eyes have been called the "mirror of the soul" because they reveal emotions to others. You may cry, blink, and widen or narrow your gaze to express your feelings.

When are you most likely to establish eye contact with another person? Researchers have found that you are more likely to make eye contact with someone if you like or love the other person, are listening rather than talking, are discussing pleasant topics, are an extrovert, have a high need to be liked, are trying to dominate the conversation, are interested in what your partner may say or do, or have nothing else especially interesting to look at.[47]

When people do establish eye contact with others, it may seem that their gaze is constant. Yet research suggests that they actually spend the majority of their time looking at something other than the person's eyes. One research team found that people focus on something else, including their partner's mouth, 57 percent of the time.[48] Not surprisingly then, facial expressions are another rich source of information in your communication with others.

Facial Expression

The Palo Alto, California, city council may well have the distinction of being the first legislative body to try to regulate facial expression. They proposed a code of conduct banning facial expressions that show "disagreement or disgust."[49] The controversy generated by the proposal attests to the importance of facial expressions in the communication process. So, too, does our reliance on *emoticons,* the "smiley faces" and other symbols created with combinations of keyboard characters to communicate facial expression via e-mail. The face is the exhibit gallery for emotional displays.

To interpret a partner's facial expressions accurately, you need to put your other-orientation skills to work, focusing on what the other person may be thinking or feeling. It helps if you know the person well, can see his or her whole face, have plenty of time to watch it, and understand the situation that prompted the emotion.[50] There is also evidence that you can more accurately decode the facial expressions and other emotional expressions of someone who comes from the same racial or ethnic background as you do.[51] Generally speaking, the more characteristics you have in common with another person, the greater the chance that you will accurately interpret that person's facial expression. In addition to having a similar background, you also need to know the cues for "reading" facial expressions.

Your face is versatile. According to Ekman and Friesen, it is capable of producing over 250,000 different expressions.[52] Research suggests that women have greater variety in their emotional expressions and spend more time smiling than men.[53] But all facial expressions can be grouped in six primary emotional categories; the following list describes the changes that occur on your face for each one.[54]

Surprise:	Wide-open eyes; raised and wrinkled brow; open mouth
Fear:	Open mouth; tense skin under the eyes; wrinkles in the center of the forehead
Disgust:	Raised or curled upper lip; wrinkled nose; raised cheeks; lowered brow; lowered upper eyelid
Anger:	Tensed lower eyelid; either pursed lips or open mouth; lowered and wrinkled brow; staring eyes

BEING Other-ORIENTED

The face is the single most important source of information about which specific emotion someone may be expressing. Compare a situation in which you accurately decoded someone's emotion based on his or her facial expression and a situation in which your inference was inaccurate. What factors increase the accuracy of your ability to interpret someone else's facial expressions?

Happiness: Smiling; mouth may be open or closed; raised cheeks; wrinkles around lower eyelids.

Sadness: Lip may tremble; corners of the lips turn downward; corners of the upper eyelid may be raised.

The face can shift between the six categories rapidly, as is evident on the NASA videotape of activity inside Mission Control at the Johnson Space Center during the final minutes of the doomed flight of the space shuttle *Columbia* in February 2003. *New York Times* reporter John Schwartz describes how

> though the voices of the mission controllers remained steady, their faces and body language showed a marked transition from the cool professionalism to wide-eyed alertness to dread and, finally, tears.[55]

How accurately do people interpret emotions expressed on the face? Several studies have attempted to measure subjects' skill in identifying emotional expressions of others. They have found that reading facial expression is a tricky business. According to Ekman and Friesen, even though faces provide a great deal of information about emotions, people can learn how to control facial expressions.[56] In addition, facial expressions seem to be contagious. One researcher who showed his subjects video clips of President Reagan giving speeches discovered that they were likely to smile when Reagan smiled and frown when Reagan appeared angry or threatening.[57] There is evidence that the tendency to smile when others are smiling is a cross-cultural characteristic—responding and reacting to others' nonverbal expressions may be universal. Researchers have found, for example, that Japanese subjects were more likely to smile when they could see others smiling during interpersonal interactions.[58] Another study found that people were better able to judge the accuracy of facial expressions when the expressions were more complex.[59] The distinctiveness of a facial expression with compound meanings may be what makes interpretation easier. It is also probable that people have more practice interpreting facial expressions with compound meanings than they do those that communicate a single emotion such as sadness or happiness. Yet despite the complexity of some facial expressions, we seem to be able to determine whether someone is really happy or merely offering a phony smile. One research team found that a genuine smile is more fleeting than a forced smile, which tends to last a bit too long.[60]

At the opposite end of the spectrum from complex facial expressions are what Ekman calls "microexpressions," fleeting facial expressions that may last only .05 of a second. Most of Ekman's test groups, including policemen and judges, have difficulty detecting microexpressions. On the other hand, some Buddhists, whom Ekman calls "gymnasts of the mind," were surprisingly sensitive to microexpressions.[61]

Vocal Cues

Vocal cues are another category of nonverbal code that we respond to. Vocal cues communicate emotions and help us manage conversations. And even the lack of vocal cues communicates information.

We're able to make a variety of inferences about other people based on the pitch, rate, volume, and quality of their voices and on their skill in pronouncing words and articulating speech sounds. We make guesses about a person's personality, power, credibility, and sexuality based only on vocal cues. One group of speech and language researchers found subtle differences between gay and lesbian speakers' vocal cues compared to those of straight individuals.[62] Another research team found that people use stereotyped vocal cues to make inferences about a person's sexual orientation.[63] Although people tend to agree on which voices sound gay or straight, they are not always accurate. According to the research, gay males have a tendency to rate a voice as "gay sounding" more than straight males. So is "gaydar" that is based on only vocal cues accurate? Not really: Although researchers have documented some recognizable differences in the vocal cues of gay and straight individuals, we're not always accurate in using the cues to determine a person's sexual orientation, unless the cues are stereotypically pronounced or exaggerated.

Our Vocal Cues Communicate Emotions. Whether you are an infant or an adult, your voice is a major vehicle for communicating your emotions and a primary tool for communicating information about the nature of relationships between you and others.[64] As an adult, you use your voice to present one message on the surface (with words) and usually a more accurate expression of your feelings with your vocal quality. Say the following sentence out loud, as if you really mean it: "This looks great." Now say it sarcastically, as if you really don't think it looks great. Clearly, your vocal cues provide the real meaning.

Laughter is contagious.

One team of nonverbal communication researchers concluded that it's primarily your voice that communicates your level of intimacy with others when you express your ideas.[65] The words you use may communicate explicit ideas and information, but it is your vocal cues that provide the primary relational cues, which truly indicate the degree of liking and trust that you feel toward others.

Some vocal expressions of emotion are easier to identify than others. Expressions of joy and anger are obvious ones, whereas shame and love are the most difficult emotions to identify based on vocal cues alone.[66] People are also likely to confuse fear with nervousness, love with sadness, and pride with satisfaction.

Laughter is another vocal cue that you probably express every day; your laugh not only reflects your emotional state but, according to research, has a strong impact on the emotions of others. Laughter is contagious.[67] When you laugh, you are not only expressing your emotions but you also increase the likelihood that others will laugh as well.

Your voice also provides information about your self-confidence and your knowledge of the subject matter in your messages. Most of us would conclude that a speaker who mumbles, speaks slowly, consistently mispronounces words, and uses "uhs" and "ums" is less credible and persuasive than one who speaks clearly, rapidly, and fluently.[68] Even though mispronunciations and vocalized pauses ("ums" and "ahs") seem to have a negative effect on credibility, they do not seem to be a major impediment to attitude change. People may, for example, think that you are less knowledgeable if you stammer, but you may still be able to get your persuasive message across.

Not only "ums" and "ahs" but also speaking rate influences our perception of others. One team of researchers found that North Americans evaluated speakers with a moderate to slightly faster speaking rate as more "socially attractive" than speakers who had a slow rate of speech.[69] North American listeners also seem to prefer a speaking rate that is equal to or slightly faster than their own speaking rate.

Vocal Cues Help Us Manage Conversations. In addition to providing information about emotions, self-confidence, and knowledge, vocal cues known as **backchannel cues** can serve a regulatory function in interpersonal situations, signaling when we want to talk and when we don't. When we are finished talking, we may lower the pitch of our final word. When we want to talk, we may start by interjecting sounds such as "I . . . I . . . I . . ." or "Ah . . . Ah . . . Ah . . ." to interrupt the speaker and grab the verbal ball. We also may use such cues as "Sure," "I understand," "Uh-huh," or "Okay" to signal that we understand the message of the other person and now we want to talk or end the conversation. These backchannel cues are particularly useful in telephone conversations when we have no other nonverbal cues to help us signal that we would like to get off the phone.

backchannel cues Vocal cues that signal your wish to speak or not to speak.

Our Use of Silence Speaks Volumes.   Sometimes it is not what we say, or even how we say it, that communicates our feelings. Being silent may communicate volumes.[70] One researcher, in commenting about the importance of silence in speech, said, "Silence is to speech as white paper is to this print. . . . The entire system of spoken language would fail without [people's] ability to both tolerate and create sign sequences of silence–sound–silence units."[71]

Would you be comfortable just sitting silently with a good friend? Sidney Baker's theory of silence suggests that the more at ease you are when you share a silence with a close friend, the more comfortable you are with just being together and enjoying each other's companionship. People need to talk until there is nothing left to say; by that point, the uncertainty as been managed. In most long-term relationships, partners may not feel a need to fill the air with sound. Just being together to enjoy each other's company may be most fulfilling. Baker calls such moments "positive silence."[72] While

Communication and Emotion

How to Accurately Interpret the Nonverbal Expression of Emotions

Are you skilled at accurately interpreting the emotions others are expressing? Since emotions are primarily communicated via nonverbal cues, the more skilled you are at interpreting nonverbal messages in general, the more likely it is that you will be able to accurately interpret the emotions other people are expressing. And there is evidence that if you are skilled in accurately interpreting the emotional expressions of others, then you will generally have more positive interpersonal relationships with others. People who are more sensitive in interpreting emotions expressed nonverbally tend to be more popular, to have a wider circle of friends, and to be less likely to experience relationship anxiety. The following research conclusions may help you enhance both your ability and your confidence in interpreting the emotional expressions of others.[73]

Facial Expression

- You are more likely to be skilled at interpreting positive emotional expressions (happiness) than negative emotional expressions (sadness, anger, disgust).[74]

- You are more likely to confuse the expression of fear with surprise or anger because of the similar position of the eyes and especially the area around the brow.

- Because facial expressions can be grouped based on the dimensions of activity, intensity, and pleasantness,

similar expressions are more likely to be confused. The more dramatically different the emotions being expressed, the more likely you are to accurately identify the emotions based on facial expression alone.

Vocal Cues

- It's generally easier to interpret anger, sadness, happiness, and nervousness from vocal cues alone and harder to identify disgust, shame, fear, jealousy, love, satisfaction, and sympathy.[75]

- People sometimes have difficulty distinguishing love from sympathy, fear from sadness, and interest from happiness.[76]

- Knowing more about the context or reason for someone's nonverbal communication helps you interpret what emotion is being expressed by vocal cues.

General Principles of Interpreting Emotions

- How you interpret emotions in others is strongly influenced by your culture; although there is some common basis for expressing emotions, there are cultural variations in how emotions are interpreted.[77]

- You are more likely to accurately interpret emotions expressed by people who are from your own cultural or ethnic background.

- You are more likely to accurately interpret emotional expression in someone

from a culture other than your own if the emotional expression is static (for example, a photograph of a facial expression) rather than dynamic (an in-person expression or a video of the expression).

- You are more likely to accurately interpret someone's emotional expression if it is genuine than if it is fake.

- Your ability to interpret emotions improves as you get older; your skill declines as age begins to have an effect on your ability to accurately see and hear others.[78]

- A person's facial expression and vocal cues communicate a specific emotional response; his or her posture and gestures communicate the *intensity* of the emotion expressed.

- In general, women are more likely to accurately interpret emotions in others than are men.

- Research suggests that women are typically more nonverbally expressive than are men in social situations.[79]

- Your ability to accurately interpret emotions is a skill that does not appear to be related to race, education, or cognitive intelligence level.

- People who more accurately interpret the emotional expressions of others tend to work at people-oriented jobs more than people who do not have such skill.[80]

Every culture has fairly rigid ways of regulating space in social interactions. People may consider violations of these implicit rules threatening.

watching a sunset with a close friend, for example, there may be no need to narrate what you are seeing—it's enough just to experience it.

Personal Space

Imagine that you are sitting alone in a booth at your local pizza parlor. As you sit munching your thin-and-crispy pepperoni pizza, you are startled when a complete stranger sits down in your booth directly across from you. With several empty tables and booths in the restaurant, you feel very uncomfortable that this unknown individual has invaded "your" area.

Normally, people do not think much about the rules of personal space, but in fact every culture has fairly rigid ways of regulating space in social interactions. Violations of these rules can be alarming and, as in the preceding scenario, even threatening. How close you are willing to get to others relates to how well you know them and to considerations of power and status.

One pioneer in helping people understand the silent language of personal space was Edward T. Hall. His study of **proxemics** investigated how close or how far away from people and things we arrange ourselves.[81] Hall identified four spatial zones that speakers in Western cultures sometimes define for themselves unconsciously, as shown in Figure 7.1.

When we are between 0 and $1\frac{1}{2}$ feet from someone, we are occupying **intimate space.** This is the zone in which the most intimate interpersonal communication occurs. It is open only to those with whom we are well acquainted, unless we are forced to stand in an elevator, a fast-food line, or some other crowded space.

proxemics Study of how close or far away from people and objects people position themselves.

intimate space Zone of space most often used for very personal or intimate interactions, ranging from 0 to $1\frac{1}{2}$ feet between individuals.

199

FIGURE 7.1

Edward T. Hall's Four Zones of Space

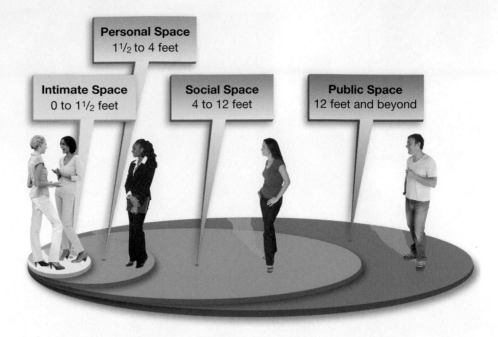

Personal Space
1¹/₂ to 4 feet

Intimate Space
0 to 1¹/₂ feet

Social Space
4 to 12 feet

Public Space
12 feet and beyond

personal space Zone of space most often used for conversations with family and friends, ranging from 1¹/₂ to 4 feet between individuals.

social space Zone of space most often used for group interactions, ranging from 4 to 12 feet between individuals.

public space Zone of space most often used by public speakers or anyone speaking to many people, ranging beyond 12 feet from the individual.

territoriality Study of how animals and humans use space and objects to communicate occupancy or ownership of space.

territorial markers Tangible objects that are used to signify that someone has claimed an area or space.

The second zone, which ranges from 1¹/₂ to 4 feet from each person, is called **personal space.** Most conversations with family and friends occur in this zone. If someone you don't know well invades this space on purpose, you may feel uncomfortable.

Zone three, called **social space,** ranges from 4 to 12 feet from a person. Most group interaction, as well as many professional relationships, takes place in this zone. The interaction tends to be more formal than that in the first two zones.

Public space, the fourth zone, begins 12 feet from a person. Interpersonal communication does not usually occur in this zone, and many public speakers and teachers position themselves even more than 12 feet from their audience.

Don't get the idea that these special zones described by Hall *always* occur precisely in the measurements that we've described. They don't. The specific space that you and others choose depends on several variables.[82] The more you like someone, the closer you will stand to the person. We allow individuals with high status to surround themselves with more space than we allow for people with lower status. Large people also usually have more space around them than smaller people do, and women stand closer to others than men do.[83] All of us tend to stand closer to others in a large room than we do in a small room. And our culture plays a significant role in determining how close to others we work or stand, as well as the power and status of individuals with whom we interact.

In a group, who's in charge, who's important, and who talks to whom are reflected by the spatial arrangement people select. The more dominant group members tend to select seats at the head of a table, while shyer individuals often select a corner seat at a rectangular table.[84]

Territory

Territoriality is the study of how animals (including humans) use space and objects to communicate occupancy or ownership of space. Earlier, we gave the example of a stranger sitting down with you in a pizza parlor. In that case, you had assumed "ownership" of the booth in the pizza parlor and the accompanying "right" to determine who sat with you, because you and your pizza were occupying the booth. In addition to invading your personal space, the intrusive stranger broke the rules that govern territoriality.

People announce ownership of space with **territorial markers**—things that signify the area has been claimed—much as explorers once planted flags claiming uncharted

RECAP Edward T. Hall's Classification of Spatial Zones

	Distance from the Individual	Examples
Zone One	0 to $1\frac{1}{2}$ feet	Communicating with our most intimate acquaintances
Zone Two	$1\frac{1}{2}$ feet to 4 feet	Conversing with good friends and family members
Zone Three	4 feet to 12 feet	Working with others in small groups and in professional situations
Zone Four	12 feet and beyond	Public speaking situations

land for their kings. When you are studying at the library, for example, and need to hop up and check a reference in the card catalog, you might leave behind a notebook or a pencil. In rural areas, landowners post signs at the borders of their property to keep hunters off their territory. Signs, locks, electronic security systems, and other devices secure home and office territories.

You also use markers to indicate where your space stops and someone else's starts. "Good fences make good neighbors," wrote the poet Robert Frost. When someone sits too close, you may try to erect a physical barrier, such as a stack of books or a napkin holder, or you might use your body as a shield by turning away. If the intruder does not get the hint that "this land is my land," you may ultimately resort to words to announce that the space is occupied.

Touch

Standing elbow to elbow in a crowded elevator, you may find yourself in physical contact with total strangers. As you stiffen your body and avert your eyes, a baffling sense of shame floods over you. If you are sitting at a conference table and you accidentally brush the toes of your shoes against your colleague's ankle, you may jerk away and even blush or apologize. Why do people react this way to unpremeditated touching? Normally, you touch to express intimacy. When intimacy is not your intended message, you instinctively react to modify the impression.

Countless studies have shown that intimate touching is vital to your personal development and well-being.[85] Infants and children need to be touched to confirm that they are valued and loved. Many hospitals invite volunteers in to hold and rock newborns whose mothers cannot do it themselves. Advocates of breastfeeding argue that the intimate touching it entails strengthens the bond between mother and child.[86]

The amount of touch you need, tolerate, receive, and initiate depends on many factors. The amount and kind of touching you receive in your family is one big influence. If your mom or dad greets you with hugs, caresses, and kisses, then you probably do this to others. If your family is less demonstrative, you may be restrained yourself. Studies by researcher Nancy Henley show that most of us are more likely to touch people when we are feeling friendly or happy, or under some of the following specific circumstances:[87]

- When we ask someone to do something for us
- When we share rather than ask for information
- When we try to persuade someone to do something
- When we are talking about intimate topics

"Well, are you going to invade my space or not?"

- When we are in social settings that we choose rather than in professional settings that are part of our job
- When we are thrilled and excited to share good news
- When we listen to a troubled or worried friend

Research has identified differences in the amount of touch men and women prefer to give and receive.[88] In general, women have less positive attitudes about being touched by members of the opposite sex than do men. Men are more likely than women to initiate touch in casual romantic heterosexual relationships, yet women are more likely to reach out and touch their spouses than are men. As a general rule, men are more likely to initiate touch with a woman before they are married than after they are married. Nonverbal communication scholars Laura Guerrero and Peter Anderson found that people in long-term relationships touched each other *less* often than people who were in the earlier stages of dating and developing a relationship.[89] Quantity of touch is apparently more important when establishing a new relationship than in maintaining a marital or long-term relationship. North American men are more uncomfortable with being touched by other men than women are with being touched by other women. In addition to one's sex, personal preferences determine how much touch a person prefers to initiate or receive. Some people just don't like to be touched; they are what researchers call high-touch-avoidance individuals; to be touched by anyone simply makes them feel uncomfortable.

Appearance

In all interactions with others, appearance counts. American culture places a high value on how much you weigh, the style of your hair, and the clothes you wear; these things are particularly important in the early stages of relationship development. Attractive females have an easier time persuading others than do those who are perceived as less attractive. In general, Americans think attractive people are more credible, happier, more popular, more sociable, and even more prosperous than less attractive people.[90] There is also evidence that if you believe that others think a person is attractive, you'll be more likely to evaluate that person as attractive as well.[91]

The shape and size of your body also affects how others perceive you. Heavier and rounder individuals are often perceived to be older, more old-fashioned, less good-looking, more talkative, and more good-natured than thin people, who are perceived to be more ambitious, more suspicious of others, more uptight and tense, more negative, and less talkative. Muscular and athletically fit folks are seen as better looking, taller, and more adventurous. These perceptions are, in fact, so common that they have become easily recognizable stereotypes on which casting directors for movies, TV shows, and plays rely in selecting actors and actresses.

Aside from keeping you warm and within the legal bounds of decency, your clothes also affect how others perceive you. The clothes you wear are a way of communicating to others how you want to be treated. One classic study found that a man who jaywalked while dressed in nice clothes attracted more fellow violators than he could when he was shabbily attired.[92] Although studies have attempted to identify a "power" look, and magazines are constantly giving prescriptions for ways to be attractive and stylish, there is no formula for dressing for success.[93]

Interpreting Nonverbal Communication

So what does it all mean? How do you make sense out of the postures, movements, gestures, eye contact, facial expressions, uses of space and territory, touch, and appearance of others? Albert Mehrabian has found that people synthesize and interpret nonverbal cues along three primary dimensions: *immediacy, arousal,* and *dominance.*[94]

Relating to Others in the 21st Century / Communicating Nonverbal Meta-Messages Online

Metacommunication, as you recall from Chapter 1, is communication about communication—one channel of communication, such as nonverbal cues, provides information about another channel of communication, the words used. Because many, if not most, people communicate online using only text, it may seem odd to discuss the role of nonverbal communication as meta-messages when you tap out words to others. But even a lean communication medium such as instant messaging or e-mail offers subtle (and sometimes not-so-subtle) nonverbal cues that provide meta-messages—information about the nature of your relationship with your communication partner.

In Chapter 1 we noted that social information processing theory suggests that we have a smaller "bandwidth" when communicating online; electronically mediated communication (EMC) tends to emphasize content over relationship messages. Relational cues are nonetheless present and provide meta-messages to others. Over time a considerable amount of relational metacommunication influences how you interact with others online. Understanding how nonverbal messages are evident in all forms of EMC, including text messages, can help you maintain an other-oriented perspective by interpreting the relational cues that are present. Here are several examples of how nonverbal messages, sometimes explicit yet often implicit, provide a meta-message when you relate to others online.

Emoticons

One obvious way we express nonverbal messages that influence the meaning of our words is with the now-ubiquitous emoticon. Emoticons are used to express a range of emotions from happiness :) to surprise :0, anger :<, and even flirtatious winks ;). Even when used minimally, emoticons provide a shorthand way of expressing your feelings. Emoticons can also signal when you're making a sarcastic remark, as when you write "I was thrilled to see her there :/." Researchers have found that we use emoticons in text messages in places where we would pause or establish eye contact with others when talking face to face.[95]

Punctuation

An exclamation mark (!) provides a powerful emotional punch to whatever message you've expressed. Writing "Nice to hear from you!!" with a double exclamation mark upgrades a normal greeting to an enthusiastic declaration. Other punctuation marks also provide relational information: commas, colons, semicolons, and periods signal the language rhythm the writer had in mind as he or she was composing the message, just as our use of pauses does when we talk to others. A message dashed off with no punctuation communicates a metamessage of informality.

Underlining and Italics

Just as gestures add emphasis to spoken words, underlining and *italicizing* words help the reader know what the writer wants to emphasize. Both underlining and italics take an additional second or two to add to your message; the extra effort of italicizing a word sends a message that you have thought about how you'd like to emphasize your idea.

Capitalization

Like the volume control on your TV, capitalization serves as a way to increase the volume of your message. Capitalizing letters has the same effect as shouting. When typed all in capital letters, the phrase "HEY, LET'S GET TO IT" communicates greater urgency that "Hey, let's get to it." Overuse of all capital letters would be like constantly raising your voice. So be careful to "shout" only when you need to add emphasis.

Message Length

If you send someone a chatty, fairly long e-mail message describing the details of your day, and you get a short and simple reply that says "Thanks," the unverbalized meta-message may be that your communication partner wasn't all that interested in you or your message. If you send a lengthy message, you probably expect a long message in response. Or, if you send a text message to simply announce "I'm here" and you get a long-winded, detailed written response, your expectations are likely violated. And you might feel some pressure to respond with an equally long response. Reciprocation or nonreciprocation of message length provides meta-message cues about interest in your message.

Response Time

In addition to how long a return message is, you will likely make inferences about the other person's interest in hearing from you based on how quickly you get a response. The shorter the response time, the more likely you will be to conclude that the other person is interested in the conversation. Of course, if you know the other person is not available when you send your message, a sluggish response time is understandable. But if you know the other person checks messages frequently or usually has his or her phone on, a long response time may signal a cooler, less-involved relationship.

Media Choice

You send a meta-message to someone based on which communication medium you use. Canadian communication theorist Marshall McLuhan famously said, "The medium is the message." Whether you choose to send a text message, make a phone call, or schedule a time to connect via webcam provides information about the relationship. A richer medium (such as a webcam session, which allows you to see images and converse in real time when immediate feedback is possible) signals that the message you wish to convey is relatively important. *Flaming* is any type of antisocial or negative message or behavior exhibited online. There is evidence that you are more likely to flame when using a relatively lean medium such as text or e-mail than you are when using a webcam or interacting in person.[96]

Emoticons :), punctuation (!!), underlining, *italicizing*, CAPITALIZATION, message length, response time, choice of medium, and even your attention to spelling and proofreading all provide meta-messages. Monitoring the way you encode EMC and the subtle relational cues you send can help ensure that the message you intended to express is the message received.

These three dimensions provide a useful way to summarize how nonverbal cues may be interpreted.

Immediacy: Communicating Liking

Sometimes, we cannot put a finger on the precise reason we find a person likable or unlikable. Mehrabian believes that immediacy cues are a likely explanation. Immediacy cues are behaviors that communicate liking and engender feelings of pleasure. The principle underlying the communication of our feelings of **immediacy** is simple: We move toward persons and things we like and avoid or move away from those we dislike. Immediacy cues increase our sensory awareness of others. Use of space and territory is not the only cue that contributes to positive or negative feelings. Mehrabian has noted several other nonverbal cues that increase immediacy. One of the most powerful is touch; others include a forward lean, increased eye contact, and an open body orientation. The meaning of these behaviors is usually implied rather than explicitly spelled out in words.

Not surprisingly, communication researcher Lois Hinkle found that spouses who reported high feelings of affection for their mates reported that their mates responded by expressing more immediacy cues toward them.[97] There is also evidence that when someone expresses immediate or pleasant nonverbal messages toward us, we reciprocate by responding in a pleasant manner. Researchers Judee Burgoon and Beth Le Poire found that people adapt their nonverbal messages to others.[98] When people express immediacy or liking toward you, you are more likely to reciprocate and express a similar sentiment toward them. Immediacy is contagious. Yet another research study found that expressions of nonverbal immediacy on the part of someone trying to offer support and comfort to another person, such as closer personal distance, touching, and forward lean, helped reduce the other person's stress and tension.[99]

In brief, we use the following cues to communicate that we like someone:[100]

Proximity:	Close, forward lean
Body orientation:	Typically face to face, but could be side by side
Eye contact:	Mutual eye contact
Facial expression:	Smiling
Gestures:	Head nods, movement
Posture:	Open, arms oriented toward others
Touch:	Cultural- and context-appropriate touch
Voice:	Higher pitch, upward pitch

Arousal: Communicating Responsiveness

The face, voice, and movement are primary indicators of **arousal.** If we sense arousal cues, we conclude that another person is responsive to and interested in us. If the person acts passive or dull, we conclude that he or she is uninterested.

When you approach someone and ask whether he or she has a minute or two to talk, that person may signal interest with a change in facial expression and more animated vocal cues. People who are aroused and interested in you show animation in their face, voice, and gestures. Forward lean, a flash of the eyebrows, and a nod of the head are other cues that implicitly communicate arousal. Someone who says, "Sure, I have time to talk with you" in a monotone and with a flat, expressionless face is communicating the opposite. Think of arousal as an on-off switch. Sleeping is the ultimate switched-off state.

immediacy Feelings of liking, pleasure, and closeness communicated by such nonverbal cues as increased eye contact, forward lean, touch, and open body orientation.

arousal Feelings of interest and excitement communicated by such nonverbal cues as vocal expression, facial expressions, and gestures.

Dominance: Communicating Power

The third dimension of Mehrabian's framework for implicit cues communicates the balance of power in a relationship. **Dominance** cues communicate power, status, position, and importance.[101] Raising the head while looking someone in the eye is perceived as communicating greater dominance than lowering the head.[102] A person of high status tends to have a relaxed body posture when interacting with a person of lower status.[103] When you talk to a professor, he may lean back in his chair, put his feet on the desk, and fold his hands behind his head during the conversation. But unless your professor is a colleague or a friend, you will maintain a relatively formal posture during your interaction in his office.

Shaking hands is a centuries-old greeting or farewell ritual that communicates power or lack of it. Alan and Barbara Pease report that people in leadership positions are more likely to be the ones who initiate a handshake than are non-leaders.[104] The person who feels the most power in a relationship is more likely to shake hands with his or her palm facing down; a submissive handshake, reports nonverbal communication researcher Peter Collett, is offered with the palm facing up. Collett has meticulously analyzed handshakes of politicians and other leaders to reveal that the person who feels the most power literally takes the upper hand when shaking hands.[105]

A person's surroundings can communicate her degree of power just as clearly as her clothing and behavior do.

Another dominance cue is the use of space. High-status individuals usually have more space around them; they have bigger offices and more "barriers" protecting them. A receptionist in an office is usually easily accessible, but to reach the president of the company, you may have to navigate through several corridors, past several secretaries and administrative assistants who are "guarding" the door.

Are most people aware of the power cues they express or receive from others? Your ability to detect nonverbal expressions of power may relate to whether you think you are powerful or not. One research team found that subordinates were better at interpreting power cues from their supervisors than supervisors were at interpreting power cues from their subordinates.[106] What this means is that if you think you have less power in a relationship, you are more likely to be aware of the more dominant power of others' nonverbal cues. If you think you do have power, you may be less sensitive to nonverbal expressions of power.

Other power cues that communicate dominance include use of furniture, clothing, and locations. You study with others at a table in the library; the college president has a large private desk. You may wear jeans and a T-shirt to class; the head of the university wears a business suit. Your dorm may be surrounded by other dorms; the president's residence may be a large house surrounded by a lush, landscaped garden in a prestigious neighborhood. People use space, territory, posture, and artifacts such as clothing and furniture to signal feelings of dominance or submissiveness in the presence of others.

Research confirms that we have certain expectations about how people who are perceived to have power will behave nonverbally.[107] People who are thought to have more power, for example, are thought to more freely express their anger and disgust than are people who have less power and status. British social psychologist Michael Argyle summarizes the nonverbal cues that communicate dominance:[108]

Use of space:	Height (on a platform or standing)
	Facing a group
	More space surrounding a person

dominance Power, status, and control communicated by such nonverbal cues as a relaxed posture, greater personal space, and protected personal space.

205

Eye contact:	More when initially establishing dominance
	More when staring to establish power
	More when talking
Face:	Frown, no smile
Touch:	Initiating touch
Voice:	Loud, low pitch, greater pitch range
	Slow, more interruptions, more talk
	Slight hesitation before speaking
Gesture:	Pointing at the other or at his or her property
Posture:	Standing, hands on hips, expanded chest, more relaxed

▶ RECAP   Dimensions for Interpreting Nonverbal Behavior

Dimension	Definition	Nonverbal Cues
Immediacy	Cues that communicate liking and pleasure	Eye contact, touch, forward lean, closeness to partner
Arousal	Cues that communicate active interest and emotional involvement	Eye contact, varied vocal cues, animated facial expressions, forward lean, movement
Dominance	Cues that communicate status and power	Protected space, relaxed posture, status symbols

Improving Your Skill in Interpreting Nonverbal Messages

Advice books, magazine articles, and experts on talk shows may make it seem like it's easy to "read" someone's "body language" by applying a few simple techniques. But as we have already cautioned, there are no dictionaries to turn to that will help you accurately interpret specific nonverbal behaviors. Because nonverbal messages are ambiguous, continuous, multichanneled, and influenced by your culture and gender, they can be a challenge to interpret accurately. But there are some research-based strategies that can increase your ability to interpret unspoken messages.

We often interpret messages based on how we *expect* people to behave in a specific situation. One theory that helps explain how and why we interpret nonverbal messages the way we do is called **expectancy violation theory.** Developed by Judee Burgoon and several of her colleagues, this theory suggests that each of us interacts with others with certain preconceived expectations about their behavior.[109] Our expectations are based on our life experiences and our culture. The research conclusions that we've summarized in this book about when eye contact is likely to occur, when we'll probably smile or frown, or how most people express immediacy, dominance, or arousal are based on the general expectations we have about how other people behave. For example, most Westerners expect that when meeting a business colleague for the first time, a person will smile, extend a hand, and say, "Hello, I'm . . ." and then say his or her name. If, instead, the person clasps two hands together and bows demurely without uttering a word, the nonverbal behavior is not what we expect. This violation

expectancy violation theory
Theory that you interpret the messages of others based on how you expect others to behave.

of our expectation would cause us to wonder what the "violator" of our expectations might mean by bowing instead of offering to shake our hand. When our expectations are violated, we may feel uncomfortable.

But when people behave nonverbally in ways that we may not expect, we adapt our behavior, especially if we are other-oriented and skilled in responding to other people.[110] If your new business colleague greets you with a bow rather than a handshake, it is appropriate to offer a bow in return, rather than trying to shake the person's hand. So, we're constantly making observations and comparing what we expect with what we get, and then adapting our behavior based on what happens.

Some people are simply better at interpreting nonverbal cues than others. The ability to interpret nonverbal cues is *not* related to a person's race, amount of education, or intelligence, but it *is* related to certain personality traits. And, in general, women have been found to be more interpersonally sensitive than men when interpersonal sensitivity was measured as the ability to accurately *recall* the nonverbal behavior of another person.[111] Research offers some clues as to who is most skilled at encoding nonverbal messages.[112]

1. People who are better at accurately expressing their feelings and emotions are also better able to interpret nonverbal expressions from others.

2. People who are skilled in interpreting one channel of information (for example, facial expression or vocal cues) are likely to be more accurate at interpreting nonverbal messages from other channels (such as posture or use of space).

3. People with certain personality characteristics have been found to interpret nonverbal messages more accurately. For instance, people who are extroverted, have high self-esteem, are nondogmatic, are not shy, and are expressive typically do a better job of interpreting nonverbal messages than do people who do not have these personality characteristics.

4. People who select such people-oriented jobs as teachers, salespersons, and nurses often have more skill in interpreting nonverbal messages.

Even if you don't have a natural talent for interpreting nonverbal cues, with training and practice, you can enhance your sensitivity to and accuracy in interpreting them. Several principles and key skills can help you to interpret others' nonverbal messages.

Consider Nonverbal Cues in Context

Just as quoting someone out of context can change the meaning of a statement, trying to draw conclusions from an isolated snatch of behavior or a single cue can lead to misinterpretations. Beware of looking at someone's folded arms and concluding that he or she does not like you or is not interested in what you are saying. It could be that the air conditioner is set too low and the person is just trying to keep warm.

> **BEING Other-ORIENTED**
>
> The ability to accurately interpret the nonverbal expressions of others is both a natural talent and a skill that can be enhanced. How would you assess your own ability to accurately interpret the nonverbal messages of others, on a scale from 1 to 10, with 1 being low and 10 being high?

Look for Clusters of Nonverbal Cues

Instead of focusing on a specific cue, look for corroborating cues that can lead you to a more accurate conclusion about the meaning of a behavior. Is the person making eye contact? Is he or she facing you? How far away is he or she standing from you? Always consider nonverbal behaviors in conjunction with other nonverbal cues, the environment, and the person's verbal message.

Consider Past Experiences When Interpreting Nonverbal Cues

It may be that "familiarity breeds contempt," as the old saying goes, but familiarity with another person also increases your ability to interpret his or her nonverbal behavior. You may have learned, for example, that when your mother starts crying when you play the piano, it signals pride, not melancholy. Family members can probably interpret each other's nonverbal cues more accurately than can those outside the family. But after knowing someone over a period of time, you begin to increase your sensitivity to certain glances, silences, movements, and vocal cues that might be overlooked or misunderstood by others.

Check Your Perceptions with Others

perception checking Asking someone whether your interpretation of his or her nonverbal behavior is accurate.

In Chapter 3 we discussed the key skill of **perception checking.** You can follow three steps to check your perception of someone's nonverbal behavior. First, observe the nonverbal cues, making a point to note such variables as eye contact, posture, use of gestures, facial expression, and tone of voice. Second, try to interpret what the individual is expressing through his or her nonverbal behavior. Finally, check your perception by asking him or her if it is accurate. Of course, we are not suggesting that you need to go through life constantly checking everyone's nonverbal cues. Overusing this skill would be irritating to most people. We are suggesting, however, that when you are uncertain of how someone feels, and it is important to know, a perception check may be in order. Consider the following example.

Building Your Skills   Practicing Nonverbal Perception Checking

We have identified several strategies to improve your skill at interpreting the nonverbal messages of others, including being able to check your perceptions of others. Accurately perceiving others gets to the heart of becoming other-oriented.

Look at the photographs. First, note the nonverbal behavior of the target person in the picture. Next, form a mental impression of what you think the person is thinking and feeling. Finally, compose a perception-checking question that the other person in the photo could ask to confirm the target person's thoughts and feelings.

Photo 1

A. Describe the student's nonverbal behavior.

B. What do you think the student is thinking and feeling?

C. What is a perception-checking question the teacher could ask her student?

Photo 2

A. Describe the customer's nonverbal behavior.

B. What do you think the customer is thinking and feeling?

C. What is a perception-checking question the salesman could ask the customer?

Deonna: Mom, I wanted to let you know that Erik and I are going to have to miss the family reunion next weekend. Life has been so hectic lately that we and the kids haven't had much time together, so we're going to spend the weekend home relaxing.

Muriel: (Frowns, avoids eye contact, folds her arms, and uses a flat voice.) Oh, don't worry about it.

Deonna: Well, you say not to worry about it, Mom, but it looks like you are upset. I know that look of yours. I also hear in your voice that you are not really pleased. Is it really OK, or are you a little miffed?

Muriel: Well, yes, to be honest, Dad and I were really looking forward to getting all the kids together.

Deonna: I'm sorry, Mom. We will make an effort to be at the next one. Thanks for admitting how you really feel.

Asking about a specific nonverbal cue will help you interpret your partner's behavior in future interactions as well. As we noted earlier, evidence suggests that the longer couples are married, the more they rely on nonverbal behavior to communicate. One study claims that some couples spend less than eleven minutes a week in sustained conversation.[113] Even in marriages of fifty years, however, conversation is still required occasionally to clarify nonverbal responses.

▶ RECAP   How to Check Your Perceptions of Others' Nonverbal Cues

Steps	Consider . . .
1. Observe their nonverbal behavior	Are they frowning?
	Do they make eye contact?
	Are their arms crossed?
	What is their tone of voice?
	What is their posture?
2. Form a mental impression of what you think they mean.	Are they happy, sad, angry?
	Is the nonverbal message contradicting the verbal message?
3. Ask questions to check whether your perception is accurate.	"Are you upset? You look angry."
	"Your expression and your voice suggest you don't believe me. Do you think I'm lying?"
	"The look on your face tells me you really like it. Do you?"

Be Aware That the Nonverbal Expression of Emotion Is Contagious

Have you ever noticed that when you watch a funny movie, you are more likely to laugh out loud if other people around you are laughing? That when you are around people who are sad or remorseful, you are more likely to feel and express sadness? There's a reason this happens. Nonverbal emotional expressions are contagious. People often display the same emotions that a communication partner is displaying. **Emotional contagion theory** suggests that people tend to "catch" the emotions of others.[114] Interpersonal interactions with others can affect your nonverbal expression of emotions.[115] The ancient Roman orator Cicero knew this when he gave advice to public speakers. He said if you want your audience to experience joy, you must be a joyful speaker. Or, if you want to communicate fear, then you should express fear when you speak.

emotional contagion theory
Theory that emotional expression is contagious; people can "catch" emotions just by observing others' emotional expressions.

Look for Cues That May Communicate Lying

In a *60 Minutes* TV broadcast, baseball superstar Alex Rodriguez boldly claimed he had not taken steroids to enhance his athletic performance. Yet nonverbal communication expert Paul Ekman, after analyzing videotapes of the interview, found clear evidence that Rodriguez was not being truthful. Repeated shoulder shrugs, a tightened corner of his lip, as well as lengthwise stretching of his lips provided telltale signals that he was lying.[116]

When it comes to using nonverbal cues to detect deception, you have to know what to look for. Research has found that when we can both see and hear a person, we have a tendency to judge the person as telling the truth—even when the person isn't being honest.[117] Perhaps we think we're pretty good at detecting deception if we can see the person, but that's not often the case.

Several researchers have been interested in identifying nonverbal cues that indicate deceit.[118] Remember not to place too much emphasis on a single cue. As we've just noted, you'll need to look for clusters of cues rather than pointing your finger when someone has less eye contact and saying, "Ah ha! Now I know you're a liar!" Table 7.1 summarizes research conclusions about nonverbal messages, comparing liars and those who are telling the truth.[119]

Researchers have found that when communicating in electronically mediated settings, liars write more words, use more references to the senses (seeing, touching, hearing), and use fewer self-oriented pronouns ("Here's what *I* think . . .") but more other-oriented pronouns ("*You* should consider this . . .").[120] So when you're trying to detect deceit in others, don't just rely on nonverbal cues. Consider the words as well.

It would be easier to detect deception if people had noses like Pinocchio's, which would grow just a bit whenever they told a lie. But in the real world, among the best ways to detect whether someone is telling the truth are to (1) look for nonverbal clues, (2) listen to the content of what the person says, and (3) measure such physiological responses as heart rate, breathing, and other factors.[121] Although nonverbal cues (such as hand and finger movements, pauses, and increased use of illustrators) can be important in helping judges sort out truth-tellers from liars, ultimately it's better to listen to the message and monitor physiological responses (which, of course, may not always be practical).

Unless you have a portable lie detector, which measures physiological responses such as heart rate, blood pressure, and breathing rate, the best approach may be to ask other

TABLE 7.1	Who's Telling the Truth? Honest vs. Dishonest Communicators	
Nonverbal Cue	**Honest Communicators . . .**	**Dishonest Communicators . . .**
Voice	Use fewer pauses when they talk.	Pause more; they are thinking about what "story" they want to give.
	Speak fluently, smoothly.	Use more nonfluencies ("ah," "er," "um").
	Speak at a normal speaking rate.	Speak a bit faster than normal.
Facial Expression	Smile genuinely and sincerely.	Display a plastered-on, phony smile.
		May smile a bit too long.
Gestures	Are less likely to play with objects as they speak.	Are more likely to play with objects (for example, twiddle a pencil).
	Use fewer gestures.	Use more gestures, more self-adaptors, touching their face and body, shrugging their shoulders.
	Are not likely to shift body weight.	Are more likely to shift their posture.
	Generally display less nervousness.	Display increased nervousness.
Eye Contact	Maintain normal eye contact—a steady, natural gaze.	May look away, maintain less direct eye contact.
	Have a normal eye-blink rate.	Have an increased eye-blink rate, a sign of increased anxiety.

people for corroborating information.[122] Or you can do your own investigation to ferret out whether someone is really telling the truth. Nonverbal cues may be important in giving us an *initial* hunch as to whether someone is telling the truth, but personal detective work may be the real way we ultimately confirm our hunches.

Improving Your Skill in Expressing Nonverbal Messages

Although we've offered recommendations about how to accurately interpret nonverbal cues, you may wonder "What can I do to express my feelings accurately to others using nonverbal cues?" Consider the following tips.

Be Mindful of Your Nonverbal Behavior

Are you aware of your nonverbal behavior at this moment? What is your facial expression communicating to others? Are you twiddling a pen or pencil? Are your hands and feet jiggling as you read these words? Even if you may not be aware of feeling anxious or nervous, your nonverbal behaviors may send those messages unless you're mindful of what you are doing. Being aware of your nonverbal behavior is the first step in improving your skill in expressing your feelings to others. There is evidence that most people "leak" nonverbal cues—we can't completely control all aspects of our nonverbal behavior, such as the size of the pupils in our eyes or our facial expressions. However, we can control many aspects of how we present ourselves to others. For example, now that you know the nonverbal behaviors that communication liking, power, or interest, you can check to see if your behavior matches your intentions.

There's another reason to be mindful of your nonverbal expressions: As we noted earlier, if your nonverbal message doesn't match your verbal message, it's your nonverbal message that will carry the most weight in terms of influencing the meaning of the message. If your communication goal is to express an emotion, nurture a relationship, or provide support and encouragement, check to ensure that your nonverbal message is expressing the sentiment that you express verbally. You can undermine your verbalized message with an out-of-synch or contradictory nonverbal message. So be aware of what your nonverbal message may be communicating to others.

Observe Others' Reactions to Your Nonverbal Behavior

By being a keen observer of how other people respond to you, you can develop a greater understanding of how your behavior affects others. Be a detective on the lookout for clues about how your nonverbal behavior is creating meaning for others. For example, you may be in a good mood, but if others don't to be reacting positively to your positive feelings, take note of the reactions you're receiving. Are you doing something to trigger a negative reaction in others? Noting the amount and duration of eye contact you receive, the facial expressions of others with whom you interact, and even the openness of their body posture will provide clues to how other people are responding to your messages. Of course, their responses could be focused on something you've said rather than on your nonverbal behavior. So it's especially useful to monitor how people are reacting to you when you're listening and not speaking.

Ask Others About Your Nonverbal Behavior

It's good to have a close friend who can give you honest advice about the nonverbal impression you make on others. Just as you may ask a trusted confidant to give his or her reaction to what you're wearing, you can also ask people you trust for honest feedback about your nonverbal behavior. Consider asking whether your actions fit your words and whether the feeling and overall mood you have is what you're communicating nonverbally. Asking for others' perception of your nonverbal behavior—inviting perception checking—can help you evaluate your nonverbal behavior.

Practice Your Nonverbal Behavior

If you've taken a public speaking class, your instructor has undoubtedly encouraged you to practice your speech so as to polish your speech delivery. Maybe you videotaped your speech or even practiced in front of a mirror to check your delivery. We're not suggesting that you rehearse "spontaneous" interpersonal conversations; that would cause you to sound stilted and artificial. But you can observe yourself on video to gain a sense of how others perceive you. If you think you need to polish your nonverbal social skills, you could consider practicing greeting others or expressing both positive and negative emotions. Again, you need not develop a script and memorize your message, but using a video camera or even a mirror to practice facial expressions and informal gestures and observe your posture can give you some insight into how to enhance your nonverbal persona. Over 100 years ago, elocution teachers used charts and other drill and practice techniques to help their students practice how to walk, move, and express themselves. But we recommend that you approach practicing nonverbal behavior with a sense of play rather than as an assignment. Spending some time practicing and experimenting with how you express yourself nonverbally can increase your awareness of how others see you.

APPLYING AN OTHER-ORIENTATION
to Nonverbal Communication

Nonverbal cues are the primary means by which we assess the feelings and emotions of others. Nonverbal cues also provide important information about the nature of the relationships you have with others. But because nonverbal messages are more ambiguous than verbal messages, your interpretation of someone's nonverbal behavior may not always be accurate. One way to enhance your ability to interpret others' nonverbal communication is to be aware of someone's normal, baseline way of responding to others.

We noted, for example, that fidgeting fingers and tapping toes may be signs of inattention, frustration, or anxiety—but if you know that your communication partner *normally* fidgets or has a habit of tapping his fingers or wagging a pencil when listen-

ing, you have a baseline for interpreting the behavior. "Oh," you may think, "He does that all the time. So he's not nervous. It's just a habit." When trying to better interpret the meaning of someone's nonverbal messages, it's important to know what the person's normal behavior is.

How do you develop a baseline for someone's normal nonverbal behavior? You'll need to spend time with the other person. That's why we noted that the longer you know someone, the more accurately you can assess the meaning of the nonverbal messages. Perhaps a friend will say, "Oh, I'm really listening to you. I just fidget a lot." Or "I'm still interested in what you're saying; I'm just thinking." These statements give you perspective for interpreting the friend's behavior. And over time, you

can tell whether the person's interpretation of his or her own behavior is accurate.

But most people don't verbalize their nonverbal behavioral norms or typical response patterns. So interpreting the nonverbal messages of others can be like testing a scientific hypothesis. You observe someone's behavior and make a good guess about what the behavior means. But, you need a normal pattern of communication behavior with which to compare the specific behavior. Be patient: Don't jump to conclusions about the meaning of a nonverbal behavior based on a small sample of someone's behavior. Knowing a person's normal, baseline nonverbal reactions will increase your accuracy in decoding that person's nonverbal messages.

Why Learn About Nonverbal Communication and the Challenge of Interpreting Nonverbal Messages
(pages 185–191)

Nonverbal communication is behavior other than written or spoken language that creates meaning for us. Although verbal and nonverbal cues work together to create meaning, nonverbal communication is the primary way in which we communicate feelings, attitudes, and emotions. Nonverbal communication is also the primary source of relationship cues, helping us initiate, maintain, and develop relationships. Interpreting others' nonverbal messages helps us appropriately adapt our communication and navigate through our daily interpersonal interactions and conversations. However, it can be difficult to interpret nonverbal cues because nonverbal messages are ambiguous, continuous, multichanneled, and culture-based.

Key Terms

Nonverbal communication 185
Interaction adaptation theory 188
Interactional synchrony 188

Critical Thinking Questions

1. Consider a communication exchange you had recently. What nonverbal cues were present? What type of eye contact, body language, and facial expressions did you observe? Did you have difficulty interpreting the nonverbal cues of your communication partner(s)? Did the nonverbal cues communicate anything that was at odds with the spoken message? Explain.

2. Ethics: Is it appropriate to draw definitive conclusions about another's personality and attitudes based only on a reading of his or her nonverbal cues? Support your answer.

Activities

Over the next week, do some serious people watching. Spend some time observing people in a public place, such as a café or coffee shop, on campus, at a bus stop, or at the mall. Make an ongoing list of nonverbal behaviors you observe. Do these behaviors support the verbal messages that you hear, such as greeting friends, asking for service, thanking someone, and the like? Are you able to notice whether any of these behaviors are ambiguous, continuous, or multichanneled? Do you observe gender and/or cultural differences in nonverbal behaviors? Discuss your findings with your classmates.

Web Resources

http://anthro.palomar.edu/language/language_6.htm Communication is far more than spoken or written words. At this site you can read the article "Language and Culture: Hidden Aspects of Communication" to sharpen your skill in interpreting nonverbal cues.

http://www.andrews.edu/~tidwell/lead689/NonVerbal.html This site defines nonverbal communication, explains why it is important, and explores cultural differences in the expression and meaning of nonverbal communication.

Nonverbal Communication Codes
(pages 192–202)

Nonverbal cues can be categorized and studied to reveal the codes of our unspoken communication, including body movement and gestures, eye contact, facial expressions, and vocal cues. Researchers have identified five categories of body movement and gestures that contribute to interpersonal communication: emblems, illustrators, affect displays, regulators, and adaptors. Our use of personal space and territory also communicates a variety of messages, particularly those pertaining to power, status, and relational concerns. Touch and appearance can also be powerful nonverbal cues.

Key Terms

Kinesics 192	Proxemics 199
Emblems 193	Intimate space 199
Illustrators 193	Personal space 200
Affect display 193	Social space 200
Regulators 193	Public space 200
Adaptors 194	Territoriality 200
Backchannel cues 197	Territorial markers 200

Critical Thinking Questions

1. Consider some recent communication exchanges you had, either face to face or over the phone. How much information did you gather from your partner's vocal cues, including backchannel cues? Were you able to make inferences about your communication partner's mood and emotions just from the tone, pitch, rate, or quality of these vocal cues? Now compare these exchanges with some recent online communication you've had. Was it more difficult to make the same kinds of inferences about moods or emotions without vocal cues? Were there other ways in which emotions were communicated? Explain.

2. Ethics: Donald really wants to be hired as a salesperson. He hires a fashion consultant to recommend what he should wear and determine how he should look when he interviews for a job. In general, is it ethical to manipulate your appearance so that you can impress others?

Activities

Go on a nonverbal communication scavenger hunt. Observe your family members, classmates, and friends to find one or more of the following sets of nonverbal communicators:

a. Examples of emblems, illustrators, affect displays, regulators, and adaptors

b. Examples of how people use the four zones of personal space

c. Examples of the cognitive, monitoring, regulatory and expressive functions of eye contact

d. Examples of emotions expressed by facial expressions or vocal cues

e. Examples of how people use touch to communicate

f. Examples of clothing or accessories that reveal intentions or personality traits

Web Resources

http://humanresources.about.com/od/interpersonalcommunicatio1/a/nonverbal_com.htm Need help understanding nonverbal communication? This site offers tips to aid understanding and demonstrates the power of this type of communication.

Interpreting Nonverbal Communication and Improving Your Skills
(pages 202–212)

Researchers have identified three primary dimensions for interpreting nonverbal messages: immediacy, arousal, and dominance. These three dimensions provide useful information about your communication partner: level of liking or dislike, level of interest in the exchange, and the position and status of the participants. To enhance your skill in interpreting nonverbal cues, always consider the context in which you observed the cues, look for clusters of nonverbal behaviors, and consider past experiences. Being other-oriented allows you to adapt, even if others' nonverbal behaviors are not what you expect. Learning to check your perceptions and detect deception further enhance your ability to interpret others' nonverbal communication. And being aware of your own nonverbal behavior is also important in expressing your feelings and emotions to others.

Key Terms

Immediacy *204*	Expectancy violation theory *206*
Arousal *204*	Perception checking *208*
Dominance *205*	Emotional contagion theory *209*

Critical Thinking Questions

1. Describe a situation in which you made eye contact with a stranger. Was it unpleasant or disturbing? Did the stranger's behavior communicate interest or liking? How did you react? Explain.

2. Greg has been told that he sometimes comes across as cold, aloof, or standoffish. What could Greg do to communicate his desire to be warm and approachable?

3. Ethics: Is it ethical for salespeople, politicians, and others who wish to make a favorable impression to alter their nonverbal messages to get you to like them, vote for them, or buy their products? Explain.

Activities

Evaluate your classroom based on the nonverbal messages this learning space communicates. Consider the following questions:

- What does the furniture arrangement communicate about the likelihood for interaction with others?

- Based on the room arrangement, what cues provide information about who has the most power and influence in this space?

- What do the colors of the classroom communicate? For example, are they contemporary or old-fashioned? Are they conducive to learning? Do they affect interpersonal communication?

- What does research about zones of personal space reveal about interpersonal communication in the room?

- On a scale from 1 to 10 (with 1 being low and 10 being high), how would you evaluate the overall attractiveness of the furniture and room décor (posters, photos, other art)? How does the attractiveness (or lack of attractiveness) of the space influence interpersonal communication? How does it enhance or detract from learning?

- What other aspects of the room have an effect on interpersonal communication and/or learning?

Use the questions in the previous activity to evaluate another room where you spend a lot of time, such as the library or student center, or another place where you typically study when you are not in class. Describe how the room's arrangement and overall appearance influence interpersonal communication as well as learning and studying.

Web Resources

http://www.culture-at-work.com/nvnegotiation.html At this site you'll learn about the importance of nonverbal communication when negotiating with others.

Conflict
Management
Skills

" Outside noisy, inside empty. "

Chinese Proverb

Thomas E. Ricks, a journalist and author who spent a considerable amount of time in Iraq reporting on the Iraq war, reached an astounding conclusion about the strategy that he believes changed the nature of the conflict for the better. Ricks observed: "When we stopped trying to figure out new ways of killing people and began to relate to others as individuals, there was a dramatic decrease in casualties and we started coming a lot closer to achieving our mutual goals."[1] Relating to the enemy as individuals rather than plotting violence against them may seem like an overly simplistic and idealistic strategy for managing an intractable political problem, yet Ricks concluded that such an approach made a difference in changing the tone of the conflict. Could the same strategy that Ricks observed in war apply to interpersonal relationships? As you will learn in this chapter, there are times to collaborate as well as times to confront others when conflict occurs. It would be naive to assume that all conflicts can be managed by applying communication principles and techniques. Yet regardless of the conflict style employed or the conflict strategies used, being other-oriented is a useful perspective for addressing interpersonal conflict and discord.

Interpersonal conflict is a fact of life. Eventually, all relationships experience conflict. It's been estimated that people in stable, romantic relationships experience a conflict episode about twice a week.[2] And the longer you know someone, the greater the likelihood that you'll experience conflict with that person, simply because you spend time together and know more about each other.[3] The key question of this chapter is, How can you best manage the inevitable conflict that occurs in your relationships with others?

Conflict management is not a single skill, but a set of skills. But to manage conflict effectively involves more than learning simple techniques. The best route to success in resolving conflict effectively is acquiring knowledge about what conflict is, what makes it happen, and what we can do about it. We will begin by defining conflict, then examine some of the myths about it and focus on some of its constructive functions. We will also discuss the relationship among conflict, power, and conflict management styles.

In addition, we will discuss how learning about your typical style of managing conflict can give you insight into managing interpersonal differences. And finally, we will build on our discussions of listening skills and verbal and nonverbal communication in the previous chapters to help you learn to manage the inevitable interpersonal conflicts that arise even in the best of relationships.

Conflict Defined

At the bedrock of all conflicts are differences—in goals, needs, and experiences. Unresolved and poorly managed interpersonal conflict is a significant predictor of an unsatisfactory interpersonal relationship. The opposite is also true: Partners in relationships in which conflict is effectively managed report being more satisfied with the relationship.[4] But precisely what is conflict? **Interpersonal conflict,** according to communication scholars William Wilmot and Joyce Hocker, includes four elements: It is (1) an expressed struggle (2) between at least two interdependent people (3) who perceive incompatible goals, scarce resources, or interference from others (4) and who are attempting to achieve specific goals.[5]

Conflict Elements

You probably don't need a textbook definition to determine whether you are experiencing conflict in a relationship. You know you're in conflict as you feel your emotions becoming aroused, as evidenced by an increased heart rate, muscle tension, and

interpersonal conflict An expressed struggle between at least two interdependent people who perceive incompatible goals, scarce resources, or interference in the achievement of their goals.

a raised voice.[6] Yet looking at the elements of conflict can help you understand both why conflict occurs and how to manage it.

An Expressed Struggle. You typically don't know that someone is upset with you until he or she expresses displeasure with a remark or by a nonverbal behavior such as a glare, a steely facial expression, or an emotion-laden tone of voice. The intensity of a conflict (as conveyed through the intensity of the emotion expressed) often correlates with the partners' perceptions of the importance of their unmet needs or goals. Sam Keltner developed the "struggle spectrum," shown in Figure 8.1, to describe conflicts ranging from mild differences to outright fights.[7] As conflict evolves in a relationship, it has the potential to escalate into physical abuse, especially in our most intimate relationships. One research team estimated that 50–60 percent of U.S. households have experienced at least minor forms of violence; there's evidence that in one out of every six romantic relationships, one partner has stalked the other.[8] Experts surmise that one reason violence is so prevalent in many relationships is that people don't have the skills to manage conflict.[9] They don't know how to express their relational struggle effectively.

Between at Least Two Interdependent People. By **interdependent** we mean that people are dependent on each other; what one person does or says affects the other.[10] If you were truly independent of someone, then what he or she did or said would have minimal effect on you. You are more likely to have conflict with people that you spend time with because you are connected to them in some way. Yes, you might have an emotional response to the anonymous driver who cuts you off in traffic, but the conflicts that weigh most heavily on us are those with people with whom we interact most frequently. And, as the old expression "it takes two to tango," suggests, it takes at least two people to have interpersonal conflict. You can certainly have intrapersonal conflict (conflict within yourself), but interpersonal conflict is between you and at least one other person.

Incompatible Goals, Scarce Resources, and Interference. Conflict often happens because two people want the same thing, but both can't have it, or because what one person wants is the opposite of what the other wants. Or, when resources (time, money, or something else) are scarce, there is more likely to be tension.[11] Whether it's a custody battle between former spouses who both want custody of the children, or a conflict over whether you spend the holidays with your parents or with your spouse or partner's parents, when there are conflicting or incompatible goals, not enough of something to go around, or someone is blocking what you believe is rightfully yours, conflict happens.

Achieving a Goal. People in conflict want something. As we noted, many conflicts occur because both people can't (or perceive that they can't) achieve their own goals. Understanding what the individuals in conflict want is an important step toward finding a way to manage the conflict. Most problems boil down to something you want more of or less of. Figuring out what you and the other person want more of or less of provides a starting point to getting to the end of conflict.

Unresolved and poorly managed interpersonal conflict is a significant predictor of an unsatisfactory interpersonal relationship.

interdependent Dependent on each other; one person's actions affect the other person.

FIGURE 8.1

The Struggle Spectrum

Used by permission of the National Communication Association.

← Mild Differences Disagreement Dispute Campaign Litigation Fight →

Conflict as a Process

Cathy was reading the Sunday paper, enjoying a second cup of coffee, and listening to her favorite classical music station. All seemed well. Suddenly, for no apparent reason, her roommate Barb brusquely stormed into the room and shouted, "I can't stand it anymore! We have to talk about who does what around here." Cathy was taken completely off guard. She had no idea her roommate was upset about the division of household chores. To her, this outburst seemed to come out of the blue; in reality, however, several events had led up to it.

Most relational disagreements have a source, a beginning, a middle, an end, and an aftermath.[12]

Source: Prior Conditions.   The first phase in the conflict process is the one that sets the stage for disagreement; it begins when you become aware that there are differences between you and another person. The differences may stem from role expectations, perceptions, goals, or resources. In the previous example, Barb perceived that she and Cathy played different roles in caring for the household.

In interpersonal relationships, *many* potential sources of conflict may be smoldering below the surface. It may take some time before they flare up into overt conflict. Moreover, they may be compounded with other concerns, making them difficult to sort out. And it may not be just one conversation or issue that triggers conflict; multiple conflict "trip wires" may contribute to a conflict episode.[13]

Beginning: Frustration Awareness.   At this stage, at least one of you becomes aware that the differences in the relationship are increasingly problematic. You may begin to engage in self-talk, noting that something is wrong and creating frustration. Perhaps you realize that you won't be able to achieve an important goal or that someone else has resources you need to achieve it. Or you may become aware of differences in perceptions. Barb knew that Cathy's family always spent their weekends relaxing. All the members of Barb's family, in contrast, pitched in on weekends to get household chores done for the week. Barb may have recognized that difference, even as her frustration level rose.

Becoming aware of differences in perception does not always lead to increased frustration. But when the differences interfere with something you want to accomplish, your frustration level rises. Barb wanted to get the house clean so that she could turn her attention to studying for a test she had the next day. Cathy's apparent indifference to helping Barb achieve that goal was a conflict trigger.

Middle: Active Conflict.   When you bring your frustration to the attention of others, a conflict becomes an active, *expressed struggle.*[14] If frustrations remain only as thoughts, the conflict is passive, not active. Active conflict does not necessarily mean that the differences are expressed with shouting or emotional intensity. An expression of disagreement may be either verbal or nonverbal. Calmly asking someone to change an attitude or behavior to help you achieve your goal is a form of active conflict; so is kicking your brother under the table when he starts to reveal a secret to the rest of the family.

Cathy was not aware of the division of labor problem until Barb stormed into the room demanding a renegotiation of roles. Barb had been aware of her frustration for some time, yet had not acted on it. Many experts advocate not waiting until your frustration level escalates to peak intensity before you approach someone with your conflict. Unexpressed frustration tends to erupt like soda in a can that has just been shaken. Intense emotions can add to the difficulty of managing a conflict.

End: Resolution. When you begin to try to manage the conflict, it has progressed to the resolution stage. Of course, not all conflicts can be neatly resolved. Couples who divorce, business partners who dissolve their corporation, or roommates who go their separate ways have all found solutions, even though they may not be amicable ones.

After Barb's outburst, she and Cathy were able to reach a workable compromise about the division of their household labor. Cathy agreed to clean the house every other week; Barb promised not to expect her to do it on weekends.

Aftermath: Follow-Up. As Yogi Berra once said, "It ain't over 'til it's over." After a conflict has been resolved, the follow-up stage involves dealing with hurt feelings or managing simmering grudges, and checking with the other person to confirm that the conflict has not retreated into the frustration awareness stage.[15] As we noted in Chapter 1, interpersonal relationships operate as transactive processes rather than as linear, step-by-step ones. Conflict does progress in stages, but you may need to resolve the same conflict again unless you confirm your understanding of the issues with your partner.

The Friday after their discussion, Cathy proudly showed off a spotless apartment to Barb when she came home from class. Barb responded with a grin and a quick hug and privately resolved to get up early on Sunday morning so that she could go out to get Cathy pastries and the Sunday paper before she awoke. This kind of mutual thoughtfulness exemplifies a successful follow-up in a conflict.

> **RECAP** **Understanding Conflict as a Process**
>
> | | |
> |---|---|
> | **Prior Conditions Stage** | The stage is set for conflict because of differences in the individuals' actions or attitudes. |
> | **Frustration Awareness Stage** | One individual becomes aware that the differences are problematic and becomes frustrated and angry. |
> | **Active Conflict Stage** | The individuals communicate with each other about the differences; the conflict becomes an expressed struggle. |
> | **Resolution Stage** | The individuals begin seeking ways to manage the conflict. |
> | **Follow-Up Stage** | The individuals examine their own feelings and check with each other to monitor whether both are satisfied with the resolution. |

Understanding the stages of conflict can help you better manage the process. You'll also be in a better position to make the conflict a constructive rather than a destructive experience. Conflict is **constructive** if it helps build new insights and establishes new patterns in a relationship. Airing differences can lead to a more satisfying relationship in the long run. David W. Johnson lists the following as benefits of conflict in interpersonal relationships. Interpersonal conflict

- Focuses attention on problems that may have to be solved.
- Clarifies what may need to be changed.
- Focuses attention on what is important to you and your partner.
- Clarifies who you are and what your values are.
- Helps you learn more about your partner.
- Keeps relationships interesting.
- Strengthens relationships by increasing your confidence that you can manage disagreements.[16]

constructive conflict Conflict that helps build new insights and establishes new patterns in a relationship.

By focusing on the problem at hand rather than assuming a defensive attitude, this machinist and his foreman may reach a constructive solution to their conflict.

Although conflict can be constructive, we don't want to oversell the value or function of conflict in relationships with others. Conflict can also be **destructive.** The hallmark of destructive conflict is a lack of flexibility in responding to others.[17] Conflict can become destructive when people view their differences from a win–lose perspective, rather than looking for solutions that allow both individuals to gain.

Conflict Triggers

Researchers have found that just as conflict typically follows a predictable path as it evolves, there are also some common causes that trigger conflict. Being aware of the topics and issues that often create conflict can help you be on your guard when discussing these issues. Two of the biggest **conflict triggers** are entitlement and fairness. If we believe we're entitled to something and we've been denied it, conflict is likely. And if we believe we have not been treated fairly or equitably, conflict is often the result. "It's mine, not yours!" and "That's not fair!" are claims children make while playing with others in a sandbox; those same sentiments fuel conflict between adults, as well as international conflicts between nations.

Scholars have identified dialectical tensions that are common conflict triggers in many relationships. A **dialectical tension** stems from people's need for two things at the same time.[18] First, we have a desire to be both separate from other people and connected to them at the same time; we want our freedom, but we also want the comfort, predictability, and convenience of having someone who is a consistent part of our life. This can cause conflict if, for example, you want more freedom in a relationship, but your partner wants to keep closer tabs on what you are doing and where you are. You may feel this as a personal dialectical tension, because you want both things at the same time: to be close to the other person *and* to have your freedom.

A second common dialectical tension is that we want and need various degrees of both openness and closedness in our relationships. We want to share and disclose our thoughts and feelings, but we also want our privacy and to keep some things secret.

The two dialectical tensions help explain why conflict is present in virtually all relationships. Besides these two tensions, researchers have discovered there are some common issues that cause conflict for couples. Researcher Lawrence Kurdek found that regardless of whether couples were heterosexual, gay, or lesbian, several topics or issues serve as conflict triggers: (1) power (who's in charge), (2) social issues (such as politics and religion), (3) personal flaws (such as use of drugs or alcohol, smoking, or laziness), (4) distrust (concern about whether one person is telling the truth), (5) intimacy (differences about the frequency and timing of sex), and (6) personal distance (as evidenced by the amount of time each person commits to the relationship).[19] (There are many other things that couples argue about, such as money, but money conflicts are often about power.) These "big six" appear to be common conflict themes across a wide variety of relationships.

In addition to the underlying tensions and topics that trigger conflict, researchers have discovered a conflict trigger that especially affects some (but certainly not all) married men. Some husbands have a heightened sensitivity to what they perceive as criticism from women—not just their wives in particular, but women in general.[20] That is, some men have a bias of treating *any* comment from *any* female as negative. This sensitivity to criticism may lead to conflict. It's been described as "empathic inaccuracy." The greater their "empathic inaccuracy," the more likely the husbands

destructive conflict Conflict that dismantles rather than strengthens relationships.

conflict triggers Common causes of interpersonal conflict.

dialectical tension Tension arising from a person's need for two things at the same time.

were to respond to their wives with verbal aggression. Why do some men do this? It's speculated that some men may have an insecure attachment style, a concept we discussed in Chapter 2. If a husband is insecure about his relationship with others, especially women, he may be more likely to lash out verbally when receiving negative comments from women. The research found that men who could better empathize with their spouses and accurately infer that their spouses really did have specific and realistic points to make reported having more satisfying and happier relationships.

In addition to tensions, controversial topics, and bias, physical conditions can trigger conflict. When you are not at your physical best—when you're tired, stressed, or overworked—it may be wise to steer clear of situations that are likely to trigger disagreement. Before you know it, what you thought was just a casual remark can quickly escalate into conflict. The beginnings of vacations, when you and your friend, partner, or spouse may be at the peak of fatigue, are prime occasions for conflict. Or, the end of a long workweek may also be a time when it doesn't take much to turn a conversation into the Friday night fights. Not surprisingly, research has documented that being under the influence of alcohol or other substances that impair judgment increases the chances that conflict will erupt.[21] Be aware of the times when you and your partner are tired or not thinking clearly. It is best to tackle difficult topics and issues when you both are rested and can give undivided attention to listening and responding.

"How many miles before our next fight?"

Conflict Myths

Although not all conflict is destructive to relationships, many cultures have taboos against displaying conflict in public. The prime experiences in life that shape how we learn to express and manage conflict occur in the families in which we grew up. It's in our families that we learn life lessons about relationships that remain with us throughout our days.[22] According to one researcher, many of us were raised with four myths that contribute to our negative feelings about conflict.[23] As you read the following sections, you may shake your head and say, "That's not where I came from." In some American families, conflict is expressed openly and often. But even if your experience has been different, reading about these prevailing myths may help you understand your or your partner's emotional responses to conflict.

Conflict Is Always a Sign of a Poor Interpersonal Relationship

It is an oversimplification to assume that all conflict is rooted in underlying relational problems. Conflict is a normal part of any interpersonal relationship.[24] Although it is true that constant bickering and sniping can be symptomatic of deeper problems, disagreements do not necessarily signal that the relationship is on the rocks. All relationships experience conflict. In fact, overly polite, stilted conversation is more likely to signal a problem than periodic disagreements.[25] The free expression of honest disagreement is often a hallmark of healthy relationships. Assertively and honestly

---

BEING Other-ORIENTED

It's hard to be focused on others when you're under stress, tired, or worried about something. Have you noticed that you tend to experience more interpersonal conflict when either you or your communication partner are not at your best? What can you do to minimize conflict when you or others are fatigued or under stress?

expressing ideas may mean that a person feels safe and comfortable enough with his or her partner to disagree. Conflict in interpersonal relationships can play a constructive role in leading people to focus on issues that may need attention. The ebb and flow of interpersonal psychological intimacy and separation inevitably lead to some degree of conflict in any relationship. When conflict happens in your relationships, don't immediately assume that the relationship is doomed.

Conflict Can Always Be Avoided

"If you can't say anything nice, don't say anything at all." Many of us were taught early in our lives that conflict is undesirable and that we should eliminate it from our conversations and relationships. Yet evidence suggests that conflict arises in virtually every relationship.[26] Because each of us has a unique perspective on our world, it would be extraordinary for us *always* to see eye to eye with another person. One study found that most romantic couples have some kind of disagreement or conflict, on average, about twice a week. Although such conflicts may not be intense, many differences of opinion punctuate our relationships with people we care about.[27]

Research suggests that contentment in marriage relates not to the amount of conflict, but to the way in which partners manage it.[28] Conflict is also a normal and productive part of interaction in group deliberations.[29] It is a myth that conflict is inherently unproductive and something to be avoided. It happens, even in the best of relationships.

Conflict Always Occurs Because of Misunderstandings

"You just don't understand what my days are like. I need to go to sleep!" shouts Janice as she scoops up a pillow and blanket and stalks off to the living room. "Oh, yeah? Well, you don't understand what will happen if I don't get this budget in!" responds Ron, who is hunched over the desk in their bedroom. It is clear that Ron and Janice are having a conflict. They have identified the cause of their problem as a lack of understanding between them, but in reality they *do* understand each other. Ron knows that Janice wants to sleep; Janice knows he wants to stay up and work. Their problem is that they disagree about whose goal is more important. This disagreement, not lack of understanding, is the source of the conflict.

Conflict Can Always Be Resolved

Consultants, corporate training experts, and authors of self-help books often offer advice about how to resolve conflicts so that all will be well and harmony will prevail. Some people claim that with the application of a few skills and how-to techniques, conflicts can disappear like a stain from a shirt laundered with the right kind of detergent. This is simply not true. Not all differences can be resolved by listening harder or paraphrasing your partner's message. Some disagreements are so intense and the perceptions so fixed that individuals may have to agree to disagree and live with it.

Conflict Types

At some time or another, many close relationships go through a conflict phase. "We're always fighting," complains a newlywed. But if she were to analyze these fights, she would discover important differences among them. According to communication researchers Gerald Miller and Mark Steinberg, most conflicts fit into one of three different categories: (1) pseudoconflict—triggered by a lack of understanding; (2) simple conflict—stemming from different ideas, definitions, perceptions, or goals; and (3) ego conflict—which occurs when conflict gets personal.[30]

Pseudoconflict: Misunderstandings

Will: Let's walk to the store.

Sean: No, it's too far. Let's drive.

Will: But the store is close.

Sean: No, it's not.

Will: Yes, it is. It's just off Market Street.

Sean: Oh, you mean the convenience store.

Will: Sure, that's exactly what I mean.

Sean: Oh, no problem. I thought you meant the supermarket.

Pseudoconflict is simply a misunderstanding. Your partner may communicate confusion by facial expressions or other nonverbal behavior. Pseudo-conflict can be resolved if partners ask for clarification, listen between the lines, and work to establish a supportive climate.

Pseudo means false or fake. **Pseudoconflict** occurs when we simply miss the meaning in a message. But unless we clear up the misunderstanding by asking for more information, a real conflict might ensue. Note that in this example, Will offers helpful information ("It's just off Market Street"), and Sean checks it with feedback ("Oh, you mean the convenience store").

How can you avoid pseudoconflict? A key strategy is to clarify the meaning of words and expressions that you don't understand. Keep the following strategies in mind to minimize misunderstandings before they occur:

- *Check your perceptions:* Ask for clarification of anything you don't understand; seek to determine whether your interpretation is the same as your partner's.

- *Listen between the lines:* Look for puzzled or quizzical facial expressions from your partner. People may not voice their misunderstanding but express their uncertainty nonverbally.

- *Establish a supportive rather than a defensive climate for conversation:* Avoid evaluating, controlling, using manipulative strategies, being aloof, acting superior, or rigidly asserting that you're always right. These classic behaviors are like pushing the button to increase defensiveness and misunderstanding.

Simple Conflict: Different Stands on the Issues

Simple conflict stems from differences in ideas, definitions, perceptions, or goals. You want to go to Disney World for your vacation; your spouse wants to go to Washington, D.C. Your spouse wants to fly; you would rather take the train. You understand each other, but you disagree.

A key to unraveling a simple conflict is to keep the conversation focused on the issues at hand so that the expression of differences does not deteriorate into a battle focusing on personalities.

The following exchange between Jason and Nick illustrates a conflict over a simple difference of opinion; notice how both partners stick to the issues and figure out a way to resolve their differences.

Jason: I want to watch *The Simpsons* tonight. It's their Christmas show.

Nick: No way, man. I have to watch a documentary about textiles for my history class. It's an assignment.

Jason: But I've worked all weekend. I'm beat. The last thing I want to watch is some stuffy old documentary on the history of weaving.

BEING **Other**-ORIENTED

Listening for the unspoken message is especially important when experiencing conflict with another person. What are nonverbal cues that you can look for to provide information about what the other person may be feeling or experiencing? How do you know whether you have made accurate inferences when "listening between the lines"?

pseudoconflict Conflict triggered by a lack of understanding and miscommunication.

simple conflict Conflict that stems from different ideas, definitions, perceptions, or goals.

UNDERSTANDING OTHERS
Adapting to Differences | Gender, Culture, and Conflict

Some research suggests that there are distinctions between feminine and masculine styles of responding to conflict. The feminine style is more likely to focus on relationship issues, whereas the masculine style typically focuses on tasks.[31] People with a feminine style often interact with others to achieve intimacy and closeness, but people with a masculine style interact to get something done or to accomplish something apart from the relationship. People employing a masculine style are often more aggressive and assertive than those employing a feminine style when pursuing a goal.[32] The following list summarizes key differences that researchers have observed between feminine and masculine styles of responding to conflict. Note that individuals of either sex may employ some characteristics of both feminine and masculine gender styles.

In addition to gender, an individual's culturally learned assumptions influence his or her conflict management behavior. In some cultures, conflict is typically **expressive,** in that it focuses on the quality of relationships and on managing interpersonal tension and hostility. In other cultures, conflict is more likely to be

Perceived Gender Differences in Responding to Conflict[33]

People with Feminine Styles . . .	People with Masculine Styles . . .
Are concerned with equity and caring; connect with and feel responsible to others.	Are concerned with equality of rights and fairness; adhere to abstract principles, rules.
Interact to achieve closeness and interdependence.	Interact to achieve specific goals; seek autonomy and distance.
Attend to interpersonal dynamics to assess relationship's health.	Are less aware of interpersonal dynamics.
Encourage mutual involvement.	Protect self-interest.
Attribute crises to problems in the relationship.	Attribute crises to problems external to the relationship.
Are concerned with the impact of the relationship on personal identity.	Are neither self- nor relationship-centered.
Respond to conflict by often focusing mainly on the relationship.	Respond to conflict by often focusing on rules and being evasive until a unilateral decision is reached.

instrumental, centering less on relationships and more on achieving a specific goal or objective.[34] Individuals from collectivist cultures, those that value group harmony and peaceful interpersonal relationships, tend to be more sensitive to expressive, relational cues, which are often expressed nonverbally. People from cultures that value achievement, especially individual achieve-

ment, are more likely to use an instrumental style of conflict management.

Another factor that influences how conflict is managed in interpersonal relationships is whether those involved are from a low-context culture (whose members derive more meaning from words than from the surrounding context) or a high-context culture (in which the context

---

expressive conflict Conflict that focuses on issues about the quality of the relationship and managing interpersonal tension and hostility.

instrumental conflict Conflict that centers on achieving a particular goal or task and less on relational issues.

Nick: Tell you what. Go ahead and watch *The Simpsons.* I'll record the documentary and watch it later. Deal?

Jason: Okay. Thanks. And I'll grill some burgers so we can have supper together first.

This next exchange between Sue and Nadiya is a bumpier one. What starts as a simple conflict deteriorates into a series of personal attacks.

Nadiya: Sue, can I borrow your skirt? I have a date tonight. It would look great with my new jacket.

Sue: Sorry, Nadiya. I'm going to wear it tonight. I've got to give a presentation to the school board about our new mentor program.

Nadiya: In case you don't remember, when you brought it home, you said I could borrow it any time. Besides, you haven't paid back the twenty bucks I loaned you to buy it.

Sue: Yes, but I bought the skirt especially for this occasion.

Nadiya: Well, don't ask to borrow anything from me ever again. You're just plain selfish.

of the conflict, including nonverbal cues, is especially important). One researcher noted that for people from low-context cultures, such as most North Americans, conflicts are most often instrumental.[35] Many Asian cultures, in contrast, are high-context cultures. They are also collectivist; they value group effort over individual achievement. For people from these cultures, conflicts often center on expressive, relational concerns. Keeping peace in the group or saving face is often a higher priority than achieving a goal.

Later in the chapter we will discuss a model that defines five styles of conflict management: collaboration, compromise, competition, accommodation, and avoidance. These five styles are determined by people's degree of concern for others and concern for self. Two communication researchers, Deborah Cai and Edward Fink, wanted to know whether people from individualistic cultures have different preferences for ways of managing conflict than people from collectivistic cultures. They found that although the collaborating (integrating) style was the overall preferred conflict management style in most cultures, people from individualistic cultures are more likely to use the avoiding style than people from collectivistic cultures. And people from collectivistic cultures are even more likely to first use a collaborative style when conflicts occur.[36]

Although we've summarized research and made some broad generalizations about culture and conflict management, don't think that everyone in a given culture manages conflict the same way. For example, one research team found that there are differences in the way older and younger Chinese adults manage conflict.[37] Older Chinese people tended to favor more accommodating approaches to managing differences, whereas younger Chinese adults used a problem-solving approach.

Researchers suggest that Americans of European descent receive little training in how to develop solutions to problems that are acceptable to an entire group.[38] Because of an emphasis on individual goals and individual achievement, they are often socialized to stick up for their own rights at any cost, and they approach conflict as a win–lose situation. In contrast, people from collectivistic cultures approach conflict situations from a win–win perspective; to them, it is important that both sides save face and avoid ridicule. Such differences in approaches provide a double challenge. In addition to disagreeing over the issue at hand, people from different cultures may also have different strategies for reaching agreement.

What are strategies that will help you manage conflict when interacting with someone who comes from a culture different from yours? Managing culture-based conflict requires a strong other-orientation. Consider these strategies:

- Don't necessarily attempt to manage the conflict based on your own cultural comfort zone; consider the cultural perspective of the other person.

- Review the strategies for intercultural competence that were presented in Chapter 4 to help enhance communication accuracy.

- When in doubt, it's best to use a collaborating style.

- Because people from collectivistic cultures prefer compromising and collaboration, which are styles that take time, it may be wise to not rush the conflict management process if you're interacting with someone from a collectivistic culture.

Sue: Oh, yeah? Well *you're* the one who hogs all the space in the refrigerator. Talk about someone who's selfish. If that's not the pot calling the kettle black!

Nadiya: All right, now that we're being honest about who hogs what, *you're* the one who monopolizes the bathroom in the morning.

And so it escalates. The original disagreement about the skirt is forgotten, and egos become attacked and bruised.

To keep simple conflict from escalating into personal vendettas, consider the following strategies:

- *Clarify your and your partner's understanding* of the issues and your partner's understanding of the source of the disagreement.

- *Keep the discussion focused* on facts and the issue at hand, rather than drifting back to past battles and unrelated personal grievances.

- *Look for more than just the initial solutions* that you and your partner bring to the discussion; generate many options.

- *Don't try to tackle too many issues at once.* Perform "issue triage"—identify the important issues, and work on those.

- *Find the kernel of truth in what your partner is saying.* Find agreement where you can.

- *If tempers begin to flare and conflict is escalating, cool off.* Come back to the discussion when you and your partner are fresh.

Ego Conflict: Conflict Gets Personal

As you can see from the preceding exchange between Sue and Nadiya, a personal attack puts your partner on the defensive, and many people behave according to the adage "The best defense is a good offense." When you launch a personal attack, you are "picking a fight." And as Sue and Nadiya's exchange illustrates, fights that begin as pseudoconflict or simple conflict can easily lapse into more vicious **ego conflict**. And as each person in the conflict becomes more defensive about his or her position, the issues become more tangled.

If you find yourself involved in ego conflict, try to refrain from hurling personal attacks and emotional epithets back and forth. Instead, take turns expressing your feelings without interrupting each other, then take time to cool off.[39] It is difficult to use effective listening skills when your emotions are at a high pitch.

Here are additional strategies to consider when conflict becomes personal:

- *Try to steer the ego conflict back to simple conflict:* Stay focused on issues rather than personalities.

- Make the issue a problem to be solved rather than a battle to be won.

- *Write down what you want to say:* It may help you clarify your point, and you and your partner can develop your ideas without interruption. But by all means avoid putting angry personal attacks in writing. Make your written summary rational, logical, and brief rather than emotion-laden.

- *When things get personal, make a vow not to reciprocate:* Use "I" messages that we talked about in Chapter 5 ("I feel uncomfortable and threatened when we yell at each other.") rather than "you" messages ("You're such a creep. You never listen.") to express how you are feeling.

ego conflict Conflict in which the original issue is ignored as partners attack each other's self-esteem.

RECAP   Types of Conflict

	Pseudoconflict	Simple Conflict	Ego Conflict
What It Is	Individuals misunderstand each other.	Individuals disagree over which action to pursue to achieve their goals.	Individuals feel personally attacked.
What to Do	Check your perceptions.	Clarify understanding.	Return to issues rather than personal attacks.
	Listen between the lines; look for nonverbal expressions of puzzlement.	Stay focused on facts and issues.	Talk about a problem to be solved rather than a fight to be won.
	Be supportive rather than defensive.	Generate many options rather than arguing over one or two options.	Write down rational arguments to support your position.
	Listen actively.	Find the kernel of truth in what your partner is saying; emphasize where you agree.	Use "I" messages rather than "you" messages.

Underlying many interpersonal conflicts is the question of who has power to make decisions.

Conflict and Power

Often what we fight about is not what we're really fighting about. The topic of your argument may be anything from deciding which movie to see to something more significant, such as whether to have children. Yet underlying the surface issue may be a question about who has the power to make the decision. If, during an argument you or your partner says, "Who made you king?" or "What gives you the right to make this decision?" those comments are indicators that underlying the conflict is an issue of power. Power and conflict go hand in hand, because people often use the sources of interpersonal power available to them to achieve their desired outcome when conflict occurs.

Interpersonal power is the degree to which a person is able to influence or control his or her relational partner. During a conflict you may not even be aware of how you are drawing on the power that you have, or that the other person is exerting power to influence you. Nonetheless, power issues are often the "back story" to the conflict. Understanding principles of power and sources of power can give you greater insight into how you are using power to influence others to achieve your goals and how others are seeking to influence or control you, especially during conflict.

Power Principles

Most of us probably don't like to think that other people have power over us, but power is a fundamental element of all our personal relationships. Understanding the role of power in our relations with others can help explain and predict our thoughts, emotions, and behaviors, especially during relational conflict.

interpersonal power Degree to which a person is able to influence his or her partner.

227

Power Exists in All Relationships. Our definition of interpersonal communication that we presented in Chapter 1 suggests that *mutual influence* is an essential element any time you relate to others. When you talk, you are attempting to exert power over other people, if for no other purpose than to get them to listen to you. By definition, being in a relationship means letting someone have some influence on you *and* having influence on the other person.

Power Derives from the Ability to Meet a Person's Needs. If you can meet someone's need, then you have power. The degree to which one person can satisfy another person's interpersonal needs (for inclusion, control, and affection) as well as other needs (for food, clothing, safety, sex, money) represents the amount of power that person has.

In a **dependent relationship,** one person has a greater need for the partner to satisfy his or her needs; the power is out of balance and the person who depends on someone else to meet his or her needs has less power. One study of heterosexual romantic couples found that the partner with less emotional involvement in the relationship had more power, and this was generally the man.[40] The more we depend on one person to satisfy our needs, the more power that person has over us.

Both People in a Relationship Have Some Power. Although sometimes one person in a relationship has more power (influence) than the other, each person has some degree of power. When you were a child, your parents clearly had more power than you did; during conflicts, especially when you were quite young, they used their power to resolve conflicts in their favor. Now the power may be more balanced (or maybe not). When two people are satisfying each other's needs, they create an interdependent relationship; each person in the relationship has some amount of power over the other.

Power Is Circumstantial. Because our needs change, so does power. As you were growing up, you were very dependent on your parents and other adults. However, as you grew and developed skills, you no longer needed your parents to meet certain needs, and thus their power diminished. So the power balance ebbs and flows in a relationship over time and depending on circumstances.

Power Is Negotiated. Partners often negotiate which individual will have decision-making responsibility over what issues. But people can disagree as to who has power to do what. If one partner wants the power to control the TV remote and the other person also wants to have channel-changing power, conflict and tension are the result, unless some negotiation occurs. "OK, you decide what we watch between 6:00 and 8:00 P.M. and I'll control the remote the next two hours" may be one couple's way of negotiating the power. With power negotiated, the conflict is managed—unless one of the individuals wants to revisit who is in charge of the remote. If the negotiation is about something more weighty than who watches which TV program (such as sex, money, or children), the conflict can be more intense, and clearly more is at stake during the power negotiation.

Power Sources

dependent relationship
Relationship in which one partner has a greater need for the other to meet his or her needs.

Why does one person in a relationship have power over the other? Understanding the sources of power can help you analyze the power that you have and that others have over you. During conflict, being mindful of how people can influence you and how you may influence others can help you understand why some conflicts are managed as they are. A classic framework for identifying the sources of power was developed by researchers John French and Bertram Raven.[41] The five sources of power they identified are legitimate (or position) power, referent power, expert power, reward power, and coercive power.

Legitimate power is power that is based on respect for a position that a person holds. Teachers, parents, law officers, store managers, and company presidents all have power because of the position they hold relative to other people. When a police officer tells you to pull off to the side of the road, you respond to this enactment of power by obeying the officer's command.

Referent power is power that comes from our attraction to another person, or the charisma a person possesses. We let people we like influence us. We change our behavior to meet their demands or desires because we are attracted to them.

Expert power is based on a person's knowledge and experience. We grant power to those who know more than we do or have some expertise we don't possess. This expertise can even include knowledge about how to manage a relationship effectively. We grant power to partners who have more experience in relationships. In many episodes of the television series *C.S.I.,* the characters often defer to the expertise of their colleagues, depending on the nature of the issue being investigated.

Reward power is based on another person's ability to satisfy your needs. There are obvious rewards, such as money and gifts, but most rewards are more interpersonal in nature. Reward power is probably the most common form of power in interpersonal relationships. Withholding rewards is actually a form of punishment, or what is called *coercive power*.

Coercive power involves the use of sanctions or punishment to influence others. Sanctions include holding back or removing rewards. If you have a high need for physical affection, your partner might withhold that affection if you do not comply with a given request. Punishment involves imposing something on another person that he or she does not want.

Power to Persuade

When we have power, we may use it to manage conflict in order to achieve our goals and meet our needs using compliance-gaining strategies. **Compliance gaining** is taking actions in interpersonal relationships to gain something from our partners—to get others to comply with our goals. Compliance gaining is persuasion in an interpersonal context. We use communication to influence others by developing and applying compliance-gaining/persuasive strategies.

People's level of power affects what compliance-gaining strategies they employ. People with more power can be more efficient in gaining compliance by using simple, more direct (and sometimes inappropriate) strategies to accomplish their goals.[42] Those with less power need to carefully consider which strategies they can use that won't result in negative consequences. For example, telling your boss that you want Friday night off or you'll quit might result in your no longer having a job. The appropriateness of compliance gaining varies according to our goals. For example, persuasive strategies involving either logic or emotion were seen as more effective in face-to-face interactions than in computer-mediated ones.[43] Communication scholar Kathy Kellerman compiled a list of fifty-six strategies that people might employ in trying to gain compliance (Table 8.1). Think about the last time you sought compliance from a friend, and see if you can identify the strategy or strategies you employed.

legitimate power Power that is based on respect for a person's position.

referent power Power that comes from our attraction to another person, or the charisma a person possesses.

expert power Power based on a person's knowledge and experience.

reward power Power based on a person's ability to satisfy our needs.

coercive power Power based on the use of sanctions or punishments to influence others.

compliance gaining Taking persuasive actions to get others to comply with our goals.

TABLE 8.1	Compliance-Gaining Strategies[44]		
Accuse	Comment	Hint	Protest
Acknowledge	Complain	Inform	Question
Advise	Compliment	Insist	Remark
Apologize	Confess	Insult	Report
Approve	Confirm	Joke	Reprimand
Argue	Criticize	Justify	Request
Ask	Demand	Offer	Ridicule
Assert	Disagree	Order	Suggest
Assure	Disclose	Permit	Summarize
Attack	Excuse	Plead	Tell
Blame	Explain	Point out	Thank
Boast	Forbid	Praise	Threaten
Challenge	Forgive	Prohibit	Vow
Claim	Give	Promise	Warn

Compliance-gaining strategies are responsive to the ongoing, transactive nature of interpersonal relationships.[45] We plot strategies that develop over a number of interactions and modify them in accordance with others' responses. For example, before you ask to borrow money from your friend, you might first do a few favors for her during the day. Then if your friend says no to your request for a loan, you might remind her that she owes you for all you've done for her. If she still says no, you might offer to help her over the weekend with her class project. The type of relationship you have established with the other person will affect your strategy selection. Often, because of our power, we face little resistance from our partners to our requests, so we have no need for any compliance-gaining strategy.

Power Negotiation

If you realize you don't have as much power as you'd like, you may want to renegotiate who has the power to do what in a relationship. Defining who has power can be a source of conflict in interpersonal relationships, potentially even bringing about the end of a relationship. When a partner abuses power, ending the relationship may be warranted. Ideally, partners negotiate a mutually acceptable and rewarding power relationship. To negotiate or renegotiate power in a relationship, consider the following strategies.

Assess Needs. The first step to negotiating a satisfactory balance of power is to identify your needs and those of your partner. Knowing what you need and what the other person needs in the relationship can help you determine whether any negotiation or renegotiation of roles, responsibilities, and assumptions is warranted. Reflecting not just on your needs but also on the needs of the other person is an other-oriented strategy that can help you honestly and realistically start the negotiation process.

Identify Power-Based Conflicts.   Examine your interpersonal conflicts for unresolved power issues. For example, in the first year of marriage, couples often argue about balancing job and family, about financial problems (including who spends money and on what), about the frequency of sexual relations, and about the division of household tasks.[46] These problems involve issues of power, control, responsibility, and decision making. Such issues exist in other relationships as well. Examine your relationships for recurring patterns of conflict, and try to determine the role that power is playing. Conflicts can result from unacceptable imbalances of power (the feeling that one or the other partner has too much), from equal amounts of power (with each partner attempting to influence the other), or as a reaction to attempts to exert control or to dominate.

Discuss Power Issues Directly.   If you're not talking about what the real, underlying issue may be during a conflict—the issue of power—the conflict is unlikely to be managed permanently. Identification of the unmet needs that are fueling conflict should be followed up with conversation about who has, wants, and expects to have influence and control. But when talking about who has power and control in a relationship, it's vital to use the principles and skills of being supportive that we discussed in Chapter 6 as well as effective listening and responding skills. Talking about who should have the power and influence in a relationship can be risky—like touching the third rail on a subway track that carries the electricity that propels the train. Some couples need a trained counselor or therapist to help them work through issues of power in their relationships. The more intense the unmet need that is affecting the power imbalance, the greater the likelihood that help may be needed to address who has the influence in a specific situation.

Conflict Management Styles

What's your approach to managing interpersonal conflict: fight or flight? Do you tackle conflict head-on or seek ways to remove yourself from it? Most of us do not have a single way of dealing with differences, but we do have a tendency to manage conflict by following patterns that we have used before.[47] The pattern we choose depends on several factors: our personality, the individuals with whom we are in conflict, the time and place of the confrontation, and other situational factors. For example, if your boss gives you an order, you respond differently from the way you do if your spouse gives you an order. Virginia Satir, author of *Peoplemaking,* a book about family communication, suggests that we learn conflict response patterns early in life.[48] Ample research evidence supports Satir's conclusion.[49] How we manage conflict with others is related to how our family of origin dealt with conflict.

One of several classifications of **conflict styles** is a five-style model based on the work of K. W. Thomas and R. H. Kilmann that includes two primary dimensions: concern for others and concern for self.[50] These two dimensions result in five conflict management styles, shown in Figure 8.2. The five styles are (1) avoidance, (2) accommodation, (3) competition, (4) compromise, and (5) collaboration.

Avoidance

One approach to managing conflict is to back off and try to side-step the conflict. Typical responses from someone who uses this style are "I don't want to talk about it," "It's not my problem," "Don't bother me with that now," or "I'm not interested in that." The **avoidance** style might indicate that a person has low concern for others as well as for himself or herself. This is sometimes called the "lose–lose" approach to

conflict style Consistent pattern or approach you use to manage disagreement with others.

avoidance Conflict management style that involves backing off and trying to side-step conflict.

FIGURE 8.2

Conflict Management Styles
The five conflict management styles in relation to concern for others and concern for self.

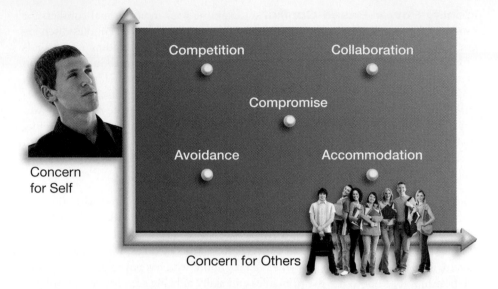

Concern for Self

Competition   Collaboration

Compromise

Avoidance   Accommodation

Concern for Others

conflict. The person using the avoidance conflict style wishes the problem or conflict would go away by itself and appears uninterested in managing the conflict or in meeting the needs of the other person involved in the disagreement. People who avoid conflict may also just not like the hassle of dealing with a difficult, uncomfortable situation. Not dealing directly with conflict may also stem from being unassertive and unable to stand up for one's own rights.

Other times, people avoid conflict because they don't want to hurt the feelings of others. There may be times when avoiding a major blowup with someone is a wise strategy, but hoping the conflict will go away on its own may not always be the best plan.

Evidence suggests that husbands are more likely to avoid confrontation as a way of managing conflict with their wives. One research team argues that males are likely to avoid conflict because of the way they process information, especially emotions.[51] Husbands may implicitly reason that it's better to keep quiet and avoid conflict than to speak up and try to sort things out; for them, the dissonance that results from speaking up is not worth the effort.

demand-withdrawal pattern of conflict management Pattern in which one person makes a demand and the other person avoids conflict by changing the subject or walking away.

One approach to managing conflict is to back off and try to avoid the conflict.

One characteristic of an avoidant conflict management style is the **demand-withdrawal pattern of conflict management.** This is a communication pattern in which one person makes a demand and the other person avoids conflict by changing the subject or just walking way—he or she withdraws from the conflict.[52] The demand-withdrawal pattern is speculated to occur because one of the partners in the relationship wants to change the relationship and the other person does not; another reason may simply be that the person who withdraws may not care about the relationship. Yet another reason people withdraw is because they simply don't like to engage in conflict.

The demand-withdrawal pattern can be found in marriages, dating relationships, and friendships, and between parents and children. Research that looked at how parents and teenagers managed their conflict found that the demand-withdrawal pattern was one of the *least* satisfying approaches to managing conflict.[53] Researchers have found that making repeated demands that aren't directly addressed, while also hurling put-downs at one another, results in a more distressed parent–teenager relationship. If you see that you're in a demand-withdrawal pattern of conflict, try to change the tone of the interaction so that it becomes a conversation rather than a shouting match or a standoff in which you both just stop talking. Make it a goal to keep the conversation going rather than making a demand that results in the other person just walking away.

In some respects, avoiding conflict could be perceived as uncooperative. However, although it may not be cooperative, there are some advantages to avoiding conflict. Doing so provides time for each person in the conflict to think about the issues, cool down, and ponder other approaches to dealing with the issues. If the conflict issue really is trivial or silly, it may also be advantageous not to throttle up the tension to make a mountain out of a molehill.

Avoiding conflict can also allow each person to save face. One of the ways people avoid conflict and try to de-escalate emotional tension is by being deliberately vague or ambiguous about what is causing the conflict. They provide general rather than specific feedback. Yet there is also evidence that in certain situations people find a direct response more honest and competent than a vague one.[54] The trick is accurately reading a situation to know when to be vague and when to be specific.

There are also several disadvantages to avoiding conflict. If you avoid the conflict, you may be sending a message that you really don't care about the other person's feelings; you're more concerned about your own needs. Avoiding the conflict may also just make things worse. A conflict that was simply simmering may boil over if it's not tended to. And, of course, another disadvantage is that the issue remains unresolved. Like a lump in the throat, the conflict just sits there.

Accommodation

To accommodate is to give in to the demands of others. Someone who accommodates believes it's OK if the other person gets what he or she wants. People may sometimes adopt an **accommodation** style because they fear rejection if they rock the boat. Sometimes, people who accommodate don't seem to get angry or upset; they just do what others want them to do. But, in reality, they also accommodate to serve their own interests—to get people to like them. This conflict management style is sometimes called the "lose–win" approach. If you consistently accommodate, you sacrifice your own needs so that someone else can win the argument.

Using the accommodation style has several advantages. For one thing, it shows that you're reasonable and you want to help. If the issue is a minor or trivial one, you may gain some credibility by just letting it slide. Of course, if you are wrong or have made a mistake, accommodation is an appropriate response.

There are disadvantages to accommodating, just as there are disadvantages to any conflict style. Throughout this book, we've stressed the importance of becoming

accommodation Conflict management style that involves giving in to the demands of others.

PEARLS BEFORE SWINE: © Stephan Pastis/Dist. by United Feature Syndicate, Inc.

other-oriented. But we've also noted that being other-oriented means considering the needs and position of the other person, without necessarily doing what the other person wants. Sometimes, a person may accommodate for self-protection rather than because he or she is genuinely interested in others. In the following exchange, note Luke's accommodation response to Martin:

Martin: Luke, I'm not in agreement with you on the QCN merger. I think the merger should be called off.

Luke: OK. Whatever you think is best. I just want you to feel good about your decision.

To accommodate can give the accommodator a false sense of security by producing a "pseudosolution"—one that doesn't really solve anything but just postpones the effort of seeking a solution to the problem. Also, if you consistently accommodate, you may diminish your power to the extent that others take advantage of you; the next time a conflict arises, the expectation may be that you'll give in and the other person will get his or her way again. In addition, if you accommodate too quickly, you short-circuit the possibility of finding a creative solution that is to everyone's liking.

Competition

"You're wrong!" shouts Ed. "Here's how to get our project in on time. We can't waste time in the library. We just have to write up what we have."

"But Ed," suggests Derrick, "the assignment calls for us to have three library sources."

"No. We don't have time. Just do it," Ed insists. Ed sees the issue as a competition that he must win.

Each of us has some need to control and also some need to be controlled by others. But people who have a **competition** conflict management style have a win–lose philosophy. They want to win at the expense of the other person, to claim victory over their opponents. They want to control others. They are typically not other-oriented; instead, they are focused on themselves.

People who compete often resort to blaming, or seeking a scapegoat, rather than assuming responsibility for a conflict. "I didn't do it," "Don't look at me," and "He made me do it" are typical blaming statements.

If these strategies do not work, people with a competitive style may try threats and warnings. Threats refer to actions that people can actually carry out.[55] Warnings are negative prophecies they cannot actually control. The boyfriend who says, "If you don't stop calling me names, I'm going to leave you," has issued a threat; he has the power to leave. If he were to say, "Don't call your parents names, or they'll write you out of their will," that would be a warning. In reality, he has no control over his partner's parents.

Obviously, threats are more powerful than warnings in changing behavior, and then only if the other person would genuinely find the threatened actions punishing or disruptive. If a parent threatens to ground a child, the child will take the threat seriously only if he or she knows the parent will carry it out. If the parent has backed down in the past, the child will probably not pay much attention to the threat.

Is it ever appropriate to compete with others? Yes, if you believe that your position is clearly the best approach and that anything short of achieving your goal would be harmful to you and to others.[56] In an election, someone will win and someone will lose. At the conclusion of a judicial trial, someone typically wins and

competition Conflict management style that stresses winning a conflict at the expense of the other person involved.

someone loses. But even hard-fought elections and controversial trials have rules designed to maintain fairness for all involved in the conflict or decision. During often-emotional periods of competition, those involved nonetheless need to maintain an ethical concern for others.

Compromise

To compromise is to attempt to find a middle ground—a solution that somewhat meets the needs of all concerned. The word *somewhat* is important. Often, when people compromise, no one gets precisely what he or she wants; each has to give up a bit of what he or she had hoped to get. When trying to craft a compromise, you're really expecting to lose something and win something simultaneously; you also expect your partner to lose and win. That's why the **compromise** style is called "a lose/win–lose/win" approach to conflict. As shown in Figure 8.2, when you compromise, you have some concern for others as well as some concern for yourself.

Compromise has some advantages. It can be a good thing if a quick resolution to the conflict is needed. And it reinforces the notion that all parties involved share in equal power. Compromise can also be useful if what is needed is a temporary solution. And it has the advantage of helping everyone save face, because everyone wins at least something.

But if compromising results in each person giving in but no person feeling pleased with the compromise, then a more collaborative approach to managing the conflict may be appropriate.

Collaboration

To collaborate is to have a high concern for both yourself and others. People who use a **collaboration** style of conflict management are more likely to view conflict as a set of problems to be solved rather than a game in which one person wins and another loses. Collaboration, which requires other-oriented strategies that foster a win–win climate, is based on the following principles offered by Harvard researchers Roger Fisher and William Ury.[57]

Separate the people from the problem. Leave personal grievances out of the discussion, describing problems without making judgmental or evaluative statements about personalities.

Focus on shared interests. Ask questions such as "What do we both want? What do we both value? Where are we already agreeing?" to emphasize common interests, values, and goals.

Generate many options to solve the problem. People who collaborate use brainstorming and other techniques to generate alternative solutions. (You will learn more about problem-solving techniques later in this chapter.)

Base decisions on objective criteria. Try to establish standards for an acceptable solution to a problem—these standards may involve cost, timing, and other factors. Suppose, for example, that you and your neighbor are discussing possible ways to stop a nearby dog from barking throughout the night. You decide on these criteria: The solution must not harm the dog; it must be easy for the owner to implement; the owner must agree to it; it should not cost more than fifty dollars; and it must keep the dog from disturbing the sleep of others. Your neighbor says, "Maybe the dog can sleep in the owner's garage at night." This solution meets all but one of your criteria, so you call the owner, who agrees to

---

BEING Other-ORIENTED

Collaboration would be impossible if you failed to consider the thoughts and feelings of the other person. What are ways to identify the interests that you have in common with the person with whom you are in conflict? How can you determine where your goal overlaps with the other person's goal?

---

compromise Conflict management style that attempts to find the middle ground in a conflict.

collaboration Conflict management style that uses other-oriented strategies to achieve a positive solution for all involved.

Those who use a collaborative style of conflict management approach the issue in a spirit of teamwork, so as to foster a win–win climate.

flaming Sending an overly negative online message that personally attacks another person.

disinhibition effect The loss of inhibitions when interacting with someone online that leads to the tendency to escalate conflict.

put the dog in the garage by 10 P.M. Now everyone wins, because the solution meets a sound, well-considered set of objective criteria.

The collaboration conflict management style is best used when those on all sides of the conflict need some new, fresh ideas. Using a collaborative approach also enhances commitment to resolution of the conflict, because all are involved in shaping the outcome. Collaborative approaches to managing conflict build rapport because everyone's concerns are at least noted, if not fully addressed. Finally, collaboration considers feelings and affirms the value of the interpersonal relationship.

It may sound as though collaboration is always the best approach to managing conflict. However, there are times when its disadvantages may outweigh the advantages.[58] One of the biggest disadvantages is the time, skill, patience, and energy required to manage conflict collaboratively. If a solution is needed quickly, other approaches such as compromise may be best.

So, which style of managing conflict is best? The short answer to this question is "It depends." It depends on the outcome you seek, the amount of time you have, the quality of the relationship you have with the other people involved, and the amount of perceived power you and others have.[59] Each style has advantages and disadvantages; no style has an inherent advantage all of the time. The competent, other-oriented communicator consciously decides whether to compete, avoid, compromise, accommodate, or collaborate. Research suggests that what most people find most uncomfortable is (1) no clear resolution to a conflict, (2) a conflict management process that is poorly managed, or (3) the avoidance of issues that they would like to discuss.[60] *There is no single conflict management style that "works" in all situations.* We do, however, strongly suggest that, when time and other factors permit, a collaborative (win–win) conflict management style is worth exploring.[61] The conflict management skills presented in the final section of this chapter are anchored in a collaborative approach to managing conflict.

Although we emphasize the value of the collaborative approach to managing conflict, your cultural background strongly influences the style of conflict management that you prefer. Communication researcher Mitchell Hammer suggests that people from highly individualistic cultures (such as the predominant U.S. culture) prefer a conflict management style that is more direct in addressing the conflict-producing issues.[62] People in collectivistic cultures—those that emphasize group and team interests over individual interests—typically prefer a more indirect approach to addressing conflict. Hammer also suggests that our cultural preferences for expressing or restraining our emotions have an important influence on our preferred conflict management style.[63] People from cultures that emphasize less explicit expression of emotions (Asian cultures, for example) will find intense emotional expressions of anger and frustration distracting and unproductive in managing conflict. Your culture has a strong influence on the degree to which you are direct or indirect when you communicate with others during conflict. Your culture also influences how emotionally expressive or restrained you are when you experience interpersonal conflict.

Relating to Others in the 21st Century | Managing Conflict Online

Our primary focus in the discussion of managing conflict has been on managing conflict in face-to-face situations, yet conflict happens in cyberspace, as well. Because we may miss some of the subtle relational cues that exist in face-to-face situations, pseudoconflict in cyberspace can escalate from a mere misunderstanding to substantive differences (simple conflict). And if those differences become personal (ego conflict), the conflict is much more difficult to unravel.

One of the ways conflict escalates online is when one person engages in flaming. **Flaming** occurs when someone sends an overly negative message that personally attacks someone else.[64] The flamer can further intensify the negative message by "shouting" the message in ALL CAPITAL LETTERS. Flaming can also include calling someone a nasty name or using R-rated language.

There is evidence that people are more likely to use flaming language online than when talking in person. This tendency to escalate conflict online is called the **disinhibition effect.** Without another person directly in front of them, and with emotional tension rising, people tend to lash out—they lose some of their inhibitions; hence the name. What should you do when you find yourself becoming enmeshed in a conflict with someone online? Some of the same strategies that you would use when interacting in person can be useful, but there are specific options to consider when you experience conflict in cyberspace.

First, because of the disinhibition effect, your first impulse may be to immediately respond with a reciprocal flaming message. It's easy to quickly dash off a return "flame." Our suggestion: Resist the temptation to fight fire with flaming fire. It may be cathartic to respond to an unfair criticism or hurtful comment, and you may feel better after you do, but escalating the conflict makes it more difficult to manage. What should you do if you receive a flaming message or if you find yourself responding to even subtle hints of disapproval? Without resorting to flaming, let

the other person know that the flaming makes it difficult for you to respond calmly. Or, simply take some time to cool off before typing a return message that you'll later regret.

Second, consider interacting with the other person in a more media-rich context. Rather than immediately typing a return message responding to the issue lobbed at you, write the other person and suggest that the two of you talk. If it's possible, talk to your communication partner in person; if that's not possible, reach for the phone to talk in real time rather than asynchronously. But before you talk in person or on the phone, take some time to calm down and gather your thoughts. Picking up the phone and shouting at someone is not likely to cool the controversy, but heat it up.

Third, before you write or say anything further, go back and read the previous text or e-mail messages. Try to read the messages while assuming the role of an impartial mediator. Rather than looking for ways to justify your actions or feelings, read the messages as if you were looking at the information for the first time. Look for clues to what may have escalated the conflict. You may discover that either you or your partner misunderstood something in a previous e-mail message. By looking for conflict escalation triggers embedded in previous messages, you can determine where you need to clarify meaning, offer an apology if you've misunderstood something or made a mistake, or ask for more information.

Fourth: Avoid tit-for-tat conflict escalation by paraphrasing what you understand your partner to be communicating. Write a summary of the issues, without trying to score any points, but rather trying to document what is causing the conflict. Then give the other person a chance to agree or disagree with your paraphrase. Don't make any further demands or requests until you're sure you comprehend the issues that are causing the controversy. Turn the conversation into one about clarification rather than hammering away at what you both want.

Fifth: Use humor with caution. In face-to-face contexts, humor can help break the tension. But when you're with someone physically you can more accurately read your partner's nonverbal behavior to know when a joke is helping to reduce the tension and when it's not. Often what makes something funny is the timing of the joke's punch line, or the vocal or physical delivery of an intended humorous comment. Online, with limited nonverbal cues, what you think might reduce tension could escalate it. What you thought was a hoot, the other person may perceive as a sarcastic remark or, even worse, an additional personal attack. So be careful when trying to use the same kind of humor that may work for you in face-to-face situations, because it could fall flat.

Sixth: Take a moment to analyze your emotional reactions. Why are you getting upset and angry? Understanding why you've become upset can help you understand how to start to manage the conflict. Of course, in the heat of conflict, taking time to be mindful of your emotions is easier said than done. When your emotions are cresting, you're *less* likely to pause and ponder the emotional triggers that are escalating the conflict.

Finally, use the other-oriented skill of decentering by asking yourself "What was the other person thinking when he or she wrote that message?" Try to identify the thoughts that may have trigged the negative comments. Then, after considering the other person's thought process, empathize by asking yourself "What was the other person feeling?" By being other-oriented you may gain a new insight into why your angry text or e-mail partner is lashing out. With this insight may come a way of managing the disagreement and moving forward rather than revisiting old wounds.

Conflict occurs both in person and online. Understanding that conflict may occur because of the disinhibition effect, and then implementing some of the suggestions presented here, may be just what you need to do to de-escalate a heated conflict and return your interaction to "room temperature."

RECAP Conflict Management Styles

	The person who uses this style . . .
Avoidance	Withdraws from conflict; tries to side-step confrontation; finds conflict uncomfortable. A lose–lose approach to conflict.
Accommodation	Easily gives in to the demands of others; typically wants to be liked by others. A lose–win approach to conflict.
Competition	Dominates the discussion and wants to accomplish the goal even at the expense of others. A win–lose approach to conflict.
Compromise	Seeks the middle ground; will give up something to get something. A lose/win–lose/win approach to conflict.
Collaboration	Views conflict as a problem to be solved; negotiates to achieve a positive solution for all involved in the conflict. A win–win approach to conflict.

Conflict Management Skills

For many people, at the heart of enhancing the quality of interpersonal relationships is learning to manage conflict.[65] Managing conflict, especially emotion-charged ego conflict, is not easy. The more stress and anxiety you feel at any given time, the more likely you are to experience conflict in your relationships with others. When you are under stress, it's more likely that conflict will become personal and degenerate into ego conflict. And just the opposite is true: When you're rested and relaxed, you're less likely to experience conflict. But even while relaxed and with a fully developed set of skills, don't expect to avoid conflict. Conflict happens. The following skills, previewed in our discussion of a collaborative approach to conflict, can help you generate options that promote understanding and provide a framework for collaboration.[66]

Manage Your Emotions

For weeks, you have been working on a brochure with a tight deadline. You turned it over to the production department with instructions two weeks ago. Today, you call to check on its progress, and you discover that it is still sitting on the production coordinator's desk. You feel your anger begin to erupt. You're tempted to march into the production coordinator's office and scream at her, or to shout at her supervisor.

Try to avoid taking action when you are in such a state. You may regret what you say, and you will probably escalate the conflict.

Often, the first sign that we are in a conflict situation is a feeling of anger, frustration, fear, or even sadness, which sweeps over us like an ocean wave.[67] If we feel powerless to control our own emotions, we will have difficulty taking a logical or rational approach to managing the conflict. Expressing our feelings in an emotional outburst may make us feel better for the moment, but it may close the door to logical, rational negotiation.

When we are emotionally charged, we experience physical changes as well. One researcher found that

"Cool! My new cell phone allows me to see your angry face as well as hear your angry voice."

. . . our adrenaline flows faster and our strength increases by about 20 percent. The liver, pumping sugar into the bloodstream, demands more oxygen from the heart and lungs. The veins become enlarged and the cortical centers where thinking takes place do not perform nearly as well. . . . The blood supply to the problem-solving part of the brain is severely decreased because, under stress, a greater portion of blood is diverted to the body's extremities.[68]

Such changes fuel our fight–flight responses. If we choose to stay, verbal or physical violence may erupt; if we flee from the conflict, we cannot resolve it. Until we can tone down (not eliminate) our emotions, we will find it difficult to apply other skills. Let's look at some specific strategies that you can draw on when an intense emotional response to conflict clouds your judgment and decision-making skills.[69]

Be Aware That You Are Becoming Angry and Emotionally Volatile. One characteristic of people who "lose it" is that they let their emotions get the best of them. Before they know it, they are saying and doing things that they later regret. Unbridled and uncensored emotional outbursts rarely enhance the quality of an interpersonal relationship. An emotional purge may make you feel better, but your partner is likely to reciprocate, which will only escalate the conflict spiral.

Before that happens, become aware of what is happening to you. As we described earlier, your body will start to react to your emotions with an increased heart rate. Be sensitive to what is happening to you physically.

Seek to Understand Why You Are Angry and Emotional. Understanding what's behind your anger can help you manage it. Realize that it is normal and natural to be angry. It's a feeling everyone experiences. You need not feel guilty about it. Anger is often expressed as a defense when you feel violated or when you are fearful of losing something that is important to you. Two powerful anger triggers are (1) feeling that you have not been treated fairly, and (2) feeling entitled to something that you are being denied. Think about the last time you became very angry. Often, you experience a sense of righteous indignation when you are angry. You are being denied something you feel you should have.

Make a Conscious Decision About Whether to Express Your Anger. Rather than just letting anger and frustration build and erupt out of control, make a conscious choice about whether you should express your frustration and irritation. We're not denying that there are valid reasons for you to express anger and frustration, or suggesting that you should not express your feelings. Sometimes, there is no way to let someone know how important an issue is to you other than by forcefully expressing your irritation or anger. As these lines from William Blake illustrate, sometimes the wisest strategy is to be honest with others and express how you feel.

I was angry with my friend:
I told my wrath, my wrath did end.
I was angry with my foe:
I told it not, my wrath did grow.

If you do decide to express your anger, don't lose control. Be direct and descriptive. The guidelines for listening and responding that we provided in Chapter 5 can serve you well. Keep your anger focused on issues rather than personalities.

Select a Mutually Acceptable Time and Place to Discuss a Conflict. If you are upset, or even tired, you risk becoming involved in an emotion-charged shouting match. If you ambush someone with an angry attack, don't expect him or her to be in a receptive frame of mind. Instead, give yourself time to cool off before you try to resolve a conflict. In the case of the lapsed deadline mentioned earlier, you could call both the

BEING Other-ORIENTED

Identifying mutually agreeable approaches to managing a conflict is also a way to manage emotions. What other strategies have worked for you in managing your emotions during conflict?

production coordinator and her boss and schedule an appointment to meet with them later in the day. By that time, you could gain control of your feelings and also think the issue through. Of course, issues sometimes need to be discussed on the spot; you may not have the luxury of waiting. But whenever practical, make sure the other person is ready to receive you and your message.

Plan Your Message. If you are approaching someone to discuss a disagreement, take care to organize your message. Consider rehearsing what you will say. Identify your goal, and determine what outcome you would like; do not barge in and pour out your emotions.

Breathe. One of the simplest yet most effective ways to avoid overheating is to breathe. As you become aware that your emotions are starting to erupt, take a slow, deep breath. Then breathe again. This can help calm you and manage the physiological changes that adrenaline creates. Deep breathing—the prime strategy women use to manage the pain of childbirth—can be a powerful way to restore calmness to your spirit. Focusing on your breathing is also one of the primary methods of meditation. We're not suggesting that you hyperventilate. But taking deep, slow breaths that not only fill your upper lungs but move your diaphragm—the muscle that moves as your lungs expand and contract—is an active strategy to help you regain rational control.

Monitor Nonverbal Messages. As you learned in Chapter 7, your actions play a key role in establishing the emotional climate in any relationship. Monitoring your nonverbal messages can help to de-escalate an emotion-charged situation. Speaking calmly, using direct eye contact, and maintaining a calm, nonthreatening facial expression will signal that you wish to collaborate rather than control. Your nonverbal message should also support your verbal response. If you say you are listening to someone, but you continue to read the paper or work on a report, you are communicating a lack of interest in the speaker and the message.

BEING Other-ORIENTED

Saving face is giving the other person a way to maintain his or her dignity, even if his or her initial ideas and proposals are not accepted in the final resolution of a conflict. What strategies have you used to help others save face and maintain their personal dignity during conflict?

Avoid Personal Attacks, Name Calling, and Emotional Overstatement. Using threats and derogatory names can turn a simple conflict into an ego conflict. When people feel attacked, they respond by protecting themselves. Research has found that when husbands and wives feel disconfirmed during conflict because of name calling or because their partner has made nasty comments, relational satisfaction significantly decreases.[70] It's not surprising that people don't like to be called names. Although you may feel hurt and angry, try to avoid exaggerating your emotions and hurling negative, personal comments at your partner.[71] If you say you are irritated or annoyed rather than furious, you can still communicate your emotions, but you take the harsh sting out of your description. We're not advocating that you be dishonest about how you are feeling; just don't overstate your emotions for dramatic effect. It may make you feel better, but it may make matters worse.[72]

Also avoid the bad habit of **gunny-sacking.** This occurs when you dredge up old problems and issues from the past, like pulling them out of an old bag or gunny sack, to use against your partner. Keep your focus on the issues at hand, not on old hurts. Gunny-sacking usually succeeds only in increasing tension, escalating emotions, and reducing listening effectiveness.

Take Time to Establish Rapport. Evidence suggests that you'll be more successful in managing conflict if you don't immediately dive in and attempt to sort out the issues with your partner.[73] Taking time to establish a positive emotional climate can pay big dividends; this is especially important if you're not well acquainted with the person you're having the conflict with. One study compared how effectively conflict was managed in two different groups.[74] In one group, the conflict negotiators spent time face to face, "schmoozing" and getting to know one another, before trying to negotiate a solution to a conflict. In the other group, the negotiators exchanged informa-

gunny-sacking Dredging up old problems and issues from the past to use against your partner.

Communication and Emotion · Tips for Managing Anger

One of the biggest obstacles to being other-oriented during conflict is the anger we often experience when we feel we're not being listened to or our rights are being violated.[75] Anger is an emotional response to fear. Stated another way, anger is an outward response to an inward feeling of fear. And fear is often about losing something or not getting something we believe is rightfully ours. We may become angry, for example, if we fear we may lose our job or if we sense a relationship that is important to us may be dissolving or becoming less important to the other person. Anger also occurs when we feel someone is keeping us from what we want and have a right to have, someone is unjustly blaming us for something, or someone is attacking us. Some people may tell you it is a good idea to express your anger to the person who is making you angry; get your anger out—don't keep it bottled up. There are times when expressing your anger is appropriate. Being assertive in expressing what bothers you is appropriate when the other person is not aware of what is bothering you. But uncensored angry words can escalate the anger you feel and also increase others' anger.[76] One research

team offers these prescriptions for managing your own anger or coping with someone else's anger during conflict.[77]

- *Be determined not to get angry yourself.* If you know you are going to face someone who is likely to tick you off, prepare yourself before you meet with him or her. Assertively express your feelings, but make a promise to yourself not to "lose it" and allow the encounter to degenerate into a shout fest.

- *Get on the same physical level as the other person.* One person should not be standing and the other sitting. Try to face each other eye to eye. You can also build rapport by trying to mirror the posture of the other person. We're not suggesting that you mimic your partner (this would probably make him or her more angry), but try to adopt a similar communication position.

- *Be silent.* If you are angry and afraid you might say something you'll regret, just be quiet and listen.

- *Express your concern nonverbally.* Because much of an emotional message is communicated nonverbally, use your facial expression and eyes to let the

other person know you care about him or her. Your communication partner will believe what you do, more than what you say.

- *Make an appropriate empathic statement.* Saying "I would probably feel angry if I had experienced what you experienced" or "I think I can see why you are so upset" may help. But be careful not to say, "I know just how you feel" or "I know where you're coming from." For many people, those statements can seem patronizing.

- *Remind yourself that you control your own emotions.* Even though others may do and say things that can upset you, you are the only person who can control yourself and your response to others. Try to respond mindfully to others rather than just reacting emotionally to them.

- *Recognize that angry emotional outbursts rarely change someone's mind.* Exploding in an angry tirade may make you feel better for a moment by "getting it off your chest," but it usually does little to advance understanding and manage the issues at hand.

---

tion via e-mail but did not meet face to face. The negotiators who spent time establishing a positive relationship in person were more successful in managing the conflict to everyone's satisfaction.

Even if you know the other person well, take some time to build rapport. Chatting about such seemingly innocuous topics as the weather or local events can help break the ice and provide a basis for a more positive conversational climate. A positive emotional climate is especially important when trying to sort through vexing, conflict-producing issues.

Several researchers also note how important it is to help the other person in the conflict save face—to not leave the conversation feeling demoralized and humiliated.

Use Self-Talk. Kosta was chairing the committee meeting when Monique accused him of falsifying the attendance numbers at the last fine arts festival. Instead of lashing back at Monique, he paused, took a slow, deep breath, and thought, "I'm tired. If I snarl back, all we will do is escalate this issue out of proportion. I'll talk with Monique later, after we have both cooled down." Perhaps you think that talking to yourself is an eccentricity. Nothing could be further from the truth. As you saw in Chapter 2, thoughts are directly linked to feelings,[78] and the messages we tell ourselves play a major

It's vital to be able to manage your emotions when you find yourself in an interpersonal conflict.

role in how we feel and respond to others. Ask yourself whether an emotional tirade and an escalating conflict will produce the results you want. When Eleanor Roosevelt noted, "No one can make you feel inferior without your consent," she was acknowledging the power of self-talk to affect your emotional response to what others say and do.

As you read the discussion about managing emotions, you may wonder if it's ever useful or productive to express negative emotions, especially anger, overtly when negotiating an issue. One research study found that expressing your anger and frustration might be a productive conflict management strategy if you are negotiating with someone who simply offers no useful alternatives.[79] The research suggests that by expressing your irritation, you may motivate the other person to come up with better alternatives. In most cases, escalating emotional tension decreases the likelihood that the conflict will be managed smoothly and effectively. But sometimes, being honest in expressing your bubbling frustration may nudge things along in a productive way, especially if there are no good options to discuss.

Manage Information

Because uncertainty, misinformation, and misunderstanding are often byproducts of conflict and disagreement, skills that promote mutual understanding are an important component of cooperative conflict management. Based on the listening and responding skills discussed in Chapter 5, the following specific suggestions can help you reduce uncertainty and enhance the quality of communication during conflict.

Clearly Describe the Conflict-Producing Events.   Instead of just blurting out your complaints in random order, think of delivering a brief, well-organized minispeech. Offer your perspective on what created the conflict, sequencing the events like a well-organized story. Describe the events dispassionately so that the other person shares your understanding of the problem.

When Marsha almost had a car accident, she came home and told her husband, "Last week, you said you would get the brakes fixed on the car. On Monday, when you still hadn't taken the car in, you said you would do it on Wednesday. Now it's Friday, and the brakes are in even worse shape. I had a close call this afternoon when the car almost wouldn't stop. We've got to get those brakes fixed before anyone drives that car again."

"Own" Your Statements by Using Descriptive "I" Language.   "I feel upset when you post the week's volunteer schedule without first consulting with me," reveals Katrina. Her statement is an example of the "I" *language* that we have discussed several times in this book. "I" language expresses how a speaker is feeling. The use of the word *I* conveys a willingness to "own" one's feelings and statements about them.

"I" language Statements that use the word *I* to express how a speaker is feeling.

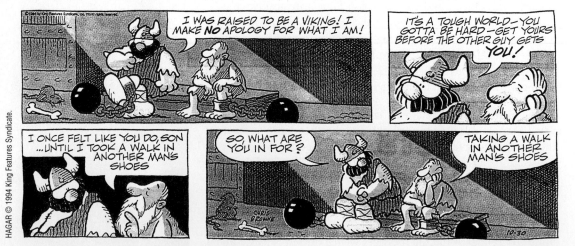

HAGAR © 1994 King Features Syndicate.

And sometimes, to make sure your communication partner doesn't miss the subtlety of your owning your feelings by using an "I" message[80] by saying, for example, "I really don't want you to take this the wrong way. I really care about you. But I want you to know that when you take food from my plate, I feel uncomfortable. My sister sometimes did that when I was a kid, and I didn't like it."

If Katrina had said, "You always prepare a schedule without telling anyone first. All of us who volunteer are mad about that," her statement would have had an accusatory sting. Beginning the statement with *you* sets the listener up for a defensive response. Also, notice that the speaker does not take responsibility for the anger; she suggests that it belongs to several unidentified people as well. If you instead narrow the issue down to a conflict between you and the other person, you put the conflict into a more manageable framework.

One final tip about using "I" messages: Monitor your "**but**" messages. What's a "but" message? It's a statement that makes it seem as though whatever you've said prior to the word *but* is not truly the way you feel. Here's an example: "I love you. I really love you. But I feel really frustrated when you leave your clothes lying on every chair." A "but" message diminishes the positive sentiment you expressed with your "I" language. We're not suggesting that you never say *but,* only that you realize how the word may create noise for the listener; it may make your entire statement seem untrue.

Use Effective Listening Skills. Managing information is a two-way process. Whether you are describing a conflict situation to someone, or that individual is bringing a conflict to your attention, good listening skills will be invaluable.

Give your full attention to the speaker and make a conscious point of tuning out your internal messages. Sometimes, the best thing to do after describing the conflict-producing events is simply to wait for a response. If you don't stop talking and give the other person a chance to respond, he or she will feel frustrated, the emotional pitch will go up a notch, and it will become more difficult to reach an understanding.

Finally, remember to not only focus on the facts or details, but also analyze them so you can understand the major point the speaker is making. Try to use your understanding of the details to interpret the speaker's major ideas. Remember to stay other-oriented and to "seek to understand rather than to be understood."[81]

Check Your Understanding of What Others Say and Do. Respond clearly and appropriately. Your response and that of your conflict partner will confirm that you have understood each other. Checking perceptions is vital when emotions run high.

If you are genuinely unsure about facts, issues, or major ideas addressed during a conflict, ask questions to help you sort through them instead of barging ahead with solutions. Then summarize your understanding of the information; do not parrot the speaker's words or paraphrase every statement, but check key points to ensure that you have understood the message. Note how Ted adeptly paraphrases to check his understanding:

Maggie: I don't like the conclusion you've written to the conference report. It doesn't mention anything about the ideas suggested at the symposium. I think you have also misinterpreted the CEO's key message.

Ted: So if I understand you, Maggie, you're saying the report missed some key information and may also include an inaccurate summary of the CEO's speech.

Maggie: Yes, Ted. Those are my concerns.

Be Empathic. Understand others not only with your head, but also with your heart. To truly understand another person, you need to do more than catch the meaning of his or her words; you need to put yourself in the person's place emotionally. Ask yourself

"but" message Statement using the word *but* that may communicate that whatever you've said prior to *but* is not really true.

these questions: What emotions is the other person feeling? Why is he or she experiencing these emotions? Throughout this book, we have stressed the importance of becoming other-oriented. It's especially important to be other-oriented when you disagree with another person.[82] Trying to understand what's behind your partner's emotions may give you the insight you need to reframe the conflict from your partner's point of view. And with this other-oriented perspective, you may see new possibilities for managing the conflict.

Manage Goals

As you've seen, conflict is goal-driven. Both individuals involved in an interpersonal conflict want something. And for some reason, be it competition, scarce resources, or lack of understanding, the goals appear to be in conflict. To manage conflict, you must seek an accurate understanding of these goals and identify where they overlap.

Communication researchers Sandra Lakey and Daniel Canary found clear support for the importance of being sensitive to and aware of your communication partner's goals when trying to manage conflict.[83] People who were focused on the other person's goals were perceived as much more competent than people who weren't aware of what the other person wanted to accomplish. Let's look at some specific strategies to help manage conflict by being aware of the other person's goals during conflict.

Identify Your Goal and Your Partner's Goal.   After you describe, listen, and respond, your next task should be to identify what you would like to have happen. What is your goal? Most goal statements can be phrased in terms of wants or desires. Consider the following examples:

Problem	Goals
Your boss wants you to work overtime; you need to pick up your son from day care.	You want to leave work on time; your boss wants the work completed ASAP.
Your spouse wants to sleep with the window open; you like a warm room and sleep better with the window closed.	You want a good night's rest; your spouse wants a good night's rest.

Often in conflicts you will face balancing your goal against the goal of maintaining the relationship that you have with your partner. Eventually, you may decide that the latter goal is more important than the substantive conflict issue.

Research by Charles Pavitt and Bradley Kemp confirms the significant role of relationships in conflict and negotiation situations.[84] If you're negotiating with someone you like, you will expect your negotiation partner to use more supportive approaches to achieve the goal. Conversely, if you're negotiating with someone you don't like, you will expect that person to use more threats and demands and be more obstinate.

Next, it is useful to identify your partner's goal. In order to manage conflict, you need to know what the other person wants. Use effective listening and responding skills to determine what each of you wants and to verbalize your goals. Obviously, if you both keep your goals hidden, it will be difficult to manage the conflict.

Identify Where Your Goals and Your Partner's Goals Overlap.   The authors of the best-selling book *Getting to Yes*, Roger Fisher and William Ury, stress the importance of focusing on shared interests when seeking to manage differences.[85] Armed with an understanding of what you want and what your partner wants, you can then determine whether the goals overlap. In the conflict over whether the window should be

Building Your Skills | Communicating with Prickly People

Some people just seem to rub us the wrong way. They generate both friction and heat when we're trying to negotiate with them. In his popular book *Getting Past No,* William Ury suggests we try to change face-to-face confrontation into side-by-side problem solving.[86] Here are Ury's tips for managing conflict with difficult people, based on his review of negotiation literature.[87]

- *Go to the Balcony.* "Going to the balcony" is a metaphor for taking a time out. Take a moment to excuse yourself to cool off when someone pushes your buttons. Staying on the "main stage" to keep banging out a solution may be counterproductive.

- *Step to the Side.* Rather than continuing to debate and refute every argument, step to the side by just asking questions and listening. Change the dynamic of the relationship from a confrontation to a conversation.

- *Change the Frame.* Reframe by trying to see more than an either/or way of managing the conflict. Try to see it from a third, fourth, or fifth point of view. Change your overall perspective for viewing the conflict by not being you: Consider how someone else may view the issue.

- *Build a Golden Bridge.* To "build a golden bridge" is a metaphor for identifying ways to help the other person say yes by saving face. Find an alternative that allows the other person his or her dignity by using objective standards to find a solution.

- *Make It Hard to Say No.* Use information to educate rather than pummel the other person. As Ury puts it, bring people to their senses, not their knees. Help the other person understand the consequences of what he or she supports and the benefits of your alternatives.

Consider a conflict that you had with a prickly person that did not have a satisfying conclusion. How could you have implemented one or more of the five suggestions we've summarized from Ury's research? If it were possible to have a "do over" with this difficult person, what would you do differently? Use the following worksheet to help you identify alternatives for dealing with the prickly person in the situation you have in mind.

Go to the Balcony. At what point in the conflict could you have suggested a cooling-off period?

_____

_____

Step to the Side. Instead of adding new ideas and arguments, when and how could you have stepped to the side to listen and paraphrase?

_____

_____

Change the Frame. How could you have changed the frame of the conflict? What would have been a different way of looking at the issue that created the conflict?

_____

_____

Build a Golden Bridge. What could you have done or said that would have helped the other person save face?

_____

_____

Make It Hard to Say No. What could you have said or done that would have helped the other person see the benefits of what you were proposing?

_____

_____

---

open or closed, the goal of both parties is the same: Each wants a good night's sleep. Framing the problem as "How can we achieve our mutual goal?" rather than arguing over whether the window should be up or down moves the discussion to a more productive level.

If you focus on shared interests (common goals) and develop objective, rather than subjective, criteria for the solution, there is hope for finding a resolution that will satisfy both parties.

Manage the Problem

If you can structure conflicts as problems to be solved rather than as battles to be won or lost, you are well on your way to finding strategies to manage the issues that confront you and your partner. Of course, as we have stressed earlier, not all conflicts can be resolved. However, approaching the core of a conflict as a problem to be managed can provide a constructive way of seeking resolution. Structuring a conflict as a problem also helps to manage the emotion and keeps the conversation focused on issues (simple conflict) rather than personalities (ego conflict). The problem-solving structure we suggest here is straightforward: Define the problem, analyze the problem's causes and effects, determine

TABLE 8.2	**Solving Problems: One Method of Organizing Problem-Solving Discussions**
1. Define the problem.	Determine the issue you disagree about.
2. Analyze the problem.	Determine the causes, symptoms, effects, and obstacles.
3. Determine the goals.	Determine what you want. Determine what your partner wants. How do the goals overlap?
4. Generate many solutions.	List many options, rather than debating one or two strategies for achieving the goal.
5. Select the best solution, and try it.	Eliminate options that are not mutually agreeable. If possible, take the best idea(s) among those generated to reach an amicable resolution.

the goals you and your partner seek, generate many possible options, then select the option that best achieves both your goals and your partner's goals.

Define the Problem. You can apply all the skills described so far to pursue a proven method for problem solving, which is shown in Table 8.2. First, *define the problem.* Most problems boil down to something you or your conflict partner want more or less of. For example, you may want more time, money, or freedom. Or you may want less interference, control, or criticism. To help you define the problem that is producing the conflict, renew your focus on your own and the other person's goals.[88] What do you want to happen, or not to happen?

Cara and Vaughn have been going together for over a year. Lately, they have been fighting over small issues, so they decide to spend some time talking about what is wrong and trying to understand one another. At the root of their conflicts, they discover, is a basic problem: Cara wants to get married to Vaughn now. Vaughn wants to stay with Cara, but he doesn't want to get married until he feels ready. He also wants to feel financially secure before he marries.

Analyze the Problem. Next, *analyze the problem.* To analyze is to break something down into its components. With your partner, begin by describing the conflict-producing events in chronological order (see page 242). Then decide whether you're facing a pseudoconflict, a simple conflict, or an ego conflict (see pages 223–226). Attempt to ferret out symptoms, effects, and obstacles; decide whether the conflict stems from several sub-problems or from one major issue. As you proceed with your analysis, you and your partner may decide that you need more information to help clarify the issues.

After some discussion, Cara and Vaughn analyze the problem. They realize they come from different family backgrounds and have different expectations about marriage. Cara's folks were high school sweethearts and got married when they were 18. Vaughn's parents are older; they met after each of them had been divorced, and they married after a long, slow-paced courtship. Cara and Vaughn's different frames of reference help explain their feelings about the timing of marriage.

Determine the Goals. The next step in managing the problem is to *determine your own and your partner's goals,* following the suggestions on pages 244–245. Also, generate objective criteria for a solution (see pages 235–236). The more measurable, verifiable, and objective the criteria, the greater the likelihood that you and your partner will be able to agree when the criteria have been met. Cara and Vaughn decide that, ultimately, they have the same goal: to get married. The issue boils down to timing. So they decide to seek a course of action that will make them both feel secure.

Generate Multiple Solutions. The next step is to *generate multiple solutions.* Simply understanding the issues and the causes, effects, symptoms, and history of a problem will not enable you to manage a conflict. It takes time and creativity to find mutually satisfactory solutions to most problems. It stands to reason that the more solutions you generate, the greater the probability that you can manage the conflict constructively. One way to generate options is through brainstorming. To use brainstorming, try the following suggestions:

1. Make sure the problem and the goals are clear to both of you.

2. Try to suspend judgment and evaluation temporarily; do not censor your thoughts.

3. Specify a certain time period for brainstorming.

4. Consider brainstorming ideas separately before meeting with your partner, or write ideas down before verbalizing solutions.

5. Try to develop at least one unique or far-out idea. You can always tame down wild ideas later.

6. Piggyback your ideas onto those of your partner. Encourage your partner to use or modify your ideas.

7. Write down all the ideas suggested.

8. Review all ideas, noting ways to combine, eliminate, or extend them.

Making efforts to structure a conflict as a problem to be solved through mutual effort can keep the conversation focused on issues, so that the conflict does not escalate.

If the goal is to find the best way to manage the difficulty, it may take only one good idea to help move the conflict forward to a constructive resolution.

When they brainstorm, Cara and Vaughn generate the following options: Save money for a year, and then get married; take turns going to college; take turns working to support each other while the other gets a degree; get married now, get jobs, and postpone college; get married now, and take out college loans.

Select the Best Solution. Finally, Cara and Vaughn decide to *select the best solution*. Sometimes, it may take several attempts at defining, analyzing, goal setting, and generating multiple ideas before a mutually agreeable solution emerges. It is always appropriate to recheck your understanding of the issues and goals. Cara and Vaughn decide to combine the best of several ideas. They agree to get engaged, but not to set a date. Instead, they set a financial goal of $5,000 in savings. When they hit that goal, they will set a wedding date. If they are both attending college, they will get part-time jobs so that they have income, and they will also apply for college loans.

If, after repeated attempts, you cannot arrive at a mutually acceptable solution, you may decide to keep trying. Or you may agree to take the issue to an impartial person who can help you identify conflict management strategies and solutions. At work, your immediate superior may be called in to help settle the matter. Or, occasionally, you may agree to disagree and drop it.

The goal of managing conflict is not just to solve a problem, but to help manage relational issues with your partner, especially if your partner thinks he or she has "lost" the conflict. When seeking a solution to interpersonal problems, try to find ways for your partner to "win" while you also achieve your goal. Help your partner save face. The concept of **face,** first introduced in Chapter 2, refers to the self-image or self-respect that you and your partner seek to maintain.[89] Communication researcher Stella Ting-Toomey has conducted studies that emphasize the importance of face-saving or maintaining a positive image, especially in collectivist cultures such as those in Asia, where maintaining face is especially important.[90] How do you help someone save face and avoid embarrassment? Sometimes you can offer genuine forgiveness. Or

face Self-image or self-respect that you and your partner seek to maintain.

247

you can offer explanations that help reframe the differences, perhaps suggesting that it was really just a misunderstanding that led to the disagreement.[91] Such face-restoring comments can help mend bruised egos. Finding ways to be gracious or allow your partner to save face is an important other-oriented approach to dealing with people. After a family feud between a mother and her teenage daughter, Mom might say, "You're right, I should not get so upset. I'm sorry I lost my temper. You're a great daughter." Admitting that you're wrong and offering an affirming, positive expression of support can begin to help heal a rift and help the other person save face.[92]

Even though we have presented these conflict management steps as prescriptive suggestions, it is important to remember that *conflict is rarely a linear, step-by-step sequence of events.* These skills are designed to serve as a general framework for collaboratively managing differences. But if your partner does not want to collaborate, your job will be more challenging.

In reality, you don't simply manage your emotions and then move neatly on to developing greater understanding with another person. Sorting out your goals and your partner's goals is not something you do once and then put behind you. It will take time and patience to balance your immediate goal with the goal of maintaining a relationship with your partner. In fact, as you try to manage a conflict, you will more than likely bounce forward and backward from one step to another. The framework we've described gives you an overarching perspective for understanding and actively managing disagreements, but the nature of interpersonal relationships means that you and your partner will respond—sometimes in unpredictable ways—to a variety of cues (psychological, sociological, physical) when communicating. Think of the skills you have learned as options to consider, rather than as hard-and-fast rules to follow in every situation.

APPLYING AN OTHER-ORIENTATION
to Conflict Management

To manage differences with others, consider the conflict-producing issue or issues from the other person's point of view. We don't claim that an other-orientation will resolve all conflicts. As we noted earlier, it's a myth that all conflict can be resolved. But being other-oriented is an important element in managing differences and disagreements. The following five strategies, drawn not only from this chapter but from the previous skill-development chapters, distill the essence of being other-oriented.

- *Stop*: Socially decenter by taking into account the other person's thoughts, feelings, values, culture, and perspective. Stop making your arguments and concentrate on your partner's points. How is your

partner "making sense" out of what has happened to him or her?

- *Look*: Monitor your partner's emotions by observing his or her nonverbal messages. Look for emotional cues in your partner's face; observe posture and gestures to gauge the intensity of the feelings being expressed.

- *Listen*: Listen both for the details and for the main points; also listen for tone of voice. Focus on the overall story your partner is telling.

- *Imagine*: Imagine how you would feel if you were in your partner's place. Based on your knowledge of the person you're in conflict with, as well as of people in general, imagine the conflict from his or her point of view.

- *Question*: If you need more information about what a partner has experienced or if there is something you don't understand, gently ask appropriate questions.

- *Paraphrase*: To confirm your understanding of your partner's point of view, briefly summarize the essence of what you think your partner is thinking or feeling.

No checklist of skills will magically melt tensions resulting from long-standing or entrenched conflicts. But honestly trying to understand both a person's position and the emotion behind it is a good beginning to developing understanding—a prerequisite to managing differences.

Conflict Defined, Myths, and Types
(pages 216–226)

Interpersonal conflict is an expressed struggle between at least two interdependent people who perceive incompatible goals, scarce resources, or interference, and who are attempting to achieve a specific goal. Conflict is a process, with a beginning, a middle, an end, and an aftermath. Conflict can be constructive if it airs differences and helps build new insights and establish new patterns that lead to a more satisfying relationship. But it can also be destructive if people have a win–lose perspective and don't look for solutions. Being aware of potential conflict triggers can help you avoid or manage sensitive topics. Most conflict fits into one of three categories: pseudoconflict, simple conflict, or ego conflict.

Key Terms

Interpersonal conflict *216*	Pseudoconflict *223*
Interdependent *217*	Simple conflict *223*
Constructive conflict *219*	Expressive conflict *224*
Destructive conflict *220*	Instrumental conflict *224*
Conflict triggers *220*	Ego conflict *226*
Dialectical tension *220*	

Critical Thinking Questions

1. Think of a recent communication exchange with a friend, spouse, or coworker that began as a seemingly casual conversation but escalated into a conflict. Can you identify a reason for this, such as one or both of you feeling tired, stressed, or anxious? Is there anything you could have done to avoid the conflict? What cues might you each have looked for to understand the other's mood?

2. Melissa and Jake always seem to end up making personal attacks and calling each other names when they get into a disagreement. What type of conflict are they experiencing when they do this, and how can they avoid it?

3. Ethics: Is it ethical to mask your true emotions in order to get along with others? Is honesty in a relationship always the best policy? Explain your response.

Activities

Based on the discussion of conflict presented on pages 218–219, think of a recent conflict you had with someone or a conflict that is still ongoing. To help you better understand and manage the process, answer the following questions:

Prior Conditions Stage
- What were the prior conditions that led to the conflict?
- How long were some of the prior conditions simmering in the background?

Frustration Awareness Stage
- When did you become aware that you were frustrated and that your needs weren't being met or that there was an issue to resolve?

- When did you perceive that the other person was aware that a conflict might exist?

Active Conflict Stage
- What caused the conflict to move from frustration to active conflict?
- What type of conflict was(is) it—pseudoconflict, simple conflict, or ego conflict?

Resolution Stage
- What conflict management skills did you use (or are you and the other person using) to manage emotions, information, goals, or the problem?
- What conflict management skills could you have used, but didn't?

Follow-Up Stage
- Has the conflict been truly managed and resolved, or not? What leads you to that conclusion?
- Did you or the other person explicitly indicate that the conflict is over?

Web Resources

http://www.cios.org.encyclopedia/conflict/index.htm This conflict management site provides an introduction to the study of conflict management through links that explain why the study of conflict is important, key elements of conflict, the nature of conflict and conflict variables, and skills for conflict managers, and offers a self-test to check your conflict management understanding.

Conflict and Power
(pages 227–231)

Conflict and power are often connected because people use interpersonal power to influence or control others. Interpersonal power is a fundamental element of our personal relationships. Understanding principles of power and sources of power can provide insight into how you and others are using power to influence the outcome of disagreements. Five sources of power suggested by researchers are legitimate power, referent power, expert power, reward power, and coercive power. Being able to negotiate and renegotiate power in a relationship can lead to a more rewarding and productive relationship.

Key Terms

Interpersonal power *227*	Expert power *229*
Dependent relationship *228*	Reward power *229*
Legitimate power *229*	Coercive power *229*
Referent power *229*	Compliance gaining *229*

Critical Thinking Questions

1. Examine several recent interpersonal conflicts for unresolved power issues. (For example, consider conflicts that have focused on managing money, household tasks, or

intimacy.) What role did power play in the conflict? What type of power is it? Does one of you have more power over the other? How might you renegotiate that power imbalance?

2. Ethics: Are certain types of power more ethical to use during a conflict than others? Explain your answer, describing conditions that would justify the use of certain types of power.

Activities

Statements About Conflict: Read each statement once, and on a separate piece of paper, indicate whether you agree (A) or disagree (D) with each statement. Take five or six minutes to do this.

1. Most people find an argument interesting and exciting.

2. In most conflicts, someone must win and someone must lose. That's the way conflict is.

3. The best way to handle a conflict is simply to let everyone cool off.

4. Most people get upset at a person who disagrees with them.

5. If people spend enough time together, they will find something to disagree about and will eventually become upset with each other.

6. Conflicts can be solved if people just take the time to listen to one another.

7. If you disagree with someone, it is usually better to keep quiet than to express your personal opinion.

8. To compromise is to take the easy way out of conflict.

9. Some people produce more conflict and tension than others. These people should be restricted from working with others.

After you have indicated whether you agree or disagree with the statements, ask a good friend, roommate, family member, or romantic partner to read each statement and indicate whether he or she agrees or disagrees. Compare answers and discuss the results. Use this activity as a way of identifying underlying assumptions you and the other person have about conflict. You could also do this activity in a small group. After comparing responses with others in the group, the entire group could seek to develop a consensus about each statement. If conflict occurs about a specific statement, use the principles of conflict management that are presented in the chapter to assist you in managing the disagreement.

Web Resources

http://www.cyberparent.com/talk/negotiations.htm Visit this site to learn tips and strategies for controlling your emotions during negotiations and when experiencing conflict.

Conflict Management Styles and Skills
(pages 231–248)

Most of us have a tendency to manage conflict by using patterns we've used before. These patterns can be classified into five conflict styles: avoidance, accommodation, competition, compromise, and collaboration. Learning to manage conflict successfully can enhance our interpersonal relationships. Strategies include managing emotions, information, and goals. Managing the problem by defining it, analyzing its causes and effects, generating possible solutions, and selecting the best of these will help you and your partner achieve your goals. As in other situations, being empathic and other-oriented is essential and will help you manage conflict.

Key Terms

Conflict style *231*	Collaboration *235*
Avoidance *231*	Flaming *236*
Demand-withdrawal pattern of conflict management *232*	Disinhibition effect *236*
	Gunny-sacking *240*
Accommodation *233*	"I" language *242*
Competition *234*	"But" message *243*
Compromise *235*	Face *247*

Critical Thinking Questions

1. Richard has an explosive temper. He consistently receives poor performance evaluations at work because he lashes out at those who disagree with him. What strategies might help him manage his emotional outbursts?

2. Have you experienced the disinhibition effect when communicating with others online? Was this in response to a blatantly negative message? Or was it your perception that you were being attacked? What was the result? How did you respond? What strategies could you have employed to avoid a conflict?

Activities

Over the next week or so, keep a list of every conflict you observe or are involved in. Make a note of what the conflict was about, whether there were underlying power issues (that you could detect), whether the conflict was resolved satisfactorily for both parties, and if so, what strategies and skills were employed. Could you identify a specific conflict management style? If the conflict involved you, did you use the style you typically use? Why or why not? Discuss your findings with your classmates.

Web Resources

http://www.mapnp.org/library/intrpsnl/conflict.htm At this site, you'll find numerous links to other sites that address interpersonal conflict, including sites that will allow you to assess your conflict management skill.

http://www.etu.org.za/toolbox/docs/building/conflict.html This site explores conflict management and how organizations use conflict management to achieve their goals. The site also touches on how to identify signs and stages of conflict as well as how to manage and resolve conflict situations.

9

Understanding Interpersonal Relationships

“You can hardly make a friend in a year, but you can lose one in an hour.”

Chinese Proverb

Pat: Hi, aren't you in my communication course?

Chris: Oh, yeah, I've seen you across the room.

Pat: What do you think about the course so far?

Chris: It's okay, but I feel a little intimidated by some of the class activities.

Pat: I know what you mean. It gets kind of scary to talk about yourself in front of everyone else.

Chris: Yeah. Plus some of the stuff you hear. I was paired up with this one student the other day who started talking about being arrested last year on a drug charge. It made me feel uncomfortable.

Pat: Really? I bet I know who that is. I don't think you have to worry about it.

Chris: Don't mention that I said anything.

Pat: It's okay. I know that guy, and he just likes to act big.

This interaction between Pat and Chris illustrates the reciprocal nature of interpersonal communication and interpersonal relationships. The character and quality of interpersonal communication are affected, in turn, by the nature of the interpersonal relationship. The conversation between Pat and Chris begins with a casual acknowledgment but quickly proceeds to a higher level of intimacy. Chris confides in Pat; Pat, an other-oriented listener, offers confirmation and support; this response encourages Chris to confide even more. In this brief encounter, Pat and Chris have laid the groundwork for transforming their casual acquaintanceship into an intimate interpersonal relationship. This chapter examines the nature of interpersonal relationships such as Pat and Chris's as well as the stages experienced in the escalation and de-escalation of interpersonal relationships.

Interpersonal Relationships Defined

In Chapter 1, we defined a **relationship** as a connection you establish when you communicate with another person. So every time you engage in interpersonal communication, you are in a relationship; but it is only through ongoing, recurring interactions that you develop interpersonal relationships. An **interpersonal relationship** is a perception shared by two people of an ongoing interdependent connection that results in the development of relational expectations and varies in interpersonal intimacy. Let's consider the four elements that constitute this definition: shared perception, ongoing interdependent connection, relational expectations, and interpersonal intimacy.

Shared Perception

To be in an interpersonal relationship, both individuals must share a perception that they have an ongoing relationship. Sometimes, only one person believes there is a relationship—a belief which, at the extreme, might lead to obsessive behavior or stalking. Even when each partner recognizes that he or she has a relationship with the other, that doesn't mean the partners think of the relationship in the same way. One difficulty often encountered in relationships is a discrepancy in how the partners see the relationship. Such discrepancies can be a source of interpersonal conflict and often necessitate heart-to-heart talks about what each person wants or expects in the relationship. Generally, the greater the similarity in perceptions of the relationship, the stronger the relationship.

relationship Connection established when we communicate with another person.

interpersonal relationship Perception shared by two people of an ongoing interdependent connection that results in the development of relational expectations and varies in interpersonal intimacy.

Ongoing Interdependent Connection

The second component of the definition, an ongoing interdependent connection, means that the interpersonal relationship is a system and a process. Interdependence occurs because each partner relies on the other to meet needs. Interdependence provides a motivation for an ongoing connection: Both partners want to continue to get together because their needs are being satisfied. As a system, an interpersonal relationship is transactional; that is, both partners affect each other simultaneously. As a result, a change in one partner has a direct impact on the relationship and on the other partner. You've probably had friends who are moody at times (or maybe you're the moody one), and when they are, it affects you and how you talk to them.

As a process, a relationship is dynamic, constantly changing and evolving. That an interpersonal relationship is a process is most apparent in relational development—the movement of a relationship through a series of stages, each representing different levels of trust, self-disclosure, and intimacy. We'll discuss the specific stages of relational development later in this chapter. Relationships are always moving to a new level or being redefined. As you interact with a person, you share a growing history together; the relationship is cumulative. That history becomes part of the relationship and affects each subsequent interaction. The *Harry Potter* books and films provide good examples of the process nature of relationships. The relationships among the three main characters—Harry, Hermione, and Ron—evolve and change as they share experiences and learn more about one another. Processes are also irreversible—once something is done, it can't be undone (unless by some wizard's magic). For example, you can't un-initiate, or take back, an argument you've had in a relationship. While you can forgive and be forgiven, the argument will always have an impact on the partners and the relationship.

In an intimate, trusting relationship, we can feel safe in telling our deepest secrets to another person.

Relational Expectations

As you continue to interact and develop your relationships, you also form relational expectations. Any time you interact with someone, you bring a set of preformed expectations based on your socialization and experiences; but as you develop an interpersonal relationship, you and your partner establish expectations specific to that relationship. Think about the expectations you have of your friends and that they have of you. For example, you might have a friend with whom you primarily play video games; thus, you know what your time together will be like, how you'll talk, what you'll talk about, and so on. These expectations are part of the relationship process and are continually developing and changing. Sometimes, expectations are violated, which can create turmoil in the relationship (this problem is discussed further in Chapter 10).

Interpersonal Intimacy

Interpersonal intimacy is the degree to which relational partners mutually confirm and accept each other's sense of self. The closer the relationship, the more you depend on a partner to accept and confirm your sense of self; your partner does the same. Think about the range of interpersonal relationships you have. You should be able to classify them according to how much interpersonal intimacy (confirmation of your self) they provide. Our closest relationships play important roles in confirming our value. And although we depend on them less, even casual relationships confirm our value; we look

interpersonal intimacy Degree to which relational partners mutually accept and confirm each other's sense of self.

Stranger ⟷ Acquaintance ⟷ Casual Friend ⟷ Friend ⟷ Close Friend ⟷ Best Friend/Spouse

FIGURE 9.1

Continuum of Interpersonal Intimacy and Friendship

for others to implicitly (and sometimes explicitly) tell us that they like who we are. As interpersonal intimacy increases, we are more and more able to just be ourselves and still feel accepted. In the most intimate relationships, our partners know our strengths and our weaknesses but still accept us; they love us in spite of our flaws—we reach a point where we don't have to hide our flaws or fear rejection because of those flaws.

We depend on intimate relationships to provide us with information about ourselves and to bolster our self-confidence. The more intimate the relationship, the more we depend on others for acceptance and confirmation of our self-image.[1] During periods when we might not have very intimate relationships, it is sometimes hard to maintain a strong positive self-image. Research confirms that having strong social support networks is related to subjective well-being.[2] Figure 9.1 orders the types of interpersonal relationships according to their relative intimacy.

Going from being strangers to being best friends involves moving through a number of relational stages that are associated with sharing information about ourselves. Our communication behaviors and strategies are directly linked to the level of relational intimacy—we communicate differently depending on the level of intimacy in a relationship. Interpersonal communication scholars Denise Solomon and Leanne Knobloch hypothesize that in more intimate relationships, people exhibit direct information-seeking behavior to reduce uncertainties, while those in less intimate relationships exhibit indirect behaviors.[3] For example, if a close friend uncharacteristically began binge drinking, you would ask him or her about it. On the other hand, you would be less inclined to ask an acquaintance so directly about his or her drinking. Solomon and Knobloch also speculate that direct information seeking creates greater clarity and understanding, thus increasing the solidarity of intimate relationships.

We communicate our sense of intimacy to others both directly, through our words, and indirectly, through actions. We might tell another person how we feel about him or her and how much we value the relationship. On the other hand, being open and honest by disclosing highly personal information is an indirect way of expressing interpersonal intimacy. We also might use nonverbal cues, such as close physical proximity, eye contact, tone of voice, touch, and time spent interacting.

BEING Other-ORIENTED

The healthiest relationships are those in which both partners have an agreed-on and clear understanding of the relationship. Think about some of your closest relationships. How close do you think those partners would say the relationship is? In what ways do they communicate the level of intimacy and the feelings they have about the relationship? What nonverbal cues do they send? Are those clear or ambiguous? What have your partners said to let you know their assessment of the relationship?

Types of Interpersonal Relationships

Interpersonal relationships vary by level of intimacy, and they vary in their origins and management of power. Relationships can be defined by circumstance or by choice, and on the basis of how partners share power and decision-making responsibilities.

Circumstance or Choice

relationship of circumstance
Interpersonal relationship that exists because of life circumstances (who your family members are, where you work or study, and so on).

relationship of choice
Interpersonal relationship you choose to initiate, maintain, and, perhaps, terminate.

Relationships of circumstance form not because we choose them, but simply because our lives overlap with others' in some way. Relationships with family members, teachers, classmates, and coworkers fall into this category. In contrast, relationships that we seek out and intentionally develop are **relationships of choice.** These relationships might include those with friends, lovers, spouses, and counselors. As German poet Emanuel von Geibel wrote, "It is chance that makes brothers but hearts that make friends."

We act and communicate differently in the two types of relationships because the stakes are different. The effect of the same behavior on different relationships can be dramatic. If we act in foolish or inappropriate ways, our friends might end the relationships. If we act the same way within the confines of our family, our relatives may not like us much, but we will still remain family.

Of course, these categories are not mutually exclusive. Relationships of circumstance can also be relationships of choice: Your brother or sister can also be your best friend. You can break off contact with family members or quit your job to sever your relationships with fellow employees. In addition, the other individual can define and redefine the relationship. Your boss might fire you, a relative might cut you off, or a lover might desert you.

In some sense, all relationships begin by circumstance; through circumstance, we become aware of another person. What we learn as a result of circumstance determines whether we then establish a relationship of choice and serves as the basis for our interpersonal attraction toward the other person. Circumstance and choice also affect the process by which we move toward and away from intimate relationships—going through a series of escalating and de-escalating stages.

Power

Relationships can also be typed according to the way partners share power or decision-making responsibilities—the relative power role that each partner plays. Each relationship type requires merging needs and styles, negotiating how decisions are made that affect both partners, and managing inevitable interpersonal conflicts. Failure to agree on roles can lead to instability, and attempts to change an agreed-on definition of the roles can meet resistance. Nonetheless, decision-making and power-sharing roles are continually tweaked. Think about how each of the following descriptions of power sharing applies to your relationships with friends, family, and coworkers and to the conflicts that arise in these relationships.

In a **complementary relationship,** one partner usually dominates or makes most of the decisions. Maybe one person likes to talk, and the other likes to listen; one person likes to decide on what movies to watch, and the other will watch anything. As a child, your relationship with your parents was probably complementary—they made the decisions. As you grew older, those roles were renegotiated, and that renegotiation might have been accompanied by some conflict. People in complementary relationships experience relatively few decision-making conflicts, because one partner readily defers to the other. In a **symmetrical relationship,** both partners behave toward power in the same way, either both wanting power or both avoiding it.[4] A **competitive symmetrical relationship** exists when both people vie for power and control of

complementary relationship Relationship in which power is divided unevenly, with one partner dominating and the other submitting.

symmetrical relationship Relationship in which both partners behave toward power in the same way, either both wanting power or both avoiding it.

competitive symmetrical relationship Relationship in which both people vie for power and control of decision making.

decision making. For example, each partner wants to play a different video game, and neither one wants to give in to the other. Equality of power is likely to result in more overt attempts at control than occur when one partner has more power than the other.[5] Effective management of decision making requires strong conflict management skills. When neither partner wants to take control or make decisions, a **submissive symmetrical relationship** is created. Because neither partner feels comfortable imposing his or her will on the other, often both partners flounder, unable to make a decision or to act. Perhaps both people want to play a video game, but neither wants to declare which video game the other should have to play.

In reflecting on your current relationships, you might find that few seem to fit the descriptions of complementary or symmetrical. Instead, most of your relationships are probably **parallel relationships** involving a shifting back and forth of the power between the partners, depending on the situation. You might defer the video game selection to your friend Riley who knows about every video game on the planet. On the other hand, Riley defers to you to decide where to get pizza. Establishing this arrangement with Riley might have involved initial conflict until you both felt comfortable with your roles. What happens when you and Riley decide to go out? Who decides where you're going? Parallel relationships often involve continual negotiation of who has decision-making power over which issues. These changes often occur in concert with movement from one stage of the relationship to another.

Genesis of Interpersonal Relationships: Attraction

A *genesis* is the coming into being of something—its origination and beginning. Attraction is the genesis of interpersonal relationships. **Interpersonal attraction** is the degree to which you want to form or maintain an interpersonal relationship. Notice that this definition identifies two forms of attraction: one that leads us to form a relationship and one that leads us to sustain it. You are constantly evaluating individuals you encounter to determine the potential for developing an interpersonal relationship; this is **short-term initial attraction.** For example, you might find one of your classmates (a relationship of circumstance) physically attractive but never move to introduce yourself. You decide, for whatever reason, that there is not much potential for a relationship and therefore you do not act on your attraction. On the other hand, as you walk out of the class, you might strike up a conversation with another classmate about an upcoming concert by one of your favorite bands, which happens to be this classmate's favorite as well. You decide it would be fun to go together. Over time, you discover lots of areas of compatibility and attraction that serve as the foundation for a long-term friendship. **Long-term maintenance attraction** is the level of liking or positive feelings that motivate us to maintain or escalate a relationship. Through interpersonal communication, self-disclosure, and continued interactions, we learn information about others that either fosters or diminishes our long-term maintenance attraction to them.

Both types of attraction involve assessing and acting on the potential value of a relationship. We try to determine how promising, viable, and rewarding the relationship might be and continue to make such assessments throughout the course of the relationship. According to communication scholar Michael Sunnafrank's theory of **predicted outcome value (POV),** we assess the potential for any given relationship to meet our need for self-image confirmation and weigh that assessment against the potential costs.[6] We are attracted to others with whom a relationship may yield a high outcome value (the rewards exceeding the costs). Over time, our assessments may change. In the movie *50 First Dates*, Henry (Adam Sandler) has a pleasant first encounter with Lucy (Drew Barrymore). The two are attracted to each other, each

---

submissive symmetrical relationship Relationship in which neither partner wants to take control or make decisions.

parallel relationship Relationship in which power shifts back and forth between the partners, depending on the situation.

interpersonal attraction Degree to which you want to form or maintain an interpersonal relationship.

short-term initial attraction Degree to which you sense a potential for developing an interpersonal relationship.

long-term maintenance attraction Degree of liking or positive feelings that motivate us to maintain or escalate a relationship.

predicted outcome value (POV) Potential for a relationship to confirm our self-image compared to its potential costs.

Interpersonal attraction leads us to form or maintain our personal relationships.

predicting a positive outcome in terms of a potential relationship that meets their social needs. Henry approaches their second encounter expecting continued positive outcomes; however, Lucy has changed her mind about her initial evaluation. Lucy's inability to sustain a positive assessment of the relationship potential produces a series of comical events, as Henry's attraction continues to grow. Not until he devises a way for her to sustain a sense of the value of the relationship can love find its way.

Like these film characters, most of us begin predicting outcome values in initial interactions and continually modify our predictions as we learn more about the other person. We pursue attractions beyond the initial interaction stage if we think they can yield positive outcomes, and generally avoid or terminate relationships for which we predict negative outcomes.[7]

Of particular interest is the role that interpersonal communication plays in attraction. Attraction and interpersonal communication are interdependent; that is, each affects the other. Short-term initial attraction acts as the impetus to communicate interpersonally—it prompts us to interact with others. The resulting interpersonal communication provides additional information that might contribute to long-term maintenance attraction. While several factors act to increase our likelihood of actually talking to another person, it is what occurs during those interactions that really determines whether we remain attracted to the person.[8]

Factors Leading to Short-Term Initial Attraction

You enter a room filled with people you don't know and proceed to the area where beverages are being served. As you stand there looking around the room, whom do you talk to? Whom do you approach? To whom are you attracted? Two factors particularly affect us in such situations: proximity and physical appearance.

Proximity. You are more likely to form relationships with classmates sitting on either side of you than with someone seated at the opposite end of the room. This is partly because physical **proximity** increases communication opportunities. We are more likely to talk, and therefore to feel attracted to, neighbors who live right next door than to those who live down the block. Any circumstance that increases the possibilities for interacting is also likely to increase attraction; proximity has been found to be a more important factor in initial attraction than in maintenance attraction.[9]

Physical Appearance. As you stand in the room full of people, you are also likely to approach people because of their physical appearance. **Physical appearance,** a form of nonverbal communication, provides us with information that again helps us make some decision about POV. It acts as a filter to reduce relationship possibilities.[10] If everyone in the room was of a different age, culture, or race than your own except for one person ten feet away, whom would you approach for conversation? Similarity with another person creates an attraction because we assume the other person will have values and interests similar to ours. We use physical appearance to make predictions about who is most likely to reciprocate our overtures for conversation—that is, who is most likely to have something in common with us. Whether a relationship escalates depends on what happens in the initial interaction and subsequent interactions.

You have probably found that even if you and another person are of a similar age, culture, or race, you won't continue a relationship if you don't have much else in common. That's one reason physical appearance is not a strong factor for long-term maintenance attraction.[11] However, researchers recently found positive social interactions increase our estimation of others' physical attractiveness.[12] Thus, not only can physical attractiveness lead to interpersonal attraction, it can also be the product of interpersonal attraction.

Sexual attraction also influences interest in forming relationships. At the most basic level, people might seek partners for physical affection and sexual gratification, to meet sexual needs.[13] In short-term sexual relationships, physical appearance tends to be more important than in long-term romantic relationships.[14] However, in the process of meeting sexual needs, people may develop long-term relationships. Indeed, research shows that sexual satisfaction is a significant factor in marital satisfaction.[15] However, sexual attraction by itself is unlikely to serve as a foundation on which to build successful long-term intimate relationships. Research also shows that strong communication is associated with marital satisfaction, regardless of sexual satisfaction, among married couples.[16]

The evolutionary theory of mate selection suggests that men and women use physical appearance to determine the adequacy of potential mates. This theory is based on biological principles and takes into account such variables as hormones, body shapes, and health. In essence, the theory asserts that people select partners for their reproductive value. Men might use appearance as a basis for determining women's fertility, receptiveness, and prospects for motherhood; women might look for men who can provide resources to raise their children.[17] Be aware that your physical attraction toward a member of the opposite sex might be stemming from basic biological and evolutionary drives rather than from a subjective impression of good looks.

Factors Leading to Both Short-Term Initial Attraction and Long-Term Maintenance Attraction

Some qualities both lead us to initiate interactions and motivate us to continue to sustain attraction as the relationship develops. These qualities are generally readily visible on first meeting another person and increase as we gather more information about the other person.

proximity Physical nearness to another that promotes communication and thus attraction.

physical appearance Nonverbal cues that allow us to assess relationship potential (POV).

Competence, Intelligence, and Credibility. Competence, intelligence, and credibility are related personal qualities that, in and of themselves, evoke attraction. Most of us are attracted to individuals who seem competent. We like those who are sure of themselves, but not full of themselves. We assume they are competent if they seem skilled, knowledgeable, and experienced. Intelligence/competence is a more important predictor of initial attraction in eventual romantic relationships than in friendships.[18] We find people credible if they display a blend of enthusiasm, trustworthiness, competence, and power.

We are attracted to people on the basis of similarity—we like people whose interests, personalities, values, and backgrounds are similar to ours.

Self-Disclosure and Reciprocation of Liking. While providing negative or intimate information about ourselves too early might have a negative impact on a developing relationship, a certain amount of openness and self-disclosure increases attraction. Similarly, an open display of attraction or liking for another person can result in a reciprocation of that attraction: We like those who like us. As relationships progress from initiation to intimacy, further openness increases attraction. In one study of newly acquainted men and women who interacted for eight minutes, participants reported favorable reactions to partners' being forthcoming about themselves, with self-disclosure being seen as communicating openness and interest.[19] Another study found that expressiveness and openness were among the most desirable qualities in a partner, regardless of the type of relationship.[20] Self-disclosure has a positive impact on liking between strangers and an even greater impact in more developed relationships.[21] In addition, our attraction to another person increases our tendency to self-disclose.[22]

Reciprocation of liking means that we like those who like us. One way to get other people to reciprocate liking, particularly in romantic relationships, is to show that we like them.[23] In a study in which participants were instructed to display liking, the frequency of their smiles, intensity of gaze, proximity during a conversation, forward leaning, and variations in vocal pitch correlated with their partners' reports of social attraction.[24] Displaying attraction toward another person seems to have the greatest impact if it is seen by the other person as being uniquely directed toward him or her, rather than as a general, indiscriminate display of interest in everyone (not being very choosey).[25] In another study, pairs of male and female college students interacting for the first time underestimated the amount of attraction that their partners felt after a brief get-acquainted conversation.[26] Perhaps we protect ourselves— "save face"—by assuming the other person doesn't like us much; it is probably less embarrassing to find out someone likes us more than we thought than to find out we've overestimated how much the person likes us.

Similarities. In general, we are attracted to people on the basis of **similarity**—we like people whose personality, values, upbringing, personal experiences, attitudes, and interests are similar to ours. We seek them out through shared activities. For example, you may join a campus environmental group because of your interests in the environment. Within the group, you would be especially attracted to those who have a similar sense of humor, who share the same attitudes on other issues, or who enjoy some of the other activities that you do. Similarly, joining a Facebook group because of a shared interest could lead to online friendships.

Results of a study by communication scholars Leslie Baxter and Lee West indicate that the main reason for placing a positive value on similarity is because it facilitates

reciprocation of liking Liking those who like us.

similarity Having comparable personalities, values, upbringing, personal experiences, attitudes, and interests.

© Randy Glasbergen.
www.glasbergen.com

"For a good relationship, I need someone who shares the same taste in music, movies, and TV...so I've started dating my iPod."

communication.[27] Similarities give people something in common to talk about, making interactions comfortable and communication effective. Similarities are also viewed as positive because they represent sources of shared fun and pleasure as well as a basis for social and emotional support. However, people also recognize that similarities can have a downside. One of the Marx Brothers comedy team, Groucho, once quipped, "I wouldn't want to belong to any club that would accept me as a member." Besides assailing the club's criteria for membership, Groucho's comment implied he didn't want to be in a club with people like himself. Being stuck with people just like us can be boring and can lead to conflicts (imagine two people who are both assertive and dominating).

In the initial stages of a relationship, we try to emphasize positive information about ourselves to create a positive and attractive image. We reveal those aspects of ourselves that we believe we have in common with the other person, and the other person does the same.[28] You save your revelations about important attitudes and issues for a later stage in the relational development process.[29] Attitude similarity is more likely to be a source of long-term maintenance attraction than of short-term initial attraction. Similarity of interests and leisure activities appears more important in same-sex friendships than in opposite-sex relationships.[30]

Differences and Complementary Needs. "Vive la différence!" "Opposites attract." "Variety is the spice of life." Such phrases reflect a positive attitude toward differences. One reason we are drawn to people who are different from us is because we learn and grow by such exposure.[31] People who are different from us expose us to new ideas, activities, and perspectives and prompt self-assessment. Differences can also lead to points of conflict and hamper our ability to effectively communicate.[32] Numerous popular books and articles have claimed that inherent differences between men and women interfere with their ability to understand and communicate with each other.

Differences can lead to long-term maintenance attraction when we find a person whose strengths complement our weaknesses. People in a relationship have **complementary needs** when each partner contributes something to the relationship that the other partner needs. We can view a pair of individuals as a team in which each person complements the other. Perhaps you're not very good at making decisions about what to do for fun on the weekend. You might form a complementary relationship with someone who always plans and does exciting things on weekends. The bottom line in terms of power in relationships is that there are no "perfect" matches, only degrees of compatibility relative to needs.

Short-term initial attraction gets relationships started, but the process of changing to long-term maintenance attraction involves working through a series of stages, each reflecting changes in attraction, self-disclosure, and intimacy. The remainder of this chapter focuses on the nature of those stages and on theories that explain how and why interpersonal attraction and intimacy increase and decrease.

complementary needs Needs that match; each partner contributes something to the relationship that the other partner needs.

relational development Movement of a relationship from one stage to another, either toward or away from greater intimacy.

Stages of Interpersonal Relationship Development

Although researchers use different terms and different numbers of stages, all agree that **relational development** proceeds in discernible stages. The stage we are in affects

▶ RECAP   Genesis of Interpersonal Relationships: Attraction

Interpersonal Attraction	Degree to which you want to form or maintain an interpersonal relationship
Short-Term Initial Attraction	Degree to which you sense a potential for developing a relationship
Long-Term Maintenance Attraction	Level of liking or positive feelings motivating you to maintain or escalate a relationship
Predicted Outcome Value (POV)	Potential for a relationship to confirm your self-image compared to its potential costs

Factors Leading to Short-Term Initial Attraction

Proximity	Physical nearness to someone that promotes communication and thus attraction
Physical Appearance	Nonverbal cues that allow you to assess relationship potential (POV)

Factors Leading to Both Short-Term Initial Attraction and Long-Term Maintenance Attraction

Competence, Intelligence, and Credibility	Personal qualities that, in and of themselves, evoke attraction
Self-Disclosure and Reciprocation of Liking	Openness; attraction toward a person who seems attracted to you
Similarity	Comparable personalities, values, upbringing, personal experiences, attitudes, and interests
Differences and Complementary Needs	Appreciation of diversity; matching needs

our interpersonal communication, and our interpersonal communication is the tool we use to move ourselves from stage to stage. Individuals in an intimate stage discuss topics and display nonverbal behaviors that do not appear in the early stages of a relationship. Outsiders usually can tell what stage a relationship is in by observing the interpersonal communication.

You can think of the stages, from first meeting to intimacy, as the floors in a highrise building. Relational development is like an elevator that stops at every floor. As you get to each floor, you might get off and wander around for a while before taking the elevator to the next floor (see Figure 9.2). Each time you get on, you don't know how many floors up the elevator will take you, or how long you will stay at any given floor. In fact, sometimes you never get back on the elevator, electing instead to stay at a particular stage of relational development. But sometimes we move quickly from floor to floor toward intimacy. Part of the time, you share this elevator with your partner, and the two of you make decisions about how far up you will go on the elevator, how long to stay at each floor, and when and whether to ride the elevator down.

Just as there are lights on a panel to let you know the elevator has moved from one floor to another, markers, or turning points, signal a move from one stage to another in a relationship. **Turning points** are specific events or interactions that are associated with positive or negative changes in a relationship.[33] A first meeting, first date, first road trip together, first sex, saying "I love you" for the first time, meeting a partner's family, making up after a conflict, becoming roommates, providing help in a crisis, or providing a favor or gift might all be turning points that indicate a relationship is moving forward. Turning points may violate expectations, which might also increase our uncertainty.[34] One way to clarify the violation and reduce uncertainty would be to discuss these turning points with our partner. One pair of researchers found that 55 percent of the time, turning points inspired a discussion about the nature of the relationship.[35] Such discussion helps the partners reach mutual agreement about the definition of the relationship.

turning point Specific event or interaction associated with a positive or negative change in a relationship.

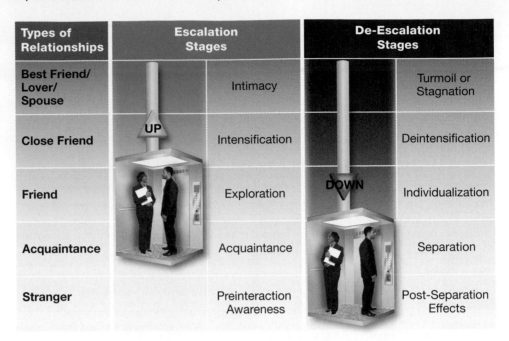

FIGURE 9.2

Model of Relational Development

Types of Relationships	Escalation Stages	De-Escalation Stages
Best Friend/ Lover/ Spouse	Intimacy	Turmoil or Stagnation
Close Friend	Intensification	Deintensification
Friend	Exploration	Individualization
Acquaintance	Acquaintance	Separation
Stranger	Preinteraction Awareness	Post-Separation Effects

Turning points can be divided into two types. **Causal turning points** are events that directly affect the relationship. Your relationships are filled with such turning points, moving you closer or further apart. Finding out that your friend has told you a significant lie might cause you to terminate the relationship. Because the event caused a change in the relationship, it is a causal turning point. On the other hand, receiving and accepting an invitation from a friend to visit his or her family for the first time is a **reflective turning point,** because it signals that a change has occurred in the definition of the relationship. The invitation and acceptance don't cause a change, but *reflect* a change in how you and your friend perceive the relationship.

causal turning point Event that brings about a change in a relationship.

reflective turning point Event that signals a change in the way a relationship is defined.

relational escalation Movement of a relationship toward intimacy through five stages: preinteraction awareness, acquaintance, exploration, intensification, and intimacy.

Relational Escalation

Relational escalation is the movement of a relationship toward greater intimacy. This movement usually goes through a series of discernible stages: preinteraction awareness,

acquaintance, exploration, intensification, and intimacy. Movement from one stage to another represents an increase in the amount of intimacy between two people. Each stage is accompanied by specific communication patterns, turning points, and relational expectations.

Preinteraction Awareness. As you can see in the model in Figure 9.2, the first floor is the *preinteraction awareness stage.* At this stage, you might observe someone or even talk with others about him or her without having any direct interaction. Gaining information about others without directly interacting with them is a *passive strategy.*[36] Through your passive observations, you form an initial impression. You might not move beyond the preinteraction awareness stage if that impression is not favorable or the circumstances aren't right. During the preinteraction awareness stage, one person might signal his or her openness to being approached by the other; but these cues, such as smiling or eye contact, can be misread.[37] Such misreadings might result in failure at the next stage.

Acquaintance. On the basis of the impression you formed in the preinteraction awareness stage, you might decide to interact with the other person. Sometimes circumstances lead to immediate interaction, and there is little or no preinteraction awareness. In either case, the very first interaction is a turning point that begins the *acquaintance stage,* in which conversations stick to safe and superficial topics and you present a "public self" to the other person. There are actually two sub-stages in the acquaintance stage: introductions and casual banter. In the **introductions** sub-stage, we tell each other our names and share basic demographic information—where we're from, what we do, and so on. In this sub-stage, the interaction typically is routine—partners usually spend the first four minutes asking each other various standard questions.[38] Except for those of us who are forgetful or who don't pay attention, we only introduce ourselves to another person once. Once we have made his or her acquaintance, we can interact without having to introduce ourselves again.

The second sub-stage is **casual banter,** talking about impersonal topics with little or no self-disclosure. You might engage only in introductions, or move from introductions to casual banter, or engage only in casual banter without even going through introductions. You've probably experienced this sub-stage in classrooms many times, as you make the acquaintance of a classmate sitting next to you, skipping introductions and just talking about casual topics. Subsequent interactions in the acquaintance stage involve continuing casual banter—discussing the weather, current events, daily news, or some common experience (what happened in class today, how the company picnic went, and the like). Many of our relationships never move beyond this stage.

Exploration. If you and your partner decide to go to the next floor, *exploration,* you will begin to share more in-depth information about yourselves. But you will have little physical contact, maintain your social distance, and limit the amount of time you spend together. This stage can occur in conjunction with the acquaintance stage. During this stage, communication becomes easier, and a large amount of low-risk disclosure occurs. Exploration entails the kind of conversation that might occur when you go out to get a bite to eat with a coworker whom you know only casually. If your conversation includes sharing more personal information about yourselves, such as your interests and hobbies, where you grew up, and what your families were like, or similar personal information, then you are in the exploration stage.

introductions Sub-stage of the acquaintance stage of relationship development, in which interaction is routine and basic information is shared

casual banter Sub-stage of the acquaintance stage of relationship development, in which impersonal topics are discussed but very limited personal information is shared.

As couples proceed from exploration to intensification, they have more physical contact and begin sharing more activities and confidences.

Intensification. If you proceed to the *intensification stage,* you will start to depend on each other for self-confirmation and engage in more risky self-disclosure. You will spend more time together, increase the variety of activities you share, adopt a more personal physical distance, engage in more physical contact, and personalize your language. Also, you may discuss and redefine the relationship often in this stage, perhaps putting a turning-point label on yourselves, such as "going steady," "good buddies," or "best friends." Other turning points associated with this stage include decisions to date each other exclusively, to become roommates, or to spend time with each other's families.

Intimacy. The "top floor" in the relational high-rise is the *intimacy stage.* In this stage, the two partners turn to each other for confirmation and acceptance of their self-concepts. Their communication is highly personalized and synchronized. They talk about anything and everything. There is a free flow of information and intimate self-disclosure. There is a commitment to maintaining the relationship that might even be formalized through marriage or some other agreement. Partners incorporate more of their own language code (nicknames, inside jokes, and special words) and use fewer words to communicate, relying more on nonverbal cues.[39] They have increased understanding of each other's words and nonverbal cues. Their roles and the relationship are discussed and more clearly defined. Physical contact increases, and their physical distance during conversations decreases. Reaching this stage takes time—time to build trust, time to share personal information, time to observe each other in various situations, and time to build a commitment and an emotional bond.

Relational De-Escalation

Relational de-escalation is the movement that occurs when a relationship decreases in intimacy or comes to an end. The process of ending a relationship is not as simple as going down the same elevator you came up on: It is not a reversal of the relationship formation process. Relational de-escalation can also involve only one or two of the stages. For example, a relationship might move from being one between good friends to a more casual friendship.[40] A **post-intimacy relationship** occurs when partners de-escalate from the intimate stage but still maintain a relationship. A couple might decide they like each other as friends but no longer want a romantic or exclusive relationship; thus, they de-escalate and maintain the relationship at the intensification or exploratory stage. Our model identifies five stages of relational de-escalation: turmoil or stagnation, deintensification, individualization, separation, and post-separation.

relational de-escalation
Movement of a relationship away from intimacy through five stages: turmoil or stagnation, deintensification, individualization, separation, and post-separation.

post-intimacy relationship
Formerly intimate relationship that is maintained at a less intimate stage.

Turmoil or Stagnation. When an intimate relationship is not going well, it usually enters the stage of either *turmoil* or *stagnation.* Turmoil involves an increase in conflict, as one or both partners tend to find more faults in the other. The definition of the relationship seems to lose its clarity, and mutual acceptance declines. The communication climate is tense, and exchanges are difficult.

Stagnation occurs when the relationship loses its vitality and the partners become complacent. Communication and physical contact between the partners decrease;

Building Your Skills | Graphing Your Relationship Changes

Think of an interpersonal relationship that you have had for at least a year. On the graph, plot the development of that relationship from stage to stage, indicating the relative amount of time you spent in each stage. You can also indicate whether you backed up to a previous stage at any point.

If possible, have your relational partner create a similar graph, and compare your perceptions of how the relationship has developed. What differences are there and why?

You also might want to compare your graph with those of classmates to see how different relationships develop. What can you tell from the graphs about the nature of their relationships?

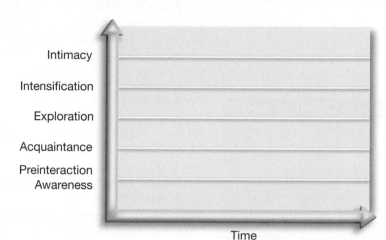

they spend less time together, but do not necessarily fight. Partners in a stagnating relationship tend to go through the motions of an intimate relationship without the commitment; they simply follow their established relational routines.

As with the up elevator, individuals can stop at this point on the down elevator and decide to quit descending. The relationship can remain in turmoil or stagnate for a long time, or the individuals can repair, redefine, or revitalize the relationship and return to intimacy.

Deintensification. If the turmoil or stagnation continues, however, the individuals might move to the *deintensification stage,* decreasing their interactions; increasing their physical, emotional, and psychological distance; and decreasing their dependence on the other for self-confirmation. They might discuss the definition of their relationship, question its future, and assess each partner's level of satisfaction or dissatisfaction. The relationship can be repaired and the individuals can move back to intensification and intimacy, but that is more difficult to accomplish at this stage.

Individualization. On the next floor down, the *individualization stage,* the partners tend to define their lives more as individuals and less as a couple. Neither views the other as a partner or significant other anymore. Interactions are limited. The perspective changes from "we" and "us" to "you" and "me," and property is defined in terms of "mine" or "yours" rather than "ours." Both partners turn to others for confirmation of their self-concepts.

Separation. In the *separation stage,* individuals make an intentional decision to eliminate or minimize further interpersonal interaction. If they share custody of children, attend mutual family gatherings, or work in the same office, the nature of their interactions will change. They will divide property, resources, and friends. For relationships that never went beyond exploration or intensification, however, the negotiation is often relatively painless. One study of post-dissolution romantic relationships found four specific patterns of commitment changes after a break-up: a *linear process,* in which commitment remained the same; a *relational decline* (the most common), in which commitment continued to decline over time; *upward relational progression,* in which commitment actually increased (perhaps re-escalating the relationship); and *turbulent relational progression*, in which the commitment went up and down several times.[41]

When intimates separate, their extensive personal knowledge about each often makes any future interaction—now limited to casual banter—awkward and uncomfortable. Over time, of course, each partner knows less about who the other person has become. For example, even after spending just a few years away from your high school friends, you might have difficulty interacting with them because your knowledge of one another is out of date.

Post-Separation Effects. Although interaction may cease altogether, the effect of the relationship is not over. The relational-stages high-rise is like something out of the old TV series *Twilight Zone*: Once you enter it, you can never leave it. The bottom floor on the down elevator, where you remain, is the *post-separation stage*. This floor represents the lasting effects the relationship has on your self and, therefore, on your other interactions and relationships. Noted relationship scholar Steve Duck claims that in this final stage of terminating relationships, we engage in "grave-dressing."[42] We create a public statement for people who ask why we broke up and also come to grips with losing the relationship. Sometimes, our sense of self gets battered during the final stages of a relationship, and we have to work hard to regain a healthy sense of self.

Of course, we are all aware of people who hop on an express elevator to get out of a relationship, bypassing all the normal stages of decline. One study found that of the various ways to terminate a relationship, abandoned partners most dislike the quick exit without discussion.[43]

Theories of Interpersonal Relationship Development

The model of relational stages provides a description of the stages you can expect to experience as you move through interpersonal relationships. However, it doesn't really provide an explanation of what motivates people to move from one stage to another. Think about some of your closer relationships. How did you move from being acquaintances to being close friends? Steve Duck suggests we go through a process of **filtering,** by which we reduce the number of partners at each stage of relational development by applying selection criteria that a potential close friend must meet.[44] In essence, a move from one stage to another toward intimacy means that a person has passed through another, finer screen or filter. These screens represent decision points in which we make some assessment of the relationship and decide how we want to proceed. We can choose to either escalate, maintain, or de-escalate the relationship. Three theories reflect the kind of decision making that might be taking place: social exchange theory, dialectical theory (or dialectics), and social penetration theory (self-disclosure).

Social Exchange Theory

Social exchange theory, an economic model of human behavior used to explain how people arrive at decisions, posits that people seek the greatest amount of reward with the least amount of cost.[45] You've probably been in a difficult relationship in which you have asked yourself, "Is this relationship really worth it?" What you are asking is whether the rewards you are gaining from the relationship are worth the trouble or expense necessary to sustain the relationship (the costs). Rewards are the positive outcomes we receive by being in the relationship, including friendship and love, fun and

---

BEING Other-ORIENTED

Relationships involve continual negotiation of the movement toward or away from intimacy. One partner often moves toward or away from intimacy before the other catches up. Not knowing what stage your partner is in creates discontent and conflict. Think about a relationship you have that has recently become closer. Who sees the relationship as closer, you or your partner? Does your partner also recognize this difference? How do you think your partner feels about it?

---

filtering Process of reducing the number of partners at each stage of relational development by applying selection criteria.

social exchange theory Theory that claims people make relationship decisions by assessing and comparing the costs and rewards.

laughter, money or favors, support and assistance, and confirmation of our value. Costs are the negative outcomes that reflect a loss, such as loss of time, loss of freedom, financial loss, denigration of our self-esteem, and even psychological or physical abuse. One factor we assess in deciding whether to pursue a relationship is the *magnitude* of the rewards or costs—the relative size of how much you put into and get out of a relationship. Another factor is how the rewards compare to the costs—the *ratio*. A relationship with high rewards (magnitude) might not be worth maintaining if the costs are also high (producing a low ratio). Perhaps you have a friend who is a lot of fun to be with, but you always have to pay that person's way, making the relationship cost as much as it rewards. On the other hand, a relationship with moderate rewards (magnitude) might be desirable if the costs are very small (producing a high ratio). You might enjoy your relationship with a coworker because you have fun working together (reward) and the relationship costs you little.

Rewards and costs affect our decisions to escalate, maintain, or terminate a relationship. For example, couples in one study who ended their romantic relationships maintained friendships when they continued to provide each other with rewards or resources (love, status, services, information, goods, or money)[46] On the other hand, those for whom there were costs or barriers (lack of support for the friendship by family and friends, involvement in new romances, or where neglect was used to end the relationship) had lower-quality friendships. A number of the issues that affect such relational development decisions are covered in the following sections.

Immediate and Forecasted Rewards and Costs. Relationships can be evaluated in terms of immediate, forecasted, and cumulative rewards and costs.[47] **Immediate rewards and costs** occur in a relationship in the present moment. You can think about your current relationships and assess their immediate value. **Forecasted rewards and costs** are based on projection or prediction. We make guesses about the potential of a relationship or its future outlook. Communication scholar Michael Sunnafrank calls this its *predicted outcome value*.[48] When you meet someone, you go through an initial assessment about whether a relationship with this person would be rewarding. You also use forecasting to decide whether to remain in existing relationships during troubled times (when costs escalate or rewards deteriorate). You can tolerate the increased costs associated with a roommate who's intolerable to live with during finals week because you know once finals are done, those costs will be gone and the relationship will be rewarding again.

Cumulative Rewards and Costs. Another reason people remain in relationships during periods of low immediate rewards has to do with cumulative rewards and costs. **Cumulative rewards and costs** represent the total rewards and costs accrued over the duration of the relationship. Just as when you have more income than expenses, you put your extra money in savings, so you build up a relational savings account of the extra rewards. You can draw on that savings account during times when the relationship is not paying off well. You hold on to a relationship because you have invested a lot in it and have gotten a lot out of it. However, just as your savings account can run out of money, cumulative rewards can lose value, and at that point you might decide to terminate the relationship. Generally, you wouldn't end a friendship with someone you've been friends with all through high school just because that friend is having personal difficulties and isn't much fun to be with. You probably would continue to be supportive until the accumulated rewards were exhausted.

Expected Rewards and Costs. People seem to construct templates in their minds for what relationships should be like. **Expected rewards and costs**

immediate rewards and costs
Rewards and costs that are associated with a relationship at the present moment.

forecasted rewards and costs
Rewards and costs that an individual assumes will occur, based on projection and prediction.

cumulative rewards and costs
Total rewards and costs accrued during a relationship.

expected rewards and costs
Expectation of how much reward we should get from a given relationship in comparison to its costs.

represent expectations and ideals about how rewarding a relationship should be relative to its costs. We have a mental model of the ideal friend, the ideal lover, the ideal coworker, and so on. We use the expected costs and rewards associated with these ideals to assess current relationships. We might abandon a relationship if we don't think it matches or has the potential to match our ideal. In essence, we set standards or criteria for our relationships by which we assess the desirability of a given relationship. Like Duck's filtering process, ideal images allow you to sort through relationships and focus on those that come closest to or exceed your ideal. The major difficulty associated with such comparisons rests in setting reasonable standards or ideals. For example, some parents adopt a philosophy of never arguing in front of their children. As the children become adults, they may have an expectation that happy marriages are ones without conflicts, and thus they may evaluate their own marriages as unsuccessful because they do not achieve this ideal. If you find that you are continually unable to find relationships that measure up to your ideals, you may need to reassess your standards.

We also compare our current relationships to the rewards and costs we forecast for other potential relationships. We reduce time spent with one friend in order to pursue another potentially more rewarding friendship. Communication researchers Gerald Miller and Malcolm Parks have proposed that we will move quickly to terminate a relationship if it falls below our expectations and we think we have an opportunity to develop a new relationship that has the potential to exceed those expectations.[49] All these comparisons work in concert with one another. We compare our current relationships to previous ones, to the ideal, and to potential ones.

Dialectical Theory

A second theory that explains relational development is dialectical theory. **Dialectical theory** looks at the human condition in terms of sets of opposing forces. When applying dialectical theory to interpersonal relationships, we can identify forces pulling us toward intimacy and opposing forces pulling us toward independence.

Three Dialectical Tensions.   Relationship researcher Leslie Baxter identified three dialectical tensions that have been widely used in interpersonal research.[50]

Connectedness versus Autonomy.   We desire to connect with others and to become interdependent, and at the same time we have a desire to remain autonomous and independent. In one study of married couples, the desire to be both connected and autonomous was found to be the most frequently occurring of the dialectical tensions.[51]

Predictability versus Novelty (Certainty versus Uncertainty).   Knowing what to expect and being able to predict the world around us helps reduce the tension that occurs from uncertainty. At the same time, we get bored by constant repetition and routine and therefore are attracted to novelty and the unexpected. Relationships that fall into routines may be comfortable, but they also suffer from a need for freshness.

dialectical theory Theory that relational development occurs in conjunction with various tensions that exist in all relationships, particularly connectedness versus autonomy, predictability versus novelty, and openness versus closedness.

Openness versus Closedness.   We wish to disclose information to others and to have those we are attracted to disclose to us. One ideal we seem to want to achieve in relationships is the ability to be totally open with our partners. However, we also value our privacy and feel a desire to hold back information. This tension was identified in the study of married couples mentioned earlier as the most important of the three tensions, although it did not occur as often as the other two.[52]

Dialectical Tensions and Relationships.

According to dialectical theory, each pair of forces in tension is present in every relationship, but the impact of each changes as a relationship progresses. Movement in relationships can be seen as a shift that occurs because of more pull from one of the two forces in tension. For example, when you begin developing a new friendship, one issue you have to address is whether you want to give up some of your autonomy (freedom to do your own things) in order to spend time with this other person (connectedness). Notice how this is similar to social exchange theory, in that you weigh costs (giving up autonomy) against rewards (becoming connected).

Both forces of autonomy and forces of connectedness can be found in even close relationships.[53] Although long-married couples have usually settled the issue of interdependence versus independence, dialectical theory asserts (and research supports) that tension from these forces is still present. Generally, such tension diminishes as we become more intimate; however, many an engagement has been called off at the last minute because of the inability of the bride or the groom to resolve this tension. The tension represents the challenge faced by individuals forming close relationships who are attempting to maintain their own identities while at the same time melding their identities.

One study of married couples found that dialectical tensions existed both at the individual level (for example, the wife or the husband trying to decide whether to be open or closed) and at the relational level (partners differing in terms of desires for autonomy, openness, or novelty).[54] In addition, the study found that extreme closedness related to greater autonomy—which makes sense, since those couples who share less information may also be likely to share less time together.

Movement in relationships can be seen as occurring because some element of tension has been resolved or overcome.[55] For example, during the initial stages of a relationship, you are restrained in your self-disclosures (closedness). As long as you remain closed, the relationship can only progress so far. You are confronted with the question of whether you should share information and increase the level of intimacy in the relationship. Thus, a tension exists until you make your decision. Once you have decided, some of the tension is relieved. If you decide on more openness, the reduction in tension is accompanied by a change in the relationship —a turning point.

Dialectical Tensions and Non-Linear Relationship Development.

You already know that few relationships progress in a nice orderly manner from acquaintance to intimacy, like an uninterrupted elevator ride. One study found that over half of the friendships studied progressed through a cycle of development, deterioration, and then development again, with each change being signaled by a turning point.[56] Dialectical theory explains these erratic movements typical of interpersonal relationships and the struggles to manage them. Your journey through relationships is more like a roller coaster ride than a trip in an elevator.

Social Penetration Theory and Self-Disclosure

Social psychologists Irwin Altman and Dalmas Taylor applied concepts about social exchange and self-disclosure to create a theory that explains the development

When a couple commits to a relationship, both partners must find a new balance between autonomy and connectedness.

269

of interpersonal relationships.[57] The main premise of their **social penetration theory** is that the movement toward intimacy is connected to increased breadth and depth of self-disclosing. They developed a model to illustrate the nature of these self-disclosures.

The Social Penetration Model. The **social penetration model** starts with a circle that represents all the potential information about yourself that you could disclose to someone (see Figure 9.3, circle A). This circle is divided into many pieces like a pie, with each piece of pie representing a particular aspect of yourself. For instance, some pieces in your pie might relate to athletic activities, religious beliefs, family, school, recreational activities, political interests, and fears. These pieces of pie represent the breadth of topics or information available about you.

In addition, the concentric circles in the pie represent the depth of information you could disclose. By depth, we mean how personal or intimate the information is; telling your friend about your fear of elevators is more intimate than telling someone that your favorite ice cream is homemade vanilla. The smallest circle represents the most personal information. Each of your relationships represents a degree of social penetration, or the extent to which the other person has penetrated your concentric circles (depth) and shared pieces of your pie (breadth). For example, the shading on circle B shows a relationship that involves a high degree of penetration, but of only one aspect of yourself. Perhaps you have a good friend with whom you study and go to the library, but you don't spend much time socializing with your friend; it's all work and no play with this friend. You might have disclosed some

social penetration theory
Theory of relational development that posits that increases in intimacy are connected to increases in self-disclosure.

social penetration model A model of the self that reflects both the breadth and the depth of information that can potentially be disclosed.

FIGURE 9.3

Social Penetration Model

A
Your "self" with all its various dimensions. The wedges represent the breadth of your "self," and the rings represent depth.

B
A limited relationship in which one dimension of your "self" has been disclosed to another person.

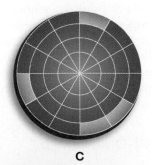

C
A relationship with greater breadth than B but with no intimacy.

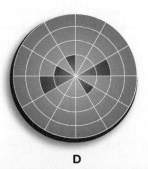

D
A highly intimate, close relationship in which there has been extensive breadth and depth of disclosure.

The social penetration model of self-disclosure suggests that self-disclosure can be described by both breadth—the number of topics we discuss—and depth—the level of intimacy we establish with others. Do cultural differences affect how much we disclose to one another? Several researchers suggest that the answer is yes. People's cultural backgrounds affect both the kinds of things they reveal and the intimacy of the information about themselves they share with others. Intercultural communication scholar William Gudykunst found that North Americans are more likely than Japanese to reveal more personal and intimate information about themselves to people whom they consider close friends.[58] Self-disclosure researcher Mie Kito found the same thing; Japanese students disclosed less about themselves than did students from North America.[59] Both Japanese and American students disclosed more about themselves in romantic relationships than with their friends. Americans were more likely than the Japanese to talk about their sex lives, dating patterns, and love interests and to reveal their emotions. A researcher investigating Korean communication patterns found that North Americans tended to disclose more than Koreans about their marital status, sexual morality, and use of birth control.[60] But Koreans were more likely than Americans to talk about issues related to education and family rules.

What are the larger implications of these studies? Simply this: The amount of self-disclosure that is considered appropriate is learned; the level of self-disclosure with which we are comfortable varies from culture to culture. Cultural norms influence how much we reveal about ourselves.

personal or intimate information to your friend about your study skills and weaknesses, but little about your family, hobbies, political views, religious beliefs, or other aspects of who you are.

Your relationships with your instructors probably look a little like circle B, with its limited breadth. In circle C, more pieces of the pie are shaded, but the information is all fairly safe, superficial information about yourself, such as where you went to school, your hometown, or your major. These would be the kind of disclosures associated with a new friendship. Circle D represents almost complete social penetration, the kind achieved in an intimate, well-developed relationship in which a large amount of self-disclosure has occurred.

Characteristics of Self-Disclosure in Relational Development.
People come to know us and even like us as we reveal who we are within the normal course of conversations.[61] However, there are rules and principles that guide the manner in which we self-disclose to others. Revealing too much, revealing too little, or making only unilateral disclosures violates disclosure norms held by most North Americans. The following is a discussion of some of the characteristics and principles involved in self-disclosing.

Self-Disclosure Usually Occurs in Small Increments.
Most people usually reveal information about themselves a little bit at a time, rather than delivering their autobiography all at once. Monitor your own self-disclosure. Are you revealing information at a greater depth sooner than you should? If you do, others may find your disclosure disquieting. Appropriate self-disclosure should be well timed to suit the occasion and the expectations of the individuals involved.

Communication privacy management theory suggests that each of us has our own boundaries and rules for sharing personal information—that is, we manage our own degree of privacy.[62] We typically don't share all that we know about ourselves to most people when we first meet them. And when we do start sharing information, we offer smaller bits and pieces, rather than revealing our entire life story to someone. Communication privacy management theory suggests that we each have

communication privacy management theory Theory that suggests that we each manage our own degree of privacy by means of personal boundaries and rules for sharing information.

individual rules about how much private information we share and with whom we share that information. What determines how much information we share with others? According to communication privacy management theory, our cultural background, our need to connect to others, and the amount of risk involved in sharing information (whether the information would embarrass us or others) are factors that determine how much and how quickly we share information about our personal lives with others.[63]

Self-Disclosure Moves from Less Personal to More Personal Information. As the social penetration model (Figure 9.3) illustrates, we can describe the depth of our self-disclosure by the intimacy level of the information we share. If we move too quickly to more intimate information before we've developed a history with someone, we violate social norms or expectations our partner may have. John Powell, author of *Why Am I Afraid to Tell You Who I Am?*, notes that the information we reveal about ourselves often progresses through the following predictable levels.[64]

Level 5: *Cliché communication.* In acknowledging the presence of another person with standard phrases such as "Hello" or the more contemporary "What's up?" we signal the desire to initiate a relationship, even if it is a brief, superficial one.

Level 4: *Facts and biographical information.* After using cliché phrases and responses to establish contact, we typically reveal nonthreatening information about ourselves, such as our names, hometowns, or majors.

Level 3: *Attitudes and personal ideas.* After noting our name and other basic information, we often begin talking about more personal information, such as our attitudes about work or school, our likes and dislikes, and noncontroversial topics.

Level 2: *Personal feelings.* After we've developed rapport and trust with someone, we share more intimate fears, secrets, and attitudes.

Relating to Others in the 21st Century — Self-Disclosure

Many of the principles and rules that guide our self-disclosure in face-to-face (FtF) interactions apply as well to electronically mediated communication (EMC). However, blogs, Facebook and MySpace pages, Internet forums, and Twitter provide different contexts for your decisions about what to share with both strangers and friends. Research suggests that we disclose more quickly in Internet interactions than in FtF ones because of anonymity, the lack of "gating features" or filters such as shyness or weak social skills, little expectation of actually meeting or sustaining a relationship, and the perception of similarity fostered by messaging in a forum devoted to a shared interest (e. g., groups discussing Dodge Neons, quilting, football, or *Grey's Anatomy*).[65] Interestingly, research found that people reveal more of their "true self" (the parts of their self they would like others to know but don't show) when interacting with strangers online than when interacting face to face.[66] Think about your own FtF and online interactions with others. Have you shared parts of yourself online that you'd like to share in your FtF interactions, but don't? What things have your friends posted on social network pages (such as photos or results of personal surveys) that you've seen as almost too personal or disclosing? Sometimes the blogs, "tweets," and text messages from friends might tell you more than you really want to know. Another research study found that in same-sex friendships, students who reported being the most comfortable self-disclosing online communicated with their friends more online and less in face-to-face interactions, compared to those who were less comfortable self-disclosing.[67] For some, seeking support or discussing difficult issues appears to be easier to do online.

Level 1: *Peak communication.* Powell calls this the ultimate level of self-disclosure that is seldom reached; his other name for level 1 communication is "gut level" communication. Only with our most intimate friends do we reveal such personal information. And it's possible, says Powell, that we may not reach this level of intimacy with our life partners, parents, or children. Peak communication is rare because of the risk and trust involved in being so open and revealing.

Our relationships develop as we disclose more and more pieces of our selves.

Self-Disclosure Is Reciprocal. In mainstream U.S. culture, one person's sharing of information about himself or herself prompts disclosure of similar information by the other person, particularly in the initial stages of relationships. This phenomenon is known as a **dyadic effect.** When we introduce ourselves and mention where we are from, we expect the other person to do likewise. Such reciprocation demonstrates trust and tends to increase liking.[68] This might be one reason strangers appear to tolerate but not necessarily to reciprocate even highly intimate information.[69] You might sometimes employ the dyadic effect as a strategy to gain information from another person: You want to know about someone's family, so you tell that person about your family first. If we don't see a relationship as having the potential to become more intimate, we are less likely to reciprocate.[70] Finally, in our closer relationships, we might not reciprocate during a given interaction, but we expect reciprocation over the course of the relationship. For example, if a friend is having difficulties in school, he might share those with you without expecting reciprocal self-disclosure; however, at some future date, you might share similar intimate information.[71]

Self-Disclosure Involves Risk. Although self-disclosure is a building block for establishing intimacy with others, it can be risky. Once you disclose something to someone, that person can now share that information with others; that person has additional power if the information is something you'd rather not have others know.

There is also the risk of rejection when you tell someone something that is personal. As Powell comments, "If I tell you who I am, and you do not like who I am, that is all that I have."[72]

Self-Disclosure Involves Trust. As we have already noted, to know something personal about someone is to have power over that person. Using personal information against others to manipulate and control is a misuse of the trust that was placed in you. According to British social psychologists Michael Argyle, Monica Henderson, and Adrian Furnham, one of the most fundamental expectations people have of their friends is that they will not reveal confidences.[73] When you say, "Oh, I won't tell anyone. Your secret's safe with me," mean it.

Perhaps the most intimate secrets are known by family members; our parents and siblings know quite a few things about us that we'd rather others not know. Interpersonal communication researchers Anita Vangelisti, John Caughlin, and Lindsay Timmerman found several factors that may help predict whether we disclose family secrets.[74] We would be *more* likely to share a family secret if . . .

- during an intimate conversation with another person, we found out that this person had a similar problem or we thought revealing the secret would help the other person

dyadic effect The reciprocal nature of self-disclosure: "You disclose to me, and I'll disclose to you."

- we thought the secret would eventually come to light even if we didn't reveal the secret

- there was some urgency or importance in revealing the secret; if we didn't reveal the secret, the concealment would create more problems than revealing the secret would cause

- we thought the family member would not mind if the secret were told; the family member would still accept us

- it seemed like a normal and natural thing to reveal, given the topic of conversation; if the topic came up, we might disclose the secret.

You might read this list and become worried that your family members might tell things they know about you that you'd rather others not know. Don't worry (too much). If sharing the secret with others would hurt the person sharing the secret, then there is less likelihood that the secret will be shared.[75] The researchers also found that there were some secrets that people would never disclose. Are there secrets in your family that you would never reveal?

Self-Disclosure Over Time: Enhancing Intimacy. As social penetration theory asserts, it is through the process of revealing information about yourself that it becomes possible for relationships to become more intimate. In an intimate friendship, we become aware of things about our friend that few if any other people may know. Intimacy grows through the process of self-disclosure. However, simply disclosing information about yourself is no guarantee that your relationship will become intimate (with *intimate* here referring to both greater depth and greater breadth of self-disclosure).[76] As we mutually self-disclose, we often discover incompatibilities or even negative information, which may lead to relational de-escalation.

As relationships move toward intimacy, they typically include periods of high self-disclosure early in the relationship. However, the *amount* of information that is disclosed decreases as the relationship becomes more and more intimate. In other words, there is generally more self-disclosing activity earlier in a relationship than later. As a relationship proceeds, we begin sharing low-risk information fairly rapidly, move on to share higher-risk information, and then finally, to share our most personal disclosures. The more intimate the relationship becomes, the more intimate the information that is disclosed. The sculpture in the photo represents the way we reveal ourselves when we are with close friends; with our best friends, we may reveal what is behind our masks. Holding back from sharing intimate information signals a reluctance to escalate the relationship. The amount of information that we have to share about ourselves is finite, so we slow down as we have less left to disclose.

Graph A in Figure 9.4 illustrates a typical disclosure pattern over the course of a long and intimate relationship. The peaks and valleys represent periods of variable disclosure. Note that most of the disclosure takes place in the beginning of the relationship. Not all relationships progress this way, however. The relationship in graph B represents two individuals who started to get to know each other but were interrupted before they became close friends.

As we develop a relationship, we reveal more of ourselves, removing the masks that we routinely use with strangers.

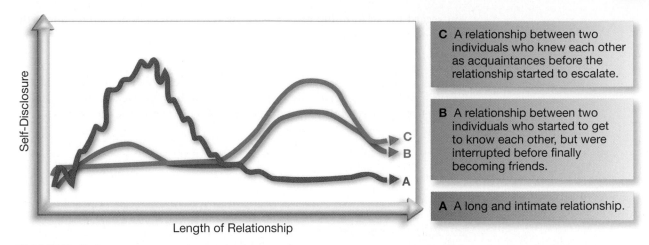

FIGURE 9.4

Self-Disclosure and Relational Development

They might have stopped because of some conflict, indecisiveness about pursuing the relationship, or external circumstances that limited opportunities for interacting. When the disclosure resumed, it became more intense. Graph C represents two individuals who probably knew each other as acquaintances for some time but never really had the opportunity or inclination to self-disclose. Once they did begin to escalate the relationship, however, there was a steep rise in self-disclosure. This graph might represent two coworkers who eventually start dating, or two students who have shared a class or two together before striking up a friendship.

Generally, a dramatic increase or decrease in self-disclosure reflects some significant change in the relationship. Even long-term relationships have significant increases and decreases in disclosure that signify changes. Before the birth of a first child, for example, both parents might disclose their fears and expectations about child rearing, and the information might have a profound effect on the relationship.

Interpersonal relationships cannot achieve intimacy without self-disclosure. Without true self-disclosure, we form only superficial relationships. You can confirm another person's self-concept, and have your self-concept confirmed, only if both you and your partner have revealed your selves to each other.

Self-Disclosure Reflects Perceptions About the Nature of Your Relationships.
What you reveal about yourself to others and what others reveal to you about themselves provide important information about how each of you perceives the nature, quality, and intimacy of your relationship.

The tricky part of interpreting the level of intimacy you have with another person, however, is to consider that what someone else thinks is very intimate and personal information you may perceive as not intimate and personal at all. For example, in a developing relationship, a friend might say, "When I was in high school, I had a crush on my English teacher." Your friend sees this as very intimate information that he is sharing because he views your relationship as having become very close. You might fail to recognize the trust being shown if you think it's no big deal to have had a crush on a high school teacher. It is difficult to know precisely what others think about a particular relationship without knowing the level of risk they associate with their disclosures. It is possible to send the wrong signal about how

BEING Other-ORIENTED

You probably have a good sense of what information you are comfortable disclosing to any given individual. But do you have a good sense of what other people are comfortable disclosing to you? Consider some of your casual and close relationships; are those partners more or less comfortable with disclosing personal information than you are? To what degree do these differences affect you, your partners, and the relationships?

you regard the relationship or to misperceive your partner's perception about the quality and nature of the relationship.

As you disclose information to another person, consider how the other person may perceive the level of intimacy and trust that you are implying when you reveal personal information. Being other-oriented means being aware that what *you* perceive as intimate and personally revealing may not be perceived as intimate information by your partner. Briefly stated, intimacy is in the mind of the listener.

Building Your Skills   Self-Disclosure as a Dance

Think of self-disclosure as a dance during which you and your partner react to each other's moves. If one is slow in disclosing, the other should follow that lead. The following are some self-disclosure dance suggestions for you to practice.

Enhancing Your Moves

Be Other-Oriented. Think about a piece of information that you have not told someone. How do you think the other person would react to that piece of information? What information about the other person are you basing your assumption on? What do you need to know about the other person to feel confident that he or she would respond positively to your disclosure?

Monitor Nonverbal Cues. Just as when dancing you focus on the other person's body movement, you need to monitor the nonverbal feedback you receive to your disclosures. For example, a person might discontinue eye contact with you, fidget, shift around in the seat, or display unexpected facial expressions. If you pick up on these, cut back on your self-disclosing. Can you recall a time when you disclosed information that appeared to make another person uncomfortable? Spend time watching other people as they interact for cues that show their level of comfort with what's being disclosed.

Disclose the Appropriate Amount. Think about the last time you had a conversation with someone new. To what degree did either of you disclose more information than the other wanted to hear, or not disclose enough? Were you uncomfortable disclosing as much information as you did? Did the other person seem uncomfortable, or maybe bored?

Disclose the Appropriate Depth. Think about times when you regret having shared information about yourself, because it was too intimate under the circumstances. To what degree were your disclosures spontaneous? What had you hoped the impact of these disclosures would be? What was the actual impact? Under what circumstances would the disclosures you made have been appropriate? Seeing a negative reaction from a partner to

a particular disclosure comes too late for retraction. Social decentering can help you in deciding what to disclose by predicting a partner's reaction to a given disclosure.

Adapt to the Other's Moves. Whether you're leading or following the dance, adjust your moves to those of your partner. Your level of disclosure should match that of your partner, but only if you are comfortable doing so. If your partner discloses information you feel is too personal, don't feel compelled to reciprocate. Ideally, your partner will sense your discomfort and adjust his or her moves to you. The two of you are creating a dance that reflects the comfort levels of both.

Promoting Your Partner's Moves

Be Trustworthy. People dance with people they trust; people open up to those they trust. Do other people see you as someone who can be trusted? What kind of signals do you send about your trustworthiness? Some trust just takes time to develop as information is shared and kept confidential. However, showing sincere interest and caring during a conversation will also build some trust. Telling the other person that you recognize the difficulty and importance of what he or she is saying, as well as expressing appreciation for his or her trust in you, shows empathy and can increase your trustworthiness.

Provide Social Support and Confirming Responses. Your dance partners want you to be there for them if they slip and to make them feel good about dancing. How do you typically react when a person shares delicate, embarrassing, or intimate information? Are you receptive, critical, indifferent, or noticeably uncomfortable? When people self-disclose negative information about themselves, they are often seeking social support and confirmation of their value. To be evaluative or judgmental of such a disclosure would be a great misstep. Apply good interpersonal listening skills, paraphrase what you've heard, and, when appropriate, don't say anything—just be there for the other person.

▶ RECAP Theories of Interpersonal Relationship Development

Theory	Definition	Application
Social Exchange Theory	People seek the greatest amount of reward with the least amount of cost.	You break up a long-distance relationship because the expense (driving time, cell phone bills) seems greater than what is gained from the relationship (fun, support).
Dialectical Theory	People must manage the tensions that result from opposing forces pulling toward intimacy and independence.	The time you spend with your new romantic partner is taking away time from your other friends. You must decide how to deal with your desire to be in the romantic relationship and still maintain your friendships.
Social Penetration Theory	Movement toward intimacy is connected to the breadth and depth of self-disclosure.	Your casual relationship with a roommate centers primarily on rent, shared bills, and housecleaning. One night your roommate shares the news that his parents are getting a divorce. You listen empathically as he shares his thoughts and feelings, sharing similar information when appropriate. From that point on, your relationship becomes closer and more intimate.

APPLYING AN OTHER-ORIENTATION
to Understanding Interpersonal Relationships

This chapter focused on the movement of relationships toward and away from intimacy; on relational costs and rewards, dialectical tensions, and self-disclosure; and on attraction. These relational elements were discussed primarily from your perspective—the rewards you may perceive, the tensions you experience, and your attraction to others. But reflecting from time to time on these elements from your relational partners' points of view can enhance these relationships. Why not start right now? Take a moment to identify a specific close friend of the same sex, a friend of the opposite sex, and a casual friend.

In what stage of development is each relationship, and how far along that stage is it? How does your perception compare to where each of your partners sees the relationship?

What cues does each partner provide to indicate how far the relationship has escalated? How sure are you of your assessment of each partner's perspective? How can you increase your certainty?

Using a scale from 0 to 100, how rewarding would you say each relationship is? How costly? Consider whether each of your three friends sees the relationship as more or less rewarding than you do. Does each see the relationship as more costly or less costly than you do?

How comfortable are you with the current balance between connectedness and autonomy in each relationship? How comfortable is each of your three friends?

What percentage (from 0 percent to 100 percent) of your "self" have you disclosed to each of your three friends? How much do you think your friends would say they have revealed about themselves to you? What differences do you think your friends perceive between what you've revealed and what they have revealed?

What was the source of your initial attraction to each of the three friends? What was the basis of each person's attraction to you? What is your long-term maintenance attraction to each person based on? What continues their attraction toward you?

Rarely do two people view their relationship in exactly the same way. If you didn't find any significant discrepancies between your views and your friends' views, you might be missing some information. Look for additional cues that might help you more completely understand your friends' perspectives, or consider sharing your views while seeking theirs.

Interpersonal Relationships: Definition and Types
(pages 252–256)

An interpersonal relationship is a perception shared by two people of an ongoing, interdependent connection resulting in the development of relational expectations and varying in interpersonal intimacy. Relationships of circumstance occur because surrounding conditions cause you to interact with someone. In contrast, you create relationships of choice when you intentionally seek to establish relationships. With respect to power and decision making, relationships can be complementary (one partner dominates and the other submits), symmetrical (both have the same amount of power, so that the relationship is competitive when both are strong or submissive when both are weak), or parallel (with power changing from situation to situation).

Key Terms

Relationship 252
Interpersonal relationship 252
Interpersonal intimacy 253
Relationship of circumstance 254
Relationship of choice 254
Complementary relationship 255

Symmetrical relationship 255
Competitive symmetrical relationship 255
Submissive symmetrical relationship 256
Parallel relationship 256

Critical Thinking Questions

1. Identify qualities beyond those cited in the text's definition of an interpersonal relationship that vary among your relationships.
2. Identify some advantages and disadvantages associated with each type of power relationship.
3. Ethics: To what degree can an individual pursue changing a relationship of circumstance into a relationship of choice if the other person rejects the initial attempt to change the relationship? What options does the person who rejects the continued attempts to change the relationship have?

Activities

Create two columns on a piece of paper. In the first column, write the names of three individuals with whom you have different relationships (for example, a parent, best same-sex friend, coworker). Using a scale of 1 (low) to 5 (high), indicate the degree to which each person likes to be in control and make decisions when you're together. In the second column, indicate the degree to which you like to be in control and make decisions when you're with each person.

Web Resources

http://www.scribd.com/doc/10195599/Interpersonal-Relationship This slideshow focuses on different qualities of relationships.

Genesis of Interpersonal Relationships
(pages 256–260)

The degree to which you wish to form or maintain a relationship represents your interpersonal attraction. Our interest in potential relationships reflects short-term initial attraction that might lead to escalating or sustaining a relationship through the development of long-term maintenance attraction. Factors that contribute to short-term initial attraction include proximity, which increases communication, and physical appearance, including sexual attraction. Some factors contribute to both short-term and long-term attraction, including the credibility, competence, and intelligence of the other person; being open and self-disclosing, which contributes to reciprocation of liking; and similarities and differences, or complementary needs.

Key Terms

Interpersonal attraction 256
Short-term initial attraction 256
Long-term maintenance attraction 256
Predicted outcome value (POV) 256

Proximity 258
Physical appearance 258
Reciprocation of liking 259
Similarity 259
Complementary needs 260

Critical Thinking Questions (POV)

1. Under what circumstances is it appropriate to act on your initial short-term attraction toward another person? Under what circumstances is it inappropriate?
2. Which source of attraction is probably the most important for sustaining a long-term relationship? Why? Which is least important? Why?

Activities

Make a list with two columns of names: people you regard as casual friends and those you regard as close friends. Identify what attracts you to the people on your list. Compare your ideas of what attracts you to casual friends and close friends with the ideas of other students. How does your list reflect the categories of attraction identified in the text?

Web Resources

http://www.solvedating.com/love.html This web site offers connections to information on soulmates, dating, love, and attraction.

Stages of Interpersonal Relationship Development
(pages 260–266)

As relationships escalate toward intimacy or de-escalate away from it, they go through identifiable stages. Each stage is marked by turning points, differences in self-disclosure, and specific verbal and nonverbal communication patterns. Escalating relationships move through preinteraction awareness, acquaintance, exploration, intensification, and intimacy. Relationships that are becoming less intimate go through turmoil or stagnation, deintensification, individualization, separation, and post-separation effects. The de-escalation of a romantic relationship does not mean that the relationship necessarily ends; sometimes couples are able to maintain rewarding post-intimacy relationships.

Key Terms

Relational development *260*	Introductions *263*
Turning point *261*	Casual banter *263*
Causal turning point *262*	Relational de-escalation *264*
Reflective turning point *262*	Post-intimacy relationship *264*
Relational escalation *262*	

Critical Thinking Questions

1. Think about three relationships you have that have remained in the exploration or intensification stage. What has prevented the relationships from escalating to the next stage? Why have you sustained the relationships?

2. Ethics: If two people have agreed to maintain a relationship below the highest level in the model of relational stages (the intimacy stage), is it ethical for one of the people to nonetheless continually try to move the relationship to the intimacy stage?

Activities

Brainstorm some of the turning points that you have experienced in both the escalation and de-escalation of your relationships. Identify the relational stages in which the turning points occurred. Identify whether each turning point is a causal or a reflective turning point. How significant an impact are turning points in your development of relationships?

Web Resources

http://www.internetromance.org/academic-research/thesis/turning-point-types-565.htm This site offers a summary of research on turning points, with charts showing some of the most common relationship turning points found in a study; includes links to other articles of interest.

Theories of Interpersonal Relationship Development
(pages 266–277)

Three theories explain relationship development. Social exchange theory posits that we make decisions about becoming more or less intimate on the basis of the rewards and costs that we perceive to be associated with the relationship. Decisions are made on the basis of forecasted and cumulative rewards and costs as well as comparisons with previous, potential, and ideal relationships. Dialectical theory sees our decisions being based on resolution of tensions between forces in our lives, particularly connectedness versus autonomy, predictability versus novelty, and openness versus closedness. Social penetration theory explains movement toward intimacy as connected to the breadth and depth of self-disclosure. Your self-disclosures are often reciprocated, involve risk and establishing trust, and reflect your perception of the relationship.

Key Terms

Filtering *266*	Dialectical theory *268*
Social exchange theory *266*	Social penetration theory *270*
Immediate rewards and costs *267*	Social penetration model *270*
Forecasted rewards and costs *267*	Communication privacy management theory *271*
Cumulative rewards and costs *267*	Dyadic effect *273*
Expected rewards and costs *267*	

Critical Thinking Questions

1. Explain (a) how social exchange theory relates to dialectical theory, (b) how social exchange theory relates to social penetration theory, and (c) how dialectical theory relates to social penetration theory and to self-disclosure.

2. Ethics: Is it ethical to intentionally increase the cost and reduce the rewards for a relational partner as a strategy for ending the relationship?

Activities

Make a list of ten pieces of information about yourself that vary in how intimate or risky the information is (its depth). Put (+) next to those you know are appropriate to disclose to a fellow student you have just met. Put (−) next to those you know are inappropriate and (?) next to those you are unsure about. Under what circumstances might the pieces of information you marked with (−) or (?) be appropriate to disclose? Your disclosures should match your level of trust in the other person. Remember that how much and what you disclose will be taken by the other person as statement of how you feel about the relationship—your level of disclosure should match your relational feelings.

Web Resources

http://www.queendom.com/tests/access_page/index.htm?idRegTest=716 This is a self-test that assesses your willingness to self-disclose to others. The questions themselves provide a good source for personal reflection.

10

Managing Relationship Challenges

Charise:	I heard you went to the new Will Smith movie last night.
Simon:	Yeah, it was pretty good.
Charise:	I thought we agreed to go see it together?
Simon:	Oh, sorry. I forgot; besides, you were busy anyway.
Charise:	Don't lie. You didn't forget—you just didn't want to go with me.
Simon:	Hey, wait a minute. It's no big deal. It was just a movie.
Charise:	Who'd you go with?
Simon:	A gang of us from work went.
Charise:	Who?
Simon:	Just some people from work.
Charise:	You're a liar! I heard it was just you and some girl.

> "Love begins with a smile, grows with a kiss, and ends with a teardrop.
>
> **Anonymous**

Throughout this book you have read about various factors that can impede effective interpersonal communication: language misunderstandings, biased perceptions, misinterpretation of nonverbal cues, weak listening skills, destructive conflict styles, and inappropriate self-disclosures. All of these factors can negatively affect interpersonal relationships. The above exchange between Charise and Simon reflects another set of issues that are covered in this chapter. Simon has obviously broken a promise he made to Charise about seeing a movie together, which places a strain on the relationship. Simon compounds the problem by being deceptive, but Charise calls him on it. Unlike the specific conflicts that you read about in Chapter 8, the challenges covered in this chapter reflect larger, more systemic relational issues. Interpersonal communication also has a dark side, in that it can be used in ways that are detrimental to others. These include being deceitful, as Simon is, and saying things that hurt other people's feelings, as Charise does. These relationship challenges and the darker aspects of interpersonal communication can contribute to relational de-escalation and termination.

Relationship Challenges

The movement toward an intimate relationship doesn't always go smoothly. Chapter 9 described some general expectations about how relationships develop, and you have your own additional set of expectations about relationships, but what happens when you encounter the unexpected? Any relationship can be challenged by one partner's failure to meet the other's expectations (a failure event), by attempts to maintain a relationship over long distances, or by social biases against certain types of relationships. Overcoming each of these challenges requires strong resolve and commitment by the relationship partners.

Violations of Relational Expectations: Failure Events and Interpersonal Transgressions

Just as relational expectations are part of the definition of relationships, violations of those expectations are an unavoidable part of relationship development. You develop sets of socially based relational expectations specific to given types of relationships, including expectations about their rewards and costs. You have sets of expectations for what a best friend should be, what a romantic partner or spouse should be like, how rewarding a relationship with an opposite-sex friend should be, and so on. Violations of these expectations arouse uncertainty and produce emotional reactions such as hurt and anger.[1] You might assess a relationship in light of your expectations and decide to de-escalate or terminate the relationship. Or, you might modify your expectations, so that what had been a violation is no longer. For example, if you held the expectation that friends lend other friends money, but your friends kept turning down your requests, you might stop seeing money lending as a quality of friendship. Finally, you might decide to discuss the violation of the expectation with the other person. How you manage relational violations affects the health of the relationship.

You also develop, in concert with your partners, sets of expectations or understandings that are specific to each relationship. These understandings can be either implicit or explicit. Implicit understandings represent an unspoken compact between the partners about the relationship and each other. Explicit understandings are stated compacts and agreements. Violations of both types of understandings arouse uncertainty and evoke various responses. For example, your roommate agrees to clean up the apartment over the weekend (an explicit understanding) and then fails to do so. Your friend says he'll meet you at the restaurant at 7:00 (an explicit understanding) but doesn't show up until 8:00. Some very personal information that you shared with only one other person (an implicit understanding) suddenly becomes common knowledge among your other friends. Your fiancée is seen out on a date with your best friend (either an implicit or an explicit understanding). These are called **failure events**—violations of understandings that occur between people in interpersonal relationships. Effective management of a failure event can lead to a clearer understanding and greater appreciation of the relationship.

Assessing Severity.   Failure events and transgressions can be thought of as occurring along a continuum of severity, with those that are least severe often being ignored altogether. The other end of that range is reflected in the behaviors people in dating relationships identify as "unfaithfulness" or as "transgressions," including spending time with another person, breaking a promise, flirting, betraying a trust or confidence, keeping secrets from the partner, or failing to return affection.[2] In fact, either offering too much affection at the wrong time or not enough affection at another can be a failure event. The most severe violations can have a traumatic impact on a relationship. In an intimate romantic relationship, partners often see sexual fidelity as a defining characteristic. Cheating on one's partner is a severe moral transgression, which often leads to the termination of the relationship.[3] What you might see as a minor failure event might be viewed more severely by your partner. Relationships can be strengthened by discussing relational expectations and violations and seeking to understand your partner's assessment of the severity of any violation.

Responding with Discussion.   The process of addressing failure events often follows the reproach-account pattern, in which both partners must make a number of decisions. The first decision is whether a failure event has actually occurred. This may be easier to determine with moral transgressions, because we expect partners to know what is appropriate, given the culture's inherent moral code. If the transgression is not a moral one, had both parties agreed to a specific rule or expectation? Did both parties understand the rule? Was the rule appropriate, applicable, and accepted?

After answering these questions, both parties must decide whether to discuss the failure.[4] If we don't care that much about the relationship or the issue, we might opt to ignore the failure, deciding it is not worth the effort. The decision to complain to or reproach a partner should be motivated by a desire to clarify relational expectations or to avoid the failure event in the future by modifying the partner's behaviors.[5] A **reproach** is a message that a failure event has occurred. Reproaches are usually

failure events Violations of understandings between people in relationships.

reproach Message that a failure event has occurred.

direct statements, but they can also be conveyed indirectly through hints or nonverbal messages. For example, if you are upset that a close friend forgot your birthday, you might act cold and distant. Reproaches range from *mitigating* (mild) to *aggravating* (threatening and severe). For example, if your friend forgets to return a book she borrowed, you might offer a mitigating reproach such as "Hey, Sally, I was wondering if you were done with that book I loaned you?" On the other hand, "Remind me to never loan you a book again, Sally; you are obviously irresponsible" is an aggravating reproach.

What would you say to each reproach if you were Sally? Which reproach would make you more likely to apologize? Which would you be more likely to ignore? The nature of the reproach affects the response, or the **account.**[6] Accounts can also be initiated without a reproach, simply because a person knows he or she has failed to live up to an expectation. Relationship scholar Frank Fincham postulated that self-initiated accounts are more likely to evoke a favorable reaction from a partner than are accounts given in response to reproaches.[7] Apologizing as you arrive late at a friend's house for dinner is more likely to appease the irritated friend than acting as though you've done nothing wrong or apologizing only *after* being reproached. The accounts people offer typically take one of five forms:

- *Apologies* include admission that the failure event occurred, acceptance of responsibility, and expression of regret.
- *Excuses* include admission that the failure event occurred, coupled with a contention that nothing could have been done to prevent the failure; it was due to unforeseen circumstances.
- *Justifications* involve accepting responsibility for the event but redefining the event as not a failure.
- *Denials* are statements that the failure event never took place.
- *Absence of an account,* or *silence,* involves ignoring a reproach or refusing to address it.

In providing an account to another person, you should examine your culpability. You should adopt an other-oriented perspective by considering the reproacher's objectives, desires, and feelings so that you can understand his or her reason for the reproach. Regardless of the legitimacy of the reproach, the person's feelings and reactions are real, and you must determine the most effective manner to address them. Sometimes simply admitting your failure and making a genuine effort to correct it is the best response.

Once they receive an account, reproachers must decide whether they find the account acceptable and can consider the issue resolved. When accounts are rejected, account givers often provide another account. However, rejection of accounts can escalate the failure event into an interpersonal conflict. Management of the conflict requires the skills and strategies discussed in Chapter 8.

Responding with Forgiveness.
Forgiveness of a failure event or interpersonal transgression was defined by respondents in one study as accepting the event, moving on, coming to terms, getting over it, letting go of negative feelings and grudges, and continuing the relationship.[8] These respondents reported forgiving others because the relationship was important or for personal health and happiness.[9] In essence, we forgive others when it is in our own best interest to do so. The same study also found that we are more likely to forgive those who apologize, are remorseful, admit their violation, and/or make restitution.[10] Intimate relationships rarely survive interpersonal transgressions that are not forgiven. Communication scholars Vincent

---

BEING Other-ORIENTED

Failure to understand another person's relational expectations can be a source of conflict and can undermine relational development. Think about how decisions are made in one of your relationships. What are *your* expectations for your role in making decisions, and your partner's role? What are your *partner's* expectations for his or her decision-making role, and for your decision-making role? To what degree are differences in these expectations the source of failure events or transgressions?

---

account Response to a reproach.

Building Your Skills | Trait Forgiveness

How forgiving a person are you? The following scale was developed to assess forgiving personalities. Be honest and objective in assessing your own behaviors. Indicate the degree to which you agree or disagree with each of the statements using the following scale:

1 – – – – – – – – 2 – – – – – – – – 3 – – – – – – – – 4 – – – – – – – – 5 – – – – – – – – 6 – – – – – – – – 7

Strongly Disagree   **Neutral/Mixed**   **Strongly Agree**

_____ 1A. I can forgive a friend for almost anything.

_____ 2A. I try to forgive others even when they don't feel guilty for what they did.

_____ 3A. I can usually forgive and forget an insult.

_____ 4A. I have always forgiven those who have hurt me.

_____ 5A. I am a forgiving person.

_____ Total of A items

_____ 1B. People close to me probably think I hold a grudge too long.

_____ 2B. If someone treats me badly, I treat him or her the same.

_____ 3B. I feel bitter about many of my relationships.

_____ 4B. Even after I forgive someone, things often come back to me that I resent.

_____ 5B. There are some things for which I would never forgive even a loved one.

_____ Total of B items

(A Total) _____ minus (−) (B Total)_____ = _____

The possible totals on this scale range from +30 to −30, with 0 being the midpoint. The more positive your total, the more likely you are to be a forgiving person. Examine your lower scores for the A items. Which ones could be improved? Examine your higher scores for the B items. What can you do to change those?

Source: J. W. Berry, E. Worthington, L. O'Connor, L. Parrott, and N. Wade, "Forgiveness, Vengeful Rumination and Affective Traits," *Journal of Personality* 73 (2005): 183–225.

Waldron and Douglas Kelley suggest taking these seven steps to achieve forgiveness:[11]

1. *Confront the transgression*: The failure event and hurt must be acknowledged by both partners.

2. *Manage emotion*: Emotions must be acknowledged, expressed, and accepted by both partners.

3. *Engage in sense making*: Both partners need to understand and empathize. As hard as it might be, the wounded partner needs to feel and understand the reasons for the transgressor's actions.

4. *Seek forgiveness*: The transgressor requests forgiveness, offers an apology, expresses regret, and acknowledges the other's hurt.

5. *Grant forgiveness*: Forgiveness can be immediate or conditional. To manage the anguish, the wounded partner may view forgiveness as a gift or as showing mercy to the transgressor.

6. *Negotiate values and rules*. Clarification, negotiation, and renewed commitment to relevant relational rules and morals are necessary.

7. *Transition, monitor, maintain, or renegotiate*. Time is needed to re-establish trust as the relationship readjusts to its pre-transgression state. Review and renegotiation of rules might be needed.

Each step addresses an important part of the forgiveness process, and some can be further broken down. For example, one study identified five forgiveness-granting strategies: nonverbal display (not directly saying that the other is forgiven, but acting in ways that show he or she is, such as showing affection, resuming interactions, and the like); conditional (expressing forgiveness but with stipulations—"You're forgiven as long as you . . ."); minimizing (shrugging off the offense as not very serious); discussion (acknowledging and talking about the failure event, sharing perspectives); and explicit (a straight declaration of forgiveness, often in combination with the other types).[12]

Whether forgiveness is achieved is ultimately dependent on a number of factors such as personality (including the ability to empathize), the quality of the relationship, the nature of the transgression (its severity), and the perceived intentionality and selfishness of the transgressor.[13]

"I don't want your apology -- I want you to be sorry."

Responding with Retaliation. Instead of a reproach, failure events might be met with retaliation. Retaliation involves an attempt to hurt the partner in response to the hurt she or he has caused—to "even the score."[14] An act of infidelity can motivate a partner to even the score by also being unfaithful.[15] We want our partner to feel the same degree of hurt that we felt, thus creating a sense of equity and balance. People also retaliate to convey how hurt they are, to regain some power, and to discourage future transgressions.[16] Retaliation behaviors can include aggressive communication (yelling, accusing, and sarcasm); active distancing (giving the partner the silent treatment or withholding affection); manipulation attempts (evoking the transgressor's jealousy or guilt, or testing his or her loyalty); contacting a rival; and violence.[17]

Physical Separation and Distance

The mobility of today's population means that we are often moving away or being separated for a time from people with whom we have formed interpersonal relationships. We tend to think of long-distance relationships primarily as dating relationships. However, you probably have or will have long-distance relationships with your parents, spouse, children, siblings, and other family members; with friends; and even with coworkers or clients. Each long-distance relationship requires specific maintenance strategies in order to be successfully managed.[18] In addition, more people are meeting and developing long-distance relationships through the Internet. Long-distance relationships vary in terms of expected length of separation, length of time between face-to-face visits, and the actual distance between the partners. Temporary separation requires adjustment and management by the partners. On the other hand, permanent physical separation produces different expectations, interactions, and relational management strategies.

How often partners are able to get together face to face also determines the impact of the physical distance. One study suggests that people who are in long-distance romantic relationships but who are able to get together at least once a week can maintain relationships similar to those between people who are geographically close.[19] Think about your own experience of being in a long-distance relationship: Was it the number of miles between you or the frequency of getting together that had the most impact? There are times when partners are relatively close geographically but are limited in how often they can get together. The infrequency of face-to-face interactions can have an

Partners in long-distance relationships must use specific maintenance strategies if the relationship is to be successful.

BEING Other-ORIENTED

Long-distance relationships add an extra obstacle to your ability to be other-oriented. The lack of face-to-face nonverbal cues limits the information you might otherwise receive to help you better understand your partner's perspective. For example, how aware are you of how your current long-distance partners (family, friends, or romantic partners) feel about how often you talk and how often you get together? What problems can be attributed to the challenge of being other-oriented in long-distance relationships?

artificially positive effect on the partners, because they work harder to be on their good behavior when they do get together.[20] This good behavior is probably one reason partners in romantic long-distance relationships report as much satisfaction and closeness as those who are geographically close.[21] Another reason for this reported satisfaction is that it is apparently easier to maintain an idealized image of a romantic relationship when you don't spend as much time with your partner.[22] Researchers Laura Stafford and James Reske found that couples in long-distance premarital relationships had less communication but surprisingly greater satisfaction and higher expectation for the likelihood of marriage than those in *proximal,* or geographically close, relationships.[23] Couples who are apart have fewer facts about their partners to get in their way. Long-distance partners report feeling "moral commitment"; they feel they "ought" to continue the relationship.[24] However, a more recent study found that when those in long-distance dating relationships moved to a proximal relationship, they were likely to terminate the relationship.[25]

In Chapter 9, social exchange theory (analysis of rewards and costs) was used to explain our decision to escalate or de-escalate a relationship. It also offers a way to analyze the survival of long-distance relationships.[26] Distance introduces added costs to maintaining a relationship, including actual monetary costs such as long-distance phone charges and expenses involved in commuting (for gasoline, airline tickets, food), as well as the expenditure of time spent commuting to see a partner and the disruption of normal routines (leaving less time available for other activities). These costs are weighed against the benefits or rewards of the relationship. The rewards depend on what you are seeking in the relationship. Obviously, if you are looking for a relationship that meets physical needs and need for affection, a permanent long-distance relationship would probably be unsatisfactory. On the other hand, if your need is for a confidant, and you don't require face-to-face interactions, a long-distance arrangement might be acceptable.[27] Or, if you perceive the costs as investments rather than losses you might sustain your commitment to the relationship.[28] Some relationships continue for a lifetime, even with little face-to-face time, because the rewards of interacting far exceed any costs.

Tensions sometimes arise when one person is trying to maintain both long-distance relationships and proximal relationships.[29] For example, the autonomy that a long-distance relationship affords provides more time for proximal relationships with others. Visits by long-distance partners can put strains on proximal partners if the two sets of friends don't get along, or if they vie for the mutual friend's time together during those visits.[30] Long-distance couples also create tensions by over-planning their time together so they don't feel they've wasted their time—planning activities, discussion topics, and even sex.[31]

Minimizing idealization and maintaining communication are probably the most important factors in sustaining strong relationships, even over long distances. The more open and honest you can keep the communication, the more similar your long-distance relationships will be to proximal ones.

Relationships That Challenge Social Norms

Each culture establishes certain norms about what are appropriate and inappropriate relationships, based on social values, biases, and prejudices. Among the types of relationships often discouraged are those between people of different races, religions, or ethnicity. In addition, many societies have social mores against romantic relationships between individuals who differ significantly in age or who are of the same sex. When norms are violated, partners face social pressure to conform or risk being ostracized. Fortunately, norms change, and in the United States the number of relational restrictions have decreased in the last thirty years; nonetheless, developing any of these types of relationships still presents challenges.

Partners in intercultural relationships face the challenge of communicating and interacting effectively, as discussed in Chapter 4. In addition, like partners in interracial relationships, they also may confront bias against the relationship itself. Movies such as *Guess Who, Save the Last Dance, Crazy/Beautiful, Remember the Titans, Jungle Fever,* and *Snow Falling on Cedars* have explored the difficulty partners in intercultural and interracial relationships have communicating with each other, as well as the negative responses they face from those around them. One aspect of many of these relationships is the clash between in-groups and out-groups. One's racial or ethnic group is one's **in-group;** cliques and gangs are also examples of in-groups. People are considered part of an in-group whenever they view themselves as such. Those who are not part of this group are part of an **out-group.**

Those outside a norm-challenging relationship might see the relationship as a threat to their respective race or ethnic group (whether they are part of the in-group or the out-group). The more different the interloper is perceived to be, the greater the threat and negative reactions.[32] For example, Catholics might feel more hostility toward a Jewish-Catholic couple than toward a Lutheran-Catholic one. Those outside the relationship have difficulty understanding the attraction between the partners and might minimize it as simply motivated by the appeal of "forbidden fruit."[33] In contrast, those in the relationship obviously have a different perspective. They can see their differences as an opportunity to learn both about others and about themselves; and they focus on the similarities in their values and personal characteristics rather than on differences.[34]

The importance of discussing and supporting the ethnic, racial, or religious identity of both members of a couple was underscored in a recent study of interracial and interethnic romantic relationships between college students. Being open about culture and faith and supporting a partner's culture and faith were associated with less relational distress.[35] However, those in intercultural and interfaith relationships also experienced more conflict related to culture and faith than did those in same-culture or same-faith relationships.[36] A discussion of cultural values helped the relationships grow; nonetheless, intercultural romantic relationships were more likely to end than were intracultural ones.[37] Religious differences did not have the same impact, as interfaith romantic relationships were just as likely to continue as intrafaith ones.[38]

Romantic homosexual relationships are increasingly accepted in U.S. culture, with a few states accepting same-sex marriage. On the other hand, some states expressly

in-group One's racial or ethnic group.

out-group A racial, cultural, religious, or ethnic group different from one's own.

Building Your Skills Friends with a Difference

Think of someone you know or imagine yourself in a friendship with someone from each of the following groups: (a) someone at least ten years older than you are; (b) someone from a country where people speak a different language than you do; (c) someone of a different sexual orientation; (d) someone of a different race; (e) someone of a different religion.

1. With which of these people is communication easiest? Why?

2. With which of these people is communication hardest? Why?

3. How do your family and friends react to this relationship? Why?

4. How have your differences affected your interpersonal communication in each friendship?

5. How does this friendship compare to friendships with those who are similar to you?

prohibit such marriages, reflecting the social hostility gay and lesbian relationships still face. This hostility is probably one reason gays and lesbians establish social networks that confirm their relationships and allow them to be forthright about them.[39] Many individuals hide their homosexual relationships from others for fear of the reactions and rejection they may face. Despite the social stigma that these are "abnormal" relationships, gay and lesbian couples engage in the same kinds of relational maintenance activities as heterosexual couples.[40]

What about relationships between heterosexuals and homosexuals? Such a relationship served as the foundation for the friendship portrayed on the TV show *Will and Grace*. An individual's sexual orientation shouldn't be a factor in whether you form a friendship, any more than a person's race, ethnicity, or age should be—but it often is. Straight people are referred to as *homophobic* when they fear interaction and friendship with gays and lesbians. While you might not find a person's sexual orientation to be a problem, one study found that heterosexual respondents reported that even if they had a lot in common with someone identified as homosexual, they were more inclined to forgo a friendship with that person and restrict themselves to relationships with heterosexuals.[41] This tendency was significantly stronger for the male respondents than for the females.

Knowing that others are likely to avoid developing friendships with them might lead gays and lesbians to hide their sexual orientation. The desire to be able to form nonsexual friendships has to be weighed against the risks of being open and self-disclosing. This scenario creates a paradox, because interactions with homosexuals positively influence the attitudes heterosexuals have toward them.[42] Regardless of your own sexual orientation, take some time to consider your attitudes and openness to forming relationships with all people, no matter how they differ from you.

The Dark Side of Interpersonal Communication and Relationships

The "dark side" of interpersonal communication is the use of interpersonal communication in damaging, unethical ways. Throughout the text, we have focused primarily on how interpersonal communication can be used for developing fulfilling relationships, for managing conflict cooperatively, for improving relationships, and for helping you meet your interpersonal needs. However, interpersonal communication can also be used to deceive and hurt people. Regrettably, the dark side of interpersonal communication and relationships is more prevalent than you might think; for example, studies focusing on deception have found that it is pervasive in interpersonal interactions.[43] There is a dark side to relationships as well, including obsessive relational intrusion, stalking, jealousy, and relational violence.

Deception

You wake up to discover you've overslept, but because an absence would hurt your grade, you come to class late and tell the instructor that you had car trouble. Your roommate is going on a date wearing an outfit that you think is nice—but not on her; when asked what you think, you say, "I've always liked that outfit," omitting the fact that you don't think it suits her. You're involved in an intimate relationship but find you no longer have strong feelings toward your partner. Your partner asks, "Do you still love me?" and you answer "Yes." You are developing a close physical relationship with someone but choose not to disclose the extent of your previous sexual relationships. In an attempt to appear "hip," you list several rock bands as favorites on your Facebook page even though they're not.

Each of these scenarios represents a situation in which there is deception, but the impact and seriousness of the deceptions differ. One way to assess the seriousness is to ask yourself, "What would happen if the other person discovered my deception?" Your instructor and your roommate might be upset, but deceiving them would probably not have the same impact as falsely declaring your love or not disclosing your sexual activity to a partner. Communication scholar Mark Knapp classifies lies as low stake and high stake lies.[44] The size of the stake represents how much might be gained by the deception and how much would be lost if the lie were detected. The lie to the instructor, the roommate, and one's Facebook friends are low stake lies, while not revealing previous sexual activity might be considered a high stake lie.

Creating a deceptive Facebook profile might not be as serious as deceiving your parents about what web sites you visit.

Interpersonal deception theory, as developed by Judee Burgoon and David Buller, is an explanation of deception and detection as processes affected by the transactional nature of interpersonal interactions.[45] A number of factors influence the process, including the context, the relationship, communication skills, suspicion, and expectations. Individuals intentionally and strategically manipulate information to achieve some goal; their audience listens and evaluates the truthfulness of the information. In other words, one person tries to get away with a lie and the other person decides whether to believe it or not. To avoid being caught, deceivers need to implement effective deception strategies and monitor listeners' responses. Listeners might accept the deception without pause, express skepticism, or blatantly challenge the deception. Each listener reaction lets the deceiver know his or her next course of action. Think about the last time you deceived someone. To what degree did you alter your strategy because of the context, the relationship, or the likely suspicion of your partner? When a listener questions your statements, you might act indignant, restate your claim more forcefully, or add more convincing evidence. Of course, you might also come clean and admit your lie.

Deception by Omission (Concealment).
Deception by omission (concealment) involves intentionally holding back some of the information another person has requested or that you are expected to share. For example, your parents ask where you were last night, and you reply that you went to the movies. While that is true, you don't tell your parents that you also went to a party at a friend's house afterwards. You have not "lied," but you have been deceptive. Determining whether an omission is deceptive depends on the intention of the deceiver. What was your reason for omitting the information about the party? Were you attempting to avoid your parents' response, or did you simply forget?

We can also present information and leave out information so as to intentionally mislead the listener. For example, telling your roommate "I've always liked that outfit" is intended to create the impression that you think the outfit is attractive on her. This deception provides you some protection if you are later called to task by your roommate for not saying the outfit looked bad. You can reply, "I never said it looked good on you." Despite your claim, your roommate would know your intention was to

interpersonal deception theory An explanation of deception and detection as processes affected by the transactional nature of interpersonal interactions.

deception by omission (concealment) Intentionally holding back some of the information another person has requested or that you are expected to share.

deceive. These types of omissions are sometimes called "half-truths," because the statements themselves are truthful, but they are not the complete truth.

Another form of deception by omission demonstrates how deceptions can be failure events. You may fail to share information that you know you should provide to another person because of relational expectations. For example, knowing that your best friend's fiancée has been having an affair but not telling your friend about it is deception by omission. Your friend's discovery that you didn't share the information is likely to create a conflict, because he will no doubt believe you owed it to him to share your "secret." Deception by omission can undermine decision making; for example, not disclosing sexual history prevents one's partner from making informed decisions about the level of risk he or she might be encountering.[46] While omitting information usually is not considered as grievous as falsifying information,[47] when the omitted information is important, omission is viewed as just as deceptive as falsifying.[48]

Deception by Commission.

Deception by commission is the deliberate presentation of false information[49]—lying. Among the types of deception by commission are white lies, exaggeration or embellishment, and baldfaced lies. **White lies** typically involve only a slight degree of falsification that has a minimal consequence. Calling these deceptions "white lies" seems to make us feel a little less guilty. Your listing on Facebook of bands as favorites when they are not would probably be considered a white lie. Sometimes we use **exaggeration**—"stretching the truth" or embellishing the facts. Telling someone you were at the library for a couple of hours when it was only twenty minutes is an exaggeration, and a lie. Most of us have stories that we've told over and over that continue to become more embellished as we tell them. **Baldfaced lies** are outright falsifications of information intended to deceive the listener. Baldfaced lies have more impact on the behavior of those who hear them than white lies or exaggeration. The emotional impact of such deception is related to the importance of the relationship, the importance of the information, and the importance of honesty to the people involved.[50] The potential negative impacts explain why we are less likely to lie to our best friends than we are to strangers.[51]

Reasons for Deception.

While there are a variety of reasons people are deceptive,[52] those reasons can be placed into two general categories: altruistic and self-serving. Altruistic motivation is a common reason we lie to a close friend. Our concerns about hurting other people may lead us to lie to protect them—for example, not telling a roommate her outfit is unbecoming. On the other hand, we might deceive others because we either gain personally through the deception or avoid some undesirable consequence. Not being truthful with the instructor about why you were late to class is an attempt to avoid a negative consequence. In general, we lie more to

deception by commission
Deliberate presentation of false information.

white lie Deception by commission involving only a slight degree of falsification that has a minimal consequence.

exaggeration Deception by commission involving "stretching the truth" or embellishing the facts.

baldfaced lie Deception by commission involving outright falsification of information intended to deceive the listener.

strangers and acquaintances than to friends, and those lies are more likely to be for personal gain or exploitation, whereas relatively more of our lies to friends are altruistic or other-centered.[53] The two categories of altruistic and self-serving lies include a number of specific reasons for deception.

1. *To gain resources.* Deception might help you acquire material resources, such as money or property. You might also use deception to achieve intangible goals, such as fostering a relationship or bolstering your self-esteem. Perhaps you intend the bands you falsely list as favorites on Facebook to make you more attractive.

2. *To avoid harm or loss of resources.* Deception may be used to prevent another person's negative reaction or to protect resources. For example, if an angry friend suspected you had broken her computer, you might lie if you were afraid she would damage something of yours in retaliation or that she would ask you to pay for repairs. Or you might avoid having to give up your free time by lying to a friend about not being able to help her move over the weekend.

3. *To protect one's self-image.* Most people attempt to present or maintain a certain image that they think others will find desirable, and people will lie if they fear their actions undermine that image. For instance, you might always be late for appointments, but you don't want people to think you are habitually late, so you lie about what made you late.

4. *For entertainment.* Teasing can be a form of deception if we tell other people things that aren't true. "I heard that Billy has a crush on you—not!" The reason for this kind of deception is to laugh at the other person's reaction.

5. *To protect another person's resources, self-image, or safety.* If you believe that certain information is harmful to another person, you might choose to keep it secret or to falsify it. In lying to protect friends from what you view as "harmful truths," you need to be honest with yourself about whether your deception is really for their benefit. Is saying "I love you" when you don't really love someone a way to avoid hurting the person—or is it a way to avoid facing conflict and threats to your resources?

Effects of Deception. While at times deception seems to be acceptable because of the benefits it provides, it can obviously also cause harm, and there are fundamental ethical questions about dishonesty. Harm either can be the direct result of the deception or can result when deception is detected or uncovered. Here are some of the more obvious ways deception can be harmful:

1. *Leading to incorrect decisions or actions.* If false information is used in decision making, then a person may take the wrong course of action.

2. *Harming relationships.* A significant impact of deception is to harm relationships, particularly if the deception is detected; it might even lead to termination of the relationship.

3. *Loss of trust.* Trust is a fundamental element of relationships, and once deception has been detected in a relationship, it may be hard for partners to regain trust.[54] Repeated deception and detection may result in one person assuming that anything the other person says is a lie.

4. *Harming innocent bystanders.* Lies often have a ripple effect, whereby other people (innocent bystanders) are harmed.

5. *Additional harm.* Other negative consequences of deception include punishment, embarrassment, a guilty conscience, and a damaged reputation.[55]

BEING Other-ORIENTED

Most of us react pretty negatively to the discovery that a friend has deceived us. Deception is seen as a violation of honesty and trust—fundamental qualities associated with friendship. But why would a friend lie to you or deceive you? Consider the most recent time you found out you had been deceived. What possible motives might your friend have had? What factors might have influenced your friend's decision (for example, your reaction to the truth, effect of the truth on the relationship, potential harm to the friend)?

The closer the relationship, the more effective people become at recognizing their partners' deceptions.[56] However, expressing suspicion can also signal inherent distrust in a partner. Interestingly, the closer the relationship, the more people know what cues their partners are suspicious of, and therefore the better equipped they are to adapt and avoid detection of their deception.[57] Deception occurs in all our relationships. We are both instigators and recipients of deception. Ethically, you should strive for honest relationships, and it would be nice to believe you could be totally honest all the time. However, honesty can be harmful too, so you are faced with weighing the harms of honesty against the harms of deception. The survival of your interpersonal relationships depends on your ability to effectively manage the challenge of deception.

Communication That Hurts Feelings

When people discover that they have been deceived, they usually feel betrayed, foolish, angry, and/or hurt. But deception is only one way in which we hurt people's feelings. As we discussed earlier, the truth can hurt, too. One of the more powerful aspects of language is that it can be used to cause emotional pain. We can be hurt by insults, criticism, or teasing about our personality, intelligence, abilities, ethnicity, relationships, or sexual behavior.[58]

Disconfirming responses (discussed in Chapter 5) are one type of message that hurts listeners by undermining their sense of self-esteem, even when that is not the speaker's intention. When we receive a hurtful message, such as a disconfirming response, we try to determine the speaker's intention. The intention affects how hurt we feel.[59] A heartfelt apology can help alleviate another person's hurt when we've said something casually that had an unintended effect: "I'm sorry, I didn't mean it like it sounded." In some instances, speakers can minimize the impact by claiming they were "just kidding." Researchers Stacy Young and Amy Bippus found that as the perceived intentionality of hurtful messages increased, so did the reported emotional pain.[60] In addition, they determined that, in general, humorously phrased hurtful messages were found to be less hurtful than comments phrased without humor. However, humorous messages were found to hurt more than nonhumorous messages when they were about abilities or intelligence, de-escalating the relationship, or about a person's hopes or plans. Apparently, there are some issues, like our abilities or dreams, about which kidding is more hurtful than straightforward comments. One study of college students in romantic relationships found that close to 88 percent reported being the recipient of a hurtful tease (a hurtful message or criticism followed by a smile, a laugh, or "just kidding"), with women reporting being teased more than men; however, they all felt there was some degree of truth to the remarks. Teasing was seen as a way to disguise the truth.[61]

Research by Anita Vangelisti and Linda Crumley identified three general categories of reactions to messages that hurt.[62] The first category, **active verbal responses,** includes reactive statements made by the hurt person, such as counterattacks, self-defense statements, sarcastic comments, and demands for explanations. The second category includes crying, conceding, or apologizing, which are considered **acquiescent responses.** Finally, **invulnerable responses** such as ignoring the message, laughing, or being silent are attempts to show that the message did not hurt. Of course, in addition to responding verbally, we are also reacting emotionally, such as by displaying anger after being criticized.[63]

active verbal responses
Reactive statements made in response to a hurtful message.

acquiescent responses Crying, conceding, or apologizing in response to a hurtful message.

invulnerable responses Ignoring, laughing, or being silent in response to a hurtful message.

What we say and how we say it can hurt other people's feelings, especially those of family members or romantic partners.

Among their other findings on hurtful messages, Van-gelisti and Crumley found that people are more hurt by messages from family members than from nonfamily members and that romantic relationships are more damaged by hurtful messages than either family or nonromantic, non-family relationships.[64] In romantic relationships, honest but hurtful messages about the relationship were found to be more hurtful than messages about a person's personality, appearance, or behaviors.[65] Such relationally oriented messages tended to threaten receivers' face, probably because such statements implied the potential loss of the relationship.[66] How the message is conveyed also affects its impact, with harsh, abrasive messages creating greater hurt.[67]

Hurtful messages are probably unavoidable in interpersonal relationships, but how you respond to and manage the impact of those messages affects the level of satisfaction and happiness you feel in your relationships. When you are the recipient of a hurtful message, you should let the speaker know that your feelings are hurt and ask the person to clarify the reasons for making such a statement. The speaker might not realize that the message was hurtful.

A strong other-orientation is needed to monitor the impact of your messages on other people. Generally, your understanding of the other person can help you select the best strategy for presenting a potentially hurtful message and the best time to deliver the message.

Jealousy is a feeling that arises when we fear a relationship is in doubt, and the feeling can lead to jealous behavior.

Jealousy

If you have ever wished that you drove as nice a car or received grades as high as those of one of your classmates, then you have experienced envy. **Envy** is a discontented feeling that arises from a desire for something someone else has. But if you have been upset because one of your good friends was spending more time working than hanging out with you, or because your boyfriend or girlfriend showed interest in another person, then you have experienced jealousy. **Jealousy** is a reaction to the threat of losing a valued relationship.[68] The future of the relationship is in doubt and the partner's loyalty is questioned.[69] Jealousy manifests itself in our thoughts, feelings, and behaviors. **Cognitive jealousy** includes thoughts about the loss of your partner, reflections on decreases in your partner's time with you, and analyses of behaviors or occurrences deemed suspicious. **Emotional or affective jealousy** includes the feelings of anger, hurt, distrust, worry, or concern aroused by the threat of losing the relationship. You can also behave in a jealous manner, such as watching your partner obsessively at social gatherings, acting aloof, or questioning your partner's whereabouts.

Sometimes concern about loss of the relationship arises because of the presence of a third party, but it can also result from outside factors that jeopardize the relationship—the partner turning to others for advice, loss of influence over the partner to someone else, or a partner's spending more time on hobbies, school, or work.[70] Jealousy presents a paradox in that, on one hand, it represents a strong display of interest and love, but on the other hand, it represents paranoia and lack of trust.[71] Sometimes people are flattered by another's jealousy and even seek to evoke it to confirm the value of a relationship. At other times, jealousy is seen as a statement of possessiveness and restriction. Interestingly, the two partners in a relationship usually have contrasting emotional reactions to the jealousy. For the person feeling jealous, the potential loss of the relationship creates fear, anger, and sadness.[72] The person's partner might also feel fearful and angry, but may also feel a wide variety of other emotions, including being amused, flattered, mistrustful, baffled, condescending, upset, or put off.

envy A feeling of discontent arising from a desire for something someone else has.

jealousy Reaction to the threat of losing a valued relationship.

cognitive jealousy Thoughts about the loss of a partner, reflections on decreases in the partner's time for the other, and analyses of behaviors or occurrences deemed suspicious.

emotional or affective jealousy Feelings of anger, hurt, distrust, worry, or concern aroused by the threat of losing a relationship.

"My boyfriend is insanely jealous. He does nothing all day but watch cartoons and plot revenge on any other men I talk to"

www.CartoonStock.com

Using Jealousy as a Tactic.   You can probably think of several TV shows or movies in which one character tries to make some other character jealous. The reasons for evoking jealousy are primarily for relational rewards (such as to test the strength of the relationship, to bolster one's self-esteem, or to improve the relationship) or to gain relational revenge (teaching the partner a lesson or punishing the partner).[73] Among the tactics people use to make another person jealous are distancing (being too busy to get together; excluding the other from plans, activities, and other friends; or ignoring the other person); *flirtation façade* (sending oneself flowers, leaving fake phone numbers and pictures of oneself with others in plain view, or expressing attraction to or sexual interest in another); and relational alternatives (letting your partner know you are thinking about other relationships by talking about past relationships, present relationships, or other people).[74]

The use of jealousy as a tactic to improve a relationship by getting the partner to pay more attention to you or display greater commitment is risky. Predicting a partner's response becomes even more complex if the partner discovers that you have intentionally evoked his or her jealousy. In general, such a discovery could have a negative impact, because, as you read in Chapter 6, manipulative behavior elicits defensiveness. Whether you feel jealousy in your relationships or a relational partner expresses jealousy to you, the way the jealousy is managed can either enhance or destroy the relationship. Use your interpersonal communication skills to address jealousy openly, honestly, and cooperatively, as a serious relational concern.

Managing Jealousy.   Concern about the possible loss of or a significant change in a relationship is neither inappropriate nor unusual. For example, the discovery (or the assumption) that a friend is spending more time on some other interest implicitly disconfirms us—the object of the friend's attention is more important than we are. While one person might simply accept the situation, another person might feel jealousy. The arousal of jealousy suggests a need for more information. Directly discussing the situation with the partner and asking for an explanation tends to evoke a more positive response than spying or seeking information from a third party.[75] A jealous partner must decide whether to even raise the issue, depending on whether he or she is interested in relational repair. How someone expresses feelings of jealousy directly affects the partner's response. Calmly expressing feelings, presenting oneself in a positive manner, and expressing caring are viewed more positively than displays of violence, being insulting or threatening, or confronting a rival.[76] Expressing jealousy arouses uncertainty about the jealous partner, particularly when the jealousy is expressed indirectly through crying or acting hurt or depressed.[77]

Obsessive Relational Intrusion and Stalking

When a person we are attracted to is no longer attracted to us, most of us move on. Our dependence on a partner in a close relationship might lead us to express some resistance to his or her decision to terminate the relationship, but eventually we accept the decision. Unfortunately, some individuals do not give up when another person fails to reciprocate their attraction, has no interest in a relationship, or desires to terminate a relationship. These individuals might engage in obsessive behaviors, trying to form or to continue a relationship. In some instances, such pursuit is simply annoying, but at its extreme, it arouses well-founded fears for personal safety.

Obsessive relational intrusion (ORI) is the term used by communication scholars William Cupach and Brian Spitzberg to describe situations in which a stranger or acquaintance who desires or assumes a close relationship with another person repeatedly invades the other person's privacy.[78] In other words, someone wants a relationship with someone else who doesn't. Unlike stalking, ORI is usually annoying and frustrating but not threatening.[79] Obsessive relational intrusion is marked by such behaviors as unregulated self-disclosing; trying to get the other person to disclose; offering unwanted gifts, notes, calls, and other expressions of affection; arranging coincidental meetings; and expressing a desire for physical contact.[80]

There is a fine line between trying to hang on to or pursue a relationship and becoming obsessive. With ORI, normal relationship development behaviors become exaggerated and are pursued obsessively, making the change from non-intrusive to intrusive difficult to pinpoint.[81] Thus, it is the repeated and sustained display of these behaviors after rejection that indicates ORI. In addition, we often negotiate relationships through indirect and implicit ways, increasing the likelihood that one partner will misunderstand the other's intentions and interest. For instance, the am-

A person who feels stalked experiences concern for her or his personal safety and fear of unwelcome intrusions.

biguity of nonverbal messages could cause your smile to be seen as an invitation for interaction rather than as a general expression of your happy mood, leading someone, even a stranger, to initiate an unwanted approach and attempt to establish a relationship. Confusion about relational goals and definitions can lead your partner to think the relationship is more intimate than you do. Such confusion can result in intrusions on your privacy. Clearly discuss your goals, interests, and desires, as well as the nature of the relationship to help clarify these confusions, and seek understanding of your partner's perspective.

Stalking involves repeated, unwelcome intrusions that create concern for personal safety and fear in the target.[82] It can be thought of as an extreme form of ORI, though sometimes stalking is motivated by revenge and not the pursuit of a relationship.[83] Stalking is an instance of the dark side of interpersonal communication, in which unwanted communication—in the form of phone calls, face-to-face meetings, letters, and e-mails—is used to instill fear. Stalking appears more prevalent on college campuses than among the general public, with studies showing almost 30 percent of males and females surveyed feeling they have been stalked.[84] Possible reasons for this prevalence are the lack of social and relational skills in young adults and the close proximity and sharing of space that occur on college campuses.

Unfortunately, there is no absolutely safe and effective way to end such behaviors, but Spitzberg and Cupach offer three recommendations for addressing ORI and stalking, based on advice from other scholars and professionals:[85]

1. *Harden the target.* "Hardening the target" involves making it harder for someone to contact you or invade your space. For example, you might get an unlisted phone number, rent a post office mail box, change locks, eliminate access information on MySpace or Facebook, and/or install a security system.

2. *Keep others apprised.* You should apprise family, friends, coworkers, employers, school administrators, and law enforcement officials of your situation. Also, consider informing people in other places you frequent (a gym, restaurant, or bar). Let everyone know you don't want contact with the person and provide photos of the person if possible.

3. *Avoidance:* After telling the intruder or stalker to leave you alone, you should avoid any further contact. Don't answer calls, don't respond to e-mails or instant messages, ignore and turn away from any approaches the person might make—don't interact. Your actions need to support your insistence that the relationship is over.

obsessive relational intrusion (ORI) Repeated invasion of a person's privacy by a stranger or acquaintance who desires or assumes a close relationship.

stalking Repeated, unwelcome intrusions that create concern for personal safety and fear in the target.

Electronically mediated communication (EMC) has many positive benefits, as we've noted: EMC allows us to quickly and easily stay in touch with our friends, colleagues, family members, and other people we love. But EMC messages can have a dark side. If personal or private information about you becomes known to others, it can be used to embarrass you or create significant negative financial consequences. And spending too much time in EMC can have a negative impact on your face-to-face relationships.

We may easily forget that some e-mails and messages posted on sites such as Facebook or MySpace can be accessed by other people. This means that information about you can be accessed not just by family members or potential employers, but also by potential stalkers—which is why there is a growing concern about teenagers posting information on MySpace, Facebook, or Twitter, as well as circulating cell phone pictures and videos.

Cyberstalkers use harassment as one of their tools for controlling and threatening others. Harassing EMC messages can come from both anonymous senders and known associates. After ending a relationship, a person might be subjected to repeated unwanted phone calls, text messages, or wall postings on Facebook from the former partner. These unwanted messages might simply be pleas for reconciliation, or they might involve threats of relational violence. Other dark uses of EMC include circulating intimate, private, or false information (slander) about an individual

(including real or manufactured images); tagging photos of someone in unflattering or compromising situations on various web sites; sending viruses or hacking into and controlling other people's computers when they log on; and posing as the other person on the Internet (identity theft), including sending messages attributed to the other person. Someone could use your name and personal information while participating in a chat room, a bulletin board, or using Facebook or MySpace, and you might never know.

The best way to handle cyberstalking and harassment is to be smart about how you use EMC. Here are some tips to consider:

- Use an alias and not your real name when participating in chat rooms or posting messages on bulletin boards.

- Avoid providing or posting personal information on web sites or social networking sites, or limit what you do post.

- Be smart about the passwords you use; nonsense combinations are best, since hackers have software that allows them to test long lists of actual words.

- Just as you are careful about whom you share your phone number with, you should be careful about sharing your e-mail address (though both are often available through an assortment of directories if a person knows your name).

- If you are faced with EMC harassment, provide a clear and assertive statement that you do *not* want to be contacted,

and keep copies of any messages you receive.

- Inform your Internet service provider, and consider changing your Internet address or service provider.

- Since many of these harassing behaviors are illegal, it is also appropriate to report the incidents to law enforcement agencies.

"Internet addiction," "Internet abuse," "Internet compulsion," "pathological Internet use," "Internet dependency," and "problematic Internet use" are phrases used to describe another dark side of Internet use: devoting endless hours to surfing the Net, social networking, or gaming. Although some people consider the term "Internet addiction" overly dramatic and misrepresentative,[86] apparently there is a point at which use of the Internet becomes "abnormal." Most of us have spent an inordinate amount of time on something—watching TV, listening to music, reading, studying (okay, maybe not studying). Does this mean we are addicted to these things? Does spending a lot of time texting, e-mailing friends, or logged on to Facebook necessarily mean you are abnormal? If you spent the same amount of time engaging in FtF conversations, would that be considered abnormal? We might be at a point in social evolution at which our conceptions of human behavior and interactions have not caught up with technology. Nonetheless, there are some potential downsides to compulsive computer and Internet use.

Relational Violence

A full discussion of violence and abuse in relationships is beyond the scope of this text. The following is only an overview, with particular attention given to the role of interpersonal communication. Stalking, obsessive relational intrusion, and jealousy can all be precursors to violent behavior in relationships, but relational violence extends beyond these behaviors. Relational violence can occur in any relationship—with a spouse, a dating partner, children, family members, friends, or coworkers. Unlike acts of violence against unknown individuals, relational violence occurs within the context of an ongoing relationship and is sometimes a defining characteristic or dynamic of the relationship.[89]

The term *violence* often connotes physical harm inflicted on another person, but we will use the term **relational violence** to refer to the full range of destructive behaviors aimed at other people, including aggressiveness, threats, violent acts, and verbal, psychological, and physical abuse. At the extreme, relational violence involves forceful

relational violence Range of destructive behaviors aimed at other people, including aggressiveness, threats, violent acts, and verbal, psychological, or physical abuse.

The most obvious impact of any excessive or compulsive behavior is the amount of time it consumes—which can prevent a person from fulfilling his or her home, school, or work responsibilities. For example, spending all night on the Internet might cause you to fall asleep in class or at work or distract you from studying. In addition to this impact, problematic Internet use can hamper or reduce human interaction. Individuals who isolate themselves all day to play computer games or surf the Net, thus passing up opportunities to socialize with others, might be cutting themselves off from personal relationships. Being alone is not, in and of itself, a negative or detrimental behavior. But if one is motivated by fear to avoid FtF human contact, such behavior could be detrimental.

But are people really isolating themselves socially when they spend hours and hours texting, posting on Facebook, e-mailing, or Twittering? In essence, such individuals have created a virtual social world that might be as effective or even more effective in meeting their interpersonal needs as FtF interactions. Individuals who are uncomfortable or shy in FtF interactions might be quite adept and comfortable engaging in online relationships. Is this a bad thing? Are FtF relationships inherently better and more desirable than EMC relationships? The answers to such questions could be a matter of personal preference rather than a matter of mental or social health.

Relying *primarily* on online relationships for social satisfaction does reduce an individual's FtF interactions and the development of interpersonal skills. People who prefer online social interactions to face-to-face interactions have been found to display other negative behaviors, including excessive and compulsive use of the Internet, social withdrawal, mood alteration, and personal, social, and professional problems attributed to Internet use.[87] One study assessed students' compulsive use of the Internet and found that in comparison to others, pathological users (those whose Internet use was causing academic, work, or interpersonal problems, distress, or alterations in mood) were lonelier and went online to relax, to meet new people, to interact with others with similar interests, and to find support.[88] However, pathological users appeared comfortable on the Internet, seeing themselves as friendlier, more open, and more themselves online than in real life compared to nonpathological users. Interestingly, the study also found that 73 percent of the participants had at least one symptom of pathological use.

Does your Internet use have negative effects on you? If you experience any of the symptoms of pathological use just mentioned, adjust your Internet use: Look for alternative activities; create a schedule for Internet use and stick to it; impose time limits on yourself; and identify your patterns and make an effort to break them. (For example, if you notice yourself spending every Friday night online, make a point to do something else on Friday nights.) If your symptoms are pathological, you might also consider professional counseling.

acts against another person. But hitting your fist through a plaster wall in rage during an argument is certainly a violent act, even though the partner is not directly abused. The act still instills fear, and the violence it represents can escalate.

Sociologist Michael Johnson separates partner violence into three types:[90]

1. *Intimate terrorism:* Using violence to control or dominate

2. *Violent resistance:* Meeting attempts at control with a violent response

3. *Situational couple violence:* Responding with violence to a specific relational conflict or tension

Males are responsible for almost all intimate terrorism, females for violent resistance, and both men and women engage in situational couple violence, which is probably the most frequently occurring form of relational violence.[91] The presence of intimate terrorism will most likely lead to the abused partner's leaving the relationship, whereas incidents of situational couple violence are usually not so severe as to end the relationship.[92]

Sadly, acts of relational violence are a form of communication—the dark side of communication. Acts of relational violence communicate anger, frustration, lack of control, and disregard for a partner and the relationship, while instilling fear and engendering retaliation, counterattacks, and subversion. The results of a study of males participating in a domestic violence program found that compared to nonviolent males, violent males engaged in more name calling, criticizing, blaming, swearing, ridiculing, and mutual verbal aggression with their partners.[93] Patterns of negative communication, ineffective conflict management and problem-solving skills, and lack of good argumentation skills all appear to contribute to an individual's propensity for relational violence. Avoiding relational violence is a strong reason for improving interpersonal communication skills. Relational violence is never acceptable, nor is it the fault of the victim; do not accept relational violence as a condition of your relationships. If you find yourself either the victim or the perpetrator of relational violence, you should seek professional help. An online search will direct you to numerous help agencies.

▶ **RECAP**   The Dark Side of Interpersonal Communication and Relationships

Deception	Using communication to deceive through false or misleading information.
Deception by Omission	Holding back information so as to leave an incorrect impression with a listener.
Deception by Commission	Deliberately presenting false information in such forms as white lies, exaggeration, or baldfaced lies.
Communication That Hurts Feelings	Causing pain to others either intentionally or unintentionally, by such means as offering unwelcome or negative information or criticizing traits or abilities.
Obsessive Relational Intrusion	Repeatedly invading a person's privacy out of a desire for or assumption of a close relationship with the other person.
Stalking	Making repeated, unwelcome intrusions that create concern for personal safety and fear in the target.
Jealousy	Reacting to the threat of losing a valued relationship.
Relational Violence	Engaging in a range of destructive behaviors aimed at other people, including aggressiveness, threats, violent acts, and verbal, psychological, and physical abuse.

De-Escalation and Termination of Relationships

The inability to effectively manage relational challenges or the dark side of interpersonal communication can contribute to the de-escalation or even termination of a relationship. For example, how likely would you be to continue a relationship after discovering that your partner had deceived you? Once a deception has been uncovered, relationships are more likely to be terminated when the offender can be avoided and there is lack of overall communication.[94] When you pick up signals of relational problems, you have four choices: You can wait and see what happens, make a decision to redefine the relationship, end the relationship, or try to repair the relationship.

Signs of Relationship Problems

Part of effective relationship management is sensitivity to cues that signal relational problems or change. Women usually sense trouble in a relationship earlier than men do—but what exactly do they sense? Because each stage in a relationship has unique communication qualities, specific verbal and nonverbal cues can tip us off when a relationship begins to de-escalate. Here are a few signs that might signal relationship problems:[95]

Less touching or physical contact	Interactions are more impersonal
Less vocal expressiveness	Separation of possessions
Less smiling	Less time talking on any given topic
Interactions don't flow as easily	Less use of present tense
Increased physical distance	More passive language
Less eye contact	Fewer references to the future
Increase in time between interactions	More qualifiers ("maybe")
	More conflict
Less sexual activity	Decreases in evaluative statements
Fewer intimate terms	Less personal language
Decreases in time together	Less self-disclosure

John Gottman, who studied couples relationships for over twenty years, identified four categories of communication behavior that indicate increasing problems in a marriage.[96]

1. *Criticisms*: Being critical of or attacking the partner's personality
2. *Contempt*: Engaging in insults and psychological abuse
3. *Defensive behaviors*: Denying responsibility by making excuses, whining, and countercomplaining
4. *Stonewalling*: Withdrawing, not responding to each other, and minimally engaging in the relationship

These behaviors undermine effective communication between couples and can lead to the end of the relationship. Among the four, stonewalling is the single strongest predictor of divorce. If all four signs are consistently present, there is a 94 percent chance the couple will eventually divorce.[97] Most couples experience some of these behaviors, but happy couples develop effective communication patterns to overcome them.

Repair and Rejuvenation of Relationships

Underlying the success of any repair effort is the degree to which both partners want to keep the relationship going. The nature of the problem, the stage of the relationship, and the commitment and motivation of the partners all affect the success of repair efforts. There is no single quick solution to relational problems because so many factors influence each one. You need to focus on the specific concerns, needs, and issues that underlie the problem; then adapt specific strategies to resolve it. Professional counseling may be one option to consider.

What if your partner wants to end the relationship and you don't? There is no pat answer for addressing this situation. If a friend stops calling or visiting, should you just assume the relationship is over and leave it alone, or should you call and ask what's up? People lose contact for a myriad of reasons. Sometimes it is beneficial to ask someone directly whether he or she is breaking off the relationship, although such direct requests place your self-esteem and face on the line. How should you react if your friend confirms a desire to end the relationship? If possible, try to have a focused discussion on what has contributed to his or her decision. You might get information you need to repair the relationship. Or you might gain information that will help you in future relationships.

Women and men differ in their management of relational challenges. Women tend to be stronger monitors of their relationships, so they often detect trouble before their male partners. In a study of married couples' initiation of relationship discussions, wives reported a higher likelihood of initiating discussions than the husbands reported.[98] And both partners underestimated their spouse's self-reports of initiating relationship discussions, which might reflect a need for increased other-centeredness. Such discussions might be spurred by failure events or transgressions by a partner, which appear to affect men and women differently. Females in romantic relationships reported more intense hurt over their partners' transgressions than males reported when their partners transgressed.[99] Men forgave the women more readily than the women forgave the men; the more intense hurt women felt might have made them less inclined to forgive.

Women's sensitivity to the health of the relationship may be one factor that makes them more likely to initiate the termination a relationship.[100] However, men who want out of a relationship might engage in behaviors that women find totally unacceptable, thus prompting the women to actually end the relationship. For example, when men avoided interaction by stonewalling and responding defensively to complaints, the couples were more likely to divorce.[101] Men also report greater likelihood of being unfaithful than women.[102] However, demonstrating commitment to the relationship was more effective in keeping it from ending when used by men than by women.[103]

Rejection in a romantic relationship has greater costs for a woman than for a man, with women experiencing greater fear and insecurity over the loss of their partners' protection.[104]

In one study of divorce, men tended to see the later part of the process as more difficult, whereas women said the period before they made the decision to divorce was more difficult. In addition, two-thirds of the women were likely to discuss marital problems with their children, as compared to only one-fourth of the men. Men were twice as likely to say that no one helped them cope with the worst part of the process.[105]

Another response to signs of relationship disintegration is to rejuvenate the relationship—to put new life back in it. The ability to rejuvenate a relationship depends on the degree to which partners recognize the reasons for relational decay and the level of their interest in rejuvenating the relationship. When only one partner wishes to rejuvenate the relationship, the first task becomes convincing the uninterested partner of the value of doing so. De-escalation can be caused by specific behavioral problems of one partner, such as not doing a fair share of the housework or no longer being a supportive listener. If so, then commitment to changing those behaviors may be one avenue for re-energizing the relationship. Because the problem behavior represents a failure event, the partner might have to provide an account, admit failure, and/or use the forgiveness-seeking strategies discussed earlier. In general, rejuvenation is usually conducted through implicit moves rather than direct discussion.[106] In other words, we change our behaviors or engage in positive behaviors that we hope our partner will recognize as an effort on our part to improve the relationship. Think about times when you have made a change or put forth extra effort for friends or family members to help reduce relational tension—cutting back on your use of swear words you know your mother dislikes, studying more, doing the dishes without being asked, washing your father's car, or baking your friend some cookies. However, another failure event might arise if your partner doesn't recognize that you've made such efforts. Explicit efforts that people have reported using include having a serious relational talk, reconnecting after separating (reconciliation), accepting or forgiving a partner's transgression, and seeking outside help.[107]

The Decision to End a Relationship

If you do choose to change the level of intimacy in a relationship, consider your goals. Do you want to continue the relationship at a less intimate level, or terminate it altogether? Do you care enough about the other person to want to preserve his or her self-esteem? Are you aware of the costs of ending the relationship? There is no one correct or best way to end a relationship. Ending relationships is also not something you can practice. But you *can* more effectively manage relational termination by decentering, being empathic, and adapting to your partner.

We rely on our social networks for support and self-confirmation when an intimate relationship comes to an end. Advice about how to handle the loss of a close relationship is plentiful, but each person must find his or her own way to compensate for the loss of intimacy and companionship. The loss of an important relationship hurts, but it need not put us out of commission if we make the most of our social support network—friends and family.

De-escalation or termination of a relationship is not inherently bad. Not all relationships are meant to endure. Ending a relationship can be a healthy move if the relationship is harmful, or if it no longer provides confirmation of the self or satisfies interpersonal needs; ending a relationship also can open the door to new ones. Sometimes we choose not to end a relationship but rather to de-escalate to a less intimate stage that offers a better balance between benefits and costs.

Partners may experience one of three types of relationship termination: fading away, in which the partners drift slowly apart; sudden death, in which separation is immediate; or incrementalism, in which conflicts gradually build until the couple reaches the breaking point.

Breaking up an intimate relationship is hard because of the degree to which you become dependent on the other person to confirm your sense of self. When a relationship ends, you may feel as if you need to redefine who you are. The most satisfying breakups are those that confirm both partners' worth rather than degrade it. "I just can't be what you want me to be"; "I'll always love you, but . . ."; or "You're a very special person, but I need other things in life" are all examples of statements intended to protect the other person's self-esteem.

The process of ending a relationship is considerably different when only one party wants out of the relationship than it is when both parties agree to the breakup.[108] In **bilateral dissolutions,** both parties are predisposed to ending the relationship; they simply need to sort out details such as agreeing on timing, dividing possessions, and defining conditions for contact after the breakup. In a **unilateral dissolution,** when one party wants the relationship to continue, the person who wants to end the relationship often tries to persuade his or her partner to break up. Sometimes, however, people simply walk out of a relationship.

How Relationships End

A declining relationship usually follows one of several paths. Sometimes a relationship loses energy slowly, like a dying battery. Instead of a single event causing the breakup, the relationship ends by **fading away**—the two partners just drift further and further apart. They spend less time together, let more time go by between interactions, and stop disclosing much about themselves. You've probably had a number of friendships that ended this way.

Some relationships end in sudden death.[109] As the name suggests, **sudden death** is the abrupt and unplanned ending of a relationship. One partner might move away or actually die; more frequently, however, a single precipitating event such as infidelity, breaking a confidence, a major conflict, or some other major relational violation precipitates the breakup. Sudden death is like taking an express elevator from the top floor to ground level.

In between fading away and sudden death lies incrementalism. **Incrementalism** is the systematic progression through each of the de-escalation stages. At each stage, the relationship reaches a threshold, at which point the relationship moves down to the next level. Turmoil or stagnation in an intimate relationship leads one or both

bilateral dissolution Ending of a relationship by mutual agreement of both parties.

unilateral dissolution Ending of a relationship by one partner, even though the other partner wants it to continue.

fading away Ending a relationship by slowly drifting apart.

sudden death Abrupt and unplanned ending of a relationship.

incrementalism Systematic progression of a relationship through each of the de-escalation stages.

partners to evaluate the relationship, and if they determine that they have reached a certain threshold of intolerance (that is, the costs exceed the rewards), the relationship moves to deintensification. Then, if and when another threshold is reached, the relationship de-escalates to individualization, and finally to separation.

Reasons for De-Escalating and Terminating Relationships

When a relationship comes to an end, we often ask ourselves, "What happened? Why did the relationship come to an end?"[110] We engage in this "postmortem" regardless of who initiated the breakup. If your partner initiated the breakup and did not provide adequate explanations, you are left to wonder and guess about what happened. You may continue behaviors that undermine future relationships because you failed to understand how you contributed to the termination of the present relationship.

Researcher Michael Cody had students assess what caused their intimate heterosexual relationships to break up.[111] "Faults" were cited as the number-one cause. These are personality traits or behaviors in one partner that the other partner dislikes. The number-two cause, "unwillingness to compromise," represents a variety of failings on the part of one or both partners, including failure to put enough effort into the relationship, a decrease in effort, or failure to make concessions for the good of the relationship. The final cause, "feeling constrained," reflects one partner's desire to be free of the commitments and constraints of a relationship. Another study found that both male and female students indicated a greater likelihood of ending a committed relationship that lacked "emotional access" or had a lack of love than a relationship that lacked "sexual access."[112] Other elements that can contribute to the breakup of both romantic and nonromantic relationships include the loss of interest in the other person, a desire for independence, and conflicting attitudes about issues affecting the relationship, such as sexual conduct, marriage, and infidelity.

Just as there are behavioral rules for making and maintaining friends, there are behaviors that, if you pursue them, will almost certainly cost you a friendship. Listed in order of offensiveness, they are as follows.[113]

1. Acting jealous or being critical of your relationship
2. Discussing with others what your friend said in confidence
3. Not volunteering help in time of need
4. Not trusting or confiding in your friend
5. Criticizing your friend in public
6. Not showing positive regard for your friend
7. Not standing up for your friend in his or her absence
8. Not being tolerant of your friend's other friends
9. Not showing emotional support
10. Nagging your friend

Friendships differ from romantic relationships in many ways, including the reasons for relational disintegration. When one researcher asked individuals to identify why their same-sex friendships ended, first on the list was physical separation.[114] Second, respondents reported that new friends replaced old friends as circumstances changed. Third, people often just grow to dislike a characteristic of the friend's behavior or personality. And finally, one friend's dating activity or romantic relationships can interfere with and contribute to the decay of a friendship. It should come as no surprise that casual friendships are more likely to end than are those between close or intimate friends. Close friendships are better able to withstand change, uncertainty, and separation.

I once volunteered as a crisis phone counselor in a large metropolitan area. We were trained to use effective counseling skills, such as empathy, in relating to the callers' crises. One night, a call came in from a very distressed and depressed man about his breakup with his homosexual partner, with whom he had a long-term intimate relationship. At first I was uncomfortable dealing with the situation. Despite extensive training and role-playing, I wondered how I, as a heterosexual male, could empathize with or relate to this caller. However, I continued to ask questions about how he felt, what he saw as his needs, and his perception of the problems. The more we talked, the more empathic I became, because I realized that his description was very familiar. I had been divorced some four years earlier, and this caller's descriptions of his feelings matched the feelings I experienced during that time. I was able to talk about some of the feelings I had experienced, and this seemed to help him understand his own situation. I realized that though the sex of our partners was different, the overriding issue was the loss of an intimate relationship. I grew a little wiser that night.

—Mark V. Redmond

A Model of Ending Relationships

Chapter 9 identified the stages of relational de-escalation and focused on changes in the interaction. Relationship scholar Steve Duck developed a model that focuses on the decision process and social network aspects of ending a relationship.[115] As Figure 10.1 shows, we first reach some threshold of dissatisfaction that prompts us to consider ending the relationship. Having passed this threshold, we enter an **intrapsychic phase,** in which we privately evaluate our partner's behaviors. Social exchange theory predicts that in this phase we would assess the relationship's costs and rewards and would be inclined to terminate a relationship that was no longer "profitable."[116] We might still remain in an unprofitable relationship if our cumulative rewards are sufficient to offset the current costs. However, as with a savings account, there is only so

intrapsychic phase First phase in relationship termination, when an individual engages in an internal evaluation of the partner.

FIGURE 10.1

A Model of Ending Relationships

Source: S. Duck, "A Typography of Relationship Disengagement and Dissolution," from *Personal Relationships, 4: Dissolving Relationships,* edited by S. Duck (London: Academic Press, 1982), p. 16.

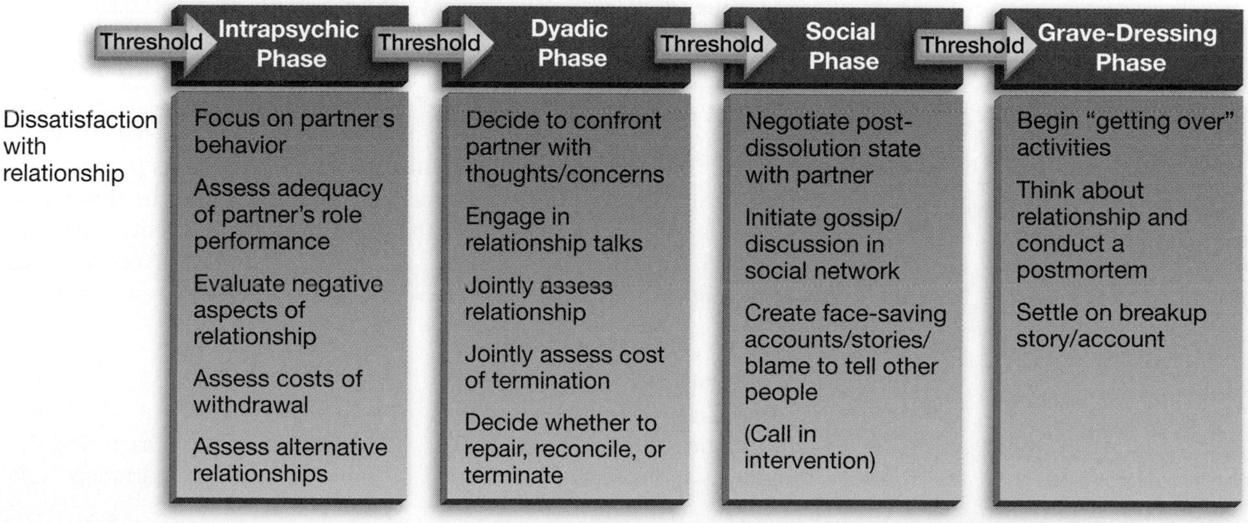

Threshold →	Intrapsychic Phase	Threshold →	Dyadic Phase	Threshold →	Social Phase	Threshold →	Grave-Dressing Phase
Dissatisfaction with relationship	Focus on partner's behavior		Decide to confront partner with thoughts/concerns		Negotiate post-dissolution state with partner		Begin "getting over" activities
	Assess adequacy of partner's role performance		Engage in relationship talks		Initiate gossip/discussion in social network		Think about relationship and conduct a postmortem
	Evaluate negative aspects of relationship		Jointly assess relationship		Create face-saving accounts/stories/blame to tell other people		Settle on breakup story/account
	Assess costs of withdrawal		Jointly assess cost of termination		(Call in intervention)		
	Assess alternative relationships		Decide whether to repair, reconcile, or terminate				

BEING Other-ORIENTED

Being other-oriented might cause you to refrain from ending a relationship because you know the pain it will cause your partner. But an other-orientation can also lead to face-saving approaches. What do you know about any of your former partners that might have helped end those relationships more positively? Being other-oriented when someone ends a relationship with you can be difficult. Consider a time someone ended a relationship with you. To what degree could you appreciate his or her perspective and feelings at the time? What about now? To what degree did your partner use his or her understanding of you to dissolve the relationship in a positive manner?

much we can withdraw before we have to close the account (end the relationship). We might also remain in an unprofitable relationship if we predict that the relationship will become profitable again.

From time to time we all become frustrated with a relationship—and for some of us the frustration may become severe enough that we consider terminating, but never proceed further than this phase. However, we might "leak" our thoughts and feelings through our communication, displaying such emotions as hostility, anxiety, stress, or guilt. We might consider various strategies for ending the relationship and/or decide to confide in our other close friends or family about our dissatisfaction. Although Duck's model does not refer to this, research indicates that we sometimes turn to friends, family, or counselors for support when a relationship is not measuring up to expectations.[117] Indeed, you might discuss your concerns with someone from your support network before you discuss them with your partner.

At some point we might decide to move from our private internal contemplations about the relationship to confronting our partner. This is the **dyadic phase** in the model. If our partner feels challenged and intimidated by our desire to end the relationship, we might have to justify our thoughts and feelings. Our partner might also criticize our behavior and identify our failings.

If we decide to end the relationship, we enter the **social phase** and begin making the information public. Sometimes a person's social network will mobilize to preserve the relationship. Friends might act as mediators, encouraging reconciliation and suggesting ways to repair the relationship. Of course, friends can also reinforce a decision to separate. Rumors and stories about what happened and what is happening can fuel bad feelings and hasten the end of the relationship.

In the **grave-dressing phase,** one or both partners may attempt to "place flowers on the grave" of their relationship to cover up the hurt and pain associated with its death. They need a public story that they can share with others about what happened: "We still love each other; we just decided we needed more in our lives." Such a story often places blame on the other partner: "I knew he had his faults, but he thought he could change, and he just wasn't able to." Most importantly, we go through an internal stage in which we try to accept the end of the relationship and let go of feelings of guilt, failure, and blame.

Strategies for Ending Relationships

dyadic phase Second phase in relationship termination, when the individual discusses termination with the partner.

social phase Third phase in relationship termination, when members of the social network around both parties are informed of and become involved in the termination process.

grave-dressing phase Final phase in relationship termination, when the partners generate public explanations and move past the relationship.

indirect termination strategies Attempts to break up a relationship without explicitly stating the desire to do so.

direct termination strategies Explicit statements of a desire to break up a relationship.

When the vitality in long marriages fades away over a period of years, the individuals move slowly through the de-escalation stages before finally divorcing. Relationships that haven't lasted as long are far more likely to end abruptly. As you saw in Chapter 9, the further up in the relational high-rise you go on the elevator, the longer the ride down.

But no matter what stage a relationship is in, partners use both direct and indirect strategies to end it. **Indirect termination strategies** represent attempts to break up a relationship without explicitly stating the desire to do so. **Direct termination strategies** involve explicit statements. The strategy that a person chooses will depend on the level of intimacy in the relationship, the level of desire to help the partner save face, the degree of urgency about terminating the relationship, and the person's interpersonal skills.

Indirect Termination Strategies. Relationship scholar Leslie Baxter identified three indirect strategies that people use to disengage: withdrawal, pseudo–de-escalation, and cost escalation. *Withdrawal* involves reducing the amount of contact and interaction without any explanation.[118] This strategy is the most dissatisfying of the three strategies for the recipient.[119] Withdrawal represents an attempt to avoid a confrontation and to protect the initiator's face.

In *pseudo–de-escalation,* one partner claims that he or she wants to redefine the relationship at a lower level of intimacy, but in reality, he or she wants to end the relationship. Statements such as "Let's just be friends" or "I think of you as more of a sister" may be sincere, or they may reflect an unspoken desire to disengage completely. When both parties want to end the relationship, they sometimes use mutual pseudo–de-escalation and enter into a false agreement to reduce the level of intimacy as they move to disengagement.

Cost escalation is an attempt to increase the costs associated with the relationship in order to encourage the other person to terminate it. A dissatisfied partner may ask for an inordinate amount of the other person's time, pick fights, criticize the other person, or violate relational rules. Men apparently use this strategy more often than women do.

"It's just not working out. I'm sure with proper medical treatment, community support and social rehabilitation you'll eventually meet that special someone."

Direct Termination Strategies. Baxter also identified four direct strategies that people use to terminate relationships: negative identity management, justification, de-escalation, and positive tone.[120] *Negative identity management* is a direct statement of the desire to terminate the relationship. It does not take into account the other's feelings, and it may even include criticisms. "I want out of our relationship," "I just can't stand to be around you anymore," and "I'm no longer happy in this relationship and I want to date other people" are examples of negative identity management.

Justification is a clear statement of the desire to end the relationship, accompanied by an honest explanation of the reasons. Justification statements may hurt the other person's feelings: "I've found someone else that I want to spend more time with who makes me happy" and "I feel as if I've grown a great deal and need more than this relationship provides." But a person who uses justification does not fault the other person, and he or she makes some attempt to protect both parties' sense of self. One researcher found that most people on the receiving end can tolerate this strategy best.[121]

De-escalation is an honest statement of a desire to redefine the relationship at a lower level of intimacy or to move toward ending the relationship. One partner might ask for a trial separation so that both people can explore other opportunities and gain a clearer understanding of their needs.[122] "Neither of us seems to be too happy with the relationship right now, so I think we should cool it for a while and see what happens."

Positive tone is the direct strategy that is most sensitive to the other person's sense of self. This strategy can seem almost contradictory, because the initiator tries to affirm the other's personal qualities and worth while nevertheless calling a halt to the relationship. "I love you; I just can't live with you," "I'm really sorry I've got to break off the relationship," and "You really are a wonderful person; you're just not the one for me" are examples of positive tone statements.

> **RECAP** Strategies for Ending Relationships

	Term	Explanation
How Relationships End	Fading away	The relationship dissolves slowly as intimacy declines.
	Sudden death	The relationship ends abruptly, usually in response to some precipitating event.
	Incrementalism	The relationship progresses systematically through each of the de-escalation stages.
Indirect Termination Strategies	Withdrawal	Reducing the amount of contact, without any explanation.
	Pseudo–de-escalation	Claiming a desire for less intimacy, when you really want out.
	Cost escalation	Increasing relational costs to encourage the other to end the relationship.
Direct Termination Strategies	Negative identity management	Directly stating a desire to end the relationship, without concern for the other person's feelings.
	Justification	Directly stating a desire to end the relationship, with an explanation of the reasons.
	De-escalation	Directly stating a desire to lower the level of intimacy or move toward termination.
	Positive tone	Directly stating a desire to end the relationship, while affirming the other person's value.

Strategies for Post-Dissolution Recovery

Our identities are often tied to our relationships, and the more intimate the relationship, the more our identity is likely to be threatened if the relationship ends. Letting go of a close relationship is not easy, and the accompanying grief and pain can be debilitating. Maintaining positive self-esteem and being able to nurture other relationships requires engaging in effective post-dissolution recovery. Keep in mind that you may experience an initial intensity bias, whereby you predict more distress than you actually experience at the end of a romantic relationship.[123] In other words, you won't really feel as bad as you fear. Relationship researcher Ann Weber created a list of strategies to help address the grief and loss of nonmarital breakups.[124] The following strategies are adapted from her list:

1. *Express your emotions.* You need to vent your feelings, if not to your "ex," then to a sympathetic listener, in a journal, or in some other forum. (There are even web sites where you can share your story.)

2. *Figure out what happened.* Understanding what occurred in the relationship is one way to get a handle on your current emotions. You need to accept the reasons for the breakup and work toward acceptance.

3. *Realize, don't idealize.* We sometimes view the end of a relationship as the death of a dream. In order to deal with a loss more realistically, Weber suggests mentally reviewing your partner's flaws.

4. *Prepare to feel better.* You might be surprised to find yourself feeling relief and joy. Finding the humor and irony in the breakup can help you cope with the grief.

5. *Expect to heal.* Some of the hardest words to accept from others are "It will get better." Although we may not want to believe it, we do recover.

6. *Talk to others.* Isolation is usually not a very healthy way to handle grief. Friends expect to provide comfort by listening to you discuss your feelings. Don't be afraid to

be direct in explaining to friends what you want or need from them; they can't read your mind.

7. *Get some perspective.* This strategy involves a little bit of wallowing in your misery by reading stories, seeing movies, or listening to songs about other people's experiences in breaking up. These can help you put your own situation into perspective.

8. *Be ready for further punishment, or maybe reward.* Weber suggests that once you've gone through the above strategies, it's time to explore potential relationships. Learn from your past experiences, hang on to pleasant memories, and move forward.

Communication and Emotion

Assessing Your Emotional Responses to Relationship Challenges

We experience certain emotions when we are first confronted with a situation; other emotions emerge as we address the issue; and still other emotions occur after the challenge has passed. This chapter could be subtitled "Experiencing Negative Emotions," because most of the issues discussed involve such negative emotions as anger, fear, sadness, jealousy, resentment, humiliation, uncertainty, disappointment, and heartbreak. However, positive feelings can arise when we successfully navigate relational challenges. Having a partner sincerely apologize for a failure event, deception, or a hurtful message can make us feel better and perhaps even increase affection for the partner. We might even feel relief

and a sense of freedom when a negative relationship finally comes to an end.

Read the list below of various topics covered in this chapter. Think of a particular time when you experienced each, and identify the positive and negative emotions that you experienced both initially and subsequently; then consider the following questions.

Questions to Consider

- Which situations produced the strongest negative emotional responses?
- What was there about the situations that caused these negative responses?

- How did you manage the negative emotional reactions?
- What could you do in the future to lessen or shorten the negative reactions?
- Which situations resulted in positive emotional responses?
- During which, if any, of the relational challenges did you discuss your emotional reactions with your partner? With a confidant?
- What impact did the discussion have on the relationships? On you? On your partner? On the confidant?

Relational Challenge	Initial Emotional Reactions	Subsequent Emotional Reactions
1. A violation of a relational expectation, a failure event, or a transgression on the part of a close friend		
2. Prolonged physical separation from a close friend or family member		
3. Negative reactions from others to a relationship of yours that was outside social norms		
4. Discovery that a friend deceived you by omission (not telling you something important)		
5. Finding out that a romantic partner lied to you		
6. Receiving criticism from a boss or teacher		
7. Being the target of obsessive relational intrusion, stalking, or relational violence		
8. Being the target of jealousy on the part of a friend, coworker, or lover		
9. Apparent de-escalation of a friendship		
10. Announcement by a romantic partner that he or she wants to end the relationship		

The ending of a relationship that has meant a great deal to you is one of the more difficult experiences you will face in your social life. The more intimate and involved you become, the more heartbreaking the end. But as the advice above suggests, there is life after the breakup of a relationship, and it is important to go through a recovery cycle that includes accepting the breakup, accepting the pain, realizing that you still have value and worth, and then moving on. Of course, all of this is easy to say and much more difficult to accomplish—which is one reason you should not isolate yourself but lean on other interpersonal relationships and family members to help you cope. Regrettably, relationships do come to an end, but just as you develop skills in initiating relationships, you can develop the ability to cope effectively with their termination, and with reflection, experience personal growth.

APPLYING AN OTHER-ORIENTATION
to Relationship Challenges

Most of the challenges discussed in this chapter can be managed more effectively if you apply an other-orientation, whether you are the perpetrator or the victim. You can use other-orientation to mediate your relationship challenges in several ways.

Avoiding or Minimizing Relational Challenges. An other-orientation might lead you to *not* engage in a behavior that could result in some harm or stress for your partner. Consider a recent failure event or interpersonal transgression that you committed. If you had considered your partner's feelings and response beforehand, would you still have committed the violation? Such preemptive other-orientation can lead us to alter what we say or do—or avoid saying or doing it at all—thus avoiding hurtful messages or deception.

Selecting Appropriate Repair Strategies. Perhaps you have considered your partner's reaction, but engaged in a failure event anyway. Intentionality makes it more difficult to achieve forgiveness or ameliorate hurt feelings. Nonetheless, by socially decentering, you anticipate your partner's thoughts and feelings about your transgression, helping you plan an appropriate repair strategy. For example, you are better able to choose between offering a simple apology or making significant reparations to restore the relationship.

Appreciating Your Partner's Reactions to Challenges. By social decentering you can better understand your partner's reactions to relationship challenges. For example, suppose your girlfriend or boyfriend returns after a semester studying abroad and acts distant and even belligerent to you after you introduce the new friends you've made. Your other-orientation would help you appreciate how your partner is affected by the change from a long-distance relationship back to a proximal one and understand why your partner feels jealous of your new friendships.

Managing Relational Termination. Being other-oriented can make de-escalating or terminating a relationship more difficult, because of an increased sensitivity to what your partner might feel about your deci-

sion. You might avoid or delay ending the relationship because you know how it will hurt the other person. On the other hand, maintaining a relationship when you no longer care about someone in the same way is a form of deception. The challenge is to use your understanding of the other to develop an approach that minimizes the hurt and best protects your partner's face, such as developing a direct, positive-tone strategy.

Forgiving. As the recipient of a partner's interpersonal transgression, deception, hurtful message, or decision to de-escalate or terminate the relationship, you might find that an other-orientation can contribute to healing and even to forgiving your partner. Suppose you know your partner's need to be independent is greater than his or her desire for an intimate relationship. If so, it should be easier to come to terms with the end of the relationship than if you failed to recognize this need. Forgiving does not mean ignoring what occurred or excusing your partner. But your own mental health generally is improved by forgiving.

Relationship Challenges
(pages 281–288)

Relationships are challenged by violations of our expectations, which create failure events and interpersonal transgressions. Such violations may evoke a reproach in which the failure is pointed out. In response, the violator may offer an account: an apology, excuse, justification, denial, or silence. We assess the severity of the violation and may opt to discuss, retaliate, or forgive. Physical separation and distance is another challenge that many relationships face. Long-distance relationships lend themselves to the maintenance of ideal images and good behavior during face-to-face interactions, creating general relationship satisfaction. Social norms challenge relationships between individuals who differ in race, religion, ethnicity, or age, or who are in a same-sex romantic relationship. Development of such relationships requires an appreciation and acceptance of people's differences and a willingness to face the social pressure to conform.

Key Terms

Failure events 282	In-group 287
Reproach 282	Out-group 287
Account 283	

Critical Thinking Questions

1. James was supposed to help clean up the apartment on Saturday, but he was gone all day. His roommate reproached him when he returned. Create three accounts that James could provide that differ in terms of how likely they are to make the situation worse.

2. Jack and Jill are in an exclusive romantic relationship, but because they attend different schools, they are living 300 miles apart. Things have not been going very smoothly recently, and Jill has gone out with a guy from her school a few times without telling Jack. Is Jill's behavior ethical?

Activities

In a group of three or four, generate a list of failure events that you have experienced and rank them in terms of their severity. What makes some failure events more injurious than others? Discuss how violators responded to these failure events.

Get together with two or three other students and identify long-distance relationships that each of you have experienced, including those with friends, lovers, and family. Discuss which relationships have continued and why. Which relationships have ended, and why? Do the reasons for breaking up a relationship change as the relationship becomes more intimate?

Web Resources

http://pnn.com/channels/21-relationships Described as the "global water cooler for women," this site includes articles and blogs with a section devoted to relationships.

http://www.soc.ucsb.edu/sexinfo/article/long-distance-relationships This site provides tips and connections to other sites addressing the challenges of long-distance relationships.

The Dark Side of Interpersonal Communication and Relationships
(pages 288–298)

The dark side of interpersonal communication refers to the ways in which communication can be harmful or detrimental. Deception varies in intent and severity and can be accomplished either by omission (leaving out information) or by commission (providing false information), including white lies, exaggeration, and baldfaced lies. People lie in their own interest and/or in the interest of others; but regardless of the reasons, lies have consequences. Messages are sometimes hurtful, either by intention or by accident. We are hurt when others (particularly family members and romantic partners) make negative comments about such things as the relationship or our personality, appearance, abilities, or dreams.

The dark side of interpersonal relationships is seen in jealousy, obsessive relational intrusion, stalking, and relational violence. Jealousy is a reaction to the threat of losing a valued relationship. People who repeatedly invade another person's privacy are engaging in obsessive relational intrusion. When such intrusions leads to concern for personal safety and fear on the part of the target, intrusion becomes stalking. Relational violence includes a range of destructive behaviors including aggressiveness, threats, violent acts, and verbal, psychological, and physical abuse.

Key Terms

Interpersonal deception theory 289	Invulnerable responses 292
Deception by omission (concealment) 289	Envy 293
Deception by commission 290	Jealousy 293
White lie 290	Cognitive jealousy 293
Exaggeration 290	Emotional or affective jealousy 293
Baldfaced lie 290	Obsessive relational intrusion (ORI) 295
Active verbal responses 292	Stalking 295
Acquiescent responses 292	Relational violence 296

Critical Thinking Questions

1. What factors would influence your reaction to the discovery that another person had deceived you?

2. Under what circumstances is it okay for you to be deceptive? Under what circumstances is it okay for your friends to lie to you?

3. You suspect a male friend is engaging in obsessive relational intrusion toward his former girlfriend. What obligation do you have to act on this? What would you do? What if your friend were a woman obsessively intruding on a former boyfriend?

Activities

Indicate with a check mark whether you have ever engaged in any of the following behaviors, and then decide if your behavior might be consider stalking. Compare your responses with those of your classmates and discuss.

_____ a. Asking someone for a date, even after being told no.

_____ b. Giving someone flowers, even though he or she doesn't want them.

_____ c. Sending text messages without signing them.

_____ d. Calling a person just to hear his or her voice on the answering machine, but not leaving a message.

_____ e. Calling someone even though you know the person doesn't want to talk to you.

_____ f. Following another person around to see where he or she goes.

_____ g. Asking someone's friend for personal information about that person.

_____ h. Taking a class just because a particular person will be there.

_____ i. Following someone in your car from a store to his or her home without his or her knowledge.

Web Resources

http://www.soc.ucsb.edu/sexinfo/article/jealousy This site presents an examination of some emotional issues surrounding jealousy and ways to manage it.

http://www.loveisnotabuse.com/ This site, sponsored by Liz Claiborne Inc. provides detailed information about and analysis of the problem of abuse and suggests action steps.

http://www.recovery-man.com/abusive/abusive.htm This site provides information on such topics as the warning signs of abuse, anger management, and help for those who are abusive.

De-Escalation and Termination of Relationships
(pages 298–308)

People react to relational problems by ignoring them, addressing and repairing them, or redefining or ending the relationship. Relationships typically end in one of three ways: fading away, sudden death, or incrementalism. In general, relationships seem to end when the costs exceed the rewards over some period of time. Reasons for ending a relationship fall into three categories: faults, unwillingness to compromise, and feeling constrained. One model of relationship termination identifies four phases: the intrapsychic phase, the dyadic phase, the social phase, and the grave-dressing phase. Partners can use direct or indirect strategies to bring a relationship to an end. Indirect strategies include withdrawal, pseudo–de-escalation, and cost escalation. Among the direct strategies for ending a relationship are negative identity management, justification, de-escalation, and positive tone. Strategies for post-dissolution recovery include expressing emotions, figuring out what happened, talking to others, and gaining perspective.

Key Terms

Bilateral dissolution *301*

Unilateral dissolution *301*

Fading away *301*

Sudden death *301*

Incrementalism *301*

Intrapsychic phase *303*

Dyadic phase *304*

Social phase *304*

Grave-dressing phase *304*

Indirect termination strategies *304*

Direct termination strategies *304*

Critical Thinking Questions

1. How do you know when it is time to get out of a relationship?

2. Think of a romantic relationship that you've had that you chose to end. How well does Duck's model of relationship dissolution fit what happened to you? What happened that is not reflected in his model?

3. Ethics: Under what circumstances is it ethical for someone to use sudden death withdrawal as a strategy for ending an intimate relationship? Under what circumstances would this behavior be unethical?

Activities

Identify two relationships that you ended and two relationships that the other person ended. In each case, try to determine which of the indirect or direct strategies were used. What differences were there in how the relationships ended? What effects do you think the choice of strategy had on you and your partner? What strategies did you use to recover from the breakup? Which was the most helpful? Least helpful? What other strategies for recovery have you used that helped?

Survey your friends to find out how they have ended close relationships and how they recovered from the termination of a close relationship. Try to identify the termination and recovery strategies they seem to have used.

Web Resources

http://love.ivillage.com/lnsproblems/lnsbreakingup/topics/0,,4tdc, 00.html This site offers lots of articles, advice, and links on breaking up, plus other advice on a variety of relationship issues.

http://www.askmen.com/dating/heidi_100/112_dating_girl.html This site, primarily aimed at men, provides articles on a wide variety of topics including breaking up and recovering from breakups.

http://breakup-songs.com/ This site lists titles and lyrics of songs about breaking up.

Interpersonal Relationships: Friendship and Romance

11

311

Chris and Lee have been friends since fourth grade. They hung out together throughout high school, sharing secrets, playing in band together, and often staying at each other's homes. In college, they roomed together and continued to depend on each other for support and companionship. During their junior year, Chris began to develop a significant romantic relationship with Jan. Chris often sought Lee's advice as the romantic relationship developed. Chris, Lee, and Jan often hung out together, and Lee became good friends with Jan. After graduation, Chris and Jan got married, with Lee providing support and assistance to both.

This scenario provides a very brief introduction to several types of relationships—same-sex best friends, romantic relationships, and opposite-sex friends. Underlying the scenario are some subtle but significant questions: Why did Chris feel the need to develop a romantic relationship? Why wasn't the relationship with Lee sufficient to meet Chris's needs for companionship and love? What needs are met by romantic relationships that aren't satisfied through friendship?

Both friendship and romance are relationships of choice; for the most part, we can opt out of them whenever we want. When we begin each relationship, we don't know how intimate it will become—although, as mentioned in Chapter 9, we probably try to predict the likelihood of an intimate and satisfying relationship. Both friendships and romantic relationships can lead to close, intimate, loving relationships.

Intimacy comes in two forms: **friendship-based intimacy,** based on feelings of warmth, understanding, and emotional connection; and **passion-based intimacy,** based on romantic and sexual feelings.[1] Friendship and romance differ in that friendships develop solely from friendship-based intimacy, whereas romantic relationships involve both friendship-based and passion-based intimacy. Chris's relationship with Lee evolved from friendship-based intimacy, whereas his relationship with Jan reflected both types.

Another obvious difference between friendship and romance is that romance includes sexual expectations and, ultimately, the prospect of creating a family. Romantic loving relationships are typified by a high degree of intimacy, attachment, and sexual activity and/or attraction.[2] Historically, marriage was considered the most intimate relationship, rooted in the goal of procreation and forming a family.[3] Today, we recognize that gays and lesbians may also form intimate romantic relationships with relational dynamics similar to those of heterosexual relationships, including marriage and child rearing.

Both friendships and romantic relationships significantly contribute to mental and physical well-being throughout our lives. This chapter discusses the qualities of each type of relationship; their similarities and differences; the role each plays in our lives; and the skills needed to initiate, escalate, and maintain them.

Friendship

Friendship is a relationship of choice that exists over time between people who share a common history.[4] A friend is someone we like and who likes us. We trust our friends. We share good and bad times with them. We want to be with them, and we make time for that purpose.

Here's a list of some of the qualities of friendship identified in a variety of research studies.[5]

- Self-disclosure/feeling free to express intimate information
- Openness/honesty/authenticity
- Compatibility/similarity

friendship-based intimacy A type of intimacy based on feelings of warmth, understanding, and emotional connection.

passion-based intimacy A type of intimacy based on romantic and sexual feelings.

- Ego-reinforcement/self-concept support
- Acceptance of one's individuality
- Respect
- Helping behavior
- Positive evaluation
- Trust
- Concern and empathy

Your own expectations of friendship probably include some of the items from this list, as well as additional qualities. How well a given person meets these expectations is one factor you use to decide whether to establish a friendship. As we noted earlier, friends represent relationships of choice. Friendship develops naturally into an interdependent relationship that is different from other interpersonal relationships; friends have no external constraints that keep them together, such as a job, school, or family, even though we often make friends with people in these situations. Usually, we form friendships with our equals, whereas we often form other types of relationships with people of different ages or social backgrounds.[6] In contrast to what we accept from our family relationships, we tend to expect equality and equity in our friendships, with both partners providing similar amounts of emotional and material support and neither one becoming overly indebted.[7]

Besides helping us enjoy a healthy life, friends help us cope with stress and take care of physical needs, and even contribute to the development of our personality. Friends significantly contribute to our social support networks, providing assistance in times of crisis.[8] Friends also help shape our attitudes and beliefs. Especially during periods of change in our lives, such as adolescence and retirement, friends help us cope with uncertainty and have a profound influence on our behavior.[9]

One of the most important functions that friends perform is to help us manage the mundane. Most friendships are not based on unusual activities. On the contrary, most of us seek out friends just to talk, share a meal, or enjoy entertainment together.

How many friends do you need? Typically, people have up to five close friends, fifteen other friends, twenty or more members in a social network (which could include family members), and many more people who are simply acquaintances.[10] In all our social interactions, we are happiest when we are in the company of our friends. Perhaps the ancient Roman orator Cicero said it best: A friend multiplies our joys and divides our sorrows.

Friends also perform other functions, such as bolstering our self-esteem. Most of us need people who provide encouragement and tell us that we are decent and likable. It is confirming to have a friend become indignant on our behalf when we have experienced an injustice. Friends can help keep a stream of positive acceptance flowing to counteract the numerous nicks and bruises that our self-worth suffers in the course of daily living.

Friends also provide material help when you need it. When you are away on vacation, you might ask a friend to feed your cat and water your plants. If you run out of gas, you might call a friend to bring you some or pick you up.

Making Friends

How do you go about making friends? The first requirement is to interact with new people. Fortunately, you are surrounded with opportunities: You can meet people at school or work; people living near you; people with whom you share activities; and people in your existing friends' social networks (mutual acquaintances). Unfortunately, making friends is like finding the perfect pair of new shoes: You might try on a lot until you find one that fits just right. Whatever your personality or interests, there are people who will like you and be open to becoming your friends, but the process of finding these people might involve discarding a lot of shoes that don't fit. An important rule of making friends is to be yourself—it needs to be your own foot you're putting in the shoe. Being yourself increases the likelihood of finding real commonalities with someone.

One factor that helps in making friends in college is that you already share similarities with people you meet there—interest in education, in bettering yourself, and pursuing a career. Repeated polling of our students who were randomly assigned dorm roommates shows that about half of them become friends. That's a pretty good success rate that can be partially attributed to shared similarities, combined with the chance to talk and learn about each other. The five factors that most affect the development of college friendships are similarity of attitudes, an expectation that the other person will like us, reciprocated self-disclosures, proximity, and accessibility or availability.[11]

Friendships at Different Stages in Life

Establishing intimacy with another person takes time, so most of us have a limited number of intimate relationships. We also have different needs for intimacy at various stages of our lives.

Psychologist Howard Markman and his colleagues found that self-disclosure, one of the most important components of friendship, did not seem to change in either depth or amount from young adulthood through age ninety-one.[12] They did report, however, that as friends get older, they engaged in more negative self-disclosure; apparently, as we age, we are more willing to tell our friends less positive things about ourselves, rather than limiting our disclosures to information that makes us "look good."

Another change that occurs as we age is the development of a more complex view of friendship. Young adults tend to lump "best friends" together, while older adults differentiate among best friends from their youth, best friends from work, best friends to do activities with, and so on.[13] Relationship scholars W. J. Dickens and Daniel Perlman examined the differences among friendships at four stages in life: childhood, adolescence, adulthood, and old age,[14] but current research suggests an additional delineation, called "young adulthood," that occurs between adolescence and adulthood.

Childhood Friendships. At about the age of two, when we start to talk, we begin parallel play with others. As toddlers, we perceive our playmates as people who can help meet our needs. Our first friendships are usually superficial and self-centered. Childhood friendships can be categorized into five sometimes overlapping stages.[15] From ages three to seven, we have *momentary playmates*—we interact with those in our presence. From ages four to nine, our friendships involve *one-way assistance*. We still view friendships from a "take" perspective, as instruments to help meet our needs, rather than from a "give" or "give-and-take" perspective.

The third stage, ages six to twelve, is the *fair-weather friend* stage. There is more give and take in friendships, but the reciprocity occurs when things are going well; the relationship is likely to end if problems and conflicts develop. The fourth stage, ages nine to fifteen, is called *mutual intimacy*. With the closeness that develops, relationships become more possessive. The last stage (beginning at about age twelve and continuing through adulthood) allows for more *independence* in friendships, as well as deepening interdependence with friends that permits greater levels of intimacy and sharing.

Adolescent Friendships. During adolescence, beginning with the onset of puberty at around age twelve, we move away from relationships with parents and other adults and toward greater intimacy with our peers. During adolescence, peer relationships significantly influence our identity and social skills.[16] We explore values, negotiate new relationships with family members, discover romantic and sexual opportunities, become more other-oriented, and seek increased intimacy. Adolescents consider spending time with friends their most enjoyable activity;[17] and they view friends as more committed, loyal, accepting, tolerant, and supportive than younger children do. In addition, adolescents place more value on personality (character, trustworthiness, similarity) and interpersonal qualities (companionship, acceptance, intimacy) in both same-sex and cross-sex friendships.[18]

In adolescence, we develop cliques of friends and form friendship networks. Boys are more likely to join groups—either socially acceptable groups such as a sports or debate team or less socially desirable groups bent on violence and destruction of property. Girls are more likely to develop intimate relationships with one or two good friends. During adolescence, boys seem to have more friends, whereas girls appear to develop closer, more intense, and more intimate relationships. The number of friendships usually peaks in late adolescence and early adulthood, before we select a mate.[19]

In adolescence we develop cliques and friendship networks.

Young Adult Friendships. Young adult friendships, those occurring in our late teens through our early thirties, are linked to a succession of significant changes in our lifestyles and goals. The post–high school experience of young adults typically includes going to college, getting a job, pursuing more serious romantic relationships, getting married, and starting a family.

Those who go directly into the workforce after high school experience different friendship experiences than those who leave home to continue their education. Those who opt out of college seek to sustain their high-school–based friendships while developing new friendships at their workplace. As a college student, you probably have such friends, and you've probably noticed your relationships with them changing.

For college students who maintain their best friendships from high school, either because they commute or because they attend the same college as their high school friends, the likelihood of forming new best friends in college is reduced.[20] Close high school friendships help new college students manage the stress and successfully adjust to college, but further adjustment requires the development of new friendships during the first year at college.[21]

For those who move away to attend college, high school relationships often de-escalate because of changing interests and the time and energy needed to maintain the friendships. The loss of these relationships, changes in family interactions, and the challenge of forming new relationships often result in feelings of loneliness; however, new friendships are usually developed that are regarded as even more satisfying than previous ones.[22]

Young adults and adolescents share some similar friendship values, such as loyalty, warmth, and having shared experiences.[23] Young adults particularly value friends who reciprocate their caring, trust, commitment, self-disclosure, helpfulness, and support, while also having strong character.[24] Finally, our friendships during this period of our lives help us learn and hone the skills needed for successful romantic relationships, as well as providing confidants with whom to discuss romantic experiences.

Adult Friendships. While the actual age ranges that define friendships is debatable, we consider adult friendships as those we have from the thirties through the sixties[25]—in essence, those relationships during the prime of our work and family lives. Some young adult friendships continue as adult friendships, with friends experiencing similar life courses that act as a foundation for mutual empathy and support. As you graduate, get married, and have children, the college friends with whom you

315

Elderly people may make new friends, but they usually rely most on their spouses and oldest friends to fulfill their need for companionship.

maintain relationships are likely having similar experiences, which can become focal points for interaction—talking about work, home life, and the kids.

Adult friendships are among our most valued relationships, providing emotional support, partners for activities, and socializing opportunities.[26] In addition to continued friendships from young adulthood, friendships emerge with coworkers, neighbors, relatives, or members of organizations we become involved in. Since these often start as relationships of circumstance, they may be temporary and fade away as circumstances change, such as when someone moves or takes a new job. The importance of the marital relationship may cause friendships to become secondary, and the likelihood of opposite-sex friendships diminishes. The number of friends married people have declines over the course of their lives.[27] On the other hand, romantic relationships and marriage introduce partners to each other's social networks, thus affording additional opportunities for new friends. Marriage can also lead to developing friendships with brothers- or sisters-in-law or other family members. You and your spouse may become friends with other couples. Unfortunately, single friends can feel left out as couples gravitate to other couples.

Late Adulthood Friendships. Although people make new friends during their late adulthood, they value their long-established friendships the most. During retirement, when people have more time for socializing, friendships become increasingly important, but older adults are less likely to form new friendships. Instead, they tend to maintain a small, highly valued network of friends. Some friendships are rekindled as the elderly act on their longing to reconnect with close friends with whom they have lost contact.[28] Late adulthood friendships keep individuals socially integrated as they reminisce, share stories, or engage in activities; in addition, their shared experiences add to their ability to be caring and supportive.[29] These friendships often provide richer interactions than older adults experience with their own family members, though family relationships remain an important part of their lives.

Same-Sex Friendships

An ongoing debate surrounds how men and women approach friendship, particularly their same-sex friendships. One claim is that women define their female friendships by intimacy, whereas men define their male friendships in terms of activities. In one study, men reported having more "best friends" than women; but women spent more hours talking with their best friends.[30] No such difference in the amount of talking was found with their "close" friends. Men also reported engaging in more physical activities in groups, whereas women spent more time discussing social relationship and school issues. However, men also value their close friendships with other men, and women do develop friendships with other women on the basis of their mutual activity.

What are your expectations for relationships with same-sex friends? The answer to this question was the focus of a study by personal relationship scholar Beverley Fehr, who examined *prototypes* (our expectations about relationships). Both men and women reported that self-disclosure, emotional support, loyalty, and trust contributed the most to a sense of intimacy in their same-sex friendships.[31] However, although men understood what contributes to intimacy, women rated all of these behaviors as more likely to produce intimacy than did men and appeared to have a stronger need or desire for intimacy in same-sex friendships. Additionally, Fehr found that friendship satisfaction for women was related to these behaviors, but they did not affect men's friendship satisfaction.[32]

Close same-sex relationships serve similar functions for both men and women. Both value intimacy, trust, interpersonal sensitivity, emotional expressiveness, and authenticity in their same-sex friendships.[33] Both men and women also value engaging in activities, conversing, having fun, and relaxing with their same-sex friends.[34] Overall, men's and women's same-sex friendships appear to differ not in the qualities they possess but in the degree to which they possess them. Compared to men, women see their same-sex friendships as more satisfying, more enjoyable, and more intimate or close. Women's same-sex friendships also involve more talk about talking (metacommunication), and are more person-centered and expressive.[35] Females in same-sex friendships have more physical affection for each other and compliment each other more, whereas men are more openly competitive.[36] While very close friends are not very interpersonally competitive, one study did find that same-sex male friends are more competitive than either same-sex female friends or cross-sex friends.[37] Men acted less interpersonally competitive in their friendships with women, but women's competitiveness increased in their friendships with males. For all friendships, being more competitive related to less friendship satisfaction.

As with all such generalizations, the conclusions of these studies don't fit every relationship. For example, a person's *preference* for same-sex or cross-sex friends might color the applicability of the conclusions. A recent study found that such preferences had a significant impact on the qualities respondents associated with each type of friendship.[38] Males who preferred being best friends with a male saw friendships with males as more caring, supportive, and trustworthy than friendships with females. Women who preferred male best friends rated friendships with men as more trustworthy, more caring, and more supportive than female friendships, and similar in closeness. We all have our own friendship preferences and expectations that we use in judging the value of each of our female and male friendships.

Cross-Sex Friendships

Perhaps as you grew up, you had close friends of the opposite sex. Adolescents often develop opposite-sex, or *cross-sex*, friendships that are not romantic.[39] However, the development of male–female friendships between heterosexual adults is sometimes a challenge because of underlying sexual attraction. In the movie *When Harry Met Sally*, Harry proclaims that "... men and women can't be friends. The sex part always gets in the way." Fortunately, research and your own experiences might indicate that Harry wasn't totally correct. We can develop cross-sex adult friendships with minimal sexual attraction or redefine romantic relationships as friendships. Adult cross-sex relationships are facilitated by opportunities for men and women to interact nonromantically—in college, at work, and in leisure activities.[40] Heidi Reeder, a communication researcher, conducted two studies on cross-sex relationships: one in which she interviewed twenty pairs of cross-sex friends, and the other in which 231 students completed questionnaires.[41] Both studies found that romantic attraction and physical/sexual attraction diminished as the relationship progressed over time, while friendship attraction increased. While sexual attraction might indeed be an issue within cross-sex relationships, it is reduced when there is a commitment to developing and maintaining the relationship as friends.

Not all cross-sex friendships are devoid of sex. Friendship, romantic relationships, and sex have been found to connect in several ways.[42] People in relationships labeled *friends with benefits (FWB)* have both sexual and nonsexual interactions but value their friendship above all; such relationships contrast with relationships that are primarily sexual and in which the couple are only minimally friends. FWB relationships are sometimes intentionally or unintentionally used as stepping stones to romantic relationships, both successfully and unsuccessfully. FWB relationships can also include instances in which going out with a mixed-sex group leads to "hooking up" at the end of the night or in which partners in a post-romantic relationship still engage in sex. Surveys of college students reveal that around half of the respondents have had such a relationship.[43] Reasons for engaging in FWB relationships include the avoidance of relational commitment, a desire to engage in sex with a friend, a perception that such relationships are simpler and less problematic than romantic ones, a desire to feel closer to the friend, and finally just a general desire to have a friends-with-benefits experience.[44] Participants in such relationships appear to discuss and establish specific relational maintenance rules, with the most frequent being emotional rules (not falling in love or being jealous) and communication rules (guidelines about honesty, topics, and phone calling).[45] However, the term *friends with benefits* seems to imply that friendships without sex do not have benefits, which misrepresents the values of same- and cross-sex friendships.

Cross-sex friendships can be important relationships, as can the other relationships that have just been discussed, because through such relationships you can gain insights into how other people think. In this case, your friends can help you better understand the opposite sex. On the basis of interviews with 300 men and women about their cross-sex friendships, psychotherapist and author Lillian Rubin found that the men reported feeling a higher level of intimacy and friendship than their female counterparts (some women were surprised to find out they were even considered friends).[46] Men seemed to gain more from their friendships with women than women did from men. Men valued their friendships with women for providing more nurturance and intimacy than their male friendships. Women did not feel their male friendships were as intimate or rewarding as their female friendships. However, women did enjoy the masculine interaction style, the fun activities, and learning about the male perspective.

In interacting with people of either sex, focus on working toward a mutual understanding and acceptance of what your expectations are for your friendship. There is great value in forming relationships with individuals who are different from you; not only can you learn about other people, but you can also gain a better sense of yourself. Learning how another person's age, race, ethnicity, or sex affects his or her values, thoughts, and behaviors can increase your awareness of how those factors have influenced you.

Diverse Friendships

Most of our friendships are with people who are fairly similar to us. Similarity makes it easier to communicate effectively and to reach mutual understanding. The more we differ from other people, the greater the challenges that must be overcome to maintain a relationship, as discussed in Chapter 4. However, both friendships and romantic relationships do develop between people who differ in culture, age, and race. Part of the success of these relationships depends on whether the difference is more superficial than profound.

Intergenerational Friendships. The impact of a ten-year age difference between you and another person is likely to be minimal if you both have the same interests and similar values. However, someone forty years older might have a very different outlook on life from yours. Usually, the older people become, the less impact age differences have on them.[47] A fifteen-year-old's interactions with a thirty-year-old represent a very different kind of relationship than that of a thirty-year-old and a forty-five-year-old.

How many close friendships do you have with anyone significantly older or younger? Developing and sustaining such relationships often requires special effort; so we are more likely to have casual intergenerational friendships. One study compared close friendships between peers of similar age and between friends who were at least ten years different in age.[48] The sample included participants who ranged from eighteen to seventy-six. Close relationships with peers, as compared to relationships with those who were of a different age, were seen as providing more companionship, satisfaction, intimacy, and nurturance and as being more likely to continue in the future.

Intercultural and Interracial Friendships. The qualities and expectations associated with being a friend differ among cultures, ethnic groups, and racial groups. You might engage in behavior that you think is appropriate in your friendship with a person from another culture, only to find that you have offended your friend by violating his or her culturally based expectations. In fact, one study that examined the qualities associated with friendship in various ethnic groups in the United States found that "Latinos emphasized relational support, Asian Americans emphasized a caring, positive exchange of ideas, African Americans emphasized respect and acceptance, and Anglo Americans emphasized recognizing the needs of the individual."[49] Realize, of course, that such generalities may not be valid for a particular member of an ethnic group. However, the study also found that in developing interethnic relationships, individuals seemed unaware of cultural or ethnic differences; rather, they developed a unique relationship defined by their own relational rules rather than by cultural rules.[50] This is similar to the notion of developing a third culture, as discussed in Chapter 4. True respect for and deep understanding of a partner's culture develops as the relationship becomes very close, at which point cultural violations are viewed less negatively and are even joked about.[51]

As in the development of most relationships, factors such as proximity and communication affect attraction in intercultural friendships. However, four factors have been identified that specifically affect the development of intercultural friendships.[52]

Couples who choose to establish relationships outside of a culture's norms face challenges and social pressures.

1. *Cultural similarities* exist across cultures, creating common ground that nurtures the development of friendship—for example, sharing the same passion for soccer as someone from Brazil or a love of anime with someone from Japan.

2. *Cultural differences* can actually heighten interest in the other person and prompt initial conversations. You might seek more information about another culture's use of arranged marriages or observance of Ramadan.

3. *Prior intercultural experiences* help reduce uncertainty about developing friendships with people from other cultures and

serve as the foundation for new friendships. Of course, this factor can be somewhat unilateral, in that you might have experience with the other person's culture, but not vice versa.

4. *Targeted socializing* occurs as partners move from acquaintanceship to friendship, socializing within the specific cultural or intercultural context of one of the partners, such as an American student attending a Chinese New Year's party with a Chinese classmate.

Opportunities to socialize also affect the development of interracial friendships. An analysis of a large national survey found that the formation of interracial friendships in the United States is associated with participation in nonreligious civic groups, socializing with coworkers, social status, shared neighborhoods, and the diversity of the community.[53] Many of these factors led to Blacks, Hispanics, and Asians being more likely than Whites to have an interracial friend. However, Whites who lived in communities with more diversity were more likely to have interracial friends. Blacks, Hispanics, and Asians were more likely to report having White friends when they belonged to nonreligious civic groups and/or socialized with coworkers. For immigrants who must bridge both cultural and racial differences, language skills and citizenship affect the ability to join groups and socialize with coworkers, thus affecting their development of interracial or interethnic friendships.

While there are similarities between forming intercultural friendships and forming interracial ones, a unique issue confronting interracial friendships is the fact that usually both members are from the same culture. Thus, they assume that they share the same cultural values, identity, and experiences and fail to appreciate the impact of race on their perspectives. Communication scholar William Rawlins identifies prerequisites for the formation of friendships between Blacks and Whites.[54] He begins with the premise that White people have difficulty seeing themselves from a racial perspective, whereas Black people have both a racial identity and feelings of being marginalized and demeaned

Building Your Skills   **Relational Expectations**

Canadian researcher Beverly Fehr found that people hold certain expectations (*prototypes*) for the kinds of interactions that lead to a sense of intimacy in friendships. People use these expected interaction patterns as a standard that helps them determine the level of intimacy in a relationship and evaluate that intimacy. Changes in the number and intensity of your prototype interaction patterns let you know whether you are moving toward or away from intimate friendships. How aware are you of your expectations? Do you have the same expectations for all relationships, or do they differ depending on the type of relationship? The statements on the facing page reflect the top patterns (*prototypes*) of relating found in Fehr's study. Think about your general expectations for each of the listed relationships. Put 2 on the line if the interaction pattern strongly reflects your explanation of what should occur in each relationship, 1 if it somewhat reflects your expectation, and 0 if it doesn't apply.

Source: Adapted from Beverly Fehr, "Intimacy Expectations in Same-Sex Friendships: A Prototype Interaction-Pattern Model," *Journal of Personality and Social Psychology* 86 (2004): 265–84.

- Examine each of the four types of relationship, and note which patterns you marked 2. How do these expectations compare to what you actually experience in these relationships? How has meeting or failing to meet your strongest expectations affected the level of intimacy in each relationship?

- Overall, for which patterns did you mark zeros across the four types of relationship? How do your low expectations affect your relationships with people who see these expectations as important?

- What patterns of interaction that you expect from each type of relationship are not listed?

- How do the rating totals relate to your level of satisfaction and closeness in each of the relationships listed?

- How do differences in the rating totals reflect differences in the relationships?

by Whites.[55] According to Rawlins, friends of different races need to recognize that racism is a reality that affects our relationships; we are all potentially racist, and racism can appear in many different forms.[56] For example, thinking you're doing a favor for someone of another race by being his or her friend might reflect an inherent belief in your superiority. Finally, friends of different races need to guard against either overaccommodating or overassimilating—each person needs to retain his or her own racial identity while appreciating that of the other.[57] Rather than changing to gain acceptance, interracial friends need to accept each other's race as part of who each person is.

Romantic Relationships

The closest relationship you ever develop with another human being will probably be a romantic one, perhaps a marriage. However, even without being married, 47 percent of students surveyed in one study indicated their closest relationships were with romantic partners.[58] This closeness is reflected in many behaviors; for example, romantic couples are more likely than friends to talk about what attracted them to each other, to celebrate anniversaries, and to mark other milestones in formal ways, such as with a card or a special dinner.

At the most rudimentary level, romantic relationships are about mating and creating a family. Your immediate reaction might be to exclaim that this was the last thing on your mind during your high school and college romances. Nonetheless, the complex process of seeking a mate begins with fairly innocuous interactions with the opposite sex. Chapter 9 provided a general model of relational stages, but romantic relationships can be further delineated along a continuum (Figure 11.1) that reflects increasing commitment, love, sex as emotional expression, exclusivity (fidelity), and self-disclosure.

Romantic relationships exist both between cross-sex couples and between same-sex couples. Gay and lesbian romantic relationships share many of the same qualities as heterosexual relationships, although homosexual couples often face added pressure of

	Close Same-Sex Friend	Close Cross-Sex Friend	Close Romantic Partner	Mother or Father
If I need to talk, this person will listen.	____	____	____	____
If I am in trouble, this person will help me.	____	____	____	____
If I need this person, he or she will be there for me.	____	____	____	____
If someone is insulting me or saying negative things behind my back, this person will stick up for me.	____	____	____	____
If I need food, clothing, or a place to stay, this person will provide it.	____	____	____	____
No matter who I am or what I do, this person will accept me.	____	____	____	____
If we have a fight or an argument, we will work it out.	____	____	____	____
Even if I feel as though no one cares, I know this person does.	____	____	____	____
If this person upsets me, I am able to let him or her know.	____	____	____	____
If something good happens to me, this person will be happy for me.	____	____	____	____
If I set a goal, this person will support and encourage me.	____	____	____	____
If I am lonely, this person will provide companionship.	____	____	____	____
Totals:	____	____	____	____

| Dating | Exclusively Dating | Pre-Engaged | Engaged | Married |

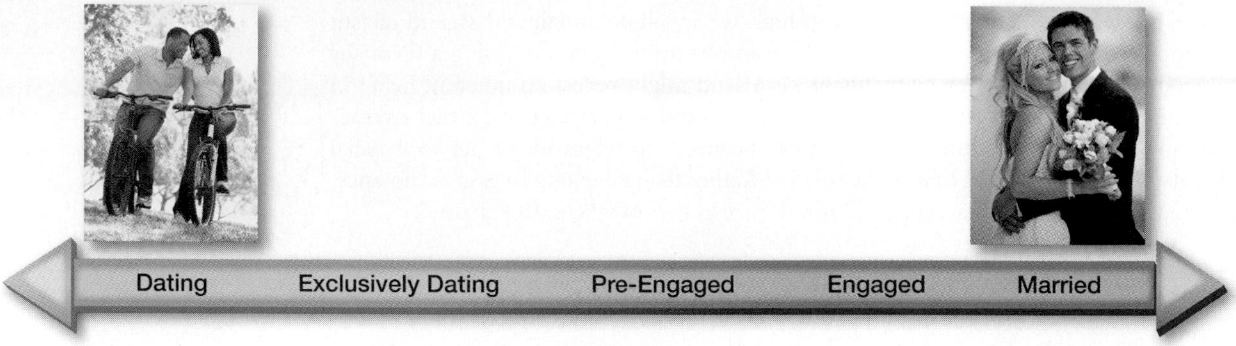

FIGURE 11.1

Continuum of Romance

social mores, restrictive laws, and condemning attitudes. Comparing married hetero-sexual couples and married homosexual couples is difficult, since homosexual couples can marry in only a few states. Nonetheless, one study found that committed gay and lesbian couples displayed patterns similar to those of married heterosexual couples in terms of change in satisfaction over a five-year period.[59] However, same-sex couples were more likely than opposite-sex married couples to end their relationships within those five years, perhaps because of social pressures or lack of social acceptance.

Qualities of Romantic Relationships

In the chapter's opening scenario, Chris's development of a romantic relationship with Jan was linked to both friendship-based and passion-based intimacy—it was a relationship that included warmth, understanding, emotional connection, romance, and sexual feelings. This section specifically examines those qualities that are most typical of romantic relationships: love, commitment, and physical affection and sex.

Love.   One pair of researchers suggests that love differs from friendship "in the iden-tity of interest that the partners share. Love exists to the extent that the outcomes en-joyed or suffered by each are enjoyed or suffered by both."[60] Love involves an increase in a sense of "we-ness," of passionate solidarity and identification with the other. Love has also been conceptualized as an individual's having the goal of preserving and pro-moting the well-being of a person who is valued.[61] Zick Rubin, a lawyer and social psy-chologist, attempted to identify differences between love and friendship by developing two scales—one to measure love and the other to measure liking.[62] He found that peo-ple describe love relationships as more passionate and intimate than friendships, but interestingly, people like their romantic partners only slightly more than they like their friends. Women make greater distinctions between love and liking than do men.

The **triangular theory of love,** developed by psychologist Robert Sternberg, iden-tifies three dimensions that can be used to describe variations in loving relationships: intimacy, commitment, and passion.[63] In this model (Figure 11.2), intimacy includes such attributes as trust, caring, honesty, supportiveness, understanding, and open-ness. The second dimension, commitment, includes loyalty, devotion, putting the other first, and needing each other. The final dimension, passion, includes excite-ment, sexual interest and activity, and extreme longing. These three dimensions relate to relationship satisfaction,[64] with passion identified as the most important dimension for developing romantic relationships.[65]

These dimensions provide a useful way of thinking about how love manifests itself in relationships. According to the triangular theory of love, the presence and strength of each of these dimensions varies from relationship to relationship, with each combi-nation defining a style of love. For example, relationships strong in intimacy and

triangular theory of love Theory that suggests that all loving relationships can be described according to three dimensions: intimacy, commitment, and passion.

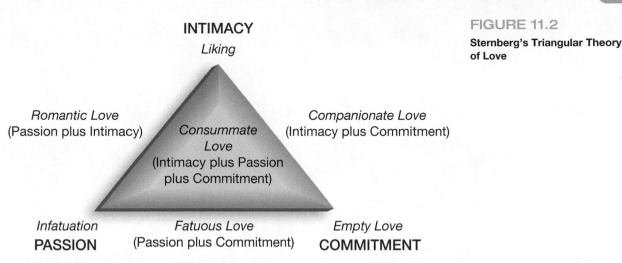

FIGURE 11.2

Sternberg's Triangular Theory of Love

commitment but weak in passion are identified as *companionate love,* and relationships strong only in passion constitute *infatuation.* Where would your current or past romantic relationship(s) be placed around the triangle? Relationships don't stay at the same place, but rather vary as each dimension ebbs and flows.

A simpler approach presents romantic love as having just two parts: passionate love and companionate love. **Passionate love** serves to establish attraction to, interest in, and focus on one person and usually, but not always, declines in the early years of marriage.[66] **Companionate love** is love that develops over time as partners become more entwined, mutually responsive to needs, and attached, while feelings of trust and caring increase.[67]

Sociologist John Alan Lee created a similar scheme that defined six types of love found in both romantic and nonromantic relationships: eros, ludis, storge, mania, pragma, and agape.[68]

Eros is sexual love based on the pursuit of beauty and pleasure. The physical need for sex brings many couples together. Erotic lovers crave sexual intimacy and passionately seek sexual activity to satisfy their need. Sexual attraction brings special needs and emotions to a relationship, sometimes obscuring other concerns. Shakespeare described this phenomenon when he wrote "But love is blind, and lovers cannot see the petty folly that themselves commit."

Ludis describes love as a game, something to pass the time. Ludic lovers are not seeking long-term relationships; rather, they seek immediate gratification and their partners' affection. Their goal is to be in love and to enjoy their partners rather than to achieve a sexual victory.

Early dating relationships are often of the ludic type. Going on a date to a junior high dance is a casual pleasure, not a prelude to a lifelong commitment. Ludis lasts as long as the partners have fun and find the relationship mutually satisfying.

Storge is the sort of love found in most friendships and in relationships with siblings and other family members. Sexual consummation is not a factor in this sort of love, although sexual attraction may be present. A storgic relationship usually develops over a long period of time, and it is solid and more resistant to change than erotic love. Trust, caring, and compassion are high; selfishness is low.

Mania describes a love relationship that swings wildly between extreme highs and lows. A manic lover is obsessed with the relationship with the other person. Each of the lovers may have an insatiable need for attention, often fueled by a low self-concept.

passionate love Romantic love that serves to establish attraction to, interest in, and focus on one person.

companionate love Romantic love that develops over time as entwinement, mutual responsiveness to needs, trust, caring, and attachment increase.

eros Sexual, erotic love based on the pursuit of physical beauty and pleasure.

ludis Game-playing love based on the enjoyment of another.

storge Solid love found in friendships and family, based on trust and caring.

mania Obsessive love driven by mutual needs.

Pragma is the root word for *pragmatic*, meaning practical. This kind of relationship works because the partners' individual requirements, personalities, backgrounds, likes, and dislikes are compatible. In some cultures, parents prearrange marriages because of pragmatic concerns, and if the couple is lucky, passion develops later on as the relationship takes its course.

Agape love is based on a spiritual ideal of love. It involves giving of yourself and expecting nothing in return. This kind of "pure" love may characterize the relationship between a parent and a child, or the relationship between a spiritual leader and his or her followers.

Commitment.   Commitment is our intention to remain in a relationship. As we progress along the continuum of romance, commitment increases and clearly differentiates even serious dating from engagement and marriage. Turning points often mark significant changes in our romantic relationship commitments—declaring our love for someone, pledging to date exclusively, proposing marriage, and making wedding vows. We also communicate our commitment to another through our behaviors. A recent study of married and romantically involved couples found that the level of commitment was related to six sets of behaviors:[69]

1. Being supportive and encouraging (e.g., listening and being courteous)

2. Reassuring our partner of our feelings (e.g., expressing love and confirming the importance of the relationship)

3. Offering tangible reminders (e.g., giving gifts and assistance)

4. Creating a relationship future (e.g., doing things together and making plans together)

pragma Practical love based on mutual benefits.

agape Selfless love based on giving of yourself for others.

5. Behaving with integrity (e.g., being honest, being faithful, and keeping promises)

6. Working on the relationship (e.g., talking out problems and expressing trust)

Women, more than men, showed commitment by being supportive, creating a relationship future, and behaving with integrity; men showed commitment by offering tangible reminders more than women. What behaviors do you display to implicitly convey commitment to your partner?

We each have specific expectations that we apply to our romantic relationships, depending on the relationship's progress. In general, we expect partners in committed relationships to be faithful, to respect us, to help maintain our face when the relationship is troubled, and to help us through hard times.[70] This list of expectations almost sounds like wedding vows, which are in essence a statement of our commitment to our partner.

Physical Affection and Sex. **Physical affection** is the use of touch to convey emotional feelings of love and caring for another person. We express affection through touch in romantic relationships, and as the relationships change, so does our physical affection. The need for touch and its relationship to intimacy is discussed in Chapter 7. As that chapter points out, more affectionate touching occurs in the earlier part of a romantic relationships than later. Touch is one way we establish intimacy; as intimacy is achieved, the need to continue displaying physical affection appears to decline.[71] Although we might engage in touching without having feelings of affection or have feelings of affection without being physically demonstrative, physical affection depends on both parts—the physical (actual behavior) and the emotional (affection). Physical affection, in and of itself, is not unique to romantic relationships. It is also a part of our interactions with friends and family—hugs, kisses, and snuggling, for example. However, physical affection can also occur as a precursor to sexual activity or in concert with sexual activity.

The ultimate goal of many romantic relationships is producing children and a family; sex is obviously the way to accomplish this goal. However, humans frequently engage in sexual intercourse with no intention of producing children, which makes the role of sex in romantic relationships complex and perplexing. Besides a desire to procreate, sex can be motivated by a desire to feel valued by the partner, to show that the partner is valued, to release stress, to show or feel power, for pleasure, and to nurture the partner.[72] Motivation to engage in sex has been linked to people's attachments styles (discussed in Chapter 2), with attachment anxiety related to engaging in sex to please a partner and express love.[73] The stronger a person's attachment avoidance, the less sex occurs as an expression of love, a show of intimacy, or to please the partner, and the more it occurs to avoid angering the partner.[74] Traditionally, sexual activity and intercourse were reserved for marriage, as they still are for some. However, romantic relationships today most often involve and are even defined by sexual activity, and sex occurs even outside the bounds of romantic relationships. Research shows that relationship satisfaction in intimate relationships (married and dating couples) positively correlates with sexual satisfaction, but this correlation might be because another variable (such as good communication) is responsible for both relationship and sexual satisfaction.[75]

Talking to your partner about sex, self-disclosure, and discussing previous sexual activity all affect both sexual and relational satisfaction. Talking about sexual intentions and desires was found to increase sexual satisfaction, relational satisfaction, and intimacy.[76] In one study, those who engaged more in nonsexual self-disclosing and those whose partners disclosed sexual information were more likely to disclose sexual expectations, which in turn related to sexual and relational satisfaction.[77] Explicit communication surrounding first sex creates a more accurate shared perception and

BEING Other-ORIENTED

Not understanding a romantic partner can have a negative impact on sustaining the relationship. Think about the period when you felt closest to a former romantic partner. What types of love would your partner say you were sharing and expressing at that time? How does that impression compare with your view? How committed would your partner say he or she was to the relationship? How committed would your partner say you were? How satisfied and comfortable was your partner with the physical affection you displayed? Your uncertainty or inability to answer these questions might reflect a need to better understand your romantic partners.

physical affection The use of touch to convey emotional feelings of love and caring for another person.

reduces uncertainty about both sexual and relational expectations.[78] You might find such open discussion about your sexual history and expectations threatening. In some instances, such disclosures might even damage the relationship. Nonetheless, informing partners about potential risks by disclosing previous sexual activity is considered a safe-sex practice. However, 32 percent of students in one survey reported withholding this information from at least one partner, and 17 percent withheld it from all their partners; in addition, 25 percent misrepresented their sexual histories.[79] Such deceptions ultimately impair relational development and intimacy. In exclusive romantic relationships, especially marriage, infidelity is a form of deception that similarly puts a partner at risk. Agreeing to an exclusive sexual relationship might be more about committing to an intimate, romantic relationship than about limiting sexual partners; infidelity thus threatens the very essence of the relationship. As you develop your own romantic relationships, strive to be as direct and explicit as you can in discussing your expectations for all aspects of the relationship, including sex.

From Friendship to Romance

Many romantic relationships begin as friendships. Establishing friendship-based intimacy first is an effective way to determine, with less risk and commitment, the potential for a more passion-based relationship. With the primary focus on compatibility, attraction, and other qualities of friendship, if the relationship fails to escalate or no romantic relationship develops, the end result is less loss of intimacy.

To move from friendship to romance involves adding passion-based intimacy to the existing friendship-based intimacy. This transition to a romantic relationship is accompanied by causal and/or reflective turning points, such as significant and intimate self-disclosure, a shared interaction that is seen as a "first date," or the occurrence of sex.[80] Such turning points might precipitate relationship talk: discussing roles and expectations, assessing the costs and rewards (benefits and risks), managing dialectical tensions (particularly the balance between autonomy and connectedness), and managing the relationship within each partner's social networks.

However, a direct statement of a desire for a romantic relationship could be face-threatening to both parties, and even a failure event, if it violates an agreement to remain platonic. The dilemma is further complicated by the fact that expressing such a desire might cause the loss of the friendship, but not expressing the desire might mean a missed opportunity for romance.[81] In such a situation, you might be better served by using *secret tests* to reduce uncertainty about the partner's feelings and to indirectly signal your interest.[82] A **secret test** is a behavior strategically chosen to indirectly determine a partner's feelings. For example, you might rely on indirect suggestions (hinting or joking about becoming romantic to test your partner's response); separation tests (decreasing or eliminating time together to see if you are missed, or not contacting your partner to see whether he or she will initiate contact); endurance tests (increasing demands on or costs to your partner to see whether he or she is willing to "pay" the price to sustain the relationship); and triangle tests (disclosing potential romantic relationships to test for jealousy, or determining your partner's interest in others to test his or her fidelity to you).[83] Each secret test is intended to determine your partner's interest and commitment to the relationship, while protecting your face and the relationship.

The First Date and Dating

So when is a social interaction with someone considered just hanging out, and when is it a date? Calling an interaction "a date" changes expectations, roles, and the relationship. When you label an interaction with someone as a date, you are usually signaling an openness to a romantic relationship with the other person. "Dating" tends to be the term for any ongoing romantic relationship that precedes "being engaged."

secret test Behavior designed to indirectly determine a partner's feelings.

We can learn the skills that can help us reduce the interpersonal tensions that most of us feel at the start of a relationship.

So what is a date? Maybe you've never been on one. Regardless of how you initiated and developed romantic relationships in high school and college, dates and dating play a significant role in the development of romantic relationships outside of school.

If you are a typical college student between the ages of 18 and 21, then most of your experiences with the opposite sex have probably occurred in group interactions and as "hooking up." Sociologist Kathleen Bogle writes that hooking up has essentially replaced dating on college campuses.[84] Although the term *hooking up* has lots of meanings, generally students use it to describe a nonromantic, short-term, physical encounter. Hooking up is like being friends with benefits, but without the friendship requirement. The level of physical intimacy ranges from kissing to sexual intercourse, and the interaction is generally without attachment, although some students, particularly women, report hoping for more.[85] Bogle found that most hookups were not one-night stands or "randoms" with strangers, but rather encounters between friends or classmates, often preceded by the consumption of alcohol. Although it happens infrequently, hookups *can* lead to romantic relationships, particularly if the hookup produced a positive emotional experience for both partners, there was some small talk and talk of future interactions, and both had similar motivations.[86]

Given the limited number of dates college students experience, it is understandable that they would have different goals for and expectations of a date than would other single adults. Both groups see dates as activity-focused events involving couples sharing information to reduce uncertainty.[87] However, college students see dates as more social, more public, and more about attraction.[88] Single adults see dates as being more about both immediate enjoyment and a future relationship, initiated by one person, and involving someone's paying for whatever activity is involved.[89] Bogle's interviews with recent graduates found that they had abandoned hooking up for dating, which for many was the first time they actually had been on a date.[90] If you are among those who have not been on a formal date, then understanding dating dynamics and your partner's expectations should help reduce your uncertainties and anxiety.

Moving from being friends to going on a date involves different issues and concerns than asking an acquaintance for a date. Students in one study were asked to imagine asking for a date with a classmate who might not even know their name.[91] The students reported they would feel anxiety, fear, and discomfort, but also excitement, a sense of pride in taking a risk, and a positive feeling for finally making the attempt. They hoped the other person would feel flattered and maybe good or great, but also saw the possibility for uncertainty, surprise, awkwardness (maybe even creepiness), or discomfort. Among the general concerns students expressed about asking for a date were the possibility of rejection, discovery that the other was already involved, uncertainty about what the person was really like, lack of reciprocal interest, and awkwardness in future class periods. Students also expressed concerns about their own physical attractiveness, as well as about appearing too pushy, too desperate, a "psycho," a fool or stupid, or a loser.

To actually ask someone for a date probably requires feeling that the risk is worth the potential loss of face, that the predicted outcome value of the relationship is high, and that you see a good chance that your request will actually be accepted. You could use secret tests to reduce some uncertainty about the other person's interest, find out what your mutual friends know about him or her, use affinity-seeking strategies (such as showing up at activities or parties you know the other person will be attending), or simply get more acquainted before seeking a date.

So what happens on a date? People bring to dates expectations about how the date will proceed. How a date proceeds depends on your relationship with the other person prior to the date, the event that is the focus of the date (a concert, a movie, a party), the cost of the date, and who initiated the date. Nonetheless, one study found that respondents shared many of the same expectations for a first date.[92] These expectations, reflecting traditional gender roles, included men picking up the women and taking them home, as well as paying for the date, even if the women initiated the date. Men were more likely to expect more than kissing, especially if the women initiated the date. Besides the expectation that the couple will engage in the agreed-on activity (going to a movie, for coffee, to a party), a significant expectation is that dating partners will talk. Talk is an important component of a date because both partners understand the need to begin self-disclosing and gaining information about each other to reduce uncertainty. As the date winds down, both have an expectation that there will be some discussion of future plans to call or text each other, an expression of interest in getting together again, and perhaps some discussion of another date, either specifically or generally. Neither partner wants to be put in a position of having to directly reject the other, so in order for each person to save face, plans for the future are usually rather vague.

The indirect manner in which we often choose to communicate, particularly when dating, causes misperceptions and awkwardness. For example, when asked why you don't ask someone out, you are likely to indicate a fear of rejection. However, you are likely to assume the reason the other person doesn't ask *you* out is because he or she lacks sufficient interest in you.[93] Sadly, the other person might be just as interested in a date but also fear rejection. Another problem is that when women confirm their attraction and affection toward their dates with smiles and other positive nonverbal affiliative cues, men may read these behaviors as cues of sexual interest.[94] Both examples reflect difficulties in reading another person's nonverbal cues and the need to practice the suggestions discussed in Chapter 7 for improving your nonverbal sensitivity. Although there is an inherent taboo about directly discussing attraction and

---

UNDERSTANDING OTHERS
Adapting to Differences

Male-Initiated versus Female-Initiated Date Requests

According to custom in the United States, men are expected to take the initiative in asking women out. While certain taboos or negative impressions have been associated with women initiating dates, more women seem to be taking this initiative. Communication scholars Paul Mongeau, Jerold Hale, Kristin Johnson, and Jacqueline Hillis examined male-initiated versus female-initiated date requests. For one part of their study, they created four written scenarios describing a male asking a female out, a male or a female initiating the date request after hints from the other, and a female asking a male out. More than four hundred student participants evaluated the females and males in these scenarios. In comparison to the woman who waited for the man to ask her out, the woman who directly asked the

man out was seen as more active, flexible, truthful, and extroverted; more of a feminist; more socially liberal; and less physically attractive (although no pictures were provided). Female students perceived the female initiator as more likeable and tactful than did the males.

What is your view of a woman who asks a man out for a first date? To what degree does your view differ if the woman asks the man to (a) go to a movie, (b) come over to her apartment for dinner, or (c) go to a party with her?

(Male students should answer these questions):

  Has a woman ever asked you out on a first date?

  How was your attitude toward her affected by her request?

(Female students should answer these questions):

  Have you ever asked a man out for a first date?

  How do you think the man's attitude toward you was affected by your request?

  If you haven't initiated a date with a man, how do you think a man would react if you did?

  Survey five or six of your male and female friends and collect their answers to the above questions. How similar are their responses? To what degree do males and females agree or disagree?

Source: P. A. Mongeau, J. L. Hale, K. L. Johnson, and J. D. Hillis. "Who's Wooing Whom? An Investigation of Female Initiated Dating," in P. J. Kalbleisch, Ed., *Interpersonal Communication: Evolving Interpersonal Relationships* (Hillsdale, NJ: Erlbaum, 1993), 51–68.

the relationship during the early part of dating, direct but tactful expression of interest, expectations, and goals by both parties contributes to clarity and understanding.

Unrequited Romantic Interest

What happens when you attempt to redefine a friendship as a romantic relationship, but your partner rejects your attempt? One partner's desire for a more intimate, romantic relationship than the other partner creates **unrequited romantic interest.** One study of college students found that unrequited romantic interest between friends was fairly common, leading to feelings of awkwardness and embarrassment; when students expressed their romantic interest, over half the relationships actually ended.[95] In friendships that persevered, both partners worked toward maintaining the friendship; the friendship was solid, long-established, open, and honest; and the partner who wanted more accepted that the feelings were not mutual. Friendships that ended did so because both partners felt embarrassed or awkward, the rejected partner felt hurt, and the other partner felt pressured to act differently. The results of this study suggest what you might do to preserve a friendship if your expression of romantic interest is not reciprocated:[96]

1. Affirm the importance of the friendship to you and continue to work on it.
2. Tell your partner you accept his or her position and then drop the issue.
3. To reduce embarrassment and awkwardness, try to go back to old relational patterns.
4. Avoid pressuring your partner to feel more than he or she does: Don't flirt, accept his or her interest in others, and give up on developing a romantic relationship.
5. Don't complain about the difference in feelings.
6. Don't suggest that maybe the relationship can be romantic sometime in the future.
7. Don't tell other friends about what happened.

On the other hand, how should you handle someone else's overtures to you if you don't feel the same way? People in this position tend to use either (1) indirect strategies—being rude or ambiguous or avoiding the other person; (2) a direct strategy without justification—simply stating a lack of reciprocal feelings; (3) a direct strategy of blaming themselves while stating lack of mutual interest ("I'm just not ready for a romantic relationship right now"); or (4) a direct strategy of blaming external factors while indicating lack of interest ("I'm involved with someone else").[97] Have you ever encountered such strategies, or have you used any of them? A study in which college students recalled times they expressed interest in developing a romantic relationship found that the results differed depending or whether the relationship was initially a friendship or was a romantic relationship that one person wished to deepen.[98] The indirect strategy was found to be the least desirable strategy for rejecting a friend's attempt to escalate the relationship, since it was seen as inappropriate. Similarly, blaming external factors was found to be undesirable for rejecting a romantic partner's attempt to escalate the relationship, perhaps because people don't expect a romantic partner to be evasive. Interestingly, students accepted rejection of their attempts to escalate friendships better than rejection of their attempts to escalate romantic relationships. We probably have expectations for romantic relationships to escalate as part of the relational development process, meaning that rejection of escalation is unexpected and disappointing. Regardless of whether you are the one whose effort to escalate a relationship is rejected or the one rejecting another's request, you both need to assess the

unrequited romantic interest
Feelings created when one partner desires a more intimate, romantic relationship than the other partner.

Relating to Others in the 21st Century

Friendship, Romance, and the Internet

Electronically mediated communication (EMC) provides avenues for initiating, maintaining, and ending both friendships and romantic relationships. A national survey of the Pew Internet & American Life Project found a growing number of adults on social networking sites like Facebook and MySpace in 2008, with 78 percent of 18–24-year-olds, 57 percent of 25–34-year-olds, and 20 percent of 35–44-year-olds surveyed reporting having an online profile.[99] However, your grandparents probably don't have online profiles, as only 7 percent of those 65 and older reported having them. Eighty-nine percent of the adults used such networks to stay in touch with friends; 57 percent used them to make plans with friends (compared with 72 percent of teens); and almost half used them to make new friends. Social networking sites provide opportunities for greatly expanding your network to include new people with whom you connect through listings of mutual friends.

Your profile provides information about you (some of which you might not even realize you are revealing) that affects other' impressions of you and that might either enhance or detract from a friendship.

For example, one study found that with everything else held constant, a person whose profile included 302 friends was rated as more socially attractive than one reporting 102, 502, 702, or 902 friends.[100] Those with 102 friends (who were perhaps seen as too aloof) and those with 902 friends (who were perhaps too indiscriminate) were the least attractive. Those with 502 friends were seen as the most extroverted, and those with 102 or 302 friends were seen as the least.

In face-to-face interactions, you control and tailor what you disclose, withholding information from those you are less interested in. Your online profile also involves self-disclosing, and you choose what to include or exclude—relationship status, attitudes, beliefs, interests, names of clubs or organizations you belong to, your online group memberships, pictures, video clips, quiz results. However, unlike your tailored, face-to-face disclosures, the information in your online profile is not restricted. Your wall and your posts are also visible. Anyone you accept as a friend—whether a new acquaintance, a romantic partner, a parent, or a best friend—has access to the same information. And those

people can cut and paste any of that information and circulate it freely to others.

Can you form intimate romantic relationships strictly through the Internet? Assuming an open and honest exchange of information, individuals can learn as much about another person through e-mail disclosures as they might in face-to-face interactions. In another survey by Pew in 2005, 11 percent of respondents reported having visited an online dating site; however, 66 percent viewed online dating as dangerous because it requires placing personal information online.[101] Nonetheless, of those visiting a dating site, 43 percent actually went on dates, and 17 percent developed long-term relationships or got married.[102] Friends can also act as go-betweens, suggesting an e-mail exchange or instant messaging between individuals they think could hit it off. EMC provides the opportunity for appropriately introduced individuals to enter the acquaintance stage of a relationship by sharing information and engaging in casual banter before moving to the exploration stage. Online networks such as Facebook can also allow people to initiate romantic relationships.

type of relationship you are willing to accept and decide whether such a relationship is possible, knowing that one of you feels more romantically inclined than the other.

Skills and Strategies for Developing Interpersonal Relationships

So far, this chapter has focused on the nature of friendship and romantic relationships. Now the focus shifts to discussing specific strategies and skills for starting, escalating, and maintaining those relationships. The skills described are not fail-safe, and the lists provided are not complete—they are intended primarily to stimulate consideration of your own thoughts and behaviors as you develop new relationships. Some skills are better suited for developing friendships and others for romance, but the foundations for both are similar.

When you meet someone you initially like, how do you go about fostering a friendship or a romance? Once you have established a relationship, how do you ensure that it remains healthy and at the level of intimacy with which you are most comfortable? The following three sections provide strategies you can use to address these questions. The first section discusses skills and strategies used primarily to initiate

So what are online romantic relationships like? In a recent study, 202 online participants described their online romantic relationships, identifying in their narratives five recurring themes:[103]

1. Experiencing intense emotions of attraction and love

2. Needing to be cautious and wary

3. Feeling a strong sense of connection based solely on words, but missing physical intimacy and becoming bored

4. Engaging in an extramarital affair through the online romance

5. Coping with negative reactions to the relationship from friends and family.

Satisfaction with online romantic relationships is affected by such factors as trust, intimacy (perceived closeness), and communication satisfaction (measured by enjoyment of conversations, perceived ease of conversations, interest, and ability to say what one wants).[104] You can easily see why communication satisfaction is a key element of EMC-based romantic relationship satisfaction, since such relationships are so dependent on

effective and satisfying communication in the absence of shared activities or direct observation of behaviors.[105] The more times online romantic couples communicate during the week, the more they appear to experience communication satisfaction, trust, intimacy, commitment, similarity, and ability to predict their partners' behaviors.[106] Couples in relationships primarily or exclusively maintained on the Internet report that they maintain their relationships using openness (self-disclosing, providing and seeking advice, and talking about the relationship) and positivity (being cheerful and making the interactions pleasant).[107]

While developing loving, romantic, online-only relationships is possible, couples often end up exchanging photos, engaging in webcam conversations, and may eventually meet face to face, as 36 percent of the participants in one study reported doing.[108] An interesting issue facing online romantic partners is whether to sustain the relationship totally online, where it might endure indefinitely, or to meet face to face, which increases the likelihood of the relationship's coming to an end if the individuals dis-

cover they are incompatible offline. The transition to offline relationships is a significant turning point in an online relationship, because it tests one's belief in the honesty of the partner and in one's own personal safety. The physical distance between partners affects the decision to meet, with partners who are in the same geographical area incurring less expense and fewer restrictions. Flying across the country or around the world to meet requires a strong sense of potential success, compared to a cross-town meeting.

interaction. The next section covers skills and strategies used in both initiating and escalating relationships. The final section focuses on skills used in either maintaining a relationship or moving it toward more intimacy once it has been established.

Skills and Strategies Used Primarily to Initiate a Relationship

There are two paths to relationship initiation, depending on whether the people involved have reached the pre-interaction awareness stage of relationship development. One path begins with interacting with a complete stranger for the very first time. The other begins after you have observed and formed an initial impression of the other person before interacting. The following sections explain some of the principles to follow as you proceed down either of these two paths.

Observe and Act on Approachability Cues. Subway riders around the world learn to avoid eye contact because it is a signal of approachability. Besides making eye contact, you can choose to signal approachability by turning toward another person, smiling, being animated, using an open body posture, winking, and waving. In the absence of these cues, we generally conclude that a person wants to be left alone. Saying hello lets people know that you are approachable, and it tests approachability.

If the other person responds with a warm smile and a few words, then the door might be open for further interaction. But if the person gives you a silent half-smile and hurries on, you can take this as a signal that the door is closed.

Identify and Use Conversation Starters.

By being observant, you can identify a certain amount of "free" information that you can use as a starting point for a conversation. If someone is walking a dog of the same breed as your childhood pet, you can open a conversation by commenting on some peculiarity of the breed. If someone is carrying a book from a class you took last semester, you might ask how the course is going. Logos on T-shirts, tags or stickers on backpacks, or even tattoos can be conversation starters. There is no perfect line to use to begin a conversation, so being direct is probably your best bet.[109]

Follow Initiation Norms.

Many of the initial interactions in a relationship are almost ritualistic, or at least scripted. In the United States, when two strangers meet for the first time, they typically follow the same general pattern of conversation:[110] greetings; introductions; discussion of initial topics such as the weather, hometown, majors, education, or occupations; followed by discussion of general topics such as sports, TV, movies, or family. If the conversation goes well, they might discuss getting together, and then end by exchanging pleasantries, closing the conversation, and saying goodbye. As you follow the script, take advantage of opportunities to expand and develop the conversation in safe ways. Listen for details about the person's background and interests that you can inquire about, and share information about your own interests.

Following a script provides some comfort and security because it reduces the uncertainties associated with meeting a stranger; deviating from the script might increase uncertainty and be a turnoff. For example, how would you react to a stranger who begins with "Nice to meet you, too. Don't you agree that television is becoming the vast wasteland of American intellect, draining the very life blood of our youth?" You might be leery of continuing this interaction.

Ask Questions.

The very act of asking questions can enhance your partner's attraction to you.[111] Asking questions shows your interest in the other person and promotes reciprocity of liking. Asking questions allows you to gain information, reduce uncertainty, and improve your ability to adapt to your partner. Ask open questions that invite elaboration and discussion, and learn to ask meaningful follow-up or probing questions without appearing to interrogate the other person. Starting with impersonal, specific questions, often about the circumstance or surroundings, encourages a response by reducing a person's reluctance to answer (for example, while standing in a movie line, you might ask "Have you heard any reviews of this movie?"). After the initial question, advance the conversation by asking open and encompassing questions related to his or her answer ("What did the reviewers have to say?").

Short responses without any reciprocal questions may be a signal that the person you're talking to is not particularly interested in interacting. If so, you're probably better off not pursing the interaction any further. Usually, however, the other person will also ask you questions. Be open and provide information about yourself that is relevant to the questions.

Recognize that the thoughts and feelings that might be evoked by your questions will differ from person to person. A question that is easy and comfortable for you to answer may not be for others. Be sensitive to how the other person responds to your questions, and be prepared to adapt your comments appropriately. Other-oriented communication skills can help you manage sensitive situations. Be prepared to adapt to any unusual response or nonverbal cues you observe.

Don't Expect Too Much from the Initial Interaction. Initial interactions do not necessarily determine the future of a relationship; the scripted nature of an initial interaction limits the opportunity to achieve an in-depth relationship. Regardless of how the first conversation might seem to go, if you sense relationship potential, you should follow up with a suggestion that the two of you get together again; the other person's response will be a gauge of his or her interest. Many relationships have started out awkwardly, with both partners feeling less than enthusiastic about the encounter, but when given the chance to interact again, they develop a more positive perspective.

Skills and Strategies Used to Initiate and/or Escalate Relationships

"No kidding! I love chocolate-covered strawberries, too." "It's nice to be able to talk to someone else who's a fan of *Survivor*." Statements like these emphasize commonalities and are used to encourage a listener to like the speaker (*affinity seeking*). We sometimes make these types of statements when we are first getting to know someone, but we also use such statements when trying to escalate a relationship. Trying to increase someone's attraction to us is just one strategy that is common to both the initiation and the escalation of interpersonal relationships.

Communicate and Cultivate Attraction. Communicating your attraction to someone increases the likelihood that your partner will reciprocate, thus cultivating his or her attraction to you. Simply spending time talking is one way to show interest and commitment. You can also use indirect strategies to communicate your liking, such as nonverbal immediacy, and direct strategies such as verbal cues. For instance, you might sit closer to someone, make more eye contact, increase your touching, lean forward, and smile more. Verbally, you might use more informal and personal language and the person's first name and increase your use of "you and I" and "we." You display and cultivate interest by asking questions and probing for details, listening responsively, and referring to previously shared information. All these behaviors confirm that you value the other person and what he or she is saying, which can be very rewarding. A more subtle approach would be to offer a compliment, such as praise for a particular trait or ability, outfit, hairstyle, or the way the person handled an irritating customer. Table 11.1 lists other ways we try to increase another person's liking of us, using what are labeled **affinity-seeking strategies.**[112] Displaying nonverbal immediacy cues and verbally confirming the other person not only communicate your attraction to the other person but also increase the likelihood that he or she will like you.

Be Open and Self-Disclose Appropriately. You need to self-disclose to other people so they can decide whether to progress with a relationship with you. Even if you have enough information about your partner and want to escalate the relationship, your partner might not know enough about you. Chapter 9 discussed the need for mutual self-disclosure to form a truly intimate relationship. Restricting the amount of self-disclosure is one way to control the development of a relationship. For example, you can reduce how much you are self-disclosing if you feel a relationship is moving too fast. The level of self-disclosure needs to be appropriate to the level of development of the relationship, and both partners must be sensitive to the timing of disclosures.

BEING Other-ORIENTED

A lack of specific knowledge about a new acquaintance means that being other-oriented involves drawing on your own thoughts, feelings, and perspective to understand the other person, and/or drawing on your understanding of people in general. Which of the affinity-seeking strategies listed in Table 11.1 would raise your attraction to another person the most? Which do you believe would raise the attraction of other people in general the most? What information are you most comfortable disclosing? What information do you think most people in general are comfortable disclosing? What do you want to learn initially to reduce your uncertainties? What do you think most people want to learn?

affinity-seeking strategy A strategy we use to increase others' liking of us.

TABLE 11.1	**Affinity-Seeking Strategies**	
	Strategies	**Examples**
1. Control	Present yourself as in control, independent, free-thinking; show that you have the ability to reward the other person.	• "I'm planning on going to grad school, and after that I'm going to Japan to teach English." • "You can borrow my notes for the class you missed if you'd like."
2. Visibility	Look and dress attractively; present yourself as an interesting, energetic, and enthusiastic person; increase your visibility to the other person.	• "Wow, that was a great show about Chinese acrobats. I do gymnastics, too. Would you like to come watch me next week in our dual meet?"
3. Mutual Trust	Present yourself as honest and reliable; display trustworthy behaviors; self-disclose to show that you trust the other person.	• "That guy you're having problems with called me and asked about you. I told him I didn't have anything to say." • "I've never told anyone this, but I've always hoped I could find my birth parents."
4. Politeness	Follow appropriate conversational rules; let the other person assume control of the interaction.	• "I'm sorry I interrupted. I thought you were done. Please, go on." • "No, you're not boring me at all; it's very interesting. Please tell me more about it."
5. Concern and Caring	Show interest in and ask questions about the other person; listen; show support and be sensitive; help the other person accomplish something or feel good about himself or herself.	• "How is your mother doing after her operation?" • "I'd like to help out at the benefit you're chairing this weekend." • "That must have been really hard for you, growing up under those conditions."
6. Other-Involvement	Put a positive spin on activities you share; draw the other person into your activities; display nonverbal immediacy and involvement with the other person.	• "This is a great party. I'm glad you came." • "A group of us are going to get a midnight snack; how about coming along?"
7. Self-Involvement	Try to arrange for encounters and interactions; engage in behaviors that encourage the other person to form a closer relationship.	• "Oh hi! I knew your class ended at two, so I thought I'd try to catch you." • "It would really be fun to go camping together this summer; I have this favorite place."
8. Commonalities	Point out similarities between yourself and the other person; try to establish equality (balanced power); present yourself as comfortable and at ease around the other person.	• I've got that computer game, too. Don't you love the robots?" • "Let's work on the project together. We're a great team." • "It's so easy to talk to you. I really feel comfortable around you."

Source: Adapted from R. A. Bell and J. A. Daly, "The Affinity Seeking Function of Communication," *Communication Monographs* 51 (1984): 91–115.

Gather Information to Reduce Uncertainty. We all seem to get uneasy when faced with the unknown or the unexpected, including interactions with strangers whose behavior we cannot predict or unexpected behaviors from our friends. According to **uncertainty reduction theory,** we want control and predictability in our lives; therefore, when we are faced with uncertainty, we are driven to gain information to reduce that uncertainty.[113] Generally, we gather as much information as we can about our partners to increase predictability and reduce anxiety. We are particularly motivated to gain information early in a relationship, when

uncertainty reduction theory
Theory that people seek information to reduce uncertainty, thus gaining control and predictability.

uncertainty is greatest and when we are trying to evaluate the relationship's predicted outcome value.[114] We also are likely to seek out information if others behave
in unexpected ways.[115] If your close friend who watches *South Park* every night
suddenly begins reading during that time slot, you'll probably want to reduce your
uncertainty about this unexpected behavior, so you'll ask why. Besides asking direct questions, we can decrease uncertainty by engaging in active perception, explicitly seeking information from other people, and using secret tests.

Sometimes we experience uncertainty about the very nature and definition of
our relationships and our partners' regard for us. Such uncertainty can hamper the
development, escalation, and maintenance of those relationships. What does your
new friend think about the relationship? How intimate a relationship does your
boyfriend or girlfriend want? Why hasn't your best friend called you in the last two
weeks? The most obvious approach to addressing these questions would be simply
to ask the other person; however, we risk "losing face" in using such direct strategies to reduce uncertainty. There are also times when uncertainty is preferable to
certainty—for example, uncertainty about your romantic partner's desire to end
the relationship can be preferable to finding out for sure. Researchers Leanne
Knobloch and Denise Solomon have conducted numerous studies on uncertainty
in relationships. In one study, they found that uncertainty hampered the ability to
identify and interpret relational information, while also making interactions more
difficult (for example, it can lead partners to be overly concerned about avoiding
certain topics).[116] However, these researchers also believe that the more intimate
the relationship, the more likely we are to use direct approaches to reduce uncertainty, which means stronger communication and the possibility of more positive
outcomes.[117] In general, our level of satisfaction in a relationship is linked to feelings of certainty,[118] because the relationships that are the most satisfying are also
those in which partners have a strong mutual understanding and a shared vision of
the relationship.

Listen Actively and Respond Confirmingly.

As you learned in Chap-
ter 5, listening is critical to effective interpersonal communication and relationships. Listening clues you in to people's needs, wants, and values, and it enables
you to respond to people in appropriate ways. You gain information by listening,
but you also demonstrate your ongoing interest in the other person. In all relationships, no matter how intimate, it is always important to stop, look, and listen—to
put down the newspaper or turn off your iPod when your close friend begins talking to you. You also need to listen actively and provide confirming responses, as
discussed in Chapter 5. Using confirming responses increases your partner's sense
of self-worth and communicates the value you place on him or her.

Socially Decenter and Adopt an Other-Oriented Perspective.

Social decentering helps you better understand your partner, and that understanding allows you to choose effective strategies for accomplishing your communication goals, adapting to your partner's current behavior, and anticipating his or her
responses. For example, on a first date, would you tell your partner about a very intimate relationship that had just ended, or would you wait? What information do
you have that can help you determine this person's reaction? Would *you* want
someone you just met to tell you about his or her recent breakup? How would most
people feel about hearing that information so early?

Even individuals weak in general social decentering skills can develop
relationship-specific social decentering—decentering skills based on the knowledge

**relationship-specific social
decentering** Other-oriented skills
based on the knowledge and
understanding gained in a specific
intimate relationship.

"You want me to talk about my feelings?
Okay – I feel like talking about sports."

and understanding they have gained in a specific intimate relationship. In studies conducted by one of your authors, respondents' relationship-specific social decentering scores were higher the more intimate the relationship, and both partners also had higher relational satisfaction.[119] The study does not show which causes which—whether increases in intimacy increase relationship-specific social decentering, or whether increases in relationship-specific social decentering lead to greater intimacy. Nonetheless, we usually expect our intimate partners to understand us and to adapt accordingly. Failure to display relationship-specific social decentering behaviors is likely to create dissatisfaction and possibly lead to an end of the relationship. As you develop intimate relationships, your interactions with your partner should reflect your understanding and appreciation of your partner's thoughts, feelings, and needs.

Skills and Strategies Used to Maintain and/or Escalate Relationships

Certain skills and strategies can be used to keep a relationship at a given stage or to further escalate it. These skills can be continually improved, and while you might not be adept at all of them, the absence of most of them will likely undermine relational satisfaction for you or your partner.

Express Emotions. Expressing emotions is a particular form of self-disclosure—sometimes the most intimate kind—which is why trust and commitment usually must be established before certain feelings can be shared. You might be uncomfortable expressing your feelings, but in order for a relationship to fully develop, you will need to share them. The more intimate the relationship, the higher the expectation and need for sharing feelings. You might show your love for someone by your behaviors, but your partner might need you to actually declare your love; the words "I love you" are powerful and enduring.

Many of the emotions you share are not related to your partner, such as your sadness over the death of a family member, or fears about what you'll do after graduation. Other feelings relate to your partner—feelings of attraction, love, anger, or disappointment. Most of us are comfortable sharing positive emotions, such as happiness and joy, but are more reserved about sharing negative emotions, such as fear or disappointment, because of a concern that we might appear weak or vulnerable. In a study of 46 committed, romantic couples, the participants reported that the number-one communication problem was partners' withholding the expression of negative feelings ("When she gets upset, she stops talking" or "He just silently pouts").[120] We generally want to know how our intimate partners are feeling, even if those feelings are negative.

However, a constant barrage of negative expressions can also alienate a partner. Not surprisingly, research has found that marital satisfaction rises with the number of positive feelings the partners disclose, not with the number of negative ones.[121] Happy couples tend to display their positive emotional state in their smiles, laughs, and affectionate behavior; distressed couples display agitation, anger, and coldness.[122]

In a balanced relationship, partners can express both positive and negative emotions at the right times in a constructive and confirming manner.

Provide Comfort and Social Support.

The ability to provide comfort, social support, and ego support is a quality associated with being a best friend.[123] We expect to be able to turn to our friends to help us through emotionally trying events. Offering social support and comfort not only directly benefits the partner but also confirms the value of the relationship and the partner. Communication scholar Brant Burleson found that being other-oriented was a key factor in being able to offer effective comforting messages. Other-oriented comforting messages confirm and accept the other person's feelings, help him or her express and examine those feelings, and help put the feelings into a broader context.[124] One research study found three outcomes of comforting messages: (1) They put the distressed person in a more positive mood, (2) they empower the person to better manage the issues, and (3) they help reduce brooding (rumination) about the problems.[125]

It can be challenging to provide social and emotional support, and sometimes our attempts even produce negative effects, making the situation worse and/or negatively affecting the other person's self-esteem.[126] For example, if you try to give a friend advice, you might be viewed as controlling or implying that your friend is incompetent at decision making (plus, the advice might be wrong!). Displaying empathy to a distressed friend by sharing your similar experiences can provide some insight but also risks disconfirming your friend, because you changed the discussion to focus on you and your life. Use social decentering to consider what you'd like to hear if you were in the other person's situation, while adapting to differences between you and the other person—what is comforting to one person can be threatening to another.

Well-adjusted couples display support and affection for each other through positive nonverbal cues.

One pair of researchers, Ruth Ann Clark and Jesse Delia, studied how people wanted to be treated by their friends in six different distressing situations.[127] Clark and Delia found that people did not have a strong desire to talk about the situations. When people were distressed, they wanted to be the ones to decide whether to bring up the issue. There was wide variation in how people wanted their friends to approach the six issues. Clark and Delia also found that people wanted their friends to keep attempts at comforting short. There are times where the best support involves saying nothing at all, but simply being with the other person or providing a hug. Another study found three behaviors on the part of comfort providers that were important in helping the partners manage the distress while maintaining face: (1) encouraging the partner to express and discuss feelings, (2) recognizing and praising the efforts already being made by the partner to cope with the problem, and (3) being pleasant and respecting the partner's autonomy to make decisions—not taking over control. How well do you do these things when providing comfort to others?[128]

Engage in Relationship Talk.

Relationship talk is talk about the nature, quality, direction, or definition of a relationship. For example, "I'm happy with how close we've become. How are you feeling about the relationship?" or "Since I'm about

relationship talk Talk about the nature, quality, direction, or definition of a relationship.

to graduate, it doesn't make too much sense to me to get very involved right now" or "I'd like to have more say in how we spend our time on the weekends." However, relationship talk is generally considered inappropriate in the early stages of a relationship, and if one partner starts talking about a relationship too early, it can scare the other person away.

Willingness to talk about the relationship is one way to implicitly signal your level of interest and commitment to it. One study of cross-sex friendships found that those in which both partners had an interest in becoming romantic included more relational talk than those in which the friends wished to maintain a platonic relationship.[129] As relationships move toward greater intimacy, the amount of direct relationship talk increases. For example, you are likely to discuss the future of the relationship, how to manage the relationship during summer break, or what will happen to the relationship after graduation. As a relationship escalates, we should be prepared to discuss our thoughts and feelings about it.

In more intimate relationships, relationship talk helps the partners resolve differences in their perceptions of the relationship that might be contributing to conflict and dissatisfaction. Although it can be difficult, expressing your concerns about whether you want the relationship to escalate or de-escalate might be unavoidable. Unwillingness to engage in relationship talk in an intimate relationship can send a negative message that ultimately drives a partner away. Relational talk appears to be viewed differently by men and women. Men tend to view talk as instrumental and as a way to fix problems. While women might share this view, they also see relationship talk as part of the routine for maintaining the relationship.[130] Relationship talk is not just about solving problems; it is an important part of maintaining the relationship.

Be Tolerant and Show Restraint. The most satisfying relationships are those in which both partners learn to accept the other and refrain from continually disagreeing, criticizing, pointing out flaws or failures, and making negative comments to each other. One study found that well-adjusted couples focus their complaints on specific behaviors, whereas maladjusted couples complain about each other's personal characteristics.[131] Well-adjusted couples are also kinder and more positive and have more humor in their interactions. They tend to agree with each other's complaints: "You're right honey, I wasn't listening—let me turn the TV off so I won't be distracted," whereas the partners in maladjusted relationships launch counter-complaints: "I *was* listening!—you just chatter on and on about the same garbage!" In addition, happy couples display more affection through positive nonverbal cues, display more supportive behaviors, and make more attempts to avoid conflict than unhappy couples do.[132]

Maintaining relationships requires tolerance. You must learn to accept your partners for who they are and put up with some things you dislike. When couples lose their tolerance, they begin focusing on and criticizing what they used to accept. Then relationships begin to deteriorate.

Manage Conflict Cooperatively. Conflicts are inevitable in interpersonal relationships. As relationships develop, the individuals share more personal information and spend more time together, so the likelihood for conflict increases. The key to successful relational development and maintenance is not to avoid conflict, but rather to manage it effectively. As we discussed in Chapter 8, a cooperative management style can actually transform conflict into an experience that strengthens a relationship. It can clarify the definition of a relationship, increase the exchange of information, and create a cooperative atmosphere for problem solving.

▶ RECAP   Skills and Strategies for Developing Interpersonal Relationships

Skills and Strategies Used Primarily to Initiate a Relationship

- Observe and act on approachability cues
- Identify and use conversation starters
- Follow initiation norms
- Ask questions
- Don't expect too much from the initial interaction

Skills and Strategies Used to Initiate and/or Escalate Relationships

- Communicate and cultivate attraction
- Be open and self-disclose appropriately
- Gather information to reduce uncertainty
- Listen actively and respond confirmingly
- Socially decenter and adopt an other-oriented perspective

Skills and Strategies Used to Maintain and/or Escalate Relationships

- Express emotions
- Provide comfort and social support
- Engage in relationship talk
- Be tolerant and show restraint
- Manage conflict cooperatively

APPLYING AN OTHER-ORIENTATION
to Friends and Romantic Partners

As you develop friendships and romantic relationships, you continue to gain more information about your partners—about their beliefs, values, attitudes, needs, interests, desires, fears, and hopes. This accumulation of knowledge provides the foundation for a better understanding and ability to predict your partners' behaviors and reactions and creates the expectation that you will anticipate and adapt to the person's behaviors and needs. From a partner's perspective, it is a failure event when you don't incorporate your accumulated knowledge and understanding of your partner into your actions. For example, forgetting that your friend dislikes horror movies when you rent a horror movie for your weekly Friday night movie is likely to evoke a comment such as "But you know I hate horror movies; I can't believe you rented it anyway." Imagine the impact on a relationship of frequently committing such failure events. Your partner might interpret your failure to be other-oriented and to adapt as a lack of caring and concern for his or

her needs and desires, or as a move toward withdrawing from the relationship.

On the other hand, increasing knowledge of your friends and romantic partners improves your ability to adapt to their behavior and to anticipate responses. Knowledge of your closest same-sex friend and closest cross-sex friend should lead you to unique interpretations of their behaviors and to adaptation of your behavior, particularly in your selection of relevant communication strategies. Such empowerment does not necessarily mean greater relational satisfaction. For example, understanding that your romantic partner's discomfort with physical affection is a result of his or her upbringing won't necessarily offset your own desire for physical affection.

The most significant challenge to being other-oriented in our friendships and romances is overcoming egocentric biases or distorted perceptions of our friends and lovers. In essence, we make errors in our mind-reading of others. The perceptual barriers identi-

fied in Chapter 3 undermine your ability to gain the accurate information needed to be other-oriented. Another error occurs when you assume similarities between you and your partner that don't really exist. Assuming similarity leads to projecting your feelings, motivations, and needs on your partner, which leads to errors when relevant differences are unaccounted for. On the other hand, when you and your partner are indeed similar, then such projecting can provide accurate understanding. A final barrier to effective other-orientation occurs when your perspective and your feelings are so strong that they prevent you from accurately recognizing your partner's perspective and feelings.[133] For example, after discovering that your partner has cheated on you, the weight of your emotional pain can prevent you from understanding your romantic partner's perspective. As a matter of fact, you might not even be motivated to try. Ultimately, the application of any other-orientation to your friendships and romantic relationships will require a motivation to do so.

Friendship
(pages 312–320)

Friends play an important part in our lives by providing support, helping us manage the mundane and cope with stress, shaping our personalities, and providing material help. Our friendships change as we move from childhood through adolescence, young adulthood, adulthood, and then late adulthood. Same-sex friendships for men and women have similarities and differences; for example, both men and women see intimacy in the same way, but women tend to view their friendships as more satisfying, enjoyable, and intimate than men do. Cross-sex friendships are generally nonsexual but some include sexual activity, as in friends with benefits. We also form intergenerational, intercultural, and interracial friendships. These friendships require a special sensitivity to how the differences affect our partner and the relationship.

Key Terms
Friendship-based intimacy *312*
Passion-based intimacy *312*

Critical Thinking Questions
1. What qualities are most important to you in a friend? Why?
2. How do your friendships with same-age friends differ from friendships you have with anyone substantially older or younger than you?
3. Ethics: What ethical responsibilities do you have toward a person you consider your best friend?
4. Ethics: Would you be okay with your spouse having a close friendship with someone of the opposite sex? Why or why not?

Activities
Write down all the qualities you can think of that you associate with being a friend. Now write down the qualities you associate with being an intimate romantic partner (lover). In groups of four or five students, compare your lists. What qualities have you listed that nobody else has? Why do you think you included that quality in your list? What qualities did everyone in the group list? To what degree are the qualities defined by your culture? Which qualities are the same for friends as for lovers? Which are different?

List five very close friendships between two TV characters. Think about those five friendships and write down the most positive qualities you see in them. Now list the negative qualities you see in those friendships. Which of the positive qualities do you exhibit the most in your own close friendships? Which of the negative qualities? How can you increase the positive qualities and reduce the negative ones?

Web Resources
http://www.queendom.com/jff_access/the_friendship_test.htm This site on relationships includes a self-test on friendship.

http://www.penpalworld.com/index.asp This web site is designed to put you in contact with pen pals throughout the world. This is a way to develop and explore online intercultural friendships.

Romantic Relationships
(pages 321–330)

Romantic relationships differ from friendships because lovers expect more, talk more about the relationship, and are more passionate, more intimate, and more committed. Three qualities particularly distinguish romantic relationships: love, commitment, and physical affection and sex. Passion, intimacy, and commitment are three dimensions that make up the triangular theory of love. Another theory defines six types of love: eros, ludis, storge, mania, pragma, and agape. Interpersonal communication plays a significant role in both relational and sexual satisfaction in romantic relationships. Some romances begin as friendships and either partner may use secret tests to determine the prospect for romance. Other romances begin with a first date, which differs from hooking up. Expectations for dating outside of college life tend to follow traditional gender roles. Some attempts to develop or escalate a romantic relationship are rejected, creating unrequited romantic interest.

Key Terms
Triangular theory of love *322*
Passionate love *323*
Companionate love *323*
Eros *323*
Ludis *323*
Storge *323*
Mania *323*
Pragma *324*
Agape *324*
Physical affection *325*
Secret test *326*
Unrequited romantic interest *329*

Critical Thinking Questions
1. Write a short answer to the question "What is love?" within the context of a romantic relationship. Why is defining love so difficult? How well do you think you know what love is? Why is love so important to humans?
2. What would be the best course of action if you found yourself becoming romantically interested in a friend with whom you had agreed not to become romantically involved?
3. Ethics: What types of secret tests to determine another person's feelings toward you are ethical? What type would you consider unethical?
4. Ethics: You are in a romantic relationship that has become physically intimate. How ethical is it for you to say, "I love you" if you really aren't sure you do? If your partner says "I love you," should you say it too, even if you don't mean it?

Activities

In your life right now, you love many things, even if you're not currently in a romantic relationship: You no doubt love your parents, siblings, and friends, and you may love beer, chocolate, vacations, or your car. Write down a list of the things you love. Now group the items together that depend on a similar meaning of love. Next, put down three words by each item or group of related items that describe your feelings without using the word *love*. Compare your results with classmates and decide the degree to which you agree on the meaning and use of the word *love*.

Web Resources

http//www.quizstop.com This site offers a wide variety of self-tests on love plus other subjects of interest.

http://www.askmen.com/dating/index.html This is a web site directed primarily to men that provides articles and advice on romance.

http://www.marsvenus.com/relationships/ This is a web site addressing a variety of relationship issues and includes self-tests. The site is associated with author John Gray, who wrote *Men Are from Mars, Women are from Venus*, and registration is required to access some material.

http://www.perfectlovestories.com/ This is a lovely site of poems, video, and music dealing with people's experiences of love.

Skills and Strategies for Developing Interpersonal Relationships
(pages 330–339)

A variety of strategies and skills can be applied to the initiation, maintenance, and escalation of interpersonal relationships. Certain skills and strategies are used primarily during the initiation of a relationship, including observing and acting on approachability cues, identifying and using conversation starters, following initiation norms, asking questions, and controlling expectations. Another set of skills and strategies is applicable to both the initiation of a relationship and the escalation of relationships toward greater intimacy. These include communicating and cultivating attraction with affinity-seeking strategies, being open and appropriately self-disclosing, gathering information to reduce uncertainty, listening actively and responding confirmingly, and socially decentering and adopting an other-oriented perspective. The final set of skills and strategies covered in this section are used primarily for maintaining existing relationships or moving a relationship toward greater intimacy. This set includes expressing emotions, providing comfort and

social support, engaging in talk about the relationship, being tolerant and showing restraint, and managing conflict cooperatively. All of these skills and strategies can be learned and enhanced to help you more effectively manage your interpersonal relationships.

Key Terms

Affinity-seeking strategies *333*
Uncertainty reduction theory *334*
Relationship-specific social decentering *335*
Relationship talk *337*

Critical Thinking Questions

1. Of all the skills for developing interpersonal relationships, which three are the most important? Why? Which three are the least important? Why?

2. Can a person have a happy and effective intimate relationship without having any of the interpersonal communication skills covered in this chapter? How? If not, why not?

3. Ethics: Assuming you were very skilled and adept at using strategies for developing interpersonal relationships, how ethical would it be for you to use those skills to satisfy your interpersonal needs in a given relationship, knowing that your partner was less skilled at getting his or her own needs met?

Activities

Which three of the skills for developing interpersonal relationships are your strongest? How do you know? Which three do you most need to improve? What can you do to improve them?

Describe two conversations you began with strangers that you think were successful. What made them successful? What was the outcome? Describe two conversations with strangers that you think were unsuccessful. What made them unsuccessful? Compare your responses to those of your classmates. To what degree are your answers similar or different? What did they do well that you could try? What did you learn to avoid?

Web Resources

http://www.csulb.edu/~tstevens/conversational_skills.htm This site includes a large number of tips on meeting people, carrying on conversations, and developing romance.

http://www.essortment.com/all/meetnewpeopl_rbhr.htm This site offers a list of 25 ideas and places for meeting new people.

Interpersonal Relationships: Family and Workplace

12

Think about the progression of relationships that you experience in your life: It starts with family and ends with family. In between, there's school for a few years and then work for quite a few more. You are born into a family—your first relationships are with your mother, father, siblings, grandparents, aunts and uncles, and cousins. And the longest-lasting relationships that you experience are with your siblings—longer than those with your parents or spouse. Outside the family, you form other important relationships—friendships and romantic relationships—and your workplace becomes one of the major contexts in which such relationships develop.

This chapter focuses on family and workplace relationships. In marriage, we make a public, legal commitment to another person; we seek societal recognition of an exclusive romantic relationship. Traditionally, marriage was a precursor to having children and a family. However, significant changes in what constitutes a family have occurred in the last forty years. Some of those changes and their impact on your future relationships are discussed later in this chapter.

Whereas marriage is a relationship of choice, families create relationships of circumstance. However, you can choose to be friends with other family members and thus create relationships of choice. Similarly, your workplace relationships with a boss, coworkers, or clients begin as relationships of circumstance. These relationships too can become relationships of choice if you elect to pursue them as friendships and even romantic relationships. The challenge of balancing professional and interpersonal relationships at work is another topic covered in this chapter.

> "Family isn't about whose blood you have. It's about who you care about. And that's why I feel like you guys are more than just friends. You're my family. Except for Cartman."
>
> Kyle, *South Park*

Family Relationships

Families have changed since your parents and grandparents were children. At one time, almost two-thirds of American families consisted of a working father, a stay-at-home mother, and at least two biological children. Today, according to the U.S. Bureau of the Census, around 10 percent of all American families fit that description. Divorce, single-parent families, mothers with careers outside the home, the longer wait to start families, the move from an agrarian to an industrial society, and increasing mobility all have dramatically altered the very nature of American families. Communication within the family has changed too. The way family members interact with one another has been altered by a variety of social influences, including electronically mediated communication.

Like many other entities covered in this book, families are dynamic and changing. Because the members of a family get older, roles and relationships change over time. In addition, families add members and lose others. As new children are born, or as a member moves out of the home, the dynamics of the family change. Ultimately, what is true of a family at one moment of time may not hold true later. By now you have already experienced the kinds of change that take place in families as you have become older and gone from being very dependent on your parents to becoming more independent. As you get older, you may discover that your relationship with your parents changes still more if you begin providing care for them. As you consider your own family experiences and apply the principles we discuss in this chapter, remember above all to continually monitor your family relationships and adapt accordingly.

Family Defined

You might think that because families are basic to human existence, there is no need for a formal definition of a *family*—but there is controversy as to what constitutes a family. Which of these constitute a "family" in your mind: a single mother and her child; two brothers sharing an apartment; two gay men living together and sharing a bank account; a lesbian couple raising two children; a husband and wife who have separated now that their children are grown?

Traditional definitions of a family focus on the roles of husbands, wives, and children who all live together under one roof. Here is one definition written by sociologist George Murdock in 1949:

> The family is a social group characterized by common residence, economic cooperation, and reproduction. It includes adults of both sexes, at least two of whom maintain a socially approved sexual relationship, and one or more children, of one's own or adopted, of the sexually cohabiting adults.[1]

More recently, sociologists Gilbert Nass and Gerald McDonald defined a family as

> a social group having specified roles and statuses (e.g., husband, wife, father, mother, son, daughter) with ties of blood, marriage, or adoption who usually share a common residence and cooperate economically.[2]

Other definitions of a family de-emphasize the traditional role of mother, father, and children, placing more emphasis on interpersonal relationships and personal commitment. Art Bochner's definition of a family echoes this relational emphasis. For him, the family is

> an organized, naturally occurring relational interaction system, usually occupying a common living space over an extended time period, and possessing a confluence of interpersonal images which evolve through the exchange of messages over time.[3]

Interpersonal communication scholar Mary Ann Fitzpatrick incorporates the transactional nature of interpersonal communication into her definition of family, which she defines as "groups of intimates with a history, a future, strong ties of loyalty and emotion, and a sense of identity and commitment."[4] For Fitzpatrick, communication is the key element that underlies the very existence of a family, with each of the elements in her definition rooted in and evolving from communication.

For our purposes in this chapter, we synthesize these perspectives to define the **family** as a self-defined unit made up of any number of persons who live or have lived in relationship with one another over time in a common living space, and who are usually, but not always, united by marriage and kinship.

The notion of "self-defined" is probably the most significant aspect of this definition. Two people who cohabit might think of themselves as close friends, but having a child together might cause them to redefine themselves as a family. We might also have friends about whom we declare "He's like a father to me" or "She's like a sister." Such a declaration is a statement of loyalty and commitment.[5] As the chapter opening line from *South Park* attests, the perception of any relationship as a family lies within the hearts and minds of the individuals. Maybe as you grew up, you spent so much time at a friend's house you were considered "one of the family." There is comfort in knowing that a friend can be a member of your family, and that a member of your family can be a friend.

family Self-defined unit made up of any number of persons who live or have lived in relationship with one another over time in a common living space and who are usually, but not always, united by marriage and kinship.

Family Types

The definition of *family* embraces a variety of types, and the type of family people are part of has a significant effect on the roles, relationships, and communication of the family members. As you consider some major family types, keep in mind that even within each type, there are variations. For example, a family consisting of a single mother raising two sons will have different dynamics than one composed of a single father raising two daughters.

Natural or Nuclear Family. A **natural or nuclear family** consists of a mother, a father, and their biological children. Changes in culture, values, economics, and other factors have rendered this once most traditional family type no longer typical. Today, such a family is sometimes called an *idealized natural family.*

Extended Family. An **extended family** includes additional relatives—aunts, uncles, cousins, or grandparents—as part of the family unit. Some extended families also include individuals who are not related by marriage or kinship but are treated like family.

Family of Origin. The **family of origin** type overlaps the others, since it refers to the family in which you were raised, no matter what type it is. It is in your family of origin that you learned the rules and skills of interpersonal communication and developed your basic assumptions about relationships. You may have been reared in more than one family of origin because of divorce and remarriage.

Blended Family. The increasingly common **blended family** consists of two adults and one or more children who come together as a result of divorce, separation, death, or adoption. The children are the offspring of other biological parents or of just one of the adults who are raising them. Blended families represent a multitude of possible relationship combinations. For example, in a blended family with children from two earlier families (aka *The Brady Bunch*), there are a multitude of relationship combinations generated between the biological parent, stepparent, stepchildren, biological siblings, stepsiblings, half-siblings, noncustodial biological parent, and noncustodial stepparent. Given so many relationships, communication becomes an even more significant factor in the development and maintenance of a healthy family. Although communication relates strongly to satisfaction in blended families, it is unclear whether more communication leads to greater satisfaction or whether greater satisfaction leads to more communication. Nonetheless, a recent study found that the more stepparents and stepchildren engaged in everyday talk, the more satisfied both were with the relationships.[6] At the same time, more everyday talk between the biological parent and children increased the children's relational satisfaction, but not that of the parent. The biological parent's everyday talk with the stepparent related to greater satisfaction for the stepparent, but not for the biological parent. Another study found that stepfamilies that function well not only engage in everyday talk but also spend time together having fun and developing a sense of unity and shared purpose, have clear rules and boundaries within and across families, engage in family problem solving, and promote a positive image of the noncustodial parent.[7]

Families with adopted children might struggle with creating a unified sense of family, particularly if the adopted children are physically different from other family members. Families adopting children from different ethnic or racial groups may experience a dialectical tension between creating a family identity yet still honoring the children's biological heritage. Should a family in Iowa raising a child from China raise the child with a sense of Chinese culture?

natural or nuclear family Mother, father, and their biological children.

extended family Relatives such as aunts, uncles, cousins, or grandparents and/or unrelated persons who are part of a family unit.

family of origin Family in which a person is raised.

blended family Two adults and their children. Because of divorce, separation, death, or adoption, the children are the offspring of other biological parents or of just one of the adults who are raising them.

Factors that create variation among adoptive families include the age at which the child was adopted, the presence of the parents' biological children or other adopted children, and the history or background of the adopted child. One factor that affects a sense of family is the degree to which the adoption is kept secret.[8] The social stigma that once was attached to adoption has greatly diminished, and rather than have the "big talk" in which a child is told he or she is adopted, parents are encouraged to engage in an ongoing dialogue that includes the sharing of narratives or stories about how the child came to be placed for adoption and how the parents came to adopt the child.[9] Sometimes adoptive parents have very little information to share with the child, and other times the parents might feel the background story would hurt the child's sense of self-worth. But the lack of a story can create a sense of loss for the child.[10] Results of one study of adult adoptees found that about one-third of those interviewed felt no sense of loss or uncertainty surrounding their adoption. Almost all had adoptive parents who were open about the adoption and conveyed love and closeness.[11] Interestingly, the adoptees accepted the stories they were told even when those stories didn't seem true. They were viewed as part of the family stories. A little over one-third of the adoptees in the study felt some degree of uncertainty and loss, often associated with a lack of birth records or family stories, particularly for those who differed physically from their adoptive families. The final third of the adoptees reported a high degree of uncertainty and loss that left them feeling a gap in their identity. This group did not feel a sense of belonging to their adopted families. Their unsuccessful efforts to gain information about their birth parents often led to increased uncertainty and frustration. The families of this group of adoptees tended to be more secretive and not supportive of the children's attempts to find out more. Sometimes the children did not discuss their attempts because of fear of disapproval or of hurting the adoptive parents' feelings.

Single-Parent Family. Divorce, unmarried parenthood, separation, desertion, and death make the **single-parent family,** a family with one parent and at least one child, the fastest-growing type of family unit in the United States today. The different causes of single parenthood directly affect the nature of the parent-child relationships. Children of divorced parents who share joint custody still have ongoing relationships with both parents. However, the nature of those relationships is affected by the level of involvement each parent maintains in the children's lives, the degree to which one parent attempts to block or undermine the other parent's relationship with the children, and the degree to which the child supports or resists continuation of a given relationship.[12] Many such children must navigate between two households, essentially living in two single-parent families until one or both remarries. This navigation is affected by the relationship between the divorced parents, which can be one of three types: (1) conflicted coparenting (frequent conflicts, poor conflict management, and failure to emotionally disengage); (2) parallel coparenting (low conflict, low

Extended families, blended families, and single-parent families all involve unique relationships and communication patterns.

single-parent family One parent raising one or more children.

communication, and emotional disengagement); or (3) cooperative coparenting (good communication, coordination, and some flexibility in planning).[13] The mother is often made the custodial parent, and the resulting restricted visitation for the father leaves children frequently wanting more contact with their fathers.[14] Children often have an interest in equal timesharing, and those who actually have such arrangements report less sense of loss and less focus on the divorce than those in sole custody.[15]

In 2007, nearly four out of ten children in the United States were born to unmarried women.[16] Understanding the dynamics of such families is confounded by socioeconomic issues. Birth rates are considerably higher among unmarried Hispanic and Black women than among non-Hispanic White women.[17] The average age of unmarried mothers is 25, and they have an average of 2.3 children living with them.[18] One study found that almost 80 percent of unmarried mothers were employed the year after the birth, and many women were receiving some support from the child's father as well as from family, friends, and the government.[19] Despite such support, unmarried women typically have less income and more challenges in dealing with childcare than other mothers. Unmarried working mothers have less time for their children and depend on the children for more household contributions, including childcare. All of these factors affect the nature of the mother-child relationship as well as relationships among siblings. Like other families, families of unmarried mothers might strive to adopt the communication patterns typical of functioning two-parent families that are discussed in the next section.

Two Models of Family Interaction

Regardless of the type of family you have, communication plays a major role in determining the quality of family life. As shown in Figure 12.1, one research team found that over 86 percent of the families who reported family difficulty and stress said that communication was the key source of the problem.[20] Virginia Satir thinks good family communication is so important that she calls it "the largest single factor determining the kinds of relationships [we make] with others.[21] Psychologist Howard Markman found that the more positively premarital couples rated their communication with their partners, the more satisfied they were with their marriage relationships more than five years later.[22]

Circumplex Model. The **circumplex model of family interaction** was developed to explain the dynamics of both effective function and dysfunction within family systems.[23] The model's three basic dimensions, as indicated in Figure 12.2, are adaptability,

circumplex model of family interaction Model of the relationships among family adaptability, cohesion, and communication.

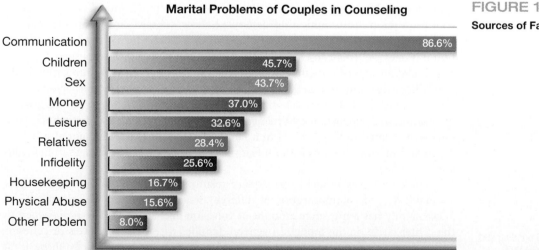

FIGURE 12.1

Sources of Family Difficulties

Marital Problems of Couples in Counseling

Communication	86.6%
Children	45.7%
Sex	43.7%
Money	37.0%
Leisure	32.6%
Relatives	28.4%
Infidelity	25.6%
Housekeeping	16.7%
Physical Abuse	15.6%
Other Problem	8.0%

FIGURE 12.2

**A Circumplex Model
of Family Interaction**

Source: Adapted from David H. L.
Olson, Candyce S. Russell, and
Douglas H. Sprenkle (Eds.), *Circumplex
Model: Systemic Assessment and
Treatment of Families* (New York:
Haworth Press, 1989). Used by
permission.

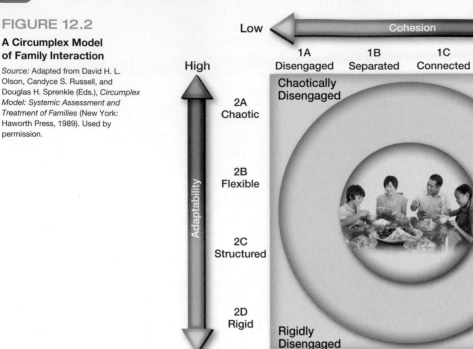

cohesion, and communication. Complete the Building Your Skills exercise about family systems to find out how these dimensions apply to your family. **Adaptability,** which ranges from chaotic to rigid, is the family's ability to modify and respond to changes in its own power structure and roles. For some families, tradition, stability, and historical perspective are important to a sense of comfort and well-being. Other families that are less tradition-bound are better able to adapt to new circumstances.

The term **cohesion** refers to the emotional bonding and feelings of togetherness that families experience. Family cohesion ranges from excessively tight, or enmeshed, to disengaged. Because family systems are dynamic, families usually move back and forth along the continuum from disengaged to enmeshed.

The third key element in the model—and the most critical one—is communication. It is not labeled in Figure 12.2 because *everything* in the model is influenced by communication. Communication determines how cohesive and adaptable families are. Communication keeps the family operating as a system. Through communication, families can adapt to change (or not) and maintain either enmeshed or disengaged relationships or something in between. The nature of the communication in the family has a direct impact on the development of family members' interpersonal communication skills. For example, one study found that the abilities to self-disclose, to offer emotional support, and to manage conflicts among friends and romantic partners were related to being raised in a family that supports learning about a diverse world and sharing opinions without fear of condemnation (a family high in flexibility and cohesion).[24]

adaptability Family's ability to modify and respond to changes in the family's power structure and roles.

cohesion Emotional bonding and feelings of togetherness that families experience.

The circumplex model helps explain relationships among family cohesiveness, adaptability, and communication at different stages of family development. A balanced family has a moderate amount of cohesion and adaptability—represented by the center circle on the model. In general, families with balanced levels of cohesion and adaptability function better across the entire family life cycle than do those at the extremes of these dimensions. Balanced families can often adapt better to changing

Building Your Skills | Identifying Your Family System

Choose the statement from each set of four that best describes the behavior typical of your family.

Level of Cohesion

1A. There is little closeness in my family. We are all pretty independent of each other. None of us have any real strong feelings of attachment to the family, and once the kids get to move out, there's not much drive to stay connected with the family.

1B. There is some closeness in my family and some interdependence, but not much—mainly we each do our own thing. The family usually gets together just for special occasions.

1C. My family is connected to each other, but we also have our independence. We get together at times besides just the holidays. There are feelings of loyalty to the family and we are pretty close to each other.

1D. My family is very close-knit and tight. We depend a lot on each other. We are always doing things together. There is nothing family members wouldn't do for each other. My family members feel a need for each other.

Level of Adaptability

2A. There are few rules about how to behave at the dinner table. My parents don't have a particular role at dinner. Family members come and go as they see fit.

2B. There are a few rules that govern dinner table behavior. My mom and dad are about equal in terms of who says what the kids should do, but the kids get a lot of say in what happens and how things are done. Both parents play a similar role.

2C. In my family, usually my mom [dad] makes most of the decisions, and my dad [mom] goes along with that. The kids get to have some input about what happens. We usually get together for dinner and have a set of rules to follow.

2D. Only one parent in my family makes the decisions and the other parent follows along. There are a lot of rules about how the kids should behave. At dinner, there are a number of rules that we follow and roles that we play—who clears the dishes, asking for things, etc.

Look at the circumplex model in Figure 12.2, and determine where the statement you chose from the first set fits along the Cohesion continuum; then locate your choice from the second set on the Adaptability continuum. Draw a vertical line down from the point you marked on the Cohesion continuum; draw a horizontal line to the right from the point you marked on the Adaptability continuum. Where the lines intersect gives a rough idea of what your family might be like in terms of its cohesion and adaptability. What communication behaviors might be evident in a family with these levels of cohesion and adaptability? Does your family exhibit these behaviors?

circumstances and manage stressful periods, such as the children's adolescence. Not surprisingly, these balanced families usually have better communication skills.

However, research suggests that *there is no single best way to be a family*. At some stages of family life, the ideal of the balanced family may not apply. Older couples, for example, seem to operate more effectively when there is more rigid structure and a lower level of cohesiveness. Families with younger children seem to function well with high levels of both cohesion and adaptability. Only one thing is constant as we go through family life: Effective communication skills play an important role in helping families change their levels of cohesiveness or adaptability. These skills include active listening, problem solving, empathy, and being supportive. Dysfunctional families—those that are unable to adapt or alter their levels of cohesion—invariably display poor communication skills. Family members blame others for problems, criticize one another, and listen poorly.

Family Communication Patterns Model. The early work of media researchers who examined families' orientation toward discussing world issues became the foundation of a theory by family communication scholars Mary Ann Fitzpatrick, L. David Ritchie, and Ascan Koerner that classifies families based on family members' openness to talking with each other. The **family communication patterns model** is based on the idea that communication in families can be described in terms of two dimensions: the level of conversation, which is the degree to which family members are encouraged to discuss any topic; and the level of conformity, which is the degree to which the family emphasizes embracing the same values, attitudes, and beliefs.[25] Families with a strong conversation orientation engage in frequent discussions, all family members share their thoughts and feelings, and they all share in decision making.

family communication patterns model A model of family communication based on two dimensions: conversation and conformity.

FIGURE 12.3

Model of Family Communication Patterns

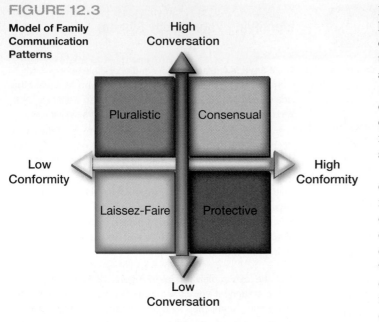

Families strong on conformity seek homogeneity, harmony, avoidance of conflict, and obedience to elders. Families range from strong to weak in their conversation and conformity orientations, as shown in the two-dimensional model in Figure 12.3. The intersection of the two dimensions produces four types of families, each type with its own unique communication patterns. As you read about each type, think which one best describes your family's communication pattern.

Consensual families, those with a high orientation toward both conversation and conformity, encourage children to talk, but the children are expected to accept their parents' explanations and values as the parents make the decisions.[26] In essence, children must give in to whatever their parents say, which undoubtedly creates stress for the children. As a matter of fact, a lot of negative feelings get expressed in consensual families, and such families rely heavily on external social support.[27]

Pluralistic families, those with a high conversation orientation and a low conformity orientation, have very open, unrestrained conversations; they emphasize talking without a concern for conforming.[28] Parents do not try to control their children's thinking, but they do expect quality arguments and support. Family members do not express many negative feelings, and hostility levels are low, probably because family members are free to discuss conflicts and are not pressured to conform.[29] Pluralistic families have the most positive family relationships among the four family types.

Protective families, those with a low conversation orientation and a high orientation toward conformity, emphasize obedience and the parents' authority in decision making without discussions or explanations.[30] Because harmony, agreement, and conformity are the goals, conflict is discouraged, and without conflict experience, family members are actually ill-equipped to manage conflict. The lack of conflict-management skills leads members of protective families to experience higher levels of hostile feelings, more venting of those feelings, and short emotional outbursts.[31]

Finally, **laissez-faire families,** those with a low orientation toward both conversation and conformity, tend to have few interactions on only a few topics. Parents support individual decision making but do not take much interest in the decisions. This pattern eventually undermines the children's confidence in their own decision-making abilities.[32] Conflicts are infrequent, as is venting of negative feelings, since there is little reason for hostility and little investment in the relationships—children feel disassociated from the family.[33]

The communication patterns in a family have a direct impact on both the well-being of family members and the development of interpersonal communication skills. One group of reviewers who analyzed research on family communication patterns discovered that the conversation orientation related more to psychosocial factors (self-esteem, mental and physical health, closeness, and relational satisfaction) than did the conformity orientation.[34] In essence, open communication appears to be one of the most significant and positive communication dynamics a family can adopt. Coming from a family with a strong conversation orientation relates to strong relationship maintenance skills, which in turn create more closeness in

consensual families Families with a high orientation toward both conversation and conformity.

pluralistic families Families with a high orientation toward conversation but a low orientation toward conformity.

protective families Families with a low orientation toward conversation but a high orientation toward conformity.

laissez-faire families Families with a low orientation toward both conversation and conformity.

friendships.[35] Conformity, on the other, hand appears to reduce the flexibility and spontaneity underlying effective relationship maintenance skills.[36]

The family communication patterns model is not a complete picture of complex family dynamics, but it does provide a foundation for an understanding of healthy family communication patterns.

Strategies for Improving Family Communication

Wouldn't it be fantastic if you could learn special techniques guaranteed to enrich your family life? But, alas, there are no sure-fire prescriptions for transforming your family system into one that a TV sitcom family would envy. Instead, we can pass on some skills and principles that researchers have either observed in healthy families or applied successfully to improve dysfunctional ones.

Virginia Satir found that in healthy families, "the members' sense of self-worth is high; communication is direct, clear, specific, and honest; rules are flexible, humane, and subject to change; and the family's links to society are open and hopeful."[37] In such families, she notes, people listen actively; they look *at* one another, not *through* one another or at the floor; they treat children as people; they touch one another affectionately regardless of age; and they openly discuss disappointments, fears, hurts, angers, and criticism, as well as joys and achievements.[38]

In his study, John Caughlin identified ten factors that were associated with families that had good communication.[39] Those factors, in order of impact, are openness, maintenance of structural stability, expression of affection, emotional/instrumental support, mind-reading (knowing what others are thinking and feeling), politeness, discipline (clear rules and consequences), humor/sarcasm, regular routine interaction, and avoidance of personal and hurtful topics. After reviewing several research studies, family communication scholars Kathleen Galvin and Bernard Brommel identified eight qualities exhibited by functional families: interactions are patterned and understood; there is more compassion and less cruelty; problems are addressed to the person who created them—other family members are not scapegoated; there is self-restraint; boundaries about safe territories and roles are clear; life includes joy and humor; misperceptions are minimal; and positive interactions outweigh negative ones.[40] Of the qualities identified in these two studies, how many are present in your family? Which qualities do you think your family could use more of?

Not all of the qualities identified in the above lists specifically involve communication, though all are certainly affected by and affect communication. The following sections explore some of the skills and strategies you can use to improve your family communication.

Take Time to Talk About Relationships and Feelings.
Healthy families talk.[41] The quantity of communication depends on family members' needs, expectations, personalities, careers, and activities. But the talking extends beyond idle chatter to focus on issues that help the family adapt to change and maintain a sense of cohesiveness.

Often, because of the crush of everyday responsibilities and tasks, family members may lapse into talking only about the task-oriented, mundane aspects of making life work: house cleaning, grocery shopping, errand running, and other uninspiring topics. Healthy families communicate about much more: their relationships, how they are feeling, and how others are feeling. They make time to converse, no matter

In terms of the circumplex model and the family communication patterns model, how would you classify this family? What cues support your classification?

BEING Other-ORIENTED

Mind-reading is identified as a factor that contributes to good communication in a family. The ability of family members to know what other members are thinking and feeling means they can more effectively adapt. How well do members of your family read each other's minds? How does this ability, or the lack of it, affect your overall family communication? What is needed to improve this ability in your family?

how busy they are. Family members have an other-orientation in these conversations, instead of focusing on themselves. In addition, they enjoy one another and don't take themselves too seriously.[42] If you haven't done so recently, try to talk to your family members about how they really are and share information about yourself.

Listen Actively and Clarify the Meaning of Messages.   Because talking about relationships is important in healthy families, it is not surprising that effective listening is also important. In the often stressful context of family life, good listening skills are essential.

Good listening requires an other-orientation. In Chapter 5, we presented fundamental skills for listening and responding to messages. Family members will communicate with greater accuracy if they learn to stop, look, and listen. Stop: Minimize mental and outside distractions; don't try to carry on a conversation over a TV blaring, a video game bleeping, or a stereo's distracting rhythmic pulse. Look: Constantly monitor the rich meaning in nonverbal messages; remember that the face and voice are prime sources for revealing emotional meaning; body posture and gestures provide clues about the intensity of an emotion. Listen: Focus on both details and major ideas. Asking appropriate follow-up questions and reflecting content and feelings are other vital skills for clarifying the meaning of messages. And remember the importance of checking your perceptions of the meaning of nonverbal messages.

Support and Encourage One Another.   A smoothly functioning family can be a supportive, encouraging sanctuary from everyday stresses. Through communication, people can let others know that they support and value them. Satir suggests that many, if not most, sources of dysfunction in families are related to feelings of low self-worth.[43] Healthy families take time to nurture one another, express confirming messages, and take a genuine interest in each person's unique contributions to the family. Researchers have found that supportive messages—those that offer praise, approval, help, and affection—can lead to higher self-esteem in children, more conformity to the wishes of the parent, higher moral standards, and less aggressive and antisocial behavior.[44] Jane Howard, who traveled extensively in search of a "good family," found that "good" families have a sense of valuing and supporting one another.[45] How can you let your family members know you value and support them?

Use Productive Strategies for Managing Conflict, Stress, and Change.   A family's inability to manage conflict and stress may be a contributing factor to family violence. In Chapter 10 you read about relational violence, which is the extreme result of what happens when people fail to resolve conflicts in a collaborative manner. Husbands and wives must learn to manage conflict in constructive ways and to manage their conflicts with their children similarly.

John Gottman has developed a set of suggestions for handling conflict between couples, some of which apply equally well to parent–child and sibling conflicts.[46] Many of his suggestions reflect recommendations made in Chapter 8 on managing conflict. Gottman suggests picking your battles carefully, scheduling the discussion, employing a structure (build an agenda, persuade and argue, resolve), and moderating your emotions. In dealing with your partner, acknowledge his or her viewpoint before presenting your own, trust your partner, communicate nondefensively, and provide comfort and positive reinforcement. Conflict might be tempered by enhancing the romance and finding enjoyment in the relationship. Gottman further suggests taking stock of the relationship and knowing when to seek help or to end the relationship.

No list of dos and don'ts will help you manage all differences in a family relationship. The suggestions offered here provide only a starting point. As we have emphasized, you will need to adapt these skills and suggestions to the context of your unique family system. But research consistently shows that listening skills and empathy are strong predictors of family satisfaction.

RECAP How to Improve Family Relationships

Take time to talk about relationships and feelings.

- Be other-oriented in your focus.
- Don't take yourself too seriously.

Listen actively and clarify the meaning of messages.

- Stop, look, and listen.
- Check your interpretation of messages.

Support and encourage one another.

- Use confirming messages.
- Be selective in disclosing your feelings.

Use productive strategies for managing conflict, stress, and change.

- Pick your battles carefully and schedule discussion.
- Acknowledge your partner's viewpoint.

Specific Family Relationships

Most of you will choose a life partner and/or get married at some point in your life, and many of you will become parents. Most of you had a relationship with your parents or other adults that greatly influenced your development through childhood. And many of you grew up with at least one younger or older sibling. These relationships are the most common ones that constitute family relationships. One feature you probably recognize about your own family relationships is how they have changed and continue to change. Your current relationships with your parents and siblings are considerably different than when you were a pre-adolescent. Your relationship with your spouse will also change over the course of your marriage, as will your relationships with your own children. All of our family relationships are important to us because, among other things, they affect our self-concept and sense of self-worth.

Committed Partners. What drives people to form a lifelong commitment to a partner? What is it that makes such a commitment so appealing? Many people seek commitment as a precursor to having children and forming a nuclear family. And marriage represents the ultimate intimate, romantic relationship to which we vow lifelong commitment. Formal recognition and cultural approval of one's relationship through the ritual of marriage adds additional meaning and challenges to the relationship. Gaining public and legal recognition is one reason some gay and lesbian committed partners seek the right to marry.

Marriage has other significant benefits. On average, married people live longer than unmarried ones, for a variety of reasons. One reason is that marriage has generally been linked to psychological well-being. A recent study found that spouses in marriages that weren't completely satisfying still enjoyed some psychological well-being if they had positive relationships with other family members and a best friend.[47] Nevertheless, those positive relationships were not enough to overcome the negative impact of a poor-quality marriage, demonstrating that although friends contribute to our daily well-being, marriage maintains our overall well-being.[48]

Most of us take the commitment of marriage very seriously. When two people enter into marriage, they spend a lot of time defining their roles and working through the trials of cohabitation. The nature of their relationship depends on a variety of factors, such as how they distribute power and make decisions (symmetric, complementary, or parallel) and what roles they each assume. Despite the variety of differences, couples can be classified according to how the partners communicate with one another.

Researcher Mary Anne Fitzpatrick identified four types of married couples found in American society: traditional, independent, separate, and mixed.[49] According to Fitzpatrick, **traditional couples** are interdependent, exhibit a lot of sharing and companionship, follow a daily routine, are not assertive, have conflicts, emphasize stability over spontaneity, and follow traditional community customs (such as the wife taking the husband's last name). **Independent couples** share and exhibit companionship but allow each other individual space; they believe the relationship should not limit their individual freedoms. They are psychologically interdependent but have a hard time matching schedules, and they also engage in conflict. **Separate couples** hold somewhat opposing values; on the one hand, they support traditional marriage and family values; on the other hand, they stress the individual over the couple. They have low interdependence and avoid conflict. This means that by maintaining their autonomy, they display less companionship and sharing than the other couple types, but they still try to keep a daily routine. In each of the preceding three types of married couples, both the wife and the husband share the same perspective about the nature of their relationship. When the husband and the wife have divergent perspectives on their roles, they are a **mixed couple** (the fourth type). There are six possible combinations that make up the mixed category:

- Husband independent and wife traditional
- Husband separate and wife traditional
- Husband traditional and wife independent
- Husband independent and wife separate
- Husband separate and wife independent
- Husband traditional and wife separate

If you're thinking that the separate style sounds appealing, you should know that research shows traditional couples are the most satisfied, whereas separate couples are the least.[50] One explanation for this is that traditional partners are the most likely to meet each other's relational expectations.[51]

traditional couples Married partners who are interdependent and who exhibit a lot of sharing and companionship.

independent couples Married partners who exhibit sharing and companionship and are psychologically interdependent but allow each other individual space.

separate couples Married partners who support the notion of marriage and family but stress the individual over the couple.

mixed couples Married couples in which the husband and wife each adopt a different perspective (traditional, independent, separate) on the marriage.

You might be wondering what it takes to ensure that you have a happy marriage. A number of factors affect marital satisfaction: approaches to conflict management, uncertainty, power, equity, decision making patterns, sexual activity, empathy, age, education, social status, presence of children, similarities, differences, marital expectations, and of course, communication. The complexity of the factors that lead to marital satisfaction has prevented the identification of a definitive set of skills or behaviors. Generally, research has done a better job of explaining what will lead to the failure of a marriage than what will ensure its success. Chapter 10 lists the four communication markers identified by marriage researcher John Gottman as highly predictive of divorce: criticism, contempt, defensive behaviors, and stonewalling. But the absence of these behaviors does not ensure happiness. What is known is that the behaviors Gottman identified—poor communication in general and the inability to manage conflict constructively—are likely to lead to dissatisfaction, dysfunction, and/or relational termination.

If you are good at communicating and managing conflict, will you have a happy marriage? Not necessarily. Communicating does not guarantee increased happiness; you might not like what you hear. Good communication just means openly sharing more information—information that has the potential to have a positive or negative effect, depending on what you learn. Hearing your spouse's constant complaints about family members, financial issues, personal distress, doubts about the marriage, or desires to engage in activities you dislike might reduce your relational satisfaction. Nonetheless, the negative impact of *not* communicating seems much greater than the negative impact of communicating. Partners should strive to establish effective communication and use that communication to honestly share and explore each other's expectations.

Wise parents use support and encouragement rather than coercion as a primary strategy for shaping their children's behavior. The challenge is to find a middle ground that tempers support with appropriate control.

Parents and Children. A great deal of study has been done on the nature of the interaction between parents and their children. Most studies focus on identifying the most effective ways for parents to communicate with their children or on describing the nature of parent–child interactions. And some studies have examined the impact of a parent's communication on the development of the child's communication skills as an adult. Your parents have affected your interpersonal communication development in three ways: by interacting with you, by providing instruction about communication rules and principles, and by engaging in communication that you observed.

Children Learn Through Interacting. The way your parents interacted with you affects your behavior and attitudes, although the effect is not always straightforward. One study found a correlation between mothers' self-reports of aggressive communication styles and the styles of their college-aged children, but did not find such a relationship between fathers' communication styles and those of their children.[52] Another study found that seventh-graders' views on openness in sharing thoughts and feelings were similar to the views of their mothers, and their views on conformity and authority were similar to those of their fathers. By the eleventh grade, however, children's views on openness matched those of their fathers, whereas their views on conformity matched those of their mothers.[53] Students' views on sex and alcohol use were not found to correlate with their parents' attitudes, but the more open the communication about sex and alcohol in the family, the more likely students were to engage in safe behavior.[54]

Children Learn Through Instruction. Your parents affected your communication development by providing you with specific instructions. They overtly conveyed such communication rules as not to interrupt others, to be polite, and to maintain eye contact when talking.

A recent study examined how parents might instill gender roles (being feminine or masculine) in their children.[55] Both male and female respondents reported that their mothers were more likely to emphasize being soft-spoken, sympathetic, compassionate, and cheerful (typically considered feminine communication qualities). Fathers were more likely to emphasize to their sons being self-reliant, dominant, aggressive, competitive, and ambitious (typically masculine qualities). Mothers emphasized the masculine traits equally to their sons and daughters.

Children Learn Through Observation. Your communication behaviors are also affected by observing your parents' interactions, notably, your parents' approaches to handling conflict. Observing destructive and hostile conflicts between parents can lead children to adopt similar styles in marriage. Similarly, your observations of how your parents interacted with their friends and coworkers and their interactions with strangers all served as potential models for your own communication behaviors. Parents who engage in ego conflicts, gunny-sacking, and other destructive conflict behaviors can either instill those styles in their children or instill a fear of conflict, leading children to avoid or accommodate. Parents who avoid conflict or who hide their conflict interactions from their children might be teaching their children to repress conflict issues or creating an expectation of a conflict-free marriage. On the other hand, children who observe their parents managing conflicts constructively are more prosocial—considerate, empathic, cooperative, and sharing.[56]

Each parent has his or her own communication strengths and weaknesses. Since interpersonal relationships are transactional, it is the combination of both parents' communication styles that affects your communication development. Take a moment to consider how each of your parents or other significant relatives has had an impact on your communication behavior. To what degree have they shaped your response to

Relating to Others in the 21st Century | Networked Families

Technology has had a tremendous effect on families. Here are a few facts from the Pew Internet & American Life Project from 2008 concerning the impact of technology on families:

- Compared to single adults or other family types, families with children at home have the highest percentage (94 percent) of ownership of home computers. Fifty-eight percent have more than one computer.

- Sixty-five percent of families with a mother, father, and a child between 7 and 17 years old living at home report that all members of the family use the computer(s).

- Eighty-nine percent of families with children between 7 and 17 have multiple cell phones, and in 57 percent of those families the children have their own cell phones.

- Families with more than one cell phone, as well as families with more than one computer, are less likely to have dinner together and are less satisfied with family time. In those families, both parents are more likely to be working, providing the funds and creating the need for technology, but re-

ducing available time (though parents tend to cut back more on leisure time than on family time). Still, 51 percent have dinner together every day.

- How does the Internet affect family leisure time activities? Internet users were just as likely to socialize in person with family and friends as non-Internet users. However, 25 percent of adults report their Internet use has decreased their TV viewing.

- Spouses who both have cell phones are more likely to contact each other daily to say hello and chat (70 percent), as well as to coordinate their schedules (64 percent), compared to other couples (54 percent and 47 percent, respectively).

- Among couples with children between 7 and 17 years old, 42 percent contact the children by cell phone every day, 35 percent by landline phone, 7 percent by text message, and 1 percent by instant message or social network pages.

- Fifty-seven percent of couples with children under 18 share equally in contacting the children; for 36 percent, the mother is the primary

communicator; and for 6 percent, the primary communicator is the father.

- The Internet and cell phones were seen as increasing the quality of communication with family members who do not reside with them by 53 percent of respondents, and increasing the quality of communication with those who did reside with them by 47 percent of the respondents. A decrease in quality was reported by less than 4 percent of respondents.

How much do the results of the Pew survey reflect your family? Since you were probably raised with computers and cell phones in your household from an early age, you might not be able to appreciate how their introduction changed communication in your family. Nonetheless, you should be able to identify some of their impact. How often do you e-mail, text-message, or call your parents? Your siblings? Other relatives? How often do they contact you? How does EMC affect interactions in your household when you are home? When you have your own family, will you set guidelines for your children regarding their use of the Internet or cell phones?

Source: B. Wellman, A. Smith, A. T. Wells, and T. L. M. Kennedy, "Networked Families," Pew Internet & American Life Project, October 19, 2008. Retrieved June 29, 2009, from *http://www.pewinternet.org/Reports/2008/Networked-Families.aspx*.

interpersonal conflict? How have they affected your ability to express caring, love, warmth, and affection? What impact have they had on your listening skills, respect for others, and openness? Some of your communication behaviors might not match those of your parents because you developed them as a reaction to your parents' patterns. For example, your dislike for your parents' aggressiveness might lead you to be passive. Finally, some of your qualities might not be learned at all but are communibiological—passed down genetically. Nonetheless, when you have your own children, be sensitive to the impact of how you communicate with them and with those around you on the development of their communication skills.

Siblings.   Although relationships with brothers and sisters tend to be the most enduring relationships in our lives, generalizing about communication between siblings is difficult, because so many factors influence the nature of the relationships, including the sex, age, and number of siblings. Overall, however, we are motivated to communicate with our siblings because of feelings of intimacy—a desire to sustain the relationship, to keep in touch, to show caring and concern, and to encourage.[57] Sibling communication

Communication and Emotion   Emotions at Home and in the Workplace

The two communication contexts covered in this chapter differ in that we experience and express emotions differently in each context. We probably express and experience more emotions within the context of our families than in any other interpersonal situation. In the majority of families, the feeling and expression of love—between a wife and husband, between parents and children, between siblings—is pervasive. Some emotions are present at birth, but the process of interpreting and managing those emotions is learned.[58] Our initial emotional socialization comes from observing our parents' emotional behavior, from direct instruction from our parents ("You should be happy about that" or "Don't be afraid of the dark"), from subtly conveyed parental expectations about their children's emotional behaviors, and from reinforcement of emotional behavior by the parents (giving a piece of candy if a child stops crying or reciprocating a child's hug).[59] Boys in the United States are often taught to be emotionally guarded, whereas girls are expected to give and receive emotional support.[60] The types of families and related family communication patterns vary in terms of openness toward emotional expression and the likelihood of positive or negative emotional expressions.

In contrast to the open expression of emotions in the family, we tend to hold our emotions in check in many of our workplace interactions; if we do express emotions, they are generally positive or related specifically to the interpersonal relationships we have established. In U.S. culture, there is an expectation that people in organizations will act "professional,"

between the ages of 18 and 34 differs from such communication during later years because we are more motivated to do something with our siblings, to get something from them, escape from doing something else, accomplish things together, get information, or simply continue a routine or habit.[61] Besides changes in our motives, additional changes occur as we move through the three of stages of sibling relationships: childhood and adolescence, early and middle adulthood, and late adulthood and old age.[62] During the first stage, siblings live together, engage in daily interactions, compete and share resources (like bedrooms and bathrooms), and probably face greater demands and more pressing tasks than in the latter stages. During the early and middle adulthood stage, siblings begin independent lives, starting their own nuclear families and pursuing careers. Sibling interactions become voluntary and perhaps more intermittent, due to such factors as geographic distance. In the late adulthood stage, siblings retire and their children are grown up, so siblings once again turn to each other.

Childhood and Adolescence.   During childhood and adolescence, siblings provide companionship, emotional support, surrogate caretaking, and protection and assistance (even forming coalitions against parents).[63] Often, children's first playmates are their brothers and sisters. Through interactions with siblings, children gain valuable psychosocial skills that translate into how they interact with friends and peers. When there is a large age difference between siblings, the older children may play nurturing roles and learn parenting skills. In divorced families, the older sibling might be particularly nurturing, although the younger children may tend to resent the older siblings' control.[64] Family communication researcher Patricia Noller notes that warm sibling relationships help us maintain positive self-evaluations. Siblings provide emotional support and advice. One study found that high school and college students were more likely to turn to their siblings than to their parents to discuss such things as their dating experiences and life problems.[65] In addition, these students preferred talking to a same-sex sibling about sexual matters, rather than talking to any other family member, because they felt less fear of evoking disappointment or disapproval from a sibling than from a parent.[66]

Children without siblings may be somewhat at a disadvantage as a result of missing the opportunity to practice and develop certain interpersonal skills. One study of first- through sixth-graders found that only children were not any different from those with siblings in terms of the number or quality of friends; however, only children were which implies emotional restraint. Unfortunately, examples of employees or customers acting in rage or anger, sometimes with devastating effects on others, are all too common. Our workplace friendships are often vital to our emotional support. Being able to discuss your frustration with a colleague who understands and shares that emotion can help you effectively cope with and manage the emotion. Most organizations are concerned with the emotions of their members, because they wish to maintain positive employee morale and create positive relationships with customers. Attempts to create a positive corporate emotional image are reflected in such slogans as "A smile in every aisle," used by some grocery-store chains, or "Fly the friendly skies of United."

Take a minute to think about your own experiences with emotions in your family and in the workplace. Identify a situation in each setting when you experienced and expressed a positive emotion. In what ways are the two situations similar and in what ways are they different? How did others respond to you when you expressed yourself? Now identify a situation in each setting when you experienced and expressed a negative emotion. In what ways are the two situations similar and in what ways are they different? How did others respond?

Think about emotions you experienced during a family gathering and at work that you did not express explicitly. What inhibited your expression? What did you expect the effect of expressing the emotion would be? How adept were those around you at picking up any cues about your emotional state?

---

less well liked, more aggressive, and victimized by their peers.[67] The researchers suggest that these problems reflect only children's difficulty in managing interpersonal conflict. But having siblings is not without its drawbacks. Differential treatment of children by their parents is likely to undermine warm, supportive sibling relationships.[68] During childhood, sibling rivalry often occurs as children vie for their parents' love or compete with one another. This rivalry can last throughout the siblings' lifetime. Nonetheless, if today you have effective conflict management skills, perhaps they were nurtured as you were forced to work through sibling squabbles in your childhood.

Early and Middle Adulthood.   A number of significant changes occur in sibling relationships as siblings leave home and begin their adult lives. You probably have experienced or are experiencing some of those changes already. Without day-to-day contact, communication and other interactions tend to decrease. The continuation and intimacy of the sibling relationship become more a question of choice than circumstance. You decide how much contact and interaction you want with your siblings. Closeness at this stage is affected by how close you were in the earlier stage, by commonalities, and by life events, such as having to care for aging parents, divorce, or a family member's death.[69] Family reunions and visits occur during this stage. Perhaps you can recall from your childhood when your parents were at this stage with their siblings—getting together, everyone bringing their kids, the storytelling and reminiscing; for you these opportunities meant developing relationships with your aunts, uncles, and cousins.

During early and middle adulthood, you and your siblings are likely to provide one another with strong emotional support (caring and assistance) rather than help with specific tasks, with sisters giving more emotional support than brothers.[70] Receiving emotional support from siblings increases the relational satisfaction of the recipient.[71] However, support tends to be directed to those perceived to need it the most, with single, divorced, or widowed siblings receiving support and support decreasing as siblings get married and have children.[72]

Siblings can provide companionship, emotional support, protection, and assistance.

Building Your Skills | Other-Orientation at Home and Work

Throughout this book we have advocated taking an other-oriented approach to interpersonal communication. But there are times when taking an other-oriented perspective or being empathic could be disadvantageous, if you ignore your own needs, values, or priorities. Look at the following situations and consider how being other-oriented might be counterproductive or lead to poor decisions. How can you be other-oriented and still make good decisions in each situation?

- You receive a call from the middle-school principle, who tells you that your seventh-grade son is being suspended for two days for fighting with another student. Because you are other-oriented, you understand the following about your son: He is very self-conscious about being overweight, and the other kids make fun of him for it. He has been struggling with his studies because he has a hard time concentrating and reading material. He has low self-esteem and does not feel that other kids like him. What would you say to your son about his suspension? What actions would you take? How would being other-oriented affect your decisions?

- You are a manager and one of your subordinates is increasingly arriving late to work, is missing deadlines and appointments, and is turning in poor work. Taking an other-oriented approach, you remind yourself that this employee is facing a divorce, has a child who was recently arrested, and is suffering from panic attacks. What would you say to the employee? What actions would you take toward the employee? How would being other-oriented affect your decisions?

Late Adulthood.   As you grow older and move out of the workforce, family relationships, including those with siblings, become increasingly important. Even with infrequent interactions over the course of a lifetime, siblings share a special bond. Communication among siblings increases during this stage.[73] Although important family events (weddings, christenings, funerals) still bring siblings together, factors such as poor health, limited income or mobility, and distance can reduce visits. An important function of sibling relationships in late adulthood is reminiscing and validating memories—activities linked to higher self-esteem, less depression, and higher morale.[74] Before they can engage in reminiscing, siblings might need to resolve any long-standing issues, such as their rivalries. For example, siblings might have to address feelings of envy over one sibling's preferential treatment from the parents. During this stage of our lives, we are often faced with the death of a spouse, death of another family member, or personal health challenges. Thus, another function of these sibling relationships is to provide psychological support during times of crisis.[75] Depending on who else (spouses, children, or friends) is around to provide instrumental support (cooking, cleaning, nursing), siblings might pitch in to help one another. For example, a brother might take care of his widowed sister's house if she has no children; or a sister might cook meals for her brother.

Close sibling relationships can enhance your lifelong emotional, psychological, and physical well-being. Maintaining close sibling relationships is no different than maintaining other intimate relationships—you need to communicate, be open, be supportive, and adapt. If you are not as close to a sibling as you would like to be, examine any issues that might be hampering that relationship, and consider which communication skills and strategies you might use to address the issues. Positive sibling relationships provide a lifetime of rewards. Although your sibling relationships exist because of circumstance, having a sibling as a friend is a rewarding choice that requires the same commitment and effort as other friendships.

Workplace Relationships

Organizations look for employees who can relate effectively to other people—bosses, subordinates, peers, and clients. All the skills you have been studying throughout this book can improve your effectiveness in organizational relationships.

After you graduate, the workplace becomes a major source for developing interpersonal relationships. You make friends with the people with whom you work. You will socialize on the job with various people from the organization and may socialize with them outside of work. Your interactions in the workplace typically vary according to their degree of task versus social orientation. This variation is the source of both personal satisfaction and conflict. Conflicts arise when job-related decisions affect personal relationships, and vice versa. As a manager, you might become friends with some of your subordinates, but if the work performance of one of those subordinates falls below a satisfactory level, the friendship could interfere with your ability to address that problem. Many companies used to have policies prohibiting socializing among employees; however, such policies created strong dissatisfaction and discontent. Organizational policies that nurture relationships among employees build camaraderie and a supportive work atmosphere.

Workplace Friendships

Interpersonal communication skills help in interactions with coworkers. Developing satisfying interpersonal relationships in an organization is often a rewarding part of a job.

The TV show *The Office* frequently focuses on the ebb and flow of friendships in the workplace. As the show often illustrates, workplace friendships can develop with anyone in an organization, though generally friendship is most likely between coworkers who are at the same status level. However, friendships also develop between supervisors and subordinates, between employees and clients, and between members of totally different departments within an organization. Friendships at work are like any other relationships in terms of their dimensions and development. One study in which coworkers were interviewed extensively identified three distinct transitions: from acquaintance to friend, from friend to close friend, and from close friend to "almost best" friend.[76] Interestingly, the researchers found respondents hesitant to refer to a coworker as a "best" friend, opting instead for "best friend at work" or "very close." The initial development of workplace friendships occurred for a variety of reasons, such as proximity, sharing tasks, sharing a similar life event, or perceiving similar interests.[77] As the relationships developed, the changes identified in this study were similar to those typically found in any developing friendship—easier and more flexible communication, increased self-disclosing, more frequent interactions, more socializing, and increased discussion of both work problems and nonwork topics.[78]

Workplace Friendships and Context. Workplace friendships might be limited to a particular context: a shared lunch hour or a project assignment. One of your authors once worked the night shift at a hospital, a schedule that limited opportunities for evening activities with friends outside of the hospital. Sometimes a group of night-shift workers from several departments would go out for breakfast together, which led to development of breakfast friendships. Outside the workplace, friendships usually find us associating with people who are similar to us in age, status, and the like; however, workplace friendships often involve people who differ in age or status.[79] For example, you may find yourself becoming friends with a supervisor or subordinate who is considerably older or younger than you. Sometimes this friendship begins within the context of a mentorship, in which the veteran employee either formally or informally provides advice and support to a new hire.

Having a friend of the opposite sex may be more likely at work than it is outside work, where such relationships might be expected to become romantic or might threaten existing intimate relationships. Results of one study indicated that men felt that socializing outside the workplace was more important to their friendships with male coworkers than to friendships with female coworkers.[80] In addition, as their workplace relationships became more intimate, same-sex friends continued and expanded their relationships

Workplace friendships can develop with anyone in the organization.

outside of the workplace; however, cross-sex relationships continued to be defined specifically as "workplace friendships."

Values and Functions of Workplace Friendships. Besides the typical benefits associated with friendships, workplace friendships help individuals with their organizational lives, and also help the organization. Workplace friendships provide the following values and functions:

1. *Information exchange*: One of the primary functions of workplace friendships is information exchange.[81] Information within an organization flows more openly between friends. You are more likely to share critical and even private news you hear because of friendship and trust. Your organizational friendship network is an informal information network that alerts you to important information such as reorganizations, job openings, cutbacks, or reviews.

2. *Social support*: Workplace friends are in a position to help you manage the stress and challenges unique to your workplace, such as a hostile boss, cutbacks in hours, or working overtime. They provide empathy, insight, comfort, support, and advice because they understand the dynamics and demands of the company and of your position.[82]

3. *Organizational support*: Workplace friends are allies and advocates who, because of friendship, will help you address organizational challenges or conflicts. A boss who is also your friend will probably argue harder on your behalf for your promotion than a boss who is indifferent. Friends can form alliances and become a team to challenge unjust or questionable organizational policies.

4. *Newcomer assimilation*: The tension that comes from a new job can be greatly reduced if you are able to form friendships with those with whom you work. Friendship formation helps you adjust socially and integrate into a new organization. Being accepted into an existing social network within an organization can be challenging, because others do not have the same needs you do, so people who are new to an organization often form friendships with other new hires.

5. *Improved performance*: Workplace friends can help ensure you do a better job. Besides giving you important information, friends provide objective advice and feedback, help you make decisions, provide resources, and lend a hand when needed. Friendships also provide "social capital," the benefit you accrue because of whom you know.[83] For example, in a meeting with coworkers, your friendship with the boss provides extra "capital" as you argue for adoption of your ideas.

6. *Retention*: Once you are settled into your job, friendship increases the likelihood that you will stay in it. One study of workers at a fast food restaurant found that the number of friends was more significant than the depth of those friendships in employee retention.[84] Perhaps you've had jobs that you didn't particularly like but kept because you enjoyed the camaraderie and friendships.

7. *Organizational change*: The trust and sense of identity that develop from friendship networks can help the distribution and adoption of organizational

changes.[85] We are more amenable to changes that our friends support and help us understand. For example, you might resist management's introduction of a new computer system and software, but if your friends like the plan, you'll probably be more accepting of the change.

8. *Organizational enhancement*: The above seven functions and values of workplace friendships combine to enhance the overall quality and efficiency of an organization by increasing information exchange and improving employee satisfaction, thus reducing turnover.

Deterioration of Workplace Friendships. Like any friendship, workplace friendships can deteriorate and end. However, unlike other friendships, these continue as relationships of circumstance with coworkers, superiors, or subordinates. Some reasons for the deterioration of workplace friendships are personality issues, interference of personal life with work, problems created by different expectations for friend and work roles, promotion of one person to a position of authority over the other, and betrayal of trust.[86] How do you go about ending workplace friendships? Chapter 10 discussed some direct and indirect strategies for ending relationships that also apply to workplace friendships. Specific indirect strategies for the workplace include keeping all conversations focused on work topics; nonverbally distancing from the other (through the use of a condescending tone or disapproving facial expressions); escalating the cost of maintaining the friendship by being more independent or making more demands (although this strategy might have a negative impact on the continuing work relationship); and avoiding socializing outside the workplace.[87] When all else fails, some of our students have reported quitting their jobs to end a workplace relationship. The ability to redefine a friendship as only a work-based relationship requires strong relationship management skills to minimize the stress and the potential resentment of a coworker or a subordinate.

Workplace Romances

The workplace provides an opportune arena for the development of intimate relationships because of the convenience and exposure to a pool of potential partners. Surveys indicate that 40 to 80 percent of respondents have dated a coworker.[88] Many people find their future spouses in the workplace. A 2009 Valentines Day national survey for Careerbuilder.com found that 31 percent of workers surveyed had married a person they dated at work. Some companies even hire married couples because they see a value in having both partners working for the same company. On the other hand, some companies have policies prohibiting dating coworkers—but how can a policy prevent people from becoming attracted?

In the workplace, you interact with people in a safe and defined context that affords the opportunity to learn about others and share information about yourself. Trust evolves, similarities are discovered, attraction develops, and the interactions increase in intimacy. Office flings, one-night stands, and hooking up are not typically about forming loving, romantic relationships, but instead satisfying sexual needs or needs for power and influence. However, most people consider almost any sexual relationship in an organization to be a workplace romance. The same principles and factors discussed in the last chapter on romantic relationships apply to workplace romances, and the processes of self-disclosing and moving toward intimacy, physical affection and sex, and even marriage are at work in workplace romances.

Reasons for and Values of Workplace Romance. Several factors inherent in the workplace foster attraction and relational development.[89] The proximity afforded by work spaces such as offices or cubicles increases the likelihood of personal interactions. Meetings and other collaborative tasks require you to interact with others. And, incidental interactions can occur in shared space such as a coffee room, cafeteria, lobby, or elevator. All of these circumstances provide the opportunity for initiating relationships. In fact, many lead to repeated interactions, which increase the opportunity for sharing information. In the 2009 survey sponsored by Careerbuilders.com, workers mentioned the following situations as leading to a relationship: 12 percent of respondents cited running into each other outside of work, 11 percent cited working late at the office, 10 percent cited meeting at happy hour, and 10 percent cited meeting at lunch.[90] Since the survey was for Valentine's Day, respondents provided examples of romantic activities they had pursued at work, including going to the office roof for a drink together, dancing in the halls to elevator music, having a candlelit picnic in the office after everyone had left, and leaving romantic sticky notes for each other.

The values and functions associated with friendships also apply to romantic relationships. For example, in TV shows such as *Grey's Anatomy, ER,* or *House,* workplace romantic partners are often seen sharing organizational, professional, and personal information; providing emotional comfort and understanding; pitching in and helping on a given task; or acting as advocates. These shows also illustrate how workplace romances can energize the partners as well as their work associates, as they all share the joy and excitement of the relationship, which bolsters workplace morale. On the downside, however, such romances can also be the source of jealousy.[91] Unlike friendships, workplace romances offer the additional prospect of becoming intimate, loving relationships and of leading to marriage.

The Challenges and Dark Side of Workplace Romances.

In general, dating in the workplace is not particularly problematic when those involved work in different units of the company or when they have no job-related power issues to deal with. Dating among members of the same unit can be a problem if it interferes with the ability of the couple to perform their jobs. If you are involved in such a situation, your interactions with your partner at work need to remain professional. Coworkers are sometimes uncomfortable around romantic partners and may worry about inappropriate sharing of information, unequal work distribution, or other potential problems. A survey of coworkers in several insurance companies found that only 14 percent felt uncomfortable about colleagues being romantic partners and only 18 percent felt the romantic partners were less productive;[92] These low percentages might be because of the level of professionalism those in the romance displayed. There is still a stigma attached to dating coworkers, with women in workplace romances being perceived more negatively than men, suffering more negative consequences, and being berated for taking the romance too seriously.[93]

The most significant problems in workplace romances occur when the relationship is between a boss and his or her employee. The employee might feel coerced into the romantic relationship, which constitutes sexual harassment. Even if the superior does not threaten or show favoritism to the subordinate, the subordinate could believe that rejecting the superior's advances would be professionally detrimental. This type of sexual harassment is usually referred to as **quid pro quo harassment.** *Quid pro quo* is a Latin phrase that basically means "You do something for me and I'll do something for you." A supervisor who says or implies "Have sex with me or your job will be in jeopardy" or "If you want this promotion, you should have sex with me" is obviously using his or her power as a boss to gain sexual favors in exchange for something the employee wants. To avoid these situations, organizations often develop extensive sexual harassment policies. You should learn the policies of any organization where you are employed and assert your rights if you find yourself being sexually harassed.

quid pro quo harassment
Implied or explicit promise of reward in exchange for sexual favors or threat of retaliation if sexual favors are withheld, given to an employee by a coworker or a superior. The Latin phrase *quid pro quo* roughly means "You do something for me and I'll do something for you."

UNDERSTANDING OTHERS
Adapting to Differences

Male and Female Interactions in the Workplace

The following six scenarios reflect some of the general ways men and women differ in their approach to communication in the workplace. These scenarios are based on U.S. stereotypes about men and women in the workplace. As you read each one, see if the description of your sex's approach actually reflects how you behave. Also think about the degree to which you believe the stereotype presented for the opposite sex. The author of these scenarios does a good job of taking an other-oriented approach to helping improve communication, and the principles she offers apply regardless of the sex of those involved.

Power Plays

Her way: Women tend to ask lots of questions before beginning work.

His way: Men simply roll up their sleeves.

The result: Men assume women aren't up to the job. If they were competent, reason men, then women wouldn't be asking so many questions. But in fact, women typically verify and validate data before starting tasks, sometimes to improve their performance. If you're a male boss, listen to the questions women ask. Sometimes, these may add information or clarify things for everyone.

The reverse scenario is that men hate to ask for directions (big news, right?). But women assume that if men don't ask questions, they must know enough to complete a job. That's often not the case. For women bosses, it's a good idea to verify that men have enough knowledge to complete a task. Oversee the work in the early phases or offer help without being asked.

Picture Imperfect

Her way: Women frequently use anecdotes or illustrations about home or relationships.

His way: Men rely on metaphors about sports or war.

The result: Dialogue can hit a dead end. Women often do not follow the touchdown, full-court-press images, and vice versa. Don't simply gender-reverse images to communicate. Instead, consider your audience and use gender-neutral images (of nature, movies, or weather, for example). Or use images you like, but with an explanation of what you mean.

Command Conflicts

Her way: Growing up, girls tend to establish relationships.

His way: Boys usually vie for leadership.

The result: Men and women impose authority differently. "Women tend to be more collaborative in the workplace, putting relationships first," says Roz Usheroff, a business trainer and author of *Customize Your Career.* "Men routinely challenge and expect to be challenged." Each often finds the other's style ineffective or insulting. To jump the divide, borrow a bit from the other's style. Men can try a more collaborative approach. Women need to take over more often.

Detailed Disputes

Her way: Women like to tell and hear stories, including stories about trials and errors, turnings and returnings.

His way: Men "cut to the chase."

The result: Each sex becomes too impatient to hear the other. "Women push for details generally for three reasons: to show concern, to vicariously participate in an experience or conversation, and to verify assumptions," says Dianna Booher, author of *Communicate with Confidence.* "Men tend to gather details just long enough to get the big-picture message and then dump them as trivial."

Again, each sex can benefit from the other's behavior. Men ought to explain their thinking and not simply jump to conclusions. Women need to get to the bottom line more quickly.

Emotional Exchanges

Her way: She tends to treat male colleagues like her husband or boyfriend.

His way: He often handles women associates like his wife or girlfriend.

The result: Subtle and tricky gender miscommunication. Typically, men and women bring into the office some version of the sexual dynamics they have at home. We also gravitate to workplace confidants, mentors, or employees who resemble the intimates in our personal lives, especially spouses. If you're in some kind of standoff or you feel like he or she "doesn't understand" you, take a break to think it through. Make sure you're not importing a personal issue into the workplace environment.

Decision Drivers

Her way: Women are generally more comfortable talking about their feelings.

His way: Men prefer to dwell on the facts and skip the feelings.

The result: Communication trouble. Every communication has both an intellectual and an emotional component; misunderstandings arise when we ignore one of the two dimensions. A man can acknowledge the emotional dimension: "I know this is a difficult conversation for you. It's difficult for me, too." A woman might dial down emotional intensity by increasing her focus on problem analysis: "I think there are three pieces to the issues we've been discussing."

The definition of a diverse work force, of course, is an environment where people accept differences rather than deny them. If we pay attention to gender differences, we just might untangle the gender communications knots—and get the job done faster, too.

Management's Response to Workplace Romances. Managers are responsible for maintaining a safe and efficient workplace. Generally, it is inappropriate for a manager to intercede in the personal lives of employees; however, if those personal lives interfere with the workplace climate or performance, then a manager has a responsibility to intercede. Managers should know their companies' policies for dating between coworkers and apply them consistently. Not only do managers need to ensure that their units are unaffected by ongoing workplace romances, but the aftermath of dissolved relationships might also require intercession. Break-ups can be the source of ill feelings and can undermine the former romantic partners' working relationship, as well as their relationships with their coworkers. Managers should also be prepared to provide conflict mediation if needed.

Guidelines for Workplace Romances. Interactions in the workplace are expected to be professional, with employees' interactions reflecting their roles. Employees who date need to keep their romantic relationship from interfering with their professional roles and be prepared to manage the possible fallout over their romance from fellow employees. In the TV show *The Office*, Dwight and Angela go to great lengths to hide their romantic relationship. For example, on Valentine's Day, Dwight is excited about the gift of a bobble-head of himself that he receives from Angela, and he tells her someone "rocked his house" so that she'll know he liked it but others won't detect their relationship. There can be dialectical tension regarding whether to reveal or conceal a relationship, but unless there are company policies against dating coworkers, you generally don't have to keep the relationship secret. Some companies actually have policies requiring that romantic relationships be revealed and even have partners sign "love contracts" indicating the relationship is consensual, thus limiting the company's liabilities. Human resource experts Cindy Schaefer and Thomas Tudor offer the following guidelines for those involved in workplace romances:[94]

1. Conduct yourself in a professional manner at all times. Be discreet and avoid public displays of affection.
2. Do not take long lunches or extended breaks with your partner, and avoid returning to work looking disheveled. Love may be blind, but your coworkers aren't.
3. Avoid romances with clients, suppliers, or vendors. These potential conflict-of-interest situations can damage the company and your career.
4. It is acceptable to ask a coworker for a date if the employer's policies allow it, but do not persist if you are rejected. Persistence may develop into harassing behavior. Harassment is strictly prohibited.
5. Exercise prudence when using the employer's communication systems for personal messages. Electronic mail, voice mail, and telephone calls might be monitored.

6. Do not call in sick on the same day. People who know about the relationship—and most coworkers do—will suspect you are not ill. The result will be a loss of reputation with your boss and coworkers, and they will resent having to pick up your slack.

7. If you are employed by an international firm, be familiar with cultural differences in dating and acceptable behavior between males and females.

Formal Relationships and Communication Directions in the Workplace

So far you have read about the formation of informal interpersonal relationships in organizations, but the organizational structure also creates a set of communication expectations and prescribes specific, formal relationships among its members. The reasons a manager talks to an employee differ from the reasons an employee seeks out a manager. The following sections describe the four directions in which communication flows within an organization: upward (from subordinate to supervisor), downward (from supervisor to subordinate), horizontally (from peer to peer), and outward (from members of an organization to clients or vendors). These formal channels of communication coexist with the informal, personal channels discussed earlier, sometimes enhancing them and sometimes interfering with them. A boss who is friends with an employee might be reluctant to reprimand or evaluate the employee, thus failing to perform one of the formal functions expected of a supervisor. The quality of the formal relationships and communication directly affect the efficiency and effectiveness of an organization.

Upward Communication: Talking with Your Boss. "Please place your suggestions in the suggestion box," announces the boss. The suggestion box is the symbol for upward communication. **Upward communication** is communication that flows from subordinates up to superiors. Today's organizations recognize that good communication improves the quality of goods and services, and thus many organizations encourage communication from lower levels to higher levels; however, effective upward communication is still far from the norm. Many employees fear that candid comments will not be well received. Others may wonder "Why bother?" If managers offer no incentive for sharing information up the line, it is unlikely that their subordinates will make the effort. In 1952, organizational researcher Donald Pelz discovered an effect that was subsequently named for him; the **Pelz effect** describes the phenomenon that subordinates are more satisfied in their jobs when they feel their immediate supervisor has influence on decisions made at higher levels.[95] Subsequent research by organizational communication scholar Fred Jablin found when subordinates perceived their supervisors as supportive, the Pelz effect was particularly strong in creating a sense of openness and satisfaction.[96] Having a supportive and influential superior enhances communication because employees are more open to sharing information.

If there is little upward communication, the organization may be in a precarious situation. Those lower down in the organization are often the ones who make contact with the customer, make the product, or develop and deliver the product or service; they hear feedback about the product's virtues and problems. If supervisors remain unaware of these problems, productivity or quality may suffer. In addition, if employees have no opportunities to share problems and complaints with their boss, their frustration level may be dangerously high. Upward communication helps managers deal quickly with problems and gather suggestions for

upward communication Communication that flows from subordinates to superiors.

Pelz effect Subordinates' feeling more satisfied in their jobs the more their supervisors are able to influence higher-level decisions.

Workplace satisfaction is related to the quality of the communication between boss and employees.

Relating to Others in the 21st Century

Networked Workers

Almost everyone seems to have a cell phone and access to the Internet both at home and at work. Electronically mediated communication (EMC) has changed the way people perform their jobs, affecting their effectiveness and their lives. Here are some results from another Pew Internet & American Life Project survey, this one concerning the impact of technology on the workplace:

- Of those working, 89 percent own a cell phone and 87 percent use the Internet or e-mail at least occasionally.

- The Internet seems to play a significant role in many jobs, with 60 percent of employees using it every day and only 28 percent never using it. The remaining workers use it a few times a week or less.

- On the plus side, 80 percent of workplace EMC users think it has improved their ability to do their job; 73 percent say it improves sharing ideas with coworkers, and 58 percent say it gives them more job hour flexibility.

- On the minus side, 46 percent of workplace EMC users say it increases their hours, 49 percent say it adds to their job stress, and 49 percent indicate it makes it harder to disconnect from work when at home in the evening or on the weekends.

- Professionals, managers, and executives are the most likely to own laptops and/or BlackBerrys or Palm Pilots.

- Fifty-three percent of workers have both personal and professional e-mail accounts, and 54 percent of those check their personal e-mail accounts at least once a day while at work.

- In 2007–2008, 37 percent of those with work e-mail accounts reported checking them constantly at work, which compares with 22 percent in 2002; 50 percent with work e-mail accounts checked them on the weekends.

- Twenty-two percent of workers said their employers expect them to check and respond to work-related e-mail even when they are not at work.

- Those who work more than 50 hours a week, those who supervise others, and those who belong to several work teams have the highest ownership of laptops and BlackBerrys (or other personal digital assistants).

- Forty-seven percent of text messages are predominantly or completely personal, and only 2 percent are predominantly or completely work-related. Of those who send text messages, 28 percent send them from work to friends and family at least once a day, compared to only 17 percent sending text messages to work colleagues.

- Twenty-two percent of respondents have made online purchases while at work, 15 percent have viewed online videos, 18 percent have engaged in instant messaging, 10 percent have gone to a networking site like Facebook or LinkedIn (a professional network), and 11 percent have read blogs, but only 3 percent report engaging in online gaming.

- E-mail is seen as the most effective way to schedule meetings (60 percent) and edit or review documents (62 percent), compared to scheduling meetings or reviewing documents in person (21 percent and 30 percent, respectively) or over the phone (17 percent and 3 percent). On the other hand, meeting face to face is seen as the best choice for asking work questions (65 percent), dealing with sensitive issues (88 percent), and bringing up a problem to a supervisor (79 percent).

What expectations do companies have for employees' use of EMC? As a supervisor, how would you feel about employees using their computers to surf the Internet for fun, to send personal e-mails, to shop online, or log on to Facebook? Should you call, text, or e-mail a coworker or your boss with a work question? The rules governing appropriate use are often vague or nonexistent. When you begin a new job, find out the formal and informal rules governing EMC use.

Source: M. Madden and S. Jones, "Networked Workers," Pew Internet & American Life Project, September 24, 2008. Retrieved June 29, 2009 from http://www.pewinternet.org/Reports/2008/Networked-Workers.aspx

improving processes and procedures. One pair of researchers suggests that subordinates can "manage up" by being sensitive to the needs of supervisors.[97] By being other-oriented you can use your knowledge of your boss's most important goals, along with his or her strengths, weaknesses, and preferred working style, to establish a more meaningful relationship that will benefit both of you.

If you are a manager, encourage your subordinates to share both good news and bad. Be visible and cultivate their trust by developing a system that elicits feedback and comments. Use a suggestion box (paper or electronic), informal discussions, or more formal meetings and presentations. Formal meetings with structured agendas appear more conducive to problem solving and negotiation than informal meetings, which seem less focused and task oriented.[98] Making time for these exchanges will pay off in the long run.

Having open communication between managers and employees does create the risk of emotional confrontations. However, in most organizations there is an unwritten rule that employees will control and restrain expressions of anger toward supervisors or subordinates. Indeed, a low level of outward expression of anger was reported by 560 respondents to a recent survey; somewhat surprisingly though, lower-status employees were more likely to express anger to higher-status members than vice versa.[99] Despite the stereotype of women being more emotional, lower-status males were more likely to express anger than lower-status females; however, no significant difference was found between men and women at the higher-status level.[100] These results suggest that lower-status males are slow to conform to the organizational rules that govern expression of anger in the workplace. Your career success is affected by your understanding of and your willingness to adapt to the organizational communication expectations and rules that affect your communication, both upward and downward.

Downward Communication: Talking with Your Subordinates.

The owner of the local movie theater tells the manager that she plans to change the theater format to specialize in international and independent films. During a weekly meeting, the manager tells the shift supervisors of the impending change. Your supervisor then tells you and the rest of the crew working Friday nights about the new format. This sequence of interactions represents **downward communication,** the flow of information from those higher up in an organization to those of lower rank. It can happen via memo, phone call, newsletter, poster, e-mail or, of course, face to face. Most downward communication consists of

- instructions about how to do a job;
- rationales for doing things;
- statements about organizational policies and procedures;
- feedback about job performance; and
- information that helps develop the mission or vision of the organization[101]

Leader-member exchange (LMX) theory recognizes that supervisors develop different types of relationships with different subordinates and seeks to explain those differences. LMX theory recognizes that, like relationships outside of work, relationships between supervisors and subordinates vary in type and quality. As strangers, supervisors and subordinates stay within their roles and task responsibilities; as acquaintances, their relationship becomes more personal; and at the strongest level (the *maturity* or *partner* level), their relationship is characterized by mutual trust, respect, and support.[102] LMX research focuses on why leader-member relationships vary and on their impact on subordinates' satisfaction and productivity. Employees in one study were given a hypothetical situation and asked to describe how their supervisor would communicate with them in that situation.[103] Those who described more person-centered communication (PCC) by their supervisor also reported stronger leader-member relationships and higher job

downward communication Communication that flows from superiors to subordinates.

leader-member exchange (LMX) theory Theory that supervisors develop different types of relationships with different subordinates and that seeks to explain those differences.

satisfaction. Besides higher job satisfaction, strong PCC and LMX relationships improve employee commitment, autonomy, and negotiation latitude, and benefit supervisors and organizations by reducing turnover and increasing productivity.[104] Besides such other-centeredness, the amount and quality of the information a manager provides to subordinates determine the quality of the relationship between them and the attitude of the employees. Information that is timely, useful, and accurate results in a better relationship and fosters more satisfaction and commitment to the organization among employees.[105] The manager also stands to gain from effective communication with his or her employees. In a national survey of managers, almost 60 percent identified good interpersonal communication skills as an important criterion for managers' promotions.[106]

What is the best way to communicate with employees—in writing or face to face? It depends on the situation. Often it is best to communicate orally, with a written follow-up. If you need immediate employee action, face-to-face communication followed by a written reminder is the most effective; sending only a written memo is the least effective.[107] On the other hand, if you are communicating about long-term actions, a written message is the most effective. Certain situations, such as reprimanding an employee or settling a dispute, are best handled in face-to-face interactions rather than through the use of any written messages.[108] The best managers take care to develop and send ethical, other-oriented messages. Then they follow up to ensure that the receiver understood the message and that it achieved its intended effect. Managers need to be especially other-oriented when they are sharing sensitive information or broaching personal topics.

As mentioned earlier, behaviors by supervisors that involve using power against subordinates for sexual favors constitute sexual harassment. However, supervisors also have a responsibility to eliminate a second type of sexual harassment that represents another dark side of interpersonal communication: a hostile environment. An employee in a **hostile environment** feels his or her rights are being violated because of working conditions or offensive behavior on the part of other workers. Telling lewd or obscene stories or jokes about members of the opposite sex, using degrading terms to describe women or men, or displaying risqué photographs of nude or seminude people can contribute to a hostile working environment. A supervisor who either creates or fails to change work situations that are threatening to a subordinate is a party to sexual harassment. Jokes are not innocent and pictures are not "all in fun" if they make an employee feel degraded. Supervisors must adopt an other-oriented approach with respect to this issue, as it is the receiver, not the sender, of the message who determines whether the behavior is hostile. Defendants have won court cases by proving that a supervisor tolerated a hostile work environment, even if the supervisor did not directly participate in the offensive behavior. As a supervisor, do not wait for a problem to occur; take a proactive approach. You can schedule seminars on how to avoid engaging in sexually offensive behavior and what actions workers should take if they become the victims of sexual harassment.

Horizontal Communication: Talking with Your Colleagues. You poke your head into your coworker's office and say, "Did you hear about the possible merger between Byteware and Datamass?" Or, while you are tossing pizza dough at the Pizza Palace, one of your fellow workers asks how much pepperoni to put on a Super Duper Supreme. Both situations illustrate horizontal communication. **Horizontal communication** refers to communication among coworkers at the same level within an organization. In larger organizations, you may talk with other workers in different departments or divisions who perform similar jobs at a similar level; that, too, is horizontal communication. Most often horizontal communication is used to

- coordinate job tasks;
- share plans and information;
- solve problems;

hostile environment Type of sexual harassment in which an employee's rights are threatened through offensive working conditions or behavior on the part of other workers.

horizontal communication Communication among colleagues or coworkers at the same level within an organization.

- make sure you understand procedures;
- manage conflict; or
- get emotional support on the job.[109]

Information travels through a workplace the way gossip travels through "the grapevine." And sometimes errors creep into workplace information that is spread this way. Although grapevine errors can cause problems for an organization, most continue to encourage coworker communication because it enhances teamwork and allows the work group to develop a certain degree of independence. Some organizations even try to formalize horizontal communication by forming *quality circles,* or groups of employees who meet together on a regular basis. These groups usually talk about such issues as how to improve the quality of services or products, reduce mistakes, lower costs, improve safety, or develop better ways of working together. Such active participation in the work process encourages workers to do a better job. Moreover, the training they receive to participate in these groups—training in group problem solving, decision-making skills, listening, relating, speaking, and managing conflict—applies to other areas of their work as well.

UNDERSTANDING OTHERS
Adapting to Differences

Intercultural Bargaining and Deal-Making

Given the global nature of today's businesses, you are likely to be involved in intercultural transactions. In Chapter 4 you read about some general qualities of intercultural communication, but cultures also vary in their business interactions. The following are a few samples of some of those variations. Whether you travel to another country to do business or do business in the United States with someone from another country, you should seek information about that other culture to enhance your interactions.

In Japan

Silence is acceptable during a meeting. Because of face issues, if asked something directly, Japanese will rarely say no but rather will say something like "I will consider this" or even "Yes," to avoid threatening your face by saying no. Given Japanese collectivistic values, you should offer compliments to the group or company rather than to an individual. Senior members of firms are expected to negotiate; having junior members conduct negotiations would be insulting. Talking with your hands (making lots of gestures) is considered distracting. Avoid touching or public displays of emotion.

In France

The approach to business is generally formal and conservative, and you will need to dress with style. You are expected to be on time, although the French might be late for meetings. Informality at a meeting might be seen as disrespectful—if you're a man, leave your jacket on. Many objections will be raised to any proposal you make as people examine all the possibilities; this is just the French way of doing business. Relationships are important, so networking is beneficial. Employers have family-like relationships with employees. Employees have strict job descriptions to which they adhere.

In Saudi Arabia

You should learn and use the Arabic greeting "Salaam." Use appropriate titles to show respect. After shaking your hand, a man might place his left hand on your right shoulder; you might be lightly kissed on both cheeks and your hand might be held for a prolonged time. A Saudi might offer to shake a women's hand, but that is all; women should adapt to their hosts. Business hierarchy is important. If you are meeting with someone higher up, that person may interrupt your meeting to focus on other things that need attention. Meetings might be scheduled around or interrupted for prayers. Eye contact is common, but people tend not to make eye contact with superiors. Gift giving is customary, but be sensitive to Muslim laws and customs—for example, do not give liquor, pig products, or pictures of women as gifts. Men accept gifts from men; women from women. A woman should not offer a gift on her own behalf to a man; it must be on behalf of another male.

In Mexico

Men usually exchange one quick, firm, handshake pump upon meeting; those who have known each other for a long time might embrace with a strong hug. Women might kiss each other on the cheek. Using some Spanish, as well as using "Señor" or "Señorita" or the person's title along with his or her last name, shows respect. Wait to be introduced by a third party; women will be introduced first, then the highest-ranking or eldest men. Meetings do not begin on time, but arrive promptly nonetheless; being an hour late for social events is typical. Business attire tends to be more European: conservative yet stylish, and highlighted by accessories. An easy-going and friendly manner, family, and friendship are highly valued. You need to establish friendship and mutual trust before you can work on business concerns.

Source: Adapted primarily from Dan Blacharski, *The Savvy Business Traveler's Guide to Customs and Practices in Other Countries: The Dos and Don'ts to Impress Your Hosts and Make the Sale* (Ocala, FL: Atlantic Publishing Group, 2008).

Outward Communication: Talking with Your Customers. More and more companies are becoming service oriented; one of the most important factors for success in such companies is building positive relationships with customers and clients. This pursuit has been formalized by organizations as "relationship marketing." Company members are taught many of the lessons contained in this book about building relationships. Successful organizations are other-oriented; they focus on the needs of those they serve through **outward communication.** They train their staffs to develop more empathy, better listening skills, and more awareness of nonverbal messages from customers.

outward communication
Communication that flows to those outside an organization (such as customers).

APPLYING AN OTHER-ORIENTATION
to Family and Workplace Relationships

Your parents probably will like this part of the text if the other-orientation exercise described below results in increased appreciation for them on your part. For you, the benefit is a better understanding of arguably the most influential family members in your life: your parents.

Effective other-orientation requires a consideration of your parents' backgrounds: their treatment as children by their parents, siblings, and other relatives; their educational and work experiences; and finally, the community and historical era in which they were raised. Imagine that you are writing a biography of your parents. Ask them about their upbringing, their childhood experiences, their education, their friends, their challenges—doing so, of course, while using your best listening skills. Talk to your uncles, aunts, grandparents, parent's friends, or older siblings to gain a more complete perspective on your parents. Socially decenter by putting yourself in their situation, imagining what it would have been like to grow up as they did, to work and raise a family. The goal of such reflections is to understand your parents' behaviors

and the choices they have made in creating a family and raising you.

Adopting an other-orientation puts you in a position to better understand those with whom you interact so that you more effectively manage those relationships and ultimately accomplish your personal goals. Applying an other-orientation to your understanding of coworkers, managers, subordinates, and clients can enhance your workplace effectiveness. One of our colleagues used to announce to his large lecture classes that the key to succeeding in his class was to figure out what he wanted and to give it to him—a pretty simple application of an other-orientation. Similarly, by figuring out what your boss, employees, or clients want, you are in a better position to adapt. Unlike the lecture situation however, you do have options about how to respond in the workplace. For example, knowing that an employee is having difficulty at home with his family doesn't mean you simply give the person lots of time off, since you also have a responsibility to the company to ensure that various jobs get done. In some ways, this is a situation in which being empathetic

can make a manager's decision making more difficult.

In business negotiation simulations with MBA students, those who thought about the interests and goals of their counterparts (perspective-taking) gained more benefits for themselves and the counterparts than did those who were concerned with the others' feelings (empathy), or those who negotiated without considering either.[110] Empathy was less effective and sometimes even detrimental to gaining benefits for the negotiators. However, since empathy creates the greatest satisfaction for the other person, the positive relationship it builds could be beneficial in future interactions.[111] These findings suggest that considering the other person's perspective can help you develop creative solutions that take into account both your goals and the goals of your partners (a principle of collaborative conflict management). Given that many of your organizational relationships will be long-term, showing empathy can help establish trust and satisfaction for others, but perspective-taking is also needed to help ensure that both parties benefit.

Family Relationships
(pages 343–360)

A family unit is made up of any number of people who live in relationship with one another over time in a common living space and are usually, but not always, united by marriage and kinship. The circumplex model of family interaction describes families according to their cohesion and adaptability, and considers the role of communication in affecting family members' roles and relationships. The family communication patterns model uses two dimensions, conversation orientation and conformity orientation, to identify four family types: pluralistic, consensual, protective, and laissez-faire. Several skills and strategies can enhance the quality of family life: taking time to talk with other family members about relationship issues, listening to others, supporting and encouraging one another, and using productive strategies for managing conflict and stress.

Committed partners be categorized as traditional (interdependent, sharing, and compassionate); independent (allowing for individual space but exhibiting sharing and compassion); separate (supporting marriage but putting the individual above the couple); or mixed (displaying different styles). Children are affected by and learn many communication skills from their parents through interaction, instruction, and observation. Your sibling relationships will change throughout your lifetime. During childhood and adolescence, siblings provide companionship, protection, support, and caretaking. Siblings provide more emotional and task help during early and middle adulthood. In late adulthood, siblings appreciate their special bond and their relationships become more important, communication increases, and assistance is provided when needed.

Key Terms

Family *344*

Natural or nuclear family *345*

Extended family *345*

Family of origin *345*

Blended family *345*

Single-parent family *346*

Circumplex model of family interaction *347*

Adaptability *348*

Cohesion *348*

Family communication patterns model *349*

Consensual families *350*

Pluralistic families *350*

Protective families *350*

Laissez-faire families *350*

Traditional couples *354*

Independent couples *354*

Separate couples *354*

Mixed couples *354*

Critical Thinking Questions

1. Do you think the institution of the family is deteriorating, or is it just changing? Support your answer.

2. Family communication changes throughout the life of the family: The married couple has a certain communication style that changes with the arrival of the first child and subsequent children. How might changes over the lifetime of a typical family cause it to evolve from one type of family to another in each of the two models of family communication?

3. Ethics: Is it ethical to withhold thoughts and feelings from family members? Should family members always "tell it like it is"? Should parents encourage their children to tell everything they know and feel?

Activities

What are your attitudes about families? Indicate whether you agree or disagree with the following statements. Talk to other class members and find out which items you agree and disagree on. Try to find reasons for differences of opinion. Decide together how you might reword statements to make ones on which you'd both agree.

_____ 1. Most family members know how to communicate effectively; they just don't take the time to practice what they know.

_____ 2. Family conflict is a symptom rather than a cause of deteriorating family relationships.

_____ 3. Family conflict is harmful to family harmony, and conflict should be avoided at all costs.

_____ 4. Most family conflict occurs because we don't understand the other family member; we fail to communicate effectively.

_____ 5. Families function best if there is one leader of the family.

_____ 6. Ineffective communication is the single most important cause of family conflict, divorce, and family tension.

_____ 7. Nonverbal communication (facial expression, eye contact, tone of voice, posture, and so on) is more important than verbal communication; what you do is more important than what you say.

_____ 8. It is sometimes necessary to ignore the feelings of others in order to reach a family decision.

_____ 9. The best way to love your spouse is to care more for your partner than you care for yourself.

_____ 10. Generally speaking, the quality of family life is deteriorating today.

_____ 11. There is one best approach or set of rules and principles that will ensure an effectively functioning family.

Do a family inventory: Assess your own family's communication behavior using the list of qualities of healthy families on page 351 and the skills and strategies for improving family communication. Which qualities are (were) strongest? Which need(ed) the most improvement? When you get married and have children, what qualities do you feel will be most important for your family to have? How will you accomplish that?

Some people develop relationships of choice with their family members. In groups of five or six, identify someone who has developed such a relationship with (a) a sibling, (b) a parent, and (c) another relative. Discuss why some students have developed friendships with these family members and why other students have not. Explore how these relationships are likely to change over the next ten to twenty years.

Web Resources

http://www.nncc.org/Parent/sf.series.html This site offers information on qualities that make up a strong family and recommended activities for families to do together.

http://www.youtube.com Conduct a search by entering "John Gottmann." You'll find several videos in which the noted marriage researcher talks about marriage.

http://www.lhj.com/lhj/quiz.jsp?quizId=/templatedata/lhj/quiz/data/TVFamilyQuiz.xml This site offers a *Ladies Home Journal* quiz that matches your family to a TV family, as well as lots of advice on families, married couples, love, and work.

Workplace Relationships (pages 360–372)

Workplace friendships follow typical relational development patterns but are affected by the context. These friendships provide a number of values and functions, including information exchange, social support, organizational support, newcomer assimilation, improved performance, retention, and organizational change and enhancement. Workplace romances are fairly common, fostered by proximity and similarities. Their dark side includes the impact on performance, dealing with relational termination, and sexual harassment. While companies might have guidelines for such relationships, those in workplace romances should act professional at all times, avoid conflicts of interest, and be prudent when using office communications.

Formal relationships in organizations determine the direction in which communication flows. Through upward communication (subordinates to supervisors) you can share ideas and strategies for improving the work process; you can also enhance your relationship with your boss. Downward communication (supervisors to subordinates) involves making contact with those who work for you. Decide whether you will send messages in writing, in person, or through mediated channels. Leader-member exchange theory identifies different factors that affect the relationships between managers and subordinates. Horizontal communication (among peers) is communication you have with colleagues on your level throughout an organization; most of the time, however, horizontal communication occurs with those who work in your immediate vicinity. Most organizations are encouraging better communication with customers and clients (through outward communication). Contacting those outside the organization who receive the organization's goods and services is an important way to ensure that what the organization offers is of high quality.

Key Terms

Quid pro quo harassment *364*
Upward communication *367*
Pelz effect *367*
Downward communication *369*
Leader-member exchange (LMX) theory *369*
Hostile environment *370*
Horizontal communication *370*
Outward communication *372*

Critical Thinking Questions

1. In what ways are workplace friendships different from friendships outside the workplace? In what ways are they similar? Which kind of relationship is more challenging to maintain? Why?

2. Jerry is president of Southwest Technical Computing. He has a sense that his managers are not tapping the wealth of ideas and suggestions that lower-level employees might have for improving productivity. What specific strategies could Jerry implement to improve upward communication?

3. Ethics: You've become very attracted to one of your subordinates with whom you get along with very well. You work well together and have had lunch and drinks together. You suggest pursuing a romantic relationship, but the subordinate feels that would create conflict of interest. If you really think this could be a special long-term relationship, should you continue to convince the subordinate, or return to a purely professional relationship? Why?

4. Ethics: Clayton has e-mail service at work but not at home. Is it ethical for Clayton to use the computer at work on company time to send and receive e-mail messages from his brother three or four times a week?

Activities

What values or functions of a workplace friendship are most important to you? Make a list and compare it with those of your classmates.

You believe your boss is treating you unfairly because you have not responded to what you interpreted as romantic overtures (though no explicit request for a date or affection has ever been made). How can you best address this issue?

Think about the best manager or supervisor you have worked for or observed. Make a list of the qualities that you think made this manager so effective. Think about the worst manager or supervisor you've worked for or observed. Make a list of the qualities that made the manager so ineffective. Compare your lists with those of your classmates and identify the five best and five worst qualities. To what degree does communication play a role in these qualities?

Web Resources

http://www.microsoft.com/education/competencies/comp_managingrelationships.mspx This Microsoft consulting web site describes a set of competencies for managing relationships in the workplace and includes reflective questions.

http://www.workrelationships.com/site/quiz/ This fifteen-item quiz, the *Appropriate Workplace Behavior Test*, is designed to test your knowledge of ethical relational behavior in the workplace.

http://www.uky.edu/~drlane/orgcomm/325ch11.ppt#263,7, This site offers a PowerPoint presentation on workplace relationship challenges.

Notes

Chapter 1

1. For a discussion of the role of communication and intentionality, see J. B. Bavelas, "Forum: Can One Not Communicate? Behaving and Communicating: A Reply to Motley," *Western Journal of Speech Communication* 54 (Fall 1990): 593–602.

2. E. T. Klemmer and F. W. Snyder, "Measurement of Time Spent Communicating." *Journal of Communication* 20 (June 1972): 142; also see L. Barker et al., "An Investigation of Proportional Time Spent in Various Communication Activities of College Students," *Journal of Applied Communication Research* 8 (1981): 101–09; R. Emanuel, J. Adams, K. Baker, E. K. Daufin, C. Ellington, E. Fitts, J. Himsel, L. Holladay, and D. Okeowo, "How College Students Spend Their Time Communicating," *International Journal of Listening* 22 (2008): 12–28.

3. E. E. Graham and C. K. Shue, "Reflections on the Past, Directions for the Future: A Template for the Study and Instruction of Interpersonal Communication," *Communication Research Reports* 17 (Fall 2000): 337–48.

4. F. E. X. Dance and C. Larson, *Speech Communication: Concepts and Behavior* (New York: Holt, Rinehart and Winston, 1972).

5. Dance and Larson, *Speech Communication*.

6. J. T. Masterson, S. A. Beebe, and N. H. Watson, *Invitation to Effective Speech Communication* (Glenview, IL: Scott, Foresman, 1989).

7. L. M. Webb and M. E. Thompson-Hayes, "Do Popular Collegiate Textbooks in Interpersonal Communication Reflect a Common Theory Base? A Telling Content Analysis," *Communication Education* 51 (April 2002): 210–24.

8. W. Carl and S. Duck, "How to Do Things with Relationships . . . and How Relationships Do Things with Us," *Communication Yearbook* 28 (2004): 1–35.

9. M. Buber, *I and Thou* (New York: Scribners, 1958); also see M. Buber, *Between Man and Man* (New York: Macmillan, 1965). For a detailed discussion of perspectives on interpersonal communication and relationship development, see G. H. Stamp, "A Qualitatively Constructed Interpersonal Communication Model: A Grounded Theory Analysis," *Human Communication Research* 25 (June 1999): 531–47; J. P. Dillard, D. H. Solomon, and M. T. Palmer, "Structuring the Concept of Relational Communication," *Communication Monographs* 66 (March 1999): 49–65.

10. Buber, *I and Thou*.

11. Buber, *I and Thou*.

12. K. Domenici and S. W. Littlejohn, *Facework: Bridging Theory and Practice* (Thousand Oaks, CA: Sage, 2006), 91.

13. V. Satir, *Peoplemaking* (Palo Alto, CA: Science and Behavior Books, 1972); J. B. Miller and P. A. deWinstanley, "The Role of Interpersonal Competence in Memory for Conversation," *Personality and Social Psychology Bulletin* 28 (January 2002): 78–89.

14. K. E. Davis and M. Todd, "Assessing Friendship: Prototypes, Paradigm Cases, and Relationship Description," in *Understanding Personal Relationships*, edited by S. W. Duck and D. Perlman (London: Sage, 1985); B. Wellman, "From Social Support to Social Network," in *Social Support, Theory, Research and Applications*, edited by I. G. Sarason and B. R. Sarason (Dordrecht, Netherlands: Nijhoff, 1985); R. Hopper, M. L. Knapp, and L. Scott, "Couples' Personal Idioms: Exploring Intimate Talk," *Journal of Communication* 31 (1981): 23–33; S. Pendell, "Affection in Interpersonal Relationships: Not Just 'A Fond or Tender Feeling,'" in *Communication Yearbook* 26, edited by W. B. Gudykunst (Mahwah, NJ: Erlbaum, 2002): 71–115.

15. M. Argyle and M. Hendershot, *The Anatomy of Relationships* (London: Penguin Books, 1985), 14.

16. R. E. Riggio, "Assessment of Basic Social Skills," *Journal of Personality and Social Psychology* 51, no. 3 (1986): 649–60.

17. See J. L. Winsor, D. B. Curtis, and R. D. Stephens, "National Preferences in Business and Communication Education: A Survey Update," *Journal of the Association for Communication Administration* 3 (September 1997), 174; *The Wall Street Journal*, September, 9, 2002: 1A.

18. K. Martell and S. Carroll, "Stress the Functional Skills When Hiring Top Managers," *HRMagazine* 39 (1994): 85–87; E. Tanyel, M. Mitchell, and H. G. McAlum, "The Skill Set for Success of New Business School Graduates: Do Prospective Employers and University Faculty Agree?" *Journal of Education for Business* 75 (1999): 33–37; W. J. Wardrope, "Department Chairs' Perceptions of the Importance of Business Communication Skills," *Business Communication Quarterly* 65 (2002): 60–72.

19. M. Argyle, *The Psychology of Happiness* (London: Routledge, 1987).

20. J. J. Lynch, *The Broken Heart: The Medical Consequences of Loneliness* (New York: Basic Books, 1977).

21. R. Korbin and G. Hendershot, "Do Family Ties Reduce Mortality: Evidence from the United States 1968," *Journal of Marriage and the Family* 39 (1977): 737–45.

22. D. P. Phillips, "Deathday and Birthday: An Unexpected Connection," in *Statistics: A Guide to the Unknown*, edited by J. M. Tanur (San Francisco: Holden Day, 1972).

23. Argyle, *The Psychology of Happiness*.

24. B. L. Fredrickson and M. F. Losada, "Positive Affect and the Complex Dynamics of Human Flourishing," *American Psychologist* (October 2005): 678–86.

25. For a comprehensive overview of the history of the study of interpersonal communication, see M. L. Knapp, J. A. Daly, K. F. Albada, and G. R. Miller, "Background and Current Trends in the Study of Interpersonal Communication," in *Handbook of Interpersonal Communication*, edited by M. L. Knapp and J. A. Daly (Thousand Oaks, CA: Sage, 2002), 3–20.

26. Among the first scholars to identify a link between the sender of a message and message context was Kurt Lewin in K. Lewin, *A Dynamic Theory of Personality* (New York: McGraw-Hill, 1935); Carl and Duck, "How to Do Things with Relationships."

27. I. Reed, "The World Is Here," in *Writin' Is Fightin'* (New York: Atheneum, 1988).

28. See V. E. Cronen, W. B. Pearce, and L. M. Harris, "The Coordinated Management of Meaning: A Theory of Communication," in *Human Communication Theory: Comparative Essays,* edited by F. E. X. Dance (New York: Harper & Row, 1982), 61–89.

29. N. S. Baron, *Always On: Language in an Online and Mobile World* (New York: Oxford University Press, 2008), 24; also see D. Crystal, *txtng: The gr8 db8* (Oxford: Oxford University Press, 2008).

30. L. C. Tidwell and J. B. Walther, "Computer-Mediated Communication Effects on Disclosure, Impressions, and Interpersonal Evaluations: Getting to Know One Another a Bit at a Time," *Human Communication Research* 28 (July 2002): 317–48.

31. Baron, *Always On*, 25.

32. Baron, *Always On*, 26.

33. Chris DeWolfe and Tom Anderson, co-founders of MySpace, interviewed by Charlie Rose, *The Charlie Rose Show*, PBS (February 3, 2009).

34. Y. Amichai-Hamburger, *The Social Net: Human Behavior in Cyberspace* (Oxford, England: Oxford University Press, 2005), v.

35. Baron, *Always On*, 28.

36. D. Knox, V. Daniels, L. Sturdivant, and M. E. Zusman, "College Student Use of the Internet for Mate Selection," *College Student Journal* 35 (March 2001): 158.

37. K. M. Cornetto, "Suspicion in Cyberspace: Deception and Detection in the Context of Internet Relay Chat Rooms," paper presented at the annual meeting of the National Communication Association, Chicago (November 1999).

38. J. B. Walther and J. K. Burgoon, "Relational Communication in Computer-Mediated Interaction," *Human Communication Research* 19 (1992): 50–88.

39. Cornetto, "Suspicion in Cyberspace."

40. R. R. Provine, R. J. Spencer, and D. L. Mandell, "Emotional Expression Online: Emoticons Punctuate Website Text Message," *Journal of Language and Social Psychology* 26 (2007): 299–307.

41. J. P. Walther, B. Van Der Heide, S.-Y. Kim, D. Westerman, and S. T. Tong, "The Role of Friends' Appearance and Behavior on Evaluations of Individuals on Facebook: Are We Known by the Company We Keep?" *Human Communication Research* 34 (2008): 28–49; also see Baron, *Always On*, 64–70; N. Chesley, "Blurring Boundaries? Linking Technology Use, Spillover, Individual Distress, and Family Satisfaction," *Journal of Marriage and Family* 67 (December 2005): 1237–48; D. K.-S. Chan and G. H.-L. Cheng, "A Comparison of Offline and Online Friendship Qualities at Different Stages of Relationship Development," *Journal of Social and Personal Relationships* 21 (2004): 305–20; Provine, Spencer, and Mandell, "Emotional Expression Online."

42. J. Shuler, "E-Mail Communication and Relationships," in *The Psychology of Cyberspace*, www.rider.edu/users/suler/psycyber/psycyber.html (August 1998).

43. R. Kraut, S. Kiesler, B. Boneva, J. Cummings, V. Helgeson, and A. Crawford, "Internet Paradox Revisited," *Journal of Social Issues*, 58 (2002): 49–74; P. E. N. Howard, L. Raine, and S. Jones, "Days and Nights on the Internet: The Impact of a Diffusing Technology," *American Behavioral Scientist*, 45 (2001): 383–404.

44. September 2005 Daily Tracking Survey/Online Dating Extension, Pew Internet & American Life Project, http://www.pewinternet.org/pdfs/Online_Dating_Questions.pdf.

45. J. B. Walther, "Computer-Mediated Communication: Impersonal, Interpersonal, and Hyperpersonal Interaction," *Communication Research* 23 (1996): 3–43. J. B. Walther, C. L. Slovacek, and L. C. Tidwell, "Is a Picture Worth a Thousand Words? Photographic Images in Long-Term and Short-Term Computer-Mediated Communication," *Communication Research* 28 (2001): 105–34.

46. Tidwell and Walther, "Computer-Mediated Communication Effects on Disclosure, Impressions, and Interpersonal Evaluations."

47. N. S. Baron, *Always On,* 27.

48. I. Sproull and S. Kiesler, "Reducing Social Context Cues: Electronic Mail in Organizational Communication," *Management Science* 32 (1986): 1492–1513.

49. L. K. Trevino, R. L. Draft, and R. H. Lengel, "Understanding Managers' Media Choices: A Symbolic Interactionist Perspective," in *Organizations and Communication Technology,* edited by J. Fulk and C. Steinfield (Newbury Park, CA: Sage, 1990), 71–74.

50. Tidwell and Walther, 2002.

51. N. Silver, *Age Sex Location* (Colchester, England: tXt café, 2006).

52. As cited by D. Crystal, *txtng: The gr8 db8.*

53. Cheil Communications, *Exploring P-Generation* (Seoul, Korea, 2003).

54. R. Ling and P. Pedersen (Eds.), *Mobile Communications: Renegotiation of the Social Sphere* (London: Springer, 2005): 335–49.

55. Crystal, *txtng: The gr8 db8,* 42.

56. Ling and Pedersen, *Mobile Communications,* 335.

57. Research summarized by Crystal, *txtng: The gr8 db8,* 91.

58. Adapted from Crystal, *txtng: The gr8 db8.*

59. N. Silver, *Laugh Out Loud :-D* (Colchester, England: tXt café, 2008).

60. Walther and Burgoon, "Relational Communication in Computer-Mediated Interaction."

61. W. S. Sanders, "Uncertainty Reduction and Information-Seeking Strategies on Facebook," paper presented to the National Communication Association, San Diego, CA (November 2008).

62. Tidwell and Walther, 2002.

63. J. B. Walther and L. Tidwell, "When Is Mediated Communication Not Interpersonal?" in K. Galvin and P. Cooper, *Making Connections* (Los Angeles, CA: Roxbury Press, 1996).

64. C. R. Berger and J. J. Bradac, *Language and Social Knowledge: Uncertainty in Interpersonal Relations* (London: Arnold, 1982); C. R. Berger and R. J. Calabrese, "Some Explorations in Initial Interaction and Beyond: Toward a Developmental Theory of Interpersonal Communication," *Human Communication Research* 1 (1975): 99–112.

65. See D. Barnlund, *Interpersonal Communication: Survey and Studies* (Boston: Houghton Mifflin, 1968).

66. O. Wiio, *Wiio's Laws—and Some Others* (Espoo, Finland: WelinGoos, 1978).

67. S. B. Shimanoff, *Communication Rules: Theory and Research* (Beverly Hills: Sage, 1980).

68. M. Argyle, M. Hendershot, and A. Furnham, "The Rules of Social Relationships," *British Journal of Social Psychology* 24 (1985): 125–39.

69. B. Parkinson, A. H. Fischer, and A. S. R. Manstead, *Emotion in Social Relations: Cultural, Group, and Interpersonal Processes* (New York: Psychology Press, 2004).

70. W. Gerrod Parrott, "The Nature of Emotion," in M. B. Brewer and M. Hewston, *Emotion and Motivation* (Oxford, England: Blackwell Publishing, 2004), 6.

71. M. S. Clark, J. Fitness, and I. Brissette, "Understanding People's Perceptions of Relationships Is Crucial to Understanding Their Emotional Lives," in M. B. Brewer and M. Hewston, *Emotion and Motivation* (Oxford, England: Blackwell Publishing, 2004), 21–46.

72. D. Matsumoto, J. LeRoux, C. Wilson-Cohn, J. Raroque, K. Kooken, P. Ekman, N. Yrizarry, S. Loewinger, H. Uchida, A. Yee, L. Amo, and A. Goh, "A New Test to Measure Emotion Recognition Ability: Matsumoto and Ekman's Japanese and Caucasian Brief Affect Recognition Test (JACBART)," *Journal of Nonverbal Behavior* 24 (Fall 2000): 179–209; F. Trompenaars and C. Hampden-Turner, *Riding the Waves of Culture* (New York: McGraw Hill, 1988); M. R. Hammer, "The Intercultural Conflict Style Inventory: A Conceptual Framework and Measure of Intercultural Conflict Resolution Approaches," *International Journal of Intercultural Relations* 29 (2005): 675–95.

73. P. Ekman and W. Friesen, "Constants Across Cultures in the Face and Emotion," *Journal of Personality and Social Psychology* 12 (1971): 124–29.

74. For an excellent review of emotional contagion, see E. Hatfield, J. T. Cacioppo, and R. L. Rapson, *Emotional Contagion* (New York: Cambridge University Press, 1994).

75. See J. C. McCroskey and M. J. Beatty, "The Communibiological Perspective: Implications for Communication in Instruction," *Communication Education* 49 (January 2000): 1–6; M. J. Beatty and J. C. McCroskey, "Theory, Scientific Evidence, and the Communibiological Paradigm: Reflections on Misguided Criticism," *Communication Education* 49 (January 2000): 36–44. Also see J. C. McCroskey, J. A. Daly, M. M. Martin, and M. J. Beatty (eds.), *Communication and Personality: Trait Perspectives* (Cresskill, NJ: Hampton Press, 1998); and M. J. Beatty, A. D. Heisel, A. E. Hall, T. R. Levine, and B. H. La France, "What Can We Learn from the Study of Twins about Genetic and Environmental Influences on Interpersonal Affiliation, Aggressiveness, and Social Anxiety? A Meta-Analytic Study," *Communication Monographs* 69 (March 2002): 1–18.

76. For additional information about the role of biology in influencing social behavior, see S. Pinker, "My Genome, My Self," *The New York Times Magazine,* January 11, 2009: 24–31.

77. See J. Ayres and T. S. Hopf, "The Long-Term Effect of Visualization in the Classroom: A Brief Research Report," *Communication Education* 39 (1990): 75–78; and J. Ayres and T. S. Hopf, "Visualization: A Means of Reducing Speech Anxiety," *Communication Education* 34 (1985): 318–23.

78. For a discussion of criticism of the communibiological approach, see C. M. Condit, "Culture and Biology in Human Communication: Toward a Multi-Causal Model," *Communication Education* 49 (January 2000): 7–24.

79. A. Bandura, *Social Learning Theory* (Englewood Cliffs, NJ: Prentice-Hall, 1977).

80. S. R. Wilson and C. M. Sabee, "Explicating Communicative Competence as a Theoretical Term," in *Handbook of Communication and Social Interaction Skills,* edited by J. O. Greene and B. R. Burleson (Mahwah, NJ: Erlbaum, 2003), 3–50.

81. M. J. Collier, "Researching Cultural Identity: Reconciling Interpretive and Postcolonial Approaches," in *Communication and Identity Across Cultures,* edited by D. Tanno and A. Gonzalez (Thousand Oaks, CA: Sage, 1998), 142. Also see S. DeTurk, "Intercultural Empathy: Myth, Competency, or Possibility for Alliance Building?" *Communication Education* 50 (October 2001): 374–84.

82. G. A. Hullman, "Interpersonal Communication Motives and Message Design Logic: Exploring Their Interaction on Perceptions of Competence," *Communication Monographs* 71 (2004): 208–25.

83. E. P. Almeida, "A Disclosure Analysis of Student Perceptions of Their Communication Competence," *Communication Education* 53, no. 4 (2004): 357–64.

84. Miller and deWinstanley, 2002.

85. L. Carrell and S. C. Wilmington, "A Comparison of Self-Report and Performance Data in Assessing Speaking and Listening Competence," *Communication Reports* 9, no. 2 (1996): 185–91.

86. M. Argyle, *The Psychology of Interpersonal Behavior* (London: Penguin, 1983).

87. J. Hakansson and H. Montgomery, "Empathy as an Interpersonal Phenomenon," *Journal of Social and Personal Relationships* 20 (2003): 267–84; Y. Nakatani, "The Effects of Awareness-Raising Training on Oral Communication Strategy Use," *The Modern Language Journal* 89 (2005): 76–91.

88. For additional information about the importance of self-preservation and evolution, see R. Dawkins, *The Selfish Gene* (Oxford: Oxford University Press, 1976).

89. K. J. K. Asada, E. Lee, T. R. Levine, and M. H. Ferrara, "Narcissism and Empathy as Predictors of Obsessive Relational Intrusion," *Communication Research Reports* 21 (2004): 379–90.

90. J. M. Twenge, *Generation Me: Why Today's Young Americans Are More Confident, Assertive, Entitled—and More Miserable Than Ever Before.* New York: Free Press (2006): 69.

91. Twenge, 2006.

92. M. V. Redmond, "Adaptation in Everyday Interactions," paper presented at the annual meeting of the National Communication Association (November 1997).

93. M. Argyle is widely acknowledged as the first scholar to suggest a systematic approach to applying learning theory to the development of social skills, including interpersonal communication skills. See Argyle, 1983.

Chapter 2

1. K. Horney, *Neurosis and Human Growth* (New York: Norton, 1950), 17.

2. Our definition is based on a discussion of mindfulness in K. Domenici and S. W. Littlejohn, *Facework: Bridging Theory and Practice* (Thousand Oaks, CA: Sage, 2008), 158.

3. R. A. Baron and D. Byrne, *Social Psychology* (Boston: Allyn & Bacon, 2003).

4. E. Goffman, *The Presentation of Self in Everyday Life* (Garden City, NY: Doubleday, Anchor Books, 1959). Also see E. Goffman, *Frame Analysis: An Essay on the Organization of Experience* (Cambridge, MA: Harvard University Press, 1974).

5. Goffman, *Frame Analysis,* 508.

6. W. James, *The Principles of Psychology* (New York: Holt, 1890).

7. Adapted from W. Ham, *Man's Living Religions* (Independence, MO: Herald Publishing House, 1966), 39–40.

8. C. H. Cooley, *Human Nature and the Social Order* (New York: Scribners, 1902).

9. G. H. Mead, *Mind, Self, and Society* (Chicago: University of Chicago Press, 1934).

10. H. S. Sullivan, *The Interpersonal Theory of Psychiatry* (New York: Norton, 1953).

11. B. R. Sarason, G. R. Pierce, and I. G. Sarason, "Social Support: The Sense of Acceptance and the Role of Relationships," in *Social Support: An Interactional View,* edited by B. R. Sarason, I. G. Sarason, and G. R. Pierce (New York: Wiley, 1990), 97–128.

12. See M. D. S. Ainsworth, M. C. Blehar, E. Waters, and S. Wall, *The Patterns of Attachment: A Psychological Study of the Strange Situation* (Hillsdale, NJ: Erlbaum, 1978); J. Bowlby, *Attachment and Loss: Volume 1* (London: Hogarth Press, 1969); C. Hazan and P. R. Shaver, "Romantic Love Conceptualized as an Attachment Process," *Journal of Personality and Social Psychology* 52 (1987): 511–24; K. Bartholomew,

"Avoidance of Intimacy: An Attachment Perspective," *Journal of Social and Personal Relationships* 7 (1990): 147–78; A. J. Z. Henderson, K. Bartholomew, J. S.Trinkle, and M. J. Kwong, "When Loving Means Hurting: An Exploration of Attachment and Intimacy Abuse in a Community Sample," *Journal of Family Violence* 20 (2005): 219–30.

13. Ainsworth, Blehar, Waters, and Wall, *The Patterns of Attachment*; Bowlby, *Attachment and Loss*.

14. K. D. Mickelson, R. Kessler, and P. R. Shaver, "Adult Attachment in a Nationally Representative Sample," *Journal of Personality and Social Psychology* 73 (1997): 1092–1106.

15. Mickelson, Kessler, and Shaver, "Adult Attachment in a Nationally Representative Sample."

16. Mickelson, Kessler, and Shaver, "Adult Attachment in a Nationally Representative Sample."

17. J. T. Masterson, *Speech Communication in Traditional and Contemporary Marriages* (doctoral dissertation, University of Denver, 1977). Also see S. A. Beebe and J. T. Masterson, *Family Talk: Interpersonal Communication in the Family* (New York: Random House, 1986), 91–100.

18. B. Marcus, F. Machilek, and A. Schutz, "Personality in Cyberspace: Personal Web Sites as Media for Personality Expressions and Impressions," *Journal of Personality and Social Psychology* 90, no. 6 (2006): 1014–31; J. B. Walther, B. Van Der Heide, S. Y. Kim, D. Westerman, and S. T. Tong, "The Role of Friends' Appearance and Behavior on Evaluations of Individuals on Facebook: Are We Known by the Company We Keep?" *Human Communication Research* 34 (2008): 28–49.

19. L. C. Tidwell and J. B. Walther, "Computer-Mediated Communication Effects on Disclosure, Impressions, and Interpersonal Evaluations: Getting to Know One Another a Bit at a Time," *Human Communication Research* 28, (July 2002): 317–48.

20. B. Cornwell and D. C. Lundgren, "Love on the Internet: Involvement and Misrepresentation in Romantic Relationships in Cyberspace vs. Realspace," *Computers in Human Behavior* 17 (2001): 197–211.

21. D. Knox, V. Daniels, L. Sturdivant, and M. E. Zusman, "College Student Use of the Internet for Mate Selection," *College Student Journal* 35 (March 2001): 158.

22. M. K. Matsuba, "Searching for Self and Relationships Online," *CyberPsychology & Behavior* 3 (2006): 275–84.

23. D. G. Ancona, "Groups in Organizations: Extending Laboratory Models," in *Annual Review of Personality and Social Psychology: Group and Intergroup Processes*, edited by C. Hendrick (Beverly Hills, CA: Sage, 1987), 207–31. Also see D. G. Ancona and D. E. Caldwell, "Beyond Task and Maintenance: Defining External Functions in Groups," *Group and Organizational Studies* 13 (1988): 468–94.

24. S. L. Bem, "The Measurement of Psychological Androgyny," *Journal of Consulting and Clinical Psychology* 42 (1974): 155–62.

25. L. A. Lefton, *Psychology* (Boston: Allyn & Bacon, 2000).

26. J. C. McCroskey and M. J. Beatty, "The Communibiological Perspective: Implications for Communication Instruction," *Communication Education* 49 (January 2000): 1–28.

27. C. M. Condit, "Culture and Biology in Human Communication: Toward a Multi-Causal Model," *Communication Education* 49 (January 2000): 7–24. Also see K. Floyd, A. C. Mikkelson, and C. Hesse, *The Biology of Human Communication* (Mason, OH: Cengage Learning), 2008. For a contrasting view of the importance of biology in shaping our behavior, see S. Begley, "When DNA Is Not Destiny," *Newsweek* (December 1, 2008): 14.

28. P. Zimbardo, *Shyness: What It Is, What to Do About It* (Reading, MA: Addison-Wesley, 1977).

29. S. Booth-Butterfield, "Instructional Interventions for Situational Anxiety and Avoidance," *Communication Education* 37 (1988): 214–23.

30. W. Gerrod Parrott, "The Nature of Emotion," in *Emotion and Motivation*, edited by M. B. Brewer and M. Hewston (Oxford, England: Blackwell Publishing, 2004), 6. Also see R. A. Baron, B. Earhard, and M. Ozier, *Psychology* (Toronto: Pearson Education, 2001).

31. See W. James, "What Is an Emotion?" *Mind* 9 (1884) 188–205. Also see B. Parkinson, A. H. Fischer, and A. S. R. Manstead, *Emotion in Social Relations: Cultural, Group, and Interpersonal Processes* (New York: Psychology Press, 2004).

32. S. Schacter and J. E. Singer, "Cognitive, Social, and Physiological Determinants of Emotional States," *Psychological Review* 69 (1962): 379–99.

33. J. C. McCroskey and V. P. Richmond, *Fundamentals of Human Communication: An Interpersonal Perspective* (Prospect Heights, IL: Waveland Press, 1996).

34. Booth-Butterfield, "Instructional Interventions."

35. Zimbardo, *Shyness*.

36. E. Sahlstein and M. Allen, "Sex Differences in Self-Esteem: A Meta-Analytic Assessment," in *Interpersonal Communication Research: Advances Through Meta-Analysis*, edited by M. Allen, R. W. Preiss, B. M. Gayle, and N. A. Burrell (Mahwah, NJ: Erlbaum, 2002), 59–72; K. Dindia, "Self-Disclosure Research: Knowledge Through Meta-Analysis," in *Interpersonal Communication Research: Advances Through Meta-Analysis*, edited by M. Allen, R. W. Preiss, B. M. Gayle, and N. A. Burrell (Mahwah, NJ: Erlbaum, 2002), 169–85; G. V. Caprara and P. Steca, "Self-Efficacy Beliefs as Determinants of Prosocial Behavior Conducive to Life Satisfaction Across Ages," *Journal of Social and Clinical Psychology* 24 (2005): 191–217.

37. S. M. Pottebaum, T. Z. Keith, and S. W. Ehly, "Is There a Casual Relation Between Self-Concept and Academic Achievement?" *Journal of Educational Research* 79, no. 3 (January/February 1986): 140–44.

38. R. F. Baumeister, J. D. Campbell, J. I. Krueger, and K. D. Vohs, "Does High Self-Esteem Cause Better Performance, Interpersonal Success, Happiness, or Healthier Lifestyles?" *Psychological Science in the Public Interest* 4, no. 1 (May 2003): 1–44; also see S. Lyubomirsky, C. Tkach, and M. R. Dimatteo, "What Are the Differences Between Happiness and Self-Esteem?" *Social Indicators Research* 78 (2006): 363–404.

39. E. Berne, *Games People Play* (New York: Grove Press, 1964).

40. S. Ting Toomey, J. G. Oetzel, and K. Yee-Jung, "Self-Construal Types and Conflict Management Styles," *Communication Reports* 14 (Summer 2001): 87–104.

41. For a comprehensive discussion of the history of facework, see Domenici and Littlejohn, *Facework*.

42. Goffman, *The Presentation of Self in Everyday Life*.

43. Domenici and Littlejohn, *Facework*.

44. Domenici and Littlejohn, *Facework*.

45. P. Brown and S. C. Levinson, *Politeness: Some Universals in Language Use* (Cambridge, England: Cambridge University Press, 1987).

46. Domenici and Littlejohn, *Facework*.

47. L. Armstrong, *It's Not About the Bike: My Journey Back to Life* (New York: Putnam's, 2000), 146.

48. J. L. S. Borton, L. J. Markowitz, and J. Dieterich, "Effects of Suppressing Negative Self-Referent Thoughts on Mood and Self-Esteem," *Journal of Social and Clinical Psychology* 24 (2005): 172–90.

49. D. B. Feldman and C. R. Snyder, "Hope and the Meaningful Life: Theoretical and Empirical Associations Between Goal-Directed Thinking and Life Meaning," *Journal of Social and Clinical Psychology* 24 (2005): 401–21.

50. J. Ayres and T. S. Hopf, "The Long-Term Effect of Visualization in the Classroom: A Brief Research Report," *Communication Education* 39 (1990): 75–78.

51. J. W. Younger, R. L. Piferi, R. L. Jobe, and K. A. Lawler, "Dimensions of Forgiveness: The Views of Laypersons," *Journal of Social and Personal Relationships* 21 (2004): 837–55.

52. K. Weber, A. Johnson, and M. Corrigan, "Communicating Emotional Support and Its Relationship to Feelings of Being Understood, Trust, and Self-Disclosure," *Communication Research Reports* 21 (2004): 316–23.

53. F. E. X. Dance and C. Larson, *The Functions of Human Communication* (New York: Holt, Rinehart and Winston, 1976), 141.

54. Mead, *Mind, Self and Society*.

55. P. A. Siegel, J. Scillitoe, and R. Parks-Yancy, "Reducing the Tendency to Self-Handicap: The Effect of Self-Affirmation," *Journal of Experimental Social Psychology* 41, no. 6 (2005): 589–97.

56. G. V. Caprara and P. Steca, "Self-Efficacy Beliefs as Determinants of Prosocial Behavior Conducive to Life Satisfaction Across Ages," *Journal of Social and Clinical Psychology* 24 (2005): 191–217.

57. H. Brody. *The Placebo Response: How You Can Release Your Body's Inner Pharmacy for Better Health* (New York: HarperCollins, 2000). Also see H. Brody, "Tapping the Power of the Placebo," *Newsweek* (August 14, 2000): 68.

58. A. A. Milne, "Pooh Does a Good Deed," in *Pooh Sleepytime Stories* (New York: Golden Press, 1979), 44.

59. *Looking Out/Looking In*, edited by R. B. Adler and N. Towne (Fort Worth, TX: Harcourt Brace Jovanovich, 1993). Also see C. R. Berger, "Self Conception and Social Information Processing," in *Personality and Interpersonal Communication*, edited by J. C. McCroskey and J. A. Daly (1986): 275–303.

60. A. A. Milne, "Owl Finds a Home," in *Pooh Sleepytime Stories* (New York: Golden Press, 1979), 28.

61. D. E. Hamachek, *Encounters with the Self* (New York: Holt, Rinehart and Winston, 1982); Berger, "Self-Conception."

62. W. C. Schutz, *FIRO: A Three-Dimensional Theory of Interpersonal Behavior* (New York: Holt, Rinehart and Winston, 1958).

63. Dindia, "Self-Disclosure Research."

64. J. Luft, *Group Process: An Introduction to Group Dynamics* (Palo Alto, CA: Mayfield, 1970).

65. C. G Jung, *Psychological Types* (Princeton, NJ: Princeton University Press, 1976).

66. For a review of applied social style research, see R. Bolton and D. G. Bolton, *People Styles at Work: Making Bad Relationships Good and Good Relationships Better* (New York: AMACOM, 1996). For an excellent review of communication and social style research literature, see W. B. Snavely and J. D. McNeill, "Communicator Style and Social Style: Testing a Theoretical Interface," *Journal of Leadership and*

Organizational Studies 14, no. 3 (February 2008): 219–32:

67. Snavely and McNeill, "Communicator Style and Social Style," 220.

68. Snavely and McNeill, "Communicator Style and Social Style," 219.

69. Bolton and Bolton, *People Styles at Work*, 82.

70. Bolton and Bolton, *People Styles at Work*, 83.

Chapter 3

1. I. P. R. Hinton, *The Psychology of Interpersonal Perception* (New York: Routledge, 1993).

2. M. Gladwell, *Blink: The Power of Thinking Without Thinking* (New York: Little, Brown and Company, 2005).

3. J. Gottman with N. Silver, *Why Marriages Succeed or Fail* (New York: Simon and Schuster, 1994); also see J. M. Gottman and J. S. Gottman, *10 Lessons to Transform Your Marriage* (New York: Crown Publishers, 2006).

4. P. Watzlawick, J. Bevelas, and D. Jackson, *The Pragmatics of Human Communication* (New York: Norton, 1967).

5. A. L. Sillars, "Attribution and Communication: Are People Naive Scientists or Just Naive?" in *Social Cognition and Communication,* edited by M. E. Roloff and C. R. Berger (Beverly Hills: Sage, 1982), 73–106.

6. Watzlawick et al., *The Pragmatics of Human Communication.*

7. S. Bruner and R. Tagiuri, "The Perception of People," in *Handbook of Social Psychology,* edited by G. Lindzey (Cambridge, MA: Addison-Wesley, 1954).

8. G. A. Kelly, *The Psychology of Personal Constructs* (New York: Norton, 1995).

9. C. R. Berger and J. J. Bradac, *Language and Social Knowledge* (Baltimore: Edward Arnold, 1982).

10. S. Asch, "Forming Impressions of Personality," *Journal of Abnormal and Social Psychology* 41 (1946): 258–90.

11. D. M. Wegner and R. R. Vallacher, *Implicit Psychology: An Introduction to Social Cognition* (New York: Oxford University Press, 1977).

12. A. L. Sillars, "Attributions and Communication in Roommate Conflicts," *Communication Monographs* 47 (1980): 180–200.

13. D. A. Infante and A. S. Rancer, "Argumentativeness and Verbal Aggressiveness: A Review of Recent Theory and Research," in *Communication Yearbook 19,* edited by B. R. Burleson (Thousand Oaks, CA: Sage, 1996), 319–52.

14. D. Hample, "The Life Space of Personalized Conflicts," in *Communication Yearbook 23,* edited by M. E. Roloff (Thousand Oaks, CA: Sage, 1999), 171–208.

15. F. Heider, *The Psychology of Interpersonal Relations* (New York: Wiley, 1958). Also see E. E. Jones and K. E. Davis, "From Acts to Dispositions: The Attribution Process in Person Perception," in *Advances in Experimental Social Psychology,* vol. 2, edited by L. Berkowitz (New York: Academic Press, 1965).

16. G. A. Kelly, *The Psychology of Personal Constructs* (New York: Norton, 1955).

17. D. F. Henson and K. C. Dybvig-Pawelko, "The Effects of Loneliness on Relational Maintenance Behaviors: An Attributional Perspective," *Communication Research Reports,* 21 (2004): 411–19.

18. A. L. Vangelisti and S. L. Young, "When Words Hurt: The Effects of Perceived Intentionality on Interpersonal Relationships," *Journal of Social and Personal Relationships* 17 (2000): 393–424.

19. G. W. F. Hegel, *Phenomenology of Mind* (Germany: Wurzburg & Bamburg, 1807).

20. R. M. Kowalski, S. Walker, R. Wilkinson, A. Queen, and B. Sharpe, "Lying, Cheating, Complaining, and Other Aversive Interpersonal Behaviors: A Narrative Examination of the Darker Side of Relationships," *Journal of Social and Personal Relationships* 20 (2003): 472–90.

21. P. Cateora and J. Hess, *International Marketing* (Homewood, IL: Irwin, 1979), 89; as discussed by L. A. Samovar and R. E. Porter, *Communication Between Cultures* (Belmont, CA: Wadsworth, 2001), 52.

22. F. T. McAndrew, A. Akande, R. Bridgstock, L. Mealey, S. C. Gordon, J. E. Scheib, B. E. Akande-Adetoun, F. Odewale, A. Morakinyo, P. Nyahete, and G. Mubvakure, "A Multicultural Study of Stereotyping in English-Speaking Countries," *The Journal of Social Psychology* 140 (2000): 487–502.

23. D. G. Embrick, C. S. Walther, and C. M. Wickens, "Working Class Masculinity: Keeping Gay Men and Lesbians Out of the Workplace," *Sex Roles* 56 (2007): 757–66; P. C. Hughes and J. R. Baldwin, "Communication and Stereotypical Impressions," *The Howard Journal of Communications* 13 (2002): 113–28.

24. A. Lyons and Y. Kashima, "How Are Stereotypes Maintained Through Communication? The Influence of Stereotype Sharedness," *Journal of Personality and Social Psychology* 85, no. 6 (2003): 989–1005.

25. E. E. Jones and R. Nisbett, "The Actor and the Observer: Divergent Perceptions of the Causes of Behavior," in *Attribution: Perceiving the Causes of Behavior,* edited by E. E. Jones et al. (Morristown, NJ: General Learning Press, 1972), 79–94; D. E. Kanouse and L. R. Hanson, Jr., "Negativity in Evaluations," in Jones et al., *Attribution,* 47–62.

26. A. Joinson, "Causes and Implications of Disinhibited Behavior on the Internet," in *Psychology and the Internet: Intrapersonal, Interpersonal, and Transpersonal Implications,* edited by J. Gackenback (San Diego, CA: Academic Press, 1998), 43–60.

27. J. B. Walther and M. B. Parks, "Cues Filtered Out, Cues Filtered In: Computer Communication and Relationships," in *Handbook of Interpersonal Communication,* edited by M. L. Knapp and J. A. Daly (Thousand Oaks, CA: Sage, 2002), 529–63.

28. See E.-J. Lee, "Effects of Gendered Language on Gender Stereotyping in Computer-Mediated Communication: The Moderating Role of Depersonalization and Gender-Role Orientation," *Human Communication Research* 33 (2007): 515–35.

29. N. Epley and J. Kruger, "When What You Type Isn't What They Read: The Perseverance of Stereotypes and Expectancies over Email," *Journal of Experimental Social Psychology* 41 (2005): 414–22.

30. E.-J. Lee, "Effects of the Influence Agent's Sex and Self-Confidence on Informational Influence in Computer-Mediated Communication: Quantitative vs. Verbal Presentation," *Communication Research* 32 (2005): 29–58.

31. J. B. Walther, B. Van Der Heide, S. Y. Kim, D. Westerman, and S. T. Tong, "The Role of Friends' Appearance and Behavior on Evaluations of Individuals on Facebook: Are We Known by the Company We Keep?" *Human Communication Research* 34 (2008): 28–49.

32. Walther, Van Der Heide, Kim, Westerman, and Tong, "The Role of Friends' Appearance and Behavior on Evaluations of Individuals on FaceBook."

33. R. Nisbett and L. Ross, *Human Inference: Strategies and Shortcomings of Social Judgment* (Englewood Cliffs, NJ: Prentice Hall, 1980).

34. F. F. Jordan-Jackson and K. A. Davis, "Men Talk: An Exploratory Study of Communication Patterns and Communication Apprehension of Black and White Males," *The Journal of Men's Studies* 13 (2005): 347–67.

35. A. G. Greenwald, D. E. McGhee, and J. L. K. Schwartz, "Measuring Individual Differences in Implicit Cognition: The Implicit Association Test," *Journal of Personality and Social Psychology* 74, no. 6 (1998): 1464–80; A. H. Eagly, M. G. Makhijani, R. D. Ashmore, and L. C. Longo, "What Is Beautiful Is Good, But. . . : A Meta-Analytic Review of Research of the Physical Attractiveness Stereotype," *Psychological Bulletin* 110, no. 1 (1991): 109–28.

36. See G. W. Allport, *The Nature of Prejudice* (Reading, MA: Addison-Wesley, 1979); Hughes and Baldwin, "Communication and Stereotypical Impressions."

37. Embrick, Walther, and Wickens, "Working Class Masculinity;" Hughes and Baldwin, "Communication and Stereotypical Impressions;" T. Mottet, "The Role of Sexual Orientation in Predicting Outcome Value and Anticipated Communication Behaviors," *Communication Quarterly* 43 (Summer 2000): 223–39.

38. Nisbett and Ross, *Human Inference.*

39. Asch, "Forming Impressions of Personality."

40. K. Floyd, "Attributions for Nonverbal Expressions of Liking and Disliking: The Extended Self-Serving Bias," *Western Journal of Communication* 64 (Fall 2000): 388.

41. N. Epley, T. Gilovich, and K. Savitsky, "Empathy Neglect: Reconciling the Spotlight Effect and the Correspondence Bias," *Journal of Personality and Social Psychology* 83, no. 2 (2002): 300–12.

42. E. Goffman, *The Presentation of Self in Everyday Life* (New York: Doubleday, 1959).

43. P. Brown and S. C. Levinson, *Politeness: Some Universals in Language Use* (Cambridge, England: Cambridge University Press, 1987).

44. M. V. Redmond, "The Functions of Empathy (Decentering) in Human Relations," *Human Relations* 42, no. 4 (1993): 593–606.

Chapter 4

1. J. Kantor, "Nation's Many Faces in Extended First Family," *The New York Times,* (January 21, 2009): A1.

2. W. B. Gudykunst and Y. Y. Kim, *Communicating with Strangers: An Approach to Intercultural Communication.* (New York: McGraw-Hill, Inc. 1997). Also see W. B. Gudykunst, "Similarities and Differences in Perceptions of Initial Intracultural and Intercultural Encounters," *Southern Speech Communication Journal* 49 (1983): 49–65; W. B. Gudykunst, "Theorizing in Intercultural Communication: An Introduction," in *Intercultural Communication Theory: Current Perspectives,* edited by W. B. Gudykunst (Beverly Hills, CA: Sage, 1983), 13–20; W. B. Gudykunst, "A Model of Uncertainty Reduction in Intercultural Encounters," *Journal of Language and Social Psychology* 4 (1985): 79–97; W. B. Gudykunst, E. Chua, and A. Gray, "Cultural Dissimilarities and Uncertainty Reduction Processes," in *Communication Yearbook 10,* edited by M. L. McLaughlin (Beverly Hills, Sage, 1987), 456–69; W. B. Gudykunst and T. Nishida, "Individual and Cultural Influences on Uncertainty Reduction," *Communication Monographs* 51 (1984): 23–36; W. B. Gudykunst, S.-M. Yang, and T. Nishida, "Cultural Differences in Self-Consciousness and Self-Monitoring," *Communication Monographs* 14 (1987): 7–14; J. R. Baldwin and S. K. Hunt, "Information-Seeking Behavior in Intercultural and Inter-

group Communication," *Human Communication Research* 28 (April 2002): 272–86.

3. Gudykunst and Kim, *Communicating with Strangers*, 20.

4. M. E. Ryan, "Another Way to Teach Migrant Students," *Los Angeles Times*, March 31, 1991, B20, as cited by M. W. Lustig and J. Koester, *Intercultural Competence: Interpersonal Communication Across Cultures* (Boston: Allyn & Bacon, 2009), 11.

5. Lustig and Koester, *Intercultural Competence*, 8.

6. G. Chen and W. J. Starosta, "A Review of the Concept of Intercultural Sensitivity," *Human Communication* 1 (1997): 7.

7. Lustig and Koester, *Intercultural Competence*, 10.

8. *Newsweek*, July 12, 1999, 51.

9. U.S. Bureau of the Census, *Statistical Abstract of the United States: 1996*, 116th ed. (Washington, DC: 1996), as cited by Lustig and Koester, *Intercultural Competence*, 8.

10. Los Angeles Almanac, http:// www. laalmanac.com/population/po55.htm, retrieved May 26, 2008.

11. Yankelovich, Inc. 2003, "Beyond the Boomers: Millennials and Generation X," http:// resources.ketchum.com/web/boomers.pdf, retrieved May 26, 2008.

12. "One Nation, One Language?" *U.S. News & World Report*, September 25, 1995, 40, as cited by Lustig and Koester, *Intercultural Competence*, 10.

13. United States Census Bureau. Retrieved December 10, 2002 from http:// www.prb.org/ AmeristatTemplate.

14. S. Roberts, *Who We Are Now: The Changing Face of America in the Twenty-First Century* (New York: Henry Holt, 2004), 122.

15. Roberts, *Who We Are Now*, 126.

16. We acknowledge and appreciate the contributions in this section of D. Ivy, from her work in D. K. Ivy and P. Backlund, *GenderSpeak: Personal Effectiveness in Gender Communication* (Boston: Allyn & Bacon, 2009); S. A. Beebe, S. J. Beebe, and D. K. Ivy, *Communication: Principles for a Lifetime* (Boston: Allyn & Bacon, 2010); W. Wood and A. H. Eagly, "A Cross-Cultural Analysis of the Behavior of Women and Men: Implications for the Origins of Sex Differences," *Psychological Bulletin* 128, no. 5 (2002): 699–727.

17. J. Gray. *Men Are from Mars, Women Are from Venus* (New York: HarperCollins, 1992).

18. J. T. Wood, "A Critical Response to John Gray's Mars and Venus Portrayals of Men and Women," *The Southern Communication Journal* 67 (2002): 201–11.

19. R. Edwards and M. A. Hamilton, "You Need to Understand My Gender Role: An Empirical Test of Tannen's Model of Gender and Communication," *Sex Roles* 50, no. 7/8 (2004): 491–504.

20. D. Tannen, *You Just Don't Understand* (New York: William Morrow, 1990).

21. Tannen, *You Just Don't Understand*.

22. S. Sprecher and M. Toro-Morn, "A Study of Men and Women from Different Sides of Earth to Determine if Men Are from Mars and Women Are from Venus in Their Beliefs About Love and Romantic Relationships," *Sex Roles* 46, no. 5/6 (March 2002): 131–47.

23. P. Gibson, "Gay Male and Lesbian Youth Suicide," *Report of the Secretary's Task Force on Youth Suicide*, edited by M. R. Feinleib (Washington, DC: U.S. Department of Health and Human Services, January 1989).

24. T. Mottet, "The Role of Sexual Orientation in Predicting Outcome Value and Anticipated Communication Behaviors," *Communication Quarterly* 43 (Summer 2000): 223–39.

25. G. M. Herek, "Heterosexuals' Attitudes Toward Lesbian and Gay Men: Correlates and Gender Differences," *The Journal of Sex Research* 25 (1988): 451–77.

26. G. M. Herek, "Heterosexuals' Attitudes Toward Lesbian and Gay Men"; M. S. Weinberg and C. J. Williams, *Male Homosexuals: Their Problems and Adaptations* (New York: The Free Press, 1974); T. Mottet, "The Role of Sexual Orientation in Predicting Outcome Value and Anticipated Communication Behaviors."

27. APA Style.org, "Removing Bias in Language: Sexuality." Retrieved March 2006 from www.apastyle.org/sexuality.html.

28. *Random House Webster's Unabridged Dictionary* (New York: Random House, 1998), 1590.

29. R. Lewontin, "The Apportionment of Human Diversity," *Evolutionary Biology* 6 (1973): 381–97.

30. D. Matsumoto and L. Juang, *Culture and Psychology* (Belmont, California: Wadsworth/Thomson, 2004), 16; also see H. A. Yee, H. H. Fairchild, F. Weizmann, and E. G. Wyatt. "Addressing Psychology's Problems with Race," *American Psychologist* 48 (1994): 1132–40.

31. B. J. Allen, *Differences Matter: Communicating Social Identity* (Long Grove, IL: Waveland Press, Inc., 2004), 68.

32. Allen, *Differences Matter*.

33. Matsumoto and Juang, *Culture and Psychology*, 80–81.

34. A. Williams and P. Garrett, "Communication Evaluations Across the Life Span: From Adolescent Storm and Stress to Elder Aches and Pains," *Journal of Language and Social Psychology* 21 (June 2002): 101–126; also see D. Cai, H. Giles, and K. Noels, "Elderly Perceptions of Communication with Older and Younger Adults in China: Implications for Mental Health," *Journal of Applied Communication Research* 26 (1998): 32–51.

35. J. Montepare, E. Koff, D. Zaitchik, and M. Albert, "The Use of Body Movements and Gestures as Cues to Emotions in Younger and Older Adults," *Journal of Nonverbal Behavior* 23 (Summer 1999): 133–52.

36. J. Harwood, E. B. Ryan, H. Giles, and S. Tysoski, "Evaluations of Patronizing Speech and Three Response Styles in a Non-Service-Providing Context," *Journal of Applied Communication Research* 25 (1997): 170–95.

37. C. Segrin, "Age Moderates the Relationship Between Social Support and Psychosocial Problems," paper presented at the International Communication Association, San Diego, California (2003).

38. N. Howe and W. Strauss, *Millennials Rising: The Next Great Generation* (New York: Vintage Books, 2000).

39. Howe and Strauss, *Millennials Rising*.

40. Our discussion of generational differences and communication is also based on J. Smith, "The Millennials Are Coming," workshop presented at Texas State University, San Marcos, TX (2006).

41. Howe and Strauss, *Millennials Rising*.

42. H. Karp, C. Fuller, and D. Sirias, *Bridging the Boomer-Xer Gap: Creating Authentic Teams for High Performance at Work* (Palo Alto, CA: Davies-Black Publishing, 2002).

43. Howe and Strauss, *Millennials Rising*.

44. M. Argyle, *The Psychology of Social Class* (London: Routledge, 1994).

45. B. J. Allen, *Differences Matter*, 113.

46. P. Henry, "Modes of Thought That Vary Systematically with Both Social Class and Age," *Psychology & Marketing* 17 (2000): 421–40.

47. Argyle, *The Psychology of Social Class*, 62.

48. Allen, *Differences Matter*, 100.

49. G. Hofstede, *Culture's Consequences: International Differences in Work-Related Values* (Beverly Hills, CA: Sage, 1980); G. Hofstede and G. J. Hofstede, *Cultures and Organizations: Software of the Mind* (New York: McGraw-Hill, 2005).

50. Hofstede, *Culture's Consequences*.

51. W. B. Gudykunst, *Bridging Differences: Effective Intergroup Communication* (Newbury Park, CA: Sage, 1998), 45.

52. Gudykunst, *Bridging Differences*.

53. E. T. Hall, *Beyond Culture* (Garden City, NY: Doubleday, 1976).

54. L. A. Samovar and R. E. Porter, *Communication Between Cultures* (Belmont, CA: Wadsworth, 2001), 234.

55. Hofstede, *Culture's Consequences;* also see G. Hofstede, "Cultural Dimensions in Management and Planning," *Asia Pacific Journal of Management* (January 1984): 81–98.

56. For an extensive review of communication gender differences see L. H. Turner, K. Dindia, and J. C. Pearson, "An Investigation of Female/Male Verbal Behaviors in Same-Sex and Mixed-Sex Conversations," *Communication Reports* 8 (Summer 1995): 86–96.

57. Hofstede and Hofstede, *Cultures and Organization*.

58. Hofstede, "Cultural Dimensions in Management and Planning"; Hofstede and Hofstede, *Cultures and Organizations*.

59. For a discussion of long- and short-term oriented national cultures, see Hofstede and Hofstede, *Cultures and Organizations*, 210–238.

60. J. L. Allen, K. M. Long, J. O'Mara, and B. B. Judd, "Verbal and Nonverbal Orientations Toward Communication and the Development of Intracultural and Intercultural Relationships," *Journal of Intercultural Communication Research* 32 (2003): 129–60.

61. H. Z. Li, "Communicating Information in Conversations: A Cross-Cultural Comparison," *International Journal of Intercultural Relations* 23, no. 3 (1999): 387.

62. Peter Coy, "The Future of Work," *Business Week* (August 20 and 27, 2007), p. 43.

63. M. V. Redmond and J. M. Bunyi, "The Relationship of Intercultural Communication Competence with Stress and the Handling of Stress as Reported by International Students," *International Journal of Intercultural Relations* 17 (1993): 235–54; R. Brislen, *Cross-Cultural Encounters: Face-to-Face Interaction* (New York: Pergamon Press, 1981).

64. Adapted from Peter Rose, "Prejudice," in *Cultural Tapestry: Readings for a Pluralistic Society*, edited by F. B. Evans, B. Gleason and M. Wiley (New York: HarperCollins, 1992), 420.

65. W. G. Sumner, *Folkways* (Boston: Ginn, 1906), as cited by James W. Neuliep, *Intercultural Communication: A Contextual Approach* (Boston: Houghton Mifflin, 2000), 160.

66. Lustig and Koester, *Intercultural Competence*.

67. J. W. Neuliep and J. C. McCroskey, "The Development of a U.S. and Generalized Ethnocentrism Scale," *Communication Research Reports* 14 (1997): 385–98.

68. W. B. Gudykunst, *Bridging Differences: Effective Intergroup Communication.* (Newbury Park, CA: Sage, 1991), 2.

69. R. K. Dillon and N. J. McKenzie, "The Influence of Ethnicity on Listening, Communication Competence, Approach, and Avoidance," *International Journal of Listening* 12 (1998): 106–21.

70. R. E. Axtell, *Do's and Taboos of Hosting International Visitors* (New York: John Wiley & Sons, 1989), 118.

71. F. T. McAndrew, A. Akande, R. Bridgstock, L. Mealey, S. C. Gordon, J. E. Scheib, B. E. Akande-Adetoun, F. Odewale, A. Morakinyo, P. Nyahete, and G. Mubvakure, "A Multicultural Study of Stereotyping in English-Speaking Countries," *The Journal of Social Psychology* 140 (2000): 487–502.

72. J. A. Richeson and J. N. Shelton, "Brief Report: Thin Slices of Racial Bias," *Journal of Nonverbal Behavior* 29 (2005): 75–85.

73. C. Kluckhohn and H. A. Murry, 1953 as quoted by J. S. Caputo, H. C. Hazel, and C. McMahon, *Interpersonal Communication* (Boston: Allyn & Bacon, 1994), 304.

74. L. Mae and D. E. Carlston, "Hoist on Your Own Petard: When Prejudiced Remarks Are Recognized and Backfire on Speakers," *Journal of Experimental Social Psychology* 41 (2005): 240–55.

75. L. C. Aguilar, *Ouch! That Stereotype Hurts: Communicating Respectfully in a Diverse World* (Dallas, TX: Walk the Talk, 2006), 20–21.

76. S. Kamekar, M. B. Kolsawalla, and T. Mazareth, "Occupational Prestige as a Function of Occupant's Gender," *Journal of Applied Social Psychology* 19 (1988): 681–88.

77. F. F. Jordan-Jackson and K. A. Davis, "Men Talk: An Exploratory Study of Communication Patterns and Communication Apprehension of Black and White Males," *Journal of Men's Studies* 13 (2005): 347–67.

78. D. E. Brown, "Human Universals and Their Implications," in *Being Humans: Anthropological Universality and Particularity in Transdisciplinary Perspectives,* edited by N. Roughley (New York: Walter de Gruyter, 2000). For an applied discussion of these universals, see Steven Pinker, *The Blank Slate: The Modern Denial of Human Nature* (London: Penguin Books, 2002).

79. D. W. Kale, "Ethics in Intercultural Communication," in *Intercultural Communication: A Reader,* 6th ed., edited by L. A. Samovar and R. E. Porter (Belmont, CA: Wadsworth, 1991).

80. Samovar and Porter, *Communication Between Cultures,* 29.

81. S. Pinker, "The Moral Instinct," *The New York Times Magazine* (January 13, 2008): 36–42.

82. Pinker, "The Moral Instinct," 36.

83. M. Obernauer, "Lessons on Values to Go Beyond Schools," *Austin-American Statesman* (March 30, 2005): B1, B5.

84. Eleanor Roosevelt, as cited by Lustig and Koester, *Intercultural Competence.*

85. M. R. Hammer, M. J. Bennett, and R. Wiseman, "Measuring Intercultural Sensitivity: The Intercultural Development Inventory," *International Journal of Intercultural Relations* 27 (2003): 422.

86. B. H. Spitzberg and W. R. Cupach, "Interpersonal Skills," in *Handbook of Interpersonal Communication,* edited by M. L. Knapp and J. A. Daly (Thousand Oaks, CA: Sage, 2002), 564–611.

87. R. Plutchick, *Emotion: A Psychoevolutionary Synthesis* (New York: Harper & Row, 1980).

88. See, for example, M. Biehl, D. Matsumoto, P. Ekman, V. Hearn, K. Heider, T. Kudoh, and V. Ton, "Matsumoto and Ekman's Japanese and Caucasian Facial Expressions of Emotion (JACFEE): Reliability Data and Cross-National Differences," *Journal of Nonverbal Behavior* 21 (1997): 3–21; J. D. Boucher and G. E. Carlson, "Recognition of Facial Expressions in Three Cultures," *Journal of Cross-Cultural Psychology* 11 (1980): 263–80; D. Keltner and J. Haidt, "Social Functions of Emotions at Four Levels of Analysis," *Cognition and Emotion* 13 (1999): 505–21.

89. C. Darwin, with contributions by P. Ekman, *The Expression of the Emotions in Man and Animals,* 3rd ed. (London: Oxford University Press, 1998), 391.

90. J. A. Russell, "Is There Universal Recognition of Emotion from Facial Expressions?: A Review of the Cross-Cultural Studies," *Psychological Bulletin* 115 (1994): 102–41.

91. E. Suh, E. Diener, S. Oishi, and H. C. Triandis, "The Shifting Basis of Life Satisfaction Judgments Across Cultures: Emotions versus Norms," *Journal of Personality and Social Psychology* 74 (1998): 482–93.

92. See B. Parkinson, A. H. Fischer, and A. S. R. Manstead, *Emotion in Social Relations: Cultural, Group, and Interpersonal Processes* (New York: Psychology Press, 2004).

93. S. A. Myers and R. L. Knox, "The Relationship Between College Student Information Seeking Behaviors and Perceived Instructor Verbal Responses," *Communication Education* 50 (2001): 343–56; Baldwin and Hunt, "Information-Seeking Behavior."

94. For an excellent discussion of worldview and the implications for intercultural communication, see C. H. Dodd, *Dynamics of Intercultural Communication* (New York: McGraw-Hill, 2007).

95. R. Berger and R. J. Calabrese, "Some Explorations in Initial Interactions and Beyond," *Human Communication Research* 1 (1975): 99–125.

96. B. J. Broome, "Building Shared Meaning: Implications of a Relational Approach to Empathy for Teaching Intercultural Communication," *Communication Education* 40 (1991): 235–49.

97. F. L. Casmir, "Foundations for the Study of Intercultural Communication Based on a Third-Culture Building Model," *International Journal of Intercultural Relations,* 23 (1999): 91–116; also see S. DeTurk, "Intercultural Empathy: Myth, Competency, or Possibility for Alliance Building?" *Communication Education* 50 (October 2001): 374–84.

98. F. L. Casmir and N. C. Asuncion-Lande, "Intercultural Communication Revisited: Conceptualization, Paradigm Building, and Methodological Approaches," in *Communication Yearbook 12,* edited by J. A. Anderson (Newbury Park, CA: Sage, 1989), 278–309.

99. Broome, "Building Shared Meaning."

100. Gudykunst and Kim, *Communicating with Strangers;* Gudykunst, *Bridging Differences.*

101. L. B. Szalay and G. H. Fisher, "Communication Overseas," in *Toward Internationalism: Readings in Cross-Cultural Communication,* edited by E. C. Smith and L. E Luce (Rowley, MA: Newbury House, 1979); also see P. E. King and C. R. Sawyer, "Mindfulness, Mindlessness and Communication Instruction," *Communication Education* 47 (October 1998): 326–36.

102. P. Brown and S. Levinson, *Politeness: Some Universals in Language Usage* (Cambridge, England: Cambridge University Press, 1987).

103. C. S. Lewis, *The Abolition of Man* (New York: Macmillan Publishing Company, 1947).

104. R. F. Chapdelaine and L. R. Alexitch, "Social Skills Difficulty: Model of Culture Shock for International Graduate Students," *Journal of College Student Development* 45, no. 2 (March/April 2004): 167–83.

105. K. Domenici and S. Littlejohn, *Facework: Bridging Theory and Practice* (Thousand Oaks, CA: Sage, 2006), 159.

106. DeTurk, "Intercultural Empathy."

107. Also see J. B. Stiff, J. P. Dillard, L. Somera, H. Kim, and C. Sleight, "Empathy, Communication, and Prosocial Behavior," *Communication Monographs* 55 (June 1988): 198–213.

108. See H. Giles, A. Mulack, J. J. Bradac, and P. Johnson, "Speech Accommodation Theory: The First Decade and Beyond," in *Communication Yearbook 10,* edited by M. L. McLaughlin (Newbury Park, CA: Sage, 1987), 13–48. For an excellent summary and application of accommodation theory, see R. West and L. H. Turner, *Introducing Communication Theory: Analysis and Application* (Mountain View, CA: Mayfield, 2000).

109. L. J. Carrell, "Diversity in the Communication Curriculum: Impact on Student Empathy," *Communication Education* 46 (October 1997): 234–44.

110. M. J. Bennett, "Overcoming the Golden Rule: Sympathy and Empathy," in *Communication Yearbook 3,* edited by D. Nimmo (Beverly Hills, CA: Sage, 1979), 407–22.

111. Bennett, "Overcoming the Golden Rule."

112. This exercise is adapted from an activity conducted in a diversity seminar presented at 3M, Austin, Texas, 1994.

Chapter 5

1. H. J. M. Nouwen, *Bread for the Journey* (San Francisco: HarperCollins, 1997), entry for March 11.

2. Nouwen, *Bread for the Journey,* March 11.

3. "The Most Valued Workplace Skills," *The Wall Street Journal,* September 9, 2002: 1A.

4. R. W. Young and C. M. Cates, "Emotional and Directive Listening in Peer Mentoring," *International Journal of Listening* 18 (2004): 21–33; also see D. A. Romig, *Side by Side Leadership* (Marietta, GA: Bard, 2001).

5. L. Barker et al., "An Investigation of Proportional Time Spent in Various Communication Activities of College Students," *Journal of Applied Communication Research* 8 (1981): 101–09; K. Dindia and B. L. Kennedy, "Communication in Everyday Life: A Descriptive Study Using Mobile Electronic Data Collection," paper presented at the annual conference of the National Communication Association, Chicago, IL (November 2004).

6. Adapted from the International Listening Association's definition of *listening,* which may be found on their web site at http://www.listen.org

7. W. G. Powers and G. D. Bodie, "Listening Fidelity: Seeking Congruence Between Cognitions of the Listener and the Sender," *International Journal of Listening* 17 (2003): 20–31.

8. L. A. Janusik, "Listening and Cognitive Processing: Is There a Difference?" paper presented at the annual conference of the National Communication Association, New Orleans, LA (November 2002). Janusik suggests that it's important to include a behavioral component, such as responding to a message, in any definition of listening.

9. L. A. Janusik, "Building Listening Theory: The Validation of the Conversational Listening Span," *Communication Studies* 58, no. 2 (June 2007): 139.

10. K. W. Watson, L. L. Barker, and J. B. Weaver, *The Listener Style Inventory* (New Orleans: SPECTRA, 1995).

11. For support of the validity and reliability of the Listening Styles Profile, see D. L. Worthington, "Exploring the Relationship Between Listening Style Preference and Personality," *International Journal of Listening* 17 (2003): 68–87; also see J. B. Weaver, K. W. Watson, and L. L. Barker, "Individual Differences in Listening Styles: Do You Hear What I Hear?" *Personality and Individual Differences* 20 (1996): 381–87; S. Sargent, J. B. Weaver, and C. Kiewitz, "Correlates Between Communication Apprehension and Listening Style Preferences," *Communication Research Reports* 14 (1997): 74–78; M. K. Johnston, J. B. Weaver, K. W. Watson, and L. B. Barker, "Listening Styles: Biological or Psychological Differences?" *International Journal of Listening* 14 (2000): 32–46.

12. R. K. Dillon and N. J. McKenzie, "The Influence of Ethnicity on Listening, Communication Competence, Approach, and Avoidance," *International Journal of Listening* 12 (1998): 106–21.

13. Sargent and Weaver, "Correlates Between Communication Apprehension and Listening Style Preferences"; G. D. Bodie and W. A. Villaume, "Aspects of Receiving Information: The Relationship Between Listening Preferences, Communication Apprehension, Receiver Apprehension, and Communicator Style," *International Journal of Listening* 17 (2003): 48–67.

14. Worthington, "Exploring the Relationship Between Listening Style Preference and Personality."

15. D. L. Worthington, "Exploring Jurors' Listening Processes: The Effect of Listening Style Preference on Juror Decision Making," *International Journal of Listening* 15 (2001): 20–37.

16. M. D. Kirtley and J. M. Honeycutt, "Listening Styles and Their Correspondence with Second Guessing," *Communication Research Reports* 13 (1996): 174–82.

17. Sargent and Weaver, "Correlates Between Communication Apprehension and Listening Style Preferences."

18. Bodie and Villaume, "Aspects of Receiving Information."

19. L. L. Barker and K. W. Watson, *Listen Up* (New York: St. Martin's Press: 2000); also see M. Imhof, "Who Are We as We Listen? Individual Listening Profiles in Varying Contexts," *International Journal of Listening* 18 (2004): 36–45.

20. Imhof, "Who Are We as We Listen?"

21. W. Winter, A. J. Ferreira, and N. Bowers, "Decision-Making in Married and Unrelated Couples," *Family Process* 12 (1973): 83–94.

22. J. Stauffer, R. Frost, and W. Rybolt, "The Attention Factor in Recalling Network News," *Journal of Communication* 33, no. 1, (1983): 29–37.

23. O. E. Rankis, "The Effects of Message Structure, Sexual Gender, and Verbal Organizing Ability upon Learning Message Information," doctoral dissertation, Ohio University, 1981; C. H. Weaver, *Human Listening. Process and Behavior* (New York: Bobbs-Merrill, 1972); R. D. Halley, "Distractibility of Males and Females in Competing Aural Message Situations: A Research Note," *Human Communication Research* 2 (1975): 79–82. Our discussion of gender-based differences and listening is also based on a discussion by S. A. Beebe and J. T. Masterson, *Family Talk: Interpersonal Communication in the Family* (New York: Random House, 1986); J. Lurito, "Listening and Gender," paper presented to the Radiological Society of North America, Chicago (2000), as cited by L. Tanner, "Listening Study Finds Difference in the Sexes," *Austin American-Statesman,* November 29, 2000: A11.

24. S. L. Sargent and J. B. Weaver III, "Listening Styles: Sex Differences in Perceptions of Self and Others," *International Journal of Listening* 17 (2003): 5–18.

25. Rankis, "The Effects of Message Structure, Sexual Gender, and Verbal Organizing Ability upon Learning Message Information."

26. This discussion is based on A. Vangelisti, M. Knapp, and J. Daly, "Conversational Narcissism," *Communication Monographs* 57 (1990): 251–74.

27. ABC News, *20/20,* January 12, 1998, featuring the research of communication researcher Kittie Watson.

28. S. L. Sargent and J. B. Weaver III, "Listening Styles: Sex Differences in Perceptions of Self and Others."

29. J. T. Wood, "A Critical Response to John Gray's Mars and Venus Portrayals of Men and Women," *The Southern Communication Journal* 67 (2002): 201–11.

30. B. L. Fredrickson and C. Branigan, "Positive Emotions Broaden the Scope of Attention and Thought-Action Repertoires," *Cognition and Emotion* 19, no. 3 (2005): 313–32.

31. R. Montgomery, *Listening Made Easy* (New York: Amacom, 1981); O. Hargie, C. Sanders, and D. Dickson, *Social Skills in Interpersonal Communication* (London: Routledge, 1994); O. Hargie, Ed., *The Handbook of Communication Skills* (London: Routledge, 1997). Also see S. W. Littlejohn and K. Domenici, *Engaging Communication in Conflict: Systemic Practice* (Thousand Oaks, CA: Sage, 2001), 105–08.

32. R. G. Owens, "Handling Strong Emotions," in *A Handbook of Communication Skills,* edited by O. Hargie (London: Croom Helm/New York University Press, 1986).

33. R. G. Nichols, "Factors in Listening Comprehension," *Speech Monographs* 15 (1948): 154–63; G. M. Goldhaber and C. H. Weaver, "Listener Comprehension of Compressed Speech When the Difficulty, Rate of Presentation, and Sex of the Listener Are Varied," *Speech Monographs* 35 (1968): 20–25.

34. M. Fitch-Hauser, L. A. Barker, and A. Hughes, "Receiver Apprehension and Listening Comprehension: A Linear or Curvilinear Relationship?" *The Southern Communication Journal* (1988): 62–71; P. Schrodt and L. R. Wheeless, "Aggressive Communication and Informational Reception Apprehension: The Influence of Listening Anxiety and Intellectual Inflexibility on Trait Argumentativeness and Verbal Aggressiveness," *Communication Quarterly* 49 (Winter 2001): 53–69.

35. A. Mulanx and W. G. Powers, "Listening Fidelity Development and Relationship to Receiver Apprehension and Locus of Control," *International Journal of Listening* 17 (2003): 69–78.

36. D. Carnegie, *How to Win Friends and Influence People* (New York: Holiday House, 1937).

37. K. K. Halone and L. L. Pecchioni, "Relational Listening: A Grounded Theoretical Model," *Communication Reports* 14 (2001): 59–71.

38. Halone and Pecchioni, "Relational Listening."

39. K. Ruyter and M. G. M. Wetzels, "The Impact of Perceived Listening Behavior in Voice-to-Voice Service Encounters," *Journal of Service Research* 2 (February 2000): 276–84.

40. J. Harrigan, "Listeners' Body Movements and Speaking Turns," *Communication Research* 12 (1985): 233–50.

41. S. Strong et al., "Nonverbal Behavior and Perceived Counselor Characteristics," *Journal of Counseling Psychology* 18 (1971): 554–61.

42. Halone and Pecchioni, "Relational Listening."

43. M. Imhof, "How to Listen More Efficiently: Self-Monitoring Strategies in Listening," *International Journal of Listening* 17 (2003): 2–19.

44. See R. G. Nichols and L. A. Stevens, "Listening to People," *Harvard Business Review* 35 (September–October 1957): 85–92.

45. A. D. Wovin and C. G. Coakley, "Listening Education in the 21st Century," *International Journal of Listening* 14 (2001): 143–52; S. C. Bentley, "Listening in the 21st Century," *International Journal of Listening* 14 (2000): 129–42; D. A. Schwartz, "Listening Out of the Box: New Perspectives for the Workplace," *International Journal of Listening* 18 (2004): 47–55.

46. J. Hakansson and H. Montgomery, "Empathy as an Interpersonal Phenomenon," *Journal of Social and Personal Relationships* 20 (2003): 267–84.

47. M. V. Redmond, "The Functions of Empathy (Decentering) in Human Relations," *Human Relations* 42 (1993): 593–606; also see M. V. Redmond, "A Multidimensional Theory and Measure of Social Decentering," *Journal of Research in Personality* 29 (1995): 35–58. For an excellent discussion of the role of emotions in establishing empathy, see D. Goleman, *Emotional Intelligence* (New York: Bantam, 1995).

48. Hakansson and Montgomery, "Empathy as an Interpersonal Phenomenon."

49. For an excellent review of research about expressing affection and empathy, see K. Floyd, *Communicating Affection: Interpersonal Behavior and Social Context* (Cambridge, England: Cambridge University Press, 2006); also see K. Floyd and M. T. Morman, "Affection Received from Fathers as a Predictor of Men's Affection with Their Own Sons: Tests of the Modeling and Compensation Hypotheses," *Communication Monographs* 67, no. 4 (2000): 347–61.

50. See D. Grewal and P. Salovey, "Feeling Smart: The Science of Emotional Intelligence," *American Scientist* 93 (2005): 330–39.; D. Goleman, *Emotional Intelligence* (New York: Bantam, 1995).

51. Hargie, Sanders, and Dickson, *Social Skills in Interpersonal Communication*; Hargie, *The Handbook of Communication Skills.*

52. D. F. Barone, P. S. Hutchings, H. J. Kimmel, H. L. Traub, J. T. Cooper, and C. M. Marshall, "Increasing Empathic Accuracy Through Practice and Feedback in a Clinical Interviewing Course," *Journal of Social and Clinical Psychology* 24 (2005): 156–71.

53. For a review of the role of empathy in enhancing the quality of interpersonal relationships as well as in addressing social and political problems, see J. D. Trout, *The Empathy Gap: Building Bridges to the Good Life and the Good Society* (New York: Viking, 2009).

54. J. B. Weaver and M. B. Kirtley, "Listening Styles and Empathy," *The Southern Communication Journal* 60 (1995): 131–40.

55. C. Rogers, *Client-Centered Therapy* (Boston: Houghton Mifflin, 1951).

56. Goleman, *Emotional Intelligence.*

57. For a comprehensive review of emotional intelligence that served as the basis for our summary of emotional intelligence, see Grewal and Salovey, "Feeling Smart."

58. J. E. Barbuto, Jr. and M. E. Burbach, "The Emotional Intelligence of Transformational Leaders: A Field Study of Elected Officials," *The Journal of Social Psychology* 146, no. 1 (2006): 51–64.

59. H. Gardner, *Frames of Mind: The Theory of Multiple Intelligences* (New York: BasicBooks, 1983).

60. See Grewal and Salovey, "Feeling Smart."

61. P. Salovey and J. D. Mayer, "Emotional Intelligence," *Imagination, Cognition and Personality* 9 (1990): 185–211.

62. Grewal and Salovey, "Feeling Smart"; Salovey and Mayer, "Emotional Intelligence."

63. Goleman, *Emotional Intelligence*; Grewal and Salovey, "Feeling Smart."

64. M. A. Brackett and J. D. Mayer, "Convergent, Discriminate, and Incremental Validity of Competing Measures of Emotional Intelligence," *Personality and Social Psychology Bulletin* 29 (2003): 1147–58.

65. Grewal and Salovey, "Feeling Smart."

66. Goleman, *Emotional Intelligence*.

67. J. B. Bavelas, L. Coates, and T. Johnson, "Listeners as Co-Narrators," *Journal of Personality and Social Psychology* 79, no. 6 (2000): 941–52.

68. C. W. Ellison and I. J. Fireston, "Development of Interpersonal Trust as a Function of Self-Esteem, Target Status and Target Style," *Journal of Personality and Social Psychology* 29 (1974): 655–63.

69. S. Gilbert, "Self-Disclosure, Intimacy, and Communication in Families," *Family Coordinator* 25 (1976).

70. J. Gottman and J. DeClaire, *The Relationship Cure* (New York: Crown, 2001), 198–201.

71. Hargie, Sanders, and Dickson, *Social Skills;* R. Boulton, *People Skills* (New York: Simon & Schuster, 1981).

72. R. Lemieux and M. R. Tighe, "Attachment Styles and the Evaluation of Comforting Responses: A Receiver Perspective," *Communication Research Reports* 21 (2004): 144–53; also see W. Samter, "How Gender and Cognitive Complexity Influence the Provision of Emotional Support: A Study of Indirect Effects," *Communication Reports* 15 (2002): 5–16.

73. Our discussion of the appropriate and inappropriate social support responses is taken from B. D. Burleson, "Emotional Support Skill," in *Handbook of Communication and Social Interaction Skills,* edited by J. O. Greene and B. R. Burleson (Mahwah, NJ: Erlbaum, 2003), 566–68.

74. E. Sieburg and C. Larson, "Dimensions of Interpersonal Response," paper delivered at the annual conference of the International Communication Association, Phoenix, Arizona, (April 1971); K. Ellis, "Perceived Teacher Confirmation: The Development and Validation of an Instrument and Two Studies of the Relationship to Cognitive and Affective Learning," *Human Communication Research* 26 (2000): 264–91.

75. S. DeTurk, "Intercultural Empathy: Myth, Competency, or Possibility for Alliance Building?" *Communication Education* 50 (October 2001): 374–84.

76. Boulton, *People Skills*. We also acknowledge others who have presented excellent applications of listening and responding skills in interpersonal and group contexts: D. A. Romig and L. J. Romig, *Structured Teamwork Guide* (Austin, TX: Performance Resources, 1990); S. Deep and L. Sussman, *Smart Moves* (Reading: MA. Addison-Wesley, 1990); P. R. Scholtes, *The Team Handbook* (Madison, WI: Joiner Associates, 1992); Hargie, Sanders, and Dick-son, *Social Skills;* Littlejohn and Domenici, *Engaging Communication in Conflict.*

77. Lemieux and Tighe, "Attachment Styles and the Evaluation of Comforting Responses"; also see J. M. Gottman and J. S. Gottman, *10 Lessons to Transform Your Marriage* (New York: Crown Publishers, 2006).

Chapter 6

1. B. Spitzberg and J. P. Dillard, "Social Skills and Communication," in *Interpersonal Communication Research: Advances Through Meta-Analysis,* edited by M. Allen, R. W. Preiss, B. M. Gayle, and N. Burrell (Mahwah, NJ: Erlbaum, 2002), 89–107.

2. K. Kellermann and N. A. Palomares, "Topical Profiling: Emergent, Co-Occurring, and Relationally Defining Topics in Talk," *Journal of Language and Social Psychology* 23 (2004): 308–37.

3. C. K. Ogden and I. A. Richards, *The Meaning of Meaning* (London: Kegan, Paul Trench, Trubner, 1923).

4. *The American Heritage Dictionary of the English Language* (Boston: Houghton Mifflin, 1969), 1162.

5. A. Liptak, "Must It Always Be About Sex?" *The New York Times* (November 2, 2008): WK4.

6. S. I. Hayakawa and A. R. Hayakawa, *Language in Thought and Action* (New York: Harcourt, Brace, Jovanovich, 1990).

7. C. F. Hockett, *A Course in Modern Linguistics* (New York: Macmillan, 1958).

8. C. S. Lewis, *Studies in Words* (Cambridge, England: Cambridge University Press, 1960).

9. B. Towner, "What Are They Talking About: 50 Words That Kids Think You Don't Know," *AARP Bulletin* (October 2008): 39.

10. See G. H. Mead, *Mind, Self and Society* (Chicago: University of Chicago Press, 1934); H. Blumer, *Symbolic Interactionism: Perspective and Method* (Englewood Cliffs, NJ: Prentice Hall, 1969).

11. D. Tannen, *You Just Don't Understand: Women and Men in Conversations* (New York: Morrow, 1990).

12. R. Edwards, "The Effects of Gender, Gender Role, and Values on the Interpretation of Messages," *Journal of Language and Social Psychology* 17 (1998): 52–71.

13. A. Korzybski, *Science and Sanity* (Lancaster, PA: Science Press, 1941).

14. G. Gusdorff, *Speaking* (Evanston, IL: Northwestern University Press, 1965), 9.

15. A. Ellis, *A New Guide to Rational Living* (North Hollywood, CA: Wilshire Books, 1977); also see W. Glaser, *Choice Theory* (New York: HarperCollins, 1998).

16. R. C. Martin and E. R. Dahlen, "Irrational Beliefs and the Experience and Expression of Anger," *Journal of Rational-Emotive & Cognitive-Behavior Therapy* 22 (2004): 3–20.

17. C. Peterson, M. E. P. Seligman, and G. E. Vaillant, "Pessimistic Explanatory Style Is a Risk Factor for Physical Illness: A 35-Year Longitudinal Study," *Journal of Personality and Social Psychology* 55 (1988): 23–27.

18. See J. K. Barge and M. Little, "A Discursive Approach to Skillful Activity," *Communication Theory* 18 (2008): 505–34.

19. E. K. Heussenstaunn, "Bumper Stickers and Cops," *Transaction* 35 (1971): 32–33.

20. C. S. Areni and J. R. Sparks, "Language Power and Persuasion," *Psychology & Marketing* 22 (2005): 507–25.

21. W. M. O'Barr. *Linguistic Evidence* (New York: Academic Press, 1982).

22. B. L. Whorf, "Science and Linguistics," in *Language, Thought and Reality,* edited by J. B. Carroll (Cambridge, MA: MIT Press, 1956), 207. This discussion of the Sapir–Whorf hypothesis is based on D. Crystal, *The Cambridge Encyclopedia of Language* (Cambridge, England: Cambridge University Press, 1997).

23. We thank an anonymous reviewer for this example.

24. W. Johnson, *People in Quandaries* (New York: Harper & Row, 1946).

25. A fascinating article, "The Melting of a Mighty Myth" in *Newsweek* (July 22, 1991) explores the topic of Eskimos' words for snow.

26. J. Coupland, "Small Talk: Social Function," *Research on Language and Social Interaction* 36 (2003): 1–6; M. M. Step and M. O. Finucane, "Interpersonal Communication Motives in Everyday Interactions," *Communication Quarterly* 50 (2002): 93–100.

27. M. McCarthy, "Talking Back: 'Small' Interactional Response Tokens in Everyday Conversation," *Research on Language and Social Interaction* 36 (2003): 33–63.

28. S. Duck, "Talking Relationships into Being," *Journal of Social and Personal Relationships*" 12 (1995): 535–40.

29. J. K. Alberts, C. G. Yoshimura, M. Rabby, and R. Loschiavo, "Mapping the Topography of Couples' Daily Conversation," *Journal of Social and Personal Relationships* 22 (2005): 299–322.

30. R. L. Howe, *The Miracle of Dialogue* (New York: The Seabury Press, 1963), 23–24.

31. C. C. Kopecky and W. G. Powers, "Relational Development and Self-Image Communication Accuracy," *Communication Research Reports* 19 (2002): 283–90.

32. S. Emling, "NuSrvc2 OffrGr8 Litr8tr On YrFon," *Austin American-Statesman* (November 26, 2005): A1, A6.

33. T. M. Karelitz and D. V. Budescu, "You Say 'Probable' and I Say 'Likely': Improving Interpersonal Communication with Verbal Probability Phrases," *Journal of Experimental Psychology* 10 (2004): 25–41.

34. H. S. O'Donnell, "Sexism in Language," *Elementary English* 50 (1973): 1067–72.

35. See D. K. Ivy and P. Backlund, *Exploring Genderspeak* (Boston: Pearson/Allyn & Bacon, 2009).

36. *Newsweek,* November 20, 1995, 81.

37. We acknowledge and appreciate D. K. Ivy's contribution to this section on biased language. For an expanded discussion on this topic, see Ivy and Backlund, *Genderspeak.*

38. J. Gray. *Men Are from Mars, Women Are from Venus* (New York: HarperCollins, 1992).

39. J. T. Wood, "A Critical Response to John Gray's Mars and Venus Portrayals of Men and Women," *The Southern Communication Journal* 67 (2002): 201–11.

40. J. Wood, *Gendered Lives: Communication, Gender and Culture,* (Mason, OH: Cengage Learning, 2008).

41. J. Wood, *Gendered Lives.*

42. J. Wood, *Gendered Lives*

43. M. R. Mehl, S. Vazire, N. Ramirez-Esparza, R. B. Slatcher, and J. W. Pennebaker, "Are Women Really More Talkative Than Men?" *Science* 317, no. 5834 (2007): 82.

44. A. Mulac, "The Gender-Linked Language Effect: Do Language Differences Really Make A Differ-

ence?" In *Sex Differences and Similarities in Communication: Critical Essays and Empirical Investigations of Sex and Gender in Interaction* edited by D. J. Canary and K. Dindia. (Mahwah, NJ: Erlbaum, 1998), 127–55.

45. Tannen, *You Just Don't Understand.*

46. J. S. Seiter, J. Larsen, and J. Skinner, "'Handicapped' or 'Handi-capable'? The Effects of Language About Persons with Disabilities on Perceptions of Source Credibility and Persuasiveness," *Communication Reports* 11, no. 1 (1998): 21–31.

47. D. O. Braithwaite and C. A. Braithwaite, "Understanding Communication of Persons with Disabilities as Cultural Communication," in *Intercultural Communication: A Reader,* 8th ed., edited by L. A. Samovar and R. E. Porter (Belmont, CA: Wadsworth, 1997), 154–64.

48. D. Yankelovich, *The Magic of Dialogue: Transforming Conflict into Cooperation* (New York: Simon & Schuster, 1999).

49. J. R. Gibb, "Defensive Communication," *Journal of Communication* 11 (1961): 141–48. Also see R. Boulton, *People Skills* (New York: Simon & Schuster, 1979), 14–26; O. Hargie, C. Sanders, and D. Dickson, *Social Skills in Interpersonal Communication* (London: Routledge, 1994); O. Hargie, Ed., *The Handbook of Communication Skills* (London: Routledge, 1997); S. W. Littlejohn and K. Domenici, *Engaging Communication in Conflict* (Thousand Oaks, CA: Sage, 2001).

50. S. M. Yoshimura, "Emotional and Behavioral Responses to Romantic Jealousy Expressions," *Communication Reports* 17 (2004): 85–101.

51. K. K. Sereno, M. Welch, and D. Braaten, "Interpersonal Conflict: Effects of Variations in Manner of Expressing Anger and Justifications for Anger upon Perceptions of Appropriateness, Competence, and Satisfaction," *Journal of Applied Communication Research* 15 (1987): 128–43; J. Gottman, *A Couples Guide to Communication* (Champaign, IL; Research Press, 1976); E. S. Kubany, G. B. Bauer, M. E. Pangilinan, M. Y. Muraoka, and V. G. Enriquez, "Impact of Labeled Anger and Blame in Intimate Relationships: Cross-Cultural Extension of Findings," *Journal of Cross-Cultural Psychology* 26 (1995): 65–83; E. S. Kubany, G. B. Bauer, M. Muraoka, D. C. Richard, and P. Read, "Impact of Labeled Anger and Blame in Intimate Relationships," *Journal of Social and Clinical Psychology* 14 (1995): 53–60; M. R. Leary, C. Springer, L. Negel, E. Ansell, and K. Evans, "The Causes, Phenomenology, and Consequences of Hurt Feelings," *Journal of Personality and Social Psychology* 74 (1998): 1225–37.

52. A. M. Bippus and S. L. Young, "Owning Your Emotions: Reactions to Expressions of Self-versus Other-Attributed Positive and Negative Emotions," *Journal of Applied Communication Research* 33 (2005): 26–45.

53. C. Rogers, *On Becoming a Person: A Therapist's View of Psychotherapy* (Boston: Houghton Mifflin, 1961); C. Rogers, *A Way of Being* (Boston: Houghton Mifflin, 1980); C. Rogers, "Comments on the Issue of Equality in Psychotherapy," *Journal of Humanistic Psychology* 27 (1987): 38–39.

54. A. M. Bippus, "Recipients' Criteria for Evaluating the Skillfulness of Comforting Communication and the Outcomes of Comforting Interactions," *Communication Monographs* 68 (2001): 301–13.

55. B. R. Burleson, "Comforting Messages: Features, Functions, and Outcomes," in *Strategic Interpersonal Communication,* edited by J. A. Daly and J. M. Wiemann (Hillsdale, NJ: Erlbaum, 1994), 135–61.

56. B. M. Gayle and R. W. Preiss, "An Overview of Interactional Processes in Interpersonal Communication," in *Interpersonal Communication Research: Advances Through Meta-Analysis,* edited by M. Allen, R. W. Preiss, B. M. Gayle, and N. Burrell (Mahwah, NJ: Erlbaum, 2002), 213–26.

57. M. Allen, "A Synthesis and Extension of Constructivist Comforting Research," in *Interpersonal Communication Research,* 237–45.

58. D. J. Dolin and M. Booth-Butterfield, "Reach Out and Touch Someone: Analysis of Nonverbal Comforting Responses," *Communication Quarterly* 41 (1993): 383–93.

59. A. M. Bippus, "Human Usages in Comforting Episodes: Factors Predicting Outcomes," *Western Journal of Communication* 54 (Fall 2000): 359–84; A. M. Bippus, "Recipients' Criteria for Evaluating the Skillfulness of Comforting Communication and the Outcomes of Comforting Interactions," *Communication Monographs* 68 (September 2001): 301–13; A. M. Bippus, "Humor Motives, Qualities, and Reactions in Recalled Conflict Episodes," *Western Journal of Communication* 67 (2003): 413–26.

60. K. Ohbuchi, M. Kameda, and N. Agarie, "Apology as Aggression Control: Its Role in Mediating Appraisal of and Response to Harm," *Journal of Personality and Social Psychology* 56 (1989): 219–27.

61. M. McCollough, K. Rachal, J. Steven, E. Worthington, S. Brown, and T. Hight. "Interpersonal Forgiving in Close Relationships II: Theoretical Elaboration and Measurement," *Journal of Personality and Social Psychology* 75 (1998): 1586–1603.

62. J. R. Meyer and K. Rothenberg, "Repairing Regretted Messages: Effects of Emotional State, Relationship Type, and Seriousness of Offense," *Communication Research Reports* 21 (2005): 348–56.

63. B. W. Darby and B. R. Schlenker, "Children's Reactions to Transgressions: Effects of the Actor's Apology, Reputation and Remorse," *British Journal of Social Psychology* 28 (1989): 353–64.

64. S. J. Scher and J. M. Darley, "How Effective Are the Things People Say to Apologize? Effects of the Realization of the Apology Speech Act," *Journal of Psycholinguistic Research* 26 (1997): 127–40.

65. C. McPherson Frantz and C. Bennigson, "Better Late Than Early: The Influence of Timing on Apology Effectiveness," *Journal of Experimental Social Psychology* 41 (2005): 201–07.

66. N. S. Baron, *Always On: Language in an Online and Mobile World* (New York: Oxford University Press, 2008).

67. V. Boogart, "Discovering the Social Impacts of Facebook on a College Campus" (master's thesis, Kansas State University, 2006), 38, as cited in Baron, *Always On,* 97.

68. R. Wright, "E-Mail and Prozac," *The New York Times* (April 17, 2007): A23.

69. Baron, *Always On,* 226.

70. Our prescriptions for assertiveness are based on a discussion by R. Boulton, *People Skills.* Also see J. S. St. Lawrence, "Situational Context: Effects on Perceptions of Assertive and Unassertive Behavior," *Behavior Therapy* 16 (1985): 51–62; D. Borisoff and D. A. Victor, *Conflict Management: A Communication Skills Approach* (Boston: Allyn & Bacon, 1999).

71. D. Cloven and M. E. Roloff, "The Chilling Effect of Aggressive Potential on the Expression of Complaints in Intimate Relationships," *Communication Monographs* 60 (1993): 199–219.

Chapter 7

1. E. Lipton, "Faces, Too, Are Searched as U.S. Airports Try to Spot Terrorists," *The New York Times* (August 17, 2006): A1.

2. J. Kabat-Zinn, *Wherever You Go, There You Are: Mindfulness Meditation in Everyday Life* (New York: Hyperion Books, 1994).

3. J. V. Cordova, C. B. Gee, and L. Z. Warren, "Emotional Skillfulness in Marriage: Intimacy as a Mediator of the Relationship Between Emotional Skillfulness and Marital Satisfaction," *Journal of Social and Clinical Psychology* 24 (2005): 218–35.

4. A. Mehrabian, *Nonverbal Communication* (Chicago: Aldine Atherton, 1972), 108.

5. D. Lapakko, "Three Cheers for Language: A Closer Examination of a Widely Cited Study of Nonverbal Communication," *Communication Education* 46 (1997): 63–67. Although other researchers suggest that nonverbal messages may not carry as much as 93 percent of the emotional weight of our communication, *all* nonverbal communication researchers agree that nonverbal communication is the most significant means of expressing emotions to others.

6. D. Matsumoto, J. LeRoux, C. Wilson-Cohn, J. Raroque, K. Kooken, P. Ekman, N. Yrizarry, S. Loewinger, H. Uchida, A. Yee, L. Amo, and A. Goh, "A New Test to Measure Emotion Recognition Ability: Matsumoto and Ekman's Japanese and Caucasian Brief Affect Recognition Test (JACBART)," *Journal of Nonverbal Behavior* 24 (Fall 2000): 179–209; J. K. Burgoon and A. E. Bacue, "Nonverbal Communication Skills," in *Handbook of Communication and Social Interaction Skills,* edited by J. O. Greene and B. R. Burleson (Mahwah, NJ: Erlbaum, 2003), 179–219; B. H. LaFrance, A. D. Heisel, and M. J. Beatty, "Is There Empirical Evidence for a Nonverbal Profile of Extraversion?" A Meta-Analysis and Critique of the Literature," *Communication Monographs* 71 (2004): 28–48.

7. M. Zuckerman, D. DePaulo, and R. Rosenthal, "Verbal and Nonverbal Communication of Deception," *Advances in Experimental Social Psychology* 14 (1981): 1–59.

8. P. Ekman and W. V. Friesen, "The Repertoire of Nonverbal Behavior: Categories, Origins, Usage and Coding," *Semiotica* 1 (1969): 49–98.

9. E. Hess, *The Tell-Tale Eye* (New York: Van Nostrand Reinhold, 1975).

10. P. Ekman, "Communication Through Nonverbal Behavior: A Source of Information About an Interpersonal Relationship," in *Affect Cognition and Personality,* edited by S. S. Tomkins and C. E. Izard (New York: Springer, 1965).

11. J. K. Burgoon, J. A. Bonito, A. Ramirez Jr., N. E. Dunbar, K. Kam, and J. Fischer, "Testing the Interactivity Principle: Effects of Mediation, Propinquity, and Verbal and Nonverbal Modalities in Interpersonal Interaction," *Journal of Communication* 52, no. 3 (2002): 657–77.

12. J. K. Burgoon, L. A. Stern, and L. Dillman, *Interpersonal Adaptation: Dyadic Interaction Patterns* (Cambridge, England: Cambridge University Press, 1995).

13. A. S. E. Hubbard, "Interpersonal Coordination in Interactions: Evaluations and Social Skills," *Communication Research Reports* 17 (Winter 2000): 95–104.

14. R. L. Birdwhistell, *Kinesics and Context* (Philadelphia: University of Pennsylvania Press, 1970).

15. N. Zunin and M. Zunin, *Contact: The First Four Minutes* (New York: Signet, 1976).

16. J. H. Bert and K. Piner, "Social Relationships and the Lack of Social Relations," in *Personal Relationships and Social Support,* edited by S. W. Duck with R. C. Silver (London: Sage, 1989).

17. S. M. Jones and L. K. Guerrero, "The Effects of Nonverbal Immediacy and Verbal Person Cen-

teredness in the Emotional Support Process," *Human Communication Research* 27 (October 2001): 567–96.

18. A. F. Koerner and M. A. Fitzpatrick, "Nonverbal Communication and Marital Adjustment and Satisfaction: The Role of Decoding Relationship Relevant and Relationship Irrelevant Affect," *Communication Monographs* 69 (2002): 3351.

19. Koerner and Fitzpatrick, "Nonverbal Communication and Marital Adjustment and Satisfaction."

20. Cordova, Gee, and Warren, "Emotional Skillfulness in Marriage."

21. Burgoon and Bacue, "Nonverbal Communication Skills."

22. B. M. DePaulo and H. S. Friedman, "Nonverbal Communication," in *The Handbook of Social Psychology,* edited by D. T. Gilbert, S. T. Fiske, and G. Lindzey (New York: McGraw-Hill, 1998).

23. M. Argyle, *Bodily Communication* (New York: Methuen, 1988).

24. W. G. Woodal and J. K. Burgoon, "The Effects of Nonverbal Synchrony on Message Comprehension and Persuasiveness," *Journal of Nonverbal Behavior* 5 (1981): 207–23.

25. Argyle, *Bodily Communication.*

26. K. N. Blurton-Jones and G. M. Leach, "Behavior of Children and Their Mothers at Separation and Parting," in *Ethological Studies of Child Behavior,* edited by N. Blurton-Jones (Cambridge, England: Cambridge University Press, 1972).

27. P. Ekman and W. V Friesen, "Constants Across Cultures in the Face and Emotion," *Journal of Personality and Social Psychology* 17 (1971): 124–29; Argyle, *Bodily Communication,* 157; I. Eibl-Eibesfeldt, "Similarities and Differences Between Cultures in Expressive Movements," in *Nonverbal Communication,* edited by R. A. Hinde (Cambridge, England: Royal Society & Cambridge University Press, 1972); P. Collett, "History and Study of Expressive Action," in *Historical Social Psychology,* edited by K. Gergen and M. Gergen (Hillsdale, NJ: Erlbaum, 1984); E. T. Hall, *The Silent Language* (Garden City, NY: Doubleday, 1959); R. Shuter, "Gaze Behavior in Interracial and Intraracial Interaction," *International and Intercultural Communication Annual* 5 (1979): 48–55; R. Shuter, "Proxemics and Tactility in Latin America," *Journal of Communication* 26 (1976): 46–52; E. T. Hall, *The Hidden Dimension* (New York: Doubleday, 1966). For an excellent discussion of worldview and the implications for intercultural communication, see C. H. Dodd, *Dynamics of Intercultural Communication* (Dubuque, IA: Brown & Benchmark, 1995); G. W. Beattie, *Talk: An Analysis of Speech and Non-Verbal Behavior in Conversation* (Milton Keynes: Open University Press, 1983); O. Hargie, C. Sanders, and D. Dickson, *Social Skills in Interpersonal Communication* (London: Routledge, 1994); O. Hargie (Ed.), *The Handbook of Communication Skills* (London: Routledge, 1997); H. A. Elfenbein and N. Ambady, "On the Universality and Cultural Specificity of Emotion Recognition: A Meta-Analysis," *Psychological Bulletin* 128, no. 2 (2002): 203–35.

28. Several studies offer evidence of the universality of facial expressions. See P. Ekman, "Strong Evidence for Universals in Facial Expressions: A Reply to Russell's Mistaken Critique," *Psychological Bulletin* 115 (1994): 268–87; Ekman and Friesen, "Constants Across Culture in the Face and Emotion"; P. Ekman and W. Friesen, *Facial Action Coding System: Investigator's Guide* (Palo Alto, CA: Consulting Psychologists Press, 1978); P. Ekman and W. Friesen, "A New Pan-Cultural Facial Expression of Emotion," *Motivation & Emotion* 10 (1986): 159–68; P. Ekman,

E. R. Sorenson, and W. Friesen, "Pancultural Elements in Facial Displays of Emotion," *Science* 164 (1969): 86–88; D. Matsumoto, "Scalar Ratings of Contempt Expressions," *Journal of Nonverbal Behavior* 29 (2005): 91–104.

29. C. M. J. Beaulieu, "Intercultural Study of Personal Space: A Case Study," *Journal of Applied Social Psychology* 34, no. 4 (2004): 794–805.

30. Beaulieu, "Intercultural Study of Personal Space."

31. For a review of culture and touch, see R. Dibiase and J. Gunnoe, "Gender and Cultural Differences in Touching Behavior," *The Journal of Social Psychology* 144, no. 1 (2004): 49–62.

32. For an excellent review of gender and nonverbal cues, see J. Pearson, L. Turner, and W. Todd-Mancillas, *Gender and Communication* (Dubuque, IA: William C. Brown, 1991); D. K. Ivy and P. Backlund, *Exploring GenderSpeak: Personal Effectiveness in Gender Communication* (New York: McGraw-Hill, 1994). Also see D. G. Leathers, *Successful Nonverbal Communication: Principles and Applications* (Boston: Allyn & Bacon, 1997).

33. This example originally appeared in Collett, "History and Study of Expressive Action."

34. Birdwhistell, *Kinesics and Context.* Also see Leathers, *Successful Nonverbal Communication.*

35. A. E. Scheflen, "Quasi-Courtship Behavior in Psychotherapy," *Psychiatry* 28 (1965): 245–57.

36. M. Moore, "Interpreting Nonverbal Messages," *Journal of Ethology and Sociology* (Summer 1994); also see D. Knox and K. Wilson, "Dating Behaviors of University Students," *Family Relations* 30 (1981): 255–58.

37. M. Reece and R. Whitman, "Expressive Movements, Warmth, and Verbal Reinforcement," *Journal of Abnormal and Social Psychology* 64 (1962): 234–36.

38. A. Mehrabian, *Silent Messages* (Belmont, CA: Wadsworth, 1972), 108.

39. Ekman and Friesen, "The Repertoire of Nonverbal Behavior."

40. A. T. Dittman, "The Body Movement–Speech Rhythm Relationship as a Cue to Speech Encoding," in *Studies in Dyadic Communication,* edited by A. W. Siegman and B. Pope (New York: Pergamon, 1972).

41. A. A. Cohen and R. P. Harrison, "Intentionality in the Use of Hand Illustrators in Face-to-Face Communication Situations," *Journal of Personality and Social Psychology* 28 (1973): 276–79.

42. C. Darwin, *The Expression of the Emotions in Man and Animals* (Chicago: University of Chicago Press, 1965). Originally published 1872.

43. A. Mehrabian and M. Williams, "Nonverbal Concomitants of Perceived and Intended Persuasiveness," *Journal of Personality and Social Psychology* 13 (1969): 37–58.

44. M. Argyle, E. Alkema, and R. Gilmour, "The Communication of Friendly and Hostile Attitudes by Verbal and Nonverbal Signals," *European Journal of Social Psychology* 1 (1972): 385–402.

45. D. Morris, *People Watching* (London: Vantage Press, 2002), 104; For a review of eye contact and facial expression research in intercultural settings, see M. Yuki, W. M. Maddux, and T. Masuda, "Are the Windows to the Soul the Same in the East and West? Cultural Differences in Using the Eyes and Mouth as Cues to Recognize Emotions in Japan and the United States," *Journal of Experimental Social Psychology* 43 (2007): 303–11.

46. A. Kendon, "Some Functions of Gaze-Direction in Social Interaction," *Acta Psychologica* 26 (1967): 22–63.

47. These research conclusions were summarized by M. L. Knapp and J. A. Hall, *Nonverbal Communication in Human Interaction* (Belmont, CA: Wadsworth, 1997); also see D. K. Ivy and S. T. Wahl, *The Nonverbal Self: Communication for a Lifetime* (Boston: Allyn and Bacon, 2009), 221–37.

48. P. Ekman, W. V. Friesen, and S. S. Tomkins, "Facial Affect Scoring Technique: A First Validity Study," *Semiotica* 3 (1971): 37–58; P. Ekman and W. V. Friesen, *Unmasking the Face* (Englewood Cliffs, NJ: Prentice Hall, 1975).

49. Associated Press, "Frowning Outlawed in Meeting Code of Conduct," Retrieved May 7, 2003 from www.Boston.com.

50. Ekman and Friesen, *Unmasking the Face;* Ekman, Friesen, and Tomkins, "Facial Affect Scoring Technique."

51. M. D. Weathers. E. M. Frank, and L. A. Spell, "Differences in the Communication of Affect: Members of the Same Race Versus Members of a Different Race," *Journal of Black Psychology* 28 (2002): 66–77.

52. Ekman and Friesen, *Unmasking the Face;* Ekman, Friesen, and Tomkins, "Facial Affect Scoring Technique."

53. A. Buck, R. E. Miller, and C. F. William, "Sex, Personality, and Physiological Variables in the Communication of Affect via Facial Expression," *Journal of Personality and Social Psychology* 30 (1974): 587–89.

54. Ekman and Friesen, *Unmasking the Face.*

55. J. Schwartz, "NASA Official Says He Held Out Hope in Final Moments," *The New York Times,* February 15, 2003: A14.

56. Ekman and Friesen, *Unmasking the Face.*

57. G. J. McHugo, "Emotional Reactions to a Political Leader's Expressive Displays," *Journal of Personality and Social Psychology* 49 (1985): 513–29.

58. K. Yamamoto and N. Suzuki, "The Effects of Social Interaction and Personal Relationships on Facial Expressions," *Journal of Nonverbal Behavior* 30 (2006): 167–79.

59. D. LaPlante and N. Ambady, "Multiple Messages: Facial Recognition Advantage for Compound Expressions," *Journal of Nonverbal Behavior* 24 (Fall 2000): 211–25.

60. E. Krumhuber and A. Kappas, "Moving Smiles: The Role of Dynamic Components for the Perception of the Genuineness of Smiles," *Journal of Nonverbal Behavior* 29 (2005): 3–24.

61. J. Elliott, "If You're Happy and You Know It, You're a Buddhist," *The Sunday Times* [London], May 25, 2003: 1.14.

62. B. Munson, E. C. McDonald, N. L. DeBoe, and A. R. White, "The Acoustic and Perceptual Bases of Judgment of Women and Men's Sexual Orientation from Read Speech," *Journal of Phonetics* 34 (2006): 202–40.

63. R. Smyth, G. Jacobs, and H. Rogers, "Male Voices and Perceived Sexual Orientation: An Experimental and Theoretical Approach," *Language in Society* 32 (2003): 329–50.

64. J. K. Burgoon, D. B. Buller, and W. G. Woodall, *Nonverbal Communication: The Unspoken Dialogue* (New York: McGraw-Hill, 1996).

65. B. Le Poire, C. Shepard, A. Duggan, and J. Burgoon, "Relational Messages Associated with Nonverbal Involvement, Pleasantness, and Expressiveness in Romantic Couples," *Communication Research Reports* 19 (2002).

66. R. Davitz, *The Communication of Emotional Meaning* (New York: McGraw-Hill, 1964).

67. M. J. Owren and J. Bachorowski, "Reconsidering the Evolution of Nonlinguistic Communication: The Case of Laughter," *Journal of Nonverbal Behavior* 27 (2003): 183–200.

68. K. K. Sereno and G. J. Hawkins, "The Effect of Variations in Speakers' Nonfluency upon Audience Ratings of Attitude Toward the Speech Topic and Speakers' Credibility," *Speech Monographs* 34 (1967): 58–74; G. R. Miller and M. A. Hewgill, "The Effect of Variations in Nonfluency on Audience Ratings of Source Credibility," *Quarterly Journal of Speech* 50 (1964): 36–44; Mehrabian and Williams, "Nonverbal Concomitants of Perceived and Intended Persuasiveness."

69. R. L. Street, R. M. Brady, and W. B. Putman, "The Influence of Speech Rate Stereotypes and Rate Similarity on Listeners' Evaluations of Speakers," *Journal of Language and Social Psychology* 2 (1983): 37–56.

70. K. Acheson, "Silence as Gesture: Rethinking the Nature of Communicative Silence," *Communication Theory* 18 (2008): 535–55.

71. T. Bruneau, "Communicative Silences: Forms and Functions," *Journal of Communication* 23 (1973): 17–46.

72. S. J. Baker, "The Theory of Silence," *Journal of General Psychology* 53 (1955): 145–67.

73. Our discussion of how to accurately interpret emotions in others is adapted from an excellent distillation of the research conducted by Burgoon and Bacue, "Nonverbal Communication Skills."

74. Burgoon, Buller and Woodall, *Nonverbal Communication.*

75. N. Horatcsu and B. Ekinci, "Children's Reliance on Situational and Vocal Expression of Emotions: Consistent and Conflicting Cues," *Journal of Nonverbal Behavior* 16 (1992): 231–47.

76. R. Banse and K. R. Schere, "Acoustic Profiles in Vocal Emotion Expression," *Journal of Personality and Social Psychology* 70 (1996): 614–36.

77. N. Ambady, "Cross-Cultural Perspectives on Social Judgments and Behavior," paper presented at the annual meeting of the Society of Experimental Social Psychology, St. Louis, MO (1999), as cited by Burgoon and Bacue, "Nonverbal Communication Skills."

78. J. M. Montepare and J. S. Tucker, "Aging and Nonverbal Behavior: Current Perspectives and Future Directions," *Journal of Nonverbal Behavior* 23 (1999): 105–10.

79. R. E. Riggio, B. Throckmorton, and S. DePaola, "Social Skills and Self-Esteem," *Personality and Social Psychology Bulletin* 13 (1990): 568–77.

80. Burgoon and Bacue, "Nonverbal Communication Skills."

81. Hall, *The Hidden Dimension.*

82. R. Sommer, "Studies in Personal Space," *Sociometry* 22 (1959): 247–60.

83. Sommer, "Studies in Personal Space."

84. See B. Stenzor, "The Spatial Factor in Face-to-Face Discussion Groups," *Journal of Abnormal and Social Psychology* 45 (1950): 552–55.

85. A. Montague, *Touching: The Human Significance of the Skin* (New York: Harper & Row, 1978).

86. Montague, *Touching.*

87. N. M. Henley, *Body Politics: Power, Sex, and Nonverbal Communication* (Englewood Cliffs, NJ: Prentice Hall, 1977).

88. L. K. Guerrero and P. A. Andersen, "Patterns of Matching and Initiation: Touch Behavior and Touch Avoidance Across Romantic Relationship Stages," *Journal of Nonverbal Behavior* 18 (1994): 137–53; M. M. Martin and C. M. Anderson, "Psycho-logical and Biological Differences in Touch Avoidance," *Communication Research Report* 10 (1993): 141–47.

89. L. K. Guerrero and P. A. Anderson, "The Waxing and Waning of Relational Intimacy: Touch as a Function of Relational Stage, Gender, and Touch Avoidance," *Journal of Social and Personal Relationships* 8 (1991): 147–65; Guerrero and Anderson, "Patterns of Matching and Initiation."

90. J. Kelly, "Dress as Non-Verbal Communication," paper presented at the annual conference of the American Association for Public Opinion Research, May 1969.

91. J. C. Valentine, V. Blankenship, H. Cooper, and E. S. Sullins, "Interpersonal Expectancy Effects and the Preference for Consistency," *Representative Research in Social Psychology* 25 (2001): 26–33.

92. J. Lefkowitz, R. Blake, and J. Mouton, "Status Factors in Pedestrian Violation of Traffic Signals," *Journal of Abnormal and Social Psychology* 51 (1970): 4–6.

93. J. T. Molloy, *Dress for Success* (New York: Warner Books, 1975); J. T. Molloy, *The Woman's Dress for Success Book* (Chicago: Follett, 1977).

94. Mehrabian, *Nonverbal Communication.*

95. R. R. Provine, R. J. Spencer, and D. L. Mandell, "Emotional Expression Online: Emoticons Punctuate Website Text Messages," *Journal of Language and Social Psychology* 26, no. 3 (September 2007): 299–307.

96. V. O. Castella, A. M. Abad, F. P. Alonso, and J. M. P. Silla, "The Influence of Familiarity Among Group Members, Group Atmosphere and Assertiveness on Uninhibited Behavior Through Three Different Communication Media," *Computers in Human Behavior* 16 (2000): 141–59; also see A. N. Joinson, *Understanding the Psychology of Internet Behavior: Virtual Worlds, Real Lives* (New York: Palgrave MacMillan, 2003), 64–65.

97. L. Hinkle, "Nonverbal Immediacy Communication Behaviors and Liking in Marital Relationships," *Communication Research Reports* 16, no. 1 (1999): 81–90.

98. J. K. Burgoon and B. A. Le Poire, "Nonverbal Cues and Interpersonal Judgments: Participant and Observer Perceptions of Intimacy, Dominance, Composure, and Formality," *Communication Monographs* 66 (1999): 105–24.

99. Jones and Guerrero, "The Effects of Nonverbal Immediacy"; also see D. J. Dolin and M. Booth-Butterfield, "Reach Out and Touch Someone: Analysis of Nonverbal Comforting Responses," *Communication Quarterly* 41 (1993): 383–93.

100. Argyle, *Bodily Communication.*

101. K. J. Tusing and J. P. Dillard, "The Sounds of Dominance: Vocal Precursors of Perceived Dominance During Interpersonal Influence," *Human Communication Research* 26 (January 2000): 148–71; N. E. Dunbar and J. K. Burgoon, "Perceptions of Power and Interactional Dominance in Interpersonal Relationships," *Journal of Social and Personal Relationships* 22 (2005): 207–33.

102. A. Mignault and A. Chaudhuri, "The Many Faces of a Neutral Face: Head Tilt and Perception of Dominance and Emotion," *Journal of Nonverbal Behavior* 27, no. 2 (Summer 2001): 111–32.

103. Mehrabian, *Nonverbal Communication.*

104. A. Pease and B. Pease, *The Definitive Book of Body Language* (London: Orion, 2005): 42.

105. P. Collett, *The Book of Tells* (London: Doubleday, 2003).

106. J. A. Hall, J. C. Rosip, L. Smith LeBeau, T. G. Horgan, and J. D. Carter, "Attributing the Sources of Accuracy in Unequal-Power Dyadic Communication: Who Is Better and Why?" *Journal of Experimental Social Psychology* 41 (2005): 1–10.

107. D. A. Carney, J. A. Hall, and L. Smith LeBeau, "Beliefs About the Nonverbal Expression of Social Power," *Journal of Nonverbal Behavior* 29 (2005): 105–23.

108. Argyle, *Bodily Communication.*

109. Burgoon, Stern, and Dillman, *Interpersonal Adaptation.*

110. B. A. Le Poire and S. M. Yoshimura, "The Effects of Expectancies and Actual Communication on Nonverbal Adaptation and Communication Outcomes: A Test of Interaction Adaptation Theory," *Communication Monographs* 66 (1999): 1–30.

111. J. A. Hall, N. A. Murphy, and M. S. Mast, "Recall of Nonverbal Cues: Exploring a New Definition of Interpersonal Sensitivity," *Journal of Nonverbal Behavior* 30 (2006): 141–55.

112. Burgoon and Bacue, "Nonverbal Communication Skills."

113. See Birdwhistell, *Kinesics and Context.*

114. E. Hatfield, J. T. Cacioppo, and R. L. Rapson, *Emotional Contagion* (New York: Cambridge University Press, 1994).

115. Hubbard, "Interpersonal Coordination in Interactions."

116. B. Marsh, "The Voice Was Lying. The Face May Have Told the Truth," *The New York Times* (February 15, 2009): WK3.

117. J. K. Burgoon, J. P. Blair, and R. E. Strom, "Cognitive Biases and Nonverbal Cue Availability in Detecting Deception," *Human Communication Research* 34 (2008): 572–99.

118. For an excellent summary of deception and nonverbal communication, see Leathers, *Successful Nonverbal Communication,* 253–74. Also see P. Ekman, M. O' Sullivan, W. V. Friesen, and K. R. Scherer, "Invited Article: Face, Voice, and Body in Detecting Deceit," *Journal of Nonverbal Behavior* 15 (1991): 125–35; P. Ekman and W. Friesen, "Detecting Deception from the Body and Face," *Journal of Personality and Social Psychology* 29 (1974): 288–98; M. Millar and K. Millar, "Detection of Deception in Familiar and Unfamiliar Persons: The Effects of Information Restriction," *Journal of Nonverbal Behavior* 19 (1995): 69–84; D. B. Buller, J. K. Burgoon, A. Buslig, and J. F. Roiger, "Interpersonal Deception: VIII. Further Analysis of the Nonverbal Correlates of Equivocation from the Bavelas et al. (1990) Research," *Journal of Language & Social Psychology* 13 (1994): 396–417.

119. Adapted from Leathers, *Successful Nonverbal Communication,* with supporting research from Ekman and Friesen, "Detecting Deception from the Face and Body"; M. Zuckerman, B. M. DePaulo, and R. Rosenthal, "Verbal and Nonverbal Communication of Deception," in *Advances in Experimental Social Psychology,* vol. 14, edited by L. Berkowitz (New York: Academic Press, 1981), 1–60.

120. J. T. Hancock, L. E. Curry, S. Goorha, and M. Woodworth, "On Lying and Being Lied To: A Linguistic Analysis of Deception in Computer-Mediated Communication," *Discourse Processed* 45 (2008): 1–23; also see J. F. George and A. Robb, "Deception and Computer-Mediated Communication in Daily Life," *Communication Reports* 21, no. 2 (July–December 2008): 92–103.

121. A. Vrij, K. Edward, K. P. Roberts, and R. Bull, "Detecting Deceit Via Analysis of Verbal and Nonverbal Behavior," *Journal of Nonverbal Communication* 24 (Winter 2000): 239–63; also see Burgoon and Bacue, "Nonverbal Communication Skills."

122. H. S. Park, T. R. Levine, S. A. McCornack, K. Morrison, and M. Ferrara, "How People Really Detect Lies," *Communication Monographs* 69 (June 2002): 144–57.

Chapter 8

1. T. E. Ricks, interviewed by Terry Gross, *Fresh Air*, National Public Radio, February 10, 2009; also see T. E. Ricks, *The Gamble: General David Petraeus and the American Military Adventure in Iraq, 2006–2008* (New York: The Penguin Press, 2009).

2. S. A. Lloyd, "Conflict in Premarital Relationships: Differential Perceptions of Males and Females," *Family Relations* 36 (1987): 290–94.

3. H. B. Braiker and H. H. Kelley, "Conflict in the Development of Close Relationships," in *Social Exchange in Developing Relationships,* edited by R. L. Burgess and T. L. Huston (New York: Academic Press, 1979), 135–68.

4. D. Cramer, "Relationship Satisfaction and Conflict Style in Romantic Relationships," *Journal of Psychology* 134 (2000): 337–41.

5. Our definition of conflict is adapted from W. Wilmot and J. Hocker, *Interpersonal Conflict* (New York: McGraw-Hill, 2007).

6. B. Fehr and C. Harasymchuk, "The Experience of Emotion in Close Relationships: Toward an Integration of the Emotion-in-Relationships and Interpersonal Script Models," *Personal Relationships* 12 (2005): 181–196.

7. J. W. Keltner, *Mediation: Toward a Civilized System of Dispute Resolution* (Annandale, VA: Speech Communication Association, 1987); also see Wilmot and Hocker, *Interpersonal Conflict.*

8. For a review of literature about violence in relationships, see L. N. Olson and T. D. Golish, "Topics of Conflict and Patterns of Aggression in Romantic Relationships," *Southern Communication Journal* 67 (Winter 2002): 180–200.

9. D. J. Canary, W. R. Cupach, and R. T. Serpe, "A Competence-Based Approach to Examining Interpersonal Conflict: Test of a Longitudinal Model," *Communication Research* 29 (February 2001): 79–104; also see L. N. Olson and D. O. Braithwaite, " 'If You Hit Me Again, I'll Hit You Back': Conflict Management Strategies of Individuals Experiencing Aggression During Conflicts," *Communication Studies* 55 (2004): 271–85; L. L. Marshall, "Physical and Psychological Abuse," in *The Dark Side of Interpersonal Communication,* edited by W. R. Cupach and B. H. Spitzberg (Hillsdale, NJ: Erlbaum, 1994), 281–311; Olson and Golish, "Topics of Conflict and Patterns of Aggression in Romantic Relationships."

10. Wilmot and Hocker, *Interpersonal Conflict,* 8–15.

11. Olson and Braithwaite, "'If You Hit Me Again, I'll Hit You Back.'"

12. A. C. Filley, *Interpersonal Conflict Resolution* (Glenview, IL: Scott Foresman, 1975); R. H. Turner, "Conflict and Harmony," *Family Interaction* (New York: Wiley, 1970); K. Galvin and B. J. Brommel, *Family Communication: Cohesion and Change* (New York: Addison Wesley Longman, 2000).

13. Olson and Golish, "Topics of Conflict and Patterns of Aggression in Romantic Relationships."

14. Wilmot and Hocker, *Interpersonal Conflict,* 10.

15. Canary, Cupach, and Serpe, "A Competence-Based Approach to Examining Interpersonal Conflict."

16. Adapted from D. W. Johnson, *Reaching Out: Interpersonal Effectiveness and Self-Actualization* (Boston: Allyn & Bacon, 2000), 314.

17. M. Deutsch, *The Resolution of Conflict* (New Haven, CT: Yale University Press, 1973).

18. L. A. Erbert, "Conflict and Dialectics: Perceptions of Dialectical Contradictions in Marital Conflict," *Journal of Social and Personal Relationships* 17 (2000): 638–59.

19. L. A. Kurdek, "Areas of Conflict for Gay, Lesbian, and Heterosexual Couples: What Couples Argue About Influences Relationship Satisfaction," *Journal of Marriage and the Family* 56 (November 1994): 923–34: L. A. Kurdek, "Conflict Resolution Styles in Gay, Lesbian, Heterosexual Nonparent, and Heterosexual Parent Couples," *Journal of Marriage and the Family* 56 (August 1994): 705–22.

20. W. E. Schweinle, W. Ickes, andI. H. Bernstein, "Empathic Inaccuracy in Husband to Wife Aggression: The Overattribution Bias," *Personal Relationships* 9 (2002): 141–58; also see W. E. Schweinle and W. Ickes, "The Role of Men's Critical/Rejecting Overattribution Bias, Affect, and Attentional Disengagement in Marital Aggression," *Journal of Social and Clinical Psychology* 26, no. 2 (2007): 173–98.

21. G. MacDonald, M. P. Zanna, and J. G. Holmes, "An Experimental Test of the Role of Alcohol in Relationship Conflict," *Journal of Experimental Social Psychology* 36 (2000): 182–93.

22. R. Dumlao and R. A. Botta, "Family Communication Patterns and the Conflict Styles Young Adults Use with Their Fathers," *Communication Quarterly* 48 (Spring 2000): 174–89; also see W. Aquilino, "From Adolescent to Young Adult: A Prospective Study of Parent-Child Relations During the Transition to Adulthood," *Journal of Marriage and the Family* 59 (1997): 670–86.

23. R. J. Doolittle, *Orientations of Communication and Conflict* (Chicago: Science Research Associates, 1976), 7–9.

24. Canary, Cupach and Serpe, "A Competence-Based Approach to Examining Interpersonal Conflict."

25. D. H. Solomon, L. K. Knoblock, and M. A. Fitzpatrick, "Relational Power, Marital Schema, and Decisions to Withhold Complaints: An Investigation of the Chilling Effect of Confrontation in Marriage," *Communication Studies* 55 (2004): 146–67.

26. D. Canary, W. Cupach, and S. Messman, *Relationship Conflict* (Thousand Oaks, CA: Sage, 1995); J. Gottman, *What Predicts Divorce? The Relationship Between Marital Process and Marital Outcomes* (Hillsdale, NJ: Erlbaum, 1994).

27. Lloyd, "Conflict in Premarital Relationships."

28. E. H. Mudd, H. E. Mitchell, and J. W. Bullard, "Areas of Marital Conflict in Successfully Functioning and Unsuccessfully Functioning Families," *Journal of Health and Human Behavior* 3 (1962): 88–93; N. R. Vines, "Adult Unfolding and Marital Conflict," *Journal of Marital and Family Therapy* 5 (1979): 5–14.

29. B. A. Fisher, "Decision Emergence: Phases in Group Decision Making," *Speech Monographs* 37 (1970): 60.

30. G. R. Miller and M. Steinberg, *Between People: A New Analysis of Interpersonal Communication* (Chicago: Science Research Associates, 1975), 264.

31. C. M. Hoppe, "Interpersonal Aggression as a Function of Subject's Sex Role Identification, Opponent's Sex, and Degree of Provocation," *Journal of Personality* 47 (1979): 317–29.

32. Wilmot and Hocker, *Interpersonal Conflict;* also see S. W. Littlejohn and K. Domenici, *Engaging Communication in Conflict: Systemic Practice* (Thousand Oaks, CA: Sage, 2001).

33. J. M. Olsen, *The Process of Social Organization* (New York: Holt, Rinehart and Winston, 1978).

34. S. Ting-Toomey, "A Face Negotiation Theory," in *Theories in Intercultural Communication,* edited by Y. Kim and W. Gudykunst (Newbury Park, CA: Sage, 1988).

35. Y. B. Zhang, J. Harwood, and M. L. Hummert, "Perceptions of Conflict Management Styles in Chinese Intergenerational Dyads," *Communication Monographs* 72 (2005): 71–91.

36. D. A. Cai and E. L. Fink, "Conflict Style Differences Between Individualists and Collectivists," *Communication Monographs* 69 (March 2002): 67–87.

37. Zhang, Harwood, and Hummert, "Perceptions of Conflict Management Styles in Chinese Intergenerational Dyads."

38. Wilmot and Hocker, *Interpersonal Conflict,* 15–16.

39. S. L. Young, "Factors That Influence Recipients' Appraisals of Hurtful Communication," *Journal of Social and Personal Relationships* 21 (2004): 291–303; S. L. Young, T. L. Kubicka, C. E. Tucker, D. Chavez-Appel, and J. S. Rex, "Communicative Responses to Hurtful Messages in Families," *The Journal of Family Communication* 5 (2005): 123–40.

40. K. Kellerman, "A Goal-Directed Approach to Gaining Compliance: Relating Differences Among Goals to Differences in Behaviors," *Communication Research* 31 (2004): 397–445.

41. J. R. P. French and B. H. Raven, "The Bases of Social Power," in *Group Dynamics,* edited by J. D. Cartwright and A. Zander (Evanston, IL: Row, Peterson, 1962), 607–22.

42. K. Kellerman, "A Goal-Directed Approach to Gaining Compliance."

43. E. V. Wilson, "Perceived Effectiveness of Interpersonal Persuasion Strategies in Computer-Mediated Communication," *Computers in Human Behavior* 19 (2003): 537–52.

44. K. Kellerman, "A Goal-Directed Approach to Gaining Compliance."

45. G. R. Miller and F. Boster, "Persuasion in Personal Relationships," in *A Handbook of Personal Relationships,* edited by S. Duck (New York: Wiley, 1988), 275–88; M. G. Garko, "Perspectives and Conceptualizations of Compliance and Compliance Gaining," *Communication Quarterly* 38, no. 2 (1990): 138–57.

46. M. G. Lawler and G. S. Risch, "Time, Sex and Money: The First Five Years of Marriage," *America* 184 (2001): 16–20.

47. M. A. Rahim and N. R. Magner, "Confirmatory Factor Analysis of the Styles of Handling Interpersonal Conflict: First-Order Factor Model and Its Invariance Across Groups," *Journal of Applied Psychology* 80, no. 1 (1995): 122–32.

48. V. Satir, *Peoplemaking* (Palo Alto, CA: Science and Behavior Books, 1972).

49. A. F. Koerner and M. A. Fitzpatrick, "You Never Leave Your Family in a Fight: The Impact of Family of Origin on Conflict Behavior in Romantic Relationships," *Communication Studies* 53 (2002): 234–51.

50. R. Kilmann and K. Thomas, "Interpersonal Conflict-Handling Behavior as Reflections of Jungian Personality Dimensions," *Psychological Reports* 37 (1975): 971–80; K. W. Thomas and R. H. Kilmann, *Thomas-Kilmann Conflict Mode Instrument* (Tuxedo, NY: XICOM, 1974).

51. A. Buysse, A. De Clercq, L. Verhofstadt, E. Heene, H. Roeyers, and P. Van Oost, "Dealing with Relational Conflict: A Picture in Milliseconds," *Journal of Social and Personal Relationships* 17 (2000): 574–79.

52. N. A. Klinetob and D. A. Smith, "Demand-Withdraw Communication in Marital Interaction: Tests of Interspousal Contingency and Gender Role Hypotheses," *Journal of Marriage and the Family* 58 (November 1996): 945–57; also see J. P. Caughlin and A. L. Vangelisti, "Desire to Change in One's Partner as a Predictor of the Demand/Withdraw Pattern of Marital Communication," *Communication Monographs* 66 (1999): 66–89

53. J. P. Caughlin and R. S. Malis, "Demand/Withdraw Communication Between Parents and Adolescents as a Correlate of Relational Satisfaction," *Communication Reports* 17 (2004): 59–71.

54. R. Bello and R. Edwards, "Interpretations of Messages: The Influence of Various Forms of Equivocation, Face Concerns, and Sex Differences," *Journal of Language and Social Psychology* 24 (2005): 160–81.

55. J. T. Tedeschi, "Threats and Promises," in *The Structure of Conflict,* edited by R. Swingle (New York: Academic Press, 1970).

56. A. M. Czopp, M. J. Monteith, and A. Y. Mark, "Standing Up for a Change: Reducing Bias Through Interpersonal Confrontation," *Journal of Personality and Social Psychology* 90, no. 5 (2006): 784–803.

57. R. Fisher and W. Ury, *Getting to Yes: Negotiating Agreement Without Giving In* (Boston: Houghton Mifflin, 1988); also see D. Yankelovich, *The Magic of Dialogue: Transforming Conflict into Cooperation* (New York: Simon & Schuster, 1999).

58. Our discussion of the advantages and disadvantages of using different conflict management styles is based on material in Wilmot and Hocker, *Interpersonal Conflict.*

59. L. Powell and M. Hickson, "Power Imbalance and Anticipation of Conflict Resolution: Positive and Negative Attributes of Perceptual Recall," *Communication Research Reports* 17 (Spring 2000): 181–90.

60. D. Cramer, "Linking Conflict Management Behaviors and Relational Satisfaction: The Intervening Role of Conflict Outcome Satisfaction," *Journal of Social and Personal Relationships* 19 (2000): 425–32.

61. Cai and Fink, "Conflict Style Differences Between Individualists and Collectivists."

62. M. R. Hammer, "The Intercultural Conflict Style Inventory: A Conceptual Framework and Measure of Intercultural Conflict Resolution Approaches," *International Journal of Intercultural Relations* 29 (2005): 675–95.

63. Hammer, "The Intercultural Conflict Style Inventory."

64. For an excellent review of the literature on flaming, see A. N. Joinson, *Understanding the Psychology of Internet Behavior: Virtual Worlds, Real Lives* (Houndsmill, England: Palgrave Macmillan, 2003), 64–77.

65. Canary, Cupach, and Serpe, "A Competence-Based Approach to Examining Interpersonal Conflict."

66. Our discussion of conflict management skills is based on several excellent discussions of conflict management prescriptions. We acknowledge Fisher and Ury, *Getting to Yes;* R. Boulton, *People Skills* (New York: Simon & Schuster, 1979); D. A. Romig and L. J. Romig, *Structured Teamwork® Guide* (Austin, TX: Performance Resources, 1990); O. Hargie, C. Saunders, and D. Dickson, *Social Skills in Interpersonal Communication* (London: Routledge, 1994); S. Deep and L. Sussman, *Smart Moves* (Reading, MA: Addison-Wesley, 1990); Wilmot and Hocker, *Interpersonal Conflict;* M. D. Davis, E. L. Eshelman, and M. McKay, *The Relaxation and Stress*

Reduction Workbook (Oakland, CA: New Harbinger Publications, 1982); W. A. Donohue and R. Kolt, *Managing Interpersonal Conflict* (Newbury Park: CA: Sage, 1992); O. Hargie (Ed.), *The Handbook of Communication Skills* (London: Routledge, 1997); Littlejohn and Domenici, *Engaging Communication in Conflict;* and M. W. Isenhart and M. Spangle, *Collaborative Approaches to Resolving Conflict* (Thousand Oaks, CA: Sage, 2000).

67. Czopp, Monteith, and Mark, "Standing Up for a Change."

68. Boulton, *People Skills,* 217.

69. For additional strategies on managing emotion, see J. Gottman, *Why Marriages Succeed and Fail: And How You Can Make Yours Last* (New York: Simon & Schuster, 1994); J. Gottman, *The Seven Principles for Making Marriage Work* (New York: Crown, 1999). Also see Johnson, *Reaching Out.*

70. J. A. Feeney, "Hurt Feelings in Couple Relationships: Towards Integrative Models of the Negative Effects of Hurtful Events," *Journal of Social and Personal Relationships* 21 (2004): 487–508.

71. Young, "Factors That Influence Recipients' Appraisals of Hurtful Communication."

72. H. Weger Jr., "Disconfirming Communication and Self-Verification in Marriage: Associations Among the Demand/Withdraw Interaction Pattern, Feeling Understood, and Marital Satisfaction," *Journal of Social and Personal Relationships* 22 (2005): 19–31.

73. J. Gottman, *What Predicts Divorce? The Relationship Between Marital Process and Marital Outcomes* (Hillsdale, NJ: Erlbaum, 1994).

74. M. Morris, J. Nadler, T. Kurtzberg, and L. Thompson, "Schmooze or Lose: Social Friction and Lubrication in E-Mail Negotiations," *Group Dynamics: Theory, Research and Practice* 6 (2002): 89–100.

75. A. Ellis, *A New Guide to Rational Living* (North Hollywood, CA: Wilshire Books, 1977).

76. Fisher and Ury, *Getting to Yes;* Boulton, *People Skills;* Romig and Romig, *Structured Teamwork® Guide;* T. Gordon, *Leader Effectiveness Training* (L.E.T.): *The No-Lose Way to Release the Productive Potential of People* (New York: Wyden Books, 1977).

77. Deep and Susman, *Smart Moves.*

78. Ellis, *A New Guide to Rational Living.*

79. M. Sinaceau and L. Z. Tiedens, "Get Mad and Get More Than Even: When and Why Anger Expression Is Effective in Negotiations," *Journal of Experimental Social Psychology* 20 (2005): 1–9.

80. A. M. Bippus and S. L. Young, "Owning Your Emotions: Reactions to Expressions of Self- versus Other-Attributed Positive and Negative Emotions," *Journal of Applied Communication Research* 33 (2005): 26–45.

81. S. R. Covey, *The 7 Habits of Highly Effective People* (New York: Simon & Schuster, 1989), 235.

82. S. G. Lakey and D. J. Canary, "Actor Goal Achievement and Sensitivity to Partner as Critical Factors in Understanding Interpersonal Communication Competence and Conflict Strategies," *Communication Monographs* 69 (2002): 217–35.

83. Lakey and Canary, "Actor Goal Achievement and Sensitivity to Partner as Critical Factors in Understanding Interpersonal Communication Competence and Conflict Strategies."

84. C. Pavitt and B. Kemp, "Contextual and Relational Factors in Interpersonal Negotiation Strategy Choice," *Communication Quarterly* 47, no. 2 (1999): 133–50.

85. Fisher and Ury, *Getting to Yes.*

86. W. Ury, *Getting Past No* (New York: Bantam Books, 1993); also see S. Hackley, "When Life Gives

You Lemons: How to Deal with Difficult People," *Harvard Business School Publishing Corporation* (2004): 3–5.

87. For an excellent review and analysis of collaborative, side-by-side leadership research, see D. Romig, *Side by Side Leadership: Achieving Outstanding Results Together* (Marietta, GA: Bard Press, 2001).

88. Lakey and Canary, "Actor Goal Achievement and Sensitivity to Partner as Critical Factors in Understanding Interpersonal Communication Competence and Conflict Strategies."

89. E. Goffman, *Interaction Rituals: Essays on Face-to-Face Interaction* (Garden City, NY: Doubleday, 1967).

90. S. Ting-Toomey, "Face and Facework: An Introduction," in *The Challenge of Facework,* edited by S. Ting-Toomey (Albany, NY: SUNY Press, 1994), 1–14; S. Ting-Toomey, "Managing Intercultural Conflicts Effectively," in *Intercultural Communication: A Reader,* edited by L. A. Samovar and R. E. Porter (Belmont, CA: Wadsworth, 1994), 360–72; also see S. Ting-Toomey and L. Chung, "Cross-Cultural Interpersonal Communication: Theoretical Trends and Research Directions," in *Communication in Personal Relationships Across Cultures,* edited by W. B. Gudykunst, S. Ting-Toomey, and T. Nishida (Thousand Oaks, CA: Sage, 1996), 237–61; Isenhart and Spangle, *Collaborative Approaches to Resolving Conflict,* 19–20.

91. V. Manusov, J. K. Kellas, and A. R. Trees, "Do Unto Others? Conversational Moves and Perceptions of Attentiveness Toward Other Face in Accounting Sequences Between Friends," *Human Communication Research* 30 (2004): 514–39.

92. M. L. McLaughlin, M. J. Cody, and H. D. O'Hair, "The Management of Failure Events: Some Contextual Determinants of Accounting Behavior," *Human Communication Research* 9 (1983): 102–25; Manusov, Kellas, and Trees, "Do Unto Others?"

Chapter 9

1. F. E. Millar and L. E. Rogers, "A Relational Approach to Interpersonal Communication," in *Explorations in Interpersonal Communication,* edited by G. R. Miller (Newbury Park, CA: Sage, 1976), 87–103.

2. K. Chow, "Social Support and Subjective Well-Being Among Hong Kong Chinese Young Adults," *Journal of Genetic Psychology* 160 (September 1999): 319–31.

3. L. K. Knobloch and D. H. Solomon, "Information Seeking Beyond Initial Interaction: Negotiating Relational Uncertainty within Close Relationships," *Human Communication Research* 28 (April 2002): 243–57.

4. F. E. Millar and L. E. Rogers, "Relational Dimensions of Interpersonal Dynamics," in *Interpersonal Processes: New Directions in Communication Research,* edited by M. E. Roloff and G. R. Miller (Newbury Park, CA: Sage, 1987), 117–39.

5. N. E. Dunbar and J. K. Burgoon, "Perceptions of Power and Interactional Dominance in Interpersonal Relationships," *Journal of Social and Personal Relationships* 22 (2005): 207–33.

6. M. Sunnafrank, "Predicted Outcome Value During Initial Interaction: A Reformulation of Uncertainty Reduction Theory," *Human Communication Research* 13 (1986): 3–33.

7. Sunnafrank, "Predicted Outcome Value During Initial Interaction."

8. M. Sunnafrank, "Interpersonal Attraction and Attitude Similarity: A Communication Based Assessment," in *Communication Yearbook 14,* edited by J. A. Anderson (Newbury Park, CA: Sage, 1991), 451–83.

9. S. Sprecher, "Insiders' Perspectives on Reasons for Attraction to a Close Other," *Social Psychology Quarterly* 61 (1998): 287–300.

10. S. W. Duck, *Personal Relationships and Personal Constructs: A Study of Friendship Formation* (New York: Wiley, 1993).

11. Sprecher, "Insiders' Perspectives."

12. K. F. Albada, M. L. Knapp, and K. E. Theune, "Interaction Appearance Theory: Changing Perceptions of Physical Attractiveness Through Social Interaction," *Communication Theory* 12 (2002): 8–40.

13. P. A. Mongeau and K. L. Johnson, "Predicting Cross-Sex First-Date Sexual Expectations and Involvement: Contextual and Individual Difference Factors," *Personal Relationships* 2 (1995): 301–12.

14. P. C. Regan, L. Levin, S. Sprecher, F. S. Christopher, and R. Cate, "Partner Preferences: What Characteristics Do Men and Women Desire in Their Short-Term Sexual and Long-Term Romantic Partners?" *Journal of Psychology and Human Sexuality* 12 (2000): 1–21.

15. S. Litzinger and K. Gordon, "Exploring Relationships Among Communication, Sexual Satisfaction, and Marital Satisfaction," *Journal of Sex and Marital Therapy* 31 (2005): 409–24; S. Sprecher, F. S. Christopher, and R. Cate, "Sexuality in Close Relationships," in *The Cambridge Handbook of Personal Relationships,* edited by A. L. Vangelisti and D. Perlman (New York: Cambridge University Press, 2006), 463–84.

16. Litzinger and Gordon, "Exploring Relationships Among Communication, Sexual Satisfaction, and Marital Satisfaction."

17. W. G. Graziano and J. W. Bruce, "Attraction and the Initiation of Relationships: A Review of the Empirical Literature," in *Handbook of Relationship Initiation,* edited by S. Sprecher, A. Wenzel, and J. Harvey (New York: Psychology Press, 2008), 269–95.

18. Sprecher, "Insiders' Perspectives."

19. R. A. Clark, M. Dockum, H. Hazeu, M. Huang, N. Luo, J. Ramsey, and A. Spyrou, "Initial Encounters of Young Men and Women: Impressions and Disclosure Estimates," *Sex Roles* 50 (2004): 699–709.

20. S. Sprecher and P. C. Regan, "Liking Some Things (in Some People) More Than Others: Partner Preferences in Romantic Relationships and Friendships," *Journal of Social and Personal Relationships* 19 (2002): 463–81.

21. N. L. Collins and L. C. Miller, "Self-Disclosure and Liking: A Meta-Analytic Review," *Psychological Bulletin* 116 (1994): 457–75.

22. Collins and Miller, "Self-Disclosure and Liking."

23. Sprecher, "Insiders' Perspectives."

24. G. B. Ray and K. Floyd, "Nonverbal Expressions of Liking and Disliking in Initial Interaction: Encoding and Decoding Perspectives," *Southern Communication Journal* 71 (2006): 45–65.

25. P. W. Eastwick, E. J. Finkel, D. Mochon, and D. Ariely, "Selective Versus Unselective Romantic Desire: Not All Reciprocity Is Created Equal," *Psychological Science* 18 (2007): 317–19.

26. M. V. Redmond and D. A. Vrchota, "The Effects of Varying Lengths of Initial Interaction on Attraction and Uncertainty Reduction," paper presented at the annual meeting of the National Communication Association, New Orleans (1994).

27. L. A. Baxter and L. West, "Couple Perceptions of Their Similarities and Differences: A Dialectical Perspective," *Journal of Social and Personal Relationships* 20 (2003): 491–514.

28. Sunnafrank, "Interpersonal Attraction and Attitude Similarity."

29. Sunnafrank, "Interpersonal Attraction and Attitude Similarity."

30. Sprecher, "Insiders' Perspectives."

31. Baxter and West, "Couple Perceptions of Their Similarities and Differences."

32. Baxter and West, "Couple Perceptions of Their Similarities and Differences."

33. L. A. Baxter and C. Bullis, "Turning Points in Developing Romantic Relationships," *Communication Research* 12 (1986): 469–93.

34. L. K. Guerrero and P. A. Mongeau, "On Becoming 'More Than Friends': The Transition from Friendship to Romantic Relationship," in *Handbook of Relationship Initiation,* edited by S. Sprecher, A. Wenzel, and J. Harvey (New York: Psychology Press, 2008), 175–96.

35. Baxter and Bullis, "Turning Points."

36. C. R. Berger and J. J. Bradac, *Language and Social Knowledge: Uncertainty and Interpersonal Relations* (Baltimore: Edward Arnold, 1982).

37. M. R. Cunningham and A. P. Barbee. "Prelude to a Kiss: Nonverbal Flirting, Opening Gambits, and Other Communication Dynamics of the Initiation of Romantic Relationships," in *Handbook of Relationship Initiation,* edited by S. Sprecher, A. Wenzel, and J. Harvey (New York: Psychology Press, 2008), 97–120.

38. W. Douglas, "Question Asking in Same and Opposite Sex Initial Interactions: The Effects of Anticipated Future Interactions," *Human Communication Research* 14 (1987): 230–45.

39. M. Parks, *Personal Relationships and Personal Networks* (Mahwah, NJ: Erlbaum, 2007).

40. S. W. Duck, "A Topography of Relationship Disengagement and Dissolution," in *Personal Relationships 4: Dissolving Personal Relationships,* edited by S. W. Duck (London: Academic Press, 1982), 1–29.

41. J. K. Kellas, D. Bean, C. Cunningham, and K. Y. Cheng. "The Ex-Files: Trajectories, Turning Points, and Adjustment in the Development of Post-Dissolutional Relationships," *Journal of Social and Personal Relationships* 25 (2008): 23–50.

42. Duck, "A Topography of Relationship Disengagement and Dissolution."

43. D. DeStephen, "Integrating Relational Termination into a General Model of Communication Competence," paper presented at the annual meeting of the National Communication Association, Denver (1985).

44. S. Duck, "Interpersonal Communication in Developing Relationships," in *Explorations in Interpersonal Communication,* edited by G. R. Miller (Newbury Park, CA: Sage, 1976), 127–47.

45. J. W. Thibaut and H. H. Kelley, *The Social Psychology of Groups* (New York: Wiley, 1959).

46. A. L. Busboom, D. M. Collins, M. D. Givertz, and L. A. Levin, "Can We Still Be Friends? Resources and Barriers to Friendship Quality after Romantic Relationship Dissolution," *Personal Relationships* 9 (2002): 215–23.

47. I. Atlman and D. A. Taylor, *Social Penetration: The Development of Interpersonal Relationships* (New York: Holt, Rinehart and Winston, 1973).

48. M. Sunnafrank, "Predicted Outcome Value During Initial Interactions."

49. G. R. Miller and M. R. Parks, "Communicating in Dissolving Relationships," in *Personal Relationships 4: Dissolving Personal Relationships,* edited by S. W. Duck (London: Academic Press, 1982), 127–54.

50. L. A. Baxter, "Dialectical Contradictions in Relationship Development," in *Handbook of Personal Relationships,* edited by S. W. Duck (Chichester, England: Wiley, 1988), 257–73; L. A. Baxter and B. M. Montgomery, "Rethinking Communication in Personal Relationships from a Dialectical Perspective," in *Handbook of Personal Relationships,* 2nd ed., edited by S. W. Duck (Chichester, England: Wiley, 1997), 325–49.

51. D. R. Pawlowski, "Dialectical Tensions in Marital Partners' Accounts of Their Relationships," *Communication Quarterly* 46 (1998): 396–416.

52. Pawlowski, "Dialectical Tensions."

53. L. A. Baxter, "Interpersonal Communication as Dialogue: A Response to the 'Social Approaches' Forum," *Communication Theory* 2 (1992): 330–38.

54. A. Hoppe-Nagao and S. Ting-Toomey, "Relational Dialectics and Management Strategies in Marital Couples," *Southern Communication Journal* 67 (Winter 2002): 142–59.

55. Baxter, "Interpersonal Communication as Dialogue."

56. A. J. Johnson, E. Wittenberg, M. M. Villagran, M. Mazur, and P. Villagran, "Relational Progression as a Dialectic: Examining Turning Points in Communication among Friends," *Communication Monographs* 70 (2003): 230–49.

57. I. Altman and D. A. Taylor, *Social Penetration: The Development of Interpersonal Relationships* (New York: Holt, Rinehart and Winston, 1973).

58. W. B. Gudykunst and T. Nishida, "Social Penetration in Japanese and American Close Friendships," in *Communication Yearbook 7,* edited by R. N. Bostrom (Beverly Hills, CA: Sage, 1963), 592–611.

59. M. Kito, "Self-Disclosure in Romantic Relationships and Friendships Among American and Japanese College Students, *The Journal of Social Psychology* 145 (2005): 127–40.

60. J. C. Korn, "Friendship Formation and Development in Two Cultures: Universal Constructs in the United States and Korea," in *Interpersonal Communication in Friend and Mate Relationships,* edited by A. M. Nicotera (Albany: State University of New York Press, 1993), 61–78.

61. K. Dindia, "Self-Disclosure Research: Knowledge through Meta-Analsysis," in *Interpersonal Communication Research: Analysis Through Meta-Analysis,* edited by M. Allen, R. W. Preiss, B. M. Gayle, and N. A. Burrell (Mahwah, NJ: Erlbaum, 2002), 169–85.

62. S. Petronio, *Boundaries of Privacy: Dialectics of Disclosure* (Albany: State University of New York Press, 2000).

63. J. P. Caughlin and T. D. Afifi, "When Is Topic Avoidance Unsatisfying? Examining Moderators of the Association Between Avoidance and Dissatisfaction," *Human Communication Research* 30 (2004): 479–513.

64. J. Powell, *Why Am I Afraid to Tell You Who I Am?* (Niles, IL: Argus Communications, 1969), 12.

65. V. J. Derlega, B. A. Winstead, and K. Greene, "Self-Disclosure and Starting a Close Relationship," in *Handbook of Relationship Initiation,* edited by S. Sprecher, A. Wenzel, and J. Harvey (New York: Psychology Press, 2008), 153–194.

66. J. A. Bargh, K. Y. A. McKenna, and G. M. Fitzsimons, "Can You See the Real Me? Activation and Expression of the 'True Self' on the Internet." *Journal of Social Issues* 58 (2002) 33–48.

67. A. M. Ledbetter, "Measuring Online Communication Attitude: Scale Development and Validation," *Communication Monographs* (in press).

68. B. Fehr, "Friendship Formation," in *Handbook of Relationship Initiation,* edited by S. Sprecher, A. Wenzel, and J. Harvey (New York: Psychology Press, 2008), 29–54.

69. J. J. Weisel and P. E. King, "Involvement in a Conversation and Attributions Concerning Excessive Self-Disclosure." *Southern Communication Journal* 72 (2007) 345–54, Fehr, "Friendship Formation."

70. Fehr, "Friendship Formation."

71. Fehr, "Friendship Formation."

72. Powell, *Why Am I Afraid.*

73. M. Argyle, M. Henderson, and A. Furnham, "The Rules of Social Relationships," *British Journal of Social Psychology* 24 (1985): 125–39.

74. A. L. Vangelisti, J. P. Caughlin, and L. Timmerman, "Criteria for Revealing Family Secrets," *Communication Monographs* 68 (March 2001): 1–27.

75. T. D. Afifi, L. N. Olson, and C. Armstrong, "The Chilling Effect and Family Secrets: Examining the Role of Self Protection, Other Protection, and Communication Efficacy," *Human Communication Research* 31 (2005): 564–98.

76. A. P. Bochner, "On the Efficacy of Openness in Close Relationships," in *Communication Yearbook 5,* edited by M. Burgoon (New Brunswick, NJ: Transaction Books, 1982), 109–24.

Chapter 10

1. P. Noller, "Bringing It All Together: A Theoretical Approach," in *The Cambridge Handbook of Personal Relationships,* edited by A. L. Vangelisti and D. Perlman (New York: Cambridge University Press, 2006), 769–89.

2. S. Metts, "Relational Transgressions," in *The Dark Side of Interpersonal Communication,* edited by W. R. Cupach and B. H. Spitzberg (Hillsdale, NJ: Erlbaum, 1994), 217–39.

3. A. P. Buunk and P. Dijkstra, "Temptation and Threat: Extradyadic Relations and Jealousy," in *The Cambridge Handbook of Personal Relationships*, edited by A. L. Vangelisti and D. Perlman (New York: Cambridge University Press, 2006), 533–56.

4. F. D. Fincham, "The Account Episode in Close Relationships," in *Explaining One's Self to Others: Reason-Giving in a Social Context,* edited by M. L. McClaughlin, M. J. Cody, and S. J. Read (Hillsdale, NJ: Erlbaum, 1992), 167–82.

5. G. Makoul and M. E. Roloff, "The Role of Efficacy and Outcome Expectations in the Decision to Withhold Relational Complaints," *Communication Research* 25 (1998): 25–30.

6. M. L. McLaughlin, M. J. Cody, and H. D. O'Hair, "The Management of Failure Events: Some Contextual Determinants of Accounting Behavior," *Human Communication Research* 9 (1983): 208–24.

7. Fincham, "The Account Episode in Close Relationships."

8. J. W. Younger, R. L. Piferi, R. L. Jobe, and K. A. Lawler, "Dimensions of Forgiveness: The Views of Laypersons," *Journal of Social and Personal Relationships* 21 (2004): 837–55.

9. Younger, Piferi, Jobe, and Lawler, "Dimensions of Forgiveness."

10. Younger, Piferi, Jobe, and Lawler, "Dimensions of Forgiveness."

11. V. R. Waldron and D. L. Kelley, *Communicating Forgiveness* (Thousand Oaks, CA: Sage, 2008).

12. V. R. Waldron and D. L. Kelley, "Forgiving Communication as a Response to Relational Transgressions," *Journal of Social and Personal Relationships* 22 (2005): 723–42.

13. S. Metts and W. R. Cupach, "Responses to Relational Transgressions: Hurt, Anger, and Sometimes Forgiveness," in *The Dark Side of Interpersonal Communication*, 2nd ed., edited by B. H. Spitzberg and W. R. Cupach (Mahwah: NJ: Erlbaum, 2007), 243–274.

14. L. K. Guerrero and W. A. Afifi, "Toward a Goal-Oriented Approach for Understanding Communicative Responses to Jealousy," *Western Journal of Communication* 63 (1999): 216–48.

15. M. A. Tofoya and B. H. Spitzberg, "The Dark Side of Infidelity: Its Nature, Prevelance, and Communicative Functions," in *The Dark Side of Interpersonal Communication*, 2nd ed., edited by B. H. Spitzberg and W. R. Cupach (Mahwah: NJ: Erlbaum, 2007), 201–42.

16. J. Fitness and J. Peterson, "Punishment and Forgiveness in Close Relationships: An Evolutionary, Social-Psychological Perspective," in *Social Relationships: Cognitive, Affective, and Motivational Processes,* edited by J. P. Forgas and J. Fitness (New York: Psychology Press, 2008), 255–69.

17. Noller, "Bringing It All Together"; Guerrero and Afifi, "Toward a Goal-Oriented Approach."

18. L. Stafford, *Maintaining Long-Distance and Cross-Residential Relationships* (Mahwah, NJ: Erlbaum, 2005).

19. M. Dainton and B. Aylor, "A Relational Uncertainty Analysis of Jealousy, Trust, and Maintenance in Long-Distance Versus Geographically Close Relationships," *Communication Quarterly* 49 (Spring 2001): 172–88.

20. Dainton and Aylor, "A Relational Uncertainty Analysis."

21. G. T. Guldner and C. H. Swensen, "Time Spent Together and Relationship Quality: Long-Distance Relationships as a Test Case," *Journal of Social and Personal Relationships* 12 (1995): 313–20; A. J. Johnson, "Examining the Maintenance of Friendships: Are There Differences Between Geographically Close and Long-Distance Friends?" *Communication Quarterly* 49 (Fall 2001): 424–35.

22. L. Stafford and J. R. Reske, "Idealization and Communication in Long-Distance Premarital Relationships," *Family Relations* 39 (July, 1990): 274–79.

23. Stafford and Reske, "Idealization and Communication in Long-Distance Premarital Relationships."

24. J. Lyndon, T. Pierce, and S. O'Regan, "Coping with Moral Commitment to Long-Distance Dating Relationships," *Journal of Personality and Social Psychology* 73 (1997): 104–13.

25. L. Stafford and A. J. Merolla, "Idealization, Reunions, and Stability in Long-Distance Dating Relationships," *Journal of Social and Personal Relationships* 24 (2007): 37–54.

26. Stafford, *Maintaining Long-Distance and Cross-Residential Relationships.*

27. B. Le and C. R. Agnew, "Need Fulfillment and Emotional Experience in Interdependent Romantic Relationships," *Journal of Social and Personal Relationships* 18 (2001): 423–40.

28. Lyndon, Pierce, and O'Regan, "Coping with Moral Commitment to Long-Distance Dating Relationships."

29. E. M. Sahlstein and T. Truong, "Proximal and Long-Distance Relations: A Web of Contradictions," paper presented at the annual meeting of the National Communication Association (2002).

30. Sahlstein and Truong, "Proximal and Long-Distance Relations."

31. E. M. Sahlstein, "Making Plans: Praxis Strategies for Negotiating Uncertainty-Certainty in Long-Distance Relationships," *Western Journal of Communication* 70 (2006): 147–65.

32. S. O. Gaines, Jr. and W. Ickes, "Perspectives on Interracial Relationships" in *The Social Psychology of Personal Relationships,* edited by W. Ickes and S. Duck, (New York: Wiley, 2000), 55–78.

33. Gaines and Ickes, "Perspectives on Interracial Relationships."

34. Gaines and Ickes, "Perspectives on Interracial Relationships."

35. M. J. Reiter and C. B. Gee, "Open Communication and Partner Support in Intercultural and Interfaith Romantic Relationships: A Relational Maintenance Approach," *Journal of Social and Personal Relationships* 25 (2008): 539–59.

36. Reiter and Gee, "Open Communication and Partner Support."

37. Reiter and Gee, "Open Communication and Partner Support."

38. Reiter and Gee, "Open Communication and Partner Support."

39. S. M. Haas and L. Stafford, "An Initial Examination of Maintenance Behaviors in Gay and Lesbian Relationships," *Journal of Social and Personal Relationships* 15 (1998): 846–55.

40. Haas and Stafford, "An Initial Examination of Maintenance Behaviors in Gay and Lesbian Relationships."

41. T. P. Mottet, "The Role of Sexual Orientation in Predicting Outcome Value and Anticipated Communication Behaviors," *Communication Quarterly* 48 (Summer 2000): 223–39.

42. Mottet, "The Role of Sexual Orientation in Predicting Outcome Value and Anticipated Communication Behaviors."

43. D. O'Hair and W. Cody, "Deception," in *The Dark Side of Interpersonal Communication,* edited by W. R. Cupach and B. H. Spitzberg (Hillsdale, NJ: Erlbaum, 1994), 181–213.

44. M. Knapp, "Lying and Deception in Close Relationships," in *The Cambridge Handbook of Personal Relationships,* edited by A. L. Vangelisti and D. Perlman (New York: Cambridge University Press, 2006), 517–32.

45. J. K. Burgoon and D. B. Buller, "Interpersonal Deception Theory: Purposive and Interdependent Behavior during Deception," in *Engaging Theories in Interpersonal Communication: Multiple Perspectives,* edited by L. A. Baxter and D. O. Braithwaite (Thousand Oaks, CA: Sage, 2008), 227–39.

46. A. E. Lucchetti, "Deception in Disclosing One's Sexual History: Safe-Sex Avoidance or Ignorance?" *Communication Quarterly* 47 (1999): 300–14.

47. O'Hair and Cody, "Deception."

48. T. R. Levine, K. J. K. Asada, and L. L. Massi Lindsey, "The Relative Impact of Violation Type and Lie Severity on Judgments of Message Deceitfulness," paper presented at the annual meeting of the National Communication Association (2002).

49. M. V. Redmond, *Human Communication: Theories and Applications* (Boston: Houghton Mifflin, 2000).

50. S. A. McCornack and T. R. Levine, "When Lies Are Uncovered: Emotional and Relational Outcomes of Discovered Deception," *Communication Monographs* 57 (1990): 119–38.

51. D. A. DePaulo and B. M. Kashy, "Everyday Lies in Close and Casual Relationships," *Journal of Personality and Social Psychology* 74 (1998): 63–80.

52. D. B. Buller and J. K. Burgoon, "Deception: Strategic and Nonstrategic Communication," in *Strategic Interpersonal Communication,* edited by J. A.

Daly and J. M. Wiemann (Hillsdale, NJ: Erlbaum, 1994), 191–223; O'Hair and Cody, "Deception."

53. DePaulo and Kashy, "Everyday Lies in Close and Casual Relationships."

54. O'Hair and Cody, "Deception."

55. O'Hair and Cody, "Deception."

56. Knapp, "Lying and Deception in Close Relationships."

57. Knapp, "Lying and Deception in Close Relationships."

58. A. L. Vangelisti, "Messages That Hurt," in *The Dark Side of Interpersonal Communication*, edited by W. R. Cupach and B. H. Spitzberg (Hillsdale, NJ: Erlbaum, 1994), 181–213.

59. Vangelisti, "Messages That Hurt."

60. S. L. Young and A. M. Bippus, "Does It Make a Difference If They Hurt You in a Funny Way? Humorously and Non-Humorously Phrased Hurtful Messages in Personal Relationships," *Communication Quarterly* 49 (Winter 2001): 35–52.

61. P. E. Madlock and M. Booth-Butterfield, "Hurtful Teasing Between Romantic Couples: The Truth in Disguise?" paper presented at the annual meeting of the National Communication Association, San Diego (2008).

62. A. L. Vangelisti and L. P. Crumley, "Reactions to Messages That Hurt: The Influence of Relational Contexts," *Communication Monographs* 65 (1998): 173–96.

63. J. A. Feeney, "Hurt Feelings in Couple Relationships: Towards Integrative Models of the Negative Effects of Hurtful Events," *Journal of Social and Personal Relationships* 21 (2004): 487–508.

64. Vangelisti and Crumley, "Reactions to Messages That Hurt."

65. S. Zhang and L. Stafford, "Perceived Face Threat of Honest but Hurtful Evaluative Messages in Romantic Relationships," *Western Journal of Communication* 72 (2008): 19–39.

66. Zhang and Stafford, "Perceived Face Threat of Honest but Hurtful Evaluative Messages."

67. S. L. Young, "Factors that Influence Recipients' Appraisals of Hurtful Communication," *Journal of Social and Personal Relationships* 21 (2004): 291–303.

68. L. K. Guerrero and P. A. Anderson, "Jealousy and Envy," in *The Dark Side of Close Relationships*, edited by W. R. Cupach and B. H. Spitzberg (Hillsdale, NJ: Erlbaum, 1994), 33–70.

69. L. K. Knobloch, "Evaluating a Contextual Model of Responses to Relational Uncertainty-Increasing Events: The Role of Intimacy, Appraisals, and Emotions," *Human Communication Research* 31 (2005): 60–101.

70. J. L. Bevan and W. Samter, "Toward a Broader Conceptualization of Jealousy in Close Relationships: Two Exploratory Studies," *Communication Studies* 55 (2004): 14–28.

71. Guerrero and Anderson, "Jealousy and Envy."

72. Guerrero and Anderson, "Jealousy and Envy."

73. A. A. Fleishmann, B. H. Spitzberg, P. A. Anderson, and S. C. Roesch, "Tickling the Green Monster: Jealousy Induction in Relationships," *Journal of Social and Personal Relationships* 22 (2005): 49–73.

74. Fleishmann, Spitzberg, Anderson, and Roesch, "Tickling the Green Monster."

75. S. M. Yoshimura, "Emotional and Behavioral Responses in Romantic Jealousy Expressions," *Communication Reports* 17 (2004): 85–102.

76. Yoshimura, "Emotional and Behavioral Responses."

77. J. L. Bevan, "General Partner and Relational Uncertainty as Consequences of Another Jealousy Expression," *Western Journal of Communication* 68 (2004): 195–218.

78. W. R. Cupach and B. H. Spitzberg, "Obsessive Relational Intrusion and Stalking," in *The Dark Side of Close Relationships*, edited by B. H. Spitzberg and W. R. Cupach (Mahwah, NJ: Erlbaum, 1998), 233–64.

79. W. R. Cupach and B. H. Spitzberg, *The Dark Side of Relationship Pursuit: From Attraction to Obsession and Stalking* (Mahwah, NJ: Erlbaum, 2004).

80. Cupach and Spitzberg, *The Dark Side of Relationship Pursuit*, 29–30.

81. B. H. Spitzberg and W. R. Cupach, "The Inappropriateness of Relational Intrusion," in *Inappropriate Relationships: The Unconventional, the Disapproved, and the Forbidden*, edited by R. Goodwin and D. Cramer (Mahwah, NJ: Erlbaum, 2002), 191–220.

82. Cupach and Spitzberg, "Obsessive Relational Intrusion and Stalking."

83. Cupach and Spitzberg, *The Dark Side of Relationship Pursuit*, 69–71.

84. V. Ravensberg and C. Miller, "Stalking among Young Adults: A Review of the Preliminary Research," *Aggression and Violent Behavior* 8 (2003): 455–69; B. H. Spitzberg, A. M. Nicastro, and A. V. Cousins, "Exploring the Interactional Phenomenon of Stalking and Obsessive Relational Intrusion," *Communication Reports* 11 (1998): 33–48.

85. B. H. Spitzberg and W. R. Cupach, "Managing Unwanted Pursuit," in *Studies in Applied Interpersonal Communication*, edited by M. T. Motley (Thousand Oaks, CA: Sage, 2008), 3–26.

86. J. Morahan-Martin, "Internet Abuse: Addiction? Disorder? Symptom? Alternative Explanations?" *Social Science Computer Review* 23 (2005): 39–48.

87. S. E. Caplan, "Preference for Online Social Interaction: A Theory of Problematic Internet Use and Psychosocial Well-Being," *Communication Research* 30 (2003): 625–48; S. E. Caplan, "A Social Skill Account of Problematic Internet Use," *Journal of Communication* 55 (2005): 721–36.

88. J. Morahan-Martin and P. Schumacher, "Incidence and Correlates of Pathological Internet Use among College Students," *Computers in Human Behavior* 16 (2000): 13–29.

89. M. P. Johnson, "Violence and Abuse in Personal Relationships: Conflict, Terror, and Resistance in Intimate Partnerships," in *The Cambridge Handbook of Personal Relationships*, edited by A. L. Vangelisti and D. Perlman (New York: Cambridge University Press, 2006), 557–76.

90. Johnson, "Violence and Abuse in Personal Relationships."

91. Johnson, "Violence and Abuse in Personal Relationships."

92. Johnson, "Violence and Abuse in Personal Relationships."

93. C. M. Feldman and C. A. Ridley, "The Role of Conflict-Based Communication Responses and Outcomes in Male Domestic Violence toward Female Partners," *Journal of Social and Personal Relationships* 17 (2000): 552–73.

94. S. A. Jang, S. W. Smith, and T. R. Levine, "To Stay or to Leave? The Role of Attachment Styles in Communication Patterns and Potential Termination of Romantic Relationships Following Discovery of Deception," *Communication Monographs* 69 (2002): 236–52.

95. G. R. Miller and M. R. Parks, "Communication in Dissolving Relationships," in *Personal Relationships 4: Dissolving Personal Relationships*, edited by S. W. Duck (London: Academic Press, 1982), 127–54.

96. J. Gottman with N. Silver, *Why Marriages Succeed or Fail* (New York: Simon and Schuster, 1994).

97. Gottman and Silver, *Why Marriages Succeed or Fail*.

98. W. H. Denton and B. R. Burleson, "The Initiator Style Questionnaire: A Scale to Assess Initiator Tendency in Couples," *Personal Relationships* 14 (2007): 245–68.

99. R. J. Sidelinger, B. N. Frisby, and A. L. McMullen, "The Decision to Forgive: Sex, Gender, and the Likelihood to Forgive Partner Transgressions," *Communication Studies* 60 (2009): 164–79.

100. S. W. Duck, *Understanding Relationships* (New York: Guilford Press, 1991).

101. J. M. Gottman and S. Carrere, "Why Can't Men and Women Get Along? Developmental Roots and Marital Inequities," in *Communication and Relational Maintenance*, edited by D. J. Canary and L. Stafford (San Diego: Academic Press, 1991), 203–29.

102. C. Perilloux and D. M. Buss, "Breaking up Romantic Relationships: Costs Experienced and Coping Strategies Deployed," *Evolutionary Psychology* 6 (2008): 164–81.

103. Perilloux and Buss, "Breaking up Romantic Relationships."

104. Perilloux and Buss, "Breaking up Romantic Relationships."

105. G. O. Hagestad and M. A. Smyer, "Dissolving Long-Term Relationships: Patterns of Divorcing in Middle Age," in *Personal Relationships 4: Dissolving Personal Relationships*, edited by S. W. Duck (London: Academic Press, 1982), 155–88.

106. W. W. Wilmot, "Relationship Rejuvenation," in *Communication and Relational Maintenance*, edited by D. J. Canary and L. Stafford (San Diego, CA: Elsevier, 1994), 255–74.

107. W. W. Wilmot and D. C. Stevens, "Relationship Rejuvenation: Arresting Decline in Personal Relationships," in *Uses of "Structure" in Communication Studies*, edited by R. L. Conville (Westport, CT: Praeger, 1994), 103–24.

108. Miller and Parks, "Communication in Dissolving Relationships."

109. S. W. Duck, "A Topography of Relationship Disengagement and Dissolution," in *Personal Relationships 4: Dissolving Personal Relationships*, edited by S. W. Duck (London: Academic Press, 1982), 1–29.

110. A. Weber, "Loving, Leaving, and Letting Go: Coping with Nonmarital Breakups," in *The Dark Side of Close Relationships*, edited by B. H. Spitzberg and W. R. Cupach (Mahwah, NJ: Erlbaum, 1998), 267–306.

111. M. J. Cody, "A Typology of Disengagement Strategies and an Examination of the Role Intimacy, Reactions to Inequity and Relational Problems Play in Strategy Selection," *Communication Monographs* 49 (1982): 148–70.

112. T. J. Wade, R. Palmer, M. Dimaria, C. Johnson, and M. Multack, "Deficits in Sexual Access Versus Deficits in Emotional Access and Relationship Termination Decisions," *Journal of Evolutionary Psychology* 6 (2008): 309–19.

113. M. Argyle and M. Henderson, *The Anatomy of Relationships* (New York: Guilford Press, 1991).

114. S. M. Rose, "How Friendships End: Patterns Among Young Adults," *Journal of Social and Personal Relationships* 1 (1984): 267–77.

115. Duck, "A Typography of Relationship Disengagement and Dissolution."

116. Miller and Parks, "Communication in Dissolving Relationships."

117. A. L. Alexander, "Relationship Resources for Coping with Unfulfilled Standards in Dating Relationships: Commitment, Satisfaction, and Closeness," *Journal of Social and Personal Relationships* 25 (2008): 725–47.

118. L. A. Baxter, "Accomplishing Relationship Disengagement," in *Understanding Personal Relationships: An Interdisciplinary Approach,* edited by S. Duck and D. Perlman (Beverly Hills, CA: Sage, 1984), 243–65.

119. D. DeStephen, "Integrating Relational Termination into a General Model of Communication Competence," paper presented at the annual meeting of the Speech Communication Association, Denver (1985).

120. Baxter, "Accomplishing Relationship Disengagement."

121. DeStephen, "Integrating Relational Termination."

122. Cody, "A Typology of Disengagement Strategies."

123. P. W. Eastwick, E. J. Finkel, T. Krishnamurti, and G. Loewenstein, "Mispredicting Distress Following Romantic Breakup: Revealing the Time Course of the Affective Forecasting Error," *Journal of Experimental Social Psychology* 44 (2008): 800–07.

124. Weber, "Loving, Leaving, and Letting Go."

Chapter 11

1. L. K. Guerrero and P. A. Mongeau, "On Becoming 'More than Friends': The Transition from Friendship to Romantic Relationship," in *Handbook of Relationship Initiation,* edited by S. Sprecher, A. Wenzel, and J. Harvey (New York: Psychology Press, 2008), 175–94.

2. A. M. Nicotera, "The Importance of Communication in Interpersonal Relationships," in *Interpersonal Communication in Friend and Mate Relationships,* edited by A. M. Nicotera and Associates (Albany: State University of New York Press, 1993), 3–12.

3. Nicotera, "The Importance of Communication in Interpersonal Relationships."

4. M. Argyle, *The Social Psychology of Everyday Life* (London: Routledge, 1991).

5. Nicotera, "The Importance of Communication in Interpersonal Relationships."

6. Argyle, *The Social Psychology of Everyday Life.*

7. G. Allen, "Flexibility, Friendship, and Family," *Personal Relationships* 15 (2008): 1–16.

8. P. M. Sias and H. Bartoo, "Friendship, Social Support, and Health," in *Low-Cost Approaches to Promote Physical and Mental Health,* edited by L. L'Abate (New York: Springer, 2007), 455–72.

9. Argyle, *The Social Psychology of Everyday Life,* 49.

10. P. Marsh, *Eye to Eye: How People Interact* (Topfield, MA: Salem House, 1988).

11. B. Fehr, "Friendship Formation," in *Handbook of Relationship Initiation,* edited by S. Sprecher, A. Wenzel, and J. Harvey (New York: Psychology Press, 2008), 29–54.

12. H. J. Markman, F. Floyd, and F. Dickson, "Towards a Model for the Prediction of Primary Prevention of Marital and Family Distress and Dissolution," in *Personal Relationships 4: Dissolving Personal Relationships,* edited by S. W. Duck and R. Gilmour (London: Academic Press, 1982).

13. J. F. Nussbaum, L. L. Pecchinoni, D. K. Baringer, and A. L. Kundrat, "Lifespan Communication," in *Communication Yearbook 26,* edited by W. B. Gudykunst (Mahwah, NJ: Erlbaum, 2002), 366–89.

14. W. J. Dickens and D. Perlman, "Friendship over the Life-Cycle," in *Personal Relationships 2: Developing Personal Relationships,* edited by S. W. Duck and R. Gilmour (London: Academic Press, 1981).

15. R. L. Selman, "Toward a Structural Analysis of Developing Interpersonal Relations Concepts: Research with Normal and Disturbed Preadolescent Boys," in *Minnesota Symposia on Child Psychology,* Vol. 10, edited by A. D. Pick (Minneapolis: University of Minnesota Press, 1976).

16. W. Rawlins, *Friendship Matters: Communication, Dialectics, and the Life Course* (New York: DeGruyter, 1992).

17. W. Samter, "Friendship Interaction Skills Across the Life Span," in *Handbook of Communication and Social Interaction Skills,* edited by J. O. Greene and B. R. Burleson (Mahwah, NJ: Erlbaum, 2003), 637–84.

18. P. McDougall and S. Hymel, "Same-Gender Versus Cross-Gender Friendship Conceptions," *Merrill-Palmer Quarterly* 53 (2007): 347–80.

19. Dickens and Perlman, "Friendship over the Life-Cycle."

20. J. E. Benson, "Make New Friends but Keep the Old: Peers and the Transition to College," in *Advances in Life Course Research Vol. 12: Interpersonal Relations Across the Life Course,* edited by T. J. Owens and J. J. Suitor (Boston: Elsevier, 2007), 309–34.

21. L. M. Swenson, A. Nordstrom, and M. Hiester, "The Role of Peer Relationships in Adjustment to College," *Journal of College Student Development* 49 (2008): 551–67.

22. Rawlins, *Friendship Matters,* 105.

23. Samter, "Friendship Interaction Skills Across the Life Span."

24. Samter, "Friendship Interaction Skills Across the Life Span."

25. Rawlins, *Friendship Matters,* 157.

26. M. Dainton, E. Zelley, and E. Langan, "Maintaining Friendships Throughout the Lifespan," in *Maintaining Relationships Through Communication,* edited by D. J. Canary and M. Dainton (Mahwah, NJ: Erlbaum, 2003), 79–102.

27. M. Kalmijn, "Shared Friendship Networks and the Life Course: An Analysis of Survey Data on Married and Cohabiting Couples," *Social Networks* 25 (2003): 231–49.

28. N. Stevens, "Friendships in Late Adulthood," in *Encyclopedia of Human Relationships,* edited by H. T. Reis and S. Sprecher (Thousand Oaks, CA: Sage, 2009), 726–30.

29. Stevens, "Friendships in Late Adulthood."

30. J. M. Vigil, "Asymmetries in the Friendship Preferences and Social Styles of Men and Women," *Human Nature* 18 (2007): 143–61.

31. B. Fehr, "A Prototype Model of Intimacy Interactions in Same-Sex Friendships," in *Handbook of Closeness and Intimacy,* edited by D. J. Mahek and A. Aron (Mahwah, NJ: Erlbaum, 2004), 9–26.

32. Fehr, "A Prototype Model of Intimacy Interactions in Same-Sex Friendships."

33. P. H. Wright, "Toward an Expanded Orientation to the Comparative Study of Women's and Men's Same-Sex Friendships," in *Sex Differences and Similarities in Communication,* 2nd ed., edited by K. Dindia and D. J. Canary (Mahwah, NJ: Erlbaum, 2006), 37–57.

34. Wright, "Toward an Expanded Orientation."

35. Wright, "Toward an Expanded Orientation."

36. G. L. Greif, *Buddy System: Understanding Male Friendships* (New York: Oxford, 2009).

37. R. A. Singleton, Jr. and J. Vacca, "Interpersonal Competition in Friendships," *Sex Roles* 57 (2007): 617–27.

38. R. Baumgarte and D. W. Nelson, "Preference for Same- Versus Cross-Sex Friendships," *Journal of Applied Social Psychology* 39 (2009): 901–17.

39. W. A. Collins and S. D. Madsen, "Personal Relationships in Adolescence and Early Adulthood," in *The Cambridge Handbook of Personal Relationships,* edited by A. L. Vangelisti and D. Perlman (New York: Cambridge University Press, 2006), 191–210.

40. Allen, "Flexibility, Friendship, and Family."

41. H. M. Reeder, "'I Like You . . . as a Friend': The Role of Attraction in Cross-Sex Friendship," *Journal of Social and Personal Relationships* 17 (2000): 329–48.

42. K. Knight, P. A. Mongeau, J. Eden, C. M. Shaw, and A. Ramirez, "The (Romantic) Relational Implication of Friends with Benefits Relationships," paper presented at the annual meeting of the National Communication Association (2008).

43. M. Hughes, K. Morrison, and K. J. K. Asada, "What's Love Got to Do with It? Exploring the Impact of Maintenance Rules, Love Attitudes, and Network Support on Friends with Benefits Relationships," *Western Journal of Communication* 69 (2005): 49–66.

44. Hughes, Morrison, and Asada, "What's Love Got to Do with It?"

45. Hughes, Morrison, and Asada, "What's Love Got to Do with It?"

46. L. Rubin, *Just Friends: The Role of Friendship in Our Lives* (New York: Harper & Row, 1985).

47. S. H. Mathews, *Friendships Through the Life Course: Oral Biographies in Old Age* (Beverly Hills, CA: Sage, 1986).

48. S. J. Holladay and K. S. Kerns, "Do Age Differences Matter in Close and Casual Relationships? A Comparison of Age Discrepant and Age Peer Friendships," *Communication Reports* 12 (1999): 101–14.

49. M. J. Collier, "Communication Competence Problematics in Ethnic Relationships," *Communication Monographs* 63 (1996): 314–35.

50. Collier, "Communication Competence Problematics."

51. P. Lee, "Stages and Transitions of Relational Identity Formation in Intercultural Friendship: Implications for Identity Management Theory," *Journal of International and Intercultural Communication* 1 (2008): 51–69.

52. P. M. Sias, J. A Drzewiecka, M. Meares, R. Bent, Y. Konomi, M. Ortega, and C. White, "Intercultural Friendship Development," *Communication Reports* 21 (2008), 1–13.

53. X. de Souza Briggs, "'Some of My Best Friends Are . . .': Interracial Friendships, Class, and Segregation in America," *City & Community* 6 (2007): 263–90.

54. W. K. Rawlins, *The Compass of Friendship: Narratives, Identities, and Dialogues* (Thousand Oaks, CA: Sage, 2009).

55. Rawlins, *The Compass of Friendship.*

56. Rawlins, *The Compass of Friendship,* 149.

57. Rawlins, *The Compass of Friendship,* 151–152.

58. A. Aron and E. N. Aron, "Love," in *Perspectives on Close Relationships,* edited by A. Weber and J. Harvey (Boston: Allyn & Bacon, 1994).

59. L. A. Kurdek, "Relationship Outcomes and Their Predictors: Longitudinal Evidence from Heterosexual Married, Gay Cohabiting, and Lesbian Cohabiting Couples," *Journal of Marriage and Family* 60 (1998): 553–68.

60. J. D. Cunningham and J. K. Antill, "Love in Developing Romantic Relationships," in *Personal Relationships 2: Developing Personal Relationships,* edited by S. W. Duck and R. Gilmour (London: Academic Press, 1981).

61. J. K. Rempel and C. T. Burris, "Let Me Count the Ways: An Integrative Theory of Love and Hate," *Personal Relationships* 12 (2005): 297–313.

62. Z. Rubin, *Liking and Loving: An Invitation to Social Psychology* (New York: Holt, Rinehart and Winston, 1973).

63. R. J. Sternberg, "A Triangular Theory of Love," *Psychological Review* 93 (1986): 119–35.

64. R. Lemieux and J. L. Hale, "Intimacy, Passion, and Commitment in Young Romantic Relationships: Successfully Measuring the Triangular Theory of Love," *Psychological Reports* 85 (1999): 497–504.

65. C. Hendrick and S. S. Hendrick, "Research on Love: Does It Measure Up?" *Journal of Personality and Social Psychology* 56 (1989): 784–94.

66. H. T. Reis and A. Aron, "Love: What Is It, Why Does It Matter, and How Does It Operate?" *Perspectives on Psychological Science* 3 (2008): 80–86.

67. Ries and Aron, "Love."

68. J. A. Lee, "A Typology of Styles of Loving," *Personality and Social Psychology Bulletin* 3 (1977): 173–82.

69. D. J. Weigel, "A Dyadic Assessment of How Couples Indicate Their Commitment to Each Other," *Personal Relationships* 15 (2008): 17–39.

70. A. D. Hampel and A. L. Vangelisti, "Commitment Expectations in Romantic Relationships: Application of a Prototype Interaction-Pattern Model," *Personal Relationships* 15 (2008): 81–102.

71. P. A. Anderson, L. K. Guerrero, and S. M. Jones, "Nonverbal Behavior in Intimate Interactions and Intimate Relationships," *The Sage Handbook of Nonverbal Communication,* edited by V. Manusov and M. L. Patterson (Thousand Oaks, CA: Sage, 2006), 259–78.

72. C. A. Hill and L. K. Preston, "Individual Differences in the Experience of Sexual Motivation: Theory and Measurement of Dispositional Sexual Motives," *The Journal of Sex Research* 33 (1996): 27–45.

73. E. A. Impett, A. M. Gordon, and A. Strachman, "Attachment and Daily Sexual Goals: A Study of Dating Couples," *Personal Relationships* 15 (2008): 375–90.

74. Impett, Gordon, and Strachman, "Attachment and Daily Sexual Goals."

75. S. Sprecher, "Sexuality in Close Relationships," in *Close Relationships: Functions, Forms, and Processes,* edited by P. Noller and J. A. Feeney (New York: Psychology Press, 2006), 267–84.

76. J. A. Theiss and D. H. Solomon, "Communication and the Emotional, Cognitive, and Relational Consequences of First Sexual Encounters between Partners," *Communication Quarterly* 55 (2007): 179–206.

77. E. S. Byers and S. Demmons, "Sexual Satisfaction and Sexual Self-Disclosure within Dating Relationships," *The Journal of Sex Research* 36 (1999): 180–89.

78. Theiss and Soloman, "Communication and the Emotional, Cognitive, and Relational Consequences of First Sexual Encounters."

79. A. E. Lucchetti, "Deception in Disclosing One's Sexual History: Safe-Sex Avoidance or Ignorance?" *Communication Quarterly* 47 (1999): 300–14.

80. P. A. Mongeau, M. C. M. Serewicz, M. L. M. Henningsen, and K. L. Davis, "Sex Differences in the Transition to a Heterosexual Romantic Relationship," in *Sex Differences and Similarities in Communication,* 2nd ed., edited by K. Dindia and D. J. Canary (Mahwah, NJ: Erlbaum, 2006), 337–58.

81. Guerrero and Mongeau, "On Becoming 'More Than Friends'."

82. Guerrero and Mongeau, "On Becoming 'More Than Friends'."

83. L. A. Baxter and W. W. Wilmot, "'Secret Tests': Social Strategies for Acquiring Information About the State of the Relationship," *Human Communication Research* 11 (1984): 171–202.

84. K. A. Bogle, *Hooking Up: Sex, Dating and Relationships on Campus* (New York: New York University Press, 2008); K. A. Bogle, "The Shift from Dating to Hooking Up in College: What Scholars Have Missed," *Sociology Compass* 1/2 (2007): 775–88.

85. Bogle, *Hooking Up,* 42.

86. E. L. Paul, A. Wenzel, and J. Harvey, "Hookups: A Facilitator or a Barrier to Relationship Initiation and Intimacy Development?" in *Handbook of Relationship Initiation,* edited by S. Sprecher, A. Wenzel, and J. Harvey (New York: Psychology Press, 2008), 375–90.

87. P. A. Mongeau, J. Jacobsen, and C. Donnerstein, "Defining Dates and First Date Goals: Generalizing from Undergraduates to Single Adults," *Communication Research* 34 (2007): 526–47.

88. Mongeau, Jacobsen, and Donnerstein, "Defining Dates and First Date Goals."

89. Mongeau, Jacobsen, and Donnerstein, "Defining Dates and First Date Goals."

90. Bogle, *Hooking Up,* 131.

91. A. D. Kunkel, S. R. Wilson, J. Olufowote, and S. J. Robson, "Identity Implications of Influence Goals: Initiating, Intensifying, and Ending Romantic Relationships," *Western Journal of Communication* 67 (2003): 382–412.

92. M. C. M. Serewicz and E. Gale, "First-Date Scripts: Gender Roles, Context, and Relationship," *Sex Roles* 58 (2008): 149–64.

93. P. C. Regan, *The Mating Game,* 2nd edition, (Thousand Oaks: CA, Sage, 2008).

94. Regan, *The Mating Game.*

95. M. T. Motley, L. J. Faulkner, and H. Reeder, "Conditions that Determine the Fate of Friendships after Unrequited Romantic Disclosures," in *Studies of Applied Interpersonal Communication,* edited by M. T. Motley (Thousand Oaks, CA: Sage, 2008): 27–50.

96. Motely, Faulkner, and Reeder, "Conditions that Determine the Fate of Friendships."

97. S. L. Young, C. G. Paxman, C. L. E. Koehring, and C. A. Anderson, "The Application of a Face Work Model of Disengagement to Unrequited Love," *Communication Research Reports* 25 (2008): 56–66.

98. Young, Paxman, Koehring, and Anderson, "The Application of a Face Work Model."

99. A. Lenhart, "Adults and Social Network Websites" Pew Internet and American Life Project, 2009. Retrieved July 22, 2009 from http://www.pewinternet.org/Reports/2009/Adults-and-Social-Network-Websites. aspx?r=1

100. S. T. Tong, B. Van Der Heide, L. Langwell, and J. B. Walther, "Too Much of a Good Thing? The Relationship Between Number of Friends and Interpersonal Impressions on Facebook," *Journal of Computer-Mediated Communication* 13 (2008): 531–49

101. September 2005 Daily Tracking Survey/Online Dating Extension, Pew Internet & American Life Project. Retrieved September 2, 2009 from http://www.pewinternet.org/pdfs/Online_Dating_Questions.pdf

102. September 2005 Daily Tracking Survey/Online Dating Extension.

103. S. M. Wildermuth and S. Vogl-Bauer, "We Met on the Net: Exploring the Perceptions of Online Romantic Relationship Participants," *Southern Communication Journal* 72 (2007): 211–28.

104. T. L. Anderson and T. M. Emmers-Sommer, "Predictors of Relationship Satisfaction in Online Romantic Relationships," *Communication Studies* 57 (2006): 153–72.

105. Anderson and Emmers-Sommer, "Predictors of Relationship Satisfaction."

106. Anderson and Emmers-Sommer, "Predictors of Relationship Satisfaction."

107. K. B. Wright, "On-Line Relational Maintenance Strategies and Perceptions of Partners within Exclusively Internet-Based and Primarily Internet-Based Relationships," *Communication Studies* 55 (2004): 239–53.

108. Wildermuth and Vogl-Bauer, "We Met on the Net."

109. K. Dindia and L. Timmerman, "Accomplishing Romantic Relationships," in *Handbook of Communication and Social Interaction Skills,* edited by J. O. Greene and B. R. Burleson (Mahwah, NJ: Erlbaum, 2003), 685–22.

110. Adapted from K. Kellerman, S. Broatzman, T. S. Lim, and K. Kitao, "The Conversation MOP: Scenes in the Stream of Discourse," *Discourse Processes* 12 (1989): 27–61.

111. A. E. Lindsey and W. R. Zahaki, "Perceptions of Men and Women Departing from Conversational Sex Role Stereotypes During Initial Interaction," in *Sex Differences and Similarities in Communication,* edited by D. J. Canary and K. Dindia (Mahwah, NJ: Erlbaum, 1998), 393–412.

112. R. A. Bell and J. A. Daly, "The Affinity Seeking Function of Communication," *Communication Monographs* 51 (1984): 91–115.

113. C. R. Berger and R. J. Calabrese, "Some Explorations in Initial Interaction and Beyond: Toward a Developmental Theory of Interpersonal Communication," *Human Communication Research* 1 (1975): 99–112; C. R. Berger and J. J. Bradac, *Language and Social Knowledge: Uncertainty in Interpersonal Relations* (Baltimore: Edward Arnold, 1982).

114. M. Sunnafrank, "Predicted Outcome Value During Initial Interactions," and "Interpersonal Attraction and Attitude Similarity," in *Communication Yearbook 14,* edited by J. A. Anderson (Newbury Park, CA: Sage, 1991), 451–83.

115. Berger and Bradac, *Language and Social Knowledge,* 14–15.

116. L. K. Knobloch and D. H. Solomon, "Relational Uncertainty and Relational Information Processing: Questions Without Answers?" *Communication Research* 32 (2005): 349–88.

117. L. K. Knobloch and D. H. Solomon, "Information Seeking Beyond Initial Interaction: Negotiating Relational Uncertainty within Close Relationships," *Human Communication Research* 28 (2002): 243–57.

118. M. Dainton, "Equity and Uncertainty in Relational Maintenance," *Western Journal of Communication* 67 (2003): 164–86.

119. M. V. Redmond, "Relationship-Specific Social Decentering: Tapping Partner Specific Empathy and Partner Specific Perspective Taking," paper presented at the annual meeting of the National Communication Association (2006).

120. A. L. Vangelisti, "Communication Problems in Committed Relationships: An Attributional Analysis," in *Attributions, Accounts, and Close Rela-*

tionships, edited by J. H. Harvey, T. L. Orbuch, and A. L. Weber (New York: Springer Verlag, 1992), 144–64.

121. G. Levinger and D. J. Senn, "Disclosure of Feelings in Marriage," *Merrill-Palmer Quarterly* 12, (1967): 237–49; A. Bochner, "On the Efficacy of Openness in Close Relationships," in *Communication Yearbook 5,* edited by M. Burgoon (New Brunswick, NJ: Transaction Books, 1982), 109–24.

122. A. B. Kelly, F. D. Fincham, and S. R. H. Beach, "Communication Skills in Couples: A Review and Discussion of Emerging Perspectives," in *Handbook of Communication and Social Interaction Skills,* edited by J. O. Greene and B. R. Burleson (Mahwah, NJ: Erlbaum, 2003), 723–51.

123. S. A. Westmyer and S. A. Myers, "Communication Skills and Social Support Messages Across Friendship Levels," *Communication Research Reports* 13 (1996): 191–97.

124. B. R. Burleson and S. R. Mortenson, "Explaining Cultural Differences in Evaluations of Emotional Support Behaviors," *Communication Research* 30 (2003): 113–46; B. R. Burleson, "Comforting Messages: Features, Functions, and Outcomes," in *Strategic Interpersonal Communication,* edited by J. A. Daly and J. M. Weimann (Hillsdale, NJ: Erlbaum, 1994), 135–61.

125. A. M. Bippus, "Recipients' Criteria for Evaluating the Skillfulness of Comforting Communication and the Outcomes of Comforting Interactions," *Communication Monographs* 68 (2001): 301–13.

126. B. R. Sarason and I. G. Sarason, "Close Relationships and Social Support: Implications for the Measurement of Social Support," in *The Cambridge Handbook of Personal Relationships,* edited by A. L. Vangelisti and D. Perlman (New York: Cambridge University Press, 2006), 429–43.

127. R. A. Clark and J. G. Delia, "Individuals' Preferences for Friends' Approaches to Providing Support in Distressing Situations," *Communication Reports* 10 (1997): 115–21.

128. N. Miczo and J. K. Burgoon, "Facework and Nonverbal Behavior in Social Support Interactions within Romantic Dyads," in *Studies in Applied Interpersonal Communication,* edited by M. T. Motley (Thousand Oaks: CA, Sage, 2008), 246–66.

129. L. K. Guerrero and A. M. Chavez, "Relational Maintenance in Cross-Sex Friendships Characterized by Different Types of Romantic Intent: An Exploratory Study," *Western Journal of Communication* 69 (2005): 339–58.

130. L. K. Acitelli, "Knowing When to Shut Up: Do Relationship Reflections Help or Hurt Relationship Satisfaction?" in *Social Relationships: Cognitive, Affective, and Motivational Processes,* edited by J. P. Forgas and J. Fitness (New York: Psychology Press, 2008), 115–30.

131. J. K. Alberts, "An Analysis of Couples' Conversational Complaints," *Communication Monographs* 55 (1988): 184–97.

132. M. A. Fitzpatrick and D. M. Badzinski, "All in the Family: Interpersonal Communication in Kin Relationships," in *Handbook of Interpersonal Communication,* edited by M. L. Knapp and G. R. Miller (Beverly Hills, CA: Sage, 1985), 687–736.

133. N. Epley, "Solving the (Real) Other Minds Problem," *Social and Personality Psychology Compass* 2/3 (2008): 1455–74.

Chapter 12

1. G. P. Murdock, *Social Structure* (New York: Free Press, 1965). Originally published 1949.

2. G. D. Nass and G. W. McDonald, *Marriage and the Family* (New York: Random House, 1982), 5.

3. A. P. Bochner, "Conceptual Frontiers in the Study of Communication in Families: An Introduction to the Literature," *Human Communication Research* 2 (Summer 1976): 382.

4. M. A. Fitzpatrick, "Family Communication Patterns Theory: Observations on its Development and Application," *Journal of Family Communication* 4 (2004): 167–80.

5. G. Allan, "Flexibility, Friendship, and Family," *Personal Relationships* 18 (2008): 1–16.

6. P. Schrodt, J. Soliz, and D. O. Braithwaite, "A Social Relations Model of Everyday Talk and Relational Satisfaction in Stepfamilies," *Communication Monographs* 75 (2008): 190–217.

7. T. D. Golish, "Stepfamily Communication Strengths: Understanding the Ties That Bind," *Human Communication Research* 29 (2003): 41–80.

8. K. M. Galvin, "Joined by Hearts and Words: Adoptive Family Relationships," in *Widening the Family Circle: New Research on Family Communication,* edited by K. Floyd and M. T. Morman (Thousand Oaks, CA: Sage, 2006), 137–152.

9. Galvin, "Joined by Hearts and Words."

10. Galvin, "Joined by Hearts and Words."

11. K. A. Powell and T. D. Afifi, "Uncertainty Management and Adoptees' Ambiguous Loss of Their Birth Parents," *Journal of Social and Personal Relationships* 22 (2005): 129–151.

12. J. B. Kelly, "Children's Living Arrangements Following Separation and Divorce: Insights from Empirical and Clinical Research," *Family Process* 46 (2006): 35–52.

13. Kelly, "Children's Living Arrangements Following Separation and Divorce."

14. Kelly, "Children's Living Arrangements Following Separation and Divorce."

15. Kelly, "Children's Living Arrangements Following Separation and Divorce."

16. Centers for Disease Control and Prevention, "Changing Patterns of Nonmarital Childbearing in the United States," *NCHS Data Brief, Number 18* (2009). Retrieved online from http://www.cdc.gov/nchs/

17. Centers for Disease Control and Prevention, "Changing Patterns of Nonmarital Childbearing."

18. M. M. Livermore and R. S. Powers, "Employment of Unwed Mothers: The Role of Government and Social Support," *Journal of Family Economic Issues* 27 (2006): 479–94.

19. Livermore and Powers, "Employment of Unwed Mothers."

20. D. E. Beck and M. A. Jones, *Progress on Family Problems: A Nationwide Study of Clients' and Counselors' Views on Family Agency Services* (New York: Family Service Association of America, 1973).

21. V. Satir, *Peoplemaking* (Palo Alto, CA: Science and Behavior Books, 1972), 30.

22. H. J. Markman, "Prediction of Mental Distress: A 5-Year Follow-Up," *Journal of Consulting and Clinical Psychology* 49 (1981): 760–62.

23. D. H. L. Olson, H. L. McCubbin, H. L. Barnes, A. S. Larsen, M. J. Muxem, and M. A. Wilson, *Families: What Makes Them Work* (Beverly Hills, CA: Sage, 1983).

24. J. Koesten, "Family Communication Patterns, Sex of Subject, and Communication Competence," *Communication Monographs* 71 (2004): 226–44.

25. M. A. Fitzpatrick and L. D. Ritchie, "Communication Schemata within the Family: Multiple Perspectives on Family Interaction." *Human Communication Research* 12 (1994): 275–301, A. F.

Koerner and M. A. Fitzpatrick, "Toward a Theory of Family Communication," *Communication Theory* 12 (2002): 70–91.

26. A. F. Koerner and M. A. Fitzpatrick, "Family Communication Patterns Theory: A Social Cognitive Approach," in *Engaging Theories in Family Communication,* edited by D. O. Braithwaite and L. A. Baxter (Thousand Oaks, CA: Sage, 2006), 50–65.

27. A. F. Koerner and M. A. Fitzpatrick, "Family Type and Conflict: The Impact of Conversation Orientation and Conformity Orientation on Conflict in the Family," *Communication Studies* 48 (1997): 59–75.

28. Koerner and Fitzpatrick, "Family Communication Patterns Theory."

29. Koerner and Fitzpatrick, "Family Type and Conflict."

30. Koerner and Fitzpatrick, "Family Communication Patterns Theory."

31. Koerner and Fitzpatrick, "Family Type and Conflict."

32. Koerner and Fitzpatrick, "Family Communication Patterns Theory."

33. Koerner and Fitzpatrick, "Family Type and Conflict."

34. P. Schrodt, P. L. Witt, and A. S. Messersmith, "A Meta-Analytic Review of Family Communication Patterns and Their Associations with Information Processing, Behavioral, and Psychosocial Outcomes," *Communication Monographs* 75 (2008): 248–269.

35. A. M. Ledbetter, "Family Communication Patterns and Relational Maintenance Behavior: Direct and Mediated Associations with Friendship Closeness," *Human Communication Research* 35 (2009): 130–47.

36. Ledbetter, "Family Communication Patterns."

37. V. Satir, *The New Peoplemaking* (Mountain View, CA: Science and Behavior Books, 1988), 4.

38. Satir, *Peoplemaking,* 13–14.

39. J. P. Caughlin, "Family Communication Standards: What Counts as Excellent Family Communication and How Are Such Standards Associated with Family Satisfaction?" *Human Communication Research* 29 (January 2003): 5–40.

40. K. M. Galvin and B. J. Brommel, *Family Communication: Cohesion and Change,* 5th ed. (New York: Longman, 2000).

41. J. Stachowiak, "Functional and Dysfunctional Families," in *Helping Families to Change,* edited by V. Satir, J. Stachowiak, and H. A. Taschman (New York: Jason Aronson, 1975).

42. A. Bockner and E. Eisenberg, "Family Process: Systems in Perspectives," in *Handbook of Communication Science,* edited by C. Berger and S. Chaffee (Beverly Hills: Sage, 1987).

43. Satir, *The New Peoplemaking.*

44. P. Noller and M. A. Fitzpatrick, *Communication in Family Relationships* (Englewood Cliffs, NJ: Prentice Hall, 1993), 202.

45. J. Howard, *Families* (New York: Simon & Schuster, 1978), 286–91.

46. J. Gottman with N. Silver, *Why Marriages Succeed or Fail* (New York: Simon and Schuster, 1994).

47. K. S. Birditt and T. C. Antonucci, "Relationship Quality Profiles and Well-Being Among Married Adults," *Journal of Family Psychology* 21 (2007): 595–604.

48. Birditt and Antonucci, "Relationship Quality Profiles"

49. M. A. Fitzpatrick, *Between Husbands and Wives: Communication in Marriage* (Newbury Park, CA: Sage, 1988).

50. D. L. Kelly, "Relational Expectancy Fulfillment as an Explanatory Variable in Distinguishing Couple Types," *Human Communication Research* 25 (1999): 420–42.

51. Kelly, "Relational Expectancy Fulfillment."

52. M. M. Martin and C. M. Andersen, "Aggressive Communication Traits: How Similar Are Young Adults and Their Parents in Argumentiveness, Assertiveness, and Verbal Aggressiveness?" *Western Journal of Communication* 61 (1997): 299–314.

53. L. D. Ritchie and M. A. Fitzpatrick, "Family Communication Patterns: Measuring Intrapersonal Perceptions of Interpersonal Relationships," *Communication Research* 17 (1990): 523–44.

54. M. Booth-Butterfield and R. Sidelinger, "The Influence of Family Communication on the College-Aged Child: Openness, Attitudes and Actions About Sex and Alcohol," *Communication Quarterly* 46 (1998): 295–308.

55. S. M. Horan, M. L. Houser, and R. L. Cowan, "Are Children Communicated with Equally? An Investigation of Parent-Child Sex Composition and Gender Role Communication Differences," *Communication Research Reports* 24 (2007): 361–72.

56. K. McCoy, E. M. Cummings, and P. T. Davies, "Constructive and Destructive Marital Conflict, Emotional Security and Children's Prosocial Behavior," *The Journal of Child Psychology and Psychiatry* 50 (2009): 270–79.

57. C. Fowler, "Motives for Sibling Communication Across the Lifespan," *Communication Quarterly* 57 (2009): 51–66.

58. P. A. Anderson and L. K. Guerrero, "Principles of Communication and Emotion in Social Interaction," in *Handbook of Communication and Emotion*, edited by P. A. Anderson and L. K. Guerrero (San Diego, CA: Academic Press, 1998), 49–96.

59. Anderson and Guerrero, "Principles of Communication and Emotion."

60. L. K. Guerrero, S. M. Jones, and R. R. Boburka, "Sex Differences in Emotional Communication," in *Sex Differences and Similarities in Communication*, 2nd ed., edited by K. Dindia and D. J. Canary (Mahwah, NJ: Erlbaum, 2006), 241–62.

61. Fowler, "Motives for Sibling Communication."

62. A. Goetting, "The Developmental Tasks of Siblingship over the Life Cycle," *Journal of Marriage and the Family* 48 (1986): 703–14.

63. Fowler, "Motives for Sibling Communication."

64. P. Noller, "Sibling Relationships in Adolescence: Learning and Growing Together," *Personal Relationships* 12 (2005): 1–22.

65. L. K. Guerrero and W. A. Afifi, "Some Things Are Better Left Unsaid: Topic Avoidance in Family Relationships," *Communication Quarterly* 43 (1995): 276–96.

66. Guerrero and Afifi, "Some Things Are Better Left Unsaid."

67. K. Kitzmann, R. Cohen, and R. L. Lockwood, "Are Only Children Missing Out? Comparison of the Peer-Related Social Competence of Only Children and Siblings," *Journal of Social and Personal Relationships* 19 (2002): 299–316.

68. Noller, "Sibling Relationships in Adolescence."

69. A. C. Mikkelson, "Communication Among Peers: Adult Sibling Relationships," in *Widening the Family Circle: New Research on Family Communication*, edited by K. Floyd and M. T. Morman (Thousand Oaks, CA: Sage, 2006), 21–36.

70. S. Boland, "Social Support and Sibling Relationships in Middle Adulthood," paper presented to the Eastern Psychological Association (2007). Retrieved June 25, 2009 from http://www.lhup.edu/sboland/social_support_and_ sibling_relat.htm

71. Boland, "Social Support and Sibling Relationships in Middle Adulthood."

72. Mikkelson, "Communication Among Peers."

73. Mikkelson, "Communication Among Peers"; Goetting, "The Developmental Tasks of Siblingship."

74. M. Van Volkom, "Sibling Relationships in Middle and Older Adulthood: A Review of the Literature," *Marriage and Family Review* 40 (2006): 151–70.

75. Mikkelson, "Communication Among Peers."

76. P. M. Sias and D. J. Cahill, "From Coworkers to Friends: The Development of Peer Friendships in the Workplace," *Western Journal of Communication* 62 (1998): 273–99.

77. Sias and Cahill, "From Coworkers to Friends."

78. Sias and Cahill, "From Coworkers to Friends."

79. E. M. Berman, J. P. West, and M. N. Richter, Jr., "Workplace Relations: Friendship Patterns and Consequences (According to Managers)," *Public Administration Review* 62 (2002): 217–30.

80. P. Sias, G. Smith, and T. Avdeyeva, "Sex and Sex-Composition Differences and Similarities in Peer Workplace Friendship Development," *Communication Studies* 54 (Fall 2003): 322–40.

81. P. Sias, *Organizing Relationships: Traditional and Emerging Perspectives on Workplace Relationships* (Thousand Oaks, CA: Sage, 2009), 93–94.

82. Sias, *Organizing Relationships*, 95–97.

83. P. S. Adler and S. Woon, "Social Capital: Prospects for a New Concept," *Academy of Management Review* 27 (2002): 17–40.

84. T. H. Feeley, J. Hwang, and G. A. Barnett, "Predicting Employee Turnover from Friendship Networks," *Journal of Applied Communication Research* 36 (2008): 56–73.

85. Sias, *Organizing Relationships*, 95.

86. P. M. Sias, R. G. Heath, T. Perry, D. Silva, and B. Fix, "Narratives of Workplace Friendship Deterioration," *Journal of Social and Personal Relationships* 21 (2004): 321–40.

87. Sias et al., "Narratives of Workplace Friendship Deterioration."

88. C. M. Schaefer and T. R. Tudor, "Managing Workplace Romances," *SAM Advanced Management Journal* 66 (2001): 4–11. Careerbuilder.com annual office romance survey, February, 10, 2009. Retrieved July 27, 2009 from careerbuilder.com.

89. J. Carson and J. Barling, "Romantic Relationships at Work: Old Issues, New Challenges," in *The Individual in the Changing Working Life*, edited by K K. Näswall, J. Hellgren, and M. Sverke (New York: Cambridge, 2008), 195–210; Sias, *Organizing Relationships*, 131–35.

90. Careerbuilder.com, "Forty Percent of Workers Have Dated a Co-Worker, Finds Annual CareerBuilder.com Valentine's Day Survey," February 10, 2009. Press release. Retrieved July 27, 2009 from http://www.careerbuilder. com/share/aboutus/pressreleasesdetail.aspx?id=pr481&sd=2/10/2009&ed= 12/31/2009

91. Carson and Barling, "Romantic Relationships at Work."

92. M. J. Lecker, "Workplace Romances: A Platonic Perspective," *Research in Ethical Issues in Organizations* 7 (2007): 253–79.

93. K. Riach and F. Wilson, "Don't Screw the Crew: Exploring the Rules of Engagement in Organizational Romance," *British Journal of Management* 18 (2007): 79–92.

94. Schaefer and Tudor, "Managing Workplace Romances."

95. F. Jablin, "Superior's Upward Influence, Satisfaction, and Openness in Superior-Subordinate Communication: A Reexamination of the 'Pelz Effect'," *Human Communication Research* 6 (1980): 210–20.

96. Jablin, "Superior's Upward Influence."

97. J. Gabarro and J. Kotter, "Managing Your Boss," *Harvard Business Review* 58 (1980): 92–100.

98. E. B. Meiners and V. D. Miller, "The Effect of Formality and Relational Tone on Supervisor/Subordinate Negotiation Episodes," *Western Journal of Communication* 68 (2004): 302–21.

99. T. A. Domagalski and L A. Steelman, "The Impact of Gender and Organizational Status on Workplace Anger Expression," *Management Communication Quarterly* 20 (2007): 297–315.

100. Domagalski and Steelman, "The Impact of Gender and Organizational Status."

101. D. Katz and R. Kahn, *The Social Psychology of Organizations* (New York: Wiley, 1966).

102. Sias, *Organizing Relationships*.

103. B. Fix and P. M. Sias, "Person-Centered Communication, Leader-Member Exchange, and Employee Job Satisfaction," *Communication Research Reports* 23 (2006): 35–44.

104. Fix and Sias, "Person-Centered Communication."

105. P. M. Sias, "Workplace Relationship Quality and Employee Information Experiences," *Communication Studies* 56 (2005): 375–96.

106. C. O. Longnecker and L. S. Fink, "Key Criteria in Twenty-First Century Management Promotional Decisions," *Career Development International* 13 (2008): 241–51.

107. D. A. Level, Jr., "Communication Effectiveness: Methods and Situation," *Journal of Business Communication* 10 (Fall 1972): 19–25.

108. Level, "Communication Effectiveness: Methods and Situation."

109. R. W. Pace and D. F. Faules, *Organizational Communication* (Englewood Cliffs, NJ: Prentice Hall, 1994).

110. A. D. Galinsky, W. W. Maddux, D. Gilin, and J. B. White, "Why It Pays to Get Inside the Head of Your Opponent: The Differential Effects of Perspective Taking and Empathy in Negotiations," *Psychological Science* 19 (2008): 378–84.

111. Galinsky et al., "Why It Pays to Get Inside the Head of Your Opponent."

Glossary

A

accommodation. Conflict management style that involves giving in to the demands of others (p. 233).

account. Response to a reproach (p. 283).

acquiescent responses. Crying, conceding, or apologizing in response to a hurtful message (p. 292).

action-oriented listener. Listener who prefers information that is well-organized, brief, and error-free (p. 121).

active perception. Perception that occurs because you seek out specific information through intentional observation and questioning (p. 68).

active verbal responses. Reactive statements made in response to a hurtful message (p. 292).

adapt. To adjust one's behavior in accord with what someone else does. We can adapt based on the individual, the relationship, and the situation (p. 112).

adapt predictively. To modify or change behavior in anticipation of an event (p. 112).

adapt reactively. To modify or change behavior after an event (p. 112).

adaptability. Family's ability to modify and respond to changes in the family's power structure and roles (p. 348).

adaptors. Nonverbal behaviors that satisfy a personal need and help a person adapt or respond to the immediate situation (p. 194).

affect display. Nonverbal behavior that communicates emotions (p. 193).

affinity-seeking strategy. A strategy we use to increase others' liking of us (p. 333).

agape. Selfless love based on giving of yourself for others (p. 324).

aggressive. Expressing one's interests while denying the rights of others by blaming, judging, and evaluating other people (p. 179).

allness. Tendency to use language to make unqualified, often untrue generalizations (p. 164).

ambush listener. Person who is overly critical and judgmental when listening to others (p. 126).

androgynous role. Gender role that includes both masculine and feminine qualities (p. 41).

anxious attachment style. The style of relating to others that is characteristic of those who experience anxiety in some intimate relationships and feel uncomfortable giving and receiving affection (p. 39).

apology. Explicit admission of an error, along with a request for forgiveness (p. 177).

arousal. Feelings of interest and excitement communicated by such nonverbal cues as vocal expression, facial expressions, and gestures (p. 204).

assertive. Able to pursue one's own best interests without denying a partner's rights (p. 179).

assertiveness. Tendency to make requests, ask for information, and generally pursue one's own rights and best interests (p. 56).

asynchronous listening. Listening to a message (on an answering machine, via voice-mail, or on a cell phone) communicated at another time (p. 132).

asynchronous message. A message that is not read, heard, or seen exactly when it is sent; there is a time delay between the sending of the message and its receipt (p. 13).

attachment style. A style of relating to others that develops early in life, based on the emotional bond one forms with one's parents or primary caregiver (p. 39).

attending. Process of focusing on a particular sound or message (p. 119).

attitude. Learned predisposition to respond to a person, object, or idea in a favorable or unfavorable way (p. 33).

attribution theory. Theory that explains how you generate explanations for people's behaviors (p. 70).

avoidance. Conflict management style that involves backing off and trying to side-step conflict (p. 231).

avoidant attachment style. The style of relating to others that is characteristic of those who consistently experience discomfort and awkwardness in intimate relationships and who therefore avoid such relationships (p. 39).

B

backchannel cues. Vocal cues that signal your wish to speak or not to speak (p. 197).

baldfaced lie. Deception by commission involving outright falsification of information intended to deceive the listener (p. 290).

belief. Way in which you structure your understanding of reality—what is true and what is false for you (p. 33).

bilateral dissolution. Ending of a relationship by mutual agreement of both parties (p. 301).

blended family. Two adults and their children. Because of divorce, separation, death, or adoption, the children may be the offspring of other parents or of just one of the adults who are raising them (p. 345).

"but" message. Statement using the word *but* that may communicate that whatever you've said prior to *but* is not really true (p. 243).

bypassing. Confusion caused by the fact that the same word can mean different things to different people (p. 162).

C

casual banter. Sub-stage of the acquaintance stage of relationship development, in which impersonal topics are discussed but very limited personal information is shared (p. 263).

causal attribution theory. Theory of attribution that identifies the cause of a person's actions as circumstance, a stimulus, or the person himself or herself (p. 71).

causal turning point. Event that brings about a change in a relationship (p. 262).

channel. Pathway through which messages are sent (p. 8).

circumplex model of family interaction. Model of the relationships among family adaptability, cohesion, and communication (p. 347).

closure. Process of filling in missing information or gaps in what we perceive (p. 66).

co-culture. A microculture; a distinct culture within a larger culture (such as the gay and lesbian co-culture) (p. 94).

coercive power. Power based on the use of sanctions or punishments to influence others (p. 229).

cognitive jealousy. Thoughts about the loss of a partner, reflections on decreases in the partner's time for the other, and analyses of behaviors or occurrences deemed suspicious (p. 293).

cohesion. Emotional bonding and feelings of togetherness that families experience (p. 348).

collaboration. Conflict management style that uses other-oriented strategies to achieve a positive solution for all involved (p. 235).

communibiological approach. Theoretical perspective that suggests communication behavior can be predicted based on personal traits and characteristics that result from people's genetic or biological background (p. 25, p. 41).

communication. Process of acting on information (p. 2).

communication accommodation theory. Theory that all people adapt their behavior to others to some extent (p. 112).

communication apprehension. Fear or anxiety associated with either real or anticipated communication with other people (p. 41).

communication privacy management theory. Theory that suggests that we each manage our own degree of privacy by means of personal boundaries and rules for sharing information (p. 271).

communication social style. An identifiable way of habitually communicating with others (p. 55).

companionate love. Romantic love that develops over time as entwinement, mutual responsiveness to needs, trust, caring, and attachment increase (p. 323).

competition. Conflict management style that stresses winning a conflict at the expense of the other person involved (p. 234).

competitive symmetrical relationship. Relationship in which both people vie for power and control of decision making (p. 255).

complementary needs. Needs that match; each partner contributes something to the relationship that the other partner needs (p. 260).

complementary relationship. Relationship in which power is divided unevenly, with one partner dominating and the other submitting (p. 255).

compliance gaining. Taking persuasive actions to get others to comply with our goals (p. 229).

compromise. Conflict management style that attempts to find the middle ground in a conflict (p. 235).

confirming response. Statement that causes another person to value himself or herself more (p. 146).

conflict style. Consistent pattern or approach you use to manage disagreement with others (p. 231).

conflict triggers. Common causes of interpersonal conflict (p. 220).

connotative meaning. Personal and subjective meaning of a word (p. 154).

consensual families. Families with a high orientation toward both conversation and conformity (p. 350).

construct. Bipolar quality used to classify people (p. 68).

constructive conflict. Conflict that helps build new insights and establishes new patterns in a relationship (p. 219).

content. Information, ideas, or suggested actions that a speaker wishes to share (p. 23).

content-oriented listener. Listener who is more comfortable listening to complex, detailed information than are those with other listening styles (p. 121).

context. Physical and psychological environment for communication (p. 10).

conversational narcissism. A focus on personal agendas and self-absorption rather than on the needs and ideas of others (p. 124).

corrective facework. Efforts to correct what one perceives as a negative perception of oneself on the part of others (p. 45).

critical listening. Listening to evaluate and assess the quality, appropriateness, value, or importance of information (p. 137).

cues-filtered-out theory. Theory that suggests that communication of emotions is restricted when people send messages to others via e-mail or other electronic means because nonverbal cues such as facial expression and tone of voice are filtered out (p. 17).

cultural context. Aspects of the environment and/or nonverbal cues that convey information that is not explicitly communicated through language (p. 95).

culture. Learned system of knowledge, behaviors, attitudes, beliefs, values, and norms shared by a group of people (p. 73, p. 93).

culture shock. Feelings of stress and anxiety a person experiences when encountering a culture different from his or her own (p. 98).

cumulative rewards and costs. Total rewards and costs accrued during a relationship (p. 267).

D

deception by commission. Deliberate presentation of false information (p. 290).

deception by omission (concealment). Intentionally holding back some of the information another person has requested or that you are expected to share (p. 289).

decode. To interpret ideas, feelings, and thoughts that have been translated into a code (p. 8).

demand-withdrawal pattern of conflict management. Pattern in which one person makes a demand and the other person avoids conflict by changing the subject or walking away (p. 232).

denotative meaning. Restrictive or literal meaning of a word (p. 154).

dependent relationship. Relationship in which one partner has a greater need for the other to meet his or her needs (p. 228).

destructive conflict. Conflict that dismantles rather than strengthens relationships (p. 220).

dialectical tension. Tension arising from a person's need for two things at the same time (p. 220).

dialectical theory. Theory that relational development occurs in conjunction with various tensions that exist in all relationships, particularly connectedness versus autonomy, predictability versus novelty, and openness versus closedness (p. 268).

direct perception checking. Asking for confirmation from the observed person of an interpretation or a perception about him or her (p. 81).

direct termination strategies. Explicit statements of a desire to break up a relationship (p. 304).

disconfirming response. Statement that causes another person to value himself or herself less (p. 146).

discrimination. Unfair or inappropriate treatment of people based on their group membership (p. 91).

disinhibition effect. The loss of inhibitions when interacting with someone online that leads to the tendency to escalate conflict (p. 236).

dominance. Power, status, and control communicated by such nonverbal cues as a relaxed posture, greater personal space, and protected personal space (p. 205).

downward communication. Communication that flows from superiors to subordinates (p. 369).

dyadic effect. The reciprocal nature of self-disclosure: "You disclose to me, and I'll disclose to you" (p. 273).

dyadic phase. Second phase in relationship termination, when the individual discusses termination with the partner (p. 304).

E

ego conflict. Conflict in which the original issue is ignored as partners attack each other's self-esteem (p. 226).

egocentric communicator. Person who creates messages without giving much thought to the person who is listening; a communicator who is self-focused and self-absorbed (p. 27).

elaborated code. Conversation that uses many words and various ways of describing an idea or concept to communicate its meaning (p. 176).

electronically mediated communication (EMC). Communication that is not face to face, but rather is sent via a medium such as a cell phone or the Internet (p. 13).

emblems. Nonverbal cues that have specific, generally understood meanings in a given culture and may substitute for a word or phrase (p. 193).

emotional or affective jealousy. Feelings of anger, hurt, distrust, worry, or concern aroused by the threat of losing a relationship (p. 293).

emotional contagion. The process whereby people mimic the emotions of others after watching and hearing their emotional expressions (p. 24).

emotional contagion theory. Theory that emotional expression is contagious; people can "catch" emotions just by observing others' emotional expressions (p. 209).

emotional intelligence. The ability to be aware of, to understand, and to manage one's own emotions and those of other people (p. 137).

emotional noise. Form of communication interference caused by emotional arousal (p. 125).

empathy. Emotional reaction that is similar to the reaction being experienced by another person; empathizing is feeling what another person is feeling (p. 111, p. 132).

encode. To translate ideas, feelings, and thoughts into code (p. 8).

enculturation. The process of transmitting a group's culture from one generation to the next (p. 94).

envy. A feeling of discontent arising from a desire for something someone else has (p. 293).

episode. Sequence of interactions between individuals, during which the message of one person influences the message of another (p. 12).

eros. Sexual, erotic love based on the pursuit of physical beauty and pleasure (p. 323).

ethics. The beliefs, values, and moral principles by which a person determines what is right or wrong (p. 28).

ethnicity. Social classification based on nationality, religion, language, and ancestral heritage, shared by a group of people who also share a common geographical origin (p. 90).

ethnocentrism. Belief that your cultural traditions and assumptions are superior to those of others (p. 99).

euphemism. A mild or indirect word that is substituted for one that describes something vulgar, profane, unpleasant, or embarrassing (p. 162).

exaggeration. Deception by commission involving "stretching the truth" or embellishing the facts (p. 290).

expectancy violation theory. Theory that you interpret the messages of others based on how you expect others to behave (p. 206).

expected rewards and costs. Expectation of how much reward we should get from a given relationship in comparison to its costs (p. 267).

expert power. Power based on a person's knowledge and experience (p. 229).

expressive conflict. Conflict that focuses on issues about the quality of the relationship and managing interpersonal tension and hostility (p. 224).

extended family. Relatives such as aunts, uncles, cousins, or grandparents and/or unrelated persons who are part of a family unit (p. 345).

extended "I" language. Brief preface to a feedback statement, intended to communicate that you don't want your listener to take your message in an overly critical way (p. 173).

F

face. A person's positive perception of himself or herself in interactions with others; self-image or self-respect that you and your partner seek to maintain (p. 45, p. 247).

face-threatening acts. Communication that undermines or challenges someone's positive face (p. 46).

facework. Using communication to maintain your own positive self-perception or to support, reinforce, or challenge someone else's self-perception (p. 45).

fact. Something that has been directly observed to be true and thus has been proven to be true (p. 138).

fading away. Ending a relationship by slowly drifting apart (p. 301).

failure events. Violations of understandings between people in relationships (p. 282).

family. Self-defined unit made up of any number of persons who live or have lived in relationship with one another over time in a common living space and who are usually, but not always, united by marriage and kinship (p. 344).

family communication patterns model. A model of family communication based on two dimensions: conversation and conformity (p. 349).

family of origin. Family in which a person is raised (p. 345).

feedback. Response to a message (p. 10).

feminine culture. Culture in which people tend to value caring, sensitivity, and attention to quality of life (p. 95).

filtering. Process of reducing the number of partners at each stage of relational development by applying selection criteria (p. 266).

flaming. Sending an overly negative online message that personally attacks another person (p. 236).

forecasted rewards and costs. Rewards and costs that an individual assumes will occur, based on projection and prediction (p. 267).

friendship-based intimacy. A type of intimacy based on feelings of warmth, understanding, and emotional connection (p. 312).

fundamental attribution error. Error that arises from attributing another person's behavior to internal, controllable causes rather than to external, uncontrollable causes (p. 77).

G

gender. Socially learned and reinforced characteristics that include one's biological sex and psychological characteristics (femininity, masculinity, androgyny) (p. 88).

grave-dressing phase. Final phase in relationship termination, when the partners generate public explanations and move past the relationship (p. 304).

gunny-sacking. Dredging up old problems and issues from the past to use against your partner (p. 240).

H

halo effect. Attributing a variety of positive qualities to those you like (p. 69).

hate speech. Words or phrases intended to offend or show disrespect for someone's race, ethnicity, cultural background, gender, or some other aspect of their personality (p. 166).

hearing. Physiological process of decoding sounds (p. 118).

high-context culture. Culture in which people derive much information from nonverbal and environmental cues (p. 95).

horizontal communication. Communication among colleagues or coworkers at the same level within an organization (p. 370).

horn effect. Attributing a variety of negative qualities to those you dislike (p. 69).

hostile environment. Type of sexual harassment in which an employee's rights are threatened through offensive working conditions or behavior on the part of other workers (p. 370).

human communication. Process of making sense out of the world and sharing that sense with others by creating meaning through the use of verbal and nonverbal messages (p. 2).

hyperpersonal relationship. A relationship formed primarily through electronically mediated communication that becomes more personal than an equivalent face-to-face relationship because of the absence of distracting external cues, smaller amounts of personal information, and idealization of the communication partner (p. 16).

I

"I" language. Statements that use the word *I* to express how a speaker is feeling (p. 242).

illustrators. Nonverbal behaviors that accompany a verbal message and either contradict, accent, or complement it (p. 193).

immediacy. Feelings of liking, pleasure, and closeness communicated by such nonverbal cues as increased eye contact, forward lean, touch, and open body orientation (p. 204).

immediate rewards and costs. Rewards and costs that are associated with a relationship at the present moment (p. 267).

impersonal communication. Process that occurs when we treat others as objects or respond to their roles rather than to who they are as unique persons (p. 3).

implicit personality theory. Your unique set of beliefs and hypotheses about what people are like (p. 68).

impression. Collection of perceptions about others that you maintain and use to interpret their behaviors (p. 67).

impression formation theory. Theory that explains how you develop perceptions about people and how you maintain and use those perceptions to interpret their behaviors (p. 67).

incrementalism. Systematic progression of a relationship through each of the de-escalation stages (p. 301).

independent couples. Married partners who exhibit sharing and companionship and are psychologically interdependent but allow each other individual space (p. 354).

indexing. Avoiding generalizations by using statements that separate one situation, person, or example from another (p. 165).

indirect perception checking. Seeking through passive perception such as observing and listening additional information to confirm or refute interpretations you are making (p. 81).

indirect termination strategies. Attempts to break up a relationship without explicitly stating the desire to do so (p. 304).

inference. Conclusion based on speculation (p. 139).

information triage. Process of evaluating information to sort good information from less useful or less valid information (p. 138).

in-group. One's racial or ethnic group (p. 287).

instrumental conflict. Conflict that centers on achieving a particular goal or task and less on relational issues (p. 224).

interaction adaptation theory. Theory suggesting that people interact with others by adapting to their communication behaviors (p. 188).

interactional synchrony. Mirroring of each other's nonverbal behavior by communication partners (p. 188).

intercultural communication. Communication between or among people who have different cultural traditions (p. 97).

intercultural communication competence. Ability to adapt one's behavior toward another in ways that are appropriate to the other person's culture (p. 104).

interdependent. Dependent on each other; one person's actions affect the other person (p. 217).

interpersonal attraction. Degree to which you want to form or maintain an interpersonal relationship (p. 256).

interpersonal communication. A distinctive, transactional form of human communication involving mutual influence, usually for the purpose of managing relationships (p. 3).

interpersonal conflict. An expressed struggle between at least two interdependent

people who perceive incompatible goals, scarce resources, or interference in the achievement of their goals (p. 216).

interpersonal deception theory. An explanation of deception and detection as processes affected by the transactional nature of interpersonal interactions (p. 289).

interpersonal intimacy. Degree to which relational partners mutually accept and confirm each other's sense of self (p. 253).

interpersonal perception. Process of selecting, organizing, and interpreting your observations of other people (p. 62).

interpersonal power. Degree to which a person is able to influence his or her partner (p. 227).

interpersonal relationship. Perception shared by two people of an ongoing interdependent connection that results in the development of relational expectations and varies in interpersonal intimacy (p. 252).

intimate space. Zone of space most often used for very personal or intimate interactions, ranging from 0 to $1^1/_2$ feet between individuals (p. 199).

intrapersonal communication. Communication with yourself; thinking or self-talk (p. 5, 47).

intrapsychic phase. First phase in relationship termination, when an individual engages in an internal evaluation of the partner (p. 303).

introductions. Sub-stage of the acquaintance stage of relationship development, in which interaction is routine and basic information is shared (p. 263).

invulnerable responses. Ignoring, laughing, or being silent in response to a hurtful message (p. 292).

J

jargon. Another name for restricted code; specialized terms or abbreviations whose meanings are known only to members of a specific group (p. 164).

jealousy. Reaction to the threat of losing a valued relationship (p. 293).

Johari Window model. Model of self-disclosure that summarizes how self-awareness is influenced by self-disclosure and information about yourself from others (p. 54).

K

kinesics. Study of human movement and gesture (p. 192).

L

laissez-faire families. Families with a low orientation toward both conversation and conformity (p. 350).

leader-member exchange (LMX) theory. Theory that supervisors develop different types of relationships with different subordinates and that seeks to explain those differences (p. 369).

legitimate power. Power that is based on respect for a person's position (p. 229).

life position. Feelings of regard for self and others, as reflected in one's sense of worth and self-esteem (p. 44).

linguistic determinism. Theory that describes how use of language determines or influences thoughts and perceptions (p. 160).

linguistic relativity. Theory that each language includes some unique features that are not found in other languages (p. 160).

listener apprehension. The fear of misunderstanding, misinterpreting, or being unable to adjust to the spoken messages of others (p. 127).

listening. Process of selecting, attending to, creating meaning from, remembering, and responding to verbal and nonverbal messages (p. 118).

listening style. Preferred way of making sense out of spoken messages (p. 121).

long-term maintenance attraction. Degree of liking or positive feelings that motivate us to maintain or escalate a relationship (p. 256).

looking-glass self. Concept that suggests you learn who you are based on your interactions with others, who reflect your self back to you (p. 38).

low-context culture. Culture in which people derive much information from the words of a message and less information from nonverbal and environmental cues (p. 95).

ludis. Game-playing love based on the enjoyment of another (p. 323).

M

malapropism. Confusion of one word or phrase for another that sounds similar to it (p. 163).

mania. Obsessive love driven by mutual needs (p. 323).

masculine culture. Culture in which people tend to value traditional roles for men and women, achievement, assertiveness, heroism, and material wealth (p. 95).

mass communication. Process that occurs when one person issues the same message to many people at once; the creator of the message is usually not physically present, and there is virtually no opportunity for listeners to respond immediately to the speaker (p. 5).

material self. Concept of self as reflected in a total of all the tangible things you own (p. 36).

media richness theory. Theory that identifies the richness of a communication medium based on the amount of feedback it allows, the number of cues receivers can interpret, the variety of language it allows, and the potential for emotional expression (p. 17).

message. Written, spoken, and unspoken elements of communication to which people assign meaning (p. 8).

metacommunication. Verbal or nonverbal communication about communication (p. 24).

meta-message. A message about a message; the message a person is expressing via nonverbal means (such as by facial expression, eye contact, and posture) about the message articulated with words (p. 129).

mindful. Conscious of what you are doing, thinking, and sensing at any given moment; aware of cultural differences and the connection between thoughts and deeds in one's interactions with someone from a background different from one's own (p. 80, p. 108).

mindfulness. The ability to consciously think about what you are doing and experiencing (p. 35).

mixed couples. Married couples in which the husband and wife each adopt a different perspective (traditional, independent, separate) on the marriage (p. 354).

mood. A conscious, subjective state of mind (p. 24).

motivation. Internal state of readiness to respond to something (p. 104).

N

natural or nuclear family. Mother, father, and their biological children (p. 345).

need for affection. Interpersonal need to give and receive love, support, warmth, and intimacy (p. 53).

need for control. Interpersonal need for some degree of influence in our relationships, as well as the need to be controlled (p. 53).

need for inclusion. Interpersonal need to be included and to include others in social activities (p. 53).

noise. Anything literal or psychological that interferes with accurate reception of a message (p. 9).

nonverbal communication. Behavior other than written or spoken language that creates meaning for someone (p. 185).

O

objective self-awareness. Ability to be the object of one's own thoughts and attention—to be aware of one's state of mind and that one is thinking (p. 35).

obsessive relational intrusion (ORI). Repeated invasion of a person's privacy by a stranger or acquaintance who desires or assumes a close relationship (p. 295).

onomatopoeia. A word that imitates a sound associated with what is named; also, the use of such a word (p. 156).

out-group. A racial, cultural, religious, or ethnic group different from one's own (p. 287).

outward communication. Communication that flows to those outside an organization (such as customers) (p. 372).

P

parallel relationship. Relationship in which power shifts back and forth between the partners, depending on the situation (p. 256).

paraphrase. Verbal summary of the key ideas of your partner's message that helps you check the accuracy of your understanding (p. 140).

passionate love. Romantic love that serves to establish attraction to, interest in, and focus on one person (p. 323).

passion-based intimacy. A type of intimacy based on romantic and sexual feelings (p. 312).

passive perception. Perception that occurs without conscious effort, simply in response to one's surroundings (p. 67).

Pelz effect. Subordinates' feeling more satisfied in their jobs, the more their supervisors are able to influence higher-level decisions (p. 367).

people-oriented listener. Listener who is comfortable with and skilled at listening to people's feelings and emotions (p. 121).

perception. Process of experiencing the world and making sense out of what you experience (p. 62).

perception checking. Asking someone whether your interpretation of his or her nonverbal behavior is accurate (p. 268).

personal space. Zone of space most often used for conversations with family and friends, ranging from $1^1/_2$ to 4 feet between individuals (p. 200).

personality. Enduring internal predispositions and behavioral characteristics that describe how people react to their environment (p. 41).

physical affection. The use of touch to convey emotional feelings of love and caring for another person (p. 325).

physical appearance. Nonverbal cues that allow us to assess relationship potential (POV) (p. 258).

pluralistic families. Families with a high orientation toward conversation but a low orientation toward conformity (p. 350).

polarization. Description and evaluation of what you observe in terms of extremes such as good or bad, old or new, beautiful or ugly (p. 165).

politeness theory. Theory that people have positive perceptions of others who treat them politely and respectfully (p. 46).

post-intimacy relationship. Formerly intimate relationship that is maintained at a less intimate stage (p. 264).

pragma. Practical love based on mutual benefits (p. 324).

predicted outcome value (POV). Potential for a relationship to confirm our self-image compared to its potential costs (p. 256).

prejudice. A judgment or opinion of someone, formed before you know all of the facts or the background of that person (p. 102).

preventative facework. Efforts to maintain and enhance one's positive self-perceptions (p. 45).

primacy effect. Tendency to attend to the first pieces of information observed about another person in order to form an impression (p. 68).

profanity. Words considered obscene, blasphemous, irreverent, rude, or insensitive (p. 161).

protective families. Families with a low orientation toward conversation but a high orientation toward conformity (p. 350).

proxemics. Study of how close or far away from people and objects people position themselves (p. 199).

proximity. Physical nearness to another that promotes communication and thus attraction (p. 258).

pseudoconflict. Conflict triggered by a lack of understanding and miscommunication (p. 223).

psychology. Study of how thinking influences behavior (p. 41).

public communication. Process that occurs when a speaker addresses an audience in person (p. 5).

public space. Zone of space most often used by public speakers or anyone speaking to many people, ranging beyond 12 feet from the individual (p. 200).

punctuation. Process of making sense out of stimuli by grouping, dividing, organizing, separating, and categorizing information (p. 65).

Q

quid pro quo harassment. Implied or explicit promise of reward in exchange for sexual favors or threat of retaliation if sexual favors are withheld, given to an employee by a coworker or a superior. The Latin phrase *quid pro quo* roughly means "You do something for me and I'll do something for you" (p. 364).

R

race. Genetically transmitted physical characteristics of a group of people (p. 90).

receiver. Person who decodes a message and attempts to make sense of what the source has encoded (p. 9).

recency effect. Tendency to attend to the most recent information observed about another person in order to form or modify an impression (p. 69).

reciprocation of liking. Liking those who like us (p. 259).

referent. Thing that a symbol represents (p. 153).

referent power. Power that comes from our attraction to another person, or the charisma a person possesses (p. 229).

reflective turning point. Event that signals a change in the way a relationship is defined (p. 262).

reframing. Process of redefining events and experiences from a different point of view (p. 48).

regulators. Nonverbal messages that help to control the interaction or flow of communication between two people (p. 193).

relational de-escalation. Movement of a relationship away from intimacy through five stages: turmoil or stagnation, deintensification, individualization, separation, and post-separation (p. 264).

relational development. Movement of a relationship from one stage to another, either toward or away from greater intimacy (p. 260).

relational empathy. Essence of a relationship that permits varying degrees of understanding, rather than requiring complete comprehension of another's culture or emotions (p. 107).

relational escalation. Movement of a relationship toward intimacy through five stages: preinteraction awareness, acquaintance, exploration, intensification, and intimacy (p. 262).

relational violence. Range of destructive behaviors aimed at other people, including aggressiveness, threats, violent acts, and verbal, psychological, or physical abuse (p. 296).

relationship. Ongoing connection established with another person through communication (p. 4, p. 252).

relationship dimension. The implied aspect of a communication message, which conveys information about emotions, attitudes, power, and control (p. 23).

relationship of choice. Interpersonal relationship you choose to initiate, maintain, and, perhaps, terminate (p. 254).

relationship of circumstance. Interpersonal relationship that exists because of life circumstances (who your family members are, where you work or study, and so on) (p. 254).

relationship talk. Talk about the nature, quality, direction, or definition of a relationship (p. 337).

relationship-specific social decentering. Other-oriented skills based on the knowledge and understanding gained in a specific intimate relationship (p. 335).

remembering. Process of recalling information (p. 120).

reproach. Message that a failure event has occurred (p. 282).

responding. Process of confirming your understanding of a message (p. 120).

responsiveness. Tendency to be sensitive to the needs of others, including being sympathetic to others' feelings and placing the feelings of others above one's own feelings (p. 56).

restricted code. Set of words that have particular meaning to a person, group, or culture (p. 164).

reward power. Power based on a person's ability to satisfy our needs (p. 229).

rule. Followable prescription that indicates what behavior is obligated, preferred, or prohibited in certain contexts (p. 22).

S

Sapir–Whorf hypothesis. Based on the principles of linguistic determinism and linguistic relativity, the hypothesis that language shapes our thoughts and culture, and our culture and thoughts affect the language we use to describe our world (p. 160).

second-guessing. Questioning the ideas and assumptions underlying a message; assessing whether the message is true or false (p. 121).

secret test. Behavior designed to indirectly determine a partner's feelings (p. 326).

secure attachment style. The style of relating to others that is characteristic of those who are comfortable giving and receiving affection, experiencing intimacy, and trusting other people (p. 39).

selecting. Process of choosing one sound while sorting through various sounds competing for your attention (p. 119).

selective attention. Process of focusing on specific stimuli, locking on to some things in the environment and ignoring others (p. 63).

selective exposure. Tendency to put ourselves in situations that reinforce our attitudes, beliefs, values, or behaviors (p. 63).

selective perception. Process of seeing, hearing, or making sense of the world around us based on such factors as our personality, beliefs, attitudes, hopes, fears, and culture, as well as what we like and don't like (p. 63).

selective recall. Process that occurs when we remember things we want to remember and forget or repress things that are unpleasant, uncomfortable, or unimportant to us (p. 64).

self. Sum total of who a person is; a person's central inner force (p. 33).

self-awareness. A person's conscious understanding of who he or she is (p. 54).

self-concept. A person's subjective description of who he or she is (p. 33).

self-disclosure. Purposefully providing information about yourself to others that they would not learn if you did not tell them (p. 53).

self-fulfilling prophecy. Prediction about future actions that is likely to come true because the person believes that it will come true (p. 51).

self-reflexiveness. Ability to think about what you are doing while you are doing it (p. 41).

self-serving bias. Tendency to perceive our own behavior as more positive than others' behavior (p. 78).

self-worth (self-esteem). Your evaluation of your worth or value based on your perception of such things as your skills, abilities, talents, and appearance (p. 43).

separate couples. Married partners who support the notion of marriage and family but stress the individual over the couple (p. 354).

sex. Biologically based differences that determine whether one is male or female (p. 88).

short-term initial attraction. Degree to which you sense a potential for developing an interpersonal relationship (p. 256).

shyness. Behavioral tendency not to talk or interact with other people (p. 41).

similarity. Having comparable personalities, values, upbringing, personal experiences, attitudes, and interests (p. 259).

simple conflict. Conflict that stems from different ideas, definitions, perceptions, or goals (p. 223).

single-parent family. One parent raising one or more children (p. 346).

skill. Behavior that improves the effectiveness or quality of communication with others (p. 104).

small group communication. Process that occurs when a group of from three to fifteen people meet to interact with a common purpose and mutually influence one another (p. 5).

social comparison. Process of comparing yourself to others who are similar to you, to measure your worth and value (p. 43).

social decentering. The cognitive process of taking into account another person's thoughts, values, background, and perspective as you interact with the person (p. 111, p. 133).

social exchange theory. Theory that claims people make relationship decisions by assessing and comparing the costs and rewards (p. 266).

social identity model of deindividuation effects (SIDE). Theory that people are more likely to stereotype others with whom they interact online, because such interactions provide fewer relationship cues and the cues take longer to emerge than they would in face-to-face interactions (p. 75).

social information-processing theory. Theory that suggests people can communicate relational and emotional messages via the Internet, although such messages take longer to express without nonverbal cues (p. 18).

social learning theory. Theory of human behavior that suggests we can learn how to adapt and adjust our behavior toward others; how we behave is not solely dependent on our genetic or biological makeup (p. 25).

social penetration model. A model of the self that reflects both the breadth and the depth of information that can potentially be disclosed (p. 270).

social penetration theory. Theory of relational development that posits that increases in intimacy are connected to increases in self-disclosure (p. 270).

social phase. Third phase in relationship termination, when members of the social network around both parties are informed of and become involved in the termination process (p. 304).

social presence. The feeling that communicators have of engaging in unmediated, face-to-face interactions even though messages are being sent electronically (p. 14).

social self. Concept of self as reflected in social interactions with others (p. 37).

social space. Zone of space most often used for group interactions, ranging from 4 to 12 feet between individuals (p. 200).

social support. Expression of empathy and concern for others that is communicated while listening to them and offering positive, sincere, supportive messages, both verbal and nonverbal, to help them deal with stress, anxiety, or uncertainty (p. 49, p. 144).

source. Originator of a thought or emotion, who puts it into a code that can be understood by a receiver (p. 8).

spiritual self. Concept of self based on thoughts and introspections about personal values, moral standards, and beliefs (p. 37).

stalking. Repeated, unwelcome intrusions that create concern for personal safety and fear in the target (p. 295).

standpoint theory. Theory that a person's social position, power, or cultural background influences how the person perceives the behavior of others (p. 71).

static evaluation. Pronouncement that does not take the possibility of change into consideration (p. 165).

stereotype. To attribute a set of qualities to a person because of the person's membership in some category; to place a person or group of persons into an inflexible, all-encompassing category (p. 74, p. 101).

storge. Solid love found in friendships and family, based on trust and caring (p. 323).

subjective self-awareness. Ability to differentiate the self from the social and physical environment (p. 35).

submissive symmetrical relationship. Relationship in which neither partner wants to take control or make decisions (p. 256).

sudden death. Abrupt and unplanned ending of a relationship (p. 301).

superimpose. To place a familiar structure on information you select (p. 65).

symbol. Word, sound, or visual image that represents something else, such as a thought, concept, or object (p. 22, p. 153).

symbolic interaction theory. Theory that people make sense of the world based on their interpretation of words or symbols used by others and that members of a society are bound together through common use of symbols (p. 50, p. 157).

symbolic self-awareness. Uniquely human ability to think about oneself and use language (symbols) to represent oneself to others (p. 35).

symmetrical relationship. Relationship in which both partners behave toward power in the same way, either both wanting power or both avoiding it (p. 255).

sympathy. Acknowledgment of someone else's feelings (p. 135).

synchronous message. A message that is sent and received simultaneously (p. 14).

systems theory. Theory that describes the interconnected elements of a system in which a change in one element affects all of the other elements (p. 11).

T

talk therapy. Technique in which a person describes his or her problems and concerns to a skilled listener in order to better understand the emotions and issues that are creating the problems (p. 49).

territorial markers. Tangible objects that are used to signify that someone has claimed an area or space (p. 200).

territoriality. Study of how animals and humans use space and objects to communicate occupancy or ownership of space (p. 200).

thin slicing. Observing a small sample of someone's behavior and then making a generalization about what the person is like, based on the sample (p. 64).

third culture. Common ground established when people from separate cultures create a third, "new," more comprehensive and inclusive culture (p. 106).

thought. Mental process of creating an image, sound, concept, or experience triggered by a referent or symbol (p. 153).

time-oriented listener. Listener who likes messages delivered succinctly (p. 122).

traditional couples. Married partners who are interdependent and who exhibit a lot of sharing and companionship (p. 354).

triangular theory of love. Theory that suggests that all loving relationships can be described according to three dimensions: intimacy, commitment, and passion (p. 322).

turning point. Specific event or interaction associated with a positive or negative change in a relationship (p. 261).

U

uncertainty reduction theory. Theory that claims people seek information in order to reduce uncertainty, thus achieving control and predictability (p. 68, p. 334).

understanding. Process of assigning meaning to sounds (p. 119).

unilateral dissolution. Ending of a relationship by one partner, even though the other partner wants it to continue (p. 301).

unrequited romantic interest. Feelings created when one partner desires a more intimate, romantic relationship than the other partner (p. 329).

upward communication. Communication that flows from subordinates to superiors (p. 367).

V

value. Enduring concept of good and bad, right and wrong (p. 34).

visualization. Technique of imagining that you are performing a particular task in a certain way; positive visualization can enhance self-esteem (p. 47).

W

white lie. Deception by commission involving only a slight degree of falsification that has a minimal consequence (p. 290).

willingness to communicate. General term for the likelihood that an individual will communicate with others in certain situations (p. 42).

word picture. Short statement or story that illustrates or describes an emotion; word pictures often use a simile (a comparison using the word *like* or *as*) to clarify the image (p. 175).

worldview. Individual perceptions or perceptions by a culture or group of people about key beliefs and issues, such as death, God, and the meaning of life, which influence interaction with others (p. 93, p. 160).

Photo Credits

Page i, Veer Inc., Royalty Free; Page 1, Veer Inc., Royalty Free; p. 5, Bob Daemmrich/Stock Boston; p. 7, Liza Donnelly; p. 15, Marili Forastieri/Getty Images/Digital Vision; p. 18, ZITS © 2008 ZITS PARTNERSHIP, KING FEATURES SYNDICATE; p. 19, Creatas Images/Jupiter Unlimited; p. 23, Ian Shaw/Getty Images Inc. — Stone Allstock; p. 32, Ned Frisk Photography/Corbis/Veer Inc., Royalty Free; p. 41, Tom McCarthy/PhotoEdit Inc.; p. 45, B2M Productions/Getty Images/Digital Vision; p. 47, Getty Images, Inc.; p. 52, Kevin Winter/American Idol 2009/Getty Images Inc. for FOX; p. 61, Veer Inc., Royalty Free; p. 62, Norman Rockwell Family Agency, Inc.; p. 64, Photos to Go; p. 67, BananaStock/Jupiter Unlimited; p. 70, ZITS © 2000 ZITS PARTNERSHIP, KING FEATURES SYNDICATE; p. 73, Paul Thuysbaert/Grapheast/Alamy Images; p. 76, Michael Newman/PhotoEdit Inc.; p. 77, Don Bayley/iStockphoto.com; p. 81, Jon Feingersh; p. 85, © Chuck Kennedy/Pool/CORBIS. All Rights Reserved; p. 89, Liza Donnelly; p. 94, Al Bello/Octagon/Getty Images, Inc.; p. 96, Ilyas Dean/The Image Works; p. 99, Hideo Haga/The Image Works; p. 107, Bob Mahoney/The Image Works; p. 110, Robert Fried /Alamy Images; p. 117, Streeter Lecka/Getty Images, Inc.; p. 120, Dorothy Littell Greco/The Image Works; p. 123, ZITS © 2001 ZITS PARTNERSHIP, KING FEATURES SYNDICATE; p. 125, BIZARRO (NEW) © 2008 DAN PIRARO, KING FEATURES SYNDICATE; p. 127, David Young-Wolff/PhotoEdit Inc.; p. 129, ZITS © 2006 ZITS PARTNERSHIP, KING FEATURES SYNDICATE; p. 133, Charles O. Cecil/Alamy Images; p. 138, Rachel Epstein/PhotoEdit Inc.; p. 141, Comstock Images/Jupiter Unlimited; p. 148, ZITS © 1999 ZITS PARTNERSHIP, KING FEATURES SYNDICATE; p. 152, Erickson Productions, Inc.; p. 155 (left), Miguel Cuenca/Alamy Images; p. 155 (right), Greg Nicholas/iStockphoto.com; p. 160, Getty Images, Inc.; p. 161, ZITS © 2004 ZITS PARTNERSHIP, KING FEATURES SYNDICATE; p. 166, R. Sidney/The Image Works; p. 172, Jason Stitt/Shutterstock; p. 178, Creatas Images/Jupiter Unlimited; p. 184, Tim Tadder/Comet Photography/Veer Inc., Royalty Free; p. 186, ZITS © 2006 ZITS PARTNERSHIP, KING FEATURES SYNDICATE; p. 187, Art Resource, N.Y.; p. 189, SHOE – NEW BUSINESS © 2000 MACNELLY, KING FEATURES SYNDICATE; p. 192, Focus Features/The Kobal Collection/Picture Desk; p. 197, BananaStock/Jupiter Unlimited; p. 199, Photos.com/Jupiter Unlimited; p. 201, Liza Donnelly; p. 205, © Jose Luis Pelaez, Inc./CORBIS; p. 208 (top), Stephen Marks; p. 208 (bottom), Bonnie Kamin/PhotoEdit Inc.; p. 215, Stu Froster/Allsport Concepts/Getty Images; p. 217, BBC Films/Evamere/Neal Street Productions/Picture Desk, Inc./Kobal Collection; p. 220, Richard Pasley/Stock Boston; p. 223, Michael Newman/PhotoEdit Inc.; p. 227, Ingram Publishing/Alamy Images Royalty Free; p. 232, Colin Young-Wolff\PhotoEdit Inc.; p. 236, Matthew Jacques/Shutterstock; p. 238, Liza Donnelly; p. 241, Comstock Images/Jupiter Unlimited; p. 247, Roberto Schmidt/AFP Photo/Newscom; p. 251, Getty Images, Inc – Purestock Royalty Free; p. 253, Tom McCarthy/PhotoEdit Inc.; p. 255, ZITS © 2006 ZITS PARTNERSHIP, KING FEATURES SYNDICATE; p. 257, Darren Michaels/Columbia/Picture Desk, Inc./Kobal Collection; p. 259, Photos to Go; p. 260, Randy Glasbergen; p. 262, ZITS © 2000 ZITS PARTNERSHIP, KING FEATURES SYNDICATE; p. 264, Sandra Rice; p. 269, Don Smetzer/PhotoEdit Inc.; p. 273, Anderson, Colin/Getty Images Inc. – Image Bank; p. 274, Sandra Rice; p. 280, RubberBall Photography/Veer Inc., Royalty Free; p. 286, Goodshot/Jupiter Unlimited; p. 289, SuperStock, Inc.; p. 292, PhotoEdit Inc.; p. 293, Jasmin Awad/iStockphoto.com; p. 295, BrandX/Superstock Royalty Free; p. 297, Comstock Images/Jupiter Unlimited; p. 301, Donna Day/Getty Images Inc. – Stone Allstock; p. 311, John Feingersh/Blend Images/Getty Images, Inc.; p. 315, Comstock Images/Jupiter Unlimited; p. 316, Sandra Rice; p. 318, © Lynn Johnston Productions, Inc. Reproduced by permission.; p. 319, Robert W. Ginn/PhotoEdit Inc.; p. 324, Anthony Harris/Shutterstock; p. 327, Bob Daemmrich/The Image Works; p. 331, Photos to Go; p. 336, Randy Glasbergen; p. 337, Steve Mason/Getty Images, Inc. – Photodisc/Royalty Free; p. 342, Floresco Images/Veer Inc., Royalty Free; p. 346 (top), © Philip Gould/CORBIS. All Rights Reserved; p. 346 (middle), James Devaney/Getty Images – WireImage.com; p. 346 (bottom), Tetra Images/Photos to Go; p. 351, Bob Daemmrich/The Image Works; p. 352, ZITS © 2007 ZITS PARTNERSHIP, KING FEATURES SYNDICATE; p. 355, BananaStock/Jupiter Unlimited; p. 356, John Lei, Jr./Stock Boston; p. 359, Michael DeLeon/iStockphoto.com; p. 361, BananaStock/Alamy Images Royalty Free; p. 362, Chris Haston/NBCU Photo Bank; p. 366, Copyright Grantland Enterprises, www.grantland.net; p. 367, Frank Siteman/PhotoEdit Inc.; p. 368, Photos to Go.